RITUALS OF
RULE,
RITUALS OF
RESISTANCE

RITUALS OF RULE, RITUALS OF RESISTANCE

*Public
Celebrations
and
Popular
Culture
in Mexico*

**Edited by
WILLIAM H. BEEZLEY
CHERYL ENGLISH MARTIN
WILLIAM E. FRENCH**

**SR
BOOKS**

A Scholarly Resources Inc. Imprint
Wilmington, Delaware

© 1994 by Scholarly Resources Inc.
All rights reserved
First published 1994
Printed and bound in the United States of America

Scholarly Resources Inc.
104 Greenhill Avenue
Wilmington, DE 19805-1897

Sources for Illustrations

Chapter 7: Justino Fernández, *El arte del siglo XIX en México* (Mexico City, 1983), Figs. 296, 299; and Salvador Novo, *México* (Barcelona, 1968), p. 294.

Chapter 15: Elsie Clews Parsons, *Mitla: Town of the Souls* (Chicago, 1936), opposite pp. 155, 192; and Frederick Starr, *In Indian Mexico: A Narrative of Travel and Labor* (Chicago, 1908), opposite pp. 126, 238.

Library of Congress Cataloging-in-Publication Data

Rituals of rule, rituals of resistance : public celebrations and
  popular culture in Mexico / edited by William H. Beezley, Cheryl
  English Martin, and William E. French.
      p.   cm. — (Latin American silhouettes)
    ISBN 0-8420-2416-6 (alk. paper). — ISBN 0-8420-2417-4
(pbk. : alk. paper)
    1. Festivals—Mexico. 2. Rites and ceremonies—Mexico.
3. Mexico—Politics and government. 4. Popular culture—Mexico.
5. Mexico—Social life and customs. I. Beezley, William H.
 II. Martin, Cheryl English, 1945–   . III. French, William E.,
1956–   . IV. Series.
GT4814.A2R57   1994
394.2'6972—dc20   94-884
                                                                          CIP

To

Paul, John, and Mark Beezley

Jeff Martin

Evan and Leah French

Contents

Acknowledgments

The Eighth Conference of Mexican and North American Historians in San Diego, 1990, provided an opportunity for the editors to present early versions of their essays in a session called "Mentalidades in 18th-20th Century Mexico." The success of the session and the conference as a whole encouraged us to undertake this book. Consequently, we extend our thanks for creating such an excellent opportunity to the Joint Organizing Committee, headed by Jaime E. Rodríguez O. and Roberto Moreno de los Arcos, and the local organizers, Eric Van Young and Paul Vanderwood. We also thank each of the contributors to this volume. Their cooperation, patience, and confidence in the project made it a pleasure to complete.

We appreciate the assistance of Howard Campbell of the Department of Anthropology at the University of Texas, El Paso, and Robert A. J. McDonald of the Department of History, University of British Columbia. Both of them read the introduction and gave us perceptive comments that we incorporated in our revisions. Charles Reagan Wilson and Paul R. Beezley at the University of Mississippi also reviewed the introduction and provided a helpful critique. K. Steven Vincent, Department of History, North Carolina State University, shared his knowledge of French popular, labor, and revolutionary history with us. The staff at Scholarly Resources, especially Richard Hopper and Laura Huey Cunningham, has supported this book since it was no more than a glimmer of an idea. We appreciate the assistance of the staff and the enthusiastic backing of the coeditor of the Latin American Silhouettes series, Judith Ewell.

Abbreviations

AAAM	Archivo del Antiguo Ayuntamiento de México, Mexico City
Actas	*Actas de cabildo de la ciudad de México* (México: Aguilar e Hijos, 1889–1911)
AGI	Archivo General de Indias, Seville
AGN	Archivo General de la Nación, Mexico City
APD	Archivo de Porfirio Díaz, Mexico City
CSSH	*Comparative Studies in Society and History*
HAHR	*Hispanic American Historical Review*
HM	*Historia Mexicana*
JCH	*Journal of Contemporary History*
JLAS	*Journal of Latin American Studies*
LARR	*Latin American Research Review*
PO	*Periódico Oficial*
PP	*Past and Present*
SEP/AH	Secretaría de Educación Publica, Archivo Histórico, Mexico City

Introduction: Constructing Consent, Inciting Conflict

William H. Beezley
Cheryl English Martin
William E. French

Successful rulers throughout history have understood that their dominion rests on much more than force alone. Persuasion, charisma, habit, and presentations of virtue serve as familiar techniques and exhibitions of authority. In particular, those in power have grasped the crucial importance of public ritual in symbolizing and constantly recreating their hegemony. Not only do ceremonies and processions provide visual and aural dramas of the society's hierarchy, but they also afford elites an opportunity to reiterate—for their own edification and that of their subordinates—the moral values on which their authority rests. Such occasions also may shape interpretations of the society's past, mask social divisions by seeming to unite disparate groups in shared ritual, and provide opportunities for popular revelry that may defuse the potentially disruptive impulses of subordinate groups. Thus, many rituals rehearsing religious premises and celebrating milestones in royal lives have yielded to analogous civic and secular holidays that continue to consolidate state authority and represent power to its subjects.[1]

From their first arrival in the Western Hemisphere, Spaniards used rituals to help establish their authority. In contrast to the English, for example, who relied on the architectural symbolism of residences (usually building houses), the Spaniards legitimated their right to rule through language and ceremony. The relevance of ritual appeared clearly from 1512 onward in the acts of possession, because the Spaniards used the ceremonial *requerimiento* (a document, read aloud, that supposedly justified the imposition of Spanish sovereignty) to establish authority over persons, not property or trade. "Spanish colonialism," in Patricia Seed's phrase, "produced the census, British colonialism the map."[2] Spanish rulers required subject peoples to reiterate and reaffirm Spanish hegemony on a regular basis.

In Mexico, from the first encounter of the Spaniards and the Aztecs, visual displays of the desired new society—with its hierarchy of authority and status—dominated the cultural interaction of these peoples.[3] Holiday celebrations offered civic and church leaders the opportunity to organize living tableaux of virtue that served to instruct subordinate peoples. Spanish efforts to acculturate, especially to evangelize, the indigenous peoples focused on dramatic demonstrations such as rituals of government, passion plays, and Amerindian dances revised to carry Christian-European meanings. Mexico's Spanish festival heritage began with the arrival of Cortés and quickly became a unique visual, acoustic, and symbolic tradition that combined Spanish and indigenous, and some African, images and icons. In the last third of the colonial era, the Bourbon monarchs attempted to reform colonial societies in many ways, including efforts to remove the carnivalesque features of popular celebrations and give them a more formal and serious character.

These changes of the eighteenth century continued and assumed a more explicitly political character immediately after independence, when patriotic Mexicans instituted holidays and celebrations that honored the heroes of independence and attempted to make colonial residents into citizens of an emerging nation-state. Emperor Agustín de Iturbide and the first congress devised an official list of these holidays that established a celebration to honor the victims of the independence struggle, the entry of the patriotic army into the capital, and the emperor's birthday. This calendar also maintained the celebration of San Hipólito Day, marking Cortés's conquest of the Aztec capital.[4] Changes and additions, of course, continued after independence. The revolution revised many local celebrations and added new festivities that continue to the present. A 1977 survey reported that communities celebrate 5,083 civil and religious occasions throughout the year in which no more than nine days go by without a fiesta somewhere in Mexico.[5] The following essays consider public ritual in Mexico over five centuries. In one way or another, all of the authors focus on symbolic dramatizations of state power and responses of intended audiences to these rituals, and some authors also pay explicit attention to the arenas in which these ceremonial displays took place.

Rituals of rule and resistance have been recognized and studied in many regions outside of Mexico. In one celebrated example, state ceremony, rather than serving as a means to a political end, expressed the end itself. Clifford Geertz, in an analysis of what he calls the theater-state, argues that Bali's great rituals—royal cremation, noble suicides, tooth filings, temple dedications, penitential pilgrimages, and blood sacrifices—become the media for rulers to act out the drama of their power rather than to administer their realm. Balinese rulers employed the rhetoric of ritual to present the tenets of their political thought—that status is the basis of power and that statecraft is a thespian art—and to express their view of the nature of reality and thus make it actual. As Geertz adduces, "The king owned the country as he ruled it—mimetically; composing and constructing the very thing he imitated."[6] Rulers try to create a compliant, imagined reality that will be accepted by subjects.[7] Rituals establish just such virtual, compliant representations of reality because they portray the idealized social relations envisioned by those in power. Such understanding rests on the assumption that ritual actions can be read as statements because they are less cluttered and more focused in purpose than daily life and therefore more articulate.

At the same time, scholars have demonstrated that daily life is suffused with ritual performances that supposedly reinforce existing social hierarchies. Rhys Isaac explained this precept of much cultural history when he defined culture as the multichanneled system of communication comprising language, gesture, demeanor, dress, and architecture.[8] Thus society emerges as a series of images that participants have of their own and others' performances. Architectural design and church seating arrangements, for example, serve as pronouncements of social order and the expression of social ranking. At the center of Isaac's work is his concern with authority and deference in social relationships and the many ways they are asserted, communicated, recognized and contested. In face-to-face communities like those of eighteenth-century Virginia and, until recently, Mexico, action (that is, physical movement) in a social context proved more articulate in total communication than speech and written words. Most authors in the present volume share the preoccupation with power and view action as statement. Studies of brass bands, drunken scandals, civic parades, street monuments, and village fiestas provide opportunities not only to gain access to the mentalities of past peoples but also to probe these activities in order to reveal them as representations that both assert and contest power.[9]

Symbolic properties make ritual a forceful medium for representing authority and facilitating rule. Geertz's discussion of the Balinese theater-state makes apparent the capacity of ritual to model desired ends. While symbols, with their layers of meaning in condensed form, allow for immediate communication, they also evoke sensual as well as intellectual responses. Ritual relates the individual to the collective by joining the emotional to the ideological. From an elite perspective, then, ritual works by fusing the positive emotions of symbols and events with social and moral demands on the subject.[10] In other words, social norms and values acquire greater force by being

invested with emotion while basic emotions are ennobled through
association with social values. Discussing the role of ritual in enab-
ling rule in the erstwhile Soviet Union, a manager of state ceremonies revealed: "Rituals are conducted at important turning-points of
a man's life. Owing to psychic mood he is particularly receptive to
external influence [that] we must utilize in the interests of communist education."[11]

While rituals fusing the individual to the collective often revolve
around rites of initiation or passage, they also can portray the past to
the present. Just as initiation rites represent an interpenetration of
social norms and individual emotions, commemorative rites strengthen
the present by reference to the past. David Cannadine, for example,
charts the transformation in the meaning and performance of British
royal ritual from 1820 to the present. Rather unimportant at the beginning of this period, between 1918 and 1953 British monarchs came
to represent a manufactured "thousand-year-old" tradition. Cannadine
notes that those persons watching carefully orchestrated displays of
royal pageantry, with commentators stressing the real or putative historic continuity with those former days of Britain's greatness, find it
difficult to believe that such greatness has vanished.[12] Perhaps the
British monarchy best exemplified this practice, but other commemorative rites have figured prominently in the rituals used by rulers as
disparate as those of Nazi Germany and the former Soviet Union,
and surely include the leaders of the Spanish colonial empire and the
Mexican republic.

The authors in this volume analyze the importance of ritual in
Mexico from the sixteenth through the twentieth century. Linda
Curcio-Nagy (Chapter 1) and Clara García Ayluardo (Chapter 4) vividly describe and evaluate the exuberantly baroque ceremonial life
of the sixteenth and seventeenth centuries that haphazardly mingled
political symbols of Hapsburg state power, religious rituals of the
Counter-Reformation, and popular traditions of both Iberian and indigenous peoples. Although colonial rituals graphically depicted and
even celebrated distinctions of class, estate, ethnicity, and gender,
they also stressed even the humblest individual's membership in the
mystical body of Christ and his or her rhetorically filial relationship
to His Majesty.[13] The Bourbon monarchs of the eighteenth century
attempted to streamline public celebrations in Mexico and utilized
these occasions for unabashed assertions of state power, as Sergio
Rivera Ayala (Chapter 2), Susan Deans-Smith (Chapter 3), and Cheryl
English Martin (Chapter 5) amply explain.

In the decades that followed independence in 1821, Mexican leaders faced the challenge of creating new vocabularies of ritual for an
emerging national state. It was here, in the Americas, as Benedict

Anderson has demonstrated, that the imagined community of the nation-state first appeared along with republican institutions, common citizenships, and popular sovereignty. And it was ritual that provided one means of facilitating the transfer of allegiances from older, more established imaginary communities based on religion, family, and region to the new nation-state.[14] Conflicts with the church, war with the United States, the Liberal triumph in the Revolution of Ayutla in 1854, and resistance to the French Intervention of the 1860s all furnished new symbols of national solidarity—a flag, a national anthem, and a gallery of heroes—that could be immortalized in place and street names and proudly heralded on ritual occasions. In the late nineteenth and early twentieth centuries, Porfirio Díaz and his supporters continued to build and consolidate a ritual repertoire appropriate to the modernized, centralized state they were creating. They constructed impressive monuments, as Barbara Tenenbaum's essay (Chapter 7) shows, that handsomely portrayed the figures and ideals of liberalism. Meanwhile, they also staged increasingly elaborate pageants of state, culminating in the celebrations held in 1910 to commemorate the one hundredth anniversary of Mexican independence and to convince invited dignitaries from around the world that Mexico deserved a place in the ranks of civilized and progressive nations.[15]

Political leaders of twentieth-century Mexico have created a new iconography incorporating the accepted heroes of the Revolution of 1910 as well as a political culture that underscores their own self-defined roles as the effective successors of those heroes.[16] On occasion the postrevolutionary elites have also augmented the ritual vocabulary. Lázaro Cárdenas's expropriation of the foreign oil properties on March 18, 1938, gave Mexicans a new holiday and a new slogan (*"El petróleo es nuestro"*) of national solidarity. In less spectacular ways the political leaders of Mexico also built an elaborate infrastructure capable of recapitulating on a daily basis the messages more dramatically conveyed on ritual occasions. Public schools, a nationwide network of museums and cultural centers that make Mexico's history and artistic achievements accessible to a wider public, and a political party that claims to encircle all Mexicans in its paternal embrace—each of these institutions performs functions similar to those of the viceregal and religious processions in the colonial era. Like their predecessors they offer certain benefits, although social security and subsidized housing have replaced spiritual indulgences and coins tossed by passing dignitaries.

Mexico's rulers of the late twentieth century continue to follow established rituals of proven patriotic worth. Thus, each year on the night of September 15–16, the president of the republic appears on the balcony of the National Palace overlooking Mexico City's majestic central plaza, called the Zócalo. Wearing the red, white, and green sash of office that represents his direct continuity with the past, he commemorates Miguel Hidalgo y Costilla's original call to arms that ignited the struggle for independence in 1810. One by one he invokes the names of Father Hidalgo and other heroes, including President Benito Juárez and the Niños Heroes de Chapultepec, the young cadets who reportedly plunged to their deaths rather than surrender to the invading North Americans in 1847. The crowd greets each new incantation with an exuberant "Viva!" until finally the president ends the litany with a resounding "Viva México!"

Although the ceremony creates the illusion of continuity between the present and the founding of the country, changes in the manner of its celebration reveal abrupt breaks with the past. Before the Juárez presidency the *grito*, given in the reduced space of a theater on the night of September 15, served not as the central focus of the Independence ceremonies but rather as an elite event overshadowed by the popular activities, including cockfights and fireworks, that took place the following day. During the rule of Díaz not only did the *grito* itself become central, but also the ceremony afforded an opportunity for the president to insinuate himself into the pantheon of national heroes as the country began to celebrate his saint's day on September 15.[17] More recently, the Independence Day celebrations also demonstrate that Mexico's leaders have proved adept at using modern technology to dramatize their message and diffuse it to a wider audience. Brilliant, multicolored lighting illuminates the Zócalo as crowds assemble to hear the president's message, while satellite hookups stand ready to beam his image and words to Mexicans throughout the republic and abroad.

In Mexico, rulers have invented tradition and presented it as having passed down unchanged from generation to generation. Here, as elsewhere, the last two hundred years in general, and situations of rapid social and economic change in particular, have provided propitious occasions for the creation of such "tradition." As societies stratified by rank or estate were replaced by those divided along class lines, and as nation-states became increasingly secular in outlook, new methods of ensuring loyalty and acceptance of state power emerged. Colonial outposts gave way to independent nations, and the host of presidents, emperors, and praetorian dictators required affirmation of their rule and confirmation of their state.[18] Perhaps no one in the early independence period was of greater importance in inventing tradition and perpetuating national myths than Carlos María de Bustamante. Between 1821 and 1827 he provided the new republic with a "portrait gallery of its founding fathers" and conjured up the image of a Mexican nation that had existed at the time of the

Spanish Conquest, and, after three hundred years of colonial rule, was about to recover its liberty.[19] This alternative civic religion relied not only on ritual pageantry but also on primary education and public monuments to symbolize social cohesion or membership in groups, to legitimate institutions or relations of authority, and to inculcate beliefs or systems of knowledge.[20] The recent controversy over the newly written primary textbooks that depict Díaz as a fiscally prudent modernizer instead of a sellout to foreign capitalists reveals that the practice continues.[21]

Although secular and popular, invented traditions that parallel the industrial revolution can be divided into three overlapping types: those symbolizing social cohesion (or membership in groups), those legitimating institutions (or relations of authority), and those inculcating beliefs (or systems of knowledge). They legitimated—even made sacred—the origins and operations of states. Mona Ozouf, borrowing from Emile Durkheim, has shown how the festivals of the French Revolution aimed at effecting the transfer of sacrality from the Old Regime to the new. This process, she adduced, is the crucial act of institution for any new regime.[22] Christel Lane finds a similar practice in Soviet Marxist-Leninism and interprets the Soviet system of holidays and rituals in the same way. In the present volume, Adrian Bantjes (Chapter 13) analyzes the desacralization of the old cultural order and the transfer of sacrality from Catholicism to a new civic religion in revolutionary Mexico. In almost every case the process of sacralization required new rituals and ceremonies as well as the infusion of old ceremonies with new meaning. Such creative use of tradition affirms Geertz's assertion that all political authority requires a "cultural frame" in which to define itself and advance its claim to rule.[23]

Philip Corrigan and Derek Sayer extend Geertz's insight to argue that state formation must be viewed as a process of cultural revolution. For them the state orchestrates an unending project of moral regulation and rule by creating social identities. Thus, state power works within us. Influenced by Michel Foucault, Corrigan and Sayer see state formation as the long-term process of cultural revolution by which the ordinary procedures of the state become the boundaries of the possible, occupying the entire social vision. These boundaries are then sanctified in the "magnificent rituals of state."[24]

Those familiar with the Mexican state between the eighteenth and the twentieth centuries will recognize the centrality of moral reform to state formation, or *forjando patria*—forging a fatherland—as Manuel Gamio so eloquently put it.[25] The state, often through ritual, strengthens the self-discipline of the middle class, the labor discipline imposed on workers, and the broader social discipline of all but the elite class that accompany capitalist development. Susan Deans-Smith discusses the role of the Bourbon state in constructing social identities in the tobacco manufactory. As Tony Morgan (Chapter 8) illustrates in his essay, late nineteenth-century elites, while not neglecting the patriotic icons of the past, increasingly turned their attention to inculcating attitudes and behavior that would contribute to their goal of modernizing Mexico. Morgan examines Mexico City, and other studies have found similar developments in the Parral mining district of Chihuahua, Guadalajara, and Monterrey.[26] These works warn that corporations, as well as nations, construct interpretations of social reality for employees, customers, and the general public.[27]

POPULAR CELEBRATIONS

There is much more to the history of public ritual than the efforts of rulers and their surrogates to intimidate, instruct, and reform their social subordinates. Not just mere witnesses to the elaborate ceremonies of statehood, popular classes also have carried out spontaneous and planned celebrations on their own. A busy festival calendar enlivened the life of the community—celebrating represented one of the few hallowed rights of the people. Whether commemorating religious beliefs or national events, festivals displayed and represented the collective life of the community and provided an opportunity for constructing and expressing meanings not connected with ideology.[28]

A number of studies have focused on the importance of ceremonial life in rural Mexican villages, particularly those where Indians historically composed the majority of the population. William Taylor's work has helped define the function of alcohol consumption in colonial celebrations, while Nancy Farriss has shown how the religious rituals sponsored by *cofradías* (religious brotherhoods or sodalities) reveal many insights about indigenous responses to European colonization.[29] Numerous anthropological studies have also paid careful attention to the ways in which Mexican local celebrations traditionally served simultaneously to reaffirm rights in communal lands and neighborhood structures, reinforce community solidarity, and redistribute wealth by requiring sponsors to underwrite their cost.[30]

In addition, community rituals often portray appropriate cultural behavior. In a performance known simply as *La Danza*, residents of Tzintzuntzan, Michoacán, celebrate the miraculous image of the Señor del Rescate for four days each February. Participants dressed as devils and death behave in a chaotic and threatening manner, victimizing the audience and engaging in phallic rivalry, homosexual display, and scatological humor. These actors deviate from acceptable social norms in order to ridicule such behavior; in this way, children learn to acknowledge the laughable and grotesque character of uncontrolled behavior.[31] Likewise, in Tlayacapan, Morelos, the theme of reproduction dominates ritual. This motif, exemplified in events that include the celebration of virgin birth, the nine nights of *posadas* before Christmas (one for each month of Mary's pregnancy), funeral ceremonies, and the resurrection of Christ at Easter, serves as a basic or root metaphor. More than a means of inculcating cultural values, folk Catholic rituals envelop all aspects of life.[32]

Acknowledging that revelers express shared values through ritual suggests neither a harmonious nor a stagnant conception of community. Drawn from collective life and grounded in social and economic conditions at the local level, rituals represent and reinforce both the solidarity and contention found there. Conflict appears as much a part of this ritual as solidarity. Displays of virility and manly courage that take place during festive occasions in rural Mexico seem to contradict the meaning of communal ritual, but in fact they may serve to inform others not to mistake the generosity of ritual sponsors for weakness.[33]

In many places public celebrations expressing notions of community became segregated over time to reflect social and gender divisions. Occasionally, rituals have arisen to highlight these differences and distinctions. In the *compagnonnages* formed by journeymen in France from the midseventeenth to the midnineteenth century, workers celebrated the finest social distinctions. Symbolic ranking created by journeymen themselves through ceremonies of initiation and bouts of fighting came to the forefront with the abolition of legally sanctioned differences. While the rituals of the *compagnonnages* created inequalities in a world where workers had too much in common, they also made members equal in a world split by differences of age, ability, and geographic origin and, at the same time, acted as a means to exclude nonmembers.[34] Rather than a rigidly prescribed set of ritual performances, the rites of the *compagnonnages* provided a "loosely structured repertoire" that journeymen could adapt to various circumstances. In Mexico, *albures,* playful jingles, developed as language games that still persist among the popular classes. Each *albur* serves as a vehicle for transmitting ideas of social and political protest or sexual misbehavior.

In addition to taking on a certain life of their own, popular celebrations, depending on circumstances, could both threaten and reinforce relations between elites and subordinates. On the one hand, Carnival revelers sometimes found a harmless safety valve for their pent-up frustrations in temporary and symbolic reversals that "turned the world upside down." On the other hand, those same celebrants (and others at the *charivari*, a ritual originally directed toward a widow or widower upon remarriage) could use the event as the vehicle for mobilizing the population against rulers. Community celebrations could also take on political overtones in periods of repression. Marcello Carmagnani analyzed the Tehuantepec riots that broke out during Holy Week of 1660–61 and Eric Van Young pointed out that major village riots erupted on *Todos Santos* (the Feast of All Saints) in 1810.[35] In April 1909, in the Guggenheim-owned mining camp of Velardeña, Durango, a procession through town that intended to burn a Judas effigy as part of the traditional Holy Saturday celebration resulted in a clash with the rural police and an orgy of looting and burning of the company-owned buildings.[36] In instances such as these, popular festivals and rituals became the means of expressing discontent and even of destroying elements of the existing state.[37] In this volume, Linda Curcio-Nagy notes that the most important popular revolt in colonial Mexico City took place during the celebration of Corpus Christi in 1692.

Fears about the disruptive effects of popular celebrations prompted elite efforts to limit the number of local festivals and to control participation in religious and civic events. Beginning in the early modern era, authorities in Europe and elsewhere appropriated many of the traditions of Carnival and other celebrations, such as the use of fireworks, thereby transforming participants into spectators at these events.[38] At the same time, they attempted to banish genuinely popular festivities from the streets and plazas of cities and towns. This struggle for the streets also took place in Mexico City.

Colonial Spanish officials and local elites, imbued with the desire to make the city streets beautiful, rational, and secure, together sought during the second half of the eighteenth century to eliminate popular celebrations and restrict urban space for their exclusive use. Bourbon officials, as García Ayluardo and Curcio-Nagy show, viewed popular religiosity—as expressed in the sometimes unruly conduct of parading confraternity members and dragons and giants of popular celebrations—as ridiculous, even profane. Along with local elites, who had lost much of their enthusiasm for participating with the masses in such celebrations, Bourbon rulers had also lost confidence in the value of these festivals for inculcating desired attitudes and behavior.[39] In eighteenth-century Chihuahua City, the *cabildo* (city council) did not even allow popular celebrations—including Carnival—on its ritual calendar. At the dawn of independence, Mexico City boasted night lighting, paved and named streets, clearly numbered houses, and increased vigilance; the colonial regime also exercised control over popular activities. The elite and the state had triumphed at least in the urban center.[40]

In the capital and throughout Mexico the struggle over public space did not end with independence. Sporadic conflict continued throughout the nineteenth century, with national and local governments following many of the projects initiated by colonial officials to achieve a rational and orderly society. Anne Staples's essay (Chapter 6) describes in detail municipal efforts in three towns, including the capital, to execute these reforms. Moreover, during the Díaz years, municipal and state authorities, viewing city space in Victorian moralistic terms, passed legislation to drive vice from city centers as a way to preserve such areas for the *gente decente*. William E. French has undertaken the first study for Porfirian Mexico of the struggle over public space, describing the moral geography of the mining community of Parral, Chihuahua;[41] he pursues this topic in this volume (Chapter 10). Nor did this concern with vice and public space end with the fall of the Díaz regime; though underemphasized by scholars, it formed a central theme of the Mexican Revolution.[42]

Meanwhile, acknowledged elites and those who aspired to join them took advantage of ritual occasions to solidify the boundaries between themselves and their subordinates. In Mexico the appearance of women as icons of patriotism, liberty, motherhood, and virtue expressed middle-class dominance of public celebrations, replacing more popular and spontaneous elements. The essays by Tony Morgan and William Beezley (Chapter 9) discuss the development of parade floats depicting such middle-class icons in Mexico and Guadalajara, respectively. A further example comes from the Hispanic community in Tucson, Arizona Territory, during the Díaz years, when middle-class Mexicanos gave up the secular fair associated with Tucson's patron, San Agustín, to celebrate Mexico's independence day with ceremonies that included a procession featuring a triumphal float with thirty young women who represented Mexico's twenty-seven states, in addition to "America," "Liberty," and "Justice."[43]

Whenever the struggle over public space failed to drive the popular classes and their celebrations from the streets, self-styled elites simply withdrew from public, religious, and patriotic rituals. Despite the absence of the middle class, their notions of respectability, as defined in processions in which they predominated, permeated working-class parades, especially those of skilled laborers.[44] In the United States between 1825 and 1850, virtually all workers had taken part in street parades displaying their solidarity, but, after midcentury, laborers from the more prestigious occupational groups abandoned the processions. The persons who continued to parade began to express new and multiple occupational, class, religious, and ethnic loyalties. In these parades, the representation of women changed; they served as "living symbols." The emergence of females portended the end of middle-class participation in urban parades and its retreat into the private sphere.[45]

Some of the elites appropriated and transformed popular forms of celebration; more often, however, they not only shunned participation in popular rites but also fashioned their own forms of recreation patterned on the behavior of European and U.S. counterparts. Those who removed themselves from public celebrations many times created their own traditions in the refined privacy of their homes and exclusive clubs rather than observe these occasions side by side with humbler social groups.[46] Public holidays joined birthdays and other personal observances as opportunities for special family gatherings. Larissa Adler Lomnitz and Marisol Pérez-Lizaur, in *A Mexican Elite Family, 1820–1980*, show how these events came to revolve around meals prepared from closely guarded family recipes. Direct female descendants share the recipes, with one older woman serving as both the custodian of festival foods and the focus of the celebration. The sense of nationalism held by these family members includes pride in their devotion to the Virgin of Guadalupe, their fine Mexican cooking, and their traditional Mexican hospitality.[47]

RITUALS OF RESISTANCE

However impressive and colorful the rites devised by rulers and elites, abundant evidence suggests that the intended audiences often rejected the authoritarian messages conveyed in these rituals even when they failed to display their insubordination in open rebellion. Lower classes often imposed their own agendas on state-sponsored observances and rejected others entirely. Both Mary Kay Vaughan and Engracia Loyo (Chapters 11 and 12) show how individuals and local communities negotiated with agents of the revolutionary state on the nature, number, and meanings of festivals. Loyo specifically examines the reaction to the Cárdenas government's effort to establish socialist education—a plan that ultimately failed because many Mexicans did not want it. Vaughan uses a district in Puebla to examine in detail the negotiatory process involved in developing meaningful festivals from 1900 to 1946. Several others consider this theme: Bantjes, in his examination of the Calles governorship in Sonora and its efforts to impose—with violence whenever necessary—the central government's plan of festivities, shows the resourceful and continuous resistance by people acting through their communities against whatever they did not want. Guy Thomson (Chapter 15) demonstrates how brass bands have "served as a locally controlled medium for absorbing external cultural and political influences." Donald Frischmann (Chapter 14), relying largely on his own field work, examines the development of local, rural theater groups that express dramatically the community's interests and concerns. Popular classes also enacted their own rituals and articulated alternative visions of social order, often in the relative safety of "off-stage" settings—working-class neighborhoods, slave quarters, or rural villages—where elites seldom ventured. Other forms of resistance ranged from subtle lapses in deference, evident only to the initiated, to open mockery of elites and of supposedly sacred rituals.[48]

In contesting official portrayals of the world, no weapon is more subversive than laughter. Inspired by the work of Mikhail Bakhtin, Dominick LaCapra argues that popular cultures employ farce, jokes, and comedy to tease out for public inspection the ambiguities in official presentations of the world.[49] On the northern frontier, Jesuit missionaries who returned after the Tarahumara rebellions of the mid-1600s reported that the Indians often threatened them with violence but on other occasions enjoyed themselves by mocking and slandering the fathers.[50] A satirical penny press during the Porfirian years amused the working class by lampooning, among others, the upper class, the bourgeoisie, the police, the clergy, and tram conductors, thereby helping to form and express a specifically working-class perspective of society.[51] The use of humor as a cunning commentary on contemporary affairs continues in Mexico. Since the end of the post-World War II miracle, a kind of "gallows humor" that turns the labyrinthine bureaucracy, the political fraud, and the devalued currency into jokes has become prevalent. National leaders and programs—such as education—also have become targets of this humor.[52] A joke currently popular in Parral, Chihuahua, pokes fun at the patriotic messages imparted on ritual occasions, in this instance Father Miguel Hidalgo y Costilla's call for independence. It seems that a popular municipal president, charged with presiding over celebrations of September 16, exhorted the gathered crowd to shout "Vivas" to the three heroes of Mexican independence: don Miguel, don Hidalgo, and don Costilla.

In the official philosophy of the ruling classes well-established lines divide all categories, and a monotone of thought and style usually prevails. In contrast, the unofficial and informal yank life out of its usual, legitimized rut. This festive laughter, characteristic of Carnival, tests and contests all aspects of society and culture. Laughter, for Bakhtin, stands as the sole "force of life" not co-opted by the official perspective. Carnivalesque celebrations not only invert the official culture (thus remaining within the framework of the dominant hierarchy) but also go beyond this to disrupt assumptions about

everyday life. Octavio Paz, offering a Mexican example, has praised
the fiesta, in which "the very notion of order disappears" and society
"ridicules its gods, its principles, and its laws: it denies its own self."[53]
Sergio Rivera Ayala, in this volume, argues that the lower classes,
through dance and song, probed the semiotic boundary between the
language of the official culture and that of the people. In doing so
they helped destroy the official framework of the late eighteenth
century.

This and other examples of the creative use of ritual highlight its
potential as a powerful means of resisting authority and envisioning
alternatives to the status quo: in France, new gender roles were pre-
figured in the rituals of charivari;[54] in England, radical men and women
workers turned mass demonstrations into carnivals of popular sovereignty. Through the symbols and icons of ritual, radicals laid claim
to public space and advocated a new role for women in the public
sphere.[55] By generating new visions of the future, such rituals have
been an important expression of the "social creativity of the inarticu-
late." Partly, this ritual form expresses the oral nature of popular culture in which knowledge and meaning are largely controlled by present
use and present need.[56] It also affirms E. P. Thompson's argument
that culture must be considered an arena of conflictual elements and
a pool of diverse resources in which "traffic passes between the literate and the oral, the superordinate and the subordinate, the village
and the metropolis."[57] Just as the state attempted to rule by creating
social identities, the popular classes actively constructed the social
order in their imaginations. Often such popular visions have been
interpreted as mere symbolic resistance against real power, but one
insight offered by the study of ritual is that the symbolic is no less
real than any other form of exercising and resisting authority.[58]

MEXICO AND THE HISTORIOGRAPHY OF RITUAL

The swamp of symbols and quagmire of anthropological and literary
theory may seem distant from the historical terra firma. Certainly,
Geertz, in particular, and those borrowing from cultural anthropology, in general, have not been without their critics. Ronald Walters
concluded more than ten years ago that Geertz is not particularly clear
on how to avoid "the potential for silliness" in undertaking thick description. Of greater concern to Walters and many others is that in
the focus on the symbolic, the social consequences to real people
seem to get lost, as does concern with concepts such as class, exploitation, and power. As he clearly explains, it is important to remember
that "symbolic drama can serve larger purposes of power, domina-

tion, exploitation, and resistance."[59] In a more recent work addressing the relationship of text and context, Gabrielle Spiegel warns that in concentrating on the meaning of texts rather than the experience of people, the social agency of historical actors is often forgotten. In her opinion it is necessary to realize that the "full meaning of social activity is not exhausted in its symbolic significance."[60]

With such criticism in mind, historians of diverse times and places have been exploring the place of ritual in the construction of the state. Even if, as Geertz recently has said, "the signs of power and the substance of it are not so easily pried apart," attempts to probe the relationship between the form and substance of state power have yielded promising results in societies as diverse as those of the Roman Empire and contemporary Ghana.[61] In Latin America, as well, historians have taken up the challenge of putting the state and questions of power and politics back into social history.[62] This volume contributes to this undertaking by focusing on the rituals of rule and the rituals through which Mexicans accepted, refashioned, ignored, or contested authority from the arrival of the Spaniards to the present.

One difficulty in trying to master the history of Latin America, as William B. Taylor points out, is that on the surface it seems so familiar.[63] Thus, an expectation exists that Latin American developments, no matter what the nation, will be the same throughout the region and analogous to either European or U.S. patterns. Superficial appearances aside, dramatic differences occur; and, despite continuities, subtle but telling distinctions characterize Mexican cultural manifestations. We want to make Mexico's uniqueness apparent and its connections obvious.

Consequently, we have introduced each of the following essays by identifying theoretical or historiographical parallels to the selection. We have noted European and U.S. studies, but at times we also mention other Latin American examples so that the reader can make comparisons and more fully appreciate Mexico's rich cultural history.

NOTES

1. Our title was inspired by Edward S. Herman and Norm Chomsky's *Manufacturing Consent: The Political Economy of Mass Media* (New York, 1988). Several themes in this volume resonate with their thesis.

2. Patricia Seed, "Taking Possession and Reading Texts: Establishing the Authority of Overseas Empires," *William and Mary Quarterly* 49, 3d ser. (April 1992): 183–209. Examining the symbolism of possession used by the English and the Spanish, Professor Seed establishes the distinction based on the construction of

dwellings and the statement of possession fortified with signs such as flags or crosses. The quotation comes from pp. 206–7.

3. For an original attempt to examine ritual as a means of understanding Aztec society before its encounter with the Spaniards, see Inga Clendinnen, *Aztecs: An Interpretation* (Cambridge, 1991), 236–63.

4. AAAM, vol. 1058; Festividades Diversas, Legajo 1, Expediente 2. Decree, August 29, 1822.

5. Paul Friedrich, "Revolutionary Politics and Communal Ritual," in *Political Anthropology* , ed. Marc J. Swartz, Victor W. Turner, and Arthur Tuden (Chicago, 1966), 191–220; and Imelda de León, coordinator, *Calendario de Fiestas Populares* (México, 1988), vii.

6. Clifford Geertz, *Negara: The Theater-State in Nineteenth-Century Bali* (Princeton, NJ, 1980), 128.

7. Inga Clendinnen, *Ambivalent Conquests: Mayan and Spaniard in Yucatán, 1517–1570* (Cambridge, 1987), 115.

8. See the methodological appendix in Rhys Isaac, *The Transformation of Virginia, 1740–1790* (Chapel Hill, NC, 1982), 323–57.

9. While those in power try to legitimate the social order by portraying it, often through ritual, in an idealized form, such a process inevitably provides subjects with the symbolic tools for fashioning a critique. See James C. Scott, *Weapons of the Weak: Everyday Forms of Peasant Resistance* (New Haven, CT, 1985), chap. 8, esp. 338. For a discussion of this development in the Mexican context and of Scott's hypothesis for Mexico, see Alan Knight, "Peculiarities of Mexican History: Mexico Compared to Latin America, 1821–1992," *JLAS* 29 (Quincentenary Supplement, 1992): 115, 124–25; and Knight's "Weapons and Arches in the Mexican Revolutionary Landscape," in *Everyday Forms of State Formation: Revolution and the Negotiation of Rule in Modern Mexico*, ed. Gilbert M. Joseph (Durham, NC, 1994).

10. Victor Turner, *The Forest of Symbols* (Ithaca, NY, 1967), 20–30.

11. Christel Lane, *The Rites of Rulers: Ritual in Industrial Society—The Soviet Case* (Cambridge, 1981), 25. Much of the material in this paragraph is based on Lane's discussion of symbol and ritual, 191–238.

12. David Cannadine, "The Context, Performance and Meaning of Ritual: The British Monarchy and the 'Invention of Tradition,' c. 1820–1977," in *The Invention of Tradition*, ed. Eric Hobsbawm and Terence Ranger (Cambridge, 1983), 157. See also an earlier article by Cannadine, "The Transformation of Civic Ritual in Modern Britain: The Colchester Oyster Feast," *PP* 94 (February 1982): 107–30.

13. David Brading, "Tridentine Catholicism and Enlightened Despotism in Bourbon Mexico," *JLAS* 15 (1983): 1–22; Juan Pedro Viqueira Albán, *¿Relajados o reprimidos? Diversiones públicas y vida social en la ciudad de México durante el Siglo de las Luces* (México, 1987). An English translation of this volume is forthcoming from Scholarly Resources.

14. Benedict Anderson, *Imagined Communities: Reflections on the Origin and Spread of Nationalism*, rev. ed. (London, 1991), 81, 169, 205–6. See also Jean Franco's discussion of imagined communities in Mexico in *Plotting Women: Gender and Representation in Mexico* (New York, 1989), 134.

15. Annick Lempérière, "D'un centenaire de l'indépendance à l'autre (1910–1921): L'invention de la mémoire culturelle du Mexique contemporain," unpublished presentation for the Université de Paris-I.

16. Ilene V. O'Malley, *The Myth of the Revolution: Hero Cults and the Institutionalization of the Mexican State, 1920–1940* (Westport, CT, 1986).

17. Enrique Plasencia de la Parra, *Independencia y nacionalismo a la luz del discurso conmemorativo (1825–1867)* (México, 1991), 137–38; Fernando Serrano Migallón, *El Grito de Independencia: Historia de una pasión nacional* (México, 1981).

18. For Argentina, see Henry Ph. Vogel, "Elements of Nation-Building in Argentina: Buenos Aires, 1810–1828" (Ph.D. diss., University of Florida, 1987).

19. David A. Brading, *The First America: The Spanish Monarchy, Creole Patriots, and the Liberal State, 1492–1867* (Cambridge, 1991), 634–37, 645.

20. Eric Hobsbawm, "Introduction: Invention Traditions," in *The Invention of Tradition,* ed. Hobsbawm and Ranger, 4–5, 9. See also "Mass-Producing Traditions: Europe, 1870–1914," ibid., 263–307.

21. See *Mi libro de Historia de México. Quinto Grado* (México, 1992).

22. Mona Ozouf, *Festivals and the French Revolution*, trans. Alan Sheridan (Cambridge, MA, 1988), 262–82.

23. Clifford Geertz, "Centers, Kings, and Charisma: Reflections on the Symbolics of Power," in *Rites of Power: Symbolism, Ritual, and Politics since the Middle Ages*, ed. Sean Wilentz (Philadelphia, 1985), 30.

24. Philip Corrigan and Derek Sayer, *The Great Arch: English State Formation as Cultural Revolution* (Oxford, 1985), 187–88, 191, 200. On the Mexican version of the Great Arch, see Knight, "Weapons and Arches," and "Peculiarities of Mexican History," 138–44.

25. Cited in Alan Knight, *The Mexican Revolution* (Cambridge, 1986), 2:497.

26. See Chapters 9 and 10 in this volume by Beezley and French, respectively; and Steven B. Bunker, "Making the Good Old Days: Invented Tradition and Civic Ritual in Northern Mexico, 1880–1910" (Honors thesis, University of British Columbia, 1992).

27. For an example of one corporation constructing social worlds through photography, see David E. Nye, *Image Worlds: Corporate Identities at General Electric, 1890–1930* (Cambridge, MA, 1985).

28. Maurice Agulhon, *The Republic in the Village: The People of the Var from the French Revolution to the Second Republic*, trans. Janet Lloyd (Cambridge, 1982), 91.

29. William B. Taylor, *Drinking, Homicide, and Rebellion in Colonial Mexican Villages* (Stanford, CA, 1979); and Nancy M. Farriss, *Maya Society under Spanish Colonial Rule: The Collective Enterprise of Survival* (Princeton, NJ, 1984).

30. See George M. Foster, *Tzintzuntzan: Mexican Peasants in a Changing World* (Boston, 1967). More recent studies include John M. Ingham, *Mary, Michael, and Lucifer: Folk Catholicism in Central Mexico* (Austin, TX, 1986); Guillermo de la Peña, *A Legacy of Promises: Agriculture, Politics and Ritual in the Morelos Highlands of Mexico* (Austin, TX, 1981), 197–224; and Judith Friedlander, *Being Indian in Hueyapan: A Study of Forced Identity in Contemporary Mexico* (New York, 1975).

31. Stanley Brandes, *Power and Persuasion: Fiestas and Social Control in Rural Mexico* (Philadelphia, 1988), 127–39. He lists other studies that draw the same conclusions on p. 139.

32. Ingham, *Mary, Michael, and Lucifer*, 180, 189.

33. On the conflict between Protestant and Catholic rituals in a single community, see Sheldon Annis, *God and Production in a Guatemalan Town* (Austin, 1987), 90–98. In San Antonio, Guatemala, ritual activity has become so expensive that the costs incurred in Catholic ceremonial life, representing a kind of cultural tax or investment in community, amount to about one quarter of a family's income. Although in this particular community, opinion divided on the relevance of such an expense; local Protestants, as one would expect, viewed it as both a "waste" and a "sin."

34. Michael Sonenscher, in *Work and Wages: Natural Law, Politics and the Eighteenth-Century French Trades* (Cambridge, 1989), 298, describes how ritual created a "complex world of ephemeral distinctions." See the extended discussion of *compagnonnages*, 295–327.

35. Marcello Carmagnani, "Un movimiento político indio: La 'rebelión' de Tehuantepec, 1660–1661," 17–35, and Eric Van Young, "Mentalities and Collectivities: A Comment," 337–53, esp. 340–41, in *Patterns of Contention in Mexican History*, ed. Jaime E. Rodríguez O. (Wilmington, DE, 1992).

36. Paul J. Vanderwood, *Disorder and Progress: Bandits, Police, and Mexican Development,* rev. and enlarged ed. (Wilmington, DE, 1992), 148–50.

37. Agulhon says that "politics furnished the occasion and the ends while folklore provided the means of expression." See *Republic in the Village*, 164, 254, 258–59. On charivari see Alan Greer, "From Folklore to Revolution: Charivaris and the Lower Canadian Rebellion of 1837," *Social History* 15, no. 1 (January 1990); and on Carnival see Emmanuel Le Roy Ladurie, *Carnival at Romans* (New York, 1979); and Natalie Zemon Davis, *Society and Culture in Early Modern France* (Stanford, CA, 1975).

38. David Garrioch, *Neighbourhood and Community in Paris, 1740–1790* (Cambridge, 1986), 196–201; Robert Muchembled, *Popular Culture and Elite Culture in France, 1400–1750* (Baton Rouge, LA, 1985), 122–48, 171–74, 212; Peter Burke, *Popular Culture in Early Modern Europe* (New York, 1978), 207–43; and Robert A. Schneider, *Public Life in Toulouse, 1463–1789: From Municipal Republic to Cosmopolitan City* (Ithaca, NY, 1989), 353.

39. Pilar Gonzalbo Aizpuru, "Las fiestas novohispanas: Espectáculo y ejemplo," *Mexican Studies/Estudios Mexicanos* 9, no. 1 (Winter 1993): 45. For more on the Bourbon campaign against folk Catholicism, especially popular religious processions, ceremonies, and "superstition," see Brading, *The First America*, esp. 494–500, 509, 549, 558.

40. Viqueira Albán, *¿Relajados o reprimidos?* 240. See his extensive discussion of attempts to wrest public space from the masses on pp. 133–69, 222–40.

41. See "Peaceful and Working People: The Inculcation of the Capitalist Work Ethic in a Mexican Mining District (Hidalgo District, Chihuahua, 1880–1920)" (Ph.D. diss., University of Texas, 1990). For an excellent introduction to the use of symbols in the struggle over public space, see James Epstein, "Understanding the Cap of Liberty: Symbolic Practice and Social Conflict in Early Nineteenth-Century England," *PP* 12, no. 2 (February 1989): 75–118; and Patrick Joyce, *Visions of the*

People: Industrial England and the Question of Class, 1848–1914 (Cambridge, 1991), 53–54.

42. See, for example, Knight, *Mexican Revolution* 1:245–46; and Carlos Martínez Assad, *El laboratorio de la revolución: El Tabasco garridista* (México, 1979).

43. Ellen M. Litwicki, "From *Patrón* to *Patria*: *Fiestas* and *Mexicano* Identity in Late Nineteenth-Century Tucson" (Paper presented at the 1992 annual meeting of the Organization of American Historians).

44. Susan G. Davis, *Parades and Power: Street Theatre in Nineteenth-Century Philadelphia* (Philadelphia, 1986), 151–53.

45. Mary Ryan, "The American Parade: Representations of the Nineteenth-Century Social Order," in *The New Cultural History*, ed. Lynn Hunt (Berkeley, CA, 1989), 149.

46. William H. Beezley, *Judas at the Jockey Club and Other Episodes of Porfirian Mexico* (Lincoln, NE, 1987), 89–124.

47. (Princeton, NJ, 1987), 6, 34, 38, 157–91, 225. On the neglected topic of cuisine and the ways it relates public and private celebrations, expresses nationalism, and articulates national programs in local and family circumstances, see the theoretical model provided by Arjun Appadurai, "How to Make a National Cuisine: Cookbooks in Contemporary India," *CSSH* 30, no. 1 (January 1988): 3–24; and the praxis with recipes offered by Patricia Quintana with Carol Harrelson, in *Mexico's Feast of Life* (Tulsa, OK, 1989). See also Jeffrey M. Pilcher, "¡Vivan Tamales! The Creation of a Mexican National Cuisine" (Ph.D. diss., Texas Christian University, 1993).

48. James C. Scott, *Domination and the Arts of Resistance: Hidden Transcripts* (New Haven, CT, 1990); E. P. Thompson, "Patrician Society, Plebeian Culture," *Journal of Social History* 7, no. 4 (Summer 1974): 382–405. The practice of mockery as a form of resistance to outsiders, especially authorities, receives careful examination on an Apache reservation in Keith Basso, *Portraits of "The Whiteman": Linguistic Play and Cultural Symbols among the Western Apache* (Cambridge, 1979).

49. See "Bakhtin, Marxism, and the Carnivalesque" in *Rethinking Intellectual History: Texts, Contexts, Language*, by Dominick LaCapra (Ithaca, NY, 1983), esp. 301–6. For a discussion of LaCapra's influence see Lloyd S. Kramer, "Literature, Criticism, and Historical Imagination: The Literary Challenge of Hayden White and Dominick LaCapra," in Hunt, ed. *New Cultural History*, 97–128.

50. AGN, Historia 19, fol. 257v–282; and the report of May 28, 1676, from the Archivum Romanum Societatis Iesu, Mexicana, published in *Documentos para la historia de México*, 4th ser., 3: 272–94. We thank Susan Deeds for calling our attention to this information. Paul Stoller provides a stimulating examination of the way in which subject peoples use traditional cultural practices and mimicry to subvert colonial authorities in "Horrific Comedy: Cultural Resistance and the Hauka Movement in Niger," *Ethos* 12, no. 2 (Summer 1984): 165–88.

51. María Elena Díaz, "The Satiric Penny Press for Workers in Mexico, 1900–1910: A Case Study in the Politicisation of Popular Culture," *JLAS* 22, no. 3 (October 1990): 497–525. This article also appears in John A. Britton, ed., *Molding the Hearts and Minds: Education, Communications, and Social Change in Latin America* (Wilmington, DE, 1994).

52. William H. Beezley, "Mexican Political Humor," *Journal of Latin American Lore* 11, no. 2 (1985): 195–223.

53. Octavio Paz, *The Labyrinth of Solitude*, trans. Lysander Kemp (New York, 1985), 51.

54. Davis, *Society and Culture*, 124–51.

55. Epstein, "Understanding the Cap of Liberty," 100–107.

56. Joyce, *Visions of the People*, 171, 225.

57. "Introduction: Custom and Culture," in *Customs in Common*, ed. E. P. Thompson (London, 1991), 6. See also his discussion of the theatrical nature of law and politics in "The Patricians and the Plebs," ibid., 46.

58. For an early work employing the symbolic and real dichotomy in Mexico, see Ruth Behar, "Sex and Sin, Witchcraft and the Devil in Late-Colonial Mexico," *American Ethnologist* 14, no. 1 (February 1987): 34–54.

59. Ronald G. Walters, "Signs of the Times: Clifford Geertz and Historians," *Social Research* 47, no. 4 (Autumn 1980): 544, 553. Others making this point include Suzanne Desan in "Crowds, Community, and Ritual in the Work of E. P. Thompson and Natalie Davis," 68; and Aletta Biersack, "Local Knowledge, Local History: Geertz and Beyond," in Hunt, ed., *New Cultural History*, 72–96.

60. Gabrielle Spiegel, "History, Historicism, and the Social Logic of the Text in the Middle Ages," *Speculum* 65, no. 1 (January 1990): 85.

61. Clifford Geertz, "History and Anthropology," *New Literary History* 21 (1989–90): 331. See also Sean Wilentz, ed., *Rites of Power: Symbolism, Ritual, and Politics Since the Middle Ages* (Philadelphia, 1985); and David Cannadine and Simon Price, *Rituals of Royalty: Power and Ceremonial in Traditional Societies* (Cambridge, 1987).

62. For a recent example see Richard Graham, *Patronage and Politics in Nineteenth-Century Brazil* (Stanford, CA, 1990).

63. William B. Taylor, "Between Global Process and Local Knowledge: An Inquiry into Early Latin American Society History, 1500–1900," in *Reliving the Past: The Worlds of Social History*, ed. Olivier Zunz (Chapel Hill, NC, 1985), 115.

1

Giants and Gypsies: Corpus Christi in Colonial Mexico City

Linda A. Curcio-Nagy
University of Nevada

The author, in her Ph.D. dissertation at Tulane University, examines five colonial celebrations: the inaugural entrance of the viceroy into Mexico City; devotions to the Virgin of Remedios; the celebration of San Hipólito; the *jura del rey*, or public oath of allegiance to commemorate a monarch's ascension; and the devotion of Corpus Christi. She analyzes only the latter celebration in the following essay. She draws on the methodological and theoretical approach used to examine seventeenth-century Spanish spectacles by José Antonio Maraval in *The Culture of the Baroque*, who discusses spectacle as one tool of hegemonic control and institutional legitimization; the interpretations of the anthropologists Edmund Leach, who stresses the fiesta's role in social reinforcement, and Victor Turner, who emphasizes its role in social integration; and the thesis presented by Paul Veyne of the relationship between governments and public festivals as a symbolic social contract.*

" THE GREATEST SINGLE THING that the city can boast about is the frequency of its religious devotion to the Sacraments, its ostentation of so many festivals, and the generosity of spirit of all its inhabitants."[1] Thus Agustín de Ventancurt described Mexico City in 1698. Although some festival traditions were instituted in the early sixteenth century, they reached full maturity a century later, when, even by conservative estimates, Mexico City played host each year to at least ninety festivals, all of European origin.[2] Every guild, confraternity, religious order, parish, and convent, in varying degrees of

This research was made possible by a Fulbright-Hays doctoral dissertation research grant.

*The Spanish phrases translated in this article can be found in the footnotes of the author's dissertation, entitled "Saints, Sovereignty and Spectacle in Colonial Mexico."

sumptuousness and public display, celebrated its specific patron saint. The university organized its festivities surrounding graduation and the Immaculate Conception of the Virgin Mary. In addition, there were larger citywide fiestas such as Easter, Carnival, All Saints' Day, San Hipólito, and Corpus Christi, and the festivities dedicated to the Virgin of Remedios. Civil authorities sponsored specific festivals— the entrance of a new viceroy, or archbishop, the oath of allegiance to a new monarch, and funeral ceremonies for a deceased king, vice- roy, or archbishop.

During this period of multitudinous celebrations, life in the city was characterized by economic and social dislocation and haunted by the specter of rebellion. Food shortages, floods, and other natural disasters, epidemics, and economic disarray plagued the city. The increasing heterogeneity of society created concern. As early as 1580, Viceroy Martín Enríquez de Almanza, in the instructions to his suc- cessor, warned of potential instability due to the growing number of *castas* (individuals of mixed Spanish, African, and Native American descent).[3] In fact, significant uprisings took place in 1611, 1612, 1624, 1665, 1692, and 1696. Such uneasiness prevailed in the city that, in 1612, when some escaped pigs ran through the streets late one evening the inhabitants, stricken with panic, believed that mulatto rebels in- tent on toppling the government had rioted.[4] In the revolt of 1692 a large group of Native Americans and *castas* stormed the main plaza, forcing the viceroy and Spanish colonists to fear for their lives.

This perception of instability on the part of the ruling elite and associated institutions brought about political policy designed to make the inhabitants into *doctos*, or educated persons in the Spanish sense of civilized and European. Festivals were an essential component of this program. Diverse ethnic groups were captivated, entertained, and acculturated by state and church in order to combat potential dissi- dence and to reaffirm institutional legitimacy in a time of social change.[5]

The elite recognized the festival's potential acculturative func- tions as early as 1525. To celebrate the dedication of the first church in Mexico City, the Franciscan friars invited Native Americans from the city and surrounding area to a festival featuring triumphal arches, music, and dancing. Agustín de Ventancurt described the use of festi- vals in the evangelization process, saying that witnessing the way "Christians celebrated their festivals, many [natives] converted to our faith; from then on they had the motivation for the celebration of the saints with the trappings and sumptuousness that characterizes these celebrations today."[6] Certainly, clergy specifically organized festi- vals to celebrate religious devotion and reinforce the evangelization process. Festivals also maintained traditions brought from Spain, demonstrated the grandeur and power of the monarchy (through oaths of allegiance to the king and viceroy entrance ceremonies), and, finally, provided entertainment. Nonetheless, these cultural events were organized and directed toward the multitude of anonymous yet potentially disruptive individuals (that is, Native Americans and *castas*) that inhabited the city and environs. The message implicit in all these festivals encouraged integration within the confines of the Spanish system; the statement was presented in the celebration of Corpus Christi.

CORPUS CHRISTI AND COLONIAL
MEXICAN SOCIETY

Corpus Christi, or the celebration of the *Santísimo Sacramento* (Holy Eucharist), was the most significant festival in Mexico City and was recognized as such throughout Spain. The feast had first appeared in the Catholic liturgical calendar during the pontificate of Urban IV in 1264, although some type of eucharistic devotion existed prior to the thirteenth century. The propagation of this devotion came under John XXII in 1316, but not until the first quarter of the fourteenth century did the festival spread throughout Castile and Aragon, where it reached its peak during the seventeenth century.[7]

It was the largest annual festival to take place in the viceregal capital, second only, in cost and luxuriousness, to the occasional ceremonies that commemorated the entrance of a new viceroy or the *jura del rey* (oath of allegiance to a new king). By 1618 the cost of the festival of Corpus amounted to 21 percent of the disposable income of the city fathers.[8] In addition to size and cost, Corpus Christi was unique because all members of society patronized and participated in the festival. Perhaps most important, all ethnicities were represented as well. Although the festival's religious significance celebrated the transubstantiation of Christ, it also paid a proud tribute to Mexico City and its inhabitants.

Corpus Christi served as a mirror of the society. Location in the procession reinforced group and ethnic identification and the hierarchical nature of viceregal society. The compartmentalized nature of the procession promoted acceptance and reaffirmed a social system devised by the ruling elite. Altogether, it symbolically reinforced the status quo. At the same time, the procession as an entity and the festive atmosphere that pervaded it joined the city's disparate and often antagonistic groups. It defined and limited the public space of the festival; and, within this space, everyday worries and responsibilities were temporarily and symbolically suspended, further

emphasizing the extraordinary nature of the festival. This unique festive space encouraged integration and identification with a larger community, beyond one's ethnicity, social status, guild, confraternity, or
ecclesiastical affiliation, and could thereby stir a sense of civic pride
in Mexico City.[9]

Colonial officials grasped the significance of Corpus. By the late
sixteenth century the cabildo, rather than ecclesiastical officials, sponsored, organized, and funded the festival, actively encouraging and,
in some cases, mandating innovation, ostentation, and participation.
These city officials approached Corpus Christi with a particular sense
of duty; they had a responsibility not only to provide and maintain
the quality of this festival but also to improve it each year. Even during times of economic hardship, Corpus as the paramount festival
forced officials to engage in tricky financial maneuvers in order to
maintain it. Politically speaking, Corpus allowed the government to
entertain the populace as a reward for submission, for acceptance of
Spanish rule. The government fulfilled a symbolic social contract:
by providing and participating in a festival to encourage integration,
it hoped, in return, to make itself admired and obeyed.[10]

In the case of Corpus Christi, viceregal and municipal officials
went one step further than in other celebrations. By joining the procession they participated with the rest of the people, all subservient
and humble before the higher moral authority that the Host symbolized. Separate groups came together to form a larger collective; and,
for a moment, the barriers that defined the social hierarchy symbolically weakened. The government's sponsorship of this festival,
complete with symbolic humbling, furthered legitimized its rule.
How noteworthy, in this context, that in 1692—one day after the
revolt that burned down the viceregal palace—the *octava* Corpus
Christi procession took place as usual, solemnly accompanied by the
viceroy.[11]

GIANTS AND GYPSIES

Corpus festivities appear to have taken place as early as 1526 in the
viceregal capital, and by 1539 they had become a permanent feature
of the religious calendar of the city.[12] The celebration grew steadily
in size, cost, and sumptuousness, reaching its peak in the late seventeenth and early eighteenth centuries, when eighty-five confraternities participated in a procession that extended 1,531 *varas* (about
three fourths of a mile, or 1,286 meters), a procession so long that
the end of the line had yet to leave the cathedral even as the beginning returned.[13]

The procession departed, after early morning Mass, from the cathedral's side door down the nearby streets of Mexico City and reentered through the front door of the cathedral.[14] The citizens had cleaned the streets, spread sand, and scattered flowers on the path in preparation for the procession. Native Americans constructed a large thatch canopy that they then erected to cover the center of the street. Buildings along the processional route were richly adorned with tapestries and silk or velvet cloth covered with painted images or scenes. For example, in 1697 the silversmiths' guild decorated its street with tapestries that recounted the conquest of Mexico "exactly as things were in the city then, with the dress that the Indians wore back then."[15]

In addition to this decoration, some confraternities and guilds built special *posas*, or altars. For Corpus in 1683 they erected ten such altars, but, unfortunately, no specific descriptions exist.[16] Generally they were sumptuous constructions of silver decorated with large votive candles. Mirrors served as backdrops enhancing the Host when it was placed on the altar. Participants lined the steps to the *posas* with flowers. The procession stopped at each of these altars for the singing of special *cánticos eclesiásticos* (hymns).[17]

The procession also stopped at the entrance to the convent of Santa Clara, located on what today is Tacuba Street. At the moment the *custodia* (the elaborate gold or silver monstrance that housed and displayed the Eucharist) reached the entrance to their convent, the nuns tossed thousands of incense-soaked bits of paper into the crowd in honor of the Host.[18]

An unusual assortment of *gigantes*, *cabezudos*, *diablillos*, and a *tarasca* led the procession. The *gigantes* (giants), made of wood, paper, metal, fur, wigs, and cloth in the shape of huge individuals, measured at least eight *varas* (five meters) in height. They were apparently rather complicated in design and in many cases made of fine cloth, such as silk, and adorned with silver or gold trim. Although detailed descriptions of the *gigantes* are unavailable, it appears that in some years they embodied a particular theme; for example, in 1722 they represented the four parts of the world. To the delight of spectators, the giants were brought to life by people inside them.[19] In Mexico City, Africans "walked" the *gigantes* and occasionally the cabildo commissioned specially decorated *carros* (carts or floats) to carry them in the procession.[20]

Cabezudos, or big heads, referred to individuals in costume who wore huge heads, or *cabezas*, made of wood and paper. In Spain they traditionally accompanied the giants and chased after small children who taunted them as part of the procession.[21] *Diablillos* (little devils), individuals in devil costumes, sometimes accompanied the procession. In 1636, for example, the cabildo commissioned ten devil costumes and masks from one Cristobal Francisco.[22]

Although the focal point of Corpus Christi was the *Santísimo Sacramento* carried in the *custodia*, few eyes could have failed to notice the *tarasca*. This large dragon was made of painted wood and usually placed on a cart so that it could be wheeled at the head of the procession. Traditionally, the dragon symbolized "sin conquered by the Holy Spirit," and during the seventeenth century in Spain it had seven heads (symbolizing the seven deadly sins). In New Spain the *tarasca* dazzled the crowd with just one head, except in 1701 when Antonio de Robles recounted the appearance of a *tarasca* with seven heads.[23] The *tarasca* and *gigantes* must have been crowd pleasers, as it became customary for vendors to sell *tarasquitas* (little dragons) and *gigantitos* (little giants) made of paper before and during the procession.[24]

Along with the dragon, giants, devils, and big heads came costumed dancers. The three main ethnic groups of the city—Native Americans, mulattoes, and Spaniards—always danced in these performances. Others occasionally joining the list included gypsies, turks, villains, pirates, and Portuguese. It appears that particularly during the sixteenth century the dancers performed on elaborately decorated *carros* that were stored for reuse the following year. The *carros* and the dances were not merely limited to the processional route; performances also took place inside the cathedral.[25]

Behind this lively group in the procession came the guilds, solemnly carrying their patron saints adorned with flowers. One witness in 1697 reported that the guilds presented one hundred statues during Corpus.[26] Each guild carried different colored candles as well as their respective banners, and every member wore a tunic and carried a large votive candle in one hand with a bouquet of flowers and a flyswatter in the other.[27]

The confraternities with their patron saints came next, followed by the religious orders, the secular clergy, the Inquisitors, the parishes—each carrying a large cross—and the "angels," or children from the school of San Juan de Letrán who, with their candles, illuminated the *custodia* behind them. The Host was carried by a prelate or housed in the *custodia*, which was always under a *palio* (sumptuous silk canopy trimmed in gold or silver). After the *Santísimo Sacramento* marched the viceroy, the members of the *audiencia*, municipal officials, university students and professors, and all other royal officials.

Theatrical performances (*comedias*) with a biblical theme were always presented as part of the festival on Corpus day and its *octava*. Large *tablados*, or bleachers with canopies for shade, were constructed for prominent royal, municipal, and ecclesiastical officials so that they might better view the performances.[28] The general public sat on the ground without benefit of shade. On some occasions, as in 1653, the Virgin of Remedios "attended" the *comedias* seated beside the *Santísimo Sacramento*. Traditionally, plays were performed in the cemetery of the cathedral during the afternoon. In 1660, though, the location was changed to the portals of the *audiencia* that faced the central square, no doubt to accommodate the increasing number of spectators. Although no evidence exists to suggest that it was a tradition, in 1660 officials distributed candy to the audience after the play.[29]

Diversion for the general public did not end with the procession or the plays but continued well into the night with a fireworks display. In addition, various games added to the festive atmosphere in the capital, so much so that individuals purchased special licenses in order to offer games specifically during fiesta times.[30] Finally, Corpus would not have been complete without the *volteo teológico de campanas* (theological volley of bells).[31] The bells of Mexico City's many churches were rung in synchronization. Whether or not the music inspired the populace, as it was designed to do, it assuredly caught their attention.

CORPUS CHRISTI UNDER THE HAPSBURGS

The Viceroys

Faced with an increasingly heterogeneous population, Hapsburg officials recognized the social significance and potential usefulness of the festival of Corpus Christi as a mechanism to encourage integration. Several viceroys, although not specifically charged with promoting the Corpus festival, directly aided and enhanced the celebration of the *Santísimo Sacramento*, thereby facilitating its rise to the premier festival in the viceregal capital. They intervened directly to increase its sumptuousness and popular participation in an effort to influence and persuade the inhabitants to accept colonial rule. Two viceroys stand out for their contributions—Luis de Velasco, the Marquis of Salinas, and Gaspar de Zúñiga y Acevedo, the Count of Monterrey.

Viceroy Velasco, during his first tenure (1590–1595), specifically added the theatrical performance presented on the *octava* of Corpus and the dance of the Spaniards. Before this time, it appears that Native American dance groups made up the majority of musical and dance performances. With regard to the indigenous population he ordered that Indians from nearby villages play their harps and dance each day of Corpus. All Indian musicians from as far away as Huejotzingo were to perform in the city for the festival. The practice of paying Native American musicians from outside as well as those nearby the city appears to have continued into the seventeenth century. During Corpus in 1608, for example, the Indians from Malinalco and Acolmán were paid five hundred pesos to play. In addition, Velasco mandated that all guilds build *ynvenciones* (a term that broadly referred to all the creations—monsters, giants, masked and costumed revelers, and others) for the procession. This decree seemed difficult to accomplish because as early as 1585 the guilds petitioned the *audiencia* for a financial reprieve from some of the expenditures of Corpus.[32]

The Count of Monterrey fostered the expansion of Corpus Christi by ordering the cabildo to "place the pomp and ceremony of other festivals in this one" and by demanding improved dramatic performances, costumes, and better-dressed giants and *cabezudos*. Native American performers were instructed to improve their dances, and more indigenous musicians were hired. In addition, he added *juegos de cañas* (mock jousts) and three days of bullfights. He settled disputes between city fathers and troupe directors regarding cost and drama selection. Cabildo records indicate that he was the first viceroy to donate money specifically for Corpus, after the city government had spent all its funds on the funeral ceremonies of Philip II in 1599, and in 1602 he lent the council money, again specifically for the festival.[33]

During the early seventeenth-century economic decline in cabildo revenues, revealed in the municipal accounts, only the willingness of several viceroys to lend royal funds to the city government permitted Corpus to survive and grow. The Marquis of Montesclaros (1603–1607) and the Marquis of Guadalcázar (1612–1621) both made loans to the cabildo on a regular basis to maintain the quality of the festival. The Marquis of Villena (1640–1642), like his predecessor the Count of Monterrey, actively participated in the decisions regarding Corpus. In 1641 his suggestions to improve the festival called for a cloth or linen canopy to be constructed for the processional route and for all the guilds to erect altars. Only the first request appears to have been successfully implemented.[34]

Viceroys demonstrated the importance of Corpus not only by their continued financial and moral support but also by their efforts to change certain Corpus traditions even if it created a scandal. The archival records demonstrate that questions regarding honor and protocol caused concern at the viceregal court; the Corpus Christi festival did not escape disputes because the procession placed the entire city on display before a multitude of expectant onlookers. Proximity to the *Santísimo Sacramento*, the recognized place of prestige, had long been a point of contention among the guilds and confraternities, and royal officials were not immune from this rivalry.

The Count of Alba de Liste (1650–1653) grasped the symbolic importance of closeness to the Eucharist and created a major public disturbance by stopping the procession midmarch in order to implement his will. In 1651 he demanded that his pages replace the church officials in the processional line. Traditionally, the ecclesiastical cabildo followed directly behind the *custodia*, thereby serving as the entourage for the Host. Perhaps the viceroy wanted to further cement, in the minds of the public, the relationship between the Eucharist and the ruling civil authorities. The civil position was metaphorically strengthened at the expense of the clergy and further legitimized by its proximity to the higher moral authority that the Eucharist represented.

In the ensuing scandal the viceroy abandoned the procession in midstride and ordered the guilds and confraternities to stop where they were. He placed the *custodia*, which had not yet left the cathedral, under guard. When the clergy attempted to resume the procession in violation of viceregal orders a small brawl broke out in which the *custodia* was almost knocked over, and the clergy abandoned the procession. The crowd then turned unruly. Informed of the commotion at the cathedral, the viceroy ordered the procession to continue without any of the city's clergy. This attempt to alter the procession encountered strong resistance from the ecclesiastical members directly involved; they immediately fired off a series of protests to Spain.

The clergy's petitions to the king emphasized the position of the church regarding what in essence was a religious celebration. Their arguments relied on both the religious nature and tradition of the festival. The Count of Alba de Liste, for his part, claimed his role as supreme authority in New Spain and viceregal prerogative. In short, given the nature of the festival and the importance of protocol, he felt that his entourage should be closest to the Eucharist. Royal mandate reinforced the viceroy's position, thus linking the symbolic relationship between the Host and the civil and royal authority in the procession at the expense of the ecclesiastical cabildo.[35]

The Count of Baños in 1662 caused an equally scandalous disturbance, though with a different outcome. He wanted the processional route changed because his ill wife did not wish to leave the palace to view the procession as was the custom. The episcopal see was vacant and therefore the church authorities appealed to the bishop of Puebla, who issued an edict stating that the Corpus procession should follow the traditional route. The viceroy countered the edict, and the procession, escorted by the military garrison, passed directly in front of the palace. Again the clergy were conspicuous by their absence, and again the spectators were unnerved. Undoubtedly, the armed guard altered the nature of the festival. In this case the symbolic consequences were detrimental to the image of the government, and officials in Spain recognized that viceregal authority had been tarnished rather than strengthened; the king reprimanded the viceroy and penalized him twelve thousand pesos for his intervention in the festival.[36]

The Cabildo

Although several viceroys demonstrated the considerable symbolic weight of the Corpus, the cabildo's actions illustrated even better the festival's importance to the civil authorities. The cabildo, after all, was directly responsible for the success or failure of Corpus as an agent of social integration. City officials actively promoted and regulated the festival from as early as 1529.[37] They held the canopy above the Eucharist, a privilege they fought to maintain against *audiencia* encroachment. This dispute revolved around whether the cabildo or the *audiencia* had the authority to choose the individuals who would carry the poles (*varas*) that held up the *palio*. The issue first erupted in 1533 when the municipal authorities refused to walk in the procession until the king ruled on the matter. Eventually, the Crown declared that the president of the *audiencia* (the viceroy) had the authority to name who would carry the *varas*. Over time the *palio* grew in size in order to accommodate more appointees. Originally it had less than twelve *varas*, but by 1675 there were fifty. No doubt the cabildo, charged with commissioning the *palio*, managed to secure its place by enlarging the canopy with more supporting poles.[38]

The city government stored the guild flags, the *gigantes*, and the *carros* in its offices.[39] By 1540 the municipal authorities officially chose special deputies to organize Corpus, and by 1628 the cabildo elected those deputies at the beginning of the year so they would have sufficient time to make all the necessary festival preparations.[40] The cabildo defined its relationship to Corpus by a sense of duty, a special obligation to provide entertainment. In 1617, speaking of festivals in general, corregidor Alonso de Tello said that celebrations were important for making the public happy. He added that neglecting them put the "public in a bad mood" and "left their spirits forlorn."[41] Municipal authorities found it essential to provide the people with entertainment to keep them satisfied with the government and to maintain order and stability. The cabildo not only appeared to recognize the social and political value of festivals in general but also formed a particular bond with Corpus Christi.

Councilmen linked the identity of the city to the ostentation, the innovation, the grandeur of Corpus. In 1600 the city fathers criticized the poor quantity and quality in the performances and costuming of the previous year's festival. Treasurer Juan Luis Ribera declared that the city had fallen short, adding that such a poor celebration was "inexcusable" in a "noble city like ours." Councilman Gaspar de Valdez agreed—the city as viceregal capital had to serve as an "inspiration and example" for others.[42]

The city's growing identification with Corpus is further illustrated by its continued financial support of the festival from the early sixteenth century to the midseventeenth century, in some cases at the expense of a sound budget. Although financial records for Corpus Christi do not exist for the early years (1520s–1560s), cabildo documents show that city officials organized the procession, set the order in the line, and maintained it with city policemen. At that time the guilds apparently bore the cost of the *ynvenciones* and *carros*. By 1564 theatrical performances were included in the festival and the city assumed responsibility for the grandstands. The absence of payment vouchers for the actors in the municipal records suggests that this too was the responsibility of guild members. The cabildo did, however, begin a sixteenth-century tradition of offering a *joya* (prize) to the best *ynvención*.[43]

The festival apparently began to expand in the 1580s, and the city fathers took on more Corpus responsibilities. The cabildo and the *oficios* now shared equally the financial burden of the festival. The city's share for the theatrical performances in 1585 amounted to 750 pesos.[44] From 1590 to 1600, Corpus reached a financial peak for the sixteenth century, averaging over 2,000 pesos per year. During this period the cabildo's responsibilities included cleaning and preparing the streets, adorning homes with tapestries, commissioning the thatch canopy, constructing the *tablados* and the *carros*, preparing the dinner served after the procession, installing lighting and fireworks, procuring two or three theatrical performances, commissioning at least four different types of dances (one was always the *gitanas*, or gypsies), and creating the *gigantes* and other similar *ynvenciones*. Apparently only the altars remained the creative and financial contribution of the guilds and confraternities.

The seventeenth century brought financial woe to the city, and the cabildo struggled to provide necessary services. In addition it strove to maintain Corpus at its previous peak as its perceived obligation to the citizenry. At no time did the municipal government cancel the festival, not even after the 1629 flood, when all the *gigantes* and *ynvenciones* were destroyed. During this time of economic difficulty and social unrest (there were demonstrations in 1611, 1612, and 1624), Corpus, the festival that encouraged integration and acted symbolically as a social equalizer, became even more essential to the city council. During this period councilmen expanded its funding to thirty-five hundred pesos (a fifteen hundred-peso increase from the sixteenth-century peak)—or 21 percent of the city's disposable income.[45]

From 1600 to 1643 the city borrowed money exclusively for the Corpus Christi festival on thirteen separate occasions. The cabildo borrowed an average of 2,580 pesos from the *sisa de vino* (royal wine-tax fund, otherwise designated for public works). In 1605 the city continued to request permission to borrow funds for Corpus even though it owed the treasury 1,119,631 pesos and was being investigated by a royal commission led by Diego Pardo Mendoza, who, after reviewing accounts from 1597 to 1603, officially recommended that the city relinquish authority over the *sisa*. Ten years later, in 1615, officials armed with a decree demanded that the city repay some 140,935 pesos to the royal coffers over a ten-year period. For the first and only time during the seventeenth century the amount spent on Corpus dropped—to a paltry 614 pesos. Ever aware of its duty the cabildo recouped the following year thanks to a two thousand-peso gift from the viceroy, the Marquis of Guadalcázar. (Even with the gift, the municipal government still went over budget.) The *regidores* (council members) formally complimented the festival deputies for the excellent Corpus that year. In 1621 the *audiencia* was less generous. Apparently during one of the dramatic performances the *tablados* collapsed, and the *regidores* quickly pointed out that this was due to pecuniary deficit; the following year more funding was allotted. In 1624 city officials once again ran into problems with the royal government regarding Corpus Christi: when the cabildo planned to use the annual four thousand-peso payment to the royal coffers to fund the festival, royal officials placed a freeze on all Corpus spending. After some discussion and a promise to pay the four thousand pesos in December, the funds were released.[46]

When the cabildo did not or could not borrow money for Corpus, it found other ways to secure funding for the celebration. In 1605, 1608, and 1609 it rented the places on the *tablados*, and in 1609, 1610, and 1611 the city collected rent from its shopkeeper tenants one year in advance. The municipal authorities also shifted money destined for other projects to Corpus; in 1610, for example, they funded Corpus by utilizing the monies for the altar of San Gregorio.

Despite economic hardship, costly dramatic performances remained an essential element of Corpus through several strategies. The cabildo no longer hired two companies to give separate performances but rather commissioned one troupe to perform two plays, thus saving several hundred pesos. In addition, circumstances forced the theater companies to perform for less remuneration if they wished to perform at all, since their trade depended upon obtaining a permit. And, in the unusual case of 1608, Viceroy Luis de Velasco ordered the dramatic players to perform free of charge during the Corpus festival, although the cabildo did manage to produce five hundred pesos to cover the cost of costumes and props.[47]

Through borrowing and other budgetary measures the city maintained the seventeenth-century Corpus Christi at a level of sumptuousness roughly equal to that of the late sixteenth century. Whenever councilmen perceived a decline in the quality of the festival they attempted to rectify it, as they did in 1603, 1605, 1616, 1623, and 1638. The essential ingredients of the festival remained intact from the sixteenth through the seventeenth century. In the review of the accounts of 1618 the councilmen listed what they believed were the most important elements of Corpus—theatrical performances, dances, fireworks, giants and other creations, candles, and patronage of the children of San Juan de Letrán. Almost one thousand additional pesos were for other items, which no doubt included tapestries and flowers, the *tablados*, and the postprocessional meal. In only one item do the two centuries differ—the *carros*. The last entry in the council records regarding the *carros* occurred in 1601.[48] After that date no mention of them appears within the city budget discussions. Perhaps the menagerie of giants, dancers, and *cabezudos* that had led the procession now walked the entire route. Or perhaps (although unlikely) the guilds themselves resumed the tradition of building the *carros*. In difficult economic times it would have been quite a task to maintain the tradition of providing the *posas* as well as the elaborately decorated *carros*. Since seventeenth-century descriptions of the festival do not mention them, the missing *carros* probably constituted the cabildo's one acquiescence to financial necessity and thus represent a unique element of the sixteenth-century Corpus celebration.

Nonetheless, during this critical first half of the seventeenth century the dedication and importance of Corpus remains evident. No other festival received such attention and such an extraordinary proportion of the city income, except for the occasional entrance of a new viceroy or the *jura del rey*. The cabildo's intrinsic understanding of the significance of Corpus is further elucidated by a brief account of its attitude toward the other annual festive duty, the celebration of

San Hipólito and the raising of the royal flag. As early as 1587 the *regidores* chosen to host the festival and carry the flag attempted to excuse themselves based on prior personal and official commitments or poor health. In 1624 a councilman traveling to Spain narrowly escaped his duty when his fellow *regidores* sent a team of riders and canoes to catch his ship. In some instances money set aside for this festival was spent on Corpus, as was the case in what should have been the one hundredth anniversary of the festival of San Hipólito in 1621. The city fathers even recommended that the festival be offered on alternate years; as early as 1591, at the height of the Corpus festival (with a cost of 6,656 pesos), the cabildo spent only 286 pesos on the *alza del pendón* (raising of the royal banner).[49]

By midseventeenth century the economy and, consequently, the city budget improved. By the end of the seventeenth and the beginning of the eighteenth centuries Corpus reached another peak in sumptuousness. The *regidores* produced a festival even more elaborate than that of the previous century. The upswing in Corpus celebrations began as early as 1660, when the Duke of Albuquerque, overwhelmed by the sumptuousness of the festivals in Mexico City, ordered a study that reported eighty thousand pesos had been spent for the candles used in celebrations for one year.[50] That same year three distinct *comedias* (which may have required the cost of an additional theater troupe) formed part of the festival, a marked change from the two of previous years.[51] By 1683, Antonio de Robles observed that the festival proceeded with more pomp than usual, including ten altars—an amazing number considering the probable cost—as the highlight. In 1701 he described a *tarasca* with seven heads and more spectacular giants in the procession, all entailing considerably more cost than those of the first half of the century.[52] At the end of the century Corpus included a lively group of eight giants, masked and costumed figures and monsters (perhaps a reference to the *tarasca*), all reflecting a substantial expense to the city fathers.[53]

Wealthy individuals patronized the celebration during the first third of the eighteenth century. The festival in 1728 was a large affair that included eighty-five confraternities and a processional canopy that extended 1,531 *varas* (1,286 meters, or about three quarters of a mile). That same year Don Lorenzo Osorio paid twenty thousand pesos to have matinal Mass sung each day. The following year an ornate heater, unveiled in the cathedral during the festival and costing twenty-five hundred pesos, was donated by the four priests of the *sagrario* (sanctuary). In 1730 two glamorous lamps of crystal and silver, valued at fifteen hundred pesos, made their Corpus debut.[54] Whether these sumptuous personal displays of devotion indicated increasing ostentation in the larger festival remains unclear.

Native American Participation

From their arrival in Mexico ecclesiastical and civil officials sought to incorporate Native Americans into Corpus Christi. Two representatives of the ecclesiastical cabildo, for example, visited the municipal officials in 1564 specifically to discuss Corpus Christi. During this meeting they commented on the need to celebrate Corpus with all the requisite pomp, emphasizing the need for both Spanish and Native American guilds to participate with "their pennants, insignias, and honest and good creations [for the procession] as is the custom." They expressed concern that the indigenous population would not grasp the significance of their participation and of all the *ynvenciones* in the procession. They decided that eight days before Corpus all creations would be reviewed because it was essential that Native Americans understand the importance of the *ynvenciones*.[55]

The authorities, although concerned about possible misinterpretation of symbols, nevertheless continued to encourage Native American participation in Corpus. For example, mandates issued during the sixteenth century ordering *oficios* to participate in the festival specifically included indigenous guilds. To support further their participation in the festival indigenous confraternities apparently received a discount on the price of candles and were urged to build their own *ynvenciones*.[56] With that in mind, in 1564 the city created its first Corpus prize, believing that the indigenous inhabitants would then follow the example of the winning Spanish entry.[57]

Encouraged by viceregal mandate, Native Americans accounted for the majority of musical and dance performances. Viceroys Velasco and Monterrey consciously reinforced indigenous integration into the festival and, perhaps indirectly, into the Spanish social system. In 1607 the surrounding Indian communities were still performing for Corpus. Although, in 1608, the city officials commissioned the musicians from Malinalco and Acolmán for five hundred pesos, every Corpus included Native American dances except the festivals during the riot-torn years of 1612 and 1692.[58]

Native Americans also carried the *ingenio* (large platform) on which was placed the *custodia*. The clergy did not always approve, complaining in 1591 that they had to purchase a larger *ingenio* because such a "huge quantity of Indians, filthy but eager," had wished to participate in what they regarded as a prestigious task.[59] According to the *cabildo eclesiástico*, this delayed the procession and on several occasions almost caused the *custodia* to fall to the ground. Despite grousing they chose to make the *ingenio* larger and more secure rather than attempt to limit Native American participation and enthusiasm.

Although the indigenous confraternities, usually the poorest in the city, could hardly compete with the famous altars of the silversmiths' guild, Native Americans prepared for the celebration by clearing and covering the streets with sand and flowers, transporting materials for the *posas*, and hanging the ornamentation along the processional route. Their most significant "donation" to the festival, however, was the construction and installation of the thatch canopy. The indigenous neighborhoods were each responsible for a section of the canopy, and the sections were then hung one after the other, forming a series of arches.[60] Mariano Cuevas reported that they utilized flowers and fragrant herbs and that they placed colorful songbirds in the thatch.[61]

Native American feeling about the festival, even the unremunerated labor of its preparation, seems to have been positive, as the case of the Indians of Xochimilco demonstrates. In 1654 they accomplished the arduous task of bringing a new bell to the cathedral in honor of the Corpus celebration. In return they received "an ornament of silver threaded cloth, a cape and clerical tunics and stoles" to wear in the procession.[62] No doubt this sumptuous attire was a mark of prestige that fellow processional participants would have recognized as an honor. This further encouraged the integration so desired for stability.

Without a review of Native American confraternity and parish records, it is difficult to paint an accurate picture of indigenous participation and thereby demonstrate the degree to which Corpus actually functioned as a social integrator. Nonetheless, Native Americans' involvement in Corpus appears extensive, as were their voluntary contributions to the festival. Their participation was such that in the eighteenth century Bourbon officials considered the festival too popular and proceeded to eliminate many indigenous elements.

Guild Participation

From the initial celebrations of Mexico City's Corpus the guilds recognized the significance of the festival. The first notices of the celebration during the sixteenth century were the consistent mandates issued by the city regarding disturbances and placement in the procession. From 1526 to 1592 one of the municipal government's main concerns about Corpus was the order within the processional line. The guilds coveted a prestigious position near the *custodia* and each, no doubt, felt better qualified than the next to merit that esteemed location. The disputes became so intense in 1533 that municipal police were required to maintain the order of the procession. Laws were soon issued carrying a fine or ten-day jail sentence for disorderly behavior.[63] The silversmiths' guild proved particularly astute in the rivalry for position in the procession; in 1537, by proclaiming San Hipólito as their patron saint, they ensured themselves the closest position to the *custodia*.[64] Regardless of the disputes over placement, guild participation in Corpus grew as each new *oficio* was accepted into the city. In 1533 the list for the procession included an unspecified number of Native American *oficios*, the giants and other games, and eight Spanish guilds.[65] By 1572 guilds had increased to forty-three.[66]

The disputes that seemed to define Corpus in the 1500s did not continue into the next century. Nevertheless, guild rivalry remained strong, and competition over the best festival developed. The guilds attempted to win public favor by the sumptuousness of their processions, by tossing to spectators small coins minted with their insignia, and by including bullfights as part of the festivities. Popular acclaim increased their prestige and perhaps even encouraged donations.[67] Such rivalry, although no longer over position in the Corpus procession, may have shifted to altar decoration. On at least one occasion a guild attempted to alter a Corpus tradition, probably at the expense of other competing guilds. The candlemakers in 1679 included the recitation of a *loa* (tribute) at their altar, thus detaining the procession longer than usual; subsequently, the archbishop ordered the arrest of the unfortunate poet.[68]

A unique guild contribution to Corpus Christi was the patronage of sermons, which required the panegyrist to include references to the sponsoring guild. Traditionally the *fruteros*, or fruit sellers, sponsored the sermon of Corpus day and, consequently, the discourse included as many references as possible to fruit. This became a complicated verbal game. Within the same sentence, the ending of one word might be combined with the beginning of the next to form the name of a fruit. The public, aware of the intrinsic challenge in such a game, attempted to locate as many "fruits" as possible. Consider this final line of one sermon: "Consérvanos en tu gracia y plántanos en tu reino." Literally, it said, "Preserve us in your grace and plant us in your kingdom," but *plántanos* also means a bunch of bananas.[69]

FAREWELL TO GIANTS AND GYPSIES

The proliferation of festivals that characterized life in the viceregal capital and the mixture of the profane and the sacred that in many cases accompanied them were not appreciated by all of the elite during the Hapsburg period. The official emphasis on both religious and civil festivals had its critics. In the case of Corpus, as early as 1544, Bishop Juan de Zumárraga banned the dances and *ynvenciones* that had already become traditional. In addition he ordered the printing of a work by Dionisio Rickel that included a discourse on proper processional conduct.[70] The prohibition continued until the bishop's death, when the cabildo reinstated the dances, dramas, and creations.[71] Not all clergy approached Corpus with such resolution. Agustín Dávila Padilla, when describing the life of fellow Dominican González Luzero, remarked that he altered the procession so as not to draw indigenous attention away from the sacred Eucharist. Rather than ban the profane elements from the festival Luzero permitted the dances and *ynvenciones* only before or after the procession.[72]

During the seventeenth century the Spanish Crown worried about moral laxity in the viceroyalty. The four categories causing the most consternation were: 1) sexual promiscuity among the elite (specifically the culture of *don juanismo*, with the supreme conquest being a nun); 2) clerical disregard of the vow of celibacy (also known as solicitation in the confessional); 3) government fraud and corruption; and 4) the continued blurring of the social categories of the caste system.[73] The royal preoccupation did not translate into a specific policy of festival reform. Life in the city remained intricately linked to public celebrations, whether sacred, profane, or both.

The eighteenth century marked a turning point in the official interpretation of the role of festivals in viceregal society. The new century brought much change to New Spain, the most important of which was the ascension of a Bourbon monarch to the Spanish throne. In an effort to maximize efficiency and the benefits of an overseas empire, the Bourbon bureaucracy instituted a series of administrative, military, economic, and social reforms. With regard to the social reforms the Bourbon cadre of officials sought to educate and enlighten—to instill the populace with what they perceived to be modern behavior.

The Bourbon concept of modernity included a frontal attack on certain excesses that they considered vulgar, unseemly, improper, and decadent. Festivals, with that unique mixture of the sacred and the profane, were right in the line of Bourbon fire. According to the new philosophy, festivals were solemn affairs that should proceed in an orderly and respectful manner, serving as a model of decorum and reverence. Hipólito Villarroel, listing the essentials of good government as related to festivals, commented that "the first object ought to be to watch over the Indians in order to make them rational, civilized. . . . Whatever they earn by working, they spend on festivals and large dinners and drunken binges with which they celebrate these festivals, that really should be called bacchanalias rather than civilized and religious [celebrations]."[74] His opinion of Corpus reveals the new elite attitude regarding that celebration: "Nothing dishonors and stains these events as the permissiveness and tolerance, in the name of confraternities, that allows [the participation of] a crowd of drunk, miserable naked Indians wearing costumes."[75]

Memory of the revolt of 1692 added even further political impetus to the Bourbon desire to implement a new social morality. The recollection of the multitude of Native Americans and *castas* storming and setting fire to the viceregal palace had a tremendous impact on the elite. Whatever fears they might have had previously regarding the political volatility of such a heterogeneous mass were now given evidence. From that incident on, the elite and the authorities viewed all popular traditions of the *pueblo* as customs containing seeds of subversion, which had to be eliminated.[76]

Festivals, particularly Corpus, brought many villagers from miles away to the capital. So many people, so much libation, and so much licentious behavior created too volatile an atmosphere, increasing the possibility of disorder and revolt. The festive space once so conducive to reinforcing the status quo was now perceived as capable of restructuring, albeit temporarily, the social hierarchy. In some respects perhaps the Bourbon perception was well founded. There was some recognition of potential links between subversion and the Corpus Christi festival during the sixteenth century. It had been customary for spectators and participants to attend the procession wearing costumes, or at least masks. From 1529 to 1556 the cabildo repeatedly prohibited the wearing of masks to the festival. Furthermore, all male Spanish citizens were ordered to participate in the procession, and any of them found watching the procession from balconies or street corners were arrested. At this time government officials feared a revolt by Spanish colonists against royal authority. One attempted uprising actually occurred. The revolt of 1692, sparked by a food shortage and reports of grain hoarding, took place during the celebration of Corpus Christi. The rioters, however, actually abandoned their uprising because of their devotion to the Holy Eucharist.[77] Apparently, two Franciscan friars carried the Host into the furious crowd and begged the Native Americans and *castas* to put out the fire at the viceregal palace and go home, all in the name of the *Santísimo Sacramento*. In 1701 fear of a revolt once again permeated the procession.[78] Bourbon officials viewed the festival not as a symbolic means to maintain order but rather as a catalyst that could shatter stability. Festivals required reform, they concluded, to strengthen elite control of these potentially volatile festive spaces.

A variety of popular pastimes—the theater, games, bullfights, dancing, tavern life—were targets of the Bourbon social reform movement in the city. Such long-standing traditions were difficult to eradicate, as they had become part of the social fabric and collective memory. Nonetheless, over time Bourbon officials banned festivals such as Native American Carnival. They radically changed other festivals, such as All Saints' Day, Our Lady of Guadalupe, Easter, and the celebration of patron saints in indigenous and *casta* neighborhoods. Corpus Christi did not escape unscathed.[79]

Bourbon reforms affecting Corpus began with regulation and ended with prohibition. Efforts began with dances, requiring authorization and approval from the cabildo and the ecclesiastical authorities. Under this new system, officials regulated the content and quality of the performances, prohibiting any that might be labeled *indecoroso* (unseemly), and by 1744 the cabildo had stopped contracting dancers altogether. Regulations outlawed food stalls and vendors from the processional route, rigorously banned drinking from the festival, and prohibited poorly dressed individuals from the festivities.[80] Underscoring the dramatic changes, in 1777, based on the instructions of José de Gálvez, municipal expenditures for Corpus were limited to 223 pesos, or 6 percent of the Corpus budget of 1618, which was possibly lower than any other period of the celebration's history.[81] The final reform of Corpus occurred in 1790 when the Count of Revillagigedo issued a decree permanently banning the *tarasca*, *gigantes*, and *cabezudos*.[82]

The last citywide Corpus of Mexico City took place in 1866.[83] In the nineteenth century, children still continued to wave *tarasquitas* during the procession. The religious celebration dedicated to the Holy Eucharist inside the cathedral certainly continued during the rest of the 1800s, but the large procession and other outdoor activities such as the *comedias* completely disappeared. After the revolution in 1920 the Corpus celebration regained some of its former colonial splendor. Today on Corpus day folkloric Native American dance performances once again accompany the fiesta, and, once again, vendors sell miniature paper constructions of animals to excited children.

Corpus during the Hapsburg years served a myriad of functions, encouraging integration, instilling the seeds of civic pride, promoting the popular welfare, and providing a symbolic means to legitimacy. Each segment of the society participated in this festival, and, particularly for the guilds and confraternities, it represented a significant annual ritual important enough to cause rivalry and disputes. Nonetheless, Corpus put the city on display as a single entity joined by a complex of religious beliefs. Although some participants belonged to a higher stratum in the socioeconomic hierarchy than others, they all shared the festive environment, the divine presence in the Eucharist, and the lively band of monsters and dancers that led the procession. With the elimination of the latter, Corpus still remained a mirror of society, but perhaps it finally became what Bishop Zumárraga had originally intended—a solemn contemplation in honor of the King of Kings.

Corpus Christi formed part of the larger official Hapsburg policy that sought to maintain order not just by force but also through persuasion, entertainment, and manipulation of the symbolic. These officials actively promoted the festival and sought to increase Native American participation in and appreciation of the celebration. So vital a symbol to the government, Corpus was maintained at the expense of other festivals, other obligations, and even a sound budget, and authorities disputed among themselves regarding position and privileges connected with the festival. Appreciation for the significance of the fiesta was reflected clearly in the fact that the dances and *ynvenciones* of Corpus were only canceled twice during the seventeenth century— in 1612 and 1692, years when the largest popular uprisings took place in the city. The processions went forward without these crowd-pleasing features because, no doubt, the officials were leery about exciting or inciting the inhabitants any further. The elimination of these profane elements almost appears to have constituted a punishment for breaking the symbolic social contract. In each case the following year the popular traditions once again defined Corpus. Bourbon officials, however, did not share the Hapsburg interest in catering to the masses in order to maintain effective rule; they set in motion a series of reforms to alter the festival permanently. New Spain's celebration of Corpus Christi, radically changed but still the symbol of the city itself, faded from view, but not before alluding to a distinctly Mexican identity yet to appear on the Bourbon horizon.

Some historians question the European Corpus procession as a mirror of society, claiming that a significant portion of the population did not and could not participate; they point out that the procession was usually a stronghold of the guilds and the clergy. Under these circumstances Corpus did not portray the community but rather displayed in the harsh light of day the differences and inequities of society.[84] Taking these studies into account, the Mexico City Corpus was unique because Native American guilds and parishes did indeed march in the procession and did provide decorations for the festival. Although a significant portion of Mexico City's citizenry did not actually walk in the procession, the mass of heterogeneous spectators witnessed Native American and *casta* participation in the fiesta. Furthermore, the participation of the indigenous population in the Mexico City Corpus was so widespread that some elites and Bourbon officials considered the festival too popular and too profane. The differences between the European and the novohispanic Corpus inevitably must be traced to the differences in the social context of the festival.

NOTES

1. Agustín de Ventancurt, *Teatro mexicano: Descripción de los sucesos exemplares, históricos, políticos, militares, y religiosos del Nuevo Mundo Occidental de las Indias* (Madrid, 1960–61), 2:193.

2. This figure is based on the research cited in the asterisk note. Many new festivals appeared during the seventeenth century.

3. Cited in Andrés Lira and Luis Mora, "El siglo de la integración," in *Historia general de México* (México, 1977), 2:90.

4. Ventancurt, *Teatro mexicano* 2:217. Antonio Morga investigated the rumored African revolt of 1612; his findings resulted in the hanging in the main plaza of thirty-six blacks judged guilty of conspiracy against the Crown. For a more detailed analysis of the revolts and the economic dislocation of this period, see Jonathan Israel, *Race, Class and Politics in Colonial Mexico, 1610–1670* (London, 1975).

5. For Spanish royal and civil policy regarding festivals and popular pastimes, see José Antonio Maraval, *The Culture of the Baroque* (Minneapolis, 1986); J. H. Elliott, "Poder y propaganda en la España de Felipe IV," in *España y su mundo 1500–1700* (Madrid, 1990), 201–28; and Walter Cohen, *Drama of a Nation: Public Theater in Renaissance England and Spain* (Ithaca, NY, 1985).

6. Ventancurt, *Teatro mexicano* 3:88. Drama was instrumental in Native American religious conversion and acculturation. See Robert Ricard, *La conquista espiritual de México* (México, 1947), 355–74; and Adam Versényi, "Getting under the Aztec Skin: Evangelical Theatre in the New World," *New Theatre Quarterly* 5 (1989): 217–26.

7. César Oliva, "La práctica escénica en fiestas teatrales previas al barroco: Algunas referencias a nuestras hechas en la región de Murcia," in *Teatro y fiesta en el Barroco* (Barcelona, 1986), 98–114; and V. Lleo Cañal, *Arte y espectáculo: La fiesta del Corpus Christi en Sevilla en los siglos XVI y XVII* (Seville, 1975). For a description and analysis of Corpus Christi in Spain, see Frances George Very, *The Spanish Corpus Christi Procession: A Literary and Folkloric Study* (Valencia, 1962). For a detailed study of its development in medieval Europe, see Miri Rubin, *Corpus Christi: The Eucharist in Late Medieval Culture* (New York, 1991).

8. This figure comes from the cabildo's income and expenditure information presented during a review of its finances. City income was listed as 16,500 pesos and the average annual cost of Corpus 3,500 pesos in *Actas*, Libro 23, 177.

9. In this analysis the author has been guided by the works of two anthropologists: Edmund Leach's discussion of the festival as a social reinforcer or restructurer in *Culture and Communication* (New York, 1989) and Victor Turner's examination of its role as social integrator and symbolic equalizer in *The Ritual Process: Structure and Anti-Structure* (Ithaca, 1977).

10. Paul Veyne examines the relationship between governments and public festivals as a social contract in *Bread and Circuses: Historical Sociology and Political Pluralism* (New York, 1990).

11. Antonio de Robles, *Diario de sucesos notables, 1665–1703*, vol. 2, *Colección de escritores mexicanos*, ed. Antonio Castro Leal (México, 1946), 2:260. Traditionally, Corpus was an eight-day celebration; the *octava* began and ended with a procession and included a variety of other activities discussed in the text.

12. *Actas*, Libro 1, 86. The official designation of Corpus Christi is listed in the statutes, chapter twenty, of the Junta Eclesiástica celebrated in Mexico City in 1539. This chapter mandated that guilds, parishes, and confraternities participate in the procession with their crosses and candles. Cited in José María Marroquí, *La ciudad de México* (México, 1900–1903), 3:495.

13. "Gacetas de México," in *Documentos para la historia de México*, 2d series (México, 1954–55), 4:130, 205 (henceforth referred to as "Gacetas"). In this study, one *vara* equals .84 meters.

14. For the processional route, see Manuel Carrera Stampa, *Los gremios mexicanos: La organización gremial en Nueva España 1521–1861* (México, 1954), 103. A series of special sermons preached by the city's different religious orders began eight days before Corpus Christi. Robles, *Diario de sucesos notables*, 2:240–41, reports the sermons for 1678.

15. Giovanni Francesco Gemelli Careri, *Viaje a la Nueva España* (México, 1976), 114.

16. Robles, *Diario de sucesos notables*, 2:48. In Spain the individuals who carried the *custodia* rested as the Host was placed on each altar accompanied by hymns and prayers. See Very, *Spanish Corpus*, 13. No doubt, the altars in New Spain afforded the same respite for the marchers.

17. Guillermo Prieto, *Memorias de mis tiempos* (México, 1969), 222.

18. Artemio de Valle Arizpe, *Por la vieja Calzada de Tlacopan* (México, 1937), 57–58.

19. "Gacetas" 4:130; *Actas*, Libro 16, 70; Libro 20, 321; Libro 30, 169; Libro 31, 223; and "Gacetas" 4:130. Seven giants, representing the deadly sins, traditionally accompanied the *tarasca* in the European Corpus. In Madrid, Corpus giants represented the four parts of the world—America, Asia, Africa, and Europe. See Very, *Spanish Corpus*, 77–78. In Mexico, extant documentation indicates that usually more than two and, particularly in the late seventeenth and early eighteenth centuries, at least eight giants accompanied the procession. For information on giants in European festivals, see VV.AA. *Les géants processionnels en Europe* (Ath, 1983); M. F. Guesquín, "Cities, Giants and Municipal Power," *Ethnología* 17: 117–28; and José Antonio González Alcantud, "Para una interpretación etnológica de la tarasca, gigantes y cabezudos," in *Antiguallas granadinas: Las fiestas del Corpus*, ed. Miguel Garrido Atienza (Granada, 1990), xxix–xlviii.

20. *Actas*, Libro 12, 282 and Libro 13, 336.

21. González Alcantud, "Para una interpretación etnológica," xvi–xvii. No evidence exists of this tradition in Mexico.

22. *Actas*, Libro 30, 169.

23. Robles, *Diario de sucesos notables*, 3:155. The dragon did not appear in Spanish processions until the second quarter of the sixteenth century. The term

tarasca may derive from the dragon legend and celebration in Tarascon, France. There does not appear to be a direct relation between the term and Native American Tarascos. Some scholars believe that the conquerors named this indigenous group based on their misunderstanding of the pronunciation of their name. For a concise history of the *tarasca* in Spain, see J. E. Varey and N. D. Shergold, "La tarasca de Madrid," *Clavileño* 4, no. 20 (March/April 1953): 18–26; González Alcantud, "Para una interpretación etnológica," xlv; and José María Bernáldez Montalvo, *Las tarascas de Madrid* (Madrid, 1981). The author of the latter study provides color duplications of original drawings that served as guidelines for the actual three-dimensional dragons constructed during the seventeenth and eighteenth centuries in the Spanish capital.

24. Juan de Viera, *Compendiosa narración de la ciudad de México* (México, 1952), 95.

25. *Actas*, Libro 11, 147; and Libro 14, 258. The *carros* in seventeenth-century Seville were painted floats on which *autos* (short religious plays) were performed by theatrical troupes as the procession meandered through the streets. The paintings depicted scenes related to the *autos*. See Very, *Spanish Corpus*, 17–18. Mexico City records do not indicate that the sixteenth-century *carros* were similar "tableaux vivants," but they do discuss the construction of the *tablados*, implying a large performance space such as the cemetery of the cathedral.

26. Gemelli Careri, *Viaje a la Nueva España*, 114.

27. Armando de María y Campos, "Las comedias en el Corpus mexicano colonial," *Humanismo* 2, No. 11–12 (May-June 1953): 113. The flyswatters were wheels of folded paper attached to a small stick. María y Campos states that vendors sold small parasols of heavy paper to the spectators for protection from the sun.

28. *Actas*, Libro 30, 169.

29. Gregorio M. de Guijo, *Diario 1648–1664* (México, 1952–53), 2:135, 217. In seventeenth-century Valencia it did become customary for the coordinators of the Corpus festival to distribute tons of candy to the crowd. See Very, *Spanish Corpus*, 22.

30. *Ordenanza* of July 13, 1613, in Eusebio Ventura Beleña, *Recopilación sumaria de todos los autos acordados de la Real Audiencia y Sala del Crimen de esta Nueva España y providencias de su superior gobierno* (México, 1787), 1:27.

31. Carrera Stampa, *Los gremios mexicanos*, 104.

32. Councilman Gaspar de Valdes in 1600 listed Velasco's contributions to Corpus (see *Actas*, Libro 14, 102); *Actas*, Libro 17, 183; and Libro 9, 12–13

33. *Actas*, Libro 14, 105; Libro 15, 53; Libro 14, 102; Libro 13, 192, 329; and Libro 15, 53.

34. *Actas*, Libro 32, 201–2; for general economic trends, see Louisa S. Hoberman, *Mexico's Merchant Elite, 1590–1660: Silver, State, and Society* (Durham, NC, 1991).

35. AGI, Mexico, 38.

36. AGI, Mexico, 39.

37. *Actas*, Libro 1, 208. The city also issued mandates and regulations in 1531, 1533, 1537, 1555, 1557, 1560, 1572, 1573, 1595, and 1599.

38. Robles, *Diario de sucesos notables*, 1:173.

39. *Actas*, Libro 3, 202.

40. *Actas*, Libro 3, 195; Libro 27, 69.

41. *Actas*, Libro 21, 245.

42. *Actas*, Libro 14, 101–2.

43. *Actas*, Libro 3, 40; and Libro 7, 193, 198. The *Actas* show that in 1577, 1579, and 1580 a specific prize was awarded.

44. *Actas*, Libro 9, 15, 19–20.

45. *Actas*, Libro 27, 231; and Libro 23, 177.

46. *Actas*, Libro 16, 26; Libro 19, 98; Libro 20, 117; Libro 21, 59; Libro 23, 71; Libro 24, 265; and Libro 25, 133–34, 138.

47. *Actas*, Libro 16, 63; Libro 17, 139, 180, 190, 338–39, 485, 501; and Libro 14, 256.

48. *Actas*, Libro 23, 177; Libro 14, 258.

49. *Actas*, Libro 13, 217–18; Libro 25, 129; Libro 23, 72; Libro 10, 122, 127; and Libro 13, 11.

50. Ventancurt, *Teatro mexicano*, 2:193.

51. Guijo, *Diario*, 2:135.

52. Robles, *Diario de sucesos notables*, 2:48, 3:155. For the *tarasca* and giants of 1638, see *Actas*, Libro 31, 226.

53. Gemelli Careri, *Viaje a la Nueva España*, 114–16.

54. "Gacetas" 4:205, 409; 5:79–80.

55. *Actas*, Libro 7, 189–90.

56. *Ordenanza* dated from 1550, cited in Carrera Stampa, *Los gremios mexicanos*, 233.

57. *Actas*, Libro 7, 193.

58. *Actas*, Libro 17, 4, 183.

59. *Actas*, Libro 9, 56.

60. María y Campos, "Las comedias," 113.

61. Mariano Cuevas, *Historia de la Iglesia en México* (México, 1976), 3:514–15.

62. Guijo, *Diario* 1:253.

63. *Actas*, Libro 3, 40.

64. *Actas*, Libro 3, 84.

65. *Actas*, Libro 3, 40.

66. *Ordenanzas de gremios de la Nueva España. Compendio de los tres tomos de la compilación nueva de ordenanzas de la muy noble, insigne y muy leal e imperial ciudad de México. Hizólo el Lic. D. Fco. del Barrio Lorenzot* (México, 1920), 264–65.

67. Carrera Stampa, *Los gremios mexicanos*, 98.

68. Marroquí, *La ciudad de México*, 3:506.

69. Cuevas, 3:505.

70. María y Campos, "Las Comedias," 111.

71. Marroquí, *La ciudad de México*, 3:498.

72. Agustín Dávila Padilla, *Historia de la fundación y discurso de la provincia de Santiago de México de la Orden de Predicadores* (México, 1955), 246.

73. Juan Pedro Viqueira Albán, *¿Relajados o reprimidos? Diversiones públicas y vida social en la ciudad de México durante el Siglo de las Luces* (México, 1987), 31. An English translation of this volume is forthcoming from Scholarly Resources.

74. Hipólito de Villarroel, *Enfermedades políticas que padece la capital de esta Nueva España en casi todos los cuerpos de que se compone y remedios que se la deben aplicar para su curación si se quiere que sea util al rey y al público* (México, 1979), 505–6.

75. Ibid., 188–89.

76. Viqueira Albán, *¿Relajados o reprimidos?* 31–32.

77. *Actas*, Libro 3, 172; and Libro 6, 232.

78. Robles, *Diario de sucesos notables*, 3:154–55. The potential of festivals occasionally to backfire on their ecclesiastical or civil organizers is well documented in studies such as Emmanuel Le Roy Ladurie, *Carnival in Romans* (New York, 1979) and Natalie Zemon Davis, "The Rites of Violence: Religious Riots in Sixteenth-century France," *PP* 59: 51–91. See also Peter Burke, *Popular Culture in Early Modern Europe* (New York, 1978); Michael Mullet, *Popular Culture and Popular Protest in Late Medieval and Early Modern Europe* (New York, 1987); and Robles, *Diario de sucesos notables*, 2:250–58.

79. Viqueira Albán, *¿Relajados o reprimidos?* 152–60.

80. Ibid.

81. Francisco Sedano, *Noticias de México: Crónicas de los siglos XVI al XVIII* (México, 1974), 1:96.

82. José Gómez, *Diario curioso de México*, vol. 3 of *Documentos para la historia de México* (México, 1854–55), 341; and Luis González Obregón, *México viejo* (México, 1966), 438. The Bourbon measures against Corpus Christi in Spain took effect ten years earlier in 1780. See Very, *Spanish Corpus*, 107.

83. Antonio García Cubas, *El libro de mis recuerdos* (México, 1904), 370.

84. See, for example, Robert Darnton's discussion of the 1768 procession of Montpellier in *The Great Cat Massacre and Other Episodes in French Cultural History* (New York, 1985), 121–22; and the general discussion of the symbolic role of the Corpus procession presented in Rubin, *Corpus Christi*, 265–69.

2

Lewd Songs and Dances from the Streets of Eighteenth-Century New Spain

Sergio Rivera Ayala
Syracuse University

Sergio Rivera steps beyond the usual interest in colonial music and dance that examines their use in conquest and conversion—recall Padre Bartolomé de Las Casas's mission to convert unconquered peoples in Vera Paz with the help of church music as well as its use by missionaries in proselytizing. He analyzes the music of the streets with its oral and kinesic accompaniment. The essay also tests Yuri Lotman's hypothesis in *Universe of the Mind: A Semiotic Theory of Culture*, which explores the boundaries of what Lotman calls the semiosphere. Beyond reviewing this theory, Rivera explores these songs and dances—affronts to the public order—as a social analogy to insults in private encounters.[*] Moreover, he discusses several songs that associate bakers with risqué lyrics and dance steps, identifying a folkloric continuity with today: *panaderos* still have a somewhat ribald reputation.[†] He initiated this study after completing his undergraduate degree at Universidad Nacional Autónoma de México, and it now forms part of his dissertation research at Syracuse University.

I would like to thank my parents, Francisco and Amalia, and my family as well as Professor Mario Julio del Campo for his friendship and help and Professors Pedro Cuperman and Daniel Testa for their encouragement. Finally, I would like to thank my wife Sonya Lipsett-Rivera, who not only helped me with the translation of this essay, but who also has been my main support for the last six years.

[*]See Cheryl English Martin, "Popular Speech and Social Order in Northern Mexico, 1650–1830," *CSSH* 32, no. 2 (April 1990): 305–24.

[†]The reputation exists in the Chicano community in the United States. See Alicia Maria González, "Guess How Doughnuts are Made," in *"And Other Neighborly Names": Social Process and Cultural Image in Texas Folklore*, ed. Richard Bauman and Roger D. Abrahams (Austin, 1981), 104–22.

"HOW CAN IT BE! The world is so advanced that I do not wonder at the existence of heretics, but that there are so few."[1] So José Antonio Rojas, a Mexican intellectual with a passionate spirit imbued with Enlightenment ideas, sarcastically grieved in his biting critique of society in New Spain. His mock lament about the rising tide of heresy revealed that Rojas was immersed in a time of change as modern thought was increasingly superimposed over Christian doctrine. He and others like him welcomed the ideologies emanating from outside the colonial world. The influence of this external philosophy changed their perspectives regarding cultural development and made more discrete semantic boundaries.

Satire, within this social and semantic framework, acquired widespread political and religious relevance in New Spain's social life and found expression in both the traditional and the modern categories of the moment:

Parada en las cuatro esquinas,	Standing on the four corners
puesto a dos mil contigencias,	ready for any opportunity,
para ofender a mi Dios,	I am doing my utmost
ando asiendo diligencias.	to offend my God.[2]

Such intellectual trends cannot be equated with atheism; instead they represented the transformations occurring within colonial society where civil order replaced divine harmony by effecting a transformation through the influence of individual liberty. These currents reached all ranks of colonial society, ignored by some and influenced by others in varying degrees.

Mexican society in the eighteenth century was undergoing a metamorphosis. People began examining their lives through the prism of their values and using their point of view rather than that of Spain; they began to create a new model of the world. With the pride experienced at the emergence of a newborn sense of culture, distinct from that of the metropolis, came a self-consciousness of their own culture, a kind of protonationalism.[3] Dr. Juan José Eguiara y Eguren, for instance, cataloged outstanding examples of ingenuity in New Spain, beginning with the pre-Columbian era. This *Bibliotheca mexicana*, he believed, adequately responded to the attacks of a Spanish theologian who characterized Mexico as an "intellectual desert." His voice trying to pierce the armor of colonial authoritarianism, Eguiara y Eguren described with romantic passion the talent and creativity of Mexicans, especially the Indians. He spoke not only for himself but also for the community that wanted "to vindicate such a tremendous and atrocious injury to our mother land and people."[4]

During the Bourbon period New Spain became the richest colony of the Spanish empire. For the upper sector of society this wealth brought optimism, an atmosphere of promise.[5] The eighteenth century became the "century of hope," according to Fray Joaquín Bolaños, in *La portentosa vida de la muerte,* "the century of cooks, of still lifes, of idleness, of abundance, of good and generous soups."[6] Moreover, it became the century of sensuality, of earthly pleasures, of delights, and of sexual encounters "that persisted in overflowing the narrow frame of family in which [they] had been confined."[7] Fray Joaquín, infected by this attitude but aware that he suffered from the consequences of original sin, complained that he could not enjoy the pleasures of sensuality: "Posterity complains and laments painfully to their common Father [Adam], that having eaten the apple, he did not reserve even the seeds for us: well, we have paid for the duck without having tasted it."[8]

Despite the prosperity of the eighteenth century only a minority, approximately fifty thousand out of a population of six million, shared this affluence. The disparity in economic circumstances revealed the most ostentatious of riches next to crushing misery. The diffusion of Enlightenment ideas as well as an increasing nationalism in the middle classes (especially among the criollos) encouraged the spread of embryonic ideas of independence.

The social stratum with access to literary culture had the possibility of putting their ideas into written form, discussing Rousseau with friends, expressing doubt in the divine power of kings, and encouraging independence and anticolonial ideas. Outside the literate, salon world other members of the colonial society used different means to communicate their attitudes and hopes. The lower strata of society reacted to the new intellectual environment through manifestations that did not require written forms. Through remarkably articulate and often lewd songs and dances, the lower classes performed their sentiments. These expressions, like any work of art, reproduced a picture of the world from the perspective of its interpreters. The structures of these texts reveal the social responses of the groups that performed these dances, and the texts themselves provide images of the social atmosphere in which the dancers lived.

These rhythmic movements and songs formed part of a popular culture that evolved in opposition to the official conventions; it developed at society's periphery, in the places where the hegemonic classes of the viceroyalty confined marginal groups. Within a system of "constraints and prescriptions" used to protect its values, the elite rejected the groups at the bottom of this hierarchy as well as their cultural manifestations.[9] For the marginal peoples their popular songs used a language that provides a key to their position in the semiotic space of Mexican culture. These songs also reveal the cultural mechanisms that provoked their development within the "semiosphere."

The concept of the "semiosphere" resulted from Yuri Lotman's efforts to draw an analogy to Vladimir Vernadsky's "biosphere," which he explained as "the semiotic space necessary for the existence and function of languages."[10] The semiosphere has a concentric organization in which the most developed and organized languages (official culture) occupy the center and push to the periphery the multiple partial languages with unofficial existence that can only operate in certain cultural functions. From the center, the official culture creates its own models, organizes itself hierarchically, canonizes certain texts, and excludes others. Thus, the center acts as the subject, and the periphery as the object, of the system. The center dictates norms of behavior and imposes them on the periphery.

Organizing the diversity that exists in the semiosphere, the center creates an image of the world according to the binary principle, where the boundary (the outer limit of the first-person form) separates, in a hierarchical manner, "our" internal space from "their" external space, "our" inside from "their" outside. This binary principle describes "our" space as "cultured," "harmoniously organized," "united," and so forth. In contrast, "their" space is "uncultured," "primitive," "strange," "disorganized," and "savage."[11]

The application of this cultural mechanism can be seen clearly in a letter from the Mexican archbishop to King Charles III in 1768. The prelate described the indigenous languages as a potential danger to the social order: "the riots, mutinies, the civil seditions take on more importance when they develop among people of strange languages, and the distinctiveness of their customs excites them with the memory of their old lords, and, Excellency, [we remain] poorly conceived of their language, costumes, liberty, heathenism, and other vices which are their nature."[12]

The use of the pronoun "their" clearly defines the author's point of view regarding the Indians he described and ascribes to their culture (language, costumes, customs) negative values. Because they did not belong to the official culture, the Indians were not recognized at the center of the semiosphere, and, consequently, they along with their culture were banished to the periphery together with other marginal groups.

The boundary not only separates the two spheres but also serves to unite them. Since the boundary functions as a space of contact it also permits cultural exchange by the two worlds, which invade each other's semiotic spaces, and permits a dialogue between center and periphery. Because of their incomplete organization the languages of the periphery possess a greater capacity for dynamic innovation, in contrast to those of the center of the semiosphere, which oppose change. The languages of the periphery have the liberty to cross boundaries in a way that those of the center cannot, which generates revolutionary texts in the semiosphere, free of canons, and renews languages through the incorporation of the speech from everyday life.

Using information derived from Inquisition registers and other official institutional sources, the reconstruction of the marginal culture, although difficult, becomes possible. Volumes of Inquisition records reveal the peripheral manifestations that the authorities considered harmful to the social order. Through this official medium we can follow the way popular manifestations such as songs and dances spread out along the colony's streets, leaving in their wake extreme displeasure and indignation among the authorities. The tribunal deployed a series of edicts to eradicate these songs and dances—without any success. The interdictions seem to have infused the "crowd" with greater creativity since, like a malignant epidemic, new melodies and rhythms appeared daily, imbued with happiness and vitality and corresponding more to earthly pleasures than to precepts imposed by the church. The authorities received many denunciations, but, unfortunately, the informants collected only a few of the songs, which, nevertheless, allow entry into the thoughts of the lower classes.

Officials characterized the movements of the dances and the lyrics of the songs as "lewd and provocative of lasciviousness, causing grave ruin and scandal to the souls of Christendom and in prejudice to the conscience . . . and offence to edification and good customs."[13] Authorities were scandalized at midcentury by the appearance of the song and dance called the *chuchumbé*. The Holy Office of the Inquisition in 1766 threatened to excommunicate anyone who danced or sang it.[14] The inquisitors transcribed some of the couplets of this offensive refrain:

En la esquina está prado	A Mercedarian monk
un fraile de la Merced,	Is standing on the corner
con los ábitos alzados	Lifting his habit,
enceñando el chuchumbé	Showing the *chuchumbé*.
El demonio de la china	The China's[15] devilish boyfriend
del barrio de la Merced	from the Merced neighborhood
y cómo se sarandiava	and how he shook
metiéndole el chuchumbé	introducing her to the *chuchumbé*.
En la esquina hay puñaladas	There are knifings on the corner.
¡Ay Dios! ¿Qué será de mí?	Oh God! What will happen to me?
Que aguellos tontos se matan	These idiots kill each other
por esto que tengo aquí	For what I have here.

Me casé con un soldado,	I married a soldier,
lo hicieron cabo de esguadra	they made him corporal
y todas las noches quiere	and every night he wants,
su merced montar la guardia	Your Honor, to stand on guard.
En la esquina está parado	On the corner is standing
el que me mantiene a mí	The one who maintains me,
el que me paga la casa	The one who pays my rent
y el que me da de vestir	And gives me clothes to wear.
Quando se fue mi marido	When my husband left,
no me dejó que comer	He left me nothing to eat.
Y yo lo busco mejor	Rather I look for it,
bailando el chuchumbé	Dancing the *chuchumbé*.
¿Save Vuestra Merced que,	Do you know, Your Honor, that,
Save Vuestra Merced que,	Do you know, Your Honor, that
Meneadora de culo	They are calling you
Le un puesto a Vuestra Merced?	*meneadora de culo?*[16]

These lyrics and the accompanying description provided by informants provide a clear picture of the social behavior of the lower
classes, one totally opposed to the norm. Since the songs and dances
derived from popular expression, they used the dynamic language of
the lower classes that swarmed the streets and public places of New
Spain. It was there that "mulattos and people of mixed race . . . soldiers, sailors and other riffraff" danced, often touching each other in
provocative ways, even "rubbing stomach to stomach."[17] The images
within the songs reflected the social reality as experienced by the
participants.

The street constituted a privileged space in this basically public
society. Distinct social classes met in the street, where they had some
contact and interaction, and both church and state used the public
arteries for sacred and civic festivities. The streets were not only a
simple medium of communication and transport but also an important social and economic space where people accomplished a multitude of activities; merchants traded all sorts of goods, men met women,
prostitutes looked for business, drinking buddies gathered for visits
to *pulquerias*—in short, the street served as the "center of social life."[18]

Songs and dances could find no more propitious space in which
to develop than the street, where plebeians constituted the dominant
group. The authorities always identified these people with negative
characteristics, as shown in Carlos de Sigüenza y Góngora's late
seventeenth-century description:

Plebs so extremely plebeian, that they can only be of the most infamous reputation, and it is so for all the plebs, as they are composed of Indians, Blacks,
Creoles, and "bozales" of different nations, of chinos, mulattos, moriscos,
mestizos, zabaigos, lobos, and also Spaniards, who by declaring themselves
zarambullos (which is the same as a rogue, pimp, and thief) and have degener-
ated in respect to their duties, are the worst among the riffraff.[19]

Because the nature of street life had an earthy quality, the lower
classes could not escape such negative stigma. The plebeians did not
attempt to rid themselves of this reputation; rather, they tried to escape from control by the authorities. For this reason urban disturbances were part of everyday life even though government officials
tried to prevent them. These disorders became associated with the
dances that reflected the attitudes of disrespect for authority. From
the port of Acapulco came a report on the *chuchumbé:*

> During the feast of San Juan, people went out into the streets at night to sing
> the Chuchumbé and other songs. In the afternoon, during the masquerade, they
> formed groups of four, and with a type of imitation miter some pretended to
> give blessings, others imitated and ridiculed the clergy, talking dirty, despite
> having been warned with the threat of excommunication, they are ignorant of
> the implication, they do not fear it [excommunication] and only fear corporal
> punishment.[20]

Rupturing the norms of behavior allowed the plebeians to ridicule religious authorities and rituals, overcoming their fear of excommunication and even denying that it constituted a risk to them.
The invasion of the center of the semiosphere always formed part of
this disorder. The boundary that divided good or divine from bad or
profane behavior was so close that any overstepping of the line was
considered a rebellion against the official order. Celebrating a
colloquium, a kind of religious representation, for example, soon included the adoption of dances and songs, which were adapted for the
diversion they offered rather than any religious significance.[21] This
offended devout elite celebrants, one of whom affirmed that "the Holy
Scriptures were mixed with short farces, lascivious *seguidillas* and
profane *tonadillas*. They started at nine and did not end until mid-
night and on some occasions until one o'clock in the morning."[22]

The proliferation of these songs and dances throughout the
viceroyalty reflected an attack on colonial power. The loosening of
customs allowed the lower classes to escape the repressive atmosphere
that characterized their social reality by providing them with the tools
to construct their own "image of the world" and to shatter the rules
of the official world. The song entitled *Tirana* caused consternation

among authorities because it mocked the brotherhood of San Juan de Dios and affirmed the rejection of the official culture:

En San Juan de Dios de acá	In San Juan de Dios over here
son los legos tan cochinos	The lay brothers are such pigs
que cogen a las mugeres	They grab the women
y les tientan los tocinos	and grope their bacon.
En San Juan de Dios de Cadiz	In Cadiz's San Juan de Dios
el enfermo que no sana	If a patient doesn't heal
lo bajan a el camposanto	they take him to the cemetery
y le cantan la tirana	and sing him the *Tirana*.
En San Juan de Dios de México	In Mexico's San Juan de Dios
el enfermo que se quexa	If a patient complains
lo matan entre los legos	the lay brothers kill him
y le quitan lo que deja.	and steal what he leaves.
En San Juan de Dios de acá	In San Juan de Dios over here
el enfermo que no mea,	If a patient doesn't piss,
lo levantan unos legos	the lay brothers lift him
y le meten la salea.	and insert the "sheepskin."
En San Juan de Dios el Prior	In San Juan de Dios, the prior
se baja a la portería	goes down to the porter's
para sacarles a todos	to take everyone out
por detrás la porquería	to the back of the "pigsty."
Con ésta y no digo más	With this and I say no more,
que les cuadre o no les cuadre	You like it or not,
que aquí se acaba la tirana	the *Tirana* finishes here
pero no el carajo Padre	but not the "prick" Father.[23]

The images contained in the *Tirana* seem to have a simple goal: to destroy the official framework. Every couplet degrades the religious personnel, in this case, the Order of San Juan de Dios, by poking fun at their hierarchical symbols. This process gave the participants (both dancer and spectator) the capacity to demean the religious hierarchies. Within this context the religious order was removed from the center of official culture and relegated to the inferior plane. On this level, intimacies of a physical nature (sexual organs, excrement, and so on) were externalized so that the intimate became public. The modification of the official order contained within the songs implied its negation and the affirmation of a new order.

Because of the heaven/hell division of the world, any behavior in the earthly life could be considered either sinful or sacred. And, in accord with official doctrine, the diversions and distractions that the populace so ardently adopted erred more on the side of sinfulness. In fact, the popular classes began to discover that the earthly life was a part of their world and they forgot their anxieties and guilt imposed by religion. The *Pan de Jarabe*, a song transcribed by Franciscans from Pachuca in 1796, recorded this transformation:

Quando estés en los infiernos	When you are in hell
ardiendo, como tú sabes,	hot, as you know,
allá te dirán los diablos	there the devils will tell you
¡Hay hombre, no te la acabes!	Hey, man! Don't finish her off!
Quando estés en los infiernos	When you are in hell
todito lleno de moscas	all covered with flies,
allá te dirán los diablos,	there the devils will tell you
¡Ay ba, te dixe, de roscas!	There she goes, I told you,
	with those ruffians!
Quando estés en los infiernos	When you are in hell
todito lleno de llamas	all covered in flames,
allá te dirán los diablos,	there the devils will tell you
¡Ay ba la india! ¿Qué no le	There goes the Indian woman!
hablas?	Don't you speak to her?[24]

The *Pan de Jarabe* became so popular that people composed new couplets. The *Pan de Jarabe Ilustrado,* one of these variations, alluded to the philosophical current of the time:

Ya el infierno se acavó	Now Hell is finished
ya los diablos se murieron	and the devils have died,
haora si, chinita mía,	Now, my honey,
ya no nos condenaremos	we won't be condemned.[25]

In these verses hell does not entail the negative meaning assigned to it within religious discourse that placed it in opposition to heaven. In fact, in these texts hell is far from that: in a spatial axis of up and down hell does not occupy the inferior place, as it does in the religious system, but exists on the superior plane. In this transposed world it is not feared but enjoyed. Here people do not suffer but rather enjoy themselves, dance, and make love. In other words the people repossessed the concept of "hell" from the official discourse in order to make it their own "holy land," a place where they could deliberately violate the norms of behavior. In doing so, they affirmed sexual pleasure and denied religious discourse.

In another version of the *Pan de Jarabe* symbols normally considered superior were degraded and pushed into an inferior realm:

Esta noche he de pasear	Tonight I have to stroll
con la amada prenda mía	with my precious treasure
y nos tenemos de holgar	and we have to make love
hasta que Jesús se ría.	until Jesus laughs.[26]

The images represented here create a unit in which laughter, the best expression of popular language, overcomes the solemnity of religious discourse and alters the meaning of the superior symbols.[27]

The social language establishes an atmosphere of liberty in which anything could be said; there were no rules to get in the way, and there were no prohibitions or condemnations. The words had a different meaning than they did in their normal context and were related not to the official system but rather to popular speech, referring specifically to the lower classes. The implicit sexual act within the texts not only degraded the religious world but also exalted the profane world. Dances and songs allowed the lower classes to free themselves, if only for a moment or two, from the atmosphere of subjugation in which they lived. Such manifestations reflected a new perspective on life that allowed the people to approach one another and break the boundaries of the official hierarchy.

This street culture spread easily to all social spaces. The governor of Mérida in 1768 ordered that all types of dances be performed in the *saraos* (soirées), even if they were considered lewd. And, even when the religious authorities reiterated prohibitions against these dances, the governor said "no one could prohibit the *saraos*, nor publicly censure [any action]" unless he gave his consent. Similar cases occurred in the coliseo theater of Mexico City, where clergymen denounced the presentation of the tragedy *Reyna después de morir* because it included a song called *La Cosecha* as an interlude. The informer stated that "the corregidor had, in previous days, ordered that it should not be danced, but the judge of the coliseo opposed this, and when the matter was appealed to the Viceroy, he ruled that it could be danced, but with decency."[28]

The merriment of the people defeated authoritarian speech. A priest from Medellín ordered that a group of dancers be publicly reprimanded and prevented from playing the music that they had performed with "clamor and scandalous voice," including a song called *Toro nuevo, Toro Viejo*. But instead of meekly complying, the offenders responded by questioning the priest's authority, asking who was he "to reprimand and prohibit a customary dance that is performed in this city all the time"?[29]

The concept of the "prohibited" seems to have disappeared from the collective conscience, and only the devout still espoused it in their struggle to suppress all the "lewd" dances and songs emerging in the streets of New Spain. The efforts of the religious authorities to convince their parishioners that they offended God with these dances and songs were singularly unsuccessful. If the people did cease their activities for a few days, any excuse was good enough reason to resume singing and dancing. Profound religiosity, nevertheless, existed among the people, but it served only to express, in a rather contradictory manner, the rejection of official dominion. The clergy felt repugnance for this duality as they fought to protect the dogmas of the church. Songs constantly mixed sacred scriptures into their lyrics, and the people dared to sing the Our Father and the Ave Maria to the music of the *Pan de Jarabe,* or to parody the act of confession or the Ten Commandments.[30] The following verses, collected in 1796, exemplify this behavior:

Vuesa reverencia, padre,	Your Reverence, Father,
oyga mis culpas, que intento	listen to my faults, I intend
hacer de ellas penitencia	to clear my soul
con grande arrenpentimiento,	with great repentance,
pues un año poco más	because I have not confessed
hace que no me confiesco.	since over a year ago.
—¿Cumpliste la penitencia?	—Did you complete the penitence?
—Si padre, luego al momento,	—Yes, Father, already,
pues entre amigos y amigas	because among friends
reparto todo de presto.	I share everything right away.
—¿Qué orden trae de confesarse?	—How do you want to start?
—Padre, por los Mandamientos.	—Father, with the Commandments.
—Pues bien está, persinese.	—All right, you cross yourself.
—Jesús, padre, que comienzo	—Jesus, Father, I start
con el nombre de mi dama.	with the name of my lady.
—¡Jesús, que notable yerro!	—Jesus! What an error!
—No se escandalice, padre,	—Don't be shocked, Father,
téngame vmd sufrimiento	have mercy on me,
que a no ser gran pecador	if I weren't a great sinner
no me huviera a sus pies puesto.	I wouldn't be at your feet.
En el 1° me acuso	First, I accuse myself
que no amo a Dios como debo,	of not loving God as I should,
por que todas mis potencias	because all my strength
en ella puestas las tengo.	belongs to her.
De no olvidarla jamás	Never to forget her
aunque pese al mismo Cielo	though it hurts Heaven itself,
hize propósito firme,	I made a firm promise
si no es que ya no me acuerdo.	even though I don't remember it.

En el 2° he jurado
más de dos mil juramentos.

Second, I have sworn
more than two thousand times.

En el 3° me acuso,
padre, quando entro en el templo,
no estoy atento a la misa
porque en verlas me deleito.

Third, I accuse myself,
Father, when I enter the temple
I don't pay attention to mass
because I love seeing women.

En el 4°, les perdí
a mis padres el respeto.

Fourth, I lost
respect for my parents.

En el 5°, yo me acuso
que levanté gran enrredo;
pues fui a decirle que el Sol
se parece a sus cabellos.

Fifth, I accuse myself
of causing great confusion;
I told her that the sun
looks like her hair.

En el 7° me acuso . . .
—¿Hijo, que dejas el 6°?
—Espantárame que el padre
no lo hubiera hechado menos.

Seventh, I accuse myself . . .
—Son, why do you leave out six?
—I hoped that the father
would miss it.

No tengo de que acusarme
en aqueste mandamiento,
porque al fin, padre, soy hombre
y mi dama es como un cielo.

I don't have to accuse myself
in this commandment,
because, finally, Father, I am a man
and my lady is like heaven.

—¿Tan bonita es esa niña?
—Si padre, como un lucero.
—¿A donde tiene su casa?
—En los profundos infiernos.

—Is she so pretty?
—Yes, Father, like a star.
—Where is her house?
—In the deepest hell.

—Hijo, no quiero mugeres.
—Pues padre, yo si las quiero,
que como de ellas nacimos,
en no viéndolas me mero.

—Son, I don't want women.
—Well, Father, I do,
since we are born from them,
if I don't see them, I die.

En el 7° me acuso
con grande arrepentimiento
que robo los corazones
por ver si me acogen dentro.

Seventh, I accuse myself
with great repentance
that I rob hearts
to see if they take me in.

En el 8° . . .

Eighth . . .

En el 9° me acuso
que a quantas mujeres veo,
no porque las quiera yo,
sino que las apetezco.

Ninth, I accuse myself
No matter how many women I see,
it is not because I love them,
but that I lust after them.

En el 10°...	Tenth...
—¿Hay templo, como no te hundes?	—Oh, temple, why don't you sink?
—No padre, no pida vmd eso, porque si el emplo se cae, a los dos no coge dentro.	—No, Father, don't ask that, because if the temple falls, we'll both be inside.
—Levantese vmd de aquí que yo absolverle no puedo.	—Stand up and leave because I cannot absolve you.
—Pues quedese con Dios padre que confesarme no quiero y voy a ver a mi dama que ha siglos que no la veo.	—Well, stay with God, Father, because I don't want to confess, and I am going to see my lady for I haven't seen her for ages.[31]

By means of a dialogue between the priest and the parishioner, this example parodies both confession and the Ten Commandments. It places in relief the conflicting points of view of center and periphery, its dialogic interaction creating tension between the two belief systems of the religious and the profane. The song shows how the parishioner confronted and evaluated the traditional belief system, and it is he who controls the situation. His condition as a subject allows him to appropriate the religious text and give it a different significance. He destroys the structure of the Commandments by giving them a meaning in opposition to the orthodox belief system, and profane love defeats sacred love.

Nothing escaped the burlesque humor of those who violated the law. No prohibition could prevent their expressions of sarcasm or blasphemy because everything was valid within their rhetorical game. The people laughed at parodies of the belief system, even though they continued to have faith in this same system. In 1785 in Querétaro, at a cockfight that some six hundred people attended, two women danced to a song called *Las bendiciones* in which the words and movements had "little virtue" and which was punctuated with this chorus:

Por ti no tengo camisa	For you I have no shirt
Por ti no tengo capote	For you I have no cape
Por ti no he cantado misa	For you I don't sing mass
Por ti no soy sacerdote	For you I am not a priest.

When the dancers finished a stanza one would remain standing and the other knelt "with impure gestures," as they sang the chorus, saying:

Mi vida, no te enternezcas	My love, don't relent,
y porque ves que me voy	and because you see me leaving

para la última partida,	for the last time,
¡echame tu vendición!	give me your blessing!

The standing dancer then blessed the one kneeling, who stood up, and they continued the dance and song. The priest who denounced this dance paid particular attention to its choreography. With photographic vision he recounted the various movements of the dancers, one of whom "lifted her petticoats to her knees and the other, twirling violently, showed her legs to her garters."[32] All in all, a rather explicit observation for a man of the cloth.

The inquisitors frequently charged that the gestures and movements of the dances defied the norms of decency and provided a bad example for all who watched by arousing profane passions and emotions. According to one Oaxacan bishop, the dances

> are not only occasions to sin, but also are sinful in and of themselves . . . because of the lasciviousness of the words, the gestures and movements, the nudity of the dancers, the reciprocal touching of men and women, by taking place in suspicious lower class houses, in the country, in poorly lit neighborhoods at night, and at times when the judges cannot discover them.[33]

Because the dancers' movements emphasized principally the lower parts of the body, the gestures that they created, apart from the text of the song, ridiculed and parodied the sublime, thus forming an upside-down world in which the degradation of canons constituted their principal objective. The sublime—that is to say, what was considered superior by the official world—was lowered to the level of the inferior corporal world, the world of stomachs, genitals, coitus, and excretions. The denunciation of the dance of the *Panaderos* (bakers) included a graphic description of its movements, and the informant asserted that the dance had been created "by a devil [who now is gone] taking the form of a woman who came from Bayadolid and sowed this bad seed."

[Sale una mujer cantando y vaylando desembueltamente con esta copla:]	[A woman goes out singing and dancing freely with these words:]
Esta sí que es panadera	She is really a baker
que no se sabe chiquear;	who doesn't indulge herself;
que salga su compañero	her partner must come out
y la venga a accompañar.	and accompany her.
[Sale un hombre vaylando y canta:]	[A man begins dancing and singing:]
Este sí que es panadero	He is really a baker
que no se sabe chiquear;	who doesn't indulge himself;

y si usted le da un besito,	and if you give him a tiny
comensará a trabaja.	kiss, he'll start to work.

[Estos dos siguen baylando	[These two continue dancing
con todos los que fuerren saliendo:]	along with all those who
	came out to dance with them:]
Esta sí que es panadera	She is really a baker
que no se sabe chiquear;	who doesn't indulge herself;
quítese usted los calsones	take off your underpants
que me quiero festejar.	because I want to party.

[Canta el hombre:]	[The man sings:]
Este sí que es panadero	He is really a baker
que no se sabe chiquear;	who doesn't indulge himself;
levante usted más las faldas	lift your skirts higher
que me quiero festejar.	because I want to party.

[Siguen baylando los cuatro.	[The four continue dancing.
Salen otros, hembra y macho.	Others come out, man and
Canta la hembra:]	woman. The woman sings:]
Esta sí que es panadera	She is really a baker
que no se sabe chiquear;	who doesn't indulge herself;
haga usted un crucifixo	Make yourself a crucifix
que me quiero festejar.	because I want to party.

[Canta el macho	[The man sings (as only heretics
(que sólo los hereges):]	would):]
Este sí que es panadero	He is really a baker
que no se sabe chiquear;	who doesn't indulge himself;
haga usted una Dolorosa	make yourself a Madonna
que me quiero festejar.	because I want to party.

In the same manner, other couples danced and sang, with additional verses that parody the Celestial Court, dogs, turkeys, and lizards. This song provides another example of the application of everyday speech of the lower classes. The baker's vocabulary, especially the names for different shapes of bread, made a play on words in the song. Even today one finds "kisses," "shirts," "underpants," "crucifixes," "madonnas," and other bread shapes in local bakeries, and bakers continue to have a risqué reputation. The names have different connotations depending upon the social language from which they come. The same word had a different meaning (referent) for distinct audiences. Apart from their primary signification (denotation), they also refer to their secondary meaning (connotation).

In 1748 the Inquisition asked Fray Gabriel de la Madre de Dios Pérez de León, a preacher of the Convent of Pachuca, to conduct an inquiry to determine the origin and abuses of these "provocative and lewd" dances. After four years he presented his results to the Holy Office. His investigation found that people performed these dances and songs in many parts of the colony and that even when priests, speaking from the pulpit, prohibited these amusements the people defended them, "asking the musicians to perform public fandangos, to play the damned song *Pan de Jarave* as well as *seguidillas* between men and women, that some assure me are worse even than the said *jarave*."[34] Fray Gabriel declared that every day people composed new couplets for this song with the deliberate intention of extending its popularity so that it would never fade away. At the same time he complained that the distribution of the Inquisition's edicts was poor, especially in the bishoprics of Valladolid and the Huasteca. He recounted finding edicts strewn on the floors of many of the churches that he visited.

The faulty distribution of inquisitorial edicts, so frequently reported, was difficult to remedy given the vast extension of the viceroyalty and the centralization of bureaucratic power in the capital that made communication difficult within the colony.[35] Moreover, since the persons in charge of distributing the edicts were sometimes partisans of the French philosophies, they not only neglected their official duties but also defied the orders of the Inquisition and tried to "seduce others into their errors and pernicious maxims." Fray Juan Francisco Ramírez de Arellano, an "adherent of the ideas of the Enlightenment," caused an enormous scandal. Among his revolutionary actions he abolished certain elements of the religious ceremony, such as the reading of the edicts of the Inquisition, because he believed that "the Inquisition only serves to render people ignorant with their prohibitions."[36]

Consequently, it is not surprising that dances and songs found their way into churches, creating a great scandal with some and giving pleasure to others. In fact, in some cases the church itself used profane diversions to attract people to religious ceremonies. In 1796 don José Máximo Paredes, cleric and minister of Mexico City's Metropolitan Cathedral choir, denounced the impious acts committed in sanctuaries, especially during the mass called the *Aguinaldo*, the Christmas Mass. He recounted an occasion during communion when the organist began to play the song *Pan de Manteca*. Paredes got up and gave a message to stop to the organist, who had the audacity to answer that those who paid his salary enjoyed this music. The same cleric complained that this type of music lured men and women to all sorts of diversions, and, sadly, "even Our Holy Mother the Church has been using this music to attract the Christian public to the celebration of the mysteries, but where it is absent, so is the congregation." Moreover, he provided a list of such songs and dances: "Pan de Manteca, Garbanzo, Perejiles, Chimizclanes, Llovisnita, Paternita, many types of boleros, many more of Tiranas, Melorico, Catatumba, Bergantín, Suá, Fandango, Mambrú."[37]

The insertion of these dances and songs into the churches of New Spain became a widespread custom. On March 11, 1805, an informant denounced the brothers of the Franciscan convent in Toluca for numerous excesses. The denunciator reported that inside the church, with the candles all snuffed out, the brothers danced to the "son de los Panaderos." During the revelry they got drunk with women and sang the "Mandamientos," the Ten Commandments, but transposed the sixth commandment to the affirmative.[38] In the village of Tamapachi similar fandangos occurred where women, drink, and cards were the principal attractions. During the processions of Holy Week there, Lieutenant José Herber ordered the saints removed so that the dances could take place inside the church, where they also offered for sale a considerable amount of liquor.[39]

The merriment of street songs infiltrated nearly every public space in the viceroyalty. Their proliferation, along with the spread of revolutionary ideas, so imbued the atmosphere that they challenged the colonial order, especially its hierarchical system. This structure was derived from Catholic doctrine that proclaimed humanity subject to the order imposed by God. The Spanish state, in this explanation, became the tool that reinforced natural law. Anyone who denigrated the religious order also assaulted the state. The texts reproduce the social reality that inspired them and from which the revelry and disorder began to impose themselves upon the norm. Within the structure of the texts, features particular to the social reality of the people who composed them are reflected in the merriment and disorder characteristic of the streets. Contrary to the harmonious and solemn image of the official discourse, the images provided by these expressions emphasized lasciviousness, parody, laughter—all elements taken from the popular culture. The structure of the text reproduces the world of the street. The characters who populate the songs were not invented but belonged to the lower classes and to the social periphery. They represent people who, by their nature, have the capacity to move freely from one space to another, to destroy the hierarchical order, and to mock religious symbols.

The dances and songs reflected the nature of the public places from which they emerged. Their essence consisted in the destruction of the official framework, whose hierarchical symbols were seen from below, from the streets where the official norms could be disobeyed. The lower classes made the sacred symbols the object, while the people became the subject, of the songs. This point of view became a powerful tool to demolish official structure. Moreover, it was not limited to the plebeians but could be utilized by members of every social class within the colony. The people's image of the world was completely externalized and its celebration became the goal of these manifestions. Everything was displayed in the midst of noise and commotion: skirts were lifted, religious habits hoisted, bodies revealed, genitals moved to the beat of the music. Everything was exposed on the same level as the hierarchical symbols were lowered and despoiled of their ornamentation and pomp, stripped of social value and given to the spectators to be reconstructed with their own clothes, in their own places, and through their own values.

The language used in the songs possessed a greater capacity for dynamism and change, which made it freer to cross the boundaries and to destroy the norm. It corrupted the purity of the sacred, authoritarian word, destroying it with the deployment of new images. This new attitude regarding language engendered a new perspective regarding words. Because the word was a symbol of authority, the lower classes separated it from the official context and adopted it as their own. The sacred word was placed on a lower level and incorporated into popular speech. Consequently, sacred word began to take on alternate meanings. When the word was separated from its original context, it acquired another significance within everyday language. The "word of God" was transformed into the "word of the people."

NOTES

1. AGN, *Inquisición*, vol. 1357, fol. 159r.

2. AGN, *Inquisición*, vol. 725, fol. 97r. The spelling of the period is respected but modern punctuation and accents have been added throughout this essay.

3. Dorothy Tanck de Estrada, "Tensión en la Torre de Marfil. La educación en la segunda mitad del siglo XVIII mexicano," in *Ensayos sobre historia de la educación en México*, ed. Josefina Zoraida Vásquez et al. (México, 2d ed., 1985), 29.

4. Luis González, "El optimismo nacionalista como factor de la independencia de México," in *Estudios de Historiografía América* (México, 1948), 155–212.

5. Enrique Florescano, *Estructuras y problemas agrarios de México, 1500–1821* (México, 1971), 35–47. Florescano notes that although economic depression characterized Spain in the eighteenth century, New Spain enjoyed a period of prosperity; mining, agriculture, and even commerce expanded prodigiously in the viceroyalty.

6. Cited by Juan Pedro Viqueira, "El sentimiento de la muerte en el México ilustrado del siglo XVIII a través de los textos de la época," *Relaciones* 5 (Winter 1981): 27–62 (citation on p. 57); ibid., 53.

7. Ibid., 44.

8. *La portentosa vida de la muerte*, 11, in Viqueira.

9. Yuri Lotman and Boris Uspensky, "On the Semiotic Mechanism of Culture," *New Literary History* 9 (Winter 1978): 211–29. They assert that we understand "culture as the nonhereditary memory of the community, a memory expressing itself in a system of constraints and prescriptions" (213).

10. Yuri Lotman, *Universe of the Mind: A Semiotic Theory of Culture*, trans. Ann Shukman (London, 1990), 123.

11. The term "boundary" is important to understanding the semiotic mechanism of culture. Lotman defines boundary as the outer limit of the first-person form (131). Every culture divides the image of the world by means of oppositions: heaven/hell, living/dead, god/devil, up/down, or open/closed.

12. Tanck de Estrada, 45.

13. AGN, *Inquisición*, vol. 1297, fol. 19r.

14. AGN, *Edictos* 11, fol. 8r.

15. In this instance, *china* does not refer to nationality; it means "a girl from the people who used to live serving no one and with a kind of liberty at the expense of a husband or a lover or by her own industry. She was mestiza and was also distinguished for her cleanliness and beauty." Francisco J. Santamaría, *Diccionario de mejicanismos* (México, 1959), 391.

16. The expression *meneadora de culo* cannot be translated exactly, but it refers to a curvaceous woman who, as she walks, accentuates the movement of her hips; the expression has sexual connotations. The lyrics are recorded in AGN, *Edictos* 11, fols. 294–295r.

17. AGN, *Inquisición*, vol. 1502, fol. 298r.

18. Juan Pedro Viqueira Albán, *¿Relajados o reprimidos? Diversiones públicas y vida social en la ciudad de México durante el Siglo de las Luces* (México, 1987), 133. An English translation of this volume is forthcoming from Scholarly Resources.

19. Carlos de Sigüenza y Góngora, *Relaciones históricas* (México, 1972), 133. *Bozales* at first referred to recently arrived Africans, but, by extension, began to connote recently arrived immigrants of low status. The labels *chino*, *mulatto*, *morisco*, *mestizo*, *zambaigo*, and *lobo* all refer to variations in racial mixtures. For an illustration, see Don Pedro Alonso O'Crouley, *A Description of New Spain*, trans. and ed. Seán Galvin (Dublin, 1972).

20. AGN, *Inquisición*, vol. 1170, fols. 201r–202r.

21. AGN, *Inquisición*, vol. 728, fol. 261r.

22. AGN, *Inquisición*, vol. 1312, fols. 138r–144r.

23. AGN, *Inquisición*, vol. 1253, fols. 43r–44r.

24. AGN, *Inquisición*, vol. 1377, fol. 22r.

25. AGN, *Inquisición*, vol. 1297, fol. 22r.

26. AGN, *Inquisición*, vol. 1297, fol. 18r.

27. Mijail Bajtin, *La cultura popular en la Edad Media y en el Renacimiento. El contexto de François Rabelais*, trans. Julio Forcat and César Conroy (Madrid, 1988), 59–130. Bajtin emphasizes the importance of laughter within popular culture.

28. AGN, *Inquisición*, vol. 1001, fols. 130r–v; ibid., vol. 1162, fols. 382r–v.

29. AGN, *Inquisición*, vol. 1410, fols. 73r–v.

30. AGN, *Inquisición*, vol. 1297, fol. 22r; ibid., vol. 1410, fols. 96r–v; ibid., vol. 1297, fol. 128r.

31. AGN, *Inquisición*, vol. 1377, exp. 7, fols. 395v–396r.
32. AGN, *Inquisición,* vol. 1272, fol. 32v.
33. María del Carmen Velázquez, "El siglo XVIII," in *Historia documental de México* (México, 1974), 416–18.
34. AGN, *Inquisición*, vol. 1297, fols. 16r–24v; ibid., fol. 23v.
35. While denouncing the disorders in the streets of Acapulco, a cleric asserted that in the "jurisdiction of Coyuca, distant from this port (eight leagues) and also in that of Atoyac, distant twenty, the people perform the same dances, and when they are admonished that the Holy Office punishes their acts with excommunication, they responded that this is not published here. I tried to transcribe the edicts of the Inquisition and to publish them. But, I stopped since I did not have Your Illustriousness' order[;] I am waiting for your divine majesty's word" (AGN, *Inquisición*, vol. 1170, fol. 202r). This chain of events also occurred in the city of Manila, where the authorities of the Holy Office asked to receive notification of the specific comedies that were prohibited (AGN, *Inquisición*, vol. 1170, fol. 242r).
36. AGN, *Inquisición,* vol. 1024, fol. 224r; ibid., vol. 1345, fol. 70r.
37. AGN, *Inquisición*, vol. 1312, fols. 149r–150r; ibid., fol. 150r.
38. AGN, *Inquisición*, vol. 1426, fols. 82r–109v.
39. AGN, *Inquisición*, vol. 1283, fols. 85r–85v.

3

The Working Poor and the Eighteenth-Century Colonial State: Gender, Public Order, and Work Discipline

Susan Deans-Smith
University of Texas

New Spain's tobacco monopoly provides the context for Susan Deans-Smith's recent monograph examining the evolving Mexico City work force. Professor Deans-Smith began this study as a dissertation at Cambridge University. In the following essay she tests the hypotheses of several historians of Europe's preindustrial workers. In particular, she creates a Mexican case for the gender studies of Joan Wallach Scott, especially the way in which different characteristics become encoded as masculine or feminine and then serve as boundaries for appropriate behavior. Furthermore, she offers a suggestive line of argument that draws on the "docile" workers of Michelle Perrot.[*] Throughout the discussion, the author focuses on the importance of space—home, street, and manufactory—and the ways it supplied the place in which the work experience and the domestic situation could promote what Alf Luedtke called *eigensinn*, a sense of individualism.[†]

This essay is based on my book, *Bureaucrats, Planters, and Workers: The Making of the Tobacco Monopoly in Bourbon Mexico* (Austin: University of Texas Press, 1992). Material from that volume is used with the permission of the University of Texas Press. I thank Eric Van Young for his helpful comments on an earlier draft.

[*]See Scott, *Gender and the Politics of History* (New York, 1988); Bryan D. Palmer, *Descent into Discourse: The Reification of Language and the Writing of Social History* (Philadelphia, 1990); and Michelle Perrot, "On the Formation of the French Working Class," in *Working Class Formation*, ed. Ira Katznelson and Aristide Zolberg (Princeton, NJ, 1986).

[†]"Cash, Coffee-Breaks, Horseplay: Eigensinn and Politics among Factory Workers in Germany circa 1900," in *Confrontation, Class Consciousness, and the Labor Process: Studies in Proletarian Class Formation,* ed. Michael Hanagan and Charles Stephenson (Westport, CT, 1986), 65–96.

S PAIN'S REFORM-MINDED BOURBON MONARCHS attempted nothing short
of a "reconquest of America." Their efforts at economic and political changes and the consequences are generally known, contrast-
ing with the poorly understood cultural dimensions of the reforms
and the popular urban response to Bourbon state building that
attempted to reorder and reclaim public space, to engineer a "reconquest of the streets."[1] The reformers made no attempt to change the
social order in fundamental ways, but many of their economic reforms could not succeed without implementing certain alterations in
social and cultural attitudes. Bourbon absolutism promoted order,
discipline, and control, especially as it related to the urban poor in
the public streets. Special attention went to the streets, because they
serve not only "for the circulation of people and merchandise," but
also became "centers of social life, a privileged space. Here, the population worked, bargained, ate, conducted civil and religious ceremonies, sauntered, entertained themselves and got drunk. Here too they
witnessed the daily spectacle of sex and death."[2] In the streets the
mixing of classes, sexes, and ethnicities cut across the idealized social and ethnic hierarchies and their representation of order, simmer-
ing with the potential for social disturbances. Although the campaigns
met with some success, colonial state officials remained fearful of
urban disorder, and these fears were inherited by the later republican
government.[3]

Reclaiming the streets went hand in hand with the colonial
administration's attempts to discipline the urban masses and to make
them productive assets of both the wider society and the state—in
other words, to get them to work. This effort both attacked guild
powers and actively encouraged women to undertake occupations "appropriate to their sex."[4] These Bourbon reformers reasoned that the
only "appropriate" spaces for the urban population were the church,
home, and workplace.[5] The director of the tobacco monopoly, Silvestre
Díaz de la Vega, summed up these views: "The man without an occupation is a dead man for the State; those who work are like living
plants which not only produce but also propagate . . . wherein lies the
true increase of the population and prosperity of the State."[6]

These concerns may be viewed through the colonial state's mono-
polization and management of the tobacco trade, especially through
the state-managed manufactory in the late eighteenth century. This
essay examines mainly the Mexico City tobacco manufactory (one
of six in the colony), its workers, and its management by a royal
bureaucracy. This manufactory represented: 1) the creation of a new
type of space for the working poor of both sexes and various backgrounds, and 2) the attempt to open up new spaces for women—primarily work outside the home or away from the streets. The

manufactory provided the opportunity for the Bourbon bureaucrats to put their policies into practice as they tried to implement work discipline and order on the large work force. Related to the goal of work discipline and control was the construction of occupations to some extent influenced by gender within the manufactories.[7] These work arrangements enable us to see, albeit at a basic level, how specific occupational identities were constructed and legitimated based on assumptions about male and female attributes. A final and much more speculative exercise considers the ways in which critiques of the manufactories and the monopoly in general were framed not only in terms of whether something was rational or irrational, just or unjust, but also whether it was moral or immoral, and, by extension, a "threat" to public order and morality. Such criticisms shed light on attitudes toward the workers and provide insights into how the colonial government and elites thought about "order" in society.

This examination of Mexico City's tobacco industry demonstrates a good deal about actions and attitudes of both managers and workers. The lack of overt, collective confrontation between them reveals that the colonial state successfully maintained public order. In place of confrontation, workers maintained some control over their lives by daily contesting working conditions in general, particularly the use and control of time and movement. This effort enabled them to exercise some command over their lives. Such actions merely reinforced the negative stereotypes of workers held by management and led them to interpret workers' actions in defense of their customs as "impertinent." Finally, criticisms of workers and their workplace, casuistic in character, illustrate that assumptions concerning gender and class partially shaped elite attitudes about the order of society.[8] In short, the "threat" posed by the tobacco manufactories did not necessarily derive from the fact that women were working but that they worked in the same enclosed space as men. Two images emerged in the discourse of state officials and the elite, that of the "working woman" and the "nonworking man." Both these images contradicted notions about what constituted order in society.

THE CREATION OF THE WORKSPACE: THE ROYAL TOBACCO MANUFACTORIES

The tobacco monopoly, established in 1765 and managed by a cadre of Bourbon bureaucrats administered by a *dirección general* (directorate-general), became one of the colony's largest industries, along with silver mining and textiles, and employed almost twenty thousand individuals. After the silver tithe, tobacco revenues ranked as the second most valuable source of government income and accounted for almost one fifth of total state revenues at the peak of their production. The new state enterprise became the only legal producer of tobacco products. Although the monopoly sold snuff and leaf tobacco, cigars and cigarettes accounted for 95 percent of annual sales.

Given the importance of manufacturing in the monopoly's operations, the directorate-general paid considerable attention to the organization and behavior of the workers. Between 1769 and 1780, six state-managed tobacco manufactories opened in Guadalajara, Oaxaca, Orizaba, Puebla, Querétaro, and, the largest, in Mexico City. These manufactories represented the Bourbon reformers' vision of an ideal colonial industry: free of guild restrictions, based on wage labor, and offering opportunities for both men and women. Viceroy Antonio María de Bucareli (1771–1779) firmly believed that the manufactory could serve as a refuge for Mexico City's poor. José de Gálvez, as visitor-general, viewed the manufactories as fulfilling the same purpose of the best *hospicio*. Women, in particular, could support themselves by working there, avoiding the "infinite risks," that is, prostitution, to which destitution made them vulnerable.[9]

The abolition of the tobacco shops occurred over almost ten years to allow workers to adjust to the reorganization. These individuals were assured of alternative employment in the manufactories, and disgruntled tobacconists, whose businesses had been destroyed, were placated with the offer of lifetime, high-paying supervisory positions there as well. As a result, the reformers incorporated the workers as collaborators in the establishment of the manufactories and gave them a vested interest in the monopoly's existence.

These manufactories provided a miniature of the Bourbon project to reform and control the populace by inculcating habits of disciplined work and ordered behavior. It emphasized submission to and respect for authority, as the following description of the manufactory suggests: "It provides the perfect school to instruct all who work there not only in their tasks but in all those qualities which make a civil man. . . . The manufactory is a workshop in which are made honest men . . . because in the manufactory every person lives subject to the voice which commands."[10] In the minds of the bureaucrats "good" workers were synonymous with obedient servants of the state.

From its beginning the monopoly presented itself as a paternal employer willing to assure workers of employment with similar pay and privileges given to them in the private workshops. Workers' perceptions of the paternalistic character of authority were conveyed in the informal name they gave to the manufactory, the *Casa del Rey* (House of the King), and their use of the term *El Rey Padre* (the

Father-King). Working conditions and organization reflected monopoly paternalism in several ways. The manufactories offered work on a relatively regular basis. The work week and year fluctuated, but extant time sheets suggest a relatively regular working year based on a six-day week, punctuated by religious holidays.[11] The periods during which workers could be laid off coincided with shortages of paper supplies or adjustments in production levels. During fluctuations and reductions in output of cigars and cigarettes, instead of laying off workers the management divided production quotas on a pro rata basis so that everyone could earn something. If it were necessary to close the manufactory for several days or weeks, the monopoly made loans as advances to the workers. Since the demand curve continued upward into the first decade of the nineteenth century regular production ensured, relatively speaking, regular work for those men and women who wanted it. In addition the workers established, with monopoly approval, their confraternity, the Concordia, that provided rudimentary illness and burial insurance. Finally, the manufactory ordered workers to submit any grievances or petitions to management for resolution.

This paternalist ethos certainly did not prevent the directorate-general from implementing reforms that increased the monopoly's profitability at the expense of the workers or using the power of the state (including the military, in rare instances) and the church to control them. The monopoly proved to be least paternal in the gradual reduction of piecework rates for cigarette rollers during the 1790s.[12] Tobacco workers, like many other urban workers, experienced the effects of late colonial inflation. The monopoly also gradually abolished many, although not all, of the nonmonetary benefits—such as "bonuses" of chocolate and free cigarettes to smoke while working—traditionally received by cigarette and cigar rollers during the 1780s and 1790s. The management, at the same time, introduced fines to penalize workers who wasted tobacco or paper. In the long term the state's gains from the monopoly were considerable. The Bourbon bureaucrats managed an industry that experienced an increase in profits from one million to four million pesos and in production of cigarettes from 40 million to 120 million packets.

The Bourbons aimed at creating a workplace as an alternative space but one without any of the perceived disorderliness of the streets. As such, manufactory and social discipline became inseparable as illustrated in regulations designed to encourage habits of regular, diligent work, sobriety, and obedience in the workers.[13] Thus, rules focused on punctuality (stipulating arrival and departure times), careful work, and obedience to supervisors. They discouraged immoral behavior with punishments for theft of monopoly materials, drunkenness, insubordination, gossip, gambling, cardplaying in the manufactory, and other "scandalous" behavior. Punishments ranged from a stint in the stocks, recompense for materials wasted, and temporary suspension from work to permanent prohibition from employment in any state tobacco manufactory.[14]

Regulations extended to the daily appearance and dress of the workers, a result of the reformist zeal of Juan Vicente de Güemes Pacheco y Padilla, the second Count of Revillagigedo, and the absolutist penchant for uniforms. Horrified at the partially clad working population—a moral rather than functional view as the manufactories were hot, stuffy places—he ordered all workers of the Mexico City manufactory and the food vendors who supplied them to wear specified clothing. Those who did not conform risked being refused entry to work until they acquired the required shirt, trousers, stockings, hat, and shoes. The cost of the clothing totaled twenty-three pesos, four and one half reales. Money for the clothing was deducted in small amounts over four months; once the necessary amount had been accumulated the administrator handed it to the worker with express orders to purchase the necessary clothes. Workers, rarely silent over objectionable orders, expressed no outrage following this declaration. Indeed, the director-general reported to the viceroy that "making the people of this type dress well, something that has never been done in New Spain, has produced a change in them, and now they are like new workers."[15] Whether the clothing regulation endured over the following decades is not known. This regulation may well acknowledge attitudes about the poor that motivated the viceroy to make manufactory workers appear "respectable" to the public eye.[16]

In the long run the state seemed less than satisfied with its attempts to discipline these employees. Even so, the tobacco workers instigated few major confrontations or street violence—two walkouts in 1780 and 1782, and a protest in 1794—during a fifty-year period. In hindsight it appears that the colonial administrators managed to negotiate and channel potential conflict. Yet there are numerous descriptions of the "disorderly" nature of the workers that originate clearly from contemporary expectations and definitions by the monopoly bureaucrats of what morality and order entailed. In the case of the manager it was more than making sure that the workers did not constantly take to the streets: they should exhibit deference, obedience, and, it would seem, some skill at their jobs. At the beginning of the nineteenth century, Viceroy Félix Berenguer de Marquina described Mexico City's manufactory employees as "four thousand workers of both sexes, the majority of them ill-bred, arrogant, restless, difficult to control and discontented." As a result, from the director-general's perspective they produced poorly made cigars and cigarettes. He reported in 1817 that the quality still left much to be desired and resulted in constant losses to the monopoly as consumers sought out contraband products.[17]

MEXICO CITY'S TOBACCO MANUFACTORY WORKERS

Before considering the workers' response to these attempts to impose discipline and other regulations, it is worth examining the size and composition of the Mexico City manufactory workforce and the administration's perceptions of it. By 1790 tobacco workers constituted approximately 12 percent of Mexico City's economically active population.[18] Measured another way, in late eighteenth-century Mexico City the tobacco manufactory employed 12,697 (55.1 percent) of the workers engaged in industrial work who received a money wage, followed by 380 (12.8 percent) in textile workshops and 9.3 percent in food production.[19] Monopoly bureaucrats, in their assessments of the numbers dependent upon work in the manufactories, counted not only those actually employed but also the family members they helped support. They calculated the total by multiplying the number of workers by an estimated two dependents for a minimum of twenty thousand persons.[20] Based on such calculations, if we take Mexico City's 1790 estimated population of 112,926, almost one fifth of the city's inhabitants depended in some measure upon manufactory work for survival.[21] With this in mind one understands the director-general's caution when it came to implementing new policies or strategies to improve production as well as the colonial government's desire to avoid social conflict and antagonisms.

Workers in the tobacco manufactories came from a variety of social backgrounds: they ranged from former tobacco-shop owners and their employees, semi- and unskilled men and women from the urban populations of the manufactory towns, residents and migrants, and those who received patronage positions granted by the viceroy or director-general to retired bureaucrats or their relatives. The workforce was differentiated according to gender, marital status, social class, race, and skill. The former tobacco-shop owners and their families comprised, according to the director-general, "a considerable number . . . (including children) who work in the *fábrica*."[22] In 1811 a sample of the tobacco workers in the Mexico City manufactory demonstrated that the majority of males were married. In comparison the majority of females (72 percent) were either single or widowed, a figure that represents the growing concentration of impoverished women in the tobacco industry.[23] Contemporary observers believed that the manufactories acted as magnets for migrants from the surrounding countryside. José de Gálvez even claimed that the Mexico City manufactory created the "notorious increment" in the population of the city because "it has attracted, is attracting, and will attract many poor families to this capital."[24] Recent studies suggest that the manufactory hired Mexico City's under- and unemployed residents rather than provincial migrants; an estimated 69 to 76 percent of the tobacco factory employees were from the capital.[25]

The racial cartography of the tobacco workers suggests a predominance of Spanish, mainly creole, and mestizo workers. In the Mexico City manufactory, peninsulars and creoles dominated supervisory and guard positions. A sample of 1,753 cigarette rollers who worked in Mexico City in 1811 broke down into 67 percent Spanish, 16 percent Indian, and 15 percent castas.[26] Manufactory bureaucrats rarely included racial characterizations in general descriptions of workers; rather, they used class terms such as the ubiquitous "plebe" or *operarios* (workers).[27]

The manufactories reflected the structure of a large-scale concentration of labor with an elite core of supervisory staff on a fixed wage who organized and managed large numbers of semi- and unskilled workers on a piecewage. At its peak the Mexico City manufactory employed almost nine thousand workers. Despite the division of labor according to occupation, the cigarette and cigar rollers formed the overwhelming majority: labor in the state manufactories remained fundamentally manual. The organization of labor there, far from resulting in homogeneity of the work force, resulted in new identifications and boundaries based on the occupational *cuerpos*.

The *cuerpos* were organized around the different manufactory tasks such as wrapping, shredding, rolling, stamping, and packing. These groups, not the Concordia, represented workers' grievances to the manufactory administration. The existence of these corporate entities also created tensions as workers were brought together through membership in the Concordia, while the *cuerpos* divided them again according to their tasks. Even the largest group, the cigarette rollers, were not leveled by the division of labor within the manufactory. Possibly as a response to loss of control over who was hired, dilution of skills, and a general reevaluation of their status, the older cigarette rollers distinguished themselves *de la profesión* (professional cigarette workers who were, by implication, skilled) as opposed to those who were employed in later years *de la calle* (literally, "from the street," and, by implication, unskilled). Workers who considered themselves *de la profesión* pointed out the distinction on several occasions to justify complaints against reduced work quotas at a time when they perceived that workers they classified *de la calle* were still being hired.[28]

DISCIPLINE AND WORKERS' RESPONSES

Manufactory regulations transcended the limits of the workplace and demanded reform of workers' morals and social mores, a policy that impinged upon their lives in general.[29] The workers' resentment at such reforms conveyed an underlying concern with their ability to live their lives as they saw fit, not according to mandates of the colonial state. Such contestations, either implicitly or explicitly, were related to issues of movement and management of time and how they affected a worker's ability to survive.

Manufactory regulations demanded regular and ordered work, yet daily practice suggests something rather different, as illustrated in the employees' strategies to manipulate the manufactory's time and space to their best advantage. The dominance of piecework allowed for flexible time management among the workers, although monopoly bureaucrats did not appear to take such flexibility into account when discussing the "undisciplined" and "unreliable" nature of the workers and the problems of enforcing regular work habits. The manufactory administrator reported that one day approximately 4,900 *tareas* (tasks) were distributed based on the number of workers listed, but no more than 3,600 were completed, leaving 1,300 unfinished due to "the continuous and voluntary lack of attendance by workers on a regular basis." By the beginning of the nineteenth century, according to the director-general, production levels remained uncertain because of discretionary attendance by some workers.[30]

Much of the blame for the poor work habits was placed on male cigarette rollers. The director-general emphasized their "shiftlessness," demonstrated by their continuous migration and the abandonment "of their souls as well as their families so that [the women] find themselves without fathers, husbands, brothers or sons."[31] These bureaucratic observations say nothing about the frequency of worker absenteeism, which was undoubtedly less than their reports would like to suggest, given the volume of annual cigarette production. The career patterns of male supervisors, for example, imply quite the contrary; individuals worked for twenty years in the Mexico City manufactory, several beginning as cigarette rollers and working their way up to supervisory positions.[32] But the perceptions and expectations of monopoly bureaucrats prevailed over actuality. Their reports focused on the unreliability of male cigarette rollers and this perception was used as a justification for employing only women—a point to be considered later.

To manage their time in the workplace, workers devised a strategy, called *la voz de fletes*, in which they sold their *tareas* to *fleteros* (generally children, inexperienced workers, or possibly relatives) for less than the estimated full value of the *tarea* and then pocketed the difference. While their *fleteros* worked, the "employers" left the manufactory to take care of other needs, returning in time to deliver their *tareas*, "appropriating the benefit without having worked for it." Repeated prohibitions against the practice indicated its popularity and persistence.[33]

The ongoing battle between workers and monopoly management for control over time and movement is also illustrated by a lengthy and ultimately successful legal fight by the workers to prevent the director-general from abolishing their confraternity, the Concordia. Between 1770 and 1793 the Concordia's management became the target of attack and investigation. Practically from its founding, from 1770 until 1783, its council had included several members who abused and embezzled its funds. The directorate-general and the manufactory administrator immediately pressed for the Concordia's abolition, arguing that *concordantes* often failed to receive compensation in accordance with their contributions and advising that most workers neither wanted nor benefited from its operations.[34] Behind the allegations of mismanagement of funds, evidence suggests that the directorate-general feared the Concordia's collective strength, which permitted workers a "voice so inclined to influence the very movements which one tries to avoid."[35] Despite threats from the administrator, in a statement to the viceroy the workers outlined the reforms necessary to eliminate past abuses: a new election of *conciliarios* (councillors) to supervise collection, management, and investment of funds; and a reassertion of their "right" to elect officers. They also requested that the chest that held the funds be moved from the manufactory to the Hospital de San Juan de Dios and that they retain the "right" to decide whether to remain at home or enter one of the hospitals when ill.[36]

In 1791, ten years after the investigation began, Viceroy Revillagigedo ruled in favor of the Concordia and ordered the immediate implementation of revised confraternal regulations designed to prevent further abuses. While the colonial state may have taken seriously its Christian and moral duties to protect the poor and encourage them to better themselves, it did so with one eye on profit. The revisions represented a move by the directorate-general to use the Concordia as a way to impose regular work habits on the manufactory workers. Under the new rules, access to Concordia contributions increasingly depended upon both regularity at the job and the length of time worked. Death benefits were restricted to those who had worked at the manufactory for at least eight years, and all other benefits required a minimum of one year before a claim could be made. Those employees who had stopped working for at least a month, even though they had paid their weekly contributions, lost their benefits. If they chose to return to the manufactory, "benefits" time had to be built up from the date they returned. Those workers who came to the job regularly, year after year, gained access to loans, daily income when sick, and assurance of a decent burial; those who did not found themselves excluded from Concordia benefits.[37]

Interpretations of the Concordia and the colonial state's decision to permit its continuation vary. Some historians argue that it became the "tool" of the monopoly, manipulated to dominate and control the workers.[38] Acknowledging that the Concordia was used to strengthen control over the workers' movements and to enforce regular attendance requires two additional observations. First, that there was no outcry against the revised regulations may reflect the approval by many of the men and women who worked regularly, expected to receive the benefits from their contributions, and wanted more honest management of their funds. Moreover, the Concordia possessed a wider symbolic importance for the workers, transcending the reform regulations because it reinforced their sense of independence. At stake, as they saw it, was the ability to control both institutional and personal space. Two demands already discussed illustrate workers' concerns—relocation of the Concordia treasury from the manufactory to the Hospital de San Juan de Dios and the right to choose where to seek recuperation when ill. The treasury remained in the manufactory, but workers succeeded in retaining the option to be treated in a hospital or in their homes, exercising their right, in other words, to maintain control over their movements.

If these practices reflected workers' beliefs of what was fair in the disposal of time and its use for their own rather than the monopoly's needs, the same could be said of their use of monopoly materials. By far, the most widespread and controversial practice was embezzlement of paper and shredded tobacco. Opportunities abounded, despite daily searches by guards, for workers to take small quantities of tobacco and paper to sell in the streets for whatever price people would pay, supplementing the inadequate income earned from piecework. A worker who smuggled out paper could sell it, barter it, or make contraband cigarettes. Not surprisingly, the greatest losses resulted from the manufactory's practice of allowing employees to prepare cigarette paper at home for the following day's work. Workers substituted cheaper, much coarser material for the fine cigarette paper. Those supervisors who took their jobs seriously had no difficulty in detecting the substitution. From the perspective of monopoly administrators such practices amounted to theft, and they

punished them as such. From the workers' perspective, their "appro-
priations" may have indicated their expectations of a nonmonetary
perquisite.

INSUBORDINATION AND SURVIVAL: TWO SIDES OF THE SAME COIN?

Despite official rhetoric about the beneficial effects of the manufactory, some monopoly bureaucrats and supervisors harbored misgivings about the impact of the regime on the workers, given their
continued "immorality" and disorderliness. Guards and foremen complained in 1783 of the increasing insubordination of workers and the
difficulties encountered in the management of more than five thousand individuals. They described life in the manufactory as characterized more by violence than order and discipline: "It is a rare day in
which one or several of the workers do not leave [the manufactory]
bleeding from blows or wounds which have been inflicted upon them
by other workers." Requests from administrators for additional
guards—even troops—to help control the unruly behavior grew
during the last decades of the eighteenth century, although one administrator discounted the intensity and frequency of violence.[39] Nevertheless, bureaucratic assessments of tobacco workers remained, for
the most part, negative, and they were variously described as "in-
competent people, full of vices," "riotous and rebellious," and "scandalous and noisy."[40]

   Like Europe's working poor, tobacco workers became the object
of "a moralizing discourse" that focused on the paradox of their poverty juxtaposed against their expenditures on "luxury" goods (especially alcohol) and irregular work habits. Members of the Real
Tribunal y Audiencia de la Contaduría Mayor de Cuentas de México
observed that "the majority . . . lack healthy principles and good education. . . . Although they work for a daily wage which provides their
basic necessities, many prefer to indulge in vice, most commonly the
drinking of *pulque*, *aguardiente* or both, even when they cannot afford to."[41] Monopoly administrators asked, "Who among them ever
considers tomorrow, today?"[42] These observations may have contained
some truth: tobacco workers enjoyed gambling as a popular pastime
to the point that cigarette rollers were arrested for gambling twice as
often as the next most numerous group, weavers.[43] Therefore, apparent contradictions between the relative poverty of manufactory workers and their resistance to work discipline merit a close examination.

   This review will clarify issues both of economic practice and
imperatives and of social perception. Tobacco workers may have been

on the job more consistently than other skilled and low-skilled workers, but they also gambled, drank, attended bullfights, and skipped work. For the large, diverse work force at the manufactory, at least three possible explanations arise. First, some of the workers were, more than likely, shiftless and profligate. Second, manufactory administrators' complaints that some of the workers left early without finishing a full day may have resulted either because they had made enough to survive by pooling family incomes, or that the flexibility of piecework permitted them to use their job in the manufactory as a relatively secure base from which to seek other supplemental work. Third, some workers may not have relied solely on wages for subsistence.

Consider Michael Sonenscher's hypothesis about French workers in the eighteenth century. Survival, he argues, even at the margins, depended only partially on a wage income. He suggests that the paradox of luxury and debauchery can be understood only when it is recognized that eating, drinking, housing, and other consumption were not predicated exclusively on wages, so that "the business of living was bound up with their capacity to subvert the economy of time embodied by the wage rate and redefine it around their changing economy of needs."[44] In other words, money was not yet needed to buy all the necessities of life. We simply do not know what proportion of the tobacco workers' income came from their manufactory wages, although for many it was likely to be the major source. The workers, apparently, found ways in which to accommodate their needs without taking to the streets by manipulating the work regime. Discretionary movement in and out of the workplace, made possible by piecework, undoubtedly responded to the changing needs of household economies and individuals alike. Despite the regularity of manufactory work, declining wages and layoffs exacerbated the uncertainty of daily survival and created imperatives in conflict with those of the monopoly, which demanded regular attendance and careful work habits.[45] The outcome was the coexistence of competing sets of economic imperatives. The monopoly management perceived the workers' strategies to ensure survival (the economic reality) as nothing more than insubordination and an ongoing failure to internalize anything remotely resembling the work ethic (the social perception).

PETITIONS AND PROTESTS

The ability of workers to submit petitions or written grievances to the manufactory administration acted as the central safety valve between workers and the monopoly, reducing the buildup of tensions and conflict. These dispute procedures drew on long-established traditions of the Spanish state that encouraged negotiation and compromise.[46] Workers, sometimes collectively as *cuerpos*, sometimes as individuals, submitted petitions for a variety of reasons that, nevertheless, reveal five broad categories of conflict with the monopoly: management of time and work discipline; fraud and abuse of power by supervisory staff (including intimidation and physical mistreatment); wage levels; violation of customary practices (provision of nonmonetary perquisites, access to raw materials); and hiring practices (including both unfair dismissal and nepotism). The manufactory administrator complained of the toll that the daily flood of complaints and petitions took on him, saying that the grievances concentrated on "maligning others of better merit or me . . . because I refuse to accede to their requests."[47] Even taking into account possible and probable exaggeration, the administrator's complaint suggests that the workers took their bosses at their word.

Management never commended workers for using established procedures but rather interpreted their grievances as further evidence of the disorderly and impertinent nature so "characteristic" of the poor. These administrative attitudes, reflecting assessments of the usually negative worker reactions to changes in daily routine, guided management's decisions. The best example concerned the 1781 investigation into the misuse of Concordia funds, whose beginning coincided with Holy Week. Normally, workers received loans during the feast, but the directorate-general argued that with the investigation in process, no advances should be made. The administrator warned that "knowing the character and way of thinking of these people . . . we will have a riot aimed at the directorate-general or the Royal Palace to request the loan." The administrator cared little whether the action was justified—his concern was how best to avoid conflict. Workers received the loans.[48]

The monopoly did not always decide in favor of the workers' petitions, and they did not perpetually take to the streets. This suggests the employees generally accepted both the authority that made such decisions and its legitimate right to do so. Limits to compromise existed, and discontent could not always be channeled through negotiations and petitions within the safe confines of the manufactory walls. On occasion, workers disrupted public order as they took their claims into the streets, in effect "bargaining by riot."[49] The contestation, for the most part, reflects not only a conflict over management of time, place, and materials but also the conflicting economic imperatives of the tobacco monopoly as a state enterprise and the domestic economies of the workers.

The first outburst occurred on September 6, 1780, when two hundred workers from the Mexico City manufactory marched on the viceregal palace to protest an increased workload that did not, as they understood it, raise wages as well.[50] The second incident took place on December 30, 1782, when workers were ordered home so that a general inventory of stock could be taken. Immediately, "up went the cries and out they went to the Palace . . . the mass entered without respect for the Guard, occupying the patios, stairs and corridors. The extraordinary noise aroused Viceroy [Martín de] Mayorga who, on determining the cause . . . ordered the administrator to allow them to work. The workers were thus pacified and carried the order in triumph."[51]

The most serious conflict, at least from the colonial state's perspective, occurred in 1794 in what could be called the Paper Riot. The controversial reform that provoked the riot originated in the monopoly's attempts to rationalize production and reduce theft and waste of cigarette paper. This paper came from Spain, but, as wars and embargoes interrupted shipments, the situation called for efficient use and stockpiling. "Appropriation" by workers and waste through unskilled rolling exacerbated the shortage. The solution was to exercise greater control by making cigarette rollers prepare their paper at work as their first task each morning instead of allowing them to prepare it at home each evening for the following workday. After the Mexico City manufactory prohibited taking paper home at night, cigarette rollers submitted petitions in the usual manner to protest the order and ask that it not be implemented. Denial of their request provoked radical action. On Monday morning, January 13, 1794, an estimated crowd of fourteen hundred women and men, approximately one quarter of the cigarette rollers, shouted demands for a repeal of the order as they marched on the viceregal palace. Witnesses later testified that protesters stood in front of the manufactory and pelted compliant workers with stones as they passed by to enter. Troops arrived to disperse demonstrators and return them to the manufactory. By 10:30 A.M., reportedly, everybody had returned to work.

Representatives in the "name of the workers," however, continued to petition against the reform. Both men and women argued that the preparation of paper was simple but arduous, and a worker could not roll and twist in the same day without damaging his or her fingers and shoulders. Preparation at home with the help of family took from one half to several hours. The representatives conceded the occurrence of theft and substitution of poor- for high-quality paper, but they explained the disadvantage of the practice; poor-quality stock could not be worked as easily and thereby jeopardized the completion of a *tarea*.

This petition caused the directorate-general to investigate the implications of the proposed reform for the workers and for the volume of cigarette production. The manufactory administrator argued that in the long term the rate of production would decline, the quality of the product worsen. Preparation of paper at the beginning of each day placed an excessive burden on the workers, who would, as they attempted to maintain their normal output, become exhausted and ill. Two weeks after the protest management reversed the decree, restoring home preparation of paper. The workers' representatives responded with a deferential declaration of gratitude to the king: "Only with silence can we thank you. There is no other language more meaningful for a prince as perfect as your excellency."[52]

Possibly, the workers saw the issue as the defense of their domestic economies. Preparation of paper at home with family help, access to a commodity that could supplement their income, and the ability to manipulate the piecework system permitted a flexibility that allowed them to manage their time and movements to the best advantage of their own and their families' needs. After a few months of the new system, with or without worker protest, the directorate-general in all likelihood would have reestablished the old method of preparation to avoid a fall in cigarette production. Two conclusions emerge: first, the resolution was ostensibly in the workers' favor, affirming the justice of the procedure of investigation and resolving the uncertainties created by the intended reforms; second, the colonial state remained unwilling to undertake economic innovations at the price of social peace. After 1794, Bourbon administrators made no further attempts to implement reforms in the organization of production in the manufactories, and they reported no further protests comparable to the Paper Riot. Nevertheless, petitions and shouting matches continued apace as part of daily negotiations between management and workers.

GENDER AND MANUFACTORY REORGANIZATION

The Paper Riot of 1794 confirmed the monopoly bureaucracy's worst perceptions of the disorderly nature of workers, which threatened social peace. Two years later fear of future outbursts by tobacco workers resulted in bitter, protracted discussions of plans to abolish the tobacco manufactories or to reduce the size of the one in Mexico City. Defenders simultaneously emphasized the secure source of revenue and produced an expedient set of rationalizations. The ministers of the Real Tribunal y Audiencia de la Contaduría Mayor de Cuentas de México, reviewing the workers' behavior before 1796, argued that it was necessary to understand the reasons behind the "commotions." In general, the tobacco workers were happy with the little they earned, and "their ideas and thoughts do not extend to sophisticated undertakings, or to the interruption or disturbance of the rules of good order." The three outbursts expressed dissatisfaction with rulings believed to be unfair and prejudicial to their work and incomes, although that certainly did not excuse the strategies adopted. No evidence existed of any conspiracy to arouse the public or encourage violent sedition against the king or government. The ministers concluded that, with better management, the riots could have been avoided. To prevent repetition of such movements the administrator needed to abolish abuses and keep good order.[53]

Despite the observations of the ministers of the Tribunal de Cuentas, manufactory administrators sought to achieve better management simply by reducing the number and altering the gender composition of workers employed in Mexico City. A fascinating part of the directorate-general's strategy to manage this unruly work force created a program to employ only women in manufactories, particularly as cigarette rollers. The policy became practice: in 1795 women comprised 43 percent of the Mexico City manufactory work force (3,055); by 1810 they had increased to an estimated 71 percent (3,883). Although the Mexico City work force had declined in number, the percentage share still represented an absolute increase in the number of women employed.[54] Analysis of this change shows how occupational identities may be based on associations with not only skill but also "natural" moral characteristics of women, which were used to legitimate such policies. The manufactory administrator argued that cigarette rolling was an appropriate task for women, whose small hands were more deft at the work tables, and that women were more obedient, less likely to steal or to move, thus improving regular attendance. In general, women were simply the moral superiors of men. Moreover, working in the tobacco manufactory protected women from becoming victims of the streets, either as vagrants or, worse, as prostitutes. Absent from any discussion of the motivations of the monopoly bureaucracy is the lower cost of female labor; but surely more than coincidence explains why in the 1790s, when the shift to employ only women occurred, the piecework rate for cigarette rollers declined significantly.

Unfortunately, we have no evidence that provides meaningful insights into female manufactory workers' responses to their new environment that could be compared to recent studies on women factory workers. Giulia Calvi, for example, has examined the relationship between women and work in the United States, and the ways in which the relationship was "lived by the women involved, their perception of their new identity as workers, and their use of time, money, and the space in which they worked—the factory."[55] Did women manufactory workers experience, as Calvi has argued, that "their very being together, was the first and fundamental discovery that work in a factory offered to young women workers"?[56] At this point what work in the tobacco manufactory meant for the women and men in social and cultural terms remains unknown, provoking a series of questions: How did work in the tobacco manufactory affect their perceptions of themselves? of one another? of whether the manufactory did indeed offer the best—or the worst—of all possible prospects in their lives?

The decision to employ only women no doubt drew from a variety of influences, combining an idealized view of their "docility" with the Bourbon policy to encourage females of the lower classes to work. As Joan Wallach Scott has recently argued, "Gender serves . . . also to identify (and contrast) abstract qualities and characteristics. . . . These qualities and characteristics are encoded as masculine or feminine, and they do not correlate exactly with what real men and women can do. . . . Yet they are not entirely unrelated to social roles either, because they provide some of the concepts that set rules, that articulate limits and possibilities for the behavior of men and women."[57] Monopoly bureaucrats held perceptions about men and women workers to some degree at odds with the manufactory workers' everyday actions. Idealizations about the respectable female worker ignored the daily behavior of women on the job. Male workers used a number of disobedient strategies, and women also used these defiant and "unseemly" actions, which included shouting matches, fistfights, and protests. Yet, none of these was sufficient to alter the views about the moral qualities of the women. Similarly, the notion of the "shiftless" male worker prevailed over those stalwart men who toiled in the manufactory for ten, fifteen, even twenty years. Nevertheless, such perceptions helped to establish definitions of gender roles used to shape policy. Such stereotypes could also be used to critique official policies. They show how gender in practice is anything but oppositional or dichotomous, although it may be made so by official actions, as in the case of the employment policies for the Mexico City manufactory after 1794.

DOCILITY OR DEFIANCE?

Ongoing negotiation and compromise rather than sharp conflict, for the most part, characterized monopoly-work relations. Several factors help to explain this relationship. First, the manufactory provided the opportunity for negotiation. Second, the paternalistic ethos of the manufactory helped to deflect conflict. Third, the wider imperial objectives of the state-endorsed social stability in its colonies contributed to decisions in favor of workers' demands and, in turn, perpetuated the legitimate and just nature of Bourbon policy.

These explanations focus on general conditions, but New Spain's domestic economy and local community life require closer scrutiny. Though evidence is scarce, recent arguments on the formation of the French working class suggest some questions and directions for future research into Mexico's urban workers, especially those in the tobacco manufactory. Michelle Perrot has emphasized "the growing awareness of space as a strategic element in games of power, as a stake in social struggles. . . . The thesis of Ira Katznelson is particularly worthy of attention: the separation between residence and workplace provides one of the keys for understanding the formation of the modern working class." The author further suggests that the relationship between workplace and home was "complicated" and that workers resisted the introduction of new technology because it might split work and home. For the early stages of industrialization, Perrot reversed Katznelson's hypothesis: "Because the family remained the principal center of decision making, the family residence, and more broadly the local community—the village or urban neighborhood—formed the basis of a popular autonomy rooted in the structures and networks of this community." For Perrot the central relevance of family or neighborhood may account in part for the "docility" of the workers in early "paternalist" factories. She argues this was "a system for integrating manpower: it was founded on the exploitation of family work power, transported into the walls of the factory, with the father's responsibilities often reinforced. . . . In exchange for complete submissiveness, these institutions provided regular work, a certain degree of protection, for a stable nucleus of workers. . . . By means of assimilation or of fear, it often resulted in the formation of an integrated body of manpower, whose docility goes a long way toward explaining the frequent silence of factories in the early stages of industrialization."[58]

Such arguments are suggestive but may need qualification in the case of tobacco workers. First, as argued above, they did not engage in many protests or prove to be particularly militant, but neither could they be described as docile. Perhaps the lack of collective protests indicates not the "docility" or "immaturity" of labor in the eighteenth century but rather the workers' ability to pressure successfully their employer, the colonial state, in order to satisfy their demands without resorting to collective protest.[59]

Second, Perrot's argument suggests that there continued to be considerable linkage between the places and spaces of home and work. The transfer of the tobacco industry from private to public management incorporated continuity as well as change in the organization and conditions of work. As a result, daily routines associated with tobacco manufacture in the private workshops, although modified, probably continued within the manufactory and helped to bridge the home and workplace, making the impact of the regime less sharp. Perhaps the most significant bridge between work and home was the "putting out" practice described above, whereby cigarette rollers took paper home with them every evening to prepare, often with the aid of their families, for the following day's work in the manufactory. In addition, management eventually formalized the informal practice started by women the first day they began work by establishing an *escuela de amigas* in the building to take care of nursing babies and young children. The ability to bring children into the workplace and to prepare part of a day's work at home permitted flexible integration of productive and domestic labor and some continuity with past practice.

Residential patterns suggest that many of the workers and their families lived concentrated together in neighborhoods close to the manufactories. Santa Ana in Querétaro was associated with "*gente ruin* [wretched people] and workers of the Royal Tobacco Factory."[60] The parish of Santa Catalina Mártir in Mexico City was a popular neighborhood for many workers and their families, who attended mass and were confessed in the local churches. Single tobacco workers usually lived in the same *casas de vecindad* (tenement houses) as married coworkers.[61] The manufactory was physically and spatially distinct from the workers' homes but close enough to facilitate movement back and forth, to enable the "interpenetration of family and work . . . and neighborhood."[62] For some employees the home remained part of the workplace, possibly enhancing their sense of autonomy. This particular relationship was something to be protected and may partly explain workers' motivations to protest, as in the case of the proposed reform of paper preparation, which would have forced greater separation between home and workplace and thereby lessen the individual's control over management of the family economy.

Moreover, the division between home (community) and the workplace, and how it affects popular action, may require refining. The tobacco workers appear to have concentrated their actions outside the manufactory, confirming Perrot's hypothesis with regard to the link between local community and popular autonomy. Workers' testimonies gathered during the investigation of the Paper Riot repeatedly referred to conversations and petition-gathering that took place in the barrios or neighborhoods close to the manufactory, in the *pulquerias*, in local churches, and even in local hospitals, where an ailing worker unwittingly revealed the protesters' plans. But testimonies also reported that workers circulated petitions in the workplace and affixed posters criticizing management to manufactory walls. In other words, the organization of the proposed strike occurred both inside and outside the manufactory.

Clearly, multiple spaces were being used. The organization of the Paper Riot also suggests that not only "space" but also wider influences, particularly state policies and management strategies, shaped the workers' political action. Finally, the composition of the work force and the associations permitted in both workplace and residence need to be taken into account. Daily living, associations, and identities of workers were rooted in and shaped by a variety of institutional and social relations that incorporated both work and home: through the occupational *cuerpos* within the manufactory, for instance, and the trade confraternity, the Concordia; through family, neighborhood, church, and tavern. If anything, the workers' actions resemble what Alf Luedtke has identified as *eigensinn* in the case of nineteenth-century German factory workers, the phenomenon whereby work experience and domestic situation promoted a sense of individualism.[63] Such associations enabled workers to act collectively yet contributed to social cleavages among them. The organization of work and wages created divisions within the work force, which were reinforced by existing differences based on status, gender, and ethnicity, and that hindered the formation of a broader class identity among the workers.

THE MANUFACTORY AND THE STREET

Some members of the state bureaucracy and the elite criticized the workers and tobacco manufactories. Such complaints provide insights into their perspectives on public order. In selected examples, the casuistic nature of fundamentally economic critiques of the tobacco manufactories forms the common element; that is to say, they were framed within a moralizing discourse. The Consulado de México fulminated about the harmful consequences of tobacco manufactories both to the economy and to the individual: "The manufactories established in Orizaba, Oaxaca, Puebla, México, Querétaro, and Guadalajara, have left all the other towns without employment in this occupation [cigarette and cigar rolling] and taken from them a multitude of families who go to work in one of those six privileged places. In these they live . . . a most licentious life, negligent in spiritual and worldly matters."[64] The Bethlemite friar-economist Padre Antonio de San José Muro described the Mexico City manufactory as nothing more than a "house of perdition" that nurtured all the vices that offended Christian morals: "Honorable families resent it because of what occurs inside, namely the threat to the innocence of young boys and girls. They pray for its abolition so that the youth will no longer be corrupted. The public complain of the bad example set by the manufactory workers while the army and agriculture suffer from a shortage of strong labor which is wasted in the manufactories."[65] Critiques continued after Mexico's independence; during discussions in 1822 concerning what to do about the tobacco monopoly, treasury commission members declared: "If manufacture had remained in the private sector, the unhappy woman who today goes to work in the factory at 5 A.M. and not at 8 A.M. . . . would not have to abandon her sons and her house to careless neighbors. . . . Be assured that these factories have been, and are, the seedbeds from where most of the prostitution of the empire is spread."[66]

The director-general discounted such accusations and criticisms, at least in official statements, and presented alternative descriptions of moral, obedient workers: "Between six thousand and seven thousand people of both sexes work daily from 6 A.M. and 7 A.M. in the morning until 5 P.M. and 6 P.M. in the evening. They are productively employed for eleven and twelve hours daily. . . . During such hard work they recite out loud the Rosary and other Christian devotions." Rounding out this image, the director-general added that at least three workers had left the manufactory to become nuns.[67] Presumably, the manager wanted to emphasize the role of the manufactory as a place of habilitation or rehabilitation and to point out the respectable character of its employees.

The implicit discussion of morality formed the core of these opposing views. The official, idealized version presented the manufactory as a sanctuary from the moral degradation of the street and therefore contributing to an orderly society. The critics, in comparison, viewed the manufactory as an extension of the street, with all its disorder and vice that threatened the morality of society and, by extension, the recognized political and social order. The latter resemble responses to the early factories in nineteenth-century France, where discussions of morality focused on both men and women in the workplace: "The graphic portrayal of promiscuous mingling stood for the absence in industrial cities of the defining characteristics of good order: hierarchy, control, stability all expressed as a matter of the customary relationship between women and men." An implicit (albeit not clearly defined) "equivalence" developed between the street, with the mingling of classes—and, above all, sexes—and the concept of the manufactory and its association with disorder. Both were beyond the regulatory confines of the home and, by extension, beyond established order and hierarchy.[68]

Lynn Hunt, like Joan Wallach Scott, has argued the importance of gender in constructing meaning and thinking about order, "the way the political system works in terms of the kinds of implicit metaphors that have to be used in order to think about order. . . . It turns out that order—political and social—depends on gender relationships."[69] More emerges from the criticisms of the Mexico City tobacco manufactory than just the mixing of the sexes in the workplace and the figure of the working woman linked to disorder and immorality; the critics identify as well the figure of the unemployed, shiftless man. Both signified unnatural states linked to an existence outside the family and the established social order and hierarchy. Despite the creation of the physical and conceptual (that is, legal) space by the state for the woman worker, she remained controversial in colonial society, provoking hostile reactions. The ideals of the established social and political hierarchy also encompassed obedience and deference. Paradoxically, the "voice" of the tobacco workers expressed through their petitions seemed to be a cause for criticism, not praise. At the same time, when the tobacco workers chose to extend their thanks to the Crown after the reform of paper preparation was rescinded, their use of "silence" suggests contemporary acknowledgment of its importance as an authentic sign of deference. Even if language was being manipulated by the workers—what James C. Scott would term use of the public transcript—it still represents the acknowledgment of how the upper classes expect the lower classes, ideally, to behave.[70]

CONCLUSION

The tobacco workers ably defended their interests through negotiation and petition, so that the imposition of discipline by bureaucratic managers of the state monopoly met with only mixed results. The workers may have claimed their spaces both inside and outside the manufactory, but serious street conflict or violence was rare. The relative lack of protest and disruption of the social order was as much a consequence of the composition of the manufactory's work force and conditions of the workplace and community as of the state's policies and its "capacity" to maintain social control. Nevertheless, such a lack of disruption did not alter the perceptions of the elite or the monopoly administrators, whose ideas of morality and good order entailed not just obedience and acquiescence to the dictates of the colonial state and church but also sobriety and regular attendance at work. They interpreted the survival strategies devised by many of the tobacco workers as insubordination in the workplace. In Mexico City's manufactory, as in the French factories, gender implicitly shaped ideas about order, focusing on the new, unplaceable person—at least in respectable society—of the "working woman." It also identified the unemployed or undisciplined man, a figure as repugnant to traditional conceptions of society as that of the working woman. At the same time, ideals about class and status shaped the elite's and the colonial state's concerns with the behavior of the poor and unruly workers who disobeyed their "betters."

A number of questions remain unanswered. At the wider level, we need to understand more about colonial society's perceptions of the poor (particularly the working poor), about social constructions of poverty, and how they change over time. We need to explore how new social identities among both men and women were formed in the tobacco manufactories, how they represented their working identities, and how workers defined their roles and articulated their thoughts in response to the wider political culture and the moralizing discourse to which they were subjected. Appropriately, the following words, even if not penned by a "ragged-trousered philanthropist," clearly acknowledge the elite's concern for order and discipline, and its contempt, perhaps fear, for the poor: "Do you wish to tell me what sin have those committed who, like me, are born and live in poverty, in order that the rich and those of moderate wealth may oppress them from above and from below?"[71]

NOTES

1. Juan Pedro Viqueira Albán, *¿Relajados o reprimidos? Diversiones públicas y vida social en la ciudad de México durante el Siglo de las Luces* (México, 1987). An English translation of this volume is forthcoming from Scholarly Resources.

2. Quoted in Jean Franco, "The Power of the Spider Woman: The Deluded Woman and the Inquisition," in *Plotting Women: Gender and Representation in Mexico* (New York, 1989), 58. See also Gabriel Haslip Viera, "The Underclass," in *Cities and Society in Colonial Latin America*, ed. Louisa Schell Hoberman and Susan Migden Socolow (Albuquerque, NM, 1986); Michael C. Scardaville, "Alcohol Abuse and Tavern Reform in Late Colonial Mexico," *HAHR* 60, no. 4 (November 1980); D. A. Brading, "Tridentine Catholicism and Enlightened Despotism in Bourbon Mexico," *JLAS* 15 (1983).

3. See, for example, the orders regulating the Corpus Christi procession of May 3, 1809, designed to ensure "solemnity and order," which included closing off the streets to carriages, closing the taverns and cafés, and prohibiting fireworks.

AAAM, vol. 1066, Fiestas Religiosas, Garibay to Fernando Hermosa, presidente de la Junta de Policia, April 28, 1809; and ibid., Secretaria del Exmo. Ayuntamiento Constitucional de México, 1822, recorded the disorders that "have always occurred" during the annual fiesta of La Candelaria.

4. Sylvia M. Arrom, *The Women of Mexico City, 1790–1857* (Stanford, CA, 1985), 26–27.

5. Viqueira Albán, *¿Relajados o reprimidos?*, 262.

6. AGN, Tabaco 241, Díaz de la Vega to Viceroy Branciforte, August 28, 1795.

7. My discussion of gender has been greatly influenced by Scott, *Gender and the Politics of History*.

8. In this essay, class is used in the sense of a relationship. For a discussion of the current debate on the concept of class in history, see William M. Reddy, "The Concept of Class," in *Social Orders and Social Classes in Europe since 1500*, ed. M. L. Bush (London, 1982).

9. AGN, Renta del Tabaco 49, Gálvez to viceroy, December 31, 1771.

10. AGN, Renta del Tabaco 49, Manifiesto que se hace en defensa de las fábricas de cuenta de S.M. en su Real Renta del Tabaco de Nueva España, sus utilidades, y bien común de la gente operaria, de ambos sexos que trabaja en ellas y sus qualidades contra el equivocada concepto del Real Tribunal del Consulado de México (herein-after cited as Manifiesto en defensa).

11. AGN, Tabaco 356, Razon de las tareas . . ., accountant-general, July 23, 1781.

12. There were a few increases registered at the supervisory levels, and individual petitions permitted some workers to improve their wages. For detailed discussion see Deans-Smith, chapter 6 in *Bureaucrats, Planters, and Workers*.

13. See Richard Price's discussion on a similar point in *Labour in British Society: An Interpretive History* (London, 1986), 39.

14. AGN, Tabaco 146, Ordenanzas de la Real Fábrica de Puros y Cigarros, June 15, 1770; Renta del Tabaco 67, Prevenciones de la dirección general, que deben observarse exactamente en la fábrica de puros y cigarros de esta capital, asi en las oficinas de hombres, como tambien en las de las mugeres mientras no haya nuevas ordenes que deroguen algunas, March 20, 1792.

15. BN, México, MSS 1338, "Para vestir a la plebe de la ciudad de México, 1790–1792," ff. 15–43; and Norman F. Martin, "La desnudez en la Nueva España," *Anuario de Estudios Americanos* 29 (1972): 15.

16. Royal orders pertaining to "correct dress" were reissued on December 13, 1799, and on April 16, 1801. They applied not only to the tobacco manufactory workers but also to employees of the Mint and Customs House and members of the *juntas de gremios*, *cofradias* or *hermandades*, the cabildos and juntas of the Republicas de Indios. The orders stipulated that no one who was inappropriately dressed be admitted to work or to meetings of the aforementioned bodies. The same applied to walking in the streets, attendance at public places, fiestas, and religious occasions. Punishment for violating such orders was eight days in jail. AAAM, vol. 383, Artesanos y Gremios, ff. 78–79. See Stuart Woolf's discussion of the importance of external appearances in constructions about poverty and the poor in which he argues that clothing "might vary in quality and luxury according to the grade of social relationships, but precisely because of its visibility outside (and even inside)

the home, clothing was emblematic of the determination to hide the evidence of poverty." "Order, Class and the Urban Poor," in *Social Orders and Social Classes*, 192.

17. AGI, México 2294, Marquina to Crown, February 26, 1802; and AGI, 2302, report of director-general, November 10, 1817.

18. Amparo Ros, "La real fábrica de puros y cigarros: organización del trabajo y estructura urbana," in *Ciudad de México, ensayo de construcción de una historia*, ed. Alejandra Moreno de Toscano (México, 1978), 48. Ros uses a figure of 60,999 for a total working-age population for Mexico City.

19. Jorge González Angulo Aguirre, in Tables 2 and 3, *Artesanado y ciudad a finales del siglo XVIII* (México, 1983), 14–15.

20. AGN, Tabaco 241, Díaz de la Vega to viceroy, July 10, 1795.

21. The population totals for Mexico City come from Enrique Florescano, *Precios del maíz y crisis agrícolas en México, 1708–1810* (México, 1969), 171.

22. AGI, México 2264, Díaz de la Vega to Ex. Sr., January 22, 1798.

23. Gabriel Brun Martínez used a sample of 1,753 cigarette rollers from the 1811 census for his analysis in "La organización del trabajo y la estructura de la unidad doméstica de los zapateros y cigarreros de la ciudad de México en 1811," in *Organización de la producción y relaciones de trabajo en el siglo XIX en México* (México, 1978), 147.

24. Michael C. Scardaville, "Crime and the Urban Poor: Mexico City in the Late Colonial Period" (Ph.D. dissertation, University of Florida, 1977), 52.

25. Brun Martínez, "La organización del trabajo," 147.

26. Ros's analysis of the *padrón* (census) of 1800 for Mexico City indicates that only 525 of 7,074 manufactory workers (7.4 percent) were Indian tributaries. She calculated that they constituted 7 percent of the total number of pieceworkers, equivalent to 88 percent of all Indian workers. No Indians were found in the ranks of administrative personnel. "La real fábrica de puros y cigarros," 52–55; and Brun Martínez, "La organización del trabajo," 147.

27. Race certainly contributed to a role in creating hostilities between the manufactory workers. In 1819 the *maestras* of the small manufactory of Guadalupe complained to the viceroy about an order stipulating that under no circumstances were female workers of "inferior class" (that is, casta and mestizo) to be promoted to higher positions. Class and race here are conflated, but race was still the issue since the order dealt with the problem of a number of Spanish war widows being granted positions in the Mexico City manufactory as compensation for their husbands' deaths. The outcome of the incident is unknown, but the case is illustrative in itself. AGN, Tabaco 167, maestras mayores to viceroy, Nov. 5, 1819.

28. AGN Tabaco 358, accountant-general to director-general, September 11, 1797.

29. For a European example of reform against "a specific form of popular culture" see Hans-Ulrich Thamer, "Journeyman Culture and Enlightened Public Opinion," in *Understanding Popular Culture: Europe from the Middle Ages to the Nineteenth Century*, ed. Steven L. Kaplan (Berlin, 1984), 227.

30. AGN, Tabaco 241, Díaz de la Vega to Viceroy Azanza, March 31, 1799.

31. AGI, México 2264, Díaz de la Vega to Ex. Sr., January 22, 1789.

32. For further discussion of the worker turnover rate and regular attendance at the manufactory, see Deans-Smith, chapter 6, *Bureaucrats, Planters, and Work-*

ers. Clearly, the problem with work discipline was not confined to the tobacco workers. The *maestros* of the *gremio de zurradores* (tanners' guild) complained of the *libertanije* of their *oficiales*, defined as a lack of religion and respect, drunkenness, abandonment of families, and their profligacy illustrated by their indebtedness to the *maestros*. AAAM, vol. 383, Artesanos-Gremios, maestros veedores del gremio de zurradores to juez de gremios, 1804, ff. 47–50 v.

33. AGN, Renta del Tabaco 67, directorate-general to Romaña, Betasolo, September 2, 1791; and ibid., Prevenciones de la dirección general, que deben observarse exactemente en la fábrica de puros y cigarros de esta capital, March 20, 1792.

34. AGN, Tabaco 500, fiscal Ramón de Posada, April 30, 1781. The directorate-general argued in favor of abolishing the Concordia on repeated occasions, April 3 and 6, 1781, and February 13, 1783. See AGN, Tabaco 500, Bataller, assessor-general, July 24, 1781.

35. AGI, México 2264, director-general to viceroy, 1797; AGN, Tabaco 500, Testimonio de los Autos formados sobre extinción de la Concordia.

36. AGN, Tabaco 500, cuerpo de operarios de varias clases to Ex. Sr., June 11, 1781.

37. AGN, Tabaco 500, Testimonio de los Autos formados sobre extinción de la Concordia; AGI, México 2313, Viceroy Revillagigedo to Conde Lerena, July 27, 1791.

38. Ros views the Concordia as a response to the need to defend the family economy in the wake of the impact of the manufactory upon the workers, which, in the process, became an organ of control of the manufactory administration, and that it was never for the purposes of the defense of labor, salaries, or even to improve work conditions. See *La producción cigarrera a finales de la colonia: la fábrica en México* (México, 1984), 82–83. For an interpretation of the Concordia as the state's exploitative mechanism for ensuring the reproduction of the manufactory's labor force, see José González Sierra, *Monopolio del humo (elementos para la historia del tabaco en México y algunos conflictos de tabaqueros veracruzanos 1915–1930)* (Jalapa, 1987), 60–61. Yves Aguila sees the Concordia as a prelude to the formation of a trade union. See "Albores de la seguridad social en México, 1770: La Concordia de la Manufactura de Tabacos," *Jahrbuch für Geschichte* 24 (1987): 351–52.

39. AGN, Tabaco 512, guards and maestros to director-general, June 17, 1783; and ibid., administrator to fiscal, July 3, 1783.

40. AGN, Tabaco 411, administrator to director-general, September 8, 1780.

41. AGN, Tabaco 241, Real Tribunal y Audiencia de la Contaduría Mayor de Cuentas de México, March 9, 1796.

42. David Lorne McWatters, "The Royal Tobacco Monopoly in Bourbon Mexico, 1764–1810" (Ph.D. dissertation, University of Florida, 1979), 160.

43. Scardaville, "Crime and the Urban Poor," 21.

44. Michael Sonenscher, "Work and Wages in Paris in the Eighteenth Century," in *Manufacture in Town and Country before the Factory*, ed. Maxine Berg, Pat Hudson, and Michael Sonenscher (Cambridge, 1983).

45. Richard Whipp concludes about the construction of time and work that "the emphasis is on uncertain outcomes. Timing becomes crucial in the experience of work. . . . The points of intersection between an individual's or family's life cycle with wider economic movements become vital in understanding how people

experience work in a total sense." " 'A Time to Every Purpose': An Essay on Time and Work," in *The Historical Meanings of Work*, ed. Patrick Joyce (Cambridge, 1987), 222.

46. John Leddy Phelan, "Authority and Flexibility in the Spanish Imperial Bureaucracy," *Administrative Science Quarterly* 5, no. 1 (June 1960): 47–65.

47. AGN, Tabaco 482, Puchet to director-general, August 12, 1794.

48. AGI, México 2313, Isidro Romaña, Perez de Acali to director-general, April 9, 1781. This is comparable to E. P. Thompson's thesis in "The Moral Economy of the English Crowd in the Eighteenth Century," *PP* 50 (February 1971): 79.

49. Catharina Lis and Hugo Soly, "Policing the Early Modern Proletariat, 1450–1850," in *Proletarianization and Family History*, ed. David Levine (New York, 1984), 212.

50. Elsewhere, the workers from the Puebla manufactory submitted petitions protesting the decision, while workers took to the streets in Querétaro and tried to prevent their fellow workers from entering the manufactory. See AGN, Renta de Tabaco 2, viceroy to director-general, September 6, 1780.

51. AGN, Tabaco 241, Díaz de la Vega to viceroy, July 10, 1795.

52. AGN, Tabaco 376, workers' representatives to director-general, n.d.

53. AGN, Tabaco 241, Report of Real Tribunal y Audiencia de la Contaduría Mayor de Cuentas de México, March 9, 1796.

54. Overall, the total number of workers (including supervisory workers and bureaucrats) increased from an estimated 12,013 in 1795 to 13,316 in 1809. In 1795, 54 percent of the total work force was female; by 1809 that percentage had increased to 68 percent. See Deans-Smith, chapter 5, in *Bureaucrats, Planters, and Workers.*

55. "Women in the Factory: Women's Networks and Social Life in America (1900–1915)" in *Sex and Gender in Historical Perspective*, ed. Edward Muir and Guido Ruggiero (Baltimore, 1990), 200.

56. Calvi, "Women in the Factory," 201.

57. Cited in Palmer, *Descent into Discourse*, 179.

58. Perrot, "Formation of the French Working Class," 83–84, 89–90.

59. Michael Sonenscher, *Work and Wages: Natural Law, Politics, and the Eighteenth-century French Trades* (Cambridge, 1989), 367. Robert C. Davis makes a similar argument in *Shipbuilders of the Venetian Arsenal: Workers and Workplace in the Preindustrial City* (Baltimore, 1991).

60. Ruth Behar, "Sex and Sin, Witchcraft and the Devil in Late Colonial Mexico," *American Ethnologist* 14, no. 1 (1987): 49. See also Celia Wu's discussion of residential patterns of tobacco workers in "The Population of the City in Querétaro in 1791," *JLAS* 16 (1984): 277–307.

61. Ros, *La producción cigarrera*, 70–75; and Brun Martínez, "La organización del trabajo," 153.

62. Perrot, "Formation of the French Working Class," 85.

63. "Cash, Coffee-Breaks, Horseplay," 65–96.

64. AGN, Renta del Tabaco 49, Manifiesto en defensa.

65. AGN, Tabaco 476, Project of Antonio de San José Muro, 1797.

66. Memoría de la Comisión de Hacienda sobre la renta, April 30, 1822, 7.

67. AGN, Renta del Tabaco 49, Manifiesto en defensa.

68. Scott, *Gender and the Politics of History*, 151–52.

69. Lynn Hunt, in Linda K. Kerber et al., (Forum) "Beyond Roles, Beyond Spheres: Thinking about Gender in the Early Republic," *William and Mary Quarterly* 3d ser., 46 (July 1989): 577–78; Scott, *Gender and the Politics of History*.

70. For a discussion of subaltern groups using the discourse and rhetoric of the dominant classes, see Scott's *Domination and the Arts of Resistance: Hidden Transcripts* (New Haven, CT, 1990).

71. "¿Quieren ustedes decirme qué pecado han cometido los que como yo nacen, vegetan y subsisten pobres, para que los ricos y los que tienen medianas proporciones los opriman por arriba y por abajo?" El Tocayo de Clarita, *Diario de México*, vol. 13, August 22, 1810.

4

A World of Images:
Cult, Ritual, and Society
in Colonial Mexico City

Clara García Ayluardo
Dirección de Estudios Históricos
Instituto Nacional de Antropología e Historia

Investigations of Renaissance Italian city-states and rural Mexican communities have focused on confraternities as the locus for the development of civic and religious culture. Among many others, James Banker, Richard Trexler, and Brian Pullan, in their respective studies of San Sepolcro, Florence, and Venice, find in these confraternities one of the keys to Renaissance civic life.[*] Anthropologists who have undertaken studies of indigenous villages in Mexico have given special attention to these lay brotherhoods and their ladder of offices and responsibilities (called *cargos*).[†] Clara García does more than bring together these two trends to examine Mexico City's confraternities—especially the prestigious brotherhoods of the Santísima Trinidad and San Pedro—during the eighteenth century; she also provides a suggestive approach for the study of Mexican popular religion. Her essay builds on the investigation completed as a Ph.D. dissertation ("Confraternity, Cult and Crown in Colonial Mexico City: 1700–1810") in 1989 at Cambridge University.

N EW SPAIN WAS AN INTEGRAL PIECE of the Catholic world. As a part of western Christianity the clergy witnessed, at the time of the Protestant Reformation, a profound controversy, with debates over

---

[*]Banker, *Death in the Community* (Athens, 1989); Trexler, *Public Life in Renaissance Florence* (New York, 1980); Pullan, *Rich and Poor in Renaissance Venice: The Social Institutions of a Catholic State to 1620* (Oxford, 1971). Keith P. Luria provides a French case study in *Territories of Grace: Cultural Change in the Seventeenth-Century Diocese of Grenoble* (Berkeley, 1991).

[†]John K. Chance and William B. Taylor, "Cofradías and Cargos: An Historical Perspective on the Mesoamerican Civil-Religious Hierarchy," *American Ethnologist* 12, no. 1 (February 1985): 1–26.

dogma taking the forefront. Beneath these theological issues, society offered new manifestations of popular piety, particularly in Spain and its empire, where the Counter-Reformation became the battle cry.[1] The religious confraternity, brotherhood, or congregation, as it has been interchangeably called, had its origin in the popular devotional practices and cult activities of medieval Christianity.[2] As yet it is not possible to generalize about the religion of the layfolk or to estimate its intensity among different generations or social groups. Nevertheless, the confraternity, as a tangible, corporate, organized, largely secular and popular instrument of lay devotion, provides a useful means for the study of popular religion. It supplies information on the history of religious consciousness and how it shaped social behavior. In colonial Mexico the confraternity remained an effective and popular vehicle for expressing the sentiments of the Catholic laity, especially the more privileged sectors that included Spaniards in the capital city. These institutions offer a picture of the devotional and ceremonial activities that formed a part of the daily life of the laity.

CEREMONIES AND CONFRATERNITIES

Ceremony expressed the communal and corporate nature of colonial society and reflected the pervasiveness of religion within it. Confraternities were the major promoters and participants in religious festivities, but other colonial corporations, like the *consulado* (merchants' chamber), *audiencia* (city council), and the religious orders, also organized and funded religious and civil celebrations. The city council, for example, staged the Fiesta del Pendón on the feast day of San Hipólito to commemorate Cortés's triumphal entry into the city.[3] Ceremony provided the opportunity to enact the principles of fraternity on public occasions.[4] The confraternity presented brotherhood as a fundamental of Christian charity that all members should recognize. This decisive ideological precept was filtered through society at large and reflected in ceremonial and devotional activities. Public ritual made individuals of different social status brothers of the same standing, identified by tunics and banners, all in the service of Christ, the Virgin his mother, and the saints. They participated together in the public life of the viceroyalty.

Processions offered a means of reaffirming the status quo and provided one form of social control. Their distinguishing mark was the way they both preserved and enhanced the social order. In a complex, stratified society where individuals, particularly from the most privileged sectors, simultaneously formed part of different groups and where a change of status in one sphere so often could affect standing in another, ceremony played a crucial, clarifying role. It became a mechanism that ensured continuity within the structure, promoting cohesion and controlling some of the inherent conflicts; it also contributed to the worship of God and to the enjoyment of spectators. Public rituals above all required participation both by those taking part in the procession and by the onlookers. Members of society were ceremoniously interrelated in public. Ritual, moreover, reflected the pious nature of society where religion unfolded in daily life; it offered a way to express popular piety.

During Lent, Easter, and Corpus Christi celebrations, confraternities became the focus of lay ceremonial activity. Holy Week marked eight days of lavish devotional celebrations that began on Palm Sunday and ended on Easter or Resurrection Sunday.[5] With devotion came splendor, and the more splendid the outward trappings the greater the adoration of the image. One aspect of the controversy sparked by the Reformation in Europe centered around a belief that the excess of popular devotion menaced the purity of religious belief.[6] In New Spain the massive and widespread manifestations of baroque piety expressed the strong popular desire to give public expression to all the emotions accompanying religious thought.

In 1722, for example, Holy Week celebrations began with the archbishop's blessing of the palms; the long string of processions commenced with the image from Santa María la Redonda on Holy Monday; Nuestra Señora del Socorro made her exit from the Franciscan priory on San Juan de la Penitencia on Tuesday, and on the next day the image of El Tránsito de Nuestra Señora left the Hospital de San Juan de Dios. The hospital order carried the exquisite and richly adorned image in an elaborate silver and crystal case. Joining the procession, a great number of penitent brothers, the Nazarenos, marched with covered faces, wearing hair shirts and carrying crosses on their shoulders.[7]

The climax of the week came on Holy Thursday and Good Friday, the commemoration of Christ's Last Supper, his betrayal, passion, and death. One of the most notable ceremonies occurred at the church of the Santísima Trinidad—which alone housed about twelve confraternities. First, the abbot of the Congregation of San Pedro, who, by virtue of its union with the Archconfraternity of the Santísima Trinidad, was also its first councillor, performed the humbling ceremony; he washed the feet of twelve paupers who were fed beforehand and afterward provided with alms. At exactly 4 P.M. the magnificent procession left the church. About a thousand men carried ceremonial candles, and most of them wore the scarlet tunics with the silver insignias of the Archconfraternity of the Santísima

Trinidad. Ten floats depicted various devotional scenes; one presented Saint Peter, the titular saint of the congregation, accompanied by over two hundred priest-members headed by the abbot. At 8 P.M. the Confraternity of the Preciosísima Sangre de Cristo left the parish church of Santa Catalina Mártir. An immense number of candles distinguished this procession and illuminated the floats depicting decorated images of all the major and minor prophets.

On Good Friday, 1722, the city witnessed many processions. The most noteworthy involved the Confraternity of the Tres Caídas de Jesús Nazareno, based in the priory of San Francisco. The brethren displayed great devotion while walking through the principal streets of the city accompanied by members of the Franciscan first and third orders. Along the way, they constantly genuflected and made a great show of penance in commemoration of Christ's three falls on his way to Calvary. By far the most magnificent procession to take place on Good Friday—at least since 1582, it was said—belonged to the Archconfraternity of the Descendimiento y Sepulcro de Cristo, based in the Dominican priory. Established to promote the cult of the death and burial of Christ, this served as the highlight of the confraternity's devotional activities. The well-staged ceremony began at midday with the erection of a platform on the main altar on which three crosses were placed. After the sermon various priests ceremoniously took down the image of the crucified Christ. These reenactments of scenes from the Passion were designed to inspire the faithful with devotion and piety.

A small mortuary carriage with a cross at the bottom, as a symbol of death, led the procession. Three confraternity members, dressed in mourning, walked behind it, sounding dirges on great trumpets. They were followed by three more brothers carrying black silk banners, including the standard that identified the confraternity. The second section of the procession followed ten paces behind; these brothers bore different symbols of the passion of Christ on silver trays covered with black veils. Next came marshals bearing standards with the insignias of the Passion embroidered in gold on a black background. Near the end four priests dressed in black capes carried maces on their shoulders and bore silver scepters as the clear sign of authority. The final section featured a choir of Dominicans, who preceded another group of four priests carrying the main image of the inert body of Christ in an elaborate crystal, silver, and tortoise-shell coffin. A representation of the grieving Virgen de la Soledad followed, escorted by penitents whipping themselves in a bloody sign of sorrow, devotion, and compassion. These emotions were complemented by figures of a crying Peter, bitterly repenting his repudiation of Christ, and of Mary Magdalene, weeping as well. Large numbers of barefoot members of the Dominican order, a company of guards from the vice-regal palace, and three hundred candle-bearing merchants accompanied this procession.[8]

Religious penetration into all spheres of daily life meant a constant blending of the profane with the sacred. Splendor, after all, belonged to those who could pay for it. Most of the confraternities taking part in the 1722 celebrations were wealthy. Two belonged to the prestigious priories of San Francisco and Santo Domingo and one to the foremost Mexico City parish, Santa Catalina. Santísima Trinidad and San Pedro were among the wealthiest and most renowned confraternities of the eighteenth century. Public ritual, in this case, provided the dominant groups with the opportunity to demonstrate their authority and status. It manifested the solidarity of the privileged by reinforcing the hierarchical nature of society. Ritual, as practiced by confraternities, established and promoted their religious as well as their sociopolitical importance. In contrast, smaller urban brotherhoods and rural Indian or mestizo groups could just manage the burning of devotional lights. Furthermore, only those individuals who shared the major expenses of worship and association were regarded as genuine members of the community. In fact, a small core of members, usually the governing board, decided confraternity policy and handled its funds. The majority of members received spiritual and material relief, and their numbers helped to give splendor to public rituals.

THE EUCHARIST AND CONFRATERNITIES

Confraternities exercised great influence in promoting the cult of the Eucharist, which took on central ideological importance in Europe during the Reformation. The feast of Corpus Christi first received papal approbation in 1264 and thereafter became a significant liturgical celebration common to all of Christendom. A procession served as its only ceremony, and the Blessed Sacrament was performed with all possible splendor.[9] Not until the late Middle Ages did the adoration of Christ under the potent, visible symbol of the monstrance—Christ incarnate in the midst of a blazing sun—take root in the liturgy. All religious and liturgical symbols grouped around the central mystery of the Eucharist. More than symbolism, there was now identity: the Host was the visible Christ. The church attempted to focus belief and redirect devotion, and the Eucharist was stressed all the more during the Counter-Reformation.[10]

The foremost brotherhood in Mexico City was dedicated to the Blessed Sacrament and housed in the Metropolitan Cathedral. Each parish in the city was required to have a confraternity to look after and to promote the cult of the Eucharist.[11] The Bourbon reformers in the latter half of the eighteenth century, as they enacted administrative and fiscal reforms aimed at a greater centralization of power, also moved into the devotional sphere. Too many corporations had statutes that allowed them to escape royal jurisdiction and control. Crown officials attempted to channel popular religious expression. The church hierarchy also tended to look upon popular devotions as profane and sought to harness them more and more according to its own moral guidelines. Both the church and the Crown favored directing devotion toward the majestic and omnipresent image of the Eucharist and the cult of the Holy Souls in Purgatory.

The Crown demanded the formation of properly established confraternities with royal licenses and favored the creation of associations known as *caballeros*, *lacayos*, *cocheros*, or *esclavos* (knights, lackeys, coachmen, or slaves) of the Santísimo Sacramento. The last quarter of the eighteenth century saw the growth of these brotherhoods—essentially closed congregations of prominent peninsular or colonial-born Spaniards, organized according to their parish of residence, to enhance their own status and the devotion of the Blessed Sacrament. The Congregación de Caballeros del Santísimo Sacramento of the parish of Santa Veracruz provides a good illustration of this type of confraternity. Manuel Pérez, Juan José Castallanos, Pascual Flores, Simón de Lara, Francisco Morales, Martín Belcho, and José García—all Mexico City merchants—established it in 1790. The Council of the Indies, referring to them as "foremost members" of the city, granted them the license to provide personal service whenever the Eucharist was taken to an infirm member of the parish. The confraternity provided a mule-drawn carriage to transport the priest with the Blessed Sacrament and a group of brothers to act as coachmen on an alternating system. Members were also required to attend, with candles, all festivities and processions in honor of the Eucharist. While other confraternities were being amalgamated and even suppressed, coachmen brotherhoods received licenses at this time because their members could pay for the promotion and enhancement of the cult of the Blessed Sacrament. Because they supported the parish church and were self-financing, they were deemed useful institutions.[12]

The cult of the Eucharist as an object of public devotion focused on the celebration of the feast day of Corpus Christi, which provided another occasion for confraternities, the ecclesiastical and civil hierarchy, the clergy, and the religious orders to go on display. In 1722 eighty-five confraternities paraded with their respective banners and a large number of patron saints. The exposed Blessed Sacrament took the forefront as the major image in the procession, which marched down streets shaded by canopies of branches and flowers and adorned with rich hangings.[13]

FUNERALS AND CONFRATERNITIES

On a less magnificent but perhaps more significant level, funerals required another public ritual carried out by the confraternity. Funerals were the basic social service provided by most retributive brotherhoods and were an occasion for the members to come together physically and symbolically. When a member of the Congregación de San Pedro died, a confraternity crier rang a small bell as he walked the streets of Mexico City to announce the death. The crier, dressed in a black bonnet and a cape embroidered with the papal tiara between the keys of St. Peter, personally informed all resident confraternity members of the time and place of the funeral. The brotherhood's statutes required that they attend, wearing their tunic and insignia. Public announcements were posted on the doors of all churches so that everyone in the city could see that the member's death represented a significant event.

The *mayordomo* took charge, setting up the bier, pall, and candles in either the church of the Santísima Trinidad, which housed the confraternity, or another church closer to the home of the deceased. He also supervised the washing and dressing of the corpse and ensured that it was properly attired. If a member died in poverty, the confraternity provided a modest shroud for a decent burial.

The master of ceremonies supervised the actual funeral cortege that went to the home of the member, the brothers either silent or chanting prayers as they escorted the coffin to the church. He made sure that they marched at a uniform pace, preventing disorderly conduct and breaks in the procession. Previously named linesmen flanked the procession at specific intervals to keep it in order. If an individual needed to leave his place, these officials saw to it that he returned to his original position. Most confraternities stipulated within their constitutions that the masters of ceremony should carry out their duties with respect and prudence to obtain due obedience and deference. They firmly believed that without the exercise of this authority, disorderly conduct would plunge the occasion into confusion.

Once outside the home the brethren awaited the arrival of the officiating priest, who donned a black cape before the coffin, which was provided by the confraternity and borne in the midst of the procession, preceded by the guide cross and flanked by candles and incense-bearing acolytes. As the march to the church began, all candles were lit and silence maintained to increase the solemnity of the moment. The confraternity officials headed the cortege and placed the coffin in the grave once the funeral mass ended.[14]

The corporate nature of ritual was clearly manifested in this traditional ceremony common to all confraternity members. Funerals demonstrated the fundamental principle of mutual aid and brotherhood. In a society where the church or church-affiliated institutions provided most of the social welfare, these corporations acted as de facto burial societies, which was a major reason for their popularity. Most confraternities provided at least memorial masses and communal prayers for the spiritual relief of members, and many also supplied material aid. Toward the end of the eighteenth century, retributive confraternities gave amounts of twenty to twenty-five pesos, a coffin, and a shroud.[15] In 1794 the tailors' confraternity of San Homobono gave twenty-two pesos to help toward funeral costs as well as a coffin, a red cloth and cushion, and coffin bearers. Because of the union with the larger Archconfraternity of the Santísima Trinidad, the deceased was entitled to receive all the benefits from joint indulgences as well as to reap the spiritual graces derived from the 187 and 104 annual memorial masses celebrated by the Santísima Trinidad and San Homobono, respectively.[16] These benefits also applied to the confraternities of Nuestra Señora de la Guía, Jesús Nazareno, Ecce-Homo, Preciosísima Sangre de Cristo, and Santo Cristo de al Salud aggregated to San Homobono.

The ideal view of society promoted by public ceremonies, from the processions to the funerals, had its more realistic counterpart in numerous incidents of laxity, turmoil, and lack of interest. Far from demonstrating a tame obedience to rules and principles, brothers often arrived late and improperly attired for processions and became involved in shoving incidents over precedence with members of rival confraternities. In all cases, confraternity statutes attempted to preempt these outbursts, even imposing financial sanctions or more severe measures, such as expulsion in cases of extreme antisocial behavior.[17] Political rivalries, personal jealousies, and, at times, sincere ideological differences over hierarchy fueled arguments over proper professional arrangements. In anticipation of this, guards were usually posted along processional routes to prevent outbreaks of violence.

RITUALISTIC PIETY

Colonial society indulged in a great deal of ritualistic piety. The liturgical context in which processions took place sanctified the hierarchical arrangement of society, and ceremonies purported to show the unity of the Catholic monarchy and religion.

Ceremonial disputes can take one of two forms. On the one hand they can express an underlying political turmoil that contradicts outright the serenity and cohesiveness of the processional image. On the other hand, they may reveal not so much a lack of concern for the image as the overwhelming importance granted to the concept of ceremonial primacy, status, and power.[18] The contentious attitude toward ceremonial behavior repudiated this exaggerated effort to eliminate all sources of scandal and to control, order, and regiment. Such attitudes went totally against the processional nucleus that symbolized authority and sovereignty. In a society that provided few avenues of social mobility, and where official salaries were not attractive, controversy became a battle mainly over symbolic power, prestige, and preeminence in a status-oriented world.

On one occasion brothers of the confraternity attached to the Jesuit College of San Gregorio, the Archconfraternity of the Santísima Trinidad, and members of the Casta Filipino confraternity erected in San Francisco were in full Holy Thursday processional order, carrying their respective images illuminated by a large quantity of candles. As they passed the viceregal palace, tempers flared and a violent fight broke out between the Trinitarian and Filipino confraternities over the order of precedence. Confusion reigned as rival brothers attacked one another with the symbols of order and religion; wielding maces and guide crosses as weapons, they left a toll of injuries.[19]

On a more political note Holy Thursday celebrations again provided the framework for controversies. Rivalry emerged between the united confraternities of San Pedro and the Santísima Trinidad, their argument centered around which route their joint procession should take. The abbot of the largely clerical San Pedro group proposed to go from the church of the Santísima Trinidad straight down along the archbishop's palace, while the Trinitarians wanted to keep to the traditional route down the street of la Merced. As a result of the subsequent stalemate the abbot refused to take part in the procession, one of the most splendid of Holy Week, and withdrew the float carrying Saint Peter, keeping the image inside its chapel instead.[20] He had chosen a strong measure.

IMAGES AND DEVOTIONS

The veneration of saints was rooted in the forms and colors of their images, which produced as much aesthetic perception as religious fervor. In many ways fervor was a response to the gilt and jewels, the pious appearance and sumptuous apparel of the image. Effusions of piety ardently went out to the saints, especially during times of public, collective ritual.[21] Images were a potential source of power, since devotion, it was held, influenced the saint represented by the image. In this sense the confraternity rendered greater glory to the cult of the saint. By keeping the image indoors the abbot consciously prevented the Trinitarians from sharing in devotion to the patron saint and, in so doing, detracted from the luster and preeminence of the procession. Withdrawing the image and its power from the community destroyed its sense of brotherhood.

Processions were only a part (albeit the most splendid one) of confraternity life. The moral and spiritual unity of the brotherhoods, for example, was achieved through devotional meetings, submission to common rules, and the wearing of a distinctive tunic on procession days. This not only helped to standardize public behavior at the micro level, but, more important, it also promoted religiosity and devotion among members. Perhaps piety and practical reasons, not doctrine, governed the religious life of most of the colonial population. The conquering Spaniards brought with them an entire medieval tradition of thought embodying itself in images, a tradition bolstered by the Counter-Reformation.[22] Consequently, believers trusted that both spiritual and material relief could be found in the manipulation of this physical image, exchanging gifts and prayer for favors.

Collective supplication in times of general crises like plague or drought was a common feature of Mexican life. The Virgin of Remedios was particularly well known and often sought out for succor in times of drought. Other images were also widely used as the objects of collective prayer throughout the colonial period. During a crisis their power went beyond the small community of confraternity members. The image of Cristo Atado a la Columna, for example, venerated in the parish church of Santa Catalina Mártir, was revered for its ability to bring relief from plague. In 1659, after a particularly virulent measles epidemic, the archbishop ordered the brotherhood to bring this image of Christ to the cathedral. At the symbolic hour of 3 P.M. other confraternities met outside the parish with their respective banners. The procession of supplication began an hour later, led by members of the Confraternity of Cristo Atado who were dressed in black and holding candles. Religious orders and clergy of the city took part. At the cathedral the image was solemnly welcomed by the archbishop, a richly dressed cathedral chapter, the Mexico City council, and the prominent members of society. While the choir sang the litany the archbishop blessed the image as it was installed by the main altar. The canons began a novena in its honor, beseeching it for delivery from the epidemic. The archbishop further enhanced the ritual and added to the power of the prayers by celebrating Mass. Later, the public that had flocked to the cathedral had the opportunity to render homage to the image. Nine days later, at the end of the ritual, it was returned to its chapel.[23]

The mere presence of a visible image sufficed to establish its truth. No doubt existed between the sight of the images—for example, the three persons of the Trinity, the sorrowful Virgin, the innumerable saints, or, as in this case, Christ—and belief in their reality. The visible image gave personality and individuality to the saint. By associating a particular saint with an attribute, such as plague relief or the power of healing, the image became miraculous. The prayer addressed to it contributed even more to its effect. Popular devotion and divine response reflected the power of the image, making popular reverence essentially identical to its efficacy. Thus, a contract of sorts, mediated by the confraternity, existed between the saint and the supplicant. Because the promotion of cult was the distinctive feature of confraternity life it may be argued that this corporation had the responsibility both to foster the idea of prayer and to provide the means to carry it out.[24]

Popular belief formed around Christ and his Mother, in their various advocations, for example, Nuestro Señor de Las Tres Caídas, de Burgos, la Exaltación, Ecce-Homo, Dulcísimo Nombre; and Dolores, Valvanera, Carmen, la Luz, Concepción. Many beliefs also clustered around the cult of the saints. Although the Eucharist became a potent symbol of power it did not seem to weaken devotion to the saints. Both coexisted in the popular mind and saints were well represented as patrons of the various confraternities; popular advocations included Saints Joseph, Anne, Thomas, Homobono, Anastasius, Sebastian, Anthony, and John, and the archangels Michael and Raphael.[25]

The celebration of the mass flourished as the most common devotion. Confraternities promoted this central ritual, which not only provided the social benefits of congregating people and gave the laity the opportunity to take part in the fundamental sacrament of the Eucharist, but also brought about salvation through perpetual offerings. These lay confraternities, then, served as significant institutions in promoting the idea that the laity could contribute to its own salvation by setting up chantries, which expressed one side of the Christian sense of charity and good works that confraternities also fostered.[26]

Prayers and masses represented corporate acts of worship mediated by the confraternity. The regular worship and high standards of morality stipulated in brotherhood statutes further helped to legitimate authority and order. Devotion to the image, communal prayers, and the mass distinguished the daily religious life of the confraternity. These combined devotions became evident, for example, in the activities of the Santísima Trinidad, which sponsored masses honoring all living and dead members, particularly on its titular feast day, All Souls, and on the fourth Sunday of the month.[27] Supplementary masses said throughout the week leading to the Day of the Dead in honor of deceased brethren and other chantry masses were also sponsored during the year by the Santísima Trinidad. In addition, the brothers acted as patrons for the exposure of the Blessed Sacrament on the first Sunday of the month in the church of the Santísima Trinidad and funded both the sermon and the procession held on the same day. Moreover, the brotherhood encouraged the saying of a novena the nine days before its titular feast, promoting the cult through collective prayer.

Similarly, the Confraternity of the Preciosísima Sangre de Cristo celebrated two principal feast days: the Transfiguration and the Day of the Most Precious Blood. Members in a 1790 petition sought royal approval for a plenary indulgence to all those who participated in the celebrations of both days. They also requested an extension of the original fifteen-year privilege to celebrate the circular jubilee. Preciosísima Sangre, like most confraternities, asserted that devotional exercises were needed to keep up the piety of its advocation and spiritual graces to kindle the devotion of the faithful. San Homobono, together with its aggregated confraternities, stated as its fundamental aim the greater glory of the saint, which it attempted to accomplish by conducting his titular feast, celebrated on November 13, with appropriate splendor. The Confraternity of Santo Tomás Apóstol also existed to promote the cult of its saint, which it venerated together with the cult of the Blessed Sacrament.[28]

Confraternities recognized both living and dead members. The deceased received the benefits of prayer from the living, who gathered either on the day of the saint or on the Day of the Dead (November 2) for a special memorial mass, normally at the particular altar or chapel dedicated to the patron saint. In this way the brotherhood provided a special prayer force. The Confraternity of San Pedro obliged its members, for example, to pray for the souls of the deceased by reciting the Paternoster and Ave Maria in honor of the Virgin three times a day, a requirement that also encouraged the practice of daily prayer.

The prestigious Confraternity of Santiago Apóstol celebrated an annual memorial mass and sermon followed by a series of masses held on the ensuing days. During this time members were urged, as an added sign of devotion, to confess and take communion. These sacramental acts, the brotherhood maintained, would set a good example and provide indulgences for those taking part.

Devotional activities fostered a spirit of ethnic or group identity. The sense of involvement and commitment, particularly in a prominent brotherhood, enhanced the status of its members. A royal decree in 1768, for example, allowed natives of Galicia to establish the Confraternity of Santiago Apóstol within the chapel of the Franciscan Third Order in the priory of San Francisco. Founded in honor of the patron saint of Spain, Santiago Matamoros, it was linked to the confraternity of the same name in Madrid and, as such, automatically enjoyed royal protection, since the king himself was an honorary member. Because Santiago reigned as the universal patron saint of the monarchy, the confraternity had the obligation to promote his cult in every way possible. The brothers in Mexico City were the most prominent members of society, including the viceroy. The organization's policy dictated recruiting these individuals because of the contention that the greater the cult, the more wealth it needed to sustain it suitably. Renowned members added greater fame and prestige to the group. All confraternity officials were required to attend the feast of the patron, which included a unique gun salute in the portico of the church. As a sign of reverence to the image and the authority of the brotherhood, the viceroy, who presided over its governing body, arrived in a special, cushioned chair symbolizing his elevated rank, accompanied by the prefect and senior councillor of the confraternity. On this occasion devotion and prestige, splendor and preeminence went hand in hand; ceremony legitimated authority.[29]

Confraternities, preeminent ones in particular, competed with one another to provide the best spiritual and material benefits for members. Spectacle made this explicit in the public forum. Visual display provided the confraternity with a peculiar dynamic that contributed to the devotion for its saint, its continuity as a body, and its popularity. Public spectacle allowed prominent confraternities to demonstrate and to maintain their socioeconomic, cultural, political, and symbolic predominance within society.

On the other hand, confraternities were popular organizations. A basic sentiment—devotion toward a particular image more than a Roman Catholic principle of belief—brought members together. This popular aspect went over and above the mere political manipulation of the governing bodies of the brotherhoods and beyond the control of the established church. Religiosity and sense of both affiliation and identity made the confraternity come alive. The brotherhoods represented social units reflecting society, personified social identity, and mediated devotional sentiments that constituted popular piety.

It was precisely this uncontrolled sentiment and lavish display of baroque piety that eighteenth-century reform ministers found objectionable. Viceroy Juan Vicente de Güemes Pacheco y Padilla, the second Count Revillagigedo (1789–1794), launched a campaign to curb what he saw as excesses in public ceremony in the last decade of the eighteenth century. Believing public, religious ceremonies to be excessive and archaic, he used the disorderly conduct of many confraternities during processions as a justification for his restrictions. Such displays of piety, he argued, encouraged indecent behavior and pretension while failing to edify the public. Furthermore, he condemned the excessive expenditure on lavish costumes and regalia that, he claimed, impoverished many members of the confraternities.[30]

Despite growing official disapproval, enthusiasm for the celebration of Holy Week and other major feast days remained as keen as it had been throughout the colonial period. No sumptuary measures or reform seemed able to eradicate the traditional, popular, and spontaneous religious fervor and its expression incited by public, religious ceremony. Although authorities attempted to ban Holy Week processions, particularly in the countryside, in 1794 the festivities in Mexico City included twenty-one different processions with individual floats displaying the respective images.[31] Accompanying their images, confraternity members were dressed in different colored tunics and wore penitential *capirotes* (pointed hoods) that covered their faces. Some images even had ceremonial guards dressed as Roman centurions. Enlightened viceregal reformers saw this spectacle as particularly offensive and profane—even ridiculous.

Taking a long, winding route, the Archconfraternity of the Preciosísima Sangre de Cristo proceeded from its parish of Santa Catalina Mártir down the streets of El Carmen and Relox, making *visitas* (stopovers) at the convents of Santa Catarina de Siena, La Encarnación, Santa Teresa de Jesús, and, finally, at the cathedral. From there the procession turned right and proceeded to the priory of Santo Domingo for its final visit before returning to the parish.

Traditionally, the rector organized the 10 P.M. Holy Thursday procession in which he carried the banner. Because the confraternity's executive committee provided the two hundred pesos needed for the ceremony, the parish priests participated in the procession only as honored escorts. Viceregal authorities suggested late in the eighteenth century that the quota for the procession be reduced to one hundred fifty pesos so that the confraternity could finance other activities and needs. The reformers advised the rector to refrain from serving refreshments after the procession "because it is a day of abstinence and because it has been the cause of many indecencies." This counsel hinted that not only was the confraternity disturbing public order, but it was also tempting people to break their Lenten fast. Under mounting pressure, in 1790 the Preciosísima Sangre brothers asked the Council of the Indies for permission to change the date of their procession from Holy Week to the early afternoon of May 3, "owing to the disturbances which have been experienced at night and to the recent orders issued by the government."[32] The confraternity provided a more sensible reason, beyond conforming to the law, for the change: given that over the previous ten years severe drought had badly damaged crops, causing much hunger and illness, they stated that the month of May was a more practical time of the year to pray for divine intervention to bring rain.

The Bourbons increasingly attacked confraternities not only in a campaign for the centralization of power by ending corporate privilege but also, in the devotional sphere, against unbridled piety that could result in disturbances. The confraternity could represent social and religious order, but it also served as a vehicle for manifestations of popular religiosity that officials progressively viewed as indulgent and heterodox.

NOTES

1. Jean Delumeau, *Catholicism between Luther and Voltaire: A New View of the Catholic Reformation* (London, 1977); John Bossy, "The Counter-Reformation and the People of Catholic Europe," *PP* 47 (1970): 51–70.

2. Antonio Rumeu de Armas, *Historia de la previsión social en España. Cofradías-gremios-hermandades-montepíos* (Madrid, 1944), 17–37; John Bossy, *Christianity and the West, 1400–1700* (New York, 1985), esp. 57–72. For a discussion of the role of the confraternity in the late Middle Ages, especially its pious activities, see Francis Oakley, *The Western Church in the Late Middle Ages* (Ithaca, NY, 1979), 113–26.

3. For accounts of different festivities in seventeenth-century Mexico City, see Antonio de Robles, *Diario de sucesos notables, 1665–1703*, vols. 30, 31, 32, *Colección de escritores mexicanos,* ed. Antonio Castro Leal (México, 1946), passim; and Linda Curcio-Nagy, Chapter 1 in this volume.

4. Although there is scant work on colonial Mexico, numerous studies examine Europe's urban communal life through ritual. See Trexler, *Public Life in Renaissance Florence,* 240–78. Pullan shows the differentiation revealed through pomp in office between the major confraternities (*Scuole Grandi*) and the less important ones in *Rich and Poor in Renaissance Venice,* 33–193. For England, see Charles Pythian-Adams, "Ceremony and the Citizen: The Communal Year at Coventry, 1450–1550," in *The Early Modern Town: A Reader* (London, 1976), 106–28.

5. Robles, *Diario de sucesos notables,* 30:115–28, 130–31.

6. Johan Huizinga, *The Waning of the Middle Ages: A Study of the Forms of Life, Thought and Art in France and the Netherlands in the Fourteenth and Fifteenth Centuries* (London, 1955), 173–79.

7. Luis González Obregón, *México viejo, 1521–1821* (México, 1900), 463–69, quoting the "Gaceta."

8. Manuel Rivera Cambas, *México pintoresco, artístico y monumental* (México, 1967), 2:3–4.

9. H. F. Westlake, *The Parish Guilds of Medieval England* (London, 1919), 49–59; and Miri Rubin, *The Fraternities of Corpus Christi and Late Medieval Piety: Studies in Church History,* vol. 24 (London, 1986). For a description of the event in Peru, see Jorge Bernales Ballesteros, "El Corpus Christi: fiesta Barroca en el Cuzco," *Primeras Jornadas de Andalucía y América,* vol. 2 (Seville, 1981). For various descriptions of festivities in Mexico City during the seventeenth century, see Robles, *Diario de sucesos notables;* and Curcio-Nagy, in this volume.

10. Huizinga, *Waning of the Middle Ages,* 153–76, 208.

11. David A. Brading, "Tridentine Catholicism and Enlightened Despotism in Bourbon Mexico," *JLAS* 15 (1983): 11–16.

12. AGI, México 2669; and Antonio García Cubas, *El libro de mís recuerodos: Narraciones históricas, anecdóticas y de costumbres mexicanas anteriores al actual estado social* (México, 1950), 202–3.

13. González Obregón, *México viejo,* 437–44.

14. AGI, México 716, Congregación del Gloriosísimo Padre San Pedro.

15. See, for example, AGI, México 2661, Cofradía de Santo Tomás and Santísimo Sacramento; AGN, Bienes Nacionales 118, exp. 3, Archicofradía de la Santísima Trinidad.

16. AGN, Bienes Nacionales 118, exp. 2.

17. AGI, México 2679, Archicofradía del Santísimo Sacramento. On efforts to pacify quarreling members and ensure the principles of brotherhood, see Ronald F. E. Weismann, *Ritual Brotherhood in Renaissance Florence* (New York, 1982), 88–90.

18. Edward Muir, *Civic Ritual in Renaissance Venice* (Princeton, NJ, 1981), 185–210.

19. Giovanni Francesco Gemelli Careri, *Viaje a la Nueva España* (México, 1976), 72–73.

20. Robles, *Diario de sucesos notables,* 263.

21. Trexler, *Public Life in Renaissance Florence,* 47–53, 240–78; and William Christian, Jr., *Local Religion in Sixteenth-Century Spain* (Princeton, NJ, 1981).

22. Huizinga, *Waning of the Middle Ages,* 166–68. For the importance of images in the Mexican experience, see Serge Gruzinski, *La Guerre des Images de Cristophe Colomb à 'Blade Runner,' 1492–2019* (Paris, 1990). Images, whether native or syncretic, had great importance in Indian confraternities; see Charles Gibson, *The Aztecs under Spanish Rule: A History of the Indians of the Valley of Mexico, 1519–1810* (Stanford, CA, 1964), 133–35.

23. Robles, *Diario de sucesos notables,* 30:122–23.

24. J. J. Scarisbrick, *The Reformation and the English People* (Oxford, 1984), 24, 39. Julio Caro Baroja sees the image as capable of instilling devotion. See *Las formas complejas de la vida religiosa: Religión, sociedad y carácter en la España de los siglos XVI y XVII* (Madrid, 1978), 107–10. For a discussion of the power of the saint and the reciprocity between the supplicant and the image, see Christian, *Local Religion,* 23–75.

25. AGN, Bienes Nacionales 574, exp. 2; ibid., Historia 314, exp. 9; and ibid., Cofradías and Archicofradías 18, exp. 7.

26. Michael Costeloe, *Church Wealth in Mexico: A Study of the Juzgado de Capellanías in the Archbishopric of México, 1800–1856* (Cambridge, 1967), 46–65; William R. Jones, "English Religious Brotherhoods and Medieval Lay Piety: The Inquiry of 1388–1389," *Historian* 36 (1973–74): 646–59; and Scarisbrick, *Reformation and the English People,* 2–12. Christian notes the role of the confraternities in the establishment of pious foundations endowed through wills promoting interest in the afterlife. *Local Religion*, 141–46.

27. AGN, Bienes Nacionales 118, exp. 3.

28. AGI, México 2669; ibid., 2683; and ibid., 2661.

29. Ibid., 716; ibid., 2667.

30. Juan Pedro Viqueira Albán, *¿Relajados o reprimidos? Diversiones públicas y vida social en la ciudad de México durante el Siglo de las Luces* (México, 1987). An English translation of this volume is forthcoming from Scholarly Resources.

31. Brading, "Tridentine Catholicism," 16–20; and AGN, Historia 437, ff. 1–4.

32. AGI, México 2669.

5

Public Celebrations, Popular Culture, and Labor Discipline in Eighteenth-Century Chihuahua

Cheryl English Martin
University of Texas at El Paso

In the following essay Cheryl English Martin, one of the editors of this volume, draws together themes from the first four contributions and analyzes them in a case study. Using the local context of Chihuahua City during the eighteenth century, she examines the development of religious and civic festivals, the contestation for the street and other public places, and the public discourse over the work ethic, particularly the proper use of time by the laboring classes. Her discussion reveals the nuances of historians of popular and working culture such as Juan Pedro Viqueira Albán, Peter Burke, E. P. Thompson, and Natalie Z. Davis, as well as her own published work on popular speech and social order.

Professor Martin has made a departure recently into the study of Bourbon Chihuahua, following the publication of *Rural Society in Colonial Morelos.** She has degrees from Georgetown and Tulane Universities and has received the Distinguished Achievement in Teaching award from the University of Texas at El Paso.

T HE DISCOVERY OF SILVER IN 1702 at a remote and sparsely populated desert location some one thousand miles to the north of Mexico City inaugurated the eighteenth-century economic revival of New Spain. Men and women representing a microcosm of colonial society soon flocked to the area, and within two decades the bustling community of San Felipe el Real de Chihuahua had blossomed as a Spanish municipality, or *villa*, on a site where no previous permanent settlement had stood. Complete with an imposing central plaza

*(Albuquerque, NM, 1985).

and governed by a municipal council, or cabildo, the town today known as Chihuahua quickly became the foremost administrative and commercial center on the north-central frontier of New Spain.

A handful of principal miners and merchants, most of them peninsular Spaniards, soon dominated economic life in the new community and seized control of the emerging apparatus of local government as well. Among the most difficult of their official duties were those of providing the visible trappings of urban life in an inhospitable frontier setting and teaching their recalcitrant subordinates the proper attitudes and behavior of "civilized" society. Religious and civic celebrations played pivotal roles in both these endeavors, affording local elites the opportunity to flaunt their wealth, buttress their own self-confidence, and boost civic pride by imitating the rich ceremonial life they had witnessed in Spain or in Mexico City. Festive occasions also enabled them to present carefully orchestrated demonstrations of power and prestige for the presumed edification of their social inferiors.

Often local officials confronted difficult choices when planning public celebrations. Lavish ceremonial displays strained public and private resources, especially after mining productivity began to fall in the 1730s, and leading citizens proved increasingly reluctant to perform their prescribed roles in these observances. By the final three decades of the eighteenth century, local officials occasionally broached the prospect of suspending certain festivities that had occupied prominent places on the villa's calendar for two generations.[1] Moreover, lower classes often failed to grasp the lessons of subordination implied in civic ritual. Elaborate processions of local dignitaries did little to increase popular respect for authority. Even more disturbing, workers viewed major holidays as opportunities to loosen already tenuous bonds of labor discipline.

Meanwhile, representatives of the colonial state attempted to impose their own agenda on Chihuahua's ceremonial life. Spain's Bourbon kings by the eighteenth century had belatedly joined other European monarchs, both Catholic and Protestant, in attempting to suppress many genuinely popular festivals and to inject more solemn religious observances into those that remained.[2] At the same time, they mandated new observances designed to impress colonial subjects with the grandeur of the monarchy.

Civic leaders in eighteenth-century Chihuahua had to weigh all of these considerations as they went about planning local celebrations. The present study examines the ways in which they balanced civic pride against labor discipline, and patriotic duty against social control. The choices they made offer telling insights into the dynamics of late colonial society on the northern frontier of New Spain.

LOCAL HOLIDAYS IN CHIHUAHUA

Following the creation of the villa's cabildo in December 1718, council members quickly moved to provide their community with the proper amenities of urban existence. In one of its first acts the council marked the town's calendar with a regular cycle of civic observances, emulating whenever possible rituals observed in Mexico City, Guadalajara, and other cities.[3] Meanwhile, popular custom, drawing on precedents from Old and New Spain alike and following the liturgical calendar, added other festivals.

By the 1720s and for the remainder of the colonial period the most important local fiesta honored Saint Francis of Assisi, patron of Chihuahua's parent settlement of San Francisco de Cuéllar. This week-long celebration, held each year in early October, began with a religious observance that featured music and a sermon. A full round of secular amusements followed, including fireworks, horse races, comedies, and reenactments of the medieval battles between the Moors and Christians. Most exciting of all, however, were the bullfights held in the central plaza, which had been especially fenced for the occasion. People traveled to Chihuahua from great distances to observe these spectacles and to enjoy the gambling, dancing, and other entertainment that marked the San Francisco celebration.[4]

After the feast of San Francisco it was less than two months to the feast day of San Andrés on November 30, when the cabildo and other dignitaries marched in solemn procession, and bonfires and fireworks illuminated the streets at night.[5] By the late 1750s local officials had added the fiesta of Nuestra Señora de Guadalupe, on December 12, to the round of local observances, again marking the day with religious ritual and fireworks. In the early nineteenth century, horse races also took place on December 12.[6]

The Christmas season soon followed, offering a full two weeks of dancing, singing, cardplaying, and other amusements in the central plaza of Chihuahua. Only after the feast of the Three Kings on January 6 did mines reopen and other economic activities resume.[7] *Semana Santa* (Holy Week) in March or April evidently entailed a more reverential form of observance as various processions, following peninsular custom, took place. On Holy Thursday, for example, local citizens formed special honor guards to accompany the consecrated Host through the streets. Holy Week also furnished workers from the surrounding area with an excuse to leave their jobs for the ostensible purpose of fulfilling their Easter duty, and many evidently lingered in town for a few rounds of dancing and gambling.[8]

The feast of San Felipe, the villa's other patron saint, followed a few weeks later on May 1. Again, an official religious service acted as the prelude for fireworks and other forms of entertainment.[9] Corpus Christi, in late May or early June, rounded out the calendar of major ceremonial events in Chihuahua. Under penalty of stiff fines set by the corregidor and cabildo, local residents decorated the streets through which the Eucharist passed in solemn procession.[10]

Other religious holidays were celebrated in more modest fashion, with observances evidently limited to a single day and in some cases confined to a special liturgical function. Saint Joseph's Day, March 19, had already claimed a spot on the town's ritual calendar by the 1740s. In 1758 mine operators and other principal entrepreneurs in Chihuahua and the nearby mining camp of Santa Eulalia adopted Saint Joseph as the official patron of mining in the hope that the special devotions marking the occasion would breathe new life into their flagging industry. From that date forward a one-day holiday for workers and a special celebration marked this feast.[11] Other documents make passing references to religious ceremonies held in honor of Nuestra Señora de los Dolores in September and a procession on the feast of Santiago on July 25.[12]

Certain customary Mexican or Iberian festivities were evidently missing from the calendar of observances in Chihuahua, or at least they were of such minor importance that they have left few documentary traces. Although the city had a *cofradía* (confraternity) dedicated to the souls in purgatory, surviving records fail to mention any special observance of the Day of the Dead (November 2), a date on which Mexicans from colonial times to the present have honored their deceased relatives.[13] Even more striking is the absence of references to the traditional three-day Carnival that preceded Ash Wednesday. Although at present we have little information on the early history of Carnival in Mexico, by the late seventeenth century it was celebrated with considerable gusto in Spanish cities and Indian villages alike. Residents of the viceregal capital danced, drank, and went about the streets in disguise—men dressed as women, laymen as religious, the young as their elders.

Civil and ecclesiastical authorities viewed these rituals with distaste, however. Inquisition administrators began attacking Carnival customs in 1679, forbidding laymen to dress as clerics. In the decades following the Mexico City riots of June 1692, officials displayed even greater concern for maintaining order in the capital. The archbishop of Mexico outlawed transvestitism in 1722, the same year that Juan de Acuña, Marqués de Casa Fuerte, took over as viceroy and resolved to do his part to curb the worst excesses of the holiday. The viceroy published a decree in December 1731 threatening harsh penalties for anyone who observed traditional pre-Lenten customs during the upcoming season. Evidently the combined efforts of church and state succeeded in banishing many Carnival observances from Mexico City, relegating them to outlying settlements.[14]

The founding of Chihuahua coincided with these campaigns to suppress Carnival, and the villa's leaders apparently fell into step with trends set in the viceregal capital. Cabildo records from San Felipe el Real show no official provisions for any pre-Lenten celebration; and employers, always critical of their workers' propensity to find the slightest excuse to shirk their jobs, never complained of work stoppages during that period. On Wednesday, March 9, 1735, for example, mine owners and merchants gathered to discuss conditions that had resulted in the recent downturn in silver production. They grumbled that they were still recovering from the disruption of work during the Christmas holidays and that Holy Week and Easter lay ahead, but they made no mention of Carnival.[15] Ash Wednesday that year was February 23; surely if any significant merriment had preceded the start of Lent, it would have been fresh in the minds of the area's major employers when they drew up their report just two weeks later.[16]

Perhaps even more revealing, passing references to Carnival did not appear in the routine court depositions of ordinary men and women. If asked to recall when a certain event took place, people often used the ritual calendar to guide them. Phrases such as "the day before the feast of San Francisco," "during the Christmas holidays," or "shortly after *Semana Santa*" regularly appear in testimony. Though an occasional mention of Ash Wednesday can also be found, the colonial townspeople of Chihuahua apparently did not measure time in terms of Carnival, except for a single reference to "the Monday of Carnaval," made, significantly, by an Indian from the mission of Carichic in 1770.[17]

DYNASTIC OBSERVANCES IN CHIHUAHUA

Even without extensive pre-Lenten festivities, people in eighteenth-century Chihuahua enjoyed numerous opportunities to escape their usual routines. In addition to the observance of regular religious holidays, the town council of San Felipe joined city governments throughout colonial Spanish America in organizing public spectacles to mark coronations, deaths, marriages, and births in the royal family.[18] In 1720 members of the newly formed council of Chihuahua prepared themselves for such eventualities by seeking advice on proper protocol from their counterparts in Guadalajara.

Officials in the Nueva Galician capital consulted their records and extracted a detailed description of the ceremonies held there following the death of King Felipe IV in 1665. After conducting funeral rites in honor of the dead king, the city of Guadalajara had staged an elaborate ceremony in which local dignitaries and the general populace swore fealty to his successor, Carlos II. Liveried pages and coachmen accompanied local dignitaries to a platform erected in the main plaza especially for the occasion. Atop the platform stood the royal coat of arms and a full-length image of the new sovereign. In a colorful procession the royal standard bearer, or *alférez real*, carried His Majesty's banner throughout the city, stopping frequently to proclaim Guadalajara's corporate allegiance to Carlos II. Each time, church bells rang and the assembled crowd shouted their "amens" and *"vivas."*[19]

Four years after receiving these guidelines from Guadalajara, cabildo officers in Chihuahua found occasion to use them. On January 10, 1724, King Felipe V abdicated in favor of his sixteen-year-old son Luis. Government authorities promptly dispatched word of the dynastic change to every city in the empire. Although young Luis had already died of smallpox before news of his accession reached Chihuahua in early September, several more months passed before people on the northern frontier of New Spain learned that King Felipe had reassumed the throne.[20] In the interim the villa of San Felipe el Real held the first of its many ceremonies in honor of the Bourbon dynasty.

Local officials in Chihuahua, unable to match the sumptuous celebrations that Guadalajara had mounted for Carlos II, nonetheless staged a tribute to Luis I that local residents remembered for years to come. Although he initially protested that his business affairs allowed him little spare time, José de Aguirre, a prosperous miner who had recently received the coveted post of *alférez real*, eventually played a prominent role in financing and executing the local festivities. Aguirre carried the royal banner about the villa in a dignified procession, while corregidor Bartolomé García Montero presided over the public acclamation of the new king. Following a solemn Te Deum in the parish church, fireworks, comedies, *bailes populares* (popular dances), the pageant of the Moors and Christians, and bullfights—involving some two hundred bulls—entertained the crowd.[21]

The number of such externally mandated observances accelerated in the 1740s and beyond. The Chihuahua municipal council in 1741 expressed its "affection for His Majesty," King Felipe V, by spending a modest forty-three pesos for a mass and fireworks to celebrate the victory of Spanish forces over the British at Cartagena. A few years later municipal authorities received instructions to plan a public manifestation honoring the marriage of Princess María Teresa to the dauphin of France. The death of King Felipe in 1746 and the crowning of Fernando VI brought yet another royal decree reminding local residents of their ties to the Bourbon dynasty.[22]

A similar notice came just thirteen years later when Carlos III succeeded to the throne. Evidently King Carlos was as energetic in promoting official celebrations throughout his empire as he was in reorganizing colonial administration. In 1771 and again in 1779 he ordered all of his subjects to observe the birth of his newest great-grandchild; at least in the latter case the governor of Nueva Vizcaya decided that a solemn mass and three nights of *luminarias* (festival torches) would suffice. Moreover, in many places the king's much-celebrated devotion to the Immaculate Conception prompted a renewed interest in staging fiestas in honor of Mary. Then in 1790 and 1791, Chihuahua held its customary funeral and coronation rites following the death of Carlos III and the accession of Carlos IV.[23]

CIVIC PRIDE, DYNASTIC LOYALTY, AND LABOR DISCIPLINE

Local leaders throughout the eighteenth century expressed repeated concern over the effects of civic and religious celebrations on labor discipline. In the performance of their official duties and in the conduct of their own businesses, the mining entrepreneurs who dominated local politics consistently demonstrated their frustration in finding sufficient numbers of well-disciplined workers to meet the needs of the local economy. Such preoccupations strongly influenced their planning of customary celebrations.

The fiesta of San Francisco prompted the most frequent expressions of official concern for labor discipline. Local leaders feared that the week-long holiday would disrupt work routines and that even the most docile employees might be corrupted by the throngs of unruly vagabonds who converged on Chihuahua for the October festivities. The Christmas season furnished additional occasions for lapses in social control. Employers complained that excessive celebration distracted workers from their promises to return to their jobs after the holidays ended. Following the customary year-end adjustments of their accounts, many workers simply disappeared, often without paying their debts. Others demanded sizable advances in money or merchandise before they agreed to resume work in the new year.[24]

For major employers, then, prolonged fiestas, more than a nuisance, interfered with the smooth operation of their enterprises. On repeated occasions the town fathers of eighteenth-century Chihuahua voiced a preference for the kind of standardized, year-in, year-out work routines usually associated with modernization and industrialization. In some respects local circumstances favored the imposition of such habits. Because mining and refining lacked agriculture's seasonal rhythms of intense toil and relative leisure, the work cycle itself dictated no obvious opportunities for celebration. Mining called for the sharp distinction between work and play characteristic of industrialized societies rather than the mixing of labor and socializing customary during harvests and other points on the agricultural calendar.[25]

At the same time, they despaired of achieving any quasi-industrial mode of labor discipline, given the frequent shortages of workers and the unruly nature of those who were available. Employers regularly complained that their employees were so devoted to fiestas that any curtailment of the bullfights or other expected entertainments might prompt them to revolt or to migrate elsewhere. Local leaders may also have understood that a lively round of fiestas could even attract new workers from other locations. Therefore, the best that they could do was to juggle the schedule of events for San Francisco and other celebrations so that the festivities did not spill over into a second week. Regardless of when the actual feast day (October 4) of San Francisco fell, successive cabildos decreed that the fiestas would begin on one Sunday and terminate on the next, so that workers could return to their jobs on Monday morning, presumably refreshed and ready for the task ahead.[26]

Concern for the discipline of labor and the conservation of scarce resources also shaped the local celebrations of dynastic events. Whenever possible, municipal officials tried to combine these observances with regular holidays already on the calendar. When they met in October 1724 to discuss the oath of allegiance to King Luis I, for example, council members explicitly voiced their concern over any possible disruption in mining. Therefore, they set the ceremony for December 24. The bullfights, comedies, and parades in honor of the new king simply added extra glitter to that year's Christmas festivities. The fiestas in 1745 in honor of Princess María Teresa's marriage took place during Christmas week as well.[27]

On later occasions the cabildo also tried to postpone the official oath of allegiance to a new king for as long as possible. When they learned of the death of King Felipe V in the spring of 1747, council members planned an immediate funeral procession for His Majesty, complete with trumpets and kettledrums, the latter covered with black cloth. They commanded all local residents to attend, dressed in mourning if they could afford to do so.[28] Because the swearing of loyalty to King Fernando VI involved greater pomp and thus greater expense, the council showed considerably less enthusiasm for fulfilling this part of its obligation. Initially, they agreed to hold the ceremony immediately following the fiesta of San Francisco in the fall, but after further discussion they deferred it until June 1748, presumably to coincide with Corpus Christi. Several cabildo members expressed the opinion that the June date would cause the least possible disruption to mining.

On February 11, 1748, an official notice describing the planned festivities appeared on the door of Chihuahua's municipal granary. Among the events listed was a comedy to be presented by the guilds of surgeons, barbers, and apothecaries on the afternoon of June 4. Members of these organizations lost no time in protesting the expense involved. One druggist also expressed his reluctance to cooperate with mere surgeons and bloodletters, whose trade he deemed socially inferior to his own.[29] Over the next several weeks others noted that the floundering local economy could ill afford the expense or the work stoppage that the festival would entail. A smallpox epidemic at the same time diverted people's attention from planning the celebration.

Finally in May, longtime civic leader Alexandro García de Bustamante asked the council to postpone the ceremony once again. He noted that on similar occasions in the past the people of Chihuahua had always shown loyalty to their sovereign. Requiring them to stage the event in the face of their current difficulties would constitute tyranny and a disservice to His Majesty, García added. He suggested that the observances be delayed until the fall, but that two full weeks be set aside to celebrate both occasions properly. Even though they undoubtedly feared the long break in mining operations the cabildo agreed to García's proposal, setting the coronation festivities to begin on Saturday, September 21. They scheduled a full week of processions, comedies, bullfights, and mock battles of the Moors and Christians following the formal acclamation of Fernando VI, so that Chihuahua might fete the new king "with the greatest plausible ostentation." The fiesta of San Francisco would then begin on Monday, September 30.

As the fiesta approached, local guilds and militia members again complained about their projected roles in the upcoming events. Andrés de Villalba, *mayordomo* (overseer) of a silver refinery, heartily objected to his selection as captain of the Moors. He pointed out that although the cabildo had attempted to follow the example set in 1724, they had overlooked the fact that on that occasion powerful mine owners of considerably higher social status had assumed duties such as the one he had been assigned. The council overruled Villalba and the festivities proceeded as planned.[30]

Chihuahua's cabildo again in 1760 weighed conflicting considerations of economics, social order, civic pride, and their loyalty as vassals in planning observances to mark the accession of a new king. The further deterioration of mining and the escalation of Indian hostilities had already undermined plans for that year's regularly scheduled holidays even before the council received word that Fernando VI had died. As late as September 1 no one had offered to fence the plaza for the San Francisco bullfights. Traditionally, local carpenters had bid for the privilege and then profited by selling space inside the fence to spectators at the bullfights. Finally, Juan Ignacio Fernández Lechuga agreed to build the fence but explained that economic hard times forced him to demand stiffer terms than those exacted by previous concessionaires. The council reluctantly accepted his proposal, granting him the right to construct the fence for the next seven years without having to pay the customary annual fee to the town's treasury.

At the same meeting the cabildo also determined that the San Francisco celebration should begin on Monday, September 29, and conclude on the following Sunday. Over the next several days questions arose with regard to the actual number of bullfights the designated timetable would permit. Documentary evidence reveals little past clerical interference with local bullfights, but Fernández Lechuga worried that church authorities might prohibit the fights on the fiesta's opening day, which happened to be the feast of San Miguel, and on the following Friday, the day of the week dedicated to commemorating the passion of Christ and one on which churchmen had sometimes objected to the holding of bullfights. He feared that he would not have sufficient opportunity to recoup the expenses he would incur in constructing the fence. Therefore, he asked that the bullfights and other secular amusements begin on Monday, October 6, two days after the actual feast of San Francisco.

Perhaps Fernández Lechuga's sensitivity to clerical opinion can be traced to the presence of Bishop Pedro Taramón y Romeral, who had recently arrived in Chihuahua to conduct his general visit.[31] Cabildo members evidently agreed that their proposed schedule might prompt the bishop to limit the number of bullfights. Although some officials fretted that postponement of the fiestas would disrupt work routines even longer than projected, the cabildo reluctantly agreed to Fernández Lechuga's proposal. Undoubtedly, they feared that curtailment of the bullfights might prove even more damaging to labor discipline.[32]

Word of King Fernando's death finally reached Chihuahua. Now the bishop found a convenient excuse to cancel the San Francisco bullfights altogether; he persuaded the cabildo that holding them during the week of October 6 would dishonor the dead king's memory. The council members therefore decided that no bullfights would take place until Christmas and that other customary San Francisco events should be cut short. They also set funeral rites for Fernando on October 13 and 14. Despite the sorry state of town finances they allocated 557 pesos for the observances.

Again the scheduling of coronation festivities posed a problem. Some cabildo members argued that San Felipe el Real should express its formal allegiance to Carlos III as soon as possible, even though time, money, and respect for Fernando's memory dictated the postponement of the associated celebration. Partisans of the current *alférez real* felt that the ceremony should take place at least before the end of 1760. By the latter half of the eighteenth century the office of *alférez* circulated annually among the *regidores* (permanent members of the cabildo), and friends of the incumbent suggested that he should have the opportunity to perform the prestigious duties involved in swearing fealty to a new monarch.

Mateo Antonio de Mendoza, governor of Nueva Vizcaya, favored postponement of the ceremony into 1761, however, citing the cold weather that usually occurred in December. Although he recommended scheduling the celebration in April, cabildo members delayed consideration of the governor's suggestion and finally reverted to their usual strategy of combining a royal festival with the traditional San Francisco holiday. In a decree issued on July 26, 1761, they set the final agenda. The proclamation of King Carlos III would take place on Saturday morning, October 3, with official church services planned for the following day. The customary comedies, bullfights, fireworks, and parades filled the remainder of the week. Despite the usual grumbling of designated participants the festivities went off as planned, at a cost of 695 pesos to the municipal treasury.[33]

FIESTAS AND COLONIAL SOCIETY

The records of civic and religious observances shed considerable light on the operation of local society in eighteenth-century Chihuahua. Most obvious is the central role played by cabildo officers and other members of the local elite in all of the town's fiestas. Council members planned virtually all events, while they and their social peers served as directors of the *cofradías* that helped arrange and finance the accompanying religious observances.[34] As in other colonial cities the Archicofradía del Santísimo Sacramento was in charge of the feast of Corpus Christi; its officers were almost always peninsular Spaniards and, in the words of a prominent member, "the most decent people that there are in this *villa*."[35]

Indeed, cabildo officers and other members of the local elite shed all subtlety in their efforts to utilize local fiestas to bolster their own positions and to reinforce hierarchical values. They and their families celebrated festive occasions in a style befitting the social precedence they claimed. They watched the bullfights and other spectacles from platforms specially constructed for their convenience, while enjoying refreshments prepared for them at public expense.[36] In 1720 the first town council provided for its own special pew, emblazoned with His Majesty's coat of arms, in the parish church. It also took measures to bar people of *color quebrado* (literally, broken color) from preferred seating at major church observances and instructed municipal employees to clean all streets and doorways through which the council would pass en route to these functions.[37] As an additional sign of their status, cabildo officers carried the maces symbolic of their authority as they paraded through the streets. At rituals held in honor of the royal family the *alférez* and other principal participants took advantage of the opportunity to advertise their special relationship to His Majesty.[38]

Cabildo officials stipulated the roles that other groups were to play in local observances. The lowest social ranks to play an active part in staging festivities were the town's craft guilds, and the cabildo carefully dictated the nature of their participation. Guild members presented the comedies and built the floats, or *carros triunfales*, that paraded through the streets. They also may have acted in the comedies themselves, for Chihuahua records contain no references to companies of specialized actors such as those that existed in Mexico City and other major urban centers.[39] A few artisans found other outlets for their creative talents. A tailor named Pedro Nolasco Bañuelos often composed verses for the comedies presented by his guild.[40]

The artisan guilds hardly represented the lowest strata of local society. The silversmiths, for example, figured prominently in many celebrations. This group included several peninsular Spaniards, and their assigned roles in most observances reflected the elevated prestige of their craft. To honor the marriage of Princess María Teresa in 1745 the cabildo ordered the silversmiths to parade on horseback, dressed in all of the *lucimiento*, or splendor, appropriate to their calling.[41]

The bakers' guild also played a major part in Chihuahua's festive rituals, but leading businessmen, often peninsular Spaniards or foreigners, usually assumed leadership of this organization. Pedro Antonio Cadrecha, for example, was an immigrant from Asturias who began his career as a cashier for a local merchant in the late 1730s. By the following decade he had established his own bakery and had begun to serve as the *cabo de panaderos* (head of the bakers) for the San Francisco celebrations. In 1759 and again in 1766 he was elected to the one-year terms on the cabildo as an *alcalde*, or magistrate. Another leading baker was Andrés Forzán, a Frenchman who took charge of organizing his guild's comedy for San Francisco in 1761. On other occasions Félix Cuarón, a merchant originally from Genoa, assisted in planning the dramatic presentations staged at local fiestas.[42]

Artisans also played limited roles in a few of the town's *cofradías*. The tailors had their own organization and a specially designated pew in the parish church.[43] The confraternity of Nuestra Señora de los Dolores, which sponsored a religious observance each September, also had members from ranks below the elite. Juana Manuela Sarmiento, proprietor of a small store and wife of carpenter José Raimundo de Castro, was serving as its *mayordoma* at the time of her death in 1770.[44]

Other groups active in planning local observances included overseers of silver refineries and others of comparable social status. Such individuals were often recruited to play leading roles in the reenactment of the battles of the Moors and Christians.[45] Vicente Vargas sometimes played the *Gran Turco*, or Grand Turk, in these rituals; when he died in 1756 his burial notice listed him as an *español* (literally, a Spaniard, but probably one born in Mexico) but did not accord him the honorific title of *don*. His family evidently lacked the means for a lavish funeral, for he was buried *de cruz baja* (literally, with a small cross—wealthier individuals were buried "with a large cross").[46]

In theory, then, skilled artisans and their social peers had an opportunity to help shape the cultural messages that these observances conveyed to the assembled crowds. Not all of them welcomed the opportunity to do so. In 1743, José de Porras found that serving as captain of the Moors for the fiesta of San Francisco was an onerous duty. Although he had invited various people to assist him they all had given their excuses; he therefore asked the cabildo to compel them to participate. Such complaints became increasingly common after the mining boom collapsed in the late 1730s.[47]

Groups lower in social status than the skilled artisans seldom played more than passive roles in officially sponsored fiestas. Most rank-and-file workers served only as spectators or occasionally as beneficiaries of official largesse when local dignitaries tossed commemorative coins to the assembled crowd to mark the coronation of a king. On the other hand, workers were sometimes asked to help defray the costs of festivities; organizers of the funeral observances for King Carlos III solicited monetary contributions from miners. Workers might also be recruited, probably against their will, to assist if their overseer were selected to serve in some ceremonial capacity,

such as captain of the Moors or Christians.[48] But other formal channels of active participation remained closed to them. Municipal
records fail to mention *cofradiás* or other organizations for any group
lower in social status than the tailors. If such organizations even existed for workers in Chihuahua, they played no part in townwide celebrations. Nor did these events feature any ritualized, accepted outlets
for lower-class frustrations or the energies of youth. As we have seen,
Carnival rituals traditionally had offered such safety valves in Spain
and in the colonies. Other colonial customs also may have entailed a
certain amount of social inversion. In his colorful description of the
"Judas-burnings" that marked the end of Lent in Porfirian times,
William Beezley has shown that the effigies of Judas in fact often
resembled local dignitaries. Beezley traces this custom to medieval
Europe and suggests that it might have spread to Mexico during the
colonial period.[49]

As we have seen, by the early eighteenth century officials in
Mexico City had begun efforts to suppress the pre-Lenten rituals,
and the cabildo of San Felipe el Real evidently followed their lead.
Furthermore, documents from Chihuahua contain no references to
Judas-burnings or any other customs that explicitly permitted a symbolic overturning of the social order. The closest that people in colonial Chihuahua may have come to such practices were in the
processions featuring individuals *enmascarados ridiculamente* (ri-
diculously disguised), as the ironsmiths and shoemakers appeared in
the celebration honoring the marriage of Princess María Teresa in
1745. But these rituals were ordered by the cabildo; any implied social inversion must have been stylized at best.[50]

Situated atop a racially mixed society and, as they often put it, on
the "frontier of enemy Indians," cabildo members saw little reason to
encourage any parodies of social unrest. It certainly can be argued
that in many societies the performance of such charades reinforced
social stability by providing an essentially harmless safety valve for
the frustrations of subordinated groups. But such rituals gave people
a chance to envision some departure from the prevailing social order
and could explode into open rebellion.[51] Chihuahua's town fathers
evidently espoused the latter point of view. From their perspective
the social order was too precarious to chance putting dangerous ideas
into the impressionable heads of those whom they regarded as their
inferiors.

Specific features of Chihuahua's historical development facilitated the efforts of local elites to minimize the disruptive effects of
local celebrations. The villa's social evolution probably impeded the
development of the kinds of fiestas, deeply rooted in popular traditions, that characterized life in early modern Europe or in the Indian

villages of central and southern Mexico. Like many other mining communities in northern Mexico, Chihuahua flowered overnight on a site where no previous permanent settlement had stood. Following the discovery of silver in the opening years of the eighteenth century, people of all races and social ranks converged on the area in search of quick fortunes. Each no doubt brought memories of rituals celebrated back home and perhaps hopes of recreating this rich ceremonial life on the northern frontier.

Most workers, however, migrated northward individually or in small groups, leaving behind the intricate web of traditional relationships that had sustained customary rituals in their home communities. Once they arrived in Chihuahua they formed part of an ethnically diverse working class whose communities of origin spanned a wide geographical and cultural spectrum. Yaqui Indians from Sonora, drifters in perpetual migration from one northern mining center to another, refugees from the embattled New Mexico frontier, and Indians from densely settled villages in central and southern Mexico joined artisans, muleteers, itinerant vendors, and emancipated Afro-Mexicans who hailed from cities and hamlets throughout the viceroyalty.

At least during the first few generations these workers were unable to form elaborate social networks once they arrived in Chihuahua. There is no evidence that any kind of formal organizations existed among workers in mines, refineries, or other enterprises. Rather than turning to a mutual aid society to cover a relative's funeral expenses or other financial emergencies, most workers had to depend on loans from their employers. Even the town's artisan guilds were loosely organized; they seldom enforced strict standards for membership and evidently did little more than stage civic rituals at the request of local officials.

Evidence from the Nueva Vizcayan mining center of Parral, founded almost a century before San Felipe el Real, suggests that Chihuahua's rapid development from a haphazard mining settlement to a full-fledged municipality with a cabildo also retarded the formation of social networks among the working classes. Like many other communities in colonial Mexico, Parral boasted a *cofradía* of *pardos* (dark-skinned people, probably of African ancestry) dating from the seventeenth century. The organization operated out of the Hospital de San Juan de Dios and traditionally staged celebrations in honor of Nuestra Señora de la Purísima Concepción each January. These observances featured the usual round of religious devotions and secular amusements, including bullfights and the pageant of the Moors and Christians, with *pardos* serving as the *Gran Turco* and in other ceremonial capacities. Though prominent local residents periodically tried to curb various excesses associated with the *cofradía*'s activities and to confine its fiesta to the already "wasted" period between Christmas and Epiphany, for most of the colonial period Parral lacked a cabildo to assume official responsibility for local festivals. When a council finally was created in the late eighteenth century, it supplanted the *pardos' cofradía* in planning the festivities honoring Nuestra Señora de la Purísima Concepción.[52]

In Chihuahua the existence of a cabildo from its earliest days provided a vehicle for local elites to maintain tighter control over ritual celebrations, while the absence of popular organizations and traditions gave them a tabula rasa on which to set an agenda of ceremonial life. Meanwhile, their relative cultural homogeneity helped them define the content of that agenda. Virtually all of Chihuahua's eighteenth-century cabildo members were *peninsulares*, and a substantial number of them came from the geographically compact region of northern Spain. Whatever differences might have separated Basques from Galicians, Spanish immigrants faced fewer obstacles in recreating customary social networks and festive rituals than did the native Mexicans who had traveled much shorter distances to reach their new homes in Chihuahua. Their concessions to local or even colonywide custom were minimal. For example, the cabildo in 1724 agreed that mock battles of the Moors and Christians to be staged in honor of the accession of Luis I be carried out *a la usanza de la tierra* (according to local custom), but in fact most of the major planners and participants were peninsular Spaniards.[53]

CONCLUSION: THE LIMITS OF SOCIAL CONTROL

Civic leaders in eighteenth-century Chihuahua succeeded in establishing a basic calendar of observances that met the minimum requirements of "civilized" communities, while stifling popular participation and minimizing disruptions in the labor discipline that was so essential to achieving their economic goals. Yet workers still managed to assert a degree of control over their leisure time despite the lack of formal organizations or traditionally sanctioned rituals.

Workers also succeeded in defending and augmenting the amount of leisure time that local fiestas afforded them. The cabildo never considered the possibility of limiting the San Francisco festivities to fewer than seven days, presumably because workers would never settle for it. Workers also played a role in prolonging the Christmas holidays for at least a full two weeks by refusing to return to work during the short intervals that separated Christmas, New Year, Epiphany, and other special days at year's end.[54] In other words, they had learned to *hacer puente*, as their twentieth-century descendants would say— to "make a bridge" between one holiday and another.

Moreover, many mine workers evidently enjoyed a weekly holiday of their own making. Employers never succeeded in imposing a full six-day workweek. Indeed, the account books kept by administrators of mines and refineries show that many workers put in only three or four days' labor during a typical week, which in at least some cases sufficed to entitle them to the rations of maize and meat that supplemented their wages.[55] Moreover, established custom called for a half-day's labor on Saturday. Some workers managed to prolong the weekend still further by doubling up and performing extra labor on Friday so that they could have a two-day rest. On leaving their jobs, those who worked in the mines of Santa Eulalia set off on the three hours' walk to Chihuahua, where many maintained their homes and families and where weekend amusements proved livelier than in the mining camp. In Chihuahua they entertained themselves on Saturday and Sunday, and, much to their employers' disgust, many extended the weekend into an unofficial holiday on Monday.[56]

Finally, workers also shaped the manner in which they celebrated local festivals. Though they lacked formal channels of participation in these events, in due time they created their own informal traditions for festive occasions. In conjunction with officially sponsored fiestas, to honor their own weddings and saints' days, or for no particular reason at all, they organized exuberant *fandangos* (dances) that lasted far into the night, despite repeated efforts of authorities to control them.[57] Surviving records also suggest that workers regularly skipped the religious observances on the feast of San Francisco and other holidays, though they rarely missed the bullfights and other merriment. Civil and ecclesiastical authorities tried various measures to induce workers to attend the religious rites; on one occasion, for example, they prohibited cockfights before one o'clock in the afternoon on fiesta days so that spectators would not be tempted to forgo church services.[58]

But no one really assumed responsibility for seeing that workers attended mass on Sundays or other religious occasions. The villa's priests lacked the kind of patriarchal control over their parishioners that their counterparts enjoyed in Indian missions. Moreover, though local custom allowed employers substantial powers to police their workers' sexual conduct and other aspects of their personal lives, seldom did anyone suggest that employers should assert control over their religious habits. Workers thus remained free to ignore the spiritual messages supposedly formulated for their enlightenment on festive occasions. They might just as well have rejected the lessons in cultural hegemony encoded in the ritual displays of wealth and power staged by local elites.

NOTES

1. Archivo del Ayuntamiento de Chihuahua, microfilm copy in the University of Texas at El Paso Library (hereafter cited as AACh, UTEP #491), 120-5, 128-15. I have assigned *expediente*, or folder, numbers to the documents according to the order in which they appear on each reel. Citations in this study give first the reel number, followed by a hyphen and the *expediente* number.

2. On the suppression of popular festivities in early modern Europe see, for example, Peter Burke, *Popular Culture in Early Modern Europe* (New York, 1978), 207–43; Robert Muchembled, *Popular Culture and Elite Culture in France* (Baton Rouge, LA, 1985), 122–48, 171–74, 212; Robert A. Schneider, *Public Life in Toulouse, 1463–1789: From Municipal Republic to Cosmopolitan City* (Ithaca, NY, 1989), 353; and John Lynch, *Bourbon Spain, 1700–1808* (Oxford, 1989), 276–78.

3. Archivo del Ayuntamiento de Chihuahua, First Supplement, microfilm copy in the University of Texas at El Paso Library (hereafter cited as AACh, UTEP #501), 5-7.

4. Descriptions of the San Francisco festivities can be found in AACh, UTEP #491, 43-19, 80-28, 87-6, 105-20.

5. Ibid., 56-6; AACh, UTEP #501, 5-6.

6. Francisco Almada, *Resumen de la historia del estado de Chihuahua* (México, 1955), 112; AACh, UTEP #491, 109-17, 133-15.

7. Archivo Municipal de Parral (hereafter cited as AMP), microfilm copy, reel 1729c, frame 1555; AACh, UTEP #491, 62-47, 100-21.

8. AACh, UTEP #491, 27-13. For *Semana Santa* observances in Parral see AMP, reel 1780, frame 226. For these observances in eighteenth-century Spain see Antonio Domínguez Ortiz, *Hechos y figuras del siglo XVIII español* (Madrid, 1973), 101–3; and William J. Callahan, *Church, Politics, and Society in Spain, 1750–1874* (Cambridge, 1984), 54.

9. AACh, UTEP #491, 56-6, 109-17; AACh, UTEP #501, 5-7, fol. 222.

10. AACh, UTEP #491, 57-14, 72-9, 84-9.

11. Ibid., 59-43, 85-22; Almada, *Resumen*, 112.

12. AACh, UTEP #491, 103-12, 109-17.

13. See, for example, S. L. Cline's reference to the celebration of Día de los Muertos in colonial Culhuacan, in *Colonial Culhuacan, 1580–1600: A Social History of an Aztec Town* (Albuquerque, NM, 1986), 25. The visits to cemeteries characteristic of this feast were evidently more popular among Indians than among Europeans. See Juan Pedro Viqueira Albán, *¿Relajados o reprimidos? Diversiones públicas y vida social en la ciudad de México durante el Siglo de las Luces* (México, 1987), 156–58.

14. Viqueira Albán, *¿Relajados o reprimidos?*, 139–47.

15. AACh, UTEP #491, 42-18.

16. For the specific dates of Ash Wednesday, Easter, and other liturgical holidays see Jacinto Agusti y Casanovas and Pedro Voltes Bon, *Manual de cronología española y universal* (Madrid, 1952), 210.

17. AACh, UTEP #501, 3-19, 5-3.

18. For information on these celebrations in Peru see John Preston Moore, *The Cabildo in Peru under the Hapsburgs: A Study in the Origins and Powers of the Town Council in the Viceroyalty of Peru, 1530–1700* (Durham, NC, 1954), 201–4; and idem, *The Cabildo in Peru under the Bourbons: A Study in the Decline and Resurgence of Local Government in the Audiencia of Lima, 1700–1824* (Durham, NC, 1966), 101.

19. AACh, UTEP #501, 5-7.

20. Ibid.; Lynch, *Bourbon Spain*, 81–84.

21. Almada, *Resumen*, 99–100; AACh, UTEP #491, 62-11; AACh, UTEP #501, 5–7. For references to the observances honoring King Luis in Parral see AMP, reel 1724a, frame 212.

22. AACh, UTEP #491, 56-6, 94-12, 125-7.

23. Ibid., 87-6, 100-21, 126-7, 142-4; Archivo del Ayuntamiento de Chihuahua, Second Supplement, microfilm copy in the University of Texas at El Paso Library (hereafter cited as AACh, UTEP #502), 5-25; see also Callahan, *Church, Politics, and Society*, 55.

24. Cheryl E. Martin, "El trabajo minero en Chihuahua, siglo XVIII," in *Actas del Primer Congreso de Historia Regional Comparada, 1989* (Ciudad Juárez, 1990), 185–96.

25. E. P. Thompson, "Time, Work-Discipline and Industrial Capitalism," *PP* 38 (1967).

26. AACh, UTEP #491, 10-53, 109-17.

27. AACh, UTEP #501, 5-7, fol. 195; AACh, UTEP #491, 94-12.

28. AACh, UTEP #491, 84-30, 125-7. For a description of the funeral rites held in San Antonio, Texas, see Gilbert R. Cruz, *Let There Be Towns: Spanish Municipal Origins in the American Southwest, 1610–1810* (College Station, TX, 1988), 139–43.

29. AACh, UTEP #491, 125-7.

30. Ibid., 62-11.

31. For the published report of the bishop's visit see Pedro Tamarón y Romeral, *Demostración del vastísimo obispado de la Nueva Vizcaya, 1765* (México, 1937). The bishop was in the city of Chihuahua from August 6 through August 17, from September 13 through September 18, and from October 11 through October 27; during the intervening periods he visited the city's immediate environs.

32. AACh, UTEP #491, 100-9.

33. Ibid., 100-15, 100-21.

34. Ibid., 59-43, 80-28, 87-6, 100-15, 109-17.

35. Ibid., 56-6. Prominent Spanish-born residents of Chihuahua also remembered the Archicofradía in their wills. See, for example, ibid., 108-36, 109-6.

36. Ibid., 109-17, 130-38.

37. AACh, UTEP #501, 5-7.

38. Ibid., 5-6. Certainly local elites expected deference in other contexts as well. See Cheryl E. Martin, "Popular Speech and Social Order in Northern Mexico, 1650–1830," *CSSH* 32, no. 2 (1990): 305–24.

39. Viqueira Albán, *¿Relajados o reprimidos?*, 57.

40. AACh, UTEP #491, 125-12.

41. Ibid., 94-12.

42. Ibid., 8-11, 80-28, 100-21. For biographical detail on Pedro Antonio Cadrecha see ibid., 7-16, 57-15, 89-2, 89-4, 89-22, 94-12, 99-7, 100-4, 100-8, 100-13, 108-36; and AACh, UTEP #501, 4-40.

43. AACh, UTEP #491, 59-43.

44. Ibid., 110-3.

45. Ibid., 122-29.

46. Ibid., 80-28; Genealogical Society of Utah, Chihuahua Burial Registers, 1756.

47. AACh, UTEP #491, 96-36. William J. Callahan has noted the reluctance of artisans to participate in local fiestas in eighteenth-century Spain; see his *Church, Politics, and Society*, 54. For similar developments in France see Schneider, *Public Life in Toulouse*, 302–7.

48. AACh, UTEP #491, 62-11, 126-7, 130-38. In early modern France a delegation of "the poor" sometimes marched in ritual processions along with representatives of other social groups. See Schneider, *Public Life in Toulouse*, 34.

49. William H. Beezley, *Judas at the Jockey Club and Other Episodes of Porfirian Mexico* (Lincoln, NE, 1987), 89–93.

50. AACh, UTEP #491, 94-12.

51. On the question of social inversion versus social stability see Natalie Z. Davis, *Society and Culture in Early Modern France* (Stanford, CA, 1975), passim, especially pp. 103–19; Burke, *Popular Culture in Early Modern Europe*, 201–4; and Emmanuel LeRoy Ladurie, *Carnival in Romans* (New York, 1979).

52. AMP, reel 1724a, frame 212; reel 1746, frame 3; reel 1794, frame 105. For the role of *pardos* in Mexico City observances see García Folder 135, Benson Latin American Collection, University of Texas at Austin.

53. AACh, UTEP #501, 5-7.

54. Martin, "El trabajo minero."

55. AACh, UTEP #491, 30-13.

56. Martin, "El trabajo minero."

57. AACh, UTEP #491, 80-21, 116-21, 118-36; AACh, UTEP #501, 4-44; AACh, UTEP #502, 5-3.

58. AACh, UTEP #491, 23-15.

6

Policia y Buen Gobierno:
Municipal Efforts to Regulate Public Behavior, 1821–1857

Anne Staples
El Colegio de México

Definition and regulation of public space provides the focus for the following essay. Anne Staples extends to the first half-century after independence the study, initiated by Juan Pedro Viqueira Albán in *¿Relajados o reprimidos?*, of the efforts by the Bourbon reformers to establish public order in Mexico City, and she proffers a Mexican case study of contested public spaces as accomplished by David Garrioch in *Neighbourhood and Community in Paris, 1740–1790.** She gives a straightforward explanation for official concern: children and drunkards represented two of the most difficult social groups to discipline. Authorities hoped to achieve order through education of the young and regulation of alcoholic beverage sales, but, unless closely controlled, public spaces, especially during fiestas, offered tempting places for childlike and drunken behavior. Her essay also examines the efforts initiated by the Bourbon reformers to associate the baser social groups with the now-shameful functions of the lower body, which resulted in myriad urban laws on cleanliness. In this respect her essay complements the work of Pamela Voekel.[†]

After receiving degrees from the Université de Grenoble, University of Oregon, University of Texas, and the doctorate from El Colegio de México, Anne Staples has centered her research on ecclesiastical affairs in the early republic and, more recently, on the history of education, especially the demand for and the growth of literacy.

M EXICANS, DESPITE COMPLEX ETHNIC, gender, occupational, and social divisions, uniformly separated daily activity into two spheres: private life in the home and public life on the street. Each of

---

*(México, 1987) and (Cambridge, 1986), respectively.

[†]"Peeing on the Palace: Bodily Resistance to Bourbon Reforms in Mexico City," *Journal of Historical Sociology* 5, no. 2 (June 1992): 183–208.

these two traditional universes had its own rules of behavior and gender identity. The street was masculine and the home was feminine, although subject to male authority. Both of these universes and the edges where they abutted and overlapped merit careful and thorough examination, especially during the nineteenth century, when significant changes occurred.

Women, for example, had long accepted the notion that males should respect female roles within the home and that females should make no complaint about male activities outside the conjugal domicile. Toward the end of the nineteenth century, however, women became increasingly restless and sought activities beyond the circle of private life. Men reacted in a desperate effort to continue confining women by domesticity, proclaiming them *reinas del hogar*, the queens of the hearth who served as the moral arbitrator of the family and the sacred depository of virtue. By necessity, then, women were restricted in their contacts with the contaminated public world accessible in the street. Not all women accepted this discourse, which both placed them on a higher pedestal and confined them at home. These defiant women struggled to redefine the role of their gender in society. The exegesis of their efforts and the social—especially male—response remains to be done.[1]

The public sphere and civic culture during the nineteenth century likewise offer opportunities for the researcher. This essay represents a preliminary effort, looking at street life from independence in 1821 until approximately the Constitution of 1857 through case studies of Toluca, Tlacotalpan, and Mexico City.

REFORMING BEHAVIOR IN PUBLIC SPACES

Street life, with its forbidden and therefore alluring pleasures of liberty, movement, association, and access, did not exist outside the mainstream of social hierarchy and moral conduct. No free-for-all developed; even though all classes gathered physically at one time or another, they were *juntos pero no revueltos*, together but not mixed together. Each social group had its own code of behavior, reinforced by the church and the state that tried valiantly to impose on everyone at least a common denominator of decency and respectability. Out of this effort came the rules for public behavior laid down during the nineteenth century by municipal governments.

Every community included disruptive individuals—children and drunkards. These persons could not easily be controlled, but local authorities did try. Governmental efforts, for example, attempted to control the sale of alcoholic beverages, especially pulque, and to regulate drinking behavior.[2] Municipal and church officials also tried to lessen youthful rambunctiousness, particularly through the schools. Special concern existed that young boys might meet and play with little girls on their way to and from school, so schedules often were staggered to reduce this possibility.[3] Schools generally were not co-educational, but in those rare instances in which youngsters of both genders shared the same building, boys and girls used separate entrances. Parents or teachers assigned older children the responsibility of supervising their siblings on the walks to and from school, which occurred in the mornings and afternoons. They were to prevent boys and girls from playing together and to stop any disruption of public order through inappropriate horseplay, running, shouting, or worse.[4] Nevertheless, the young did violate the rules of propriety. The schools lacked bathrooms, and children simply urinated in the street.

Students were not the only ones to use public places for toilets. One of the reasons offered by the Mexico City cabildo, or city council, to order the demolition of colonial ruins was their use as urinals. Moreover, couples also huddled together in their shadows, screened from indiscreet glances, and thieves hid behind their crumbling walls before pouncing on passersby. Yet no one could be found to destroy the old monuments because they originally had been stations of the cross. No matter how desecrated or run down, the ruins retained their sacred character. Not even forced labor could be induced to attack them with picks and shovels. Finally, soldiers did the job; the threat of court-martial weakened their compunctions about razing former holy shrines.[5]

The trend to secularize society affected street culture in many ways, and the presence of foreigners created unusual problems in this Roman Catholic society. Public worship of all kinds formed part of daily life and included bowing to images of saints located in shrines at the corners of buildings or over front doors. Liturgical hours determined the rhythm of urban life, the slow progression of prayers that marked morning, noon, dusk, and bedtime at least acknowledging the presence of a patron saint, which comfortably looked down on human folly from its sculptured niche. Foreigners, usually in Mexico for business, refused to be distracted by this leisurely pace and otherworldly focus. They rushed to complete their affairs (at least that was the excuse offered for not paying proper respect to the images), neither bowing nor saying a minimal prayer as they passed. One American shoemaker paid dearly for his lack of reverence. A uniformed military officer noticed that at the moment when a carriage carrying the holy sacraments to some dying mortal passed, the shoemaker did not come out of his shop and kneel on the sidewalk, along with the other passersby, but simply knelt in his shop. To teach him proper respect the officer slit him with his sword.[6]

Concern over lack of respect and a desire to benefit from commerce eventually prompted the Mexico City government and the cathedral chapter to suggest that images be kept inside buildings. There they could be attended with greater care, and they would not be exposed to the presence of foreigners of questionable religious orthodoxy, even though the 1824 Federal Constitution expressly forbade the exercise of any religion other than the obligatory Roman Catholicism. But, as the early nineteenth-century decades passed, church and state agreed less and less about what type of religious activities should be allowed in the street. More modern, secular city life proved incompatible with the daily schedule and activities imposed by the church. Thus, for example, authorities curtailed the ringing of bells so that city residents would be less inclined to leave their productive duties for prayer.[7] Taking the last rites to the dying was no longer performed with its previous ostentation in order that people could go about their business with little interruption. Statutes restricted the gathering of alms to certain areas by specific groups.

Above all, what most dismayed the traditional Catholic society was the prohibition of pilgrimages and public religious processions. How could Corpus Christi be properly celebrated without a procession when one had taken place every year since the early colonial period? How could the stations of the cross be visited? How could all the pageantry of Catholicism be reduced to the churchyard or the temple itself? Churchmen argued that the gospel had been preached in marketplaces, village squares, and along the streets and roads for generations. How could ecclesiastics be prevented from wearing their clerical garments in public? Was it not peculiar to require clergymen to ride in their carriages with the blinds rolled down so that they would not be seen wearing their robes in the street? And yet, the reform laws of the 1850s mandated these changes and, in doing so, altered the color, form, and, of course, meaning of street culture. These regulations sought to remove the church from the street and make it invisible, as if it were no longer a vital element in public life.

As the state reduced the jurisdiction of the church, it increased its own power. It too had rules and regulations to impose, so that society would function in an orderly fashion and steadily go about the business of development. Through legislation the state tried to put into practice the basic principles of the Enlightenment, striving for the common good. Municipal governments took charge of maintaining decorum and urbanity, the essence of city living. Each town laid down its own rules, molded to the idiosyncracies of its place and people. Of the dozens of sets of regulations created during the nineteenth century, the three examples that follow show how the desire for orderly public behavior was couched in the law. The case studies come from Toluca, a high, cold agricultural town to the west of the capital; Tlacotalpan, a humid, hot trading town located on the Papaloapan River not far from the Veracruz coast; and Mexico City.

URBAN REGULATIONS

In Toluca, after the disruption caused by the U.S. invasions of 1846 and 1847, the municipal authorities tried to regain control of their city. As a first step they required all residents, including children and visitors, to register so that officials could watch out for strangers and odd behavior. Innkeepers were required to report on their guests— where they came from, where they were going, and anything suspicious about them. Moreover, the appearance of Toluca began to change. As in other cities of the republic, it became law that all houses be numbered, all streets have written names. This, of course, implied a need for litcracy that had not existed before. People, homes, and businesses now had addresses of names and numbers, not just locations such as "around the corner from the large shade tree," or, "next to Sánchez's stable." Stores had to post lists of their products and prices, thereby creating another need for literacy that had not existed previously, giving fixed prices to merchandise and promoting competition. These signs, the forerunners of advertising, added one more element of interest to the streets.

Two concerns—sanitation and easy transit—appear common to all the municipal ordinances. Sanitation was by far the more difficult problem in places that had no underground sewers, no market buildings, no zoning, and no enclosed water system. Top priority went to keeping the water supply clean. Strict injunctions existed against befouling water fountains, allowing cattle to drink from them, or breaking the main that brought water to them. Keeping the streets clean also required attention. That too proved a formidable task for people unaccustomed to thinking of the street as a shared space for which everyone had responsibility. In Toluca as of 1849, homeowners received orders to build indoor toilets and to avoid throwing the contents of chamber pots into the street. Statutes forbade the entire population, including children and Indians, from answering nature's call in the streets, cemeteries, plazas, or alleys. Many other ordinances repeated the same injunctions. Property owners were required to sweep the street and sidewalk in front of their businesses and homes every Wednesday and Saturday; shop owners had to sweep every day, between five and seven in the morning. The rules dictated that property owners should sprinkle the section with water before sweeping to prevent raising dust, that they should remove all the dirt and garbage collected, and that they should not disturb passersby in the process.

Streets, plazas, parks, and other public spaces had their specific uses, but washing clothes and putting them out to dry was not one of them. Restrictions also applied to flower pots on balconies because when they were watered, the runoff inevitably caught some pedestrian by surprise. Rules directed the construction of drains (so that rainwater from the roof did not hit the sidewalk) and prohibited both throwing garbage from the roof into the street and using the sidewalks for draining suet or curd. Foul-smelling products could not be transported in open containers. No stalls could be placed along the sidewalks, and kites could not be flown from them. People carrying large objects could not use the sidewalk but had to walk in the street; many ladies had been bumped by the oversized baskets use to carry freshly baked bread. The bakers had to discipline their delivery boys and, moreover, had to see that smoke from their ovens did not disrupt life in the neighborhood. The regulations called for each bakery oven to have a chimney at least six feet above its roof. Other city ordinances required that obstacles such as scaffolding be kept off the sidewalks and be lighted at night. New houses had to be constructed in line with the street without protruding in such a way as to interrupt the flow of pedestrian or animal traffic. In addition, the street became the object of legislation designed to facilitate urban life. Laws expressly prohibited carriage and horse races and pigs grazing in the thoroughfares. Through traffic was discouraged on market day, and at no time could mounted horses, buggies, or other vehicles use the sidewalks.

Beyond the physical aspects, other laws concerned the public morals of those who appeared on the street. Regulations governed the sale of alcoholic beverages, prohibiting them after 6 P.M., and closed cafés and social clubs at 10 P.M. Rules directed that the bar inside a tavern be located near the door in the hope that patrons would be induced to have a quick drink and leave for home. The same desire motivated prohibition of music, games, and other entertainment that might prompt a prolonged stay. Municipal authorities tried to stop stores that sold liquor from becoming gathering places; they did not want individuals to collect outside the door or stand in the doorway to chat.[8]

Toluca began improving its appearance even before its designation as the capital of the state of Mexico. Early efforts included the donation to the city in 1827 of a portion of the Franciscans' orchard for the construction of *portales*, the town's arcades; provisions in 1828 for getting water to various sections of town; improvements of the street lighting and the enlargement of the cemetery in 1830; and, in 1836, initiation of construction of the Alameda park.[9]

During the first half of the nineteenth century the reappearance of these ordinances, with only slight variations, indicated the need to remind Toluca's residents repeatedly of their obligations. Moreover, the similarity of ordinances in various communities suggests that town authorities had the same concerns, problems, and responsibilities, altered only by local circumstances.

URBAN REFORMS IN TLACOTALPAN

In proud Tlacotalpan, officials wanted to set a moral tone superior to that of the neighboring port of Alvarado, known even today for its spicy language. The first rule of its municipal code warned that any man who took the Lord's name in vain, or the name of the Virgin or any of the saints, would face the full weight of the law (that a woman would do so was unthinkable). Obscene language that offended the purity of the faith represented the most serious breach of civility that an inhabitant of Tlacotalpan could commit and would not be tolerated. Special care had to be taken to avoid contamination from the ill-speaking Alvaradoreños and to ensure that none of their vile expressions would be heard in Tlacotalpan, a town, according to its municipal government, distinguished by its higher moral character.

Other measures attempted to ensure decency, which was regarded as the characteristic sign of people governed by reason. No one was supposed to be out in the street at night after the curfew, usually 10 P.M. Beyond those running errands for doctors, midwives, or confessors, others who violated the curfew and could not offer justification of urgency were jailed for ten days and had to sweep the streets if they could not pay the fine. Discovery of someone in possession of firearms at night led to the confiscation of the weapon.

Tlacotalpan's concern for public morals extended to decrying the unbridled inclinations of the young, the majority of whom enjoyed various games unsuited to public order. Local authorities warned parents that they would take young people to court if they engaged in unruly or dangerous activities such as shooting arrows in the street.[10] Rules informed owners of food stalls, cafés, and pool halls that if they allowed minors to enter their premises they faced a heavy fine of five to fifty pesos. City fathers also felt it necessary to curb the scandalous practice followed by unconscionable boys and girls of swimming naked (*enteramente descubiertos de sus carnes*, or literally, with their flesh entirely uncovered) in the Papaloapan River that flows next to the town. The law warned that youngsters caught swimming in such a fashion or answering the call of nature in public would be taken to court, their parents fined.

The rest of the population also had to be reminded of its obligations. These duties included sweeping and, in Tlacotalpan, where lack of water is never a problem and the grass grows beautifully, weeding the streets and sidewalks. City streets had to be made presentable by Saturday night so that they could be enjoyed by everyone on Sundays before and after mass. As in Toluca, sidewalk traffic was restricted in an attempt to keep Indians off the sidewalks, reserving them for more "decent" people. Anyone carrying anything on his or her back had to walk in the street or face a two-*reales* fine or one day in jail. In practice only Indians fit this description and received punishment.

Other regulations showed a concern for the community. Stores could not open before 4 A.M., so that they would not awaken neighbors, and had to close at 3 P.M. on holidays. When someone was ill, dances or family parties that might disturb the rest and recovery of the convalescent were prohibited in the neighborhood. Private fiestas that planned to serve liquor had to inform municipal authorities as to their day and hour.

Wealthier community members were expected to improve the quality of life in Tlacotalpan and other provincial municipalities that were chronically and woefully short of funds. The local priest tried to persuade successful merchants in the river town to pave at least the section of street in front of their homes in the hope that their example and enthusiasm would influence others to do the same. Everyone, regardless of income, was obliged to hang a lantern from his door on dark, moonless nights until the municipal government could install a system of public lighting.[11]

Animals represented another ingredient of street life. As in Toluca, regulations outlawed grazing pigs, but dogs presented a greater problem.[12] The municipal government in 1850 commented on the damage caused by the excessive number of dogs and allowed residents eight days to tag and identify dogs with their masters' initials. After that time untagged animals were to be destroyed.[13] In 1851 the same authorities broadened the penalty: death for both untagged dogs and any tagged ones found on the streets after 11 P.M. Cattle rustling was and remains a problem in this ranching region of Veracruz. Many strategies tried to curtail it; one prohibited moving herds of cows without registry papers through town. Butchers could not slaughter or sell beef in the local market without certifying its origin.[14]

The church, before the reform laws, affected many aspects of street life and continually made efforts to conciliate the needs of temporal and spiritual power. District authorities had the chore of eliminating pagan elements from public pageants at Easter. They were ordered to consult the local priest as to the best way to purge processions of carnivalesque features and to revive the solemn attitudes that should accompany public worship, even if not confined inside temples.[15]

URBAN REFORM IN THE CAPITAL CITY

Mexico City, of course, had a long tradition of municipal ordinances, the most enlightened dating from the division of the city into *cuarteles*, or wards, and Viceroy Revillagigedo's efforts to clean up the city.[16] The national congress passed many regulations after independence, and the mayor issued decrees as the need arose. The detailed code decreed shortly after independence in 1825 revealed the city's urban orientation, addressing problems that did not arise in more rural settings. For example, one ordinance forbade shaking out carpets, *petates* (sleeping mats), cloths, or other large objects that might cover passersby with dust. Foodstuffs could be sifted between six and eight in the morning, with the exception of chile powder. To protect people from clouds of piquant dust, only clean chile powder could be brought into the city. The code dissuaded residents from washing dishes and bathing horses in the street. Vendors who sold fragile items that came wrapped in packing material such as dried grass (glassware, for instance) were directed not to leave it strewn about, and public eateries were enjoined from plucking fowls in or throwing the feathers and innards into public passageways. The same laws cautioned customers at restaurants not to fling leftovers onto the sidewalk or toss bones to ever-awaiting dogs.

Writing, as mentioned, became a part of daily life in the lettered signs above businesses. The government attempted to eliminate the traditional signs, whose size and shape indicated the nature of the establishment. These signs, which cluttered the facades, gradually were replaced. Often atrocious spelling and handwriting created problems, so the city council established a commission to check spelling before signs were painted, imposing fines for shopkeepers who did not consult it. City council members prohibited the incorporation of dolls, animals, or other figures as part of painted signs, allowing only letters and numbers. In this way they restricted information to the literate.

As in any community, one family's rejoicing could inconvenience others. Reunions, dances, private theater performances, baptisms, or similar celebrations, especially if accompanied by shouting or loud noises, drew the attention of municipal authorities. In many instances the city required advance permission for such fiestas and levied fines whenever the revelry became too boisterous.[17]

Municipal officials promulgated ordinances for reasons beyond keeping the streets clean. They also faced basic issues of public health, especially in calamitous times such as the cholera outbreak in 1833. On three different occasions during March 1833, decrees urged extra care in sweeping the streets and handling garbage and human waste. A new ordinance ordered the washing of the water fountains every fifteen days instead of once a month as had been previously decreed. Further efforts to instill cleanliness called for painting and maintaining walls, doors, and fences. In a vain effort to ward off the effects of the cholera epidemic, the city council tried anything that might contribute to a healthy atmosphere.

Mexico City's municipal government, under the reforming zeal of Vice President Valentín Gómez Farías in 1834, studied previous ordinances and decided that lack of compliance rather than lack of laws was responsible for the unclean conditions of the city. Previous ordinances had been decreed in December 1780, August 1790, March 1791, January 1796, and January 1822. Therefore, the council reprinted the 1822 ordinances in 1834, insisting that people observe these elementary rules of orderliness and decency.[18] No government could ensure the safety of individuals, their property, health, and comfort unless the officials in charge enforced strict obedience to the laws. Order could not be maintained if the general public did not quickly comply with authority. Of course, many vices corrupted the body politic; apathy, influence peddling, and gaining special advantages from personal connections with bureaucrats in the lower echelons of the city administration were all practices that managed to make the best plans and ordinances useless.

Life in the street featured a continuous give and take between hard-pressed inhabitants, who used the space as an extension of their living and working areas, and government officials, who yearned for an orderly, clean, behaved public that would be seen on the streets only in passing. The climate in Mexico City invited its inhabitants to spend time out of doors. People of all walks of life, but especially the urban poor, spent most of their existence in the streets. The *léperos* (homeless), who constituted a considerable portion of the capital's population in the early nineteenth century, lived in the streets begging for alms, warming themselves in the sun, washing in the fountains, and sleeping in doorways at night.[19]

Almost everyone found an excuse at some point during the day to go out into the streets, which were crowded with pedestrians, vendors, carriages, horses, dogs, and, in more rural areas, cattle and pigs.

In Enlightened fashion the municipal governments of nineteenth-century Mexico made a valiant effort to control the public behavior of their citizens; for their part, however, the people kept to their individualistic ways, accepting the view that rules were fine for everyone else but did not apply to them personally. Again and again city councils issued the same ordinances, and only with the greatest effort did they succeed in incorporating basic principles into the life of city streets.

A tour of the old neighborhoods of Mexico City on a busy day today tells of the slight effect all the worthy regulations for urban life have had over the past two centuries. The same problems exist—the same demand from the municipal government and the upper classes for reform; the same impossibility of controlling space that belongs to a community responding to its needs. Although their forms may be more complex, municipal ordinances of today address problems similar to those faced by their predecessors, the dilemmas of how to regulate public behavior.

NOTES

1. Recent studies of women and gender in nineteenth-century Mexico include Sylvia M. Arrom, *The Women of Mexico City, 1750–1850* (Stanford, CA, 1986); William E. French, "Prostitutes and Guardian Angels: Women, Work, and the Family in Porfirian Chihuahua," *HAHR* 72, no. 4 (November 1992): 529–53; Heather Fowler Salamini and Mary Kay Vaughan, eds., "Creating Spaces, Shaping Transition: Women of the Mexican Countryside, 1850–1990" (forthcoming); Asunción Lavrin, ed., *Sexuality and Marriage in Colonial Latin America* (Lincoln, NE, 1989); Julia Tuñón Pablos, *Mujeres en México: Una historia olvidada* (México, 1987); and Carmen Ramos-Escandón, *Presencia y transparencia: La Mujer en la historia de México* (México, 1987).

2. William Taylor, *Drinking, Homicide and Rebellion in Colonial Mexican Villages* (Stanford, CA, 1979); Viqueira Albán, *¿Relajados o reprimidos?*, 169–218; and William E. French, Chapter 10 in this volume.

3. "Reglamento para la educación primaria de la juventud en el departamento, 1840," in *Recopilación de los decretos y órdenes expedidos en el estado de Veracruz, desde el 4 de diciembre de 1840, al 24 de diciembre de 1852* (Xalapa, 1970), 10–11.

4. Article 10, part 7, "Reglamento para las escuelas de primera educación, dotadas de los fondos de propios y arbitrios del departamento de Jalisco, aprobado por la junta directiva de la instrucción primaria del mismo," 4 febrero 1841, in José Luis Razo Zaragoza, *Don Manuel López Cotilla, vida y obra de un ilustre jaliscense* (Guadalajara, 1961), 133–65.

5. Andrés Lira, "La creación del Distrito Federal," in *La república federal mexicana, gestación y nacimiento*, vol. 7 (México, 1974).

6. Carlos María de Bustamante, *Diario histórico de México, enero-diciembre 1824*, notes by Manuel Calvillo (México, 1981), entries 28 agosto 1824, 122; 4 septiembre 1824, 125–26; and 5 septiembre 1824, 126. See also Salvador Novo, "La vida en la ciudad de méxico en 1824," in *La república federal mexicana, gestación y nacimiento*, vol. 8 (México, 1974).

7. Anne Staples, "El abuso de las campanas en el siglo pasado," *Historia Mexicana* 27, no. 2 (octubre-diciembre 1977): 177–94.

8. Bando municipal publicado el 31 de enero de 1849 por José Jiménez de Velasco, alcalde primero constitucional de Toluca y presidente del ilustre ayuntamiento, Archivo Histórico Municipal de Toluca, ramo Presidencia, vol. 1, exp. 9.

9. *Toluca en el siglo XIX*, Exposición documental Catálogo (México, 1991).

10. Libro sesiones del ayuntamiento de Tlacotalpan, 24 octubre 1851, Municipal Archives, Tlacotalpan, Veracruz. In Mexico City, boys had to be prohibited from shooting each other with toy cannons, that nevertheless were loaded and fired. Decreto 593, "Bando de policía," 5 enero 1829, in Manuel Dublán and José María Lozano, *Legislación mexicana o colección completa de las disposiciones legislativas expedidas desde la independencia de la república* (México, 1976), 2:89.

11. Libro sesiones del ayuntamiento de Tlacotalpan, 1 julio 1853; 11 abril 1855.

12. "Parte oficial. Gobierno del estado libre y soberano de Veracruz. Circular," *El Zempoalteca*, 6 abril 1849, 2–3.

13. Libro sesiones del ayuntamiento de Tlacotalpan, 25 octubre 1850, and repeated 9 diciembre 1852.

14. Ibid., 23 noviembre 1850.

15. "Reglamento de policia 1852," aprobado según libro sesiones del ayuntamiento de Tlacotalpan, 16 abril 1852.

16. Ignacio González Polo, "La ciudad de México a fines del siglo XVIII. Disquisiciones sobre un manuscrito anónimo," *HM* 21, no. 1 (julio-septiembre 1971): 29–47. Viqueira Albán discusses the division of the city into wards in ¿*Relajados o reprimidos?*.

17. Decreto 454, "Decreto de policia y buen gobierno," 7 febrero 1825, in Dublán and Lozano, 1:764–69.

18. Decreto 1341, 15 enero 1834, in Dublán and Lozano, 2:662–66.

19. Fanny Calderon de la Barca, *Life in Mexico: The Letters of Fanny Calderon de la Barca with New Material from the Author's Private Journals*, edited and annotated by Howard T. Fisher and Marion Hall Fisher (New York, 1970), 91, 106, 175.

7

Streetwise History:
The Paseo de la Reforma and
the Porfirian State, 1876–1910

Barbara A. Tenenbaum
Hispanic Division
Library of Congress

Barbara Tenenbaum provides a Mexican complement to the historical approach initiated in general by Jacob Burckhardt's *Civilization of
the Renaissance in Italy*, in which he examined "The State as a Work
of Art," and carried forward in particular by Donald J. Olsen in *The
City as a Work of Art: London, Paris, Vienna*, who found cities "complex but legible documents that can tell us something about the values and aspirations of their rulers, designers, builders, owners, and
inhabitants."* Her research project, currently supported by the
Rockefeller Foundation, is indeed rare. Robert Quirk's introduction to
his concise history of Mexico, Gil Joseph and Allen Wells's essay on
Mérida, and Thomas Benjamin's evaluation of the Monument to the
Revolution number among the scarce parallel studies.† This endeavor
represents a shift in emphasis from the economic studies she has
executed since completing her doctoral dissertation at Harvard University and foreshadows a book promising a distinctive approach to
the capital city.‡

The author gratefully acknowledges the support of the Rockefeller Resident
Fellowship in the Humanities at the University of Maryland, 1991–1992, in the
writing of this article. She also thanks the editors for their judicious and helpful
comments.

*(New Haven, CT, 1986), ix.

†Robert Quirk, "Mexico in Its Monuments," in *Mexico* (Englewood Cliffs, NJ,
1971), 1–4; Gilbert Joseph and Allen Wells, "Chilango Blueprints and Provincial
Growing Pains: Mérida at the Turn of the Century," *Mexican Studies/Estudios
Mexicanos* 8 (Summer 1992): 167–215; and Thomas Benjamin, "The Mythic Image: Mexico's Monument to the Revolution" (unpub. ms.).

‡For an example of Tenenbaum's economic studies, see, most notably, *The Politics of Penury: Debt and Taxes in Mexico, 1821–1856* (Albuquerque, NM, 1986).

B Y THE TIME RESIDENTS of Mexico City celebrated the centennial of national independence in 1910, their city had undergone a transformation that reflected the enormous struggle of a country torn by the simultaneous need to preserve its sovereignty while trying to lure the necessary capital from abroad for economic development. In the process, "official history"—sometimes to impress foreigners, sometimes to teach the virtues the Porfirian government thought appropriate at home—was born right there for everyone to see on city streets.

The victors write the history, as the truism says; in Mexico City the winners demolished the losers' strongholds even before war had been declared. Official Mexico created the Real Academia de las Tres Nobles Artes de San Carlos de la Nueva España in 1781 as part of a frontal attack on the baroque style. It revised and corrected architectural projects and eliminated without further ado the architects associated with the old aesthetic.[1] The Royal Academy adopted neoclassicism in the name of universalism and set out to destroy the baroque churches and *palacios* built since the 1520s.[2]

Some of the new architecture would become the priceless treasures we admire today, such as José Damián Ortiz de Castro's addition of a second group of towers to the Cathedral of Mexico City that Manuel Tolsá completed with a central clock, banisters, and other embellishments. The Spanish-born Tolsá, the embodiment of this new neoclassical style, also built the palace of the Marqués del Apartado and the Palacio de Buenavista. Moreover, in this period Viceroy Revillagigedo the Second revised the layout of the capital to include four large plazas on its outskirts as satellite areas. Furthermore, city planners added the Paseos de Bucareli and Azanza and adorned the Zócalo with Tolsá's magnificent statue of Carlos IV (*El Caballito*). Although the city still retained its baroque character, it made a firm commitment to the adoption of a new, more European look.

These architectural innovations reflected both an aristocratic pursuit of classical austerity, as opposed to the syncretic and flamboyant "Mexican" (read mestizo) arts and architecture, as well as the first and perhaps most subtle weapon in the fight for national laicization. With the Bourbons came the French predilection for order, control, and precision in counterdistinction to the riotous Habsburg approach to colonial life. The effect on Mexican architecture was profound, particularly in the case of Manuel Tolsá, whose *Caballito* remains one of the city's glories.

This process undoubtedly would have continued once independence had been achieved had not bankrupt treasuries saved the city from further neoclassical renewal.[3] Nevertheless, the coming of Benito Juárez and the liberals of the 1850s added renewed impetus to the process of transforming an ecclesiastical capital into a secular one. Former convents such as that of San Francisco were taken over by the state and demolished to make way for Gante and Sixteenth of September streets; in two cases among many the chapel of the San Andrés hospital was razed for Xicoténcatl Street, while the convent of Santo Domingo became Leandro Valle Street.[4] The French occupation in the 1860s almost inadvertently accelerated the transformation of Mexico City. Apparently, Emperor Maximilian decided to build an avenue that would run directly from his Alcázar de Chapultepec to the Palacio Nacional downtown. He named his new avenue the Calzada de la Emperatriz in honor of his wife, the Empress Carlota.[5] Maximilian entrusted Francisco Somera, the well-known architect and urban developer, with all the details concerning its construction. Somera was the obvious choice. From 1850 to 1866 he served as *regidor* on the city council, or ayuntamiento, in charge of both roads and canals as well as sewers and pavement, and in 1856 he sat on a committee studying the flood problem in the Valley of Mexico. In 1862 he reorganized the *obrería mayor* (public works administration) in the capital, then controlled by untrained "administrators," into the Dirección General de Obras Públicas, staffed with civil engineers and architects from the Academia de San Carlos, Somera's alma mater. During the empire he became the chief magistrate (alcalde) of Mexico City and then head of the treasury committee of the ayuntamiento, which set rates for property taxes.

But Somera is best known as a real estate developer. In 1858 he began to lay the groundwork for one of the first subdivisions of the city to be known as the *colonia de arquitectos*, and, because of his standing in the government, he was able to provide the residents of his areas with better basic services more rapidly than those received by other city dwellers. After Maximilian announced his intention to build his new *calzada*, Somera sold part of the section that lies in the trapezoid formed by present-day Gómez Farías, Sullivan, and Miguel Schultz streets and Avenida Insurgentes to the imperial government as an adjunct to the new avenue, for which he received the highest payment in his entire career as a land speculator.[6]

After the empire had fallen in 1867 and Mexicans had regained control of their nation, President Benito Juárez made a decision that would affect the development of both Mexico and its capital city for decades—he once again suspended payment on the foreign debt. In the following year Matías Romero, former minister to the United States and now minister of the treasury, announced that Mexico would not permit any revenues to be mortgaged to pay the foreign debt and that the treasury would confine its attention to retiring its internal obligations. This policy would remain in force until 1885.[7]

While the old guard surrounding Juárez, survivors of both the War of the Reform and the Intervention, were happy with financial isolation from Europe, other leaders were eager to adopt the ways of continental progress, particularly as they had seen it displayed in Paris. The latter got their chance when Sebastían Lerdo de Tejada became president in 1872. They quickly revived interest in Maximilian's *calzada*, appropriately renamed the Paseo de la Reforma, and encouraged civic leaders to formulate plans for its beautification. These men became "francophile progressives." One of the admirers of the beauties of Paris was Ignacio Cumplido, founder of the Mexico City liberal daily, *El Siglo XIX*. He had visited the City of Light in 1848 and again in 1860 after Baron Georges-Eugène Haussmann had directed its reconstruction under the watchful eye of Emperor Napoleon III; his admiration for the city of Paris developed into a desire to see its beauties replicated in Mexico.[8] When he became the member of the ayuntamiento in charge of boulevards in 1873, Cumplido had both sides of the Paseo lined with trees in emulation of the Champs Elysées.[9]

Antonio Escandón, the famous railroad entrepreneur, was another "francophile progressive." This much younger brother of the highly successful moneylender and entrepreneur Manuel Escandón and son-in-law of the even more notorious moneylender and entrepreneur Eustaquio Barron had actively promoted the development of a railway between Mexico City and Veracruz since the 1850s. During the time of the Mexican Empire he prowled the capitals of Europe for investors to fund his dream and in so doing became quite at home in London and Paris.[10] Escandón's understanding of the new Paris as a center of highly profitable commercial space as well as the model of how a progressive and powerful city should appear to the world reflected his entrepreneurial outlook. Paris, with its Etoile, or star, formed by the juxtaposition of twelve avenues, symbolized in its very construction the centralization of national power and the rise of the *haute bourgeoisie* during the reign of Napoleon III.[11] Although Mexico, in contrast, barely had a civilian governing class in the 1870s, Escandón believed the construction of a new, beautiful city would promote its economic development and stimulate the growth of a professional bureaucracy. The Mexico City he envisioned would have many *étoiles*, to be called *glorietas*, where important streets met the new Paseo de la Reforma.

In 1871, Escandón decided to facilitate the transformation of the Paseo de la Reforma and Mexico City by presenting the capital with a special token of his esteem, a monument honoring Christopher Columbus, in commemoration of the future opening of his railroad connecting Mexico City with Veracruz. According to Justino Fernández, Emperor Maximilian had conceived the idea of the statue and had asked engineer Ramón Rodríguez Arrangoity to direct the project. At that time the sculptor Pedro Vilar imagined the figure of Columbus rising from a pedestal comprised of representations of the four seas. After the empire fell, Escandón revived the concept and called again on Rodríguez Arrangoity. His version depicted Columbus rising from a base composed in part of four friars from the colonial past—Pedro de Gante, Bartolomé de Las Casas, Juan de Torquemada, and Bartolomé de Olmedo. Escandón apparently accepted and paid for the design, creating the impression that he would have this statue executed in Paris, but the work that he commissioned in 1873 from the French sculptor Charles Cordier turned out to be significantly different. Cordier, in consultation with Escandón's nephew Alejandro Arango y Escandón, a literary figure and poet, substituted friars Juan Pérez de Marchena, Diego de Deza, and Toribio de Benavente ("Motolinía") for the original group, retaining only Bartolomé de Las Casas. The statue was shipped to Mexico in 1875 and unveiled two years later in August 1877 in the second of the *glorietas* of the Paseo

Monument to Columbus

de la Reforma, the precise spot Maximilian had had in mind. Ironically, Antonio Escandón never saw the monument; he had died in May of that year while traveling by train from Seville to Córdoba.[12]

As with all the statues that eventually graced the *glorietas* of the Reforma, this Columbus monument had its story to tell. The original Mexican design had tried to associate the Navigator with the conquest by including Fray Bartolomé de Olmedo, a Mercedarian friar who had been Cortés's chaplain throughout his journey to Tenochtitlan. Among his accomplishments, Olmedo is credited with celebrating the first mass and planting the first cross in New Spain as well as accompanying Pedro de Alvarado on his march through Guatemala. Fray Juan de Torquemada is best remembered as the author of *Twentyone Ritual Books and Indian Monarchy*, known as *Monarquía indiana*. In addition, Torquemada was well known as the architect who rebuilt the Church of Santiago Tlatelolco from 1603 to 1610. Apparently he shared something in common with Escandón, for he designed the streets of Guadelupe and Chapultepec in Mexico City. Pedro de Gante was perhaps the best known of the three figures. A Franciscan and relative of Charles V, he had been born in Flanders and in 1523 was one of the first friars to come to Mexico. Subsequently, he founded at least two major schools for the instruction of Indians at Texcoco and San Francisco de México.

The new statue shifted the focus to Spain as Escandón and his nephew finessed the issue of the conquest by deciding to concentrate on the life of Columbus and the benefits of the Christianity he had brought to the New World. Two of the new figures, Fray Juan Pérez de Marchena and Fray Diego de Deza, belong to Columbus's life before his voyages to the New World. "Fray Pérez de Marchena" was really a conflation of two historical personages—Juan Pérez and Antonio de Marchena. The former had been the guardian of the Monastery of la Rábida, who, according to García Pimentel, a prominent historian of the Porfiriato, had brought Columbus to Córdoba to meet with Queen Isabella and her court. He used his influence to win their support of the Navigator's venture.[13] The monument stresses the connection with la Rábida by including a bas-relief of Columbus visiting the rebuilding of the monastery, perhaps recognizing that he allegedly had set sail from Palos because it was only a mile away from this monastery.[14] Fray Diego de Deza, a Dominican, was acknowledged as having strongly supported Columbus at the court in his role as member of the committee to judge the project and as tutor to the heir apparent, Prince Juan. From 1499 to 1506, Deza served as inquisitor general but was removed from his post because of riots in Córdoba.[15]

The two figures that relate to Mexico emphasize the humanistic aspect of Spanish evangelization in its colonies. Fray Toribio de Benavente was honored because he had greatly respected and loved the Indians and had lived such a life of poverty that they had called him "Motolinía" ("poor little one"). Furthermore, the Escandóns singled him out because he supposedly founded the city of their birth, Puebla de los Angeles. As for Las Casas, bishop of Chiapas, his defense of the Indians was so well known that his inclusion barely needed explanation.[16]

Nevertheless, the statue is meant to honor not only individuals but also:

the Catholic faith, the religion to whose influence is owed not only a new world, but the greatest enterprise of all time. Catholics were the ones who invested in the discovery of the New World . . . the religious zeal of Marchena [*sic*] and Isabel I, who thought only in adding to the already extensive conquests of the Cross, is what America owes for its saving beliefs, its civilization, and its liberty.[17]

In effect, the message is a compromise. Fully European in content, even to the extent of having the part of Columbus's letter to the Catholic king describing the success of his voyage carved in Latin rather than in Spanish or Nahuatl (as Rodríguez Arrangoity complained), the statue indicates that some aspects of "creole nationalism" had taken root by the 1870s even among conservative supporters of the empire such as Antonio Escandón and his nephew Alejandro, who had been educated in Europe and had spent much of his life there.[18]

The reevaluation of the Aztecs, now referred to as "creole nationalism," had begun in the seventeenth century, notably with the research of the Jesuit Manuel Duarte on the Aztec god Quetzalcoatl previously attributed to Carlos Sigüenza y Góngora, professor of mathematics at the University of Mexico. In his writings, Sigüenza y Góngora contrasted the noble Aztecs with the royalty of the Greco-Roman world and even connected them with the Hebrews, the Egyptians, and the Christians. Further, he conceived the idea that the god Quetzalcoatl was really Saint Thomas the Apostle. The Jesuit priest Francisco Javier de Clavijero fleshed out the new view of the Aztecs in his *Historia antigua de México*, published in Bologna in 1780, even though he never accepted Sigüenza's belief in the Quetzalcoatl-Saint Thomas identification. Clavijero thought that God had permitted the Spanish to conquer the Aztecs as punishment for the Indians' sins, but at the same time he stressed that Aztec polytheism was superior to the Greek or Roman varieties.[19]

When creoles identified Quetzalcoatl with Saint Thomas, they effectively centered themselves between the "motivation" and the gift of the Spanish Conquest—the conversion of the Indians to Christianity as expressed on the Columbus statue. If it were true that Saint Thomas had indeed come to the New World after the Resurrection and been remembered or referred to as Quetzalcoatl in Mexico, Viracocha in Peru, and other pre-Columbian dieties, then the New World had received the word of Christ centuries before the coming of the Spaniards. And if he had been revealed as the Savior at such an early date, it put the Western Hemisphere on equal terms with Spain and was poignant evidence of creole equality with *peninsulares* at home and in Europe.

Only a few years later, in 1794, the Dominican Fray Servando Teresa de Mier delivered a sermon that affirmed the equality of the Old and New Worlds. In his pronouncement he connected the miraculous appearance of the Virgin of Guadalupe with the missionary work of Saint Thomas. In 1813, while in England, he published his *Historia de la revolución de Nueva España, antiguamente Anahuac*, which explicitly contended that Spain had contributed nothing to Mexico. The implications of that argument were clear: If Spain gave nothing to its colonies and the Aztec religion had connections to Christianity, then the conquest became illegitimate and wrong. Carlos María de Bustamante amplified Mier's arguments, and eventually the theories of these two polemicists found a home in liberal political thought.[20] Following the defeat of the French empire, they became an unquestioned part of Mexican nationalism as seen in the redesign of the Columbus monument.

During the years between the time Escandón had commissioned his statue (1873) and its unveiling (1877), Mexico had undergone another change in government. With the victory of the revolution of Tuxtepec in 1876, new men came to power with great plans for their country. One of the leaders was the minister of development, Vicente Riva Palacio, son of General Mariano Riva Palacio, a former governor of Mexico State, and María Dolores Guerrero, the only child of martyred President Vicente Guerrero (1828–29). By 1876, Vicente Riva Palacio had spent twenty years in service to his country. He had attended the Constitutional Convention of 1857 as an alternate and found employment as secretary to the Mexico City ayuntamiento. During the War of the Reform, Félix Zuloaga had imprisoned him for his liberal politics and Miguel Miramón later threw him into solitary confinement. After Juárez defeated the conservatives, Riva Palacio was elected a federal deputy, joined the staff of the newspaper *La Orquesta*, and collaborated with Juan Antonio Mateos on a series of plays. When the French invaded in 1862, Riva Palacio outfitted a band of guerrillas and fought in Puebla under General Ignacio Zaragoza; he later saw action alongside General Jésus González Ortega. When Juárez established his capital in exile at San Luis Potosí, Riva Palacio edited a newspaper there called *El Monarca* and later served as the state's republican governor. Next, he became governor of Michoacán and founded another newspaper, *El Pito Real*, where he published his stirring song, "Adíos Mamá Carlota," which became an anthem of the resistance. In August 1867 he bid farewell to his troops and returned to his former position on the editorial board of *La Orquesta*; that same year he became a magistrate of the Supreme Court.

As the Restored Republic began, Riva Palacio joined with Ignacio Altamirano to promote a national literature. He began to write novels such as the romantic *Calvario y Tabor*, exalting the national soldier, *el chicaco*, but soon switched to romances of the colonial period with special emphasis on the social problems of the church. After losing his position on the Supreme Court because his rival, José María Iglesias, had the backing of President Sebastián Lerdo, he founded the newspaper *El Ahuizote* and joined the opposition. When the followers of Porfirio Díaz were victorious in the Revolt of Tuxtepec, the new president named Riva Palacio minister of development on November 29, 1876.[21]

While in this post from 1876 to 1880, Riva Palacio embarked on an ambitious program to beautify Mexico City in general and the Paseo de la Reforma in particular as he became the champion of a new group, the "nationalist mythologizers." As he noted in the *Memoria del Ministerio de Fomento, 1876–1877*:

Public monuments exist not only to perpetuate the memory of heroes and of great men who deserve the gratitude of the people, but also to awaken in some and strengthen in others the love of legitimate glories and also the love of art, where in those monuments one of its most beautiful expressions is to be found. To create recreational areas or boulevards, is to distract members of society with licit diversions within reach of all and allow them to mingle while avoiding the isolation and the vices which are common in populations which lack those means of communication.[22]

This statement demonstrated Riva Palacio's concern for all the residents of the capital, rich and poor alike. The Paseo de la Reforma, in his view, was to educate Mexicans about the nature of the national past, or, as Justino Fernández commented, "to present living and important examples from our history to point out to future generations the names of heroes and patriots, that is, history artistically made into objects with a moral sense."[23] With this introduction, Riva Palacio opened a competition for the best "monument dedicated to Cuauhtémoc and to the other leaders who distinguished themselves in defense of the nation in the period." He planned two other monuments to keep the statue of Columbus company in the *glorietas* of the avenue: one to honor Hidalgo and the heroes of Independence; and the second to pay homage to Juárez, the patriots of the Reform, and those who distinguished themselves during the War against the French (called the Second Independence). Eventually, Riva Palacio changed his mind and, instead of the third statue, ordered two—one for Juárez and the Reform and the other for Zaragoza and the heroes of the War against the French.[24]

Only two of the proposed statues ever appeared on the Paseo de la Reforma. The first, an homage of Cuauhtémoc, was planned in 1876 and finally unveiled in 1887, despite the fact that Mexico City already had a monument to the last Aztec emperor, a bust that had been unveiled on the Paseo de la Viga on August 13, 1869, the anniversary of the conquest of Tenochtitlan. In the customary tributes given on that occasion, the speakers added three new themes to the "creole nationalism" that had already become part of Mexican patriotism.

First, the orators continued firmly in the Mier-Bustamante tradition, speaking of the Spaniards as bloodthirsty villains and Cuauhtémoc as a hero. Gerardo María Silva characterized Cortés as a leader "whose laurels if they hadn't been stained by so many vile betrayals . . . would have made him a hero, but history and legend do not grant such a title except to those who have fought for their country or have liberated the land from the monsters who oppress it, and not to those very monsters who have desolated it with their cruelties."[25] No mention here of Aztec human sacrifice and oppressive tribute collections. For the sake of consistency the speakers then came to the second theme—that those Indians, such as the Tlaxcalans, who collaborated with the Spaniards and fought against the Aztecs, must be considered traitors to the Mexican nation.[26] As a result Cuauhtémoc and the Aztecs became synonymous with the entire republic, regardless of the fact that at the time of the conquest there were perhaps as many as two or three hundred different Indian groups living in the territory that became known as New Spain. Finally, the third theme announced that day connected Cuauhtémoc to other national heroes of later periods. In his address, Antonio Carrión noted that "the public spirit of the Mexicans that was extinguished with the breath of Cuauhtémoc, certainly did not remain dead forever, but stayed dormant for three hundred years to rekindle itself again in Dolores on the night of September 15."[27]

Despite the public support for the cult of the Aztecs, these three new ideas about the pre-Columbian past and the conquest were by no means universally accepted in 1867, least of all by Vicente Riva Palacio. In an address given in the Alameda of Mexico City on September 16, 1871, the soon-to-be leader of the "nationalist mythologizers" spoke of the conquest in quite different terms. He described the pre-Columbian indigenous leaders as "monarchs, who without more law than their caprice, bloody and terrible most of the time, governed the ancient people of the Americas, [and] fell to the energy of the soldiers of Cortés, Pizarro, and the Almagros; the monarchy disappeared to give way to the colony"—a statement much more favorable to the conquest than the one that the conservative Escandones were willing to enshrine. Riva Palacio also stressed that because of *mestizaje* (which he referred to as "the amalgamation of conquerers and the conquered") the New World was the continent predestined for democracy and republicanism.[28]

By the time he announced the competition for the statue of Cuauhtémoc only six years later, Riva Palacio had undergone a startling ideological about-face and had become a firm champion of the newly enlarged cult of the Aztecs. Although there were undoubtedly many reasons for this, it seems probable that Riva Palacio had started to view the past more propagandistically, looking for potential heroes rather than for historical truth. This tendency fit the requirements of the time, for the men of Tuxtepec who had made Díaz president wanted to create something unique to proclaim their new epoch, as those of Ayutla had made the Reform.

So the government opened its competition for the best design for the Cuauhtémoc statue. Riva Palacio assembled a blue-ribbon committee of judges including the English graphic artist and design teacher at the Academy of San Carlos, Juan Santiago Baggally; the future architect of the Café Colón and the renovations of the Iturbide Palace, Emilio Dondé Preciat; the former "First Imperial Architect" who converted the ruins of Chapultepec into a palace for Maximilian, the builder of the monument to the Niños Heroes of 1847, and the manager of the original Columbus statue project, Ramón Rodríguez Arrangoity; the former architect of Mexico City, Manuel Gargollo y Parra; and, of course, Riva Palacio himself.[29]

Francisco M. Jiménez y Arias, an engineer, won the competition's prize of one thousand pesos. He knew how to write winning proposals for Riva Palacio; he also received the commission for the monument to Hidalgo in Chihuahua and the one in honor of the cosmographer Enrico Martínez that was to stand in the Palacio Nacional.[30] Jiménez curried favor with Riva Palacio in his submission for the Cuauhtémoc contract by mentioning that

> no style of architecture would be more suitable than a rebirth which would include those beautiful details which today are seen in the ruins of Tula, Uxmal, Mitla, and Palenque, conserving as much as possible the general character of the architecture of the ancient inhabitants of this Continent, architecture which contains richness and detail so beautiful and appropriate that they can be borrowed to develop a characteristic style which we can call the national style.[31]

Riva Palacio, in search of a national literary style for Mexico, saw Jiménez as a kindred spirit who offered a similar project in the visual arts.

As originally proposed, the monument was to contain three bronze figures—Cuauhtémoc (4 meters high); Cacamatzin, king of Texcoco (2.8 meters high); and Cuitlahuac, identified in the proposal as "chief of the priests and Aztecs who led the struggle on the Noche Triste" (2.8 meters high). The total budget for the proposed statue came to $152,032, approximately 20 percent of the amount that the ayuntamiento of Mexico City had collected in taxes for the year 1877. Nevertheless, Jiménez left the description of the actual statue and its pedestal rather vague while promising that it would "not only take the character of Aztec architecture, but that of the ruins of various parts of the country in order to show architectural advances in all the parts which compose the Mexican republic."[32]

By the time the statue was unveiled, its design had altered substantially. By then, Riva Palacio was no longer involved in the project. In 1880, he had been part of a group which proposed that the Ministry of Development sponsor a Universal Mexican Exposition that same year so foreign nations could exhibit their products and Mexico its own. Porfirio Díaz rejected the idea because he viewed the exposition as a way for some members of his administration to obtain the 1880 presidential nomination for themselves. Following Díaz's reaction, Riva Palacio resigned from the ministry on May 17, 1880.[33]

After leaving the presidency, Díaz became development minister on December 1, 1880, and held the post until June 1881. He was succeeded by Carlos Pacheco, who also handled all of the former president's business affairs in Mexico City. When Jiménez presented his new plans for the statue on December 9, 1881, the "sculptural part" of the monument had been reduced by more than 50 percent, allegedly for "budgetary reasons." The lion's share of the budget cuts came from a $44,637 reduction in the allotment for sculpture; the new design omitted the secondary statues of Cuitlahuac and Cacamatzin and two of the four bas-reliefs. The changes left a single figure—Cuauhtémoc on top of the substantial pedestal—and significantly altered the meaning of the statue.[34]

By the time the monument was unveiled on August 21, 1887, Jiménez, its designer, had died, and Riva Palacio, its promoter within the government, was in unofficial exile as minister plenipotentiary to Spain and Portugal. Minister of Development Pacheco had commissioned Miguel Noreña, professor of sculpture at the Escuela Nacional de Bellas Artes, to fashion the statue, and Gabriel Guerra, who remained true to the "national style" that Jiménez and Riva Palacio had envisioned, to do the two remaining bas-reliefs. The ayuntamiento organized modest festivities to inaugurate the monument. The *festividad cívica* was dedicated "to the memory of the heroic defender of the capital of Mexico during the conquest, the Immortal Cuauhtémoc, last ruler of the Nation, who valiantly preferred to see homes destroyed before he would accept a peace with the opprobrium of slavery."

At 8 A.M. on the morning of August 21, 1887, civil and military leaders, the members of the ayunta-miento, workers' societies, students, and invited commissions representing various communities gathered at the *glorieta* where the Paseo de la Reforma meets the Avenida de los Insurgentes. Upon the arrival of President Díaz, soldiers fired a twenty-one-gun salute and military bands played the national anthem. Then Lic. Alfredo Chavero, author of the first volume of the liberal history that Riva Palacio had edited, *México a través del los siglos*, delivered his address. After the chief justice of the Supreme Court unveiled the monument and another twenty-one-gun salute was fired, Francisco del Paso y Troncoso, director of the National Museum, delivered an address in Nahuatl. Francisco Sosa, Eduardo del Valle, and Amalio José Cabrera each recited poems, Demetrio Mejía read a prose selection, and the bands played. Afterward, the assembled guests sang the national anthem once more and the president departed to another twenty-one-gun salute.[35]

Monument to Cuauhtémoc

The new monument evoked the same sentiments expressed at the unveiling of the bust of Cuauh-témoc in 1869. As described by Francisco W. González in *El Monitor Republicano*, the standard identification of the Aztecs as the symbolic representation of the entire nation was stated and amplified.[36] But it was Francisco Sosa, Riva Palacio's successor as the leading proponent of official nationalism, who most explicitly identified Mexico solely with its Aztec past. In his pamphlet written on the occasion of the unveiling, Sosa noted that "our government is paying a debt of gratitude owed by the Mexican people for over three centuries by inaugurating the magnificent monument which will honor permanently the last of the Aztec emperors to whom goes the credit as the first and most illustrious of the defenders of the nationality founded by Tenoch in 1327."[37]

Sosa did not mention that the government had decided to use such a public commemoration of the Cuauhtémoc cult for its own benefit when it had eliminated the other two figures, concentrating solely on

Cuauhtémoc, and had placed the monument in such a prominent location. The Porfirians wanted the statue to inculcate an official liberal "national" history for the country and create public support for their domination of its present and future.

The design of the statue, like that of its Columbus counterpart, has a story to tell. Justino Fernández states that the monument is the first example of the "neoindigenist style" and that it opened "the possibilities for a genuine national architecture."[38] The base of the statue was formed by a replica of the pyramid of the sun from Teotihuacan, topped with designs from the Zapotec and Mixtec buildings at Mitla in Oaxaca. The middle portion contains a structure designed to resemble the Temple of the Inscriptions at the Maya site of Palenque in Chiapas but is supported by columns meant to look like those from Tula in the state of Hidalgo, thought to be the Tollan that the Aztecs believed was the center of the Toltec empire. The column formed by these structures made the pedestal for the statue of Cuauhtémoc, draped in a garment concocted from the pictographs in the codices but one that easily could have passed for something Socrates might have worn.[39] The statue vividly proclaims the government's decision that Mexico would officially identify itself with its pre-Columbian Indian past. This message is strongly conveyed in the bas-relief known as "the torment of Cuauhtémoc," carved into one side of the base by Gabriel Guerra, depicting how the Spaniards put his feet to the fire. The inclusion of such a specific incident in the monument makes an official statement—Cuauhtémoc is a national hero who was brutally treated by the villainous Spaniards.[40] Cuauhtémoc is also a martyr, as Francisco W. González notes in his essay:

> In Cuauhtémoc we do not see the last descendant of the Aztec kings . . . we view in him the hero of the fatherland. . . . Cuauhtémoc conquered, Cuauhtémoc imprisoned and enchained, Cuauhtémoc powerless to defend his throne by means of arms, defended it suffering valiantly the wicked and terrible torments which the inhuman conquistadores applied to him to extract from him the renunciation of his rights, sealing with such heroic sacrifice the most solemn protest against usurpation, which later should produce its greatest and most precious fruits.[41]

González concluded his statement with the familiar de rigueur linkage of the martyrdom of Cuauhtémoc with the insurrection of Hidalgo seen in the addresses at the Paseo de la Viga in 1869. He proclaimed, "The seed of the heroic sacrifice of Cuauhtémoc came to flower in the year 1810 under the hoe of the immortal *cura* of Dolores," thus seconding another theme of the 1869 evocation of the Aztec cult that he then converted into an identification with Jesus Christ by giving the impression that it took the noble Aztec not three days, but three centuries, for his resurrection from the dead.[42]

The statue also telescoped the Porfirian intention to assert that the rulers of Tenochtitlan henceforth would represent the entire Mexican nation. Although the statue does include elements from other Indian groups—the Zapotecs, the Mixtecs, the Maya, the Toltecs—these are shown as mere forerunners or supporters of the Aztecs, the pedestal from which the latter triumphantly rose. Through this identification not just with the Indian as opposed to the Spanish past but specifically with the Aztecs per se, the Porfirians, the then-current rulers of the Valley of Mexico, positioned themselves as heirs to their predecessors' imperial legacy. Their official version of Mexican history was to play itself out neatly down the Paseo de la Reforma as exemplified in the proposed additional statues, as Cuauhtémoc flowed into Hidalgo into Juárez into Zaragoza into, of course, the current occupant of the recently renovated Chapultepec castle, Porfirio Díaz—another hero in the war against the French and clearly its triumphal product. The official historians not only used the symbolism of the Aztecs to validate Díaz's stewardship of the country but also intended to use the monument to Cuauhtémoc and the official veneration of the Aztecs to reconfirm the power of Mexico City and its right to rule the nation by inheritance. Guerra's frieze of Cuauhtémoc's torture at the hands of the Spaniards bears the inscription "To the memory of Cuauhtémoc and of the warriors who heroically struggled in defense of their country." Yet, the Aztecs ruled over the majority of the population of Mexico in a tyrannical fashion and more Indians fought against Cuauhtémoc than with him. Therefore, the statue pays tribute to someone who "heroically struggled" *against* the majority of indigenous Mexicans and tries to legitimate him as the personification of Mexican identity and his capital of Tenochtitlan as its ancient seat of power.

The Porfirians had fiscal goals in mind as well. By insisting on Cuauhtémoc as their first ancestor, they asserted their rights over state revenues as the Aztecs had once taken tribute payments of revenue and goods by force and terror. The statue thus delivered the symbolic coup de grace to political and fiscal federalism and proclaimed the primacy of the central state as embodied in and ruled by Mexico City. It served notice that the Porfirians planned to include centralism in their definition of liberalism now that the former's original conservative proponents had been thoroughly defeated and discredited. Indeed, as early as 1873 most of the conservatives were either dead, exiled, or, like Escandón and Somera, active collaborators in the new order.

True to the program embodied in their monument, the Porfirians quickly began their assault on what remained of Mexican federalism. Although the liberal Constitution of 1857 strongly supported freedom of internal trade in article 124, declaring that eleven *alcabalas* (sales taxes) and internal tariffs cease by June 1, 1858, subsequent governments had never been able to implement the provision. Nor had they been able to enforce any of the laws affecting the freedom of internal trade passed since that time. The Porfirians reopened the war on the state *alcabala* in October 1877, two months after Riva Palacio announced the proposed construction of the monument to Cuauhtémoc. The struggle heated up near the end of the term of President Manuel González in 1883, when the state of Veracruz called a meeting of governors to discuss the issue. According to the results of a survey assembled by the representatives to that meeting, the *alcabalas* remained in place because they supplied up to 68 percent of state revenue, most of which went to the major cities. On November 22, 1886, fifteen legislatures accepted the proposition that states could not tax foreign products or keep goods from entering or leaving their territories. Although this was a step forward, most states continued to collect *alcabalas*, much to the annoyance of those like Veracruz that had abolished them. The issue dragged on until May 30, 1895, when Minister of Finance José Ives Limantour finally abolished the *alcabala* effective July 1, 1896, and with it the financial independence of the states from Mexico City.[43]

Although no editorials appeared discussing the government's motives for building this expensive monument to Cuauhtémoc, neither were Mexicans naive enough to read any *indigenista* messages in its design. On the face of it the public homage to that pre-Columbian royal Indian could have been seen as a way to inspire the Indians living at the time to lift themselves out of their degraded state. After all, the statue offered a heroic representation of what Indians had once been and could be again—strong, intelligent, leaders of nations—a kind of social Darwinism in stone that promised greatness perhaps to the lucky few. But the honor accorded to Cuauhtémoc and the Indian, or at least the Aztec past, occurred at the time Indians and their mestizo descendants were being deprived of their lands through increased use of the Reform laws, new legislation, and economic development. Furthermore, through the centuries those creole thinkers interested in glorifying the Indians of antiquity, such as Carlos Sigüenza y Góngora and the liberal ideologue José María Luis Mora, concerned themselves with Indian rulers like Cuauhtémoc rather than with real Indians living at the time. Therefore, the Greek details on Cuauhtémoc's costume and his white features are quite deliberate, as were the drawings that appeared in newspapers looking equally white, if not more so. And it is hardly accidental that the "descendant" of Cuauhtémoc is the creole priest Miguel Hidalgo.[44]

No matter what messages the Paseo de la Reforma conveyed or was supposed to convey to those Mexicans who gazed on it, it was primarily built to impress foreign capitalists. By the time of the unveiling of the monument to Cuauhtémoc in 1887, the Mexican political climate had undergone an important shift. The nation had resumed payments on its foreign debt in 1885 and shortly thereafter began receiving large loans from abroad.[45] Suddenly, the government pushed for foreign investment, foreign capital, and foreign approval. As *The Mexican Financier* noted on September 9, 1887, in an article entitled "Municipal Embellishments":

> On the world-famed Paseo de la Reforma . . . [the] unveiling of that colossal figure [of Cuauhtémoc] the other day gave Mexico one of its noblest works of art on this continent. Thus in many ways the wise rulers of the Municipality are adding to the attractions of the capital. . . . The money expended in these notable works of municipal embellishment has been most sagaciously invested, for by beautifying the city, travellers will be brought here to sojourn during the winter months and the spirit of civic pride and enthusiasm evoked. We believe in the future of this City, in the ability of its rulers to make it one of the most beautiful capitals of the world. [Such a city] has demonstrated its right to ask of capitalists the money needed to carry out great works of permanent utility.[46]

The Paseo de la Reforma had been designed as a showpiece, but it started to develop only after 1900. The *Actas del cabildo municipal* for the years 1887–1900 show a divided Mexico City. The capital up to the Alameda Park belonged to its residents while the Paseo de la Reforma seemed somehow apart. The city fathers, for example, planned no celebrations at the new monument to Cuauhtémoc except for those on August 21 while they vigorously supported those headquartered in the Alameda.[47] And despite the 1889 opening of the Café Colón, built by Emilio Dondé Preciat across from the Monumento de Colón, which became the "in place" for making business deals, few built their homes near the new avenue.

Directly following the unveiling of the Cuauhtémoc statue, Francisco Sosa proposed that each state donate two life-size statues of its patriots to be placed on the grassy areas on each side of the avenue. The government quickly adopted the idea and on October 1, 1887, Carlos Pacheco, minister of development, issued an *iniciativa* calling for each state to pay tribute to the capital of the central valley of Mexico with two statues of its heroes.

Yet once again the national government retained control over the entire process, perhaps to prevent embarrassing selections. The ayuntamiento of Mexico City, for example, never even discussed which figures should represent the Federal District and only contributed $2,000 to the project when it routinely spent $5,000 for the celebrations for May 5 and September 16. The life-size statues were erected between 1889 and 1899, but all were pedestrian and foreign-inspired, most often figures from the Reform, showing nothing of the "national style." Jesús F. Contreras, who built most of these statues, although born in Aguascalientes, received support from the Mexican government to work in Paris from 1886 to 1891. Upon his return he organized the Mexican Artistic Foundation under Díaz's sponsorship and worked on the Reforma bronzes. It is no accident that the first edition of Sosa's biographies of the men so honored was published in French and delivered immediately to its intended audience gathered at the Paris Exposition of 1900. Mexicans would have to wait an entire year for the Spanish edition.[48]

The Porfirians never hid their desire to give Mexico a real capital city in every sense of the word. As Francisco González pointed out,

> the Avenue of our most grateful memories, which begins with the truly notable work of Tolsá [the statue of Carlos IV] and ends in the castle of the ancient Mexican monarchs [Chapultepec], today converted into a recreation place for the leaders of the Republic, made lovely with the natural beauties of the soil and with national and foreign artistic creations, will later become one of our priceless treasures, which will provoke envy in other countries.[49]

The Paseo, as González notes, was built only for the elite, and indeed the vast majority of city residents probably rarely saw it until after the Revolution. As the city developed, it turned out that Antonio Escandón and Ignacio Cumplido, much more than Vicente Riva Palacio and Francisco Sosa, had achieved their purpose. The Paseo created new commercial space and excellent sites for land developers. Nevertheless, by the time the last statues were unveiled in 1899, there was still virtually no one living near the Paseo de la Reforma. True, the fashionable thing to do was to drive from the Zócalo to Chapultepec Park on a Sunday afternoon and return home around dusk, but the neighborhoods directly fronting the Paseo—America, Juárez, and Cuauhtémoc—were not built until the first decade of the twentieth century.[50]

The *colonias* known today as Roma and the Zona Rosa date from the last decade of the Porfiriato when new subdivisions were built and the Paseo de la Reforma became the choice site for a new series of mansions erected by the most prominent financiers of the day— Manterola, Scherer, Solórzano, Braniff, Aburto, and others—who all established residences there. A trolley line opened in the years from

1891 to 1902, operated first by mules and then by electricity, which ran up the avenue to Chapultepec.[51]

Porfirio Díaz laid the first stone for a new statue to grace the *glorietas* of the Paseo de la Reforma, the monument to Independence, on January 2, 1902.[52] The idea for the tribute was hardly new; in fact, it had originated even before Vicente Riva Palacio. It derived from Antonio López de Santa Anna's monumental period—October 10, 1841, to September 7, 1844—during which the president had ostentatiously buried the leg he had lost during the defense of Veracruz against the French. A statue in honor of "Independence and Liberty" was designed as early as 1843 by the distinguished Spanish architect Lorenzo de la Hidalga (1810–1872), who came to Mexico in 1838 and remained there until his death. Among his other works, de la Hidalga became famous for his Teatro Nacional (also known as the Teatro de Santa Anna), which was inaugurated in 1844.

The government opened a competition on June 27, 1843, for the best statue honoring Independence to be placed in the corner between the Palacio Nacional and the cathedral in the Zócalo. On July 7, 1843, while working on the Teatro Nacional, de la Hidalga submitted his winning entry:

> It must be a grandiose monument . . . whose artistic and philosophical composition would be the open book of history . . . to stimulate a free society to make people who remember their statues, reliefs and inscriptions.[53]

De la Hidalga divided his proposed statue into two parts. The first was to be a burial place for the remains of the heroes of the first period of independence and the rest to "show the honor and the glory of all those who fought to achieve the great goal." He suggested eight statues on the monument: "History and the wise men who make up the government should designate, in case it is necessary, the names of those who should be represented there, both in statues and in inscriptions."

Although the sculptor coyly shied away from proposing any specific figures, he advocated a particular point of view when noting those subjects he thought appropriate for bronze bas-reliefs—the Grito de Dolores, the Grito de Iguala, the Entrance of the Triumphal Army, and the Battle of Tampico. The committee from the Academia de Bellas Artes de San Carlos selected the composition of Enrique Griffón, which is currently lost to history, but Santa Anna himself awarded the commission to de la Hidalga. And no wonder, for that proposal sought to honor Iturbide (the Grito de Iguala and the Entrance of the Triumphal Army) and Santa Anna himself, who had commanded Mexican troops in the successful defeat of the Barradas' invasion

Monument to Independence

at the Battle of Tampico in 1827. Santa Anna approved the statue on August 23, 1843, and assigned Pedro García Conde, later of U.S.-Mexican boundary survey fame, to supervise its construction, but it was never built because the president was removed from office the following year.[54] Maximilian too expressed interest in such a monument; in June 1864 he asked Joaquin Velázquez de León to supervise its construction, and he laid its first stone in the Zócalo on September 16 of that year. Once again the plan remained in abeyance.[55]

Although Riva Palacio had envisioned his monument to Independence as one of those to grace the Paseo de la Reforma, the process by which the monument evolved was a far cry from the open competition for proposals generated by the Ministry of Development in 1877. In fact, the entire evolution of the statue from its beginnings to its unveiling is shrouded in mystery. In May 1878 a proposal by Ramón Rodríguez Arrangoity was approved, then in 1886 a new competition was opened and won by the Washington architectural firm of Cluss and Schultze, but once again nothing happened. Finally, in 1900 the commission went to Antonio Rivas Mercado, a Mexican architect who had been trained in France. When Porfirio Díaz laid the first stone on January 2, 1902, a date timed to coincide with the meeting of the International Pan-American Conference in Mexico City, the ceremony left no doubt as to the meaning of the event. The keynote speaker, engineer Ramón de Ibarrola, in keeping with the new Mexico of the 1900s, used the occasion to remind the audience of the glories of the patriarch:

> [The cornerstone] is about to be laid by the hand that was strong in battle and magnanimous in victory, by the hand of the citizen whose great practical sense taught him to lead his people away from barren, nay, fratricidal strife and to direct its energies into the useful avenues of public works, so as to connect the principal centers of the country by means of railroads and telegraph lines, to create and improve ports, to erect lighthouses, and multiply by these means a hundredfold the strength and efficency of his administration.

After the speech and an original poem by Juan de Dios Peza, Díaz, the hero of the hour (if not of Independence itself), took a silver trowel from a silver pail and laid the first stone.[56]

The following year, due to the Law of Public Organization, the Ministry of the Interior, now headed by Ramón Corral, took over the administration of the monument among other matters. By the middle of 1906 construction engineers working on the statue noticed that it was tilting, and the ministry established a commission to study the problem. The monument was dismantled in June 1907, its stones used to build the new national penitentiary at Lecumberri. According to *El Imparcial* the cost of dismembering and reconstructing the base came to $537,000 and was concluded only in May 1909.

By then the administration was frantic; it redoubled its efforts to have the statue ready for unveiling in time for the centenary celebrations on September 16, 1910. Its efforts paid off, for precisely on the anniversary the completed statue known today as *The Angel* was revealed. It contained four seated women representing Peace, Law, Justice, and War, and on its base were written twenty-four names of "precursors, conspirators, heroines, representatives, writers, warriors, caudillos and the makers of the Independence" including Aldama, Allende, Galeana, Matamoros, Mier y Teran, Rayon, and Victoria, and, though a far cry from de la Hidalga's two bas-reliefs, Iturbide. Four bronze statues, costing $107,000 and modeled by Enrique Alciati and cast in Florence, Italy, under his direction, depicted Morelos, Guerrero, Mina, and Nicolas Bravo. Then there stood, "forming the cumulative motif of the composition, the apotheosis of the Father of the Country, Hidalgo, with his flag in his hand." The statue concluded in a long column capped by a lovely Angel with a laurel wreath. The completed monument cost $2,150,000.[57]

By the time of *The Angel*'s unveiling, Mexico was in the midst of another movement that would change its political history forever. No one can calibrate exactly which factors in what measure provoked the Mexican Revolution but certainly the shift away from the "national style" of the 1870s and 1880s, as seen in the Cuauhtémoc monument, into the generic Europeanism, represented by the Independence column, accurately depicts more than simple artistic differences. As shown so vividly on the street, the Porfirian state had gotten lost; its search for international respectability through the worship of technology ultimately dwarfed even the mighty Hidalgo and what he had wrought.

In the end both the "francophile progressives" and the "nationalist mythologizers" won the war. The Paseo de la Reforma is perhaps the most important and most lovely avenue of the capital, and its messages, in murals of stone, continue to be instilled in generation after generation of Mexican schoolchildren. But the victory increasingly looks short-lived as the combination of technology and commerce with political centralization so extolled in the statuary of the Paseo de la Reforma continues to poison the air and darken the future of the beloved city that Cuauhtémoc defended.

NOTES

1. Jorge Alberto Manrique, "La ciudad de México en el siglo XIX," in *México-Tenochtitlán ,1325–1975: Pasado, presente y futuro de una gran ciudad* (México, 1976), 23.

2. Justino Fernández looks at this process somewhat differently. While he acknowledges the point of view expressed by Manrique, he emphasizes that "in truth its [neoclassicism's] acceptance and continuation show that it is the expression of a new attitude of renewal that led to our independence movement." See *El arte del siglo XIX en México* (México, 1983), 5.

3. This paper will note some examples of monuments and buildings planned during the 1842–1844 Santa Anna administration when discussing the monument to Independence.

4. For more on the destruction of the ecclesiastical city, see Salvador Novo, *La ciudad de México del 9 de junio al 15 de julio de 1867* (México, 1967), 18–19.

5. Salvador Novo, *Los paseos de la ciudad de México* (México, 1980), 35–36.

6. María Dolores Morales, "Francisco Somera y el primer fraccionamiento de la ciudad de México, 1840–1889," in Ciro F. S. Cardoso, *Formación y desarrollo de la burguesía en México: Siglo XIX* (México, 1978), 188–230.

7. For more information on the relationship between the foreign debt and the development of both Mexico and Mexico City, see Tenenbaum, "Mexico City and the Royal Indian," Latin American Studies Center Ser. No. 14, University of Maryland, College Park, forthcoming; and Tenenbaum, "Liberals without Money—Liberalism and Imperialism in Mexico, 1867–1885," in *Constitutional Order and State Finance in Nineteenth-Century Latin America*, ed. Vincent C. Peloso and Barbara A. Tenenbaum (Pittsburgh, forthcoming).

8. Cumplido wrote to his friend León Ortigosa, September 5, 1851: "I wish that in your trip through Europe, you take advantage of the time as you please and enjoy the magnificent spectacle of the [Paris] Exposition and how much more these truly civilized countries present." *Correspondencia de Ignacio Cumplido a León Ortigosa en la Biblioteca del Instituto Tecnológico y de Estudios Superiores de Monterrey* (Monterrey, 1969), 44.

9. Novo, *Los paseos*, 38.

10. For more on this see Barbara A. Tenenbaum, "Development and Sovereignty: Intellectuals and the Second Empire," in Roderic A. Camp, Charles A. Hale, and Josefina Z. Vásquez, eds., *Los Intelectuales y el Poder en México* (Mexico City/Los Angeles, 1991), 77–88.

11. Anthony Sutcliffe, *The Autumn of Central Paris: The Defeat of Town Planning, 1850–1970* (London, 1970), 169; David H. Pinkney, *Napoleon III and the*

Rebuilding of Paris (Princeton, NJ, 1958), 62–64; and Howard Saalman, *Haussmann: Paris Transformed* (New York, 1971), 14–15.

12. José María Marroqui, *La ciudad de México*, 3 vols. (México, 1900–1903), 1:647; Fernández, *El Arte del siglo XIX*, 170–71; Luis García Pimentel, *El Monumento elevado en la ciudad de México a Cristóbal Colón: Descripción e historia* (México, 1889). Many stories surround this statue. For example, some sources mention that Cordier delayed the shipment of the statue until he had been paid in full.

13. García Pimentel, *El Monumento*, 3–4; Espasa-Calpe, *Enciclopedia universal ilustrada: Europeo-Americana* (Barcelona, 1921), 43:654–55.

14. Christopher Columbus, *The Log of Christopher Columbus*, tr. Robert H. Fuson (Camden, ME, 1987), 37.

15. Espasa-Calpe, *Enciclopedia universal ilustrada: Europeo-Americana* 7:769.

16. García Pimentel, *El Monumento*, 2–6.

17. *Ibid.*, 5–6.

18. Rodríguez Arrangoity, *Apuntes sobre la historia del Monumento de Colón* (México, 1877) as cited in Justino Fernández, *El arte del siglo XIX*, 171–72.

19. Benjamin Keen, *The Aztec Image in Western Thought* (New Brunswick, NJ, 1971), 192–93, 292–99. For a discussion of the evolution of the creole cult, see Jacques Lafaye, *Quetzalcóatl and Guadalupe: The Formation of Mexican National Consciousness, 1531–1813*, tr. Benjamin Keen (Chicago, 1976).

20. Keen, *Aztec Image*, 317–20; Charles Hale, chapters 1 and 7, *Mexican Liberalism in the Age of Mora* (New Haven, CT, 1968).

21. Clementina Díaz y de Ovando, "Prólogo," in Vicente Riva Palacio, *Cuentos del General* (México, 1968), ix–xx.

22. *Memoria de Fomento, Colonización, Industria, y Comercio 1876–1877*, 3 vols. (México, 1877), 3:353–54.

23. Justino Fernández, *El arte del siglo XIX*, 167.

24. *Ibid.*, 358.

25. *Discursos pronunciados el día 13 de agosto de 1869 en la inauguración del busto de Cuauhtemotzin erigido en el Paso de la Viga* (México, 1869), 50.

26. *Ibid.*, 7

27. *Ibid.*, 25.

28. Vicente Riva Palacio, *Discurso Cívico pronunciado en la Alameda de México en el aniversario del glorioso grito de independencia el día 16 de septiembre de 1871* (México, 1871), 8–9.

29. *Diccionario Porrúa de historia, biografía y geografía de México*, 3d. ed. (México, 1971), 382, 1915.

30. *Memoria de Fomento 1876–1877*, 3:356; *Memoria de Fomento, Colonización, Industria y Comercio (1877–1882)*, 3 vols. (México, 1885), 3:340.

31. *Memoria de Fomento 1877–1882*, 3:332–33.

32. *Ibid.*, 332.

33. Díaz y de Ovando, "Prólogo," xx–xxi. For a different version of these events, see Ralph Roeder, *Hacia el México moderno, Porfirio Díaz*, 2 vols. (México, 1981), 1:119–25.

34. Donald Coerver, *Porfirian Interregnum: The Presidency of Manuel González of Mexico, 1880–1884* (Fort Worth, TX, 1979), 45; *Memoria de Fomento 1877–1882*, 3:332–39.

35. *El Monitor Republicano*, August 20, 1887.

36. *Ibid.*, August 23, 1887.

37. Francisco Sosa, *Apuntamientos para la historia del monumento de Cuauhtémoc* (México, 1887), 3, 27.

38. Justino Fernández, *El arte del siglo XIX*, 168.

39. *El Monitor Republicano*, August 20, 1887.

40. Esther Acevedo de Iturriaga and Eloisa Uribe, *La escultura del siglo XIX* (México, 1980), fig. 219, 42.

41. *El Monitor Republicano*, August 23, 1887.

42. *Ibid.*

43. Daniel Cosío Villegas, *Historia moderna de México,* vol. 2, *El Porfiriato: Vida económica* (México, 1972), 904–18, 1234.

44. Keen, *Aztec Image*, 192–93; Hale, *Mexican Liberalism*, 218–20. Another example is the design by Antonio Peñafiel for the Mexican exhibit at the Columbian Exhibition held in Madrid in 1892, which looks more like an ersatz Grecian temple than anything that Moctezuma would have recognized. See Ignacio Bernal, *A History of Mexican Archeology* (New York, 1980), 153.

45. Jan Bazant, *Historia de la deuda exterior de México (1823–1946)* (México, 1968), 119–35.

46. *The Mexican Financier*, September 9, 1887.

47. *Actas del cabildo municipal*, 1886–1890, "Paseos."

48. Francisco Sosa, *Los estatuas de la Reforma*, 3 vols. (México, 1974); Matthew D. Esposito, "From Cuauhtémoc to Juárez: Monuments, Myth, and Culture in Porfirian Mexico, 1876–1900" (M.A. thesis, Arizona State University, 1993).

49. *El Monitor Republicano*, August 23, 1887.

50. María Dolores Morales, "La expansión de la ciudad de México en el siglo XIX: el caso de los fraccionamientos," in *Ciudad de México: Ensayo de construcción de una historia*, coord. Alejandra Moreno Toscano (México, 1978), 190–200.

51. Salvador Novo, *Los paseos*, 41.

52. Francisco de Antuñano, *México. 75 Años. 1910–1985* (México, 1984), 138.

53. Lorenzo de la Hidalga, "Proposal for monument to Independence and Liberty," July 23, 1843, as printed in Justino Fernández, *El Arte Moderno en México* (México, 1937), 115–16.

54. *Ibid.*

55. "Columna de la independencia," in *Diccionario Porrúa de historia, biografía y geografía de México*, 2d. ed. (México, 1964), 366.

56. *The Mexican Herald*, January 2, 1902.

57. *El Imparcial*, September 16, 1910.

8

Proletarians, Politicos, and Patriarchs: The Use and Abuse of Cultural Customs in the Early Industrialization of Mexico City, 1880–1910

Tony Morgan
Anglia Polytechnic University

Tony Morgan examines paternalistic industrialism in Mexico City as exemplified by the owner of El Buen Tono cigarette factory, the rise of marketing strategies, and government-business cooperation, especially in the creation of a tame, mutualist society. Morgan, who teaches Hispanic history and the Spanish language, draws on his Ph.D. dissertation completed at Anglia Polytechnic University to provide information on the use of holidays and public spectacles in efforts to tie together government, industry, and labor. Throughout the essay are echoes of the Bourbon project of social control, the Comtian demands for order, and the Victorian industrial paternalism practiced by factory owners in England (William Lever) and the United States (George Pullman).

T HE FEDERAL DISTRICT OF MEXICO changed greatly during the years of Porfirio Díaz (1876–1910), especially during the height of the capital's industrial boom from 1890 to 1910. The population mushroomed, new occupations appeared, and old ones were transformed; modern power systems brought electric machines, lights at night, and fast transport. An urban proletariat emerged and had to subsist without adequate housing and health care. Exploitation abounded, but opportunity increased as well. Relations between the classes were strained, although not to the breaking point, as the elite created social distance by physical relocation, departing the colonial city center for their new suburban mansions to the west. The beleaguered ayuntamiento (city council) could not or would not cope with the pace and scale of change, and its shortcomings fed the frustrations that would lead the new middle and lower classes to support the insurgency of Francisco Madero in 1911. City fathers failed to provide the necessary education, welfare, and recreation that these new groups demanded.

But the traditional Mexican sense of celebration, occasion, and dignity survived these changes. Although patronized, workers retained integrity; bosses were often uncaring, but some related to their workers with grace as well as favor. The trappings of new technology appeared on the streets even if they often remained beyond the reach of the worker's purse. Leisure recreation was a scarce commodity for the new working class as well as for most of the other classes; but social events, music, a smattering of education, and some light diversions did enliven the gloomier aspects of industrialism. With so few amusements available some new industrial paymasters exploited cheap devices to curry favor without much grace and to win the new working class to their political support. In the end, having denied workers genuine political dialogue, the industrialists tried to buy their support as Porfirio Díaz's regime crumbled in 1910; but their desperate effort came too late. This essay examines the links between industry, government, and workers in the capital and the way in which cultural devices bound them together.

From 1877 to 1910 the Federal District's population grew by 120 percent, from 327,000 to 720,753.[1] In 1910 the capital—now a metropolitan financial and industrial center and melting pot of internal migrants—was a world away from the administrative and commercial center that Díaz had inherited. The 44 percent of its population who had originated elsewhere in Mexico came looking for change and chances. They often realized their hopes through new employment; but they were alienated politically and culturally. Both metropolitan elites and government authorities ignored the rising aspirations inevitably brought by industrialism. Instead, with few exceptions, the authorities sought to contain change and curtail expectation.[2] Imbued with a paternalistic ethos, they strove to retain the traditional nature of social relations that had survived from colonial days. They preferred to rely on political co-optation and social control until they ran out of ideas; in retrospect, they seemed insensitive to coming changes.[3]

The capital could scarcely be described as industrial when Díaz came to power. Only two identifiable industries existed—textiles and tobacco—each employing one thousand people and grossing in sales one million pesos per year. These activities were organized in large factories with up to three hundred workers, but most other economic activity was fundamentally artisanal.[4] The lack of coal and the consequent shortage of steam power helped to keep the area's industrial life dispersed. Some large tobacco factories were located in the city center, but, with little mechanization as yet in the 1870s, most of their product was hand rolled. Textile factories, on the other hand, were largely water-powered and therefore located mainly in the industrial hamlets scattered around the fringes of the Federal District, in Tlalpán, Contreras, San Angel, Santa Fe, Chalco, and Tlalnepantla. Here social life was dominated by the few mills around which workers clustered and in which millowners exerted a traditional social control akin to life on the hacienda.[5]

Cheaper steam and more electricity revolutionized this pattern. In 1882 the first electric-powered domestic lighting was switched on in the house of government minister Carlos Pacheco, and by 1900 facilities existed for lighting thirty thousand houses in the capital. Domestic as well as industrial life was transformed by the new power source. One can easily imagine the liberating impact created by the first commercialized electric tortilla machines, invented in 1902, with an output of five thousand tortillas per hour, supplying the capital through twenty-five franchised outlets.[6] Electrification of the tramway system transformed mobility. In 1898 the Guadalupe-San Angel line was electrified for twenty-six miles to create a rapid-transit spine running north-south through the city. The original mule-drawn line had been opened to Guadalupe in 1856 to take the faithful to the Basilica, instead of the originally planned line to Tlalpan to transport workers and those on holiday to the factories and spas of the southern hamlet. The sight of the brightly lit streetcar lurching through the night streets symbolized the changing speed of urban life, a disturbing change in several ways: the pylons bringing the power from Necaxa Falls near Puebla were shot at regularly by country people, and, in 1900, Díaz banned the use of hearse tramcars since it seemed impious to allow corpses to be carried by an "occult force."[7] Three years later he relented, and funeral processions by tram soon became de rigueur. By 1911, 213 miles of electrified track crisscrossed the capital; passenger trips rose from 11,000,000 in 1887 to 70,357,671 in 1908 as the population acquired the habit of using rapid transit both for work and pleasure.[8]

As the development boom of the 1880s and especially the 1890s unfolded, electrification as much as any other factor enabled industrial life to develop and expand in the city center instead of in the industrial hamlets of the Federal District. In particular, it transformed the traditional tobacco and textile industries and stimulated the formation of a host of others. Ernesto Pugibet's El Buen Tono, a cigarette factory opened in the center in new premises in 1894, earned the praise of visiting U.S. Secretary of State Elihu Root, who proclaimed it "the best factory in the world."[9] The opening of new textile mills such as La Perfeccionada in 1895, La Carolina in 1898, or El Salvador in 1896; new shoe factories such as Carlos Zetina's Excelsior and the United States Shoe Manufacturing Co. in 1906; or even the Palacio de Hierro clothing workshops in 1900 (employing eight hundred)—all brought modern machinery and methods into the heart of the city. This encouraged the formation of both the working and middle classes with an urban life-style of their own, free from the constraints of restrictive bosses who controlled conditions in the industrial hamlets. A wide range of other industries opened in these two decades, qualitatively changing the nature of work, residence, recreation, and social relations in the city center.

Of greatest impact, the nature of work changed. Now, unskilled workers could perform tasks previously performed only by artisans and specialists. When, for example, a modern bakery opened in 1907 at a time of acute labor agitation in the capital's bakeries, the owners chided striking bakers in an open letter: "In a few days the unskilled worker can know as much as the long-serving craftsman." When its advertisement for new workers attracted five hundred men to queue up before 9 A.M., *El Imparcial* commented on the significance of the change mechanization was bringing: "A remarkable aspect was that those applying for work were tailors, shoemakers, mechanics, a printer and a telephonist." In other words, the paper continued, "education and automation are revolutionizing work and shattering the old craft habits." Similarly, mechanization loosened the ties that traditionally had bound employers and craftsmen.[10]

The impact of electrification and the new, sharper commercial climate it brought to industry led to an incipient consumerism, the introduction of novelty, and a new frivolity that enlivened the staid industrial culture. This "modernization" was most apparent in the capital's tobacco industry. The emergence of El Buen Tono forced amalgamation of most of the other smaller companies into two other large concerns, La Cigarrera Mexicana and La Tabacalera Mexicana, each of which built modern factories in the center. They radically altered the commercial impact of business among the population by a series of stunts and initiatives designed to promote their products.

Marketing and advertising received only modest attention before 1900 and were largely restricted to restrained, factual newspaper advertising. These modest efforts only rarely included incidents such as Alfonso Labat's audacious balloon ascent to mark the opening of his new tobacco factory in 1878, with free matches distributed to introduce his new cigars, "L'Exposición de Paris."[11] Such Victorian showmanship remained rare until 1901, when Pugibet began a new era of aggressive and entertaining promotional activity that transformed the climate in the city streets. He began advertising the company's products by mounting and operating working machines in Paris and New York, investing $20,859 [$ indicates pesos in this chapter] in the Paris exhibit and $60,000 for his showroom on Broadway.[12] As possibly Mexico's first entrepreneur to make a mark overseas, he received a good deal of attention. La Cigarrera Mexicana countered Pugibet's initiative and attention by sending girls to distribute packets of its new brand, "Electra," to men and flowers to their ladies in the audience of a production of *Electra* at the Teatro Arbeu.[13] From 1904, Pugibet ran free films at his factory. In 1905, La Tabacalera Mexicana began to compete by celebrating Independence Day with a function in the Circo Orrin for smokers of its brand, "Flor de Canela"; the evening climaxed with a film documenting the receipt of the Grand Prix for the brand in the St. Louis Exhibition. Again, girls distributed free packets to the audience. Within weeks, El Buen Tono upstaged its rivals, mounting shows in Veracruz's Parque Ciriaco Vazquez, including what was claimed to be the first film advertisements in Mexico: "The method of advertising is truly ingenious, because between scenes there is a still slide, which with the most disguised modesty shows the public that El Buen Tono has $5,000,000 in capital and that with its smooth brand Canela it is the best."[14] La Tabacalera responded by launching a promotional campaign that included $100 prizes for winning coupons from its packets; mildly erotic newspaper advertisements for its new brand "Sirenas," complete with risqué lyrics in *El Imparcial* (which started a newspaper advertising war with El Buen Tono); monthly lotteries for prizes such as a crocodile; and sending its own hostesses to distribute free samples at bullfights. By 1910, El Buen Tono had stepped up its monthly lottery prizes to $12,500 and, on one occasion, awarded a new French car. This spurred La Tabacalera Mexicana later that year to offer a new house.[15]

The novel commercial combination of advertising and gambling accompanied the promotion and popularization of technical innovation. In 1907, Pugibet brought a dirigible to the capital (claimed to be the first example of controlled flight there) and, three years later, he introduced the Blériot monoplane—the first airplane in the country—to publicize his brand "Alfonso XIII." El Buen Tono's free films packed working-class audiences into the Alameda as did its free variety shows in the Plaza de San Juan, alongside the factory, including such novelties as a bicycle wall of death. Pugibet introduced the city's first delivery vans in 1908 and claimed to have brought the first radio transmitter to Mexico.[16]

The diversions were not, of course, merely diversionary, and the highest reaches of Porfirian society recognized the promotional power and political potential of the new industrialism. New, technologically advanced industries such as El Buen Tono became such potent symbols of Mexico's modernization that President Díaz's son used the factory, on occasion, rather than the Palacio Nacional, to impress visiting dignitaries. While Pugibet promoted his products and amused his female employees by feting the visiting French opera star Emma Calvé in the factory, inviting her to try her hand at the machines and dedicating a new brand to her (after all, she had made her name in Georges Bizet's *Carmen*), Díaz the son presided over lunches in the factory for visiting political and military guests.[17] Apart from Secretary of State Root and the French foreign minister, he gave dinner parties for visiting French, German, and British sailors, expecting some of the glamour of the model factory to rub off on him.[18] At the least, he had the central street running through the factory named after his father.

For its part, La Tabacalera also provided entertainment, staging circus and opera as well as nightly film shows in the 1,400-seat theater built on the factory grounds in 1907. And while the capital's elite were not renowned for their industrialism, "the cream of Porfirian society" was reported to attend the dances staged in the factory gardens.[19]

While enterprising new companies brought variety and innovation, the metropolitan world of labor experienced diversification and expanding opportunity. The growing industries displaced artisan activity but witnessed a significant rise in the capital's service sector, substantially increasing the white-collar jobs available. While the total employed in the nation's service sector rose by a mere 6 percent in the period from 1898 to 1910, in the Federal District it surged by 45 percent, from 125,374 to 178,716—a numerical increase greater than the net figure for the rest of the country. Jobs in the public services increased from 3,398 to 6,184 while the number of white-collar employees in the private sector more than doubled, from 12,040 to 25,826. Many others found occupation in railways, gas and electrical companies, telephone and telegraph companies, hotels, shops, restaurants, and offices. In the decade after 1900, although pressure on middle-class wages increased, the range of goods and services in the Federal District also expanded.[20]

At a time when the recession deepened in most other parts of the country, the fabric of society in the capital became more diverse. The newer employees, with their interest in cultural advance and education, would be the very people who would welcome Francisco Madero and his progressive, pragmatic liberal approach. Equally as important, the small but rapidly growing managerial and technical staff in the new businesses became increasingly frustrated as inadequate education and training facilities made it difficult for them to obtain promotions and advance in the companies. As *El Progreso Latino* concluded in bewilderment: "The more progress is made, the greater is the contrast between it and the intellectual and moral state of the country. The people do not identify with the authorities. . . . While the people's spirit sleeps, they work with all their strength . . . badly taught. . . . How many schools are there for the 117,992 workers of the tobacco factories and textile mills in the country? Only two."[21]

Madero's Anti-Reelectionist Manifesto of 1909 recognized this point; its first demand concerning industry called for improvement of technical training.[22] Madero's new Department of Labor, established in 1912, proposed as the first of the nine points in its action program the creation of workers' technical schools with day and evening classes, "which could be done by getting manufacturers to contribute." The British manager of the large, modern meat-packing plant El Popo, in the capital, expressed concern about the neglect of education in the city: "The relatively small but ambitious middle class was neglected . . . and they did not take effective measures to enlarge the scope of endeavor of the masses."[23]

The masses wanted to live in better conditions, too, and, while most of them could not, a significant minority did help raise the aspirations of the rest. Enlightened employers set the pace, with the authorities lamely unable to contribute. New housing developments remade the residential face of the capital as the dramatic spatial changes of settlement became evident; in 1898 the *Mexican Financier* said that the city was becoming "like a man who wears sandals, a *zárape* and a top hat . . . the top hat is . . . the electric light, the asphalt or concrete-block pavements, and the street railways, while the *zarape* and the sandals are representative of the frank barbarism of the lower classes, their sometimes repulsively unclean habits, of which the city streets bear witness, and the swarming tenements where life is lived at very close quarters and at the social level of the Hottentots."[24]

At the end of the period the millworkers of the outlying industrial hamlets still suffered primitive conditions in their company-owned cottages. As late as 1912 the workers of the Santa Teresa mill in Contreras lived in overcrowded two-room huts with leaking fabric roofs and damp floors housing not only their children but also their animals.[25] At the other end of the scale the new Paseo de la Reforma in the capital boasted the extravagance of the nouveaux riches. In between, new workers' housing developments met some of the demand for lower-class housing in areas such as Rancho del Chopo or Colonia Indianilla.[26] Undoubtedly, the mass of the lumpenproletariat eked out their lives in the severely depressed conditions of the notorious *casas de vecindad* of the city's center. Rays of light for the aspiring lower classes did appear occasionally, such as the model houses built by Ernesto Pugibet for the employees of El Buen Tono in Calle Bucareli in 1905. Company executives claimed that this represented a breakthrough as the first case of a Mexican industrial company building a "model workers' estate" with modern, sound, hygienic houses. Complete with electric lighting, running hot water, showers, and even an electric lift, they were show houses. The initiative was a rare one, but the company recognized the urgency of meeting rising aspirations in this way when it confessed in its annual report for 1907 that the construction had resulted "out of a sense of duty and solidarity, because of the situation of the working class, and in order to improve the workers' situation a little, showing them that this company is concerned for their welfare."[27]

El Buen Tono, in this respect as in so many others, was an exemplary benefactor to its employees' cultural welfare. How did workers fare at other factories? The usual description generally reports the repressive treatment of factory workers. A catalog of radical protest and labor disturbances supports this view; most of the protest concerned long hours and low wages. Generally true of the Federal District, though, this characterization did not present the entire picture. Some traditional owners did make efforts to court their workers' support and affection. One of the country's oldest cotton manufactories, for example, the Miraflores cotton mill, which dominated Chalco in the south of the Federal District, had the reputation of being run as a "model settlement" by its Scottish owners, the Robertson Brothers. Along other benefits, they provided a well-equipped school, music training, a theater, and well-paid teachers. The mill escaped industrial unrest until 1911. Ricardo Sainz, the autocratic boss of La Fama cotton mill in Tlalpán, another of the country's historic mills, received praise for the two schools, the doctor, the pharmacy, and the band he supported in Tlalpán. Two traditional woollen mills in the city's center, La Victoria and Minerva, also supported workers' associations.[28] Alfonso Labat looked after his employees and, to celebrate the opening of his new match factory in 1880, gave a generous banquet at which the five hundred workers danced until 2 A.M. Reports said these people arrived at the factory "full of joy to be going to work" where they were accustomed to "laugh and sing amongst their toil."[29] Ignacio Ferrer started a night school in his model chocolate factory, Flor de Tabasco, in 1877, and on opening his new city-center shop in 1883 he gave a champagne banquet where his workers mingled with invited dignitaries. He, too, recognized the value of the work environment, filling the factory patio with flowers, and the value of education, founding a school and distributing annual prizes to employees. Brecker, the owner of one of the country's most venerable paper mills,

Belém in Santa Fe, came from the same mould. He provided the "affectionate care of a father" to his five hundred employees, for whom he provided a school.[30]

On occasion, employers used religion to cement this kind of relationship, although it appears to be less significant in the Federal District than in other parts of the country at this time and hardly figured as an element of social relations within the city. In the industrial hamlets, religious ceremonies persisted as a means of binding workers to the mill. Ricardo Sainz, for example, when he opened the new chapel built on the grounds of La Fama in 1876, discounted workers' wages to help pay for the ceremony; in return they received a "magnificent free lunch."[31] Other established mills had chapels on their grounds, such as Belém paper mill, where co-owner Juan Benfield built a church "'to keep alive the feeling for God in his workers.'"[32] On feast days such as the Immaculate Conception on December 8, workers were encouraged to decorate archways and pathways on the grounds of La Fama. On the same day, in 1880, the owners of La Magdalena cotton mill in nearby Contreras encouraged workers to take part in processions on the mill grounds and in the village with a statue of the Virgin reputed to have cost one thousand pesos.

The labor press denounced these practices as collusion between employers and the church.[33] As late as 1911 religion was still an important element of tension in La Magdalena mill when, in a dispute connected with water rights in the village, workers from the mill complained that "a religious cult is being forced upon us." Chapel rivalries existed in the village, and a large group of La Magdalena employees protested that their wish to have a Catholic church was being denied by the authorities.[34]

The much more secular character of the city center resulted in a quite different environment. Indeed, the tone had been set by Benito Juárez when he donated the Church of San Pedro y San Pablo to the Gran Círculo de Obreros to be used as an artisans' center; in 1879 the ayuntamiento gave financial help to establish a night school and artisans' workshops there.[35] Religion scarcely appeared as a feature of employment relations in the center.

As newer companies opened in the capital in the 1890s and 1900s, a handful of enlightened entrepreneurs also reaped large rewards of loyalty from their work force for taking simple steps to encourage them. Hipólito Chambón, the Swiss-born founder of the country's most important silk mill; Alberto Lentz, the German-born designer and owner of paper mills; Carlos Zetina, the Mexican founder of the leading shoe factory; Alberto Arellano, Spanish owner of the capital's largest clothing factory, La Unión; and Pugibet were five leading examples of what industrial paternalism could achieve. Pugibet's provision of good working conditions and wages in El Buen Tono was legendary: he even introduced profit-sharing schemes. He won special praise for his treatment of women employees and encouraged them even to the extent of helping potentially subversive workers. In 1896 the leader of a major strike among women tobacco workers in the capital, Isabel Guerrero, a primary schoolteacher dedicated to improving the lot of the *cigarreras*, received an invitation to be guest poet at a Buen Tono lunch celebration in the Tivoli gardens to mark the motherhood of a popular forewoman of the factory, Lina Vega. One hundred women attended, and an orchestra played during lunch. Some of the male workers joined them later, along with friends of Pugibet. "Cries of Viva México mingled with Vivas to France and Spain, to their benefactor Sr. Pugibet, to labor and to Mexican women" before the party returned in five special coaches. They went on to a theater celebration, with city councillor Pedro Ordóñez (Díaz's coordinator with the officially approved labor organization, the Gran Congreso Obrero) as master of ceremonies for a program that included an overture, the theatrical piece *Flor de un día* by Francisco Camprodón, a Schubert serenade, recitals, and more music. The event finished at 5 A.M. The factory even hosted a birthday party for two of its forewomen, Linita and Rafaela Narva, which five hundred women operatives attended. Nor was this solidarity forced; when the popular forewoman Rita Castaño died in 1897 police had to intervene to get the cortege through the streets, so great was the crush of five hundred *cigarreras* attending. Pugibet's attention was widely agreed to have helped the *cigarreras* transform their lot: "The old cigarette girls of the *estanco* have chiselled and polished themselves into the *cigarreritas* of the factory."[36]

Hipólito Chambón founded and sustained an important silk industry in the capital that also employed a large number of women. He sponsored a theater evening in 1888 to announce plans to establish the silk business. In the presence of Díaz's wife, the press, and representatives of banking and industry, and with the backing of the Gran Congreso Obrero, he presided over an event in the Teatro Nacional to launch his scheme and attract both working-class and middle-class support and investment. His factory (with three hundred operatives) thrived, along with his plantations and sericulture training schools in Michoacán, Guerrero, Veracruz, Aguascalientes, and Mexico state. In 1901 he threw a luncheon party in the factory, with leading members of the French community and Pedro Ordóñez in attendance, to celebrate the expansion of the business.[37] His public celebration of his industry in Irapuato in 1896 even gained an enthusiastic mention in Díaz's address to Congress that year. Such was the affection of his employees (who had up to twenty-nine-years' service with him) that on his return to Mexico from a trip abroad in 1911 they organized a picnic excursion to Tizapán, where they danced to a band hired by Chambón and sang to the accompaniment of guitars throughout the afternoon. Chambón gave a silk rebozo to each woman present.[38]

Alberto Lentz had a similar relationship with the employees of his Loreto paper mill in San Angel, which he renovated and operated together with the Peña Pobre paper mill in Tlalpán. He, too, apart from building houses for his workers and providing them with doctors, medicine, and good pay and conditions, earned their appreciation for building them a school. A measure of his social impact received visible witness after his death in 1951 when three thousand workers and their families accompanied his coffin.[39] More than anyone else, Carlos Zetina was responsible for mechanizing the footwear industry in the capital. His Excelsior factory became the largest in Mexico by 1910, producing twelve hundred pairs of shoes daily. He added a gymnasium and swimming pool for employees, helped with housing, and his factory, according to the revolutionary inspectors, far exceeded "the requirements of revolutionary legislation."[40] Alberto Arellano had a reputation similar to that of Alberto Lentz and was praised for his treatment of employees. In 1911 workers celebrated his birthday with a fiesta in the Tivoli that included poetry, choral recitals, and a lunch followed by a dance. His funeral, in 1913, also attracted a large crowd of employees and their families.[41]

While these cases provide salutary examples of how well the capital's workers responded when they received minimally decent encouragement, they were the exceptions. In general the capital's elite showed little urgency to resolve the frustrations of their lower classes. As happened in other industrializing societies, the Mexico City elite preferred generally to adopt the postures established by the British Victorian industrial elite as the proletariat showed resistance to the work ethic and turned to drink and absenteeism. In this they were abetted by the largely laissez-faire stance of the administration on social issues. A few were moved to try to do something about the plight of the capital's lower orders and founded the Sociedad Filantrópica Mexicana in 1888. But the constitution of the society issued by its committee (which included Ricardo Sainz) revealed its preference for elitism and moralizing. Believing that vices permeated "all social classes," they determined "to spread morality among the people by all means possible." Their preferred method relied on didactic drama; they encouraged uplifting works of theater and distributed free tickets for performances "in which issues of dogma or politics would be strictly avoided." They particularly aimed to improve artisans and the city's poor, to whom they would distribute "simple moral instructive publications which would encourage optimism and make work seem desirable."[42] The ayuntamiento made its contribution, too, when in 1902 it helped the owners of the Manuel González Cosío workshops distribute fifteen thousand leaflets to workplaces in the city. These leaflets appealed to industrialists and workers to combat weekend drinking "so as to help a little in the regeneration of our working class" and to curb "the ancient and depraved habit of our working class . . . of getting drunk on Sundays and Mondays of each week."[43] They do not appear to have had conspicuous success.

The capital's political elites, in conjunction with the emerging elites of business and industry, made a more sustained effort to bind the city's work force into political support of the regime by displays of enthusiasm and allegiance that in superficial but spectacular form pandered to the taste for display while substituting for democracy or real dialogue. From 1891 onward, the Junta Central Porfirista mounted celebrations in honor of Díaz's birthday. This twenty-eight-member body organized by Carlos Pacheco included a selection of the "prominent people in banking, politics, industry, commerce and the army," and they merged with the existing patriotic society, the Círculo de Amigos del General Díaz. Their leading lights included city industrialists Thomas Braniff (on the board of San Ildefonso and La Victoria woollen mills, Buen Tono, and San Rafael paper mill), Iñigo Noriega (San Antonio Abad cotton mill and La Tabacalera Mexicana), José Sánchez Ramos (San Rafael), and Guillermo Landa y Escandón (future governor of the Federal District). They organized a massive celebration in the capital—probably the first such national assembly of leading political figures from all parts of the country—to demonstrate the unity of business and politics behind Díaz. Presidents of all major municipalities of the country were invited to a banquet on September 21, 1891, with free transport provided by the railway companies. Also invited to the banquet in the Teatro Nacional were "secretaries of state, ambassadors, the Mexico City ayuntamiento, consuls, governors, army generals, the proprietors of Mexico City newspapers, the directors of railway companies, commercial businesses and agricultural concerns." In all, 565 guests, surrounded by two hundred thousand flowers, enjoyed a banquet, concert, and ball that lasted until dawn. An extensive cross section of the beneficiaries of Díaz's progress assembled to pledge their support for his system. Nor were the workers forgotten; as part of the week's celebrations, ayuntamiento members and leaders of the pro-Díaz Gran Congreso Obrero (Pedro Ordóñez and José María González) dutifully organized a torchlight procession of three thousand capital-city workers, attended by banners and marching bands, to parade before Díaz at the palace. Confidence and self-congratulation formed the bond between

government and business as the major actors, while workers had a
walk-on part as the supporting cast.[44]

A regular series of such events followed until 1910, each designed
to reinforce the government-business alliance that steadily grew more
powerful. In 1892, Congress amended the constitution, allowing Díaz
to stand for reelection; one of the first voices raised in support was
that of Rafael Dondé (San Antonio Abad and Buen Tono), who suggested that to deny reelection to Díaz, a figure of "incomparable experience . . . and moreover one who had the confidence of foreign capital,"
would be unpatriotic. Even a physical assault on Díaz, made during
the Independence parade of 1892, could not spoil the powerful display of mutual societies from the capital and government employees
who led the parade in his honor. This procession has been described
as the first appearance of "the phenomenon of popular support for
Díaz . . . organized by big business."[45]

In 1896 the Junta Central Porfirista organized a celebration to
mark the twentieth anniversary of Díaz's accession. Braniff, Dondé,
and Sánchez Ramos, each now a very wealthy man from his business
dealings, again served as the leading organizers. Braniff was said to
be worth five million pesos, and the other two, one million pesos
each from their association with the industrial companies. This time
the banquet was held on the main platform of the Buenavista railway
station—the symbol of the Porfirian development with foreign capital as its hub—where "main bankers, industrialists and merchants of
the city" gathered.[46]

In 1899, as fin de siècle excitement mounted, two more celebrations in the capital sought to identify the regime with the technological developments transforming the city. In September the Círculo
de Amigos del General Díaz staged a procession of twenty-three
decorated floats, each sponsored by a company. The floats included a
maiden on a globe holding aloft an Edison bulb (sponsored by the
electric companies), a snow-covered mountain with a power source
for a model streetcar (the Federal District tramways), a tall chimney
garlanded with Mexican, Spanish, and French flags and surrounded
by mill operatives (the textile mills of the Federal District), and even
one with heads of cattle upon blocks of ice (sponsored by the new
slaughterhouse). The capital's leading industrialists, notably Indalecio
Ibáñez, Saturnino Sauto, and Antero Muñúzuri, organized the parade.
The more overt role of foreign communities as supporters of Díaz,
alluded to by the textile mills' float, was the theme of the mass
demonstrations two months later in November. This time the Círculo
arranged their most spectacular and overtly political show to date.
A huge parade was organized by the leading bankers, industrialists,
and merchants, "in a word the richest proprietors and most notable

businessmen," with Rafael Dondé giving the keynote speech on behalf of foreign business interests in the capital: "We live peacefully now; in perfect security we create companies which develop and progress. . . . You have worked like the most indefatigable industrialist."[47]

The spirit of such overt collaboration between business (foreign and national) and the government continued. In 1901 the Círculo was prepared to stage smaller events, such as a morale-boosting evening reception, when La Cigarrera Mexicana won the prize for industrial participants with its Japanese pavilion and working cigarette machines.[48] In 1904 the Círculo organized even more sophisticated technological tricks in their parade: the electric companies' float sported a model dynamo, and La Cigarrera Mexicana had a working Bonsack cigarette machine topped by a portrait of Díaz with the inscription: "He brought peace to make his people happy. The people love him. God bless him." El Buen Tono went one better by building a Moorish pavilion with three hundred working *cigarreras* in uniform.[49]

The 1910 centenary celebrations brought these staged events to a climax. On that occasion the mutual admiration offered by the Díaz administration and the capital's business community turned out to be the last rites for the regime. The National Celebration Committee was largely in the hands of the shopkeepers and industrialists of the capital, with Andrés Eizaguirre, manager of El Buen Tono, as its treasurer. The propaganda effort for consumption by the outside world relied on a joint effort between government and entrepreneurs. Workers, for example, were paraded in factory delegations before the ambassadors of the United States, Germany, Italy, and Japan, who were the first to arrive in the capital. For the main floodlit procession of September 21, the Ministry of the Interior provided five hundred mounted rurales with flaming torches, followed by "nine thousand people on foot, each bearing a flag of red, white and green, and a candle costing $1.05 each, and given out to the people—with no more requirement than that they turn up clean and wearing at least trousers and shoes." The ministry also suggested that the companies arrange for their own floats and worker delegations.[50]

In the end, Governor Landa y Escandón attempted—too late—to subsume these staged arrangements into a permanent organization when he launched the Sociedad Mutualista y Moralizadora del Distrito Federal in 1910. This was a logical extension of the attempts to give the regime an identity among the new proletariat. The propaganda possibilities of the new society became apparent in its first event, a demonstration of support for Díaz in April 1910. Before an approving Díaz paraded some five thousand workers, representing most of the large factories and mills of the Federal District and accompanied by bands and flower-decked girls.[51] The red, white, and green of the national tricolor pervaded all these events as patriotism served as the thread to stitch together the regime, big business, and the workers; but the thread would not hold a third of those groups to the banner when the regime came under fire in 1911. The workers had been offered little choice and no opportunity to debate the benefits of this partnership, but in a culture of caciquismo they knew what was sensible for their job prospects. In a rare glimpse of private misgivings about the acceptability of these managed displays of support for the regime and the misuse of public celebration for political gain, *El Obrero Mexicano* voiced its doubts as early as 1894: "It is time for our citizens to put their own interests before the music of parades, put the country before Bengal rockets, do some thinking instead of eating Salvatierra crackers. It is time our numerous workers' associations stop wasting their goodwill by parading their banners before the National Palace, meekly asking the President for permission to enter. It is time for something more dignified and practical."[52]

Indeed, there had been close paternalistic links between the regime and organized labor for some time in the capital, and the regime turned to old techniques in trying desperately to build support when it came under threat in 1910. Since the days when Benito Juárez had been the benefactor of the capital's artisans there had been a steady relationship between metropolitan labor and the government. The early working-class radicalism found in the 1870s was largely blunted by the regime's suppression of dissent by the mid-1880s, and workers in the Federal District only made rare protests later. Labor associations continued, but largely in a controlled and co-opted form. The capital's hat makers formed the first independent association in 1853, and mutual societies proliferated in the 1860s. In 1874 the Círculo de Obreros, a support vehicle for Lerdo de Tejada, organized a massive popular demonstration to back his candidature, and four thousand workers attended a celebratory banquet.[53] As they were eventually organized and patronized by Díaz's organization, the Gran Congreso Obrero, they organized their own support for the regime before the industrialists climbed literally onto the bandwagon. In 1887 three thousand members of workers' associations paraded to support the regime in the February 5 celebrations, and thirty-four hundred participated in the Independence Day parade, with Díaz emotionally embracing the leader of the Gran Congreso Obrero, Pedro Ordóñez, who had organized the event. In the reelection campaign earlier that year the government had helped the Gran Congreso Obrero purchase twelve thousand patriotic banners and hundreds of rockets to launch while ten thousand workers took one and one half hours to parade past the palace.[54]

In 1892, in response to the Comité Central Porfirista, ten thousand workers, including many mutual societies, marched past Díaz in the National Palace accompanied by twenty bands and calling for workers' support for his reelection. The mutual societies of the capital continued to turn out dutifully for the next decade to support the chief.

Paternalistic employers had encouraged mutual societies in the capital since the early Porfiriato. With the emergence of independent workers' groups, mutual societies were at times an attractive option for an employer to court the favor of his employees—and employers did not hesitate to call on culture to help in this job. In 1879, for example, Remigio Noriega, owner of the capital's largest traditional tobacco factory, El Borrego, hosted a luncheon and dance on his birthday for his workers and used the occasion to launch the company society, whose objective was to improve conditions for his female employees and to found a girls' orphanage. Four hundred couples drank wine and champagne before attending a fund-raising theater function, comprising a suitably entitled play, "Más vale maña que fuerza," a poetry reading, and the overtures from "Nora" and "Miserere del Trovador."[55] Most mutual societies had a restrained political dimension: usually they excluded discussion of politics and religion in their articles of constitution. So anodyne had they become by the 1890s, thanks to coercion and work of labor caciques such as Pedro Ordóñez and José María González, that even the weekly organ of the industrialists of the capital, *La Semana Mercantil,* could comment wryly in 1896 that "the agreement that fortunately exists between bosses and workers, labor and capital . . . makes our mutualist groups a parody of the powerful forces organized in the Old World. . . . All that they offer is a lavishly decorated banner and dinners or anniversary dances from time to time." Even with their potential for political independence emasculated, they still survived, and some fifty mutualist societies existed in the capital alone in 1906.[56]

As Madero's propaganda began to threaten the Porfirian regime, the metropolitan elites belatedly recognized they had neglected the capital's working class and its needs. They decided to make a play for the support of these workers by reviving, modernizing, and politicizing the institution of the mutualist society. There followed a remarkable effort by Landa y Escandón, governor of the Federal District, to win them over, persuade them that the regime in fact did care, and tie them to the government. It failed.

In July 1910 he announced the formation of the Sociedad Mutualista y Moralizadora del Distrito Federal. Explaining that there existed an urgent need to promote the moral and material welfare of the workers, he said that there was "no lack of money" and that the authorities would provide "unconditional help."[57] Cynics charged that this was only an effort to counter the rise of support for Francisco Madero among local textile workers.[58] The governor's official publication admitted the covert purpose of the society would be to inhibit politicalization: "The worker, properly speaking, should only think about his own well-being, dedicating himself to steady, intelligent honest work; he must reject agitators whose perfidious words make him believe in things which do not and cannot exist, and he must with equal energy reject so-called politicians who dress up with false rhetoric to confuse and subvert."[59] Landa y Escandón put enormous energy into organizing the society by staging personal visits to many of the capital's factories, publishing a weekly newspaper, and organizing many theater events. His letter to all factory owners in the Federal District explained that the society's aim would be to add "moralizing" to the role of "mutualist," by declaring its objective "to advance in general the workers' education and advance all necessary means for centers of recreation and culture for them . . . to keep them away from places of degeneration and vice."[60]

The society had clearly political purposes, yet its preferred route to attract the support of the workers was to offer cultural spectacle and diversion as a deflection of politicalization—rather a microcosm of the past twenty years. When the governor visited factories to court membership he was regularly greeted by the assembled work force, organized to cry "Viva el gobernador," and was well feted in establishments such as Hipólito Chambón's silk mill, where, in April 1910, he was regaled with a champagne lunch and speeches of welcome by representative workers. Landa y Escandón's private secretary, Antonio Peralta, also edited *El Obrero Mexicano* and faithfully reported all such visits. The techniques the tobacco firms had used successfully to stimulate public interest were adopted: free tickets to watch "moral works" in the Teatro Hidalgo were distributed to three or four factories each week, with a recommendation that they be given to "workers who are distinguished by their good behavior and diligence at work." When the society's drama group mounted its own plays to show "realities of the worker's life, to combat with example the vices and bad behavior of men," the small audience did not cover costs and the governor had to donate one hundred pesos to recover losses. After a subgroup, the Guillermo Landa y Escandón Instruction and Recreation Society, proposed a nursery for workers' children, Ramón Corral promised to pay the hundred-peso monthly rent and the cost of furniture, while Justo Sierra pledged furniture and teachers.[61]

Practical benefits were offered to entice members: in September 1910 the governor opened the Parque Obrero Hidalgo in Balbuena with twenty thousand tamales and ten thousand liters of atole distributed free. A women's group, three hundred strong, organized collections of clothing there for workers' children and ran distribution ceremonies where "those who distribute the clothing among the poor children were to be children chosen principally from the middle class." Meetings to explain the society and encourage membership offered free films that on occasion attracted eight hundred workers. At one such showing, Peralta explained that the idea for the society had been Díaz's and that he had appointed Landa y Escandón to establish it. But in November 1910, as Madero's Plan of San Luis Potosí appeared, a note of urgency crept in. One of the meetings in the Teatro Borrás had to be suspended because the owner had allowed an antireelectionist meeting beforehand and, consequently, the authorities had closed the theater. When the Círculo de Amigos del General Díaz countered this rally by offering a free banquet to thirteen thousand workers in the Balbuena Park to celebrate the reelection of Díaz and Corral, the event was suddenly canceled "because those in charge of decorating the park could not do it in time." Clearly, the threat posed by Maderistas hastened matters: in December the society held its first meeting, with 225 delegates. The firm hand of the authorities was clear from the start, as Landa y Escandón chose the five-member executive committee and claimed the group had some five thousand members. Soon, the committee was even meeting in Landa y Escandón's office, while factory managers were invited to his home to discuss collaboration.[62]

When the committee eventually made firm proposals for action the reformist conservatism of the old mutualist societies, combined with the guilty conscience of the authorities for their neglect of working-class needs, was dominant. They wanted recreation centers, libraries, schools, shelters, and gymnasiums to keep workers away from vice. When the society was formally inaugurated in April 1911, the stake in it held by local industry was formidable: El Buen Tono donated one thousand pesos, La Central matchworks five hundred pesos, and eleven other factories gave one hundred pesos each. The society became a focal point for efforts to try to swing the working class behind the government as the regime crumbled. Peralta persuaded it to organize a voluntary battalion "to defend the state," and its subgroup, the Asociación Docente de Propaganda Cívica, arranged films, recitals, and concerts for members, during which "it will be attempted to instruct the worker about his duties as a citizen of a democratic country, and how he should vote in the next election." The announcement ended with wry irony, stating that "the meetings will have no political character."[63]

Events overtook the wishes of the society. As late as February 1913 it still had 5,674 members and funds of $112,579 (Landa y Escandón had donated $100,000 to start it), making it the biggest workers' society in the capital area. But the governor had been forced to flee into exile with Díaz in 1911, and the patronage of the state evaporated. Workers preferred to form their own unions and associations under the freedom given by Madero after 1912. And they did so for a brief interlude, until the next phase of government control. In 1918 the Confederación Regional Obrera Mexicana, created with government money, once again reminded workers of what was good for them and warned them not to bite the hand that fed them.

NOTES

1. M. González Navarro, *Estadísticas sociales del porfiriato 1877–1910* (México, 1956), table 1.

2. This discussion is expanded in A. L. Morgan, "Industry and Society in the Mexico City Area 1875–1910" (Ph.D. dissertation, CNAA, London, 1984).

3. D. W. Walker, "Porfirian Labor Politics: Working Class Organizations in Mexico City and Porfirio Díaz 1876–1910," *The Americas* 37, no. 3 (January 1981): 257–90.

4. E. Busto, *Memoria de Hacienda de 1877–78* (México, 1878), anexo no. 3.

5. As late as 1912, 90 percent of the workers reportedly had been born on the grounds of the more outlying Rio Hondo cotton mill. T. de la Torre to Departamento de Trabajo, February 12, 1912. AGN Trabajo 30.13.5.

6. E. Galarza, *La Industria Eléctrica en México* (México, 1941), 16; *El Imparcial*, August 26, September 2, October 24, 1902; *Boletín Financiero y Minero* (hereinafter cited as BFM), October 21, 1904; *México Industrial* 1 (August 15, 1905).

7. Bjorklund, *Foreign Office Diplomatic and Consular Reports*, no. 2693 (August 1901); E de la Torre Villar, "La capital y sus primeros medios de transporte," *HM* 9 (1959): 215–48; F. Calderón, "La república restaurada: Vida económica," in *Historia moderna de México*, ed. D. Cosío Villegas (México, 1955–1973), 670–94; *La Semana Mercantil*, September 18, 1905.

8. For vivid depictions of the vagaries of policy, see R. Beredicio and S. Applebaum, *Posada's Popular Mexican Prints* (New York, 1972), 27; *La Semana Mercantil*, February 22, 1909; and The *Times* (London), May 5, 1906.

9. *El Imparcial*, October 1, 1907.

10. *Ibid.*, July 4, 6, 8, 1907.

11. *El Hijo del Trabajo*, November 24, 1878; and *El Socialista*, June 13, 1880.

12. BFM, February 8, 1901.

13. *El Imparcial*, April 7, 1901.

14. *Ibid.*, October 14, 1905.

15. BFM, September 10, 1907.

16. *El Imparcial*, January 8, November 30, 1907; May 17, 1910; and H. Ruíz Sandoval, "Lecciones Industriales de Excélsior," no. 11 (*Excélsior*, México, 1960).

17. *El Mundo Ilustrado*, January 5, 1908.

18. *El Imparcial*, February 15, March 7, 10, April 5, 7, October 4, December 24, 1907.

19. H. Ruíz Sandoval, "La Industria Cigarrera" (*Excélsior*, México, 1960).

20. González Navarro, *Estadísticas Sociales*, 48, 55.

21. *El Progreso Latino*, July 21, 1905.

22. M. González Ramírez, *Fuentes para la historia de la revolución mexicana* (México, 1957), 4:55–57.

23. R. Sierra, October 29, 1912. AGN Trabajo 34.3.4.11. The plant itself demonstrated the impact of electrical technology on a primitive trade; it was hailed as something of a technological wonder as it provided, among other things, a steady supply of ice for the first time. J. DeKay, *Dictators of Mexico* (London, 1914), 19–32.

24. *Mexican Financier*, February 11, 1898.

25. R. Sierra, June 17, 1912. AGN Trabajo 31.3.7.14.

26. M. Yamada, "Mexico City: Development and Urban Problems before the Revolution," *Latin American Studies* (Tsukuba, Japan), no. 7 (1983): 37; M. D. Morales, "La expansión de la Ciudad de México en el siglo XIX: El caso de los fraccionamientos," *INAH Cuadernos de Trabajo*, no. 4 (México, 1974): 71–74.

27. Annual General Meeting in BFM, March 14, 1908.

28. *El Socialista*, November 6, 19, 1876; J. Figueroa Domenech, *Guía descriptiva de la República Mexicana* (Barcelona, 1899), 188; and *La Convención Radical*, September 4, 1887.

29. *El Socialista*, June 13, 1880.

30. *El Hijo del Trabajo*, September 23, 1877, November 24, 1878, February 18, 1883; *El Socialista*, January 31, 1886.

31. *La Unión de los Obreros*, September 16, 1877.

32. Figueroa Domenech, *Guía descriptiva*, 202.

33. *El Hijo del Trabajo*, January 11, 1880.

34. Srta. Luz Sánchez, headmistress of school no. 195 in San Angel district, to Díaz, and letter from 169 workers of La Magdalena to Díaz, March 17, 1911, AAAM, 1391.1.39.

35. Sección de Fomento de Artesanos to Cabildo, July 19, 1881, AAAM, 354.10.546

36. *La Convención Radical*, October 4, 11, 1896; *ibid.*, November 3, 1895; *El Imparcial*, July 16, 1897; and *ibid.*, November 4, 1898.

37. *La Convención Radical*, April 10, 1892; *ibid.*, July 14, 1901.

38. *El Obrero Mexicano*, January 13, March 10, 1911.

39. B. Dromondo, "Lentz, un gran mexicano," *Excélsior*, December 24, 1951.

40. E. Gruening, *Mexico and Its Heritage* (New York, 1928), 355.

41. *El Obrero Mexicano*, October 20, 1911; F. Fernández del Castillo, *Historia de San Angel y sus alrededores* (México, 1913), 192–93.

42. Constitution of the Sociedad Filantrópica Mexicana, March 31, 1888, AAAM, 355.11.675.

43. Arámburu and Lago, March 11, 1902, AAAM 3643.17.1507.

44. G. Villanueva, *Las fiestas en honor del Sr. General Porfirio Díaz* (México, 1891).

45. D. Cosío Villegas, *El Porfiriato: Vida política interior*, vol. 2, *Historia Moderna*, ed. Cosío Villegas (México, 1972), 384, 599, 653, 684–87.

46. *La Semana Mercantil*, April 6, 1896; *El Mundo Ilustrado*, April 12, 1896.

47. *El Imparcial*, September 7, 1899; *ibid.*, September 16, 1899.

48. *Ibid.*, September 23, 1901.

49. *El Mundo Ilustrado*, December 11, 1904.

50. *La Semana Mercantil*, June 13, 1910; *El Imparcial*, September 5, 1910; and AGN, Gobernación, Sección 10 "Centario," April 12, 1910.

51. *El Obrero Mexicano*, April 8, 1910.

52. *Ibid.*, August 12, 1894.

53. Luis González, "La república restaurada: Vida social," in Cosío Villegas, *Historia Moderna,* 439–40.

54. Walker, 269–71.

55. *El Industrial*, October 7, 1879.

56. *La Semana Mercantil*, March 9, 1896; and Ruhland, *Directorio de la Ciudad de México, 1906–07* (México, 1907), 859.

57. *El Heraldo de Morelos*, July 18, 1909.

58. A. M. Hernández, *La mujer mexicana en la industria textil* (México, 1940), 49.

59. *Boletín del Consejo de Gobierno del Distrito Federal*, September 10, 1909.

60. Letter from Landa y Escandón to the factory owners, published in *El Obrero Mexicano*, April 29, 1910.

61. *Ibid.*, May 13, 1910; *ibid.*, May 20, 1910; and *ibid.*, July 29, 1910.

62. *Ibid.*, November 25, December 2, 1910; *ibid.*, December 9, 23, 1910; January 27, 1911.

63. *Ibid.*, August 25, 1911.

9

The Porfirian Smart Set Anticipates Thorstein Veblen in Guadalajara

William H. Beezley
Texas Christian University

This study focuses on the form or structure of festive performances, especially parades. It follows the work of such scholars as communications specialist Susan G. Davis,* historian Mary Ryan, and anthropologist Milton Sanger. The latter concludes that these events "encapsulate a culture," revealing the stratification of society, the interplay of ethnic groups, the relationship of clergy and clerisy, the official version of the past and religion, and the desirable patterns of individual behavior.† In its nuances the essay contains allusions to Jacob Burckhardt's thesis that artistic categories, here mnemonics and trompe l'oeil, have application to society, and specific references to Veblen and Robert M. Isherwood's study of Parisian entertainment and street culture. Mikhail Bakhtin's analysis of carnivalesque celebrations informs the essay throughout.

The author, a student of Michael C. Meyer, made his first foray into cultural history in *Judas at the Jockey Club* (1987).

MEXICAN HOLIDAY CELEBRATIONS have always offered church and civic leaders the opportunity to organize living tableaux of virtue. From the first encounter of the Spanish and the Aztecs, rituals

Excerpted from my current research entitled "Holidays . . . Holy Days . . . Mexican Virtue on Parade: The Nimble Mnemonics of Social Tradition, 1821–1911." I have presented portions of this study to seminars at Princeton University, the University of California-San Diego, Tulane University, and the University of Houston. I thank the participants in those sessions, especially Arcadio Díaz-Quiñones, Eric Van Young, Richard E. Greenleaf, and John Hart, and I am also grateful for the helpful comments of Tulane graduate student Karen Joyner.

*Susan G. Davis, *Parades and Power: Street Theatre in Nineteenth-Century Philadelphia* (Philadelphia, 1986).

†Mary Ryan quotes Sanger in her essay "The American Parade: Representations of the Nineteenth-Century Social Order," in *The New Cultural History*, ed. Lynn Hunt (Berkeley, CA, 1990), 132.

have dominated the cultural interaction of these peoples. Spanish efforts to rule, to hispanize to some extent, and to convert the indigenous peoples relied on the drama and music, the sights and sounds, and the emotions and sanctity provided by rituals of government, passion plays, and Amerindian dances revised to carry Christian-European meanings. A succession of Mexican governments, after the colonial period, and an eagerly aggressive church, free from Spanish control to strengthen its allegiance to the pope, used public performances of sacred and civic duties to instruct and inspire the people. Public square and thoroughfare became the classroom of Mexican and Catholic virtue.

Independence in 1821 resulted in general efforts to reshape the cycle of celebrations in Mexico. Major religious holidays remained on the calendar, but officials of the First Empire devised a new list of civic celebrations to mark the struggle for independence, honor the martyrs of the campaign, and remove the vestiges of colonialism by discarding Spanish holidays. Religious feast days posed some difficulties in the early years of independence as government officials attempted to promote industry and thrift in an effort to bring about recovery from the economic disruptions that attended the wars of independence and the break from Spanish mercantilism. Hard work and holidays collided in the numerous holy days of obligation that mandated attending mass and refraining from manual labor. As part of an effort at reconciliation between the Mexican government and the Holy See, Pope Gregory XVI, in 1839, issued a directive to the Mexican bishops which reduced the number of religious holidays that should be honored as a means of diminishing what the pope and the Mexican government regarded as an excessive number.[1]

Civil authorities followed this pattern during the nineteenth century. From 1839 until 1876, when the Porfirian regime took power, the city council of Mexico at various times attempted to regulate—usually suppress—various public celebrations to halt what it perceived as social disorder. Carnival on Shrove Tuesday and Judas burnings on Holy Saturday received particular attention from the government. Carnival celebrations posed potential threats to civic order because they generally occurred in the evening, with the revelers often disguised in masks and dominoes that obscured their identities. Thus, the celebrants acted with the encouragement and assurance of anonymity, cloaked in a way that could hide from view weapons or stolen goods. This danger soon encouraged people of the higher ranks to move their celebration of Carnival off the streets and into theaters and public halls rented for the occasion. Judas burnings, following the pattern of many other popular carnivalesque celebrations in western Europe, were suppressed as a danger to public safety (usually described as a fire hazard) or reduced to the trivial activity of children.[2]

THE PORFIRIAN HOLIDAY

The Porfirian holiday was an innovation of the regime, but it built on Mexico's long-standing practice of using celebrations as dramatic statements of the dominant culture. Porfirian ritual celebrations offer an indisputable expression of governance during the last quarter of the nineteenth century. ORDER AND PROGRESS, the slogan and the ideal of Mexico's Comtian Positivists, animated administrative policies and inspired governmental displays during Porfirio Díaz's government. Civic celebrations assumed special importance as affirmations of the regime's anticlerical politics and modernistic drive toward secularism. These government-sponsored holidays revealed the values that the dictator and his fellow travelers in the full-coach (as the public called the administration) hoped to promote and expressed the Porfirian understanding of what Mexican virtue should be.

The capital city's ayuntamiento budgeted funds during the Díaz years to celebrate three major civic festivities. The earliest holiday each year, February 5, marked the anniversary of the promulgation of the Constitution of 1857, the paramount expression of western Liberalism in Mexican society. In the spring, on May 5, the nation recognized the anniversary of the Mexican victory over invading French troops in 1862, the major military success of the Mexican army; and in the fall, on September 15 and 16, the nation celebrated the day (September 16, 1810) when Padre Miguel Hidalgo first called on Mexicans to expel the Spaniards and establish an independent government in their country.

The Porfirians celebrated these holidays in the traditional center of the capital city, the Zócalo, bounded by the houses of both civic and church authority, the presidential palace, and the national cathedral. But the Porfirians also promoted a new arena of civic virtue, the Paseo de la Reforma. This avenue's name honored the era of the Constitution of 1857 and liberal triumph, the reform years of Benito Juárez. At major intersections, *glorietas*, traffic circles reminiscent of Paris's Etoile with the Arc de Triomphe at its center, offered locations where Porfirians could present their view of history in monuments. Vicente Riva Palacio, Díaz's first minister of development, headed a group of bureaucrats intent on perpetuating in marble and bronze their conceptions of virtue. "Public monuments exist," wrote Riva Palacio to extol this Porfirian vision, "not only to perpetuate the memory of heroes and of great men who deserve the gratitude of the people, but also to awaken in some and strengthen in others the love of legitimate glories."[3] An early plan called for statues of Cuauhtémoc, Hidalgo, and Juárez to grace the *glorietas* in the center of the avenue.

The Paseo de la Reforma became the national highway of civic virtue. Along this tree-lined esplanade the dictator placed bronze statues representing the two greatest heroes of each Mexican state.[4] Of course, Díaz feted the memory of these heroes as liberal champions of state autonomy, yet he brought their statues to Mexico City to stand in obeisance along the street where he paraded. The Paseo de la Reforma became an avenue symbolic of Porfirian centralization.

The Paseo de la Reforma epitomized the planners' goal of giving major thoroughfares both metaphoric and specific significance. No church or religious building stood along this thoroughfare of deference; instead, shops, parks, homes, and government offices appeared. The Reforma, like Classical Roman streets, became a corridor for public processions that served both urban control and regulation by replacing spontaneous celebrations.[5] Moreover, the ownership of the lots along the street reflected the configuration of the national and foreign elites in Mexico. The development of property rested primarily in the owners of U.S. real estate firms, with prominent Mexican and British citizens holding titles as well.[6]

On Reforma Avenue and throughout the city, Porfirians in 1896 lengthened their list of civil holidays to emphasize the values already honored by the three major holidays and to expand the celebrations of those holidays. The proper presentation of these events required the illumination of public buildings. In earlier years, before electricity, buildings were illuminated with candles in holders of various kinds. (The luminarias used during the Christmas season in New Mexico continue this practice.) This style of illumination required a great number of people to arrange the holders and light the candles. Under Díaz, the illumination changed to an electrical display. These electric lights made spectators rather than celebrants, observers rather than participants, out of those who came to witness the marking of this anniversary. Once the lights were strung, only one person turned them on and off. Moreover, the lighting system reflected the system Porfirio hoped to create. That is, each light formed part of the system and depended upon all the others to work. This string of lights became a metaphor for how the regime had replaced independent state governments with the national government. Moreover, the electric display demonstrated better than anything else the modernization programs of the regime. Most Mexicans, for example, could only marvel at the speed and comfort offered by the newly constructed railroads, but everyone present could witness the way electricity illuminated the dark, without regard for other elements such as wind and rain.[7]

The municipal government suppressed spontaneous processions through the capital city streets in the late 1890s. These occasions, much like the Carnival celebrations, offered the opportunity to turn the world upside down in the popular social reversals that released anger and frustrations in a nondestructive way. Instead, Porfirians sponsored parades to replace Carnival, Judas burnings, and spontaneous processions. These parades included the so-called Flowery War, a romantic promenade in which young gentlemen tossed flowers at fashionably dressed young women riding in elaborately decorated coaches that drove the length of the Paseo de la Reforma. The spontaneity of Judas Day was replaced by the organization of bicycle parades in which the city council offered prizes for cycle decorations and riders' costumes. At one point it even considered clearing vagabonds and loiterers from among the spectators.

Another step toward regulating public life came in 1896 when the ayuntamiento, led by Sebastian Camacho, decided to prohibit all private persons from setting up street amusements and concessions that disrupted the flow of pedestrians through the city's streets and the Alameda's walkways. The councilmen struck at the itinerant entrepreneurs, the part-time puppeteers, the various vendors of homemade snacks and drinks, and the casual street-corner performers of magic and music for tips.[8] These hygienic measures, insofar as they were successful, may have sanitized the streets to some extent, but at the cost of the character of the culture that used them. The laws aimed to create modern antiseptic urban spaces through, in William H. Whyte's word, "dullification."[9] These statutes, moreover, helped destroy the culture of the street shared by all Mexicans of every social rank. This common experience rested on the music, magic, and mystery created by strolling charlatans who told fortunes and performed exotic tricks, by exhibitors of bizarre natural and unnatural oddities, and by acrobats who accomplished miraculous physical stunts. This world of street entertainment enabled people to dream, to recall their childhoods and escape their daily drudgery, and thereby diverted them from more politically disruptive behavior. Removing these feats from public spaces—feats that stretched from magic to science—made the world of the street flat.[10]

ENTER VEBLEN, STAGE RIGHT

As the Porfirians altered the kind, cycle, and celebration of civic and religious fiestas in the public space, they also engaged in a far more sweeping and fundamental change. These years (1876–1911) brought new wealth to Mexico's high society of political favorites, partners of foreign investors, crafty owners of new enterprises, and new rich sprung from the landed poor through conversion of family or village property to commercial agriculture. Extractive industries remained predominate and expanded greatly as fresh markets appeared for lumber, coal, copper, and cattle in the southwestern United States and overseas. Commercial agriculture boomed, replacing subsistence production and producers. Factories and railroads offered investment opportunities that hinted at profits beyond the wildest imagination. Money, and the luxuries it could buy, appeared in profusion: foreigners dumped dollars, deutsche marks, and pounds sterling in heaps, and new banks distributed both silver and paper pesos in stacks.

Mexican plutocrats, with fists full of dollars, looked to the bon ton of Paris, London, and, increasingly, New York to find models for their lives, fashions, entertainments, and attitudes. Mexico's smart set found little if anything worth retaining in their country's historic culture. Few, in post-Liberal-reform Mexico, had any special concern about traditional Catholicism; they abandoned their peninsular heritage because Spain's stature in world affairs, even before the disaster of the Spanish-American War, cast a rickety, humped shadow; they rejected folkways of food and fashion that seemed increasingly quaint, so they exchanged sombreros and ponchos, except on holidays (when they wanted to maintain a link to their past), for homburgs and business suits with vests; men shaved drooping moustaches, preferring muttonchop whiskers; white bread replaced tortillas in better homes.

Thus they began to create a Victorian society of consumers characterized by what Thorstein Veblen called ostentatious consumption of goods and leisure that would demonstrate their personal, if not Mexico's, wealth and reputation.[11] In their rush to reveal that they indeed possessed modern qualities, the self-defined chic socialites discarded many of the old ways of celebrating. The smart set no longer observed holidays as they and their ancestors had done, because those festivals seemed old fashioned and could not sufficiently serve to proclaim the status and wealth of the new rich. Community ceremonies languished, even in the small towns where a remnant of the cargo system barely hung on. In place of these communal activities that once offered the opportunity for townspeople to renew and affirm their general agreement on public virtue and the good life, the smart set turned to rituals associated with the life cycle—those that anthropologists identify as rites of passage—to display their prominence in society.[12]

The individual's rites received family celebration, usually staged for the community to witness but only from a distance. Births resulted in lavish celebrations of christening. Saints' days offered the opportunity for large private parties. *Quince años galas* became elaborate affairs for well-to-do fathers, who preened beside their well-turned-out daughters. Weddings became occasions for displays of wealth. All these events allowed bystanders to collect outside the family home or the church, though they did not participate in the activities. Even somber obsequies called for family mourning in front of watchers at the gate and along the street to the cemetery. All in all, for the Porfirian smart set, family celebrations of holidays for individuals replaced general community events.

Wealthy and powerful persons no longer sought affirmation of their prestige and status through the organization and financial sponsorship of community celebrations. As a result, these festivals languished, or at least fell into the hands of bureaucrats. Those who were literate could read about the private parties or they could gather outside the churches, halls, and homes to catch a glimpse of the select who were in attendance. But they watched as spectators, not as fellow citizens involved in the proper performance of a shared event. As family observances became more conspicuous during the Porfirian years they became the major source of reportage on newspaper society pages. The individual thus triumphed over the community.

Ostentation through consumption replaced community ceremonial sponsorship as the measure of social status. Private celebration of holidays reflected the individual character of economic activities as opportunities for personal profits increased dramatically during the dictatorship. These occasions were soon graphically recorded by the new practice of photography. Governor Manuel Alarcón of Morelos, for example, hired H. F. Schlattman, the popular U.S. photographer of capitaline society, to photograph his daughter's wedding. Photographers promptly became as essential as servants at any social gathering.[13]

The two-dimensional memory offered by photographs induced Mexicans to indulge in more expensive clothing, coaches, and furnishings so that, when posterity examined their immortality in black and white, they would not be found gauche, common, or, worst of all, traditional and therefore backward. Society-page descriptions similarly encouraged lavish consumption. Moreover, when the *tarjeta de visita*—the calling cards first used during the Maximillian era—began incorporating photographs less expensively, the elite made them all the rage as they collected and exchanged those of leading members of society. Díaz often concluded interviews by distributing signed photographs of himself or posing for pictures taken by guests with their own cameras.[14]

Private celebration of what had been community occasions occurred as well. The solemnization of Good Friday, or the Friday of Sorrows, underwent a dramatic change during the Porfirian era. To the strict religious observances of earlier years, the Porfirians of the 1880s added privately held dances. Performances of the operas *Carmen* and *La Traviata* resulted in the popularity of the Habanera, described as an obscene dance of Cuban slaves. Parties on the evening of Good Friday soon became occasions for the elite to try dancing the Habanera. Bon-ton couples who performed the bawdy dance flouted Lenten strictures that called for fasting and penitence.

Individualism created the self-serving sense of community responsibility, the sense of performing before an audience that, appreciative or not, needed an example of modern life. Díaz's birthday became one of the most important national holidays as he encouraged observance of his saint's day, September 15, to take advantage of its coincidence with the Independence Day celebration, linking the two. In this way his birthday became one of the most lavish celebrations for the capital's high society.

Honoring Díaz's birthday in 1891, a committee composed of the nation's most important government and business leaders arranged a remarkable formal dinner, concert, and dance for some five hundred guests, including municipal presidents from across the country, in the National Theater. Only honored males had seats at the tables arranged on the theater floor, although their wives and daughters enjoyed the event from theater boxes. The elaborate menu, presented in French, featured Spanish sherry followed by seven French wines and concluded with Cognac Martell. The concert, on the other hand, featured Italian composers, especially Gioacchino Rossini. The celebration included decorating the city's major streets, particularly the Avenida de Plateros, which was adorned with an elegant portal whose columns were covered with moss while beautiful and fragrant flowers covered the arch. Along the street, merchants placed posts covered with moss at intervals, displaying floral coats of arms, streamers, and tricolor flags; from one post to another waved garlands of cypress dotted with flowers. All the houses on Plateros and on San Francisco Street featured flags, streamers, and garlands, while all the public buildings in the city displayed flags and streamers. The gaudiest (or at least the most elaborate) flower displays decorated the Spanish and National Casinos and the Jockey Club. Similar celebrations, which also included the inauguration of new public works or private factories, marked the president's birthday until 1910.[15]

This celebration set an example for others, confirmed in their status as celebrities by their membership in the Jockey Club, who now had only slightly less ostentatious celebrations of their own anniversaries of birth, marriage, and so forth. While photography served to record these celebrations for the elite, the president required something grander. Soon, the new technology of moving pictures furnished documents of Porfirio's holidays, civic celebrations, and public appearances.[16] Film put even further distance between spectators at the event and the much larger number who became witnesses to the event after the fact and clearly could not influence it in any way. Thus, a privatization of holidays—with emphasis on rites of passage—and the creation of greater social space between the elite and the others followed.

Conspicuous consumption, including private celebrations, not only satisfied one's ego but also served as a goal for the aspirations of the less fortunate—or at least the elite believed this was so. The dictator himself led this social parade under the direction of his wife, Carmen Romero Rubio. Her influence, described at the time as the "bleaching" of the mestizo Porfirio, led to table manners, fashionable haberdashery, and chic celebrations of birthdays and anniversaries. Each of these fiestas featured special meals that soon became part of each family's heritage as the matriarch became the guardian of special recipes and oversaw the preparation and serving of the feast. While Mexican society for years had developed festival foods, such as the *calavera*-shaped breads and cookies for the Day of the Dead, these family recipes created space for variations on traditional (that is, colonial) dishes such as the different moles, religious concoctions such as the Virgin's Tears (a beet-juice drink prepared during Holy Week), and the de rigueur tamales of the Christmas season.[17]

Women of the elite followed the example of Doña Carmen, stressing manners, fashion, and the elaborate etiquette possible only to those with servant staffs and unlimited leisure. Charities and devotions, especially those associated with great expenditure, allowed public performances by these ladies in imported European fashions. Of all these efforts, nothing rivaled the fund-raising of Doña Carmen that finally climaxed in the crowning of the Virgin of Guadalupe in 1895. Not only did crowning the Virgin give Mexicans a new religious holiday, but it also prompted an expanded celebration of December 12, the Virgin's Day. In addition to the customary pilgrimages and devotions, such as villagers journeying to the shrine and penitents crawling on their knees for blocks to reach the basilica, new ways of celebrating the holy day appeared as well. The capital's well-to-do followed the example of the governor of the Federal District, Pedro Rincón Gallardo, who decorated his home with electric lights that he burned through the night of December 12. His neighbors, the Escandón family, and other fashionable Mexicans adopted the practice and added a variety of decorations to the electric illumination. Nearly every household had a dinner to honor a family member of close relationship who bore the name Guadalupe, and the custom became firmly established that this dinner require a meal of turkey mole. The circle around Doña Carmen inaugurated a number of charitable and devotional activities, all done so that the wives could perform for their husbands, to quote Veblen's inimitable prose, "such an amount of vicarious consumption of time and sustenance as is demanded by the standard of pecuniary decency."[18]

Few Mexicans, men or women, would accept the English aphorism that "clothes make the man." The majority might accept something like "clothes, carriage, possessions, property, and celebrations, including holiday excursions, make the man and his family." Photographs from the era show an increasingly European appearance in the clothes of the smart set; newspaper advertisements mirror the same development with announcements of imported suits, hats, shoes, and cravats. Veblen found fashion to be an expression of exaggerated consumption guided by the desire for social recognition that he identified as "pecuniary repute."[19]

Certainly, people on the margins of this "smart society" recognized it by its clothing. When the Oaxaca state government passed a new tax on villagers in 1896, San Juan Quiahiji led several Indian towns in a rebellion that aimed at expelling the oppressors they identified as "wearing pants." Once this "War Against the Pants" had been put down, federal troops executed the leaders, and, as a general punishment, the jefe político ordered villagers to adopt pants as well.[20]

Devout female socialites helped restore the church to prominence. Thus the church, bold from its new rapprochement with the Porfirian government in the 1890s and coincident with new and expanded civic celebrations and the emergence of more important personal holidays, renewed and expanded its festivities as well. The church's new vigor appeared in the form of new dioceses created during the Porfirian years and an increase in the number of Jesuit Fathers (39 in 1876 to 338 in 1910) in the country.[21] But the church's reemergence appeared most clearly in the campaign to crown the Virgin of Guadalupe that succeeded in 1895.

Had Veblen examined the end-of-century society in Mexico rather than in the United States for the inspiration to write about conspicuous consumption, he would have written the same book indeed.

PORFIRIAN GUADALAJARA

National patterns, especially as found in Mexico City, had slightly different and often more revealing twists in other cities. Guadalajara's ayuntamiento worked with Jalisco's governor in the selection of a junta patriótica—a committee of private citizens and public officials—to organize its civic celebrations. Using funds from both the city and the state and contributions from guilds, occupations groups, and government workers, this committee, like the Mexico City organization, devoted its greatest efforts to Independence Day, May 5 (Cinco de Mayo), and Constitution Day.[22]

Until the mid-1890s the patriotic committee collected funds to augment its small budget provided by the city council, usually with matching funds from the state treasury. The committee's president designated fund-raisers and the groups that each should solicit. These lists indicate what members of the community were expected to participate in the celebration. Here the impact of social stratification becomes most apparent. For example, the committee directing the 1877 Independence Day celebration raised the requisite monies by combining its allocation from the treasury ($412.38) with donations ($226.71). Physicians led the list of contributors, although some doctors identified by name gave nothing. Other contributors included federal, state, and local government bureaucrats and small shopkeepers.[23]

This pattern of celebrating Independence Day and Cinco de Mayo, the major holidays in Guadalajara, continued into the 1880s, with the committee swinging a wider net to collect funds. The list of prospective contributors in 1882 included federal and state bureaucrats, city employees, the police, the army garrison (both officers and common soldiers), and owners of shops and businesses.[24] A decade later, collection reached its highest point with the appointment of solicitors who raised monies from the Spanish, French, American, German, Italian, and Scandinavian colonies ($315.00), dry goods and general shopkeepers ($30.00), the jefe político and police ($57.01), grocers ($13.50), artisans ($88.23), clergy ($27.30), landowners, agriculturalists, and industrialists ($68.50), government employees ($45.00), lawyers ($18.75), doctors ($25.00), legislative representatives ($12.00), and judicial employees ($23.00). Altogether, in 1892 the committee received over $1,500 in donations.[25]

Especially noticeable is the absence of the archbishop and church officials as contributors before the 1890s. This serves as another indication of the timing of the rapprochement between church and state and the disregard for Liberal efforts to keep the church out of public life during the high years of the Porfirian regime. In 1892 the archbishop and his cathedral chapter donated to the fund for the Independence and Cinco de Mayo celebrations.

But we can see the shadow of Guadalajara's smart set at mid-decade. Beginning in 1895 the junta patriótica became a committee of the city council and the celebrations underwent dramatic changes. The Independence Day celebration had traditionally been held in the Plaza de Armas and the Plaza Constitución, located within a block of each other, with serenades, dramatic presentations, awards to outstanding students, and, in the evening, a torchlight parade ending in one plaza or the other followed by fireworks and a dance.

Beginning in 1895 the celebration underwent numerous changes, and the year 1895 itself offers a striking example: the evening torchlight parade was replaced by an afternoon parade of decorated carriages and floats. This alteration offers an intriguing look at Guadalajara's Porfirian smart set. Torchlight parades throughout the nineteenth century were closely associated with liberty and patriotism. Perhaps Tapatío (the nickname for residents of the Jalisco state) Porfirians sought in some general way to restrict all symbolic emblems of the values that might challenge their authority (especially as that authority came to represent less freedom of action and more slavish mimicry of European culture). Perhaps this change merely represented an adoption of European activities, such as the grand bicycle and float parades of contemporary Germany, which, in an ironic twist, were the celebrations of that country's socialist workers.[26]

This grand paseo was followed by bicycle races organized by the Club Atlético Jaliscense in the Alameda. The holiday, for the most part, was decentralized, with events organized by the police chief of each of the city's five precincts. The decentralized celebration limited the citywide torchlight parade, making the maintenance of order easier. Another revealing addition to the program was the collection of funds, clothing, and toys for distribution to poor children and families in each precinct. (Principals were instructed to submit lists of the poorest children in their schools.) This policy did give new life to community volunteerism as society ladies got together to organize donations to the less fortunate and to sponsor medical and self-help programs for the poor.

Funds were no longer solicited for the celebration; rather, the committee sent representatives who ordered community groups to build floats for the afternoon parades held in the different precincts. These representatives, who decided what kind of float each group should build and then directed its construction, were lawyers or bureaucrats.

The guilds no longer marched as collections of artisans with skills and prestige important to the community. Instead, after 1895 their floats had a general marketing message, announcing products that Guadalajara had available for the Mexican or even international market. Guild members were only along through their association with the product. The parades in this way created commodities out of what once had been celebrants. By the end of the decade in Mexico City, floats featuring industrial products sponsored by companies and foreign colonies had become part of the president's birthday celebration. Guild members continued to build Guadalajara's floats until the end of the century. Nevertheless, the celebration had become a peripatetic trade fair.[27]

A similar procession, organized by the Mexican and Mexican-American community, occurred in Tucson, Arizona. The fiesta became a celebration of middle-class values and a vehicle with which to praise Mexico. Women were made into idealized representations of virtue, and floats presented evidence of capitalist progress in Porfirian Mexico and among Mexican-Americans.[28] The celebration reveals how fiestas can present and represent a number of ideas and points of view at the same time.

The change in Guadalajara embodied a major alteration. The celebration was a kind of cultural equivalent of what Hanna Pitkin calls "descriptive representation." Before, the constituent groups in the community actually had presented themselves, rather than abstract symbols, for public view so that celebration re-presented the urban population, forming a detailed, descriptive portrait of Guadalajara's social structure.[29] Now they appeared as symbols—as wealth and prestige for the smart set.

The bon ton in Guadalajara shared the same goals as Mexico City's elites, moving toward personal celebrations and seeking more hygienic streets. In the mid-1890s the city council began hosting holiday celebrations for members of the incumbent regime—that is, regular celebrations of President Díaz's birthday, the anniversary of Governor Miguel Ahumada's inauguration in Jalisco, and so forth. In a measure to centralize activities in Guadalajara, Nicolás Espoña, the jefe político, informed the ayuntamiento that he wanted to review all licenses for public diversions and amusements in order to ensure public order.[30] This, of course, led to further regularization of these celebrations, making them more trivial and creating even more order that destroyed their value as outlets for the energies of youth, class, and ethnic groups.

Celebrations revealed the changing role of gender. Women such as the wives and daughters of city aldermen began to play some part in the celebrations beginning in the 1890s. They distributed clothing and toys to poor children identified in each precinct—making females the living metaphors of charity; some young women—today's debutantes—rode floats as symbols of beauty, youth, Jalisco, and Mexico. Some women distributed awards to outstanding students and winners of literary contests, again acting as emblems of the universal mother who rewards those who make outstanding efforts.

Nearly every contingent in civic celebrations reflected a male social or occupational role. Women were icons who represented national unity, the Mexican states, liberty, and, above all, motherhood. Denied a political role in society, women served as the symbols of unity, of a society free of fractious politics and economic divisions.[31] This creation of female icons reached its height with the crowning of the Virgin of Guadalupe in 1895.

CONCLUSION

The Porfirians wanted to dismiss traditional public celebrations because they expressed what modern bureaucrats regarded as primitive disorder and licentious freedom. The Porfirian, Veblenesque government substituted bicycle parades and military displays, both of which demonstrated order and hierarchy, bureaucracy and authority.[32] These celebrations had a didactic purpose, teaching lessons of the regime's conceptions of virtue. Everyone, the government demanded, should witness these displays; one announcement, for example, called for "everyone, the poor as well as the rich, the young as well as the old, men as well as women, and the great as well as the ordinary," to be present for holidays.[33]

In part, the Porfirian effort came as a consequence of trying to invent traditions, to give the regime a history. Celebration of historical events fixed the festivity in time and called for some representation of the affair (Cinco de Mayo, for example, is indeed celebrated on May 5). This contradicted the cycle of civil and sacred rituals previously celebrated, whose histories are unimportant to the celebrants but that require performance (which some call presentation) each year. (Carnival and Lent are the best examples.) The distinction appears clearly in the difference between a Judas burning and a bicycle parade. The difference between representation and presentation of events distinguishes between the general participation by the people in the former and the reduction of the people to an audience in the latter.[34] The Porfirian holiday tradition in Mexico encouraged celebrations, as one handbill stated, in which "parents served as an example for their children, teachers for their students, bosses for their workers, and rich for the poor."[35] Both Porfirians and their later revolutionary challengers wanted to control the conduct of these examples to regulate the content of the fiestas and, through them, their lessons of virtue. At stake was the understanding of the nation's historic culture and the formulation of its future, because these celebrations, as Marsha Bol concludes, "mediate between the past and future not only by giving its members a sense of tradition but also by providing continuity into the future."[36]

Public celebrations had been ordered and reordered since the arrival of the Spanish in 1521. These festival occasions included both those sanctioned by the church and state and those of a spontaneous nature. The latter often faced civil or clerical opposition and offered popular opportunities for disorderly merrymaking. The smart set established new and reformed holidays and forms of celebration. These Porfirians, pretending playful abandon, paraded after 1895 in Mexico City and Guadalajara at specified times, in specified order, and representing specified images. Newcomers to the city, many of them scarcely rehabilitated villagers, practiced the etiquette of urban living in public, if only as appreciative, well-behaved bystanders.[37]

Of course, regional elites in the larger cities throughout the republic quickly took up these new forms of holiday festivities. By 1906 the notables in Mérida hosted a procession in honor of Porfirio Díaz entitled the "Paseo Histórico." Floats passed by the huge crowd in a moving display of Mexico's history, ending in the glory of the Porfirian regime. The president, represented by a bronze bust, traveled through the capital accompanied by Industry, Liberty, Peace, and the liberal arts, as the icons of progress.[38] Residents of other state capitals and major towns witnessed these new holiday celebrations, which Thorstein Veblen recognized as well. For the time, Porfirians controlled public places and festivities. After 1910 the revolutionaries, particularly through their educational policies and anticlerical campaigns, tried to capture and manipulate the use of public space and the rituals of holidays.[39]

NOTES

1. Pope Gregory XVI, "Breve Pontificio sobre diminución de Días festivas en la República Mexicana," May 16, 1839, published as decree number 104, September 14, 1839, by the Mexican government in parallel Latin and Spanish. Rare Book Collection, Latin American Library, Tulane University.

2. This does not mean that no fire hazard existed in Mexico City. During the Porfirian years, fires were a major threat to life and property and were fully reported in *El Siglo XIX*. See Mikhail Bakhtin, *Rabelais and His World*, trans. Helene Iswolsky (Cambridge, MA, 1965), for the general European campaign to suppress festivals.

3. See Barbara Tenenbaum's essay (Chapter 7) in this volume; the quotation comes from p. 135.

4. Francisco Sosa, *Las estatuas de la Reforma* (México, 1974).

5. Joseph Rykwert points out that the street has always possessed an importance beyond its apparent use, "witnessed by innumerable appearances in proverbs: everybody knows that the path to salvation is straight and the gate is narrow." See his essay "The Street: The Use of Its History," in *On Streets*, ed. Stanford Anderson (Cambridge, MA, 1978), 22. In that volume, see also Anthony Vidler, "The Scenes of the Street: Transformation in Ideal and Reality, 1750–1871," 30.

6. APD, see documentos 002708-002710 in 1885 Bundle; see the correspondence of Thomas B. Lewis, who incorporated in New York City a land development company for properties along the Reforma. My thanks to John Hart, who brought these documents to my attention.

7. Rykwert, "The Street," 170–71; Thomas P. Hughes, *Networks of Power: Electrification in Western Society, 1880–1930* (Baltimore, 1983), 1–2.

8. Ayuntamiento de México, "Paseos," *Discursos y memoria documentada, 1896*, 166–67.

9. Stephen S. Hall, "Standing on those Corners, Watching All the Folks Go By," *Smithsonian* (February 1989): 123.

10. Street entertainment and the culture it helped inculcate deserves much greater attention than the few comments it has received here. Robert M. Isherwood offers a provocative introduction in "Entertainment in the Parisian Fairs in the Eighteenth Century," *Journal of Modern History* 53 (March 1981): 24–48.

11. Thorstein Veblen, *The Theory of the Leisure Class: An Economic Study of Institutions* (1899; reprint ed. New York, 1934), 84–85.

12. This argument follows Stanley Brandes, *Power and Persuasion: Fiestas and Social Control in Rural Mexico* (Philadelphia, 1988), 54–55.

13. For early photography and photographers, see *The Two Republics*, January 18, 1874; and *Mexico City Herald*, February 17, 1896.

14. Robert M. Levine, *Images of History: Nineteenth- and Early Twentieth-Century Latin American Photographs as Documents* (Durham, NC, 1989), 28–29; William Schell, Jr., "Integral Outsiders, Mexico City's American Colony (1876–1911): Society and Political Economy in Porfirian Mexico" (Ph.D. dissertation, University of North Carolina, 1992), 22–23. A small collection of these *tarjetas de visita* exists at the Amon Carter Museum in Fort Worth, Texas.

15. Gabriel Villanueva, *Las fiestas en honor del Sr. General Porfirio Díaz: Crónica completa* (México, 1891). Compare this celebration with the colonial Corpus Christi festival discussed by Linda A. Curcio-Nagy in Chapter 1 of this volume; see also Tony Morgan's essay (Chapter 8).

16. See William H. Beezley, "Popular Culture," in *Twentieth-Century Mexico*, ed. W. Dirk Raat and William H. Beezley (Lincoln, NE, 1986), 35.

17. For a study of a contemporary elite family, its private holidays, and the extensive family responsibilities—including supervision of holiday feasts, assumed by women within the family—see Larissa Adler Lomnitz and Marisol Perez-Lizar, *A Mexican Elite Family, 1820–1980* (Princeton, NJ, 1987), 36, 118, 120, 157–91. For a brief description of four generations of family celebrations and a volume of recipes, see Patricia Quintana with Carol Harrelson, *Mexico's Feast of Life* (Tulsa,

OK, 1989). See also Beverly Bundy, "The Tamale Tradition," *Fort Worth Star-Telegram*, December 18, 1991.

18. *Mexican Herald*, December 13, 1895; Veblen, *Theory*, 118.

19. *Ibid.*, 167–87.

20. James B. Greenberg, *Santiago's Sword: Chatino Peasant Religion and Economics* (Berkeley, CA, 1981), 51.

21. *The New Catholic Encyclopedia*, IX, 779.

22. See the reports of the junta patriótica in the Ramo of diversiones civicas, Archivo General Municipal, Guadalajara (hereinafter cited as AGM).

23. AAG, 1887, Caja 1224, Paquete 142, Expediente 109.

24. AAG 1882, Paquete 150, Expediente 8.

25. AAG 1892, Caja 1247, Paquete 165, Expediente 39, Fiestas cívicas y diversiones.

26. Vernon L. Lidtke, *The Alternative Culture: Socialist Labor in Imperial Germany* (New York, 1985), 75–101.

27. Roger D. Abrahams argues that parades quickly become advertisements for business in the United States, building on the frontier tradition where they were organized to show off newly arrived products from the East. Thus, the experience became "a symbolization of the forward march of commerce and industry." See "The Language of Festivals: Celebrating the Economy," in *Celebration: Studies in Festivity and Ritual*, ed. Victor Turner (Washington, DC, 1982), 161–77; the quotation is found on p. 175. Also see Tony Morgan's essay (Chapter 8) in this volume. On the general topic of the development of the commercial character of holidays in the United States, see Leigh Eric Schmidt, "The Commercialization of the Calendar: American Holidays and the Culture of Consumption, 1870–1930," *Journal of American History* 78, no. 3 (December 1991): 887–916.

28. Ellen M. Litwicki, "From *Patrón* to *Patria*: *Fiestas* and *Mexicano* Identity in Late Nineteenth-Century Tucson" (paper presented April 4, 1992, at the annual meeting of the Organization of American History).

29. Ryan, "American Parade," 137–38; Hanna Fenichel Pitkin, *The Concept of Representation* (Berkeley, CA, 1967).

30. AAG, 1889, Caja 1244, Paquete 162, Expediente 18, Espoña to Ayuntamiento, January 26, 1889.

31. Ryan, "American Parade," 148–50.

32. Iu. M. Lotman, "Theater and Theatricality in the Order of Early Nineteenth-Century Culture," in *Semiotics and Structuralism: Readings from the Soviet Union*, ed. Henryk Baran (White Plains, NY, 1974), 33–63, esp. 48–49.

33. Independence Announcement, 1889; AGM 1889, Caja 1244, Paquete 162, Expediente 124.

34. Samuel Kinser has a well-thought-out discussion of this topic in his article, "Presentation and Representation: Carnival at Nuremberg, 1450–1550," *Representations* 13 (Winter 1986): 1–41, esp. p. 6, and n. 14.

35. Independence Announcement, 1889; AAG, 1889, Caja 1244, Paquete 162, Expediente 124.

36. "The Making of a Festival," in Eliot Porter and Ellen Auerbach, *Mexican Celebrations* (Albuquerque, NM, 1990), 114.

37. Ryan, "American Parade," 131–53.

38. Rafael de Zayas Enríquez, *El Estado de Yucatán. Su pasado, su presente, su provenir* (New York, 1908), 325–27.

39. For revolutionary celebrations, see the subsequent essays in this volume; Evon Z. Vogt and Suzanne Abel, "On Political rituals in Contemporary Mexico," in *Secular Ritual*, ed. Sally F. Moore and Barbara G. Myerhoff (Amsterdam, 1977), 173–88, esp. 174–77; and Ilene V. O'Malley, *The Myth of the Revolution: Hero Cults and the Institutionalization of the Mexican State, 1920–1940* (New York, 1986).

10

Progreso Forzado: *Workers and the Inculcation of the Capitalist Work Ethic in the Parral Mining District*

William E. French
University of British Columbia

One of this volume's editors, William French uses a Chihuahua mining district as a case study of the completion of the Enlightenment Project in the late nineteenth century. His work draws on E. P. Thompson and Daniel Roche as he develops the discourse shaping work and moral behavior as part of the competition over public space and popular diversions. His analysis examines the contest that emerged when workers, as they developed and displayed their understanding of appropriate and satisfying behavior, often violated middle-class values, especially of fashion and luxury. Protecting their way of life, workers, the author demonstrates, often resorted to what James C. Scott termed the "weapons of the weak." The essay contributes to the comparative literature of the struggle over inculcation of capitalist conceptions of work, time, and leisure, the formation of gender, and the representation of self and resistance (through fashion, for example) to new social strictures.

William French received his graduate degrees from the Universities of Calgary (M.A.) and Texas (Ph.D.), where he mastered as well "the stomach Steinway of the popular classes" (the accordian)—an essential instrument in Mexican *norteño* music.

D URING THE PORFIRIATO, mining in northern Mexico became a capital-intensive proposition. Managers of large industrial establishments, known as extractories, stretching from the coal faces of northern Coahuila to the copper mines of Sonora, expanded gross output, implemented economies of scale, and embarked on a more thorough division of labor. Utilizing labor-saving machinery, including compressed-air drills, aerial trams, and mechanical crushers,

managers eliminated jobs and hired recent arrivals from the countryside to replace miners skilled in the use of traditional technology.
Many of these new entrants to the industrial labor force maintained
their links to the land, combining subsistence agriculture with seasonal wage labor in the mines and on the railroads. To mold these
peasant-workers into a disciplined and subordinated work force, managers utilized force, economic incentives, and paternalism. The transition to industrial capitalism in northern Mexico, as in many areas
of the world, took time—even generations—as it entailed the spurn-
ing of one culture and the absorption of another.[1]

Local, state, and national elites aided managers in the task of
transforming campesinos into wage laborers. Committed to the ideal
of economic progress, Porfirian rulers established new police forces
and passed measures to eliminate vice and popular celebrations. In
Chihuahua, for example, a new police force known as the Cuerpo de
Policia Rural, organized in 1902 and funded by contributions from
mining companies, escorted pay shipments to mining sites, maintained
order on paydays, and attempted to stop workers from drinking, gambling, and behaving in a disorderly manner.[2] Throughout Mexico, but
especially in the north, those in the middle class championed moral
reform in hopes of stimulating what they referred to as moral regeneration in the rest of society. Between 1900 and 1910 district and
municipal officials in Hidalgo District, Chihuahua, following the lead
of the state government in Ciudad Chihuahua, regulated gambling,
fairs, circuses, leisure activities, brothels, and the sale and consumption of alcohol. In place of these popular activities they hoped to
inculcate the values of thrift, sobriety, hygiene, and punctuality in
succeeding generations of workers. These authorities attempted mostly
to preserve public space and the street for middle-class Mexicans,
the *gente decente* (decent folk).[3]

Such a developmentalist agenda did not originate with the Mexican bourgeoisie of the late nineteenth century. As Susan Deans-Smith
makes clear in her essay in this volume (Chapter 3), a century earlier
Bourbon officials, in addition to imposing work discipline in the tobacco manufactories, had also attempted to reorder and reclaim public space in an effort to change popular practices and attitudes. They
stressed in their "moralizing discourse" that good workers were synonymous with obedient servants of the state. Successive governments
after Independence followed Bourbon precedents and utilized education to instill values of work, thrift, and initiative in future generations and attempted to reserve urban space for their exclusive use.
Working-class Mexicans in the nineteenth and twentieth centuries,
like their counterparts in the colonial tobacco factories, continued to
make streets and workplaces contested terrain. They asserted their

own values in these spaces while adopting, refashioning, and, often, thumbing their noses at officially prescribed behavior.

MINING IN HIDALGO DISTRICT, CHIHUAHUA

In the late nineteenth and early twentieth century, campesinos from nearby agricultural villages, such as Valle de Zaragoza and Balleza, joined migrants from Zacatecas and other Mexican states in the mining camps of Parral, Santa Bárbara, and Minas Nuevas (later renamed Villa Escobedo), all located in Hidalgo District. Here, the American Smelting and Refining Company and other, mostly foreign, mining companies employed them to mine the extensive deposits of low-grade silver ore that characterized the district. Instead of extracting ore with hammers and bars, black powder, and rawhide sacks, increasingly mine workers used the latest technology, operating compressed-air drills and blasting ore with dynamite. They toiled in mines equipped with electrical lighting, steam-powered hoists, and modern drainage pumps. Mule-drawn *arrastras* and the patio system of mercury amalgamation of milling gave way to giant mechanical crushers and new ore-refining methods. Technology transformed the mining industry and managers demanded more obedient and reliable, although less skilled, mine workers.[4]

Transforming campesinos and men skilled in the old ways into obedient and reliable workers was an uneven process. On the one hand, many workers retained links to subsistence agriculture, thus avoiding complete dependence on wages and the workings of the market. They infuriated managers by their transience and by dropping their picks and shovels to return home to plant or harvest. According to employers, these workers constituted a floating population that did not take a serious interest in mining but quit once they had a bag of beans and a pot of cornmeal in the house.[5] Many left their jobs to search for higher-paying ones in the United States.[6] On the other hand, some workers became completely dependent on earning a wage. Those acquiring new skills as winch operators or compressed-air drillers often began attending night schools and dressing like their social superiors. They aspired, above all else, to be recognized as members of middle-class society. Accepting and refashioning the tenets of the moralizing discourse, they often used the streets and other public spaces to violate regulations governing public behavior and proclaim their equality.

Although access to nonwage alternatives divided mine workers, common experiences, including dependence on foreign capital markets and the world-market price of silver, united them. Workers in Hidalgo District experienced several periods of boom and bust. In Parral, for example, mining boomed from 1895 to 1903, and the total population grew to sixteen thousand inhabitants. A downturn between 1904 and 1906 forced over five thousand residents to search elsewhere for work. The worst was yet to come; economic downturn in late 1907 led to an exodus of mine workers. By the end of 1909, the population in Parral had diminished to half its 1903 total.[7] Workers also shared constant danger. Mines claimed the lives of workers in premature explosions, late explosions in drill holes, equipment failures, inexperienced winch operators, falling timber and rock, floods, and falls. Three or four workers died each month of 1905, for example, in La Palmilla mine alone. The following year the local newspaper concluded that once workers went below ground they were in imminent danger of never returning. Workers agreed. In a letter to the editor, one worker claimed that miners deserved better treatment from company stores because they placed their lives in danger every day they worked.[8]

After their shifts, mine workers in Hidalgo District returned to communities composed of other workers and their families. Miners near Santa Bárbara, rather than live in town, built houses and rented rooms in their own barrio, known as El Ultimo Esfuerzo, near the mines. Although only a kilometer from the center of town, the barrio was described by local officials as remote and isolated. Apart from workers and their families, few lived in these communities. In the larger towns such as Villa Escobedo, where workers comprised an overwhelming proportion of the population, even in bad years municipal authorities spent little on public assistance. Those with no intention of working were not welcome, and men finding themselves out of a job had little choice but to leave town to search elsewhere for work. Even in Parral workers lived in barrios removed from the city center. Many rented rooms in poorly constructed adobe houses that were small and isolated and lacked latrines and running water. Most rented on a short-term basis as fluctuations in the mining economy made for a migratory existence.[9]

The work experience created shared assumptions concerning the work process and the value of worker contribution to production, and wages and daily life in miner barrios contributed to common attitudes about personal worth and the right to attend fairs and hold popular celebrations. Moreover, the popular perception of individual rights inherited from nineteenth-century Mexican liberalism informed workers' responses to capitalism and the Mexican state. By drawing on these experiences and beliefs, a heterogeneous work force made sense of the new circumstances of industrial labor and life in the mines.

WORKERS RESPOND TO THE NEW ORDER

Similar conditions in the mining towns in the neighboring state of
Sonora, according to Ramón Eduardo Ruiz, undermined the traditional foundations of life, eroded the social structure, and weakened
society's fabric—all to the detriment of the miner. Economic change
broke down rural values of home and family as "workers left behind
safe, familiar communities more conducive to family life" for life in
mining towns where they found solace in drink, gambling, and prostitutes.[10] That they committed crimes and indulged in vice confirms,
for Ruiz, the decadence of the new American-introduced cultural and
economic order.[11]

Like their counterparts in Sonora, mine workers in Hidalgo District drank, gambled, and frequented brothels. Local officials in the
mining camp of Los Azules consistently described worker behavior
as scandalous and immoral. On paydays workers gathered to drink
and gamble on games prohibited by law—games such as *ruleta*,
chuzas, *frontones*, *tatemados*. On one occasion in 1904 the chief of
public security interrupted a drinking spree and threw thirty-six workers into jail. The *presidente municipal* (of Villa Escobedo) reported
frequent nocturnal disturbances during which drinking workers shot
off their pistols. Paydays in San Francisco del Oro became occasions
for drinking and gambling that local authorities could only describe
as scandalous—prompting them to prohibit liquor sales. Workers jour-
neyed to Santa Bárbara to purchase large quantities of mescal and
frustrated local officials by drinking and committing scandals within
their own homes. In the isolated railroad construction camps of
Hidalgo District, workers celebrated paydays with alcohol, horse
racing, and cockfighting.[12]

Far from being limited to the mining camps and other areas ex-
periencing U.S. investment, this same behavior was apparent in agricultural municipalities throughout Hidalgo District. Ruiz's lament of
the breakdown of traditional social values ignores the fact that these
"vices" often characterized traditional, moral society as well. Whether
predominantly mining or agricultural, areas without a police presence experienced popular carousing. In the small ranchos surrounding Balleza, for example, local authorities found it impossible to
suppress the clandestine sale of alcohol. Drinking in such isolated
areas led to daily scandals and crimes. The owner of the nearby Hacienda de San Juán, M. Gamboa, regularly complained that his employees failed to show up to work because they were drunk. In 1909
open gambling took place during Balleza's annual fiesta. State officials were astounded that their local counterparts had sanctioned the
establishment of prohibited card games and betting. State authorities

also accused several ayuntamientos of allowing the distillation of *mezcal sotol* to take place on common lands. In another agricultural community in the district, Valle de Zaragoza, continuous clandestine alcohol sales occurred on haciendas and ranchos. Residents of San Antonio del Tule, Huejotitan, and Rosario, where legal and illegal alcohol sales were rife, petitioned for relief from the disorders, obscene shouts, and even pistol shots that accompanied drinking sprees. As in the mining towns, petitioners stated that such scandals jeopardized family life and threatened to corrupt future generations.[13]

In mining and agricultural communities alike, what authorities described as a "scandal" followed a set script. First, carousers claimed the streets either to parade or dance. In one celebrated incident in Valle de Zaragoza, for example, participants mocked another citizen through dance before marching through the city streets. On another occasion, in Santa Bárbara, a group of drinking workers paraded through the streets accompanied by music (to the great chagrin of their self-described "peaceful neighbors").[14] Loud, "inappropriate" noises marked the next phase of the scandal. Often, revelers shouted insults or obscenities or sang loudly. Pistol shots inevitably followed. Insults, if they were traded, almost always challenged the masculinity of bystanders and local officials. In the Valle de Zaragoza scandal, for example, drinkers shouted "death to cowards" while marching through the streets. In Huejotitan another transgressor of public order challenged observers to "grab him if they were men." One recalcitrant individual in Santa Bárbara repeatedly performed this ritual: drunk and with pistol in hand, he would ride through the streets, threatening and cursing those he met, entering stores on horseback, and committing—according to local officials—every class of abuse.[15]

Through scandal the laboring folk in Hidalgo District rejected elite notions of the social order. Officials perceived these actions as scandalous because, along with the district's more "respectable" residents, they regarded public space in moral terms. As *casas de tolerancia* (brothels) were the centers of immorality, so *casas de respeto* (respectable houses) embodied virtue; for the *gente decente*, space itself possessed moral characteristics. Middle-class Mexicans envisioned an urban geography of vice and attempted to remove brothels, cantinas, and popular recreations from city centers. In the mining towns of Santa Bárbara and Villa Escobedo, for example, officials designated specific zones for the sale of alcohol and the location of brothels. Parral officials, in addition to attacking vice, also attempted to eliminate unfenced lots and other sites where transients could gather.[16] As in eighteenth-century France, Hidalgo District officials intended to preserve important public space for the *gente decente* by immobilizing the popular classes in time and space.[17] They believed this could be accomplished by banishing such practices, including drinking, gambling, and other forms of popular recreation, from city centers.

By claiming the street for themselves and violating middle-class notions of respectability, popular carousers rejected the cultural framework through which Porfirian rulers advanced their claim to rule. They asserted a distinct manner of proving their own worthiness. While those belonging to *sociedad culta* (cultured society) divided society into the worthy and the worthless on the basis of family, wealth, and connections, members of the floating and working population accorded personal honor on the basis of force of arms. When discussing a petition sent from Villa Escobedo, the jefe político defined *personas de valer* (worthy people) as merchants, mine owners, and representatives of big mining companies. Those who had signed the petition, including *barreteros y operarios* (mine workers), he described as *de ninguna representación* (of no standing in the community).[18] Resort to arms, the ultimate scandalous act, revealed a distinct measure of worthiness—one that was based on independence and personal honor and the ability to protect these characteristics through the use of force. As one member of the floating population in Hidalgo District put it, "I have a pistol and a rifle with which to prove my worthiness."[19] Honor as a personal virtue could subvert the existing social order.

Moreover, cantinas, billiard halls, and brothels became important centers for the expression of popular culture. These Mexicans, like the popular classes of eighteenth-century Paris, imposed their own rules and mores in the taverns.[20] Despite reformers' efforts to banish brothels and cantinas to specified and limited zones and impose strict closing regulations, they accomplished neither. Outside Parral, in the mining towns of Santa Bárbara and Villa Escobedo, clandestine liquor sales plagued municipal officials despite the creation of new police forces and the restriction of cantinas to specified zones.[21]

In cantinas, billiard halls, and brothels, working-class drinkers rejected the time restrictions advocated by middle-class moralists and municipal officials and imposed their own schedules. After the turn of the century Parral store employees began demanding that merchants close their shops at 1:00 P.M. on Sundays and national holidays. In early 1906 the Hidalgo District jefe político implemented this policy. At the same time, state officials passed legislation requiring those selling intoxicating beverages to close on Sunday afternoons. Cantina and liquor-store owners, in part because of unlicensed and illegal competition, did not hesitate to accommodate drinkers during proscribed hours. Despite the new regulations Parral cantina

employees complained bitterly to the governor that the great majority of their employers disregarded the law and continued to sell liquor after hours and even on Sundays, and that they were forced to
work long into the night.[22] Police reports substantiate their charges.
In mid-1906 police *comandante* Trinidad Torres reported that while
clothing and produce stores closed early on Sunday afternoons, many
cantinas did not. La Internacional, Las Quince Letras, Cantina Verde,
La Central, El Paraíso, Hotel Francés, Gran Central, and two name-
less cantinas all remained open for business.[23]

Brothels proved as impervious to regulation as did cantinas and
billiard halls. Documents in the *Ramo de Tolerancia* provide a description of the legally sanctioned side of the business. Parral ac-
commodated four houses with sixty-nine prostitutes in 1902. By 1906
only twenty-four prostitutes categorized as first class and nineteen as
second class worked in brothels recognized by district authorities,
and, by the end of the following year, five first-class brothels and
two second-class houses employed sixty-eight prostitutes. Sixty
women registered as prostitutes in 1908. While most of these women
were Mexican, some of French, American, and Japanese nationality
described themselves as prostitutes. Regulations also specified the
location of brothels on Calle de Ocampo or on Calle de la Agricultura.[24] Illegal alcohol sales, failure to observe closing regulations,
and scandals frequently took place in regulated brothels. Many women
refused to submit to registration or monthly inspection by health officials; they also refused to carry the *libreta* (record book) required
by law. In late 1909 sixteen Parral brothel owners and registered prostitutes complained to the jefe político that the clandestine exercise of
prostitution was so extensive that they could not make any money.
Those not paying municipal taxes, as in the case of liquor vendors,
provided unfair competition.[25] In all houses of prostitution, as in the
cantinas and billiard halls, the floating and working population ignored the line between legal and illegal and established their own
rules.

Gambling represented another integral part of Hidalgo District
popular culture. On Sundays, holidays, and, increasingly, on paydays,
workers throughout Hidalgo District gambled. Unskilled railroad
workers bet on horses and fighting cocks; others enjoyed games of
chance during fairs and holidays, and entire Tarahumara villages
wagered on the outcomes of long-distance races. Workers also gathered in mining-camp cantinas and billiard halls to gamble on cards.
Municipal authorities in Santa Bárbara reported that gambling occurred every night, especially in one particular cantina. Even making
regular arrests during the last decade of the Porfiriato failed to stop
such behavior.[26] In addition to fairground games and cards, workers

participated in lotteries and raffles. In some cases middle-class Mexicans even sponsored these events. Employees in one Chihuahua City factory, for example, bought raffle tickets for a large cash prize put up by the boss at Christmas.

FESTIVALS AND RITES OF PASSAGE

Personal celebrations provided workers with other opportunities to express themselves and claim public space. The newspaper *El Correo* stated that the majority of those who lived by manual labor spent extravagantly on birthdays, baptisms, and wedding feasts.[27] In mining regions, family ties extended to the workplace (relatives often worked for the same mining contractor or composed a two-man drilling team), further linking workplace and home in festivities corresponding to rites of passage. Important occasions in the lives of individuals enabled workmates to celebrate together while the high death rate in the mining camps prompted workers frequently to petition district officials for the establishment of local cemeteries where their dead could properly be honored. Funerals provided the opportunity for the display of community, rather than class, solidarity. When the wife of mine owner Pedro Alvarado died in 1905, the humblest workers employed in his mine, La Palmilla, paraded her coffin through the streets to the cemetery.[28]

Middle-class observers commented on the expenditures on weddings, baptisms, and birthdays and the luxurious tastes of working-class women. They maintained that anyone observing these women on fair days or at dances and fiestas would conclude, by their dress, that they were persons who enjoyed the comforts of life. In the opinion of these editors this indulgence in luxury misled others, and, more important, caused women to go hungry, age prematurely, and become ill. To middle-class observers, such luxury did not make sense.[29] Mineworker behavior seemed equally illogical. *El Correo* questioned how men who earned their money by risking their lives at such rough work could spend it with such ease, as if it were money earned in gambling. Other observers concurred. American mine managers believed that Mexican workers only wanted to show off their clothes to their neighbors.[30] In Chihuahua, working-class spending habits seemed irrational to more affluent observers.

Public and symbolic demonstrations of a perceived superior lifestyle took place among Chihuahuan workers. By their dress, workers and their families violated, in the evocative phrase coined by Daniel Roche, the social hierarchy of appearances.[31] By doing so, they laid claim to inclusion in refined society. In using clothing to accomplish this end Mexican workers replicated the behavior of their counterparts elsewhere. In her discussion of the formation of the French working class, Michelle Perrot shows that workers' aspirations crystallized around clothing, which became the most rapidly expanding item in the French working-class budget. Dress, the most visible evidence of improvement, drew the most criticism in Mexico as in France. According to Peter Stearns, French manufacturers, dismayed that their employees could afford middle-class clothing for Sundays, spoke disapprovingly of eroding social standards. Workers used clothing to assert an equality of rank that did not exist. After 1860 many middle- and upper-class French citizens expressed outrage at the number of lower-class women dressing like their social betters.[32] Clothing played this same symbolic role in the United States. In 1908 the Ford *Times* mocked the "dude employee" described as wearing "a higher priced hat than his boss," "immaculately neat," and dressed "like a fashion plate." Editors concluded, "The dude employee who wears a high collar is not the one that knuckles down to hard work."[33] In Hidalgo District members of refined society expected clothing to correspond to station in life. Authorities regularly described wanted criminals in terms of their dress. They felt that the statement, "dressed in the clothes of a worker," was sufficient identification. By shedding their work clothes and donning Sunday suits and shoes, workers presented themselves as equal to those in the middle class.[34]

Assertions of equality did not imply that workers considered themselves to be pale imitations of the *gente decente*. Despite the transient nature of the work force and the changing nature of work, aspects of a mine workers' culture flourished. In their own spaces these men constructed chapels and shrines. In the San Pedro mines of Corralitos, Chihuahua, for example, a short passageway led from the mine entrance to a subterranean chapel. Morris Parker, a mine manager, observed that it remained a sacred place of worship often unable to accommodate all those wishing to participate in the various services.[35] In Parral at a later date mine workers recreated the world of the undergound chapel aboveground in the church of Our Lady of Fátima, constructed out of rock taken from the surrounding mines. In this church a large stone slab forms the altar and, in place of conventional lighting, bare electric bulbs protrude from the tips of gnarled wood mounted on the ceiling like chandeliers. The wood, representing tree roots reaching in from aboveground, symbolically transports parishioners into the underground work space.[36] Workers also continued to celebrate their religion in a distinct manner. While descending into the mine they often sang praises to their patron saint in hymns described by a contemporary observer as "dissonant and vulgar, yet tender, sweet, and full of faith."[37]

Like the unique practice of their faith, a distinctive ritual calendar emerged in the mining regions.[38] The most important celebration honored Santa Cruz on the third of May. Although recognized throughout Mexico the day was celebrated principally in Chihuahua. In Santa Eulalia and Santo Domingo mine workers prepared solemn religious functions in honor of their saint. The day had particular significance for residents of Parral, as the city was located at the foot of the Cerro de Santa Cruz. Also in Parral, an annual festival known as the Verbena del Rayo took place beginning on August 11. In nearby Santa Bárbara the community celebrated an annual festival September 5–12.[39] Carnival in both Ciudad Chihuahua and Parral had been the subject of strict governmental regulation in 1902 and 1903; by 1905, *El Correo* rejoiced that the farces of Carnival seemed to have passed into history.[40]

Restrictions on Carnival notwithstanding, the popular revelry associated with it continued. Shortly after the Santa Cruz celebrations in 1903, for example, *La Nueva Era* chastized inhabitants for attending festivals drunk and behaving improperly in public.[41] In another part of the state, Ojinaga, commentators dreaded the arrival of Christmas, which, in their opinion, represented little more to the masses than the opportunity for a month of drinking and gambling.[42] Reporting on the 1901 Christmas fiesta in Parral, *El Correo* noted the absence of the disorders that had characterized previous years and concluded that the culture of the people must be improving—an event truly worth celebrating.[43] The continued expression of such middle-class concern reveals that popular revelry characterized these occasions, turning them into scandals in the opinion of middle-class observers.

Mine owners used these celebrations to advance their own agendas. Pedro Alvarado in Parral seized the ceremony honoring Santa Cruz as an opportunity to cultivate paternalistic bonds with workers. After a morning of music at the Sanctuary of Guadalupe, band performances on the hill of Santa Cruz, and an evening of worship, Alvarado sponsored a display of fireworks in the Porfirio Díaz plaza. Each rocket was adorned with an image of the Holy Virgin, and one carried a cloth banner reading, "Negociación minera de la Palmilla." Afterward, he treated workers to refreshments. *El Correo* estimated that each year Alvarado spent three thousand pesos to sponsor the celebration. At least in 1904, thanks to the vigilance of local authorities and the "proper" behavior of the popular classes, order was maintained at all times. In cultivating such bonds Alvarado harked back to old, rather than new, forms of labor-management relations. In place of Virgin-bearing rockets, refreshments, and paternalistic concern, the American Smelting and Refining Company, and others like it, had offered company stores, schools, and bonuses for regular attendance at work.[44]

State authorities and mine owners also perceived that mutual-aid societies and night schools could be used to influence the behavior of workers. Established in Parral before the turn of the century, the Sociedad Cooperativa de Obreros operated a night school for workers. In 1904, sixty-seven students registered with the school and about thirty-five regularly attended meetings. *La Nueva Era* described in extremely paternalistic terms the society's goal of promoting the instruction and advancement of the working class and reported that it was succeeding in imparting, albeit on a rudimentary basis, knowledge to intelligences that lay in the most complete ignorance.[45] Mutual-aid societies also sponsored night schools for workers. In Santa Bárbara the Sociedad Mutualista de Obreros "Vicente Guerrero" established a school in 1906. In Villa Escobedo the jefe municipal formed a mutal-aid society called Protección del Hogar and promised mine workers medical care and financial assistance if illness prevented them from working.[46] Authorities saw mutual-aid societies and schools as another means of imposing morality and discipline on the working class. Despite these intentions many mining companies in Hidalgo District reported that their workers had not joined such societies.

Elsewhere in the state, those workers who did join found that through such societies they could take action on issues of importance to them. Officials of the Unión de Carpinteros Mexicanos, for example, complained of the treatment they received at the hands of foreign management. Disgruntled carpenters resented the foreign boss not so much because of his nationality but because he discriminated against them at the workplace. Not only did he pay foreign workers twice as much as he paid them, he offered to hire Mexicans only as helpers for the American workers rather than as skilled carpenters.[47] In Cananea, Sonora, the high proportion of American skilled employees and the higher wages paid to them prompted Mexican skilled workers to protest and organize unions. Unmet demands for better pay, promotion, and Mexicanization led workers there to strike in 1906.[48] Before the Mexican Revolution, skilled workers demanded equality of pay and opportunity. Through mutual-aid societies they pursued these goals.

POPULAR PERCEPTIONS AND ATTITUDES

Working conditions led to common goals among skilled workers, and residents of Hidalgo District shared beliefs about the proper role of government. All resented arbitrary local officials. In petitions tailored not to offend state leaders, signers lamented that despite honorable, clean, and just state government, local officials dreamt of absolute power and attempted to become caciques.[49] One petitioner characterized authorities in San Nicolás del Cañón (a place he described as "far from refined society") as ignorant, arbitrary, and lacking in culture and honor. Such officials, in his opinion, stained proper administration by subjecting citizens to brutal and arbitrary acts. As the petition went to state authorities, he made it clear that failure lay with the character of the individual officeholder, not with the system of government, and he expressed confidence that if state authorities could be made aware of the true situation, honorable officials would be appointed.[50] Agricultural workers in Tule de San Antonio de Arévalo made the same point. Although many were unable to sign their petition they demanded a new *comisario de policía* (police commissioner) who would stop bothering them and let them work in peace.[51]

Hidalgo District mine workers concurred. Near the end of the Porfiriato, Parral's jefe político attempted to enforce regulations requiring the installation of new sanitary plumbing in the city's houses. This municipal effort to promote hygiene and cleanliness, including threats of fines for noncompliance, led to a flood of petitions. Describing themselves as workers in Hidalgo District mines, petitioners emphasized their inability to pay for such improvements given the lack of work. Crescencio Sáenz captured the mood of many workers who had managed to acquire small properties when he protested that such compulsion represented *progreso forzado* (forced progress). Sáenz lectured authorities on the true laws of political economy. He envisioned a more humanitarian and moral definition of progress that placed the greatest possible sum of goods with the greatest possible number of individuals. Under this kinder, gentler version of progress the economy would operate in a consensual manner to develop resources without exhausting them. According to Sáenz the jefe político in Hidalgo District was corrupting true progress with his arbitrary and tyrannical local rule in which he treated inhabitants with the arrogance of a sultan.[52] Another petitioner concluded that the merits of a governing authority must be measured by the happiness that their acts and decisions brought to the poor (whom he described as the majority of the people). Given this criterion he concluded that Señor Valles was the most inadequate jefe político ever to rule Hidalgo District.[53]

Petitioners argued that all Mexicans enjoyed fundamental individual rights by virtue of citizenship, and they cited the Constitution of 1857 to support their claims. They resented arbitrary authorities precisely because these officials violated the individual rights guaranteed to them by this hallowed document. José Pallan, Indian *gobernadorcillo* of Guasárachic, believed that the constitution protected individual rights given to all sons of the Mexican soil. Enshrinement of these rights in the constitution gave Pallan "great pride at living in this blessed country."[54] In district ranchos and pueblos, petitioners, referring to the constitution as "our most holy shield" and "the fundamental document of our republic," cited specific articles in support of their claims. Mining-town residents displayed equal familiarity with the constitution. Many informed the police that they could neither be arrested nor harassed unless caught in flagrante delicto. When the jefe político arrested Victorio García, a miner, for murdering his wife, García protested to district judicial officials that the jefe político had violated the individual guarantees as set out in articles 14, 16, and 23 of the 1857 constitution. First, García maintained that he could only be judged and sentenced by a competent tribunal presided over by the judiciary, and not by the jefe político. Second, he asserted that he could not be bothered in his person or home except by virtue of written orders from competent authorities and never by the kind executed by the jefe político. Finally, fearing the *ley fuga* (that is, to be shot while "trying to flee"), he pointed out that the death penalty had been abolished.[55] Another mine worker, who had landed in the Minas Nuevas jail for failure to pay his debts, cited articles 17, 18, and 19 in his defense. Moreover, the seditious barber of Santa Bárbara, León Proa, protested his arrest as a violation of the constitution. For Proa, Benito Juárez had delivered these sacred laws to the Mexican people, and he intended to defend his rights.[56]

Such views constituted popular or folk liberalism.[57] Throughout Mexico the popular classes drew their own lessons and heroes from the past. They revered Benito Juárez, honored the Constitution of 1857, and celebrated victory against the French and the Conservatives in the 1860s; these figures both inspired and justified resistance against abusive governmental authorities. That Mexican elites had used these same events, glorified and idealized in ritual, to legitimate the social order confirms James Scott's conclusion that such a process always provides its subjects with the ideas for a critique and the symbolic tools from which resistance can be fashioned.[58] Like the eighteenth-century plebeians studied by E. P. Thompson, the popular classes borrowed the dominant themes of elite political rhetoric and turned them back against their own rulers.[59] Such a view could challenge the social order even as advocated by fellow "liberals." With the outbreak of the Mexican Revolution in 1910, for example, workers in Hidalgo District reinterpreted the message of middle-class revolutionaries in terms that made sense to them: the worst caciques who needed to be eliminated, in their opinion, were the railroad construction bosses and mine foremen, while the goals of the revolution were to include higher pay and secure jobs.[60]

As those inspired by folk liberalism came to experience the new conditions of industrial work a common consciousness of being dependent on earning a daily wage emerged, especially among those with skills. *Jornaleros* (day laborers), petitioning for relief from drainage regulations, stated that the only resources they had at their disposal came from work. For them and their families to subsist they were "subject to a daily wage, earned with most sacred work."[61] Forty-four petitioning *operarios* made the same point, revealing that they had no resources other than those they earned by working. One man from Santa Bárbara explained that "the day I don't work is the day my family doesn't eat."[62] Not surprisingly, skilled workers coalesced either to defend their earnings or to demand increased wages. In 1906 in Hidalgo District striking carpenters (skilled workers) in the Tecolotes mine made one demand—a salary increase. Moreover, shortly after the fall of the Porfirian regime an *operario* from the Tecolotes mine attempted to win election in the district by promising mine workers that his first act as an elected official would be to call a strike to demand increased salaries and fewer hours of work for miners.[63]

Above all else, workers constructed their view of the world and of themselves in response to the disparaging view of them presented by members of refined society. Those completely dependent on earning a wage perceived and resented being characterized as having no standing in the community. In mid-1911 petitioning workers lamented that many referred to the proletariat as the *pueblo bajo* (lowest people). Workers throughout the country bitterly resented the lack of respect accorded to them by the rest of society.[64] Rather than reject the moralizing discourse of middle-class rulers these workers strove to be accepted as equal members of decent society.

Other Mexican skilled workers hungered for respect. Stung by accusations in the press and from Porfirio Díaz that they did not know how to apply themselves to work, skilled members of the Unión de Mecánicos Mexicanos insisted that they had been trained since apprenticeship in the American system. Over the years they had acquired the custom of working like foreigners to the point that they believed that the work of Americans and Mexicans should be regarded as equal in efficiency and quantity. In 1908, Silvino E. Rodríguez, general president of the union, defended, in the face of stiff criticism, the mechanics' goal of obtaining a holiday that paid tribute to work. Mexico City's press pointed to the many official and unofficial holidays workers already enjoyed and to the great damage absenteeism inflicted on industry. Rodríguez's response testifies to the degree to which skilled workers accepted the dominant ideology. He maintained that his union had been one of the first to reduce to within limits the "innumerable days of fiestas" that caused the economic failure of so many industries and hardship for the working class, and he added that he hoped to reduce the total number of holidays to eight per year. Moreover, he dreamed of the education, moralization, and elevation of the working class—all concepts employed by middle-class reformers.[65]

In Ciudad Chihuahua, manifesting this desire to behave like *gente decente*, more workers began attending the theater. In place of polite applause theater audiences now responded to performances with loud whistling. For one *El Correo* contributor, this was too much. He lamented that "now there is almost no difference between the *plaza de toros* (bullring) and the theater."[66] In the mining town of Santa Eulalia, Chihuahua, the mine worker voted the most laborious and honorable by his fellows received a fifty-peso prize. While their living and working conditions contributed to the emergence of a distinctive view of the world, many workers adopted tenets of the moralizing discourse, though not without some modifications. A process of negotiation took place through which workers refashioned middle-class discourse, as in the case of folk liberalism, on the basis of their own experiences and beliefs.

CONCLUSION

Both skilled and unskilled workers shared many features of what can be called popular culture. Drinking, gambling, and prostitution flourished in the mining centers. Rather than representing the breakdown of traditional popular values, these habits reflected the continued expression and vigor of such values. The new working class imposed its own schedule and rules of behavior in cantinas, billiard halls, and brothels. Wage earners confronted municipal authorities and middle-class society over access to streets and public places and asserted individual worth, measured by honor and physical prowess rather than by family origin and wealth. Mining-town residents claimed rights as Mexican citizens under the 1857 constitution and held specific ideas concerning the proper role of governing authorities. Hidalgo District's rural residents shared many of these values. Their continuing appeal in the mining camps attests to the rural origin of the work force of the Hidalgo District mines.

Workers shared many aspects of a rebellious popular culture, yet skilled workers in particular were drawn to the moralizing discourse of the middle class. They began to dress like their social superiors, to join mutual-aid societies, and to attend night schools that promised morality, progress, and enlightenment. Although illogical to more affluent Porfirians, the consumption patterns of skilled workers symbolized their assertion of equality and helped to mitigate class differences. But even as they asserted their equality, a process of negotiation led workers to develop distinctive concepts of their own worth based largely on their dependence upon wages and pride in their role in the process of production. The continued vitality of the work culture forged in the mines and in mining communities also led them to refashion many of the tenets of middle-class reform. They advanced the notion of a fair day's wage for a fair day's work and used wages as their measure of social worth and the solution to economic problems. Arduous work could be made more palatable by higher wages. In short, they came together to struggle over wage bargaining. In contesting the worth of time rather than their control over it, skilled workers had absorbed an essential aspect of the culture of industrial capitalism. Rather than spurn popular culture, they drew from it to contest and refashion middle-class discourse.

NOTES

1. An extensive literature exists on this topic. See E. P. Thompson, "Time, Work-Discipline, and Industrial Capitalism," *PP* 38 (1967): 56–97; Sidney Pollard, *The Genesis of Modern Management: A Study of the Industrial Revolution in Great Britain* (Cambridge, MA, 1965); Herbert G. Gutman, *Work, Culture, and Society in Industrializing America: Essays in American Working-Class and Social History* (New York, 1977); and Michelle Perrot, "On the Formation of the French Working Class," in *Working-Class Formation: Nineteenth-Century Patterns in Western Europe and the United States*, ed. Ira Katznelson and Aristide R. Zolberg (Princeton, NJ, 1986). For a discussion of "extractories" in the American context, see Ronald C. Brown, *Hard-Rock Miners: The Intermountain West, 1860–1920* (College Station, TX, 1979), 65.

2. Mining company contributions to the Cuerpo de Policia Rural, located in Archivo Municipal, Hidalgo del Parral (hereafter AM). See presidente municipal, Santa Bárbara, to jefe político, Parral, 12 diciembre 1903, caja 1903I; Albino Padilla, presidente municipal, Santa Bárbara, to jefe político, Parral, 11 octubre 1904, caja 1904B; F. Villegas, jefe municipal, Santa Bárbara, 14 agosto 1906, caja 1906T; Agustín Páez, jefe municipal, Santa Bárbara, 26 diciembre 1907, caja 1907ñ; E. de la Fuente, Villa Escobedo, 8 febrero 1908, caja 1908C; J. M. Delgado, jefe municipal, Villa Escobedo, 2 abril 1908, caja 1908C; Jorge Maul, jefe municipal, Villa

Escobedo, 3 junio 1908, caja 1908ñ; Agustín Páez, 8 diciembre 1909, caja 1909A, and 10 febrero 1910, caja 1910H.

3. For a discussion of moral reform in Porfirian Chihuahua, see William E. French, "Prostitutes and Guardian Angels: Women, Work, and the Family in Porfirian Chihuahua," *HAHR* 72, no. 4 (November 1992): 529–53.

4. For a detailed description of these changes in the work process, see William E. French, "Peaceful and Working People: The Inculcation of the Capitalist Work Ethic in a Mexican Mining District (Hidalgo District, Chihuahua, 1880–1920)" (Ph.D. dissertation, University of Texas, 1990), 10–67. On this process in Sonora and Coahuila, see Juan Luis Sariego, *Enclaves y minerales en el norte de México: Historia social de los mineros de Cananea y Nueva Rosita 1900–1970* (México, 1988). The classic work on mining in Mexico remains that of Marvin D. Bernstein, *The Mexican Mining Industry, 1890–1950: A Study of the Interaction of Politics, Economics, and Technology* (Albany, NY, 1964).

5. Comments by employers found in mine manager interviews located in the Edward L. Doheny Research Fund Collection, Occidental College, Los Angeles.

6. At the end of 1908, the U.S. Bureau of Labor estimated that between 60,000 and 100,000 Mexicans entered the United States each year. Bureau of Labor figures discussed in "Mexican Labor and Its Place in this Country," *El Paso Morning Times*, December 17, 1908; Jane Dale Lloyd describes how Galeana District, Chihuahua, became a passageway for migrants on their way to the United States in *El proceso de modernización capitalista en el noroeste de Chihuahua (1880–1910)* (México, 1987), 46.

7. All figures are from the yearly reports of the jefe político, Distrito Hidalgo, and from other correspondence in AM, Hidalgo del Parral.

8. "Las minas y los mineros," *El Hijo del Parral*, 15 octubre 1899, caja 1900F, AM; "Desgracia en la mina del Refugio," *El Hijo del Parral*, 11 febrero 1906, caja 1906R, AM. El Palmilla mine discussed in "Por Hidalgo del Parral," *El Correo de Chihuahua*, September 7, 1905. This newspaper is available on microfilm in the Benson Latin American Collection, University of Texas, Austin. Other accident reports discussed in French, "Peaceful and Working People," 261–63.

9. Living conditions discussed in J. Villegas, jefe municipal, Santa Bárbara, to jefe político, Parral, 7 julio 1906, caja 1906T, AM; Agustín Páez, jefe municipal, Santa Bárbara, to jefe político, Parral, 11 febrero 1908, caja 1908C, AM; presidente municipal, Santa Bárbara, to jefe político, Parral, 13 mayo 1904, caja 1904O; and Leonidez Sapien, Parral, to c. pres. de la Junta Calificadora, 7 enero 1908, caja 1908R, AM.

10. Ramón Eduardo Ruiz, *The People of Sonora and Yankee Capitalists* (Tucson, AZ, 1988), 91.

11. See ibid., 64, 84, 90, 91, 94–99.

12. On Los Azules, see el jefe de la seguridad pública, Los Azules, to jefe político, Distrito Hidalgo, 21 junio 1904, caja 1904G; presidente municipal, Santa Bárbara, to jefe político, 25 junio 1904, caja 1904O; Agustín Páez, jefe municipal, Santa Bárbara, to jefe político, 3 octubre 1908, caja 1908AA. For Villa Escobedo, see presidente municipal, Villa Escobedo, to jefe político, 27 septiembre 1904, and 9 noviembre 1904, caja 1904C; reports from San Francisco del Oro, in presidente municipal, San Francisco del Oro, to jefe político, 13 abril 1906, caja 1906C; Agustín

Páez, jefe municipal, Santa Bárbara, to jefe político, 2 enero 1911, caja 1911B. On railroad workers, see J. J. Gutiérrez, presidente municipal, Santa Bárbara, to jefe político, 17 diciembre 1900, caja 1900SUSY, all in AM.

13. On Balleza, see Miguel Armendáriz, presidente municipal, Balleza, to jefe político, 1 octubre 1904, folder 1904, caja decade 1900A; Armendáriz to jefe político, 10 octubre 1906, caja 1906Y; Armendáriz to jefe político, 23 enero 1909, caja 1909F; and Mateo Moreno, jefe municipal, Balleza, to jefe político, 18 diciembre 1909. On Valle de Zaragoza, see presidente municipal, Valle de Zaragoza, to jefe político, 18 junio 1903, caja 1903I; and Francisco Chavez L., jefe municipal, Valle de Zaragoza, to jefe político, 16 octubre 1907, caja 1907A. See also presidente municipal, Huejotitan, to jefe político, 10 abril 1903, caja 1903J; thirty petitioners, hacienda de San José de Gracia, municipalidad de Valle del Rosario, to governor, 3 abril 1906, caja 1906N; jefe municipal, Huejotitan, to jefe político, 26 junio 1907, caja 1905G; petitioners from San Antonio del Tule, in Guillermo Porras, secretario, secretaría de gobierno del Estado, ramo de instrucción pública, 16 marzo 1909, caja 1909C, all in AM.

14. Presidente municipal, Valle de Zaragoza, to jefe político, Parral, 18 junio 1903, caja 1903I; Varios vecinos, "Escandalitos en Santa Bárbara," *La Nueva Era*, 28 julio 1904, 3:1, caja 1904A, AM.

15. Bernabé Uribe, R. 3e E. de la jefatura municipal, Santa Bárbara, to jefe político, 27 agosto 1906, caja 1906T; on Huejotitan, see jefe municipal, Huejotitan, to jefe político, 26 junio 1907, folder Huejotitan 1905–1911, caja 1905G. Many other descriptions of scandals appear in Hidalgo District records.

16. Rodolfo Valles, jefe político, to c.c. miembros de la asamblea municipal, 2 julio 1906, caja 1906N, AM.

17. Daniel Roche, *The People of Paris: An Essay in Popular Culture in the Eighteenth Century*, trans. Marie Evans (Hamburg, NY, 1987), 272.

18. Rodolfo Valles, jefe político, Distrito Hidalgo, to c. secretario del gobierno, 24 febrero 1906, caja 1906T, AM.

19. Jesús Lozano, juez, juzgado de paz del Tercero, Parral, to jefe político, 1 agosto 1904, caja 1904C, AM. Lozano quotes the individual as saying, "Tengo pistola y carabina, con que hacerme valer." Others have noted the close connection between honor and worthiness. See James Farr, *Hands of Honor: Artisans and Their World in Dijon, 1550–1650* (Ithaca, NY, 1988), 179. On honor during the colonial period in New Spain, see Patricia Seed, *To Love, Honor, and Obey in Colonial Mexico: Conflicts over Marriage Choice, 1574–1821* (Stanford, CA, 1988), 62–65.

20. Roche, *People of Paris*, 255.

21. Jorge Maul, jefe municipal, Ville Escobedo, to jefe político, 27 mayo 1908, caja 1908ñ; and Agustín Páez, jefe municipal, Santa Bárbara, to jefe político, 17 enero 1910, caja 1910B, AM.

22. Seven cantina employees, Parral to governor, Chihuahua, 22 enero 1906, caja 1906X. The Sunday-rest movement was well covered in Parral's press. See "El descanso dominical de los dependientes," *El Hijo del Parral*, 5 octubre 1902, 1, caja 1902D; and "El cierre de las casas comerciales," *El Hijo del Parral*, 26 noviembre 1905, 1, caja 1906G, all in AM.

23. Trinidad Torres, comandante, Parral, to jefe político, 22 mayo 1906, caja 1906H; and Torres to jefe político, 28 mayo 1906, caja 1906G, all in AM. Other

cantina names include La Gaviota, La Nueva Roca de Oro, La Columbia, Nuevo Siglo, La Bohemia, La Noche Buena, La Verbena, La Roca de Hielo, La Fortuna, El Porvenir, and La Fuente de Oro.

24. Number of prostitutes compiled from Padrón de las meretrices inscritas en el ramo de Tolerancia, 1902, caja 1902F; Médicos cirujanos municipales, 26 febrero 1906, caja 1906U; Partes rendidos por el Agente de Sanidad, dic. 1907, caja 1907L; Partes rendidos por el Agente de Sanidad, 2 mayo 1908, caja 1908S; and Agustín Páez, jefe municipal, Santa Bárbara, to jefe político, 10 diciembre 1907, caja 1907H, AM. (Páez counts thirty-nine registered prostitutes in Santa Bárbara in late 1907.)

25. Sixteen prostitutes and matronas of Casas de Asignación, Parral, to jefe político, 26 noviembre 1909, caja 1909Q, AM.

26. J. J. Gutiérrez, presidente municipal, Santa Bárbara, to jefe político, Parral, 9 noviembre 1900, caja 1900SUSY; Agustín Páez, jefe municipal, Santa Bárbara, to jefe político, 12 noviembre 1906, caja 1906C; and Páez to jefe político, 2 abril 1907, caja 1907J, all in AM.

27. "Uno de nuestros defectos," *El Correo*, May 12, 1905.

28. "Correspondencia del Parral," *El Correo*, May 11, 1905.

29. "Uno de nuestros defectos," *El Correo*, May 12, 1905.

30. Ibid.; Morse interview, Doheny Papers; and Labor Conditions, Southern Sinaloa, Doheny Papers.

31. Roche, *People of Paris*, 160.

32. Michelle Perrot, "On the Formation of the French Working Class," 104; Peter N. Stearns, *Paths to Authority: The Middle Class and the Industrial Labor Force in France, 1820–48* (Urbana, IL, 1978), 78; and Eugen Weber, *Peasants into Frenchmen: The Modernization of Rural France, 1870–1914* (Stanford, CA, 1976), 21. Reformers in Argentina pointed to the role of luxury in forcing women into prostitution. See Donna J. Guy, *Sex and Danger in Buenos Aires: Prostitution, Family, and Nation in Argentina* (Lincoln, NE, 1991), 49. Luxury in fashion was also linked to loss of virtue in women by nineteenth-century middle-class observers of social life. See Mariana Valverde, "The Love of Finery: Fashion and the Fallen Woman in Ninteenth-Century Social Discourse," *Victorian Studies* 32, no. 2 (Winter 1989): 169–70.

33. The Ford *Times* cited in Stephen Meyer III, *The Five-Dollar Day: Labor Management and Social Control in the Ford Motor Company, 1908–1921* (Albany, NY, 1981), 73.

34. Quotation from Juzgado 1º de Lo Penal, Parral, to jefe político, 15 mayo 1906, caja 1906D; for other arrest notices that describe clothing, see jefatura de cuartel, Ojuela, to jefe político, 4 noviembre 1902, caja 1902C; and Juzgado 1º de Letras, Parral, to jefe político, 30 julio 1902, caja 1902D, all in AM.

35. Morris B. Parker, *Mules, Mines, and Me in Mexico, 1895–1932* (Tucson, AZ, 1979), 27.

36. Personal observations of the author during visit to church, Parral, August 1987.

37. J. Trinidad Hernández y Chavez, "El barretero," *El Hijo del Parral*, 18 octubre 1903, 1: 1, caja 1903C, AM.

38. For a discussion of mining festivals in the European context, see Klaus Tenfelde, "Mining Festivals in the Nineteenth Century," *JCH* 13 (1978): 377–412.

39. On Parral, see "A traves del estado: Parral," *El Correo*, August 23, 1902; "En Hidalgo del Parral," *El Correo*, August 17, 1904; and Francisco Cordero, Parral, to jefe político, 1 julio 1911, caja 1911S, AM. On Santa Bárbara, see "Fiestas en Santa Bárbara," *La Nueva Era*, 22 agosto 1901, caja 1902G, AM.

40. "La entrada de la cuaresma," *El Correo*, March 8, 1905.

41. T. A. Clara, "Mas reverencia," *La Nueva Era*, 7 mayo 1903, caja 1903H, AM.

42. "A traves del estado: Ojinaga," *El Correo*, December 5, 1902.

43. "Notas del Parral," *El Correo*, January 15, 1902.

44. Description of the 1904 celebration in "Por el Parral," *El Correo*, May 13, 1904. For a discussion of employers looking "backward" to the old order while groping toward new, impersonal discipline, see Pollard, *Genesis of Modern Management*, p. 182, and compare this with Mexico City developments discussed by Morgan.

45. "¡Importante á los adultos!" *La Nueva Era*, 18 agosto 1901, caja 1902G, AM.

46. "Ecos de Villa Escobedo," *El Padre Padilla*, 15 noviembre 1905, caja 1906T, AM.

47. "Vejaciones a mexicanos," *El Correo*, June 8, 1907.

48. Alan Knight, *The Mexican Revolution*, 2 vols. (Cambridge, 1986), 1:146–50.

49. The term *caciques* was used by petitioners both before and after the Porfiriato. A number of vecinos wrote the new governor in 1911 that "the abuses of the *caciquillos* are still abundant in this unfortunate state." See vecinos de Hidalgo del Parral to c. gobernador, Chihuahua, 6 abril 1911, caja 1911I, AM.

50. Rafael Contreras, San Nicolas del Cañón, to jefe municipal, Olivos, 23 diciembre 1905, caja 1905K, AM.

51. Five labradores, Tule de San Antonio de Arévalo, to jefe político, Distrito Hidalgo, 4 junio 1909, caja 1909B, AM.

52. Crescencio Sáenz in el secretario, secretaría del gobierno del estado, Ramo de Fomento, to jefe político, Distrito Hidalgo, 24 junio 1908, caja 1908B, AM.

53. Rafael Díaz in el secretario, secretaría del gobierno del estado, Ramo de Fomento, to jefe político, Distrito Hidalgo, 27 mayo 1908, caja 1908A, AM.

54. José Pallan, gobernadorcillo de Pueblo de Guasárachic, to governor, found in el secretario, secretaría del gobierno del estado, Ramo de Fomento, 13 abril 1908, caja 1908J. Another description of the Constitution of 1857 is found in Rafael Contreras, San Nicolas del Cañón, to jefe municipal, Olivos, 23 diciembre 1905, caja 1905K, AM.

55. Victorio García, barretero, to juez de distrito, 4 julio 1902, caja 1902D. Lusana Lopez chastized local police and informed them that she could not be arrested as a *clandestina* unless caught in the act. See Lusana Lopez, Parral, to jefe político, 2 febrero 1909, caja 1909E, AM.

56. León Proa, Santa Bárbara, to jefe político, 2 julio 1903, caja 1903I, AM. Proa states: "Yo me amparo y mede fiendo con haquellas Sagradas Leyes que nos dejo haquel memorable—¡Benito! ¡Juárez! Esas sagradas Leyes de La Constitución! y protesto decir verdad y no hobrar de malicia y ¡Defender mi derecho!" Petition from operario in José María Muniz, Cárcel de Minas Nuevas, to jefe político, 8 agosto 1902, caja 1902M, AM.

57. Alan Knight developed "folk liberalism" in "Revolutionary Project, Recalcitrant People: Mexico, 1910–40," in *The Revolutionary Process in Mexico: Essays on Political and Social Change, 1880–1940*, ed. Jaime E. Rodríguez O. (Los Angeles, 1990), 233.

58. James C. Scott, *Weapons of the Weak: Everyday Forms of Peasant Resistance* (New Haven, CT, 1985), 338. See Scott's critique of the concept of hegemony in the same volume, pp. 304–50.

59. E. P. Thompson, "Eighteenth-Century English Society: Class Struggle without Class," *Social History* 3, no. 2 (May 1978): 158. American workers in the first half of the nineteenth century held beliefs drawn from republicanism including commonwealth, virtue, independence, citizenship, and equality. Sean Wilentz concludes that ordinary workers, faced with changes in the social relations of production, began to reinterpret their shared ideal and to struggle over the meaning of these terms. See his *Chants Democratic: New York City and the Rise of the American Working Class, 1788–1850* (New York, 1984), 14.

60. N. B. González, comisionado, Borjas, Ramal del Parral y más de cien firmas, to Sr. Abraham González, gobernador del estado, 1 agosto 1911, caja 1911S, AM.

61. Twenty-eight jornaleros, Parral, to gobernador, Chihuahua, in secretario, secretaría del gobierno del estado, Ramo de Fomento, 13 marzo 1908, caja 1908B, AM.

62. León Proa, Santa Bárbara, to jefe político, Parral, 2 julio 1903, caja 1903I, AM.

63. Striking carpenters' demands in F. Villegas, jefe municipal, Santa Bárbara, to jefe político, Distrito Hidalgo, 4 agosto 1906, caja 1906T; workers mention reduced wages in most petititions complaining of drainage requirements; and *operario* candidate discussed in M. Cavazos, jefe municipal, Santa Bárbara, to jefe político, 23 noviembre 1911, caja 1911F, AM.

64. Rodney D. Anderson, *Outcasts in their Own Land: Mexican Industrial Workers, 1906–1911* (DeKalb, IL, 1976), 68; petitioning workers in N. B. González and more than one hundred signatories to Sr. Abraham González, gobernador del estado de Chihuahua, 1 agosto 1911, caja 1911S, AM.

65. Rodríguez cited in Marcelo N. Rodea, *Historia del movimiento obrero ferrocarrilero en México (1890–1943)* (México, 1944), 120, 125, 126. Workers' response to Porfirio Díaz on p. 309. Michelle Perrot stresses that the image of the French working class in the nineteenth century was also constructed reactively. See "On the Formation of the French Working Class," in *Working-Class Formation*, ed. Katznelson and Zolberg, 96.

66. "Locales y personales," *El Correo de Chihuahua*, February 27, 1902.

11

The Construction of the Patriotic Festival in Tecamachalco, Puebla, 1900–1946

Mary Kay Vaughan
University of Illinois-Chicago

Mary Kay Vaughan engages the interpretations of popular festivals by both Judith Friedlander and Alan Knight as she examines the negotiations between local communities and government agents (such as schoolteachers and agrarian authorities) that result in the celebration of holidays. In the process she also grapples with Antonio Gramsci's constructions of hegemony and, to some extent, with Philip Corrigan and Derek Sayer, the proponents of the Great Arch. The essay addresses the rise of team sports in school, which provided another forum for male displays of aggression and physical prowess. Above all, the author demonstrates the vitality of communities in Puebla and their ability to construct an educational system that benefited them. Beyond the theoretical studies mentioned, she also provides an intriguing comparison of the development of Mother's Day in Mexico with the commercial Mother's Day that emerged in the United States.[*]

Vaughan's book, *The State, Education, and Social Class in Mexico, 1880–1928*, which resulted from her doctoral dissertation at the University of Wisconsin, remains the standard work on Mexican education.[†]

I would like to thank Judith Friedlander, Joann Martin, Barbara Tenenbaum, Elsie Rockwell, Guy P. C. Thomson, William Beezley, William French, and Marc Zimmerman for comments on this essay at various points in its writing. Any errors in fact and interpretation are my own.

[*]For a discussion of Mother's Day in the United States, see Leigh Eric Schmidt, "The Commercialization of the Calendar: American Holidays and the Culture of Consumption, 1870–1930," *Journal of American History* 78, no. 3 (December 1991): 887–916.

[†](DeKalb, IL, 1982).

We will sacrifice before allowing our rights to be denied. . . . The times we
were intimidated and subjected by brute force are long gone.

PEOPLE OF CUESTA BLANCA, February 20, 1941

ANTHROPOLOGISTS HAVE LONG IDENTIFIED the Mexican village fiesta
with collective renewal and cohesion.[1] Judith Friedlander has
provided a helpful corrective to this literature by arguing that the
villagewide fiesta, rather than an exclusively isolated event, often
has links to the state, affirming both the local collectivity and a hierarchical, extravillage order. She describes the parallels between the
religious fiesta of the sixteenth century—replete with colorful
processions, music, incense, flowers, and theater dedicated to the
Christian pantheon of saints and organized by the village elites—and
the patriotic festival celebrated in Morelos towns in the 1970s where
local notables led the Independence Day parade through the streets
carrying huge portraits of the patriot heroes Miguel Hidalgo, José
Morelos, and Emiliano Zapata. She contends that the Catholic
missionaries' construction of the religious fiesta in the sixteenth century made Indian villagers "accomplices in their own oppression"
within the Spanish colonial system. Moreover, she asserts that the
postrevolutionary Mexican state of the twentieth century adopted the
missionaries' use of ritual for similar purposes of domination. The
postrevolutionary patriotic festival, as she sees it, teaches a vocabulary appropriate to the maintenance of state power and the promotion of socioeconomic change. The festival is a state imposition
perpetrated with the assistance of schoolteachers and ambitious
local politicians on a passive and victimized audience.[2]

Her interpretation has much in common with revisionist studies
of the 1910 Mexican Revolution that have held sway since 1968.
Revisionists have made the state the major actor in that event. They
have minimized the role of popular forces and movements in the revolution to focus on ambitious politicians who manipulated the people
to create an overarching authoritarian state and a political party, the
Partido Revolucionario Institucional (PRI), divorced from popular
will and culture.[3]

Among historians, the leading challenge to this school has come
from Alan Knight, who argues that the revisionists' understanding of
the Mexican state derives from their assessment of its current strength.
He sees a weak revolutionary state until after 1940 and gives greater
credit to popular movements, demographic trends, and socioeconomic
change in the revolutionary process.[4] Knight, addressing the patriotic fiesta in the nineteenth and twentieth centuries, argues that it

was not a postrevolutionary state adaptation of sixteenth-century missionary techniques but rather a ritual typical of the liberal state in the second half of the nineteenth century. Further, he contends that the ideology of Independence Day celebrations in the Porfiriato— the oratory of schoolteachers fixed on notions of patriotism, defensive nationalism, and liberal principles linked to the Constitution of 1857—had popular appeal. It captured and gave specific meaning to real political experiences in the nineteenth-century civil wars and contributed to an oppositional ideology that fueled the Revolution of 1910.[5]

Knight suggests that the patriotic festival elaborated in the course of the Mexican Revolution (1910–1940), rather than an imposition, represented the syncretic product of an interactive process among communities, popular movements, and the emerging state. Moreover, he places less emphasis on the festival's vocabulary of socioeconomic change than does Friedlander because he deemphasizes the role of the revolutionary state in altering *mentalités*. For Knight, sociocultural change results from demographic movements and market dynamics rather than from the efforts of the state's cultural engineers, the schoolteachers.[6]

Recent work on the patriotic fiesta poses many questions. Was the fiesta simply a state imposition on resistant communities, an alien ritual falling on deaf ears, a conspiracy between representatives of the state (teachers and local and regional politicians) to confirm state power and domination? Or was the patriotic fiesta in the revolution a construction negotiated between communities as social entities, popular movements, and those allied with or incorporated into the emerging state? As a negotiated construction, did the patriotic festival simply confirm the power of separate elements in the postrevolutionary state's alliance (municipal officeholders, ejido leaders, the local economic elite, members of the Confederación Nacional Campesina and the PRI)? Or did the festival play a more creative role in changing mentalities, defining identities, and mobilizing energies around a national project?

Understanding that the elaboration of the patriotic fiesta varied locally, the following essay is a case study of Tecamachalco, an agrarian and *agrarista* district of central Puebla. Here, between 1900 and 1946, the patriotic fiesta simultaneously contributed to state and nation formation. More than a mechanism of imposed domination (state formation), it created identity and loyalty while it harnessed energies and movement (nation formation).[7] The festival facilitated the penetration of the nation-state and its regional representation (state government) but also helped to legitimize local power structures, confirm social cohesion, and enhance collective identity in relation to surrounding communities and the state. From a didactic ritual engaging reduced circles in the nineteenth century, the patriotic fiesta became inclusionary between 1910 and 1940. Inclusion was accomplished through interaction between the political processes of revolutionary upheaval and state formation and the social conditions of everyday life. In this interactive space, nation-building took place. The vocabulary and content of the patriotic festival required negotiation among representatives of the state (many of them schoolteachers), local political groups (many of them *agraristas*), and villagers as they initiated and responded to change.

The emerging patriotic festival of the 1940s did not simply disseminate ideology from above nor merely legitimate local, regional, and national powerholders; it engaged and mobilized people. The symbols, values, and behavior celebrated in the festival fused in a hegemonic discourse in which the state linked its modernizing project to a multiplicity of cultural traditions, social values, and discourses in such a way as to promote political stability, rapid socioeconomic change, and respect for local custom. Changing mentalities comprised more than the effects of demographics and market penetration. They included attitudes, values, and behavior encouraged in the patriotic festival by the state's cultural producers, the teachers.

THE PATRIOTIC FESTIVAL IN
PORFIRIAN TECAMACHALCO (1900–1910)

Tecamachalco, situated on the eastern side of the Puebla basin on Mexico's central plateau, a region of low, balding mountain ranges separating cultivated valleys, lies equidistant from Puebla city to the west and Mount Orizaba rising out of the Sierra Madre Oriental to the east. As an administrative district of Puebla state, it consisted of eight counties in 1900. Large and medium-sized properties (haciendas and ranchos) and agrarian villages (pueblos, *rancherías*, and barrios) dry-farmed cereal and produced pulque, ixtle fiber, chiles, onions, and beans. In 1900 only 4 percent of the population lived on haciendas, while the majority lived in villages in varying degrees of subordination to surrounding ranchos and haciendas. Although Tecamachalco was an area of Indian settlement at the time of the Spanish conquest, by 1910, 90 percent of its population spoke Spanish.[8]

Municipal archival data suggest that in the Porfiriato, the patriotic fiesta was most elaborately celebrated in the *cabeceras* (county seats) and a handful of other pueblos of relative size and wealth. The *fiestas patrióticas* took place on May 5, Cinco de Mayo, celebrating the day on which the republican army defeated the French invaders at Puebla in 1862—not on September 16, in honor of Mexico's independence from Spain. This focus revealed the strength of regionalism. Nevertheless, the festival articulated simultaneous, albeit incipient, processes of state and nation building. The identification of the citizen-subject-patriot referred to real experiences: the *poblanos* had fought two foreign invaders, the North Americans in 1847 and the French in 1862. The patriotic festival in the late nineteenth-century liberal state gave those experiences a specific meaning designed to create loyalties and identities. Villagers were to see themselves as part of a "democratic people," "the Mexican people," who had successfully fought and repulsed foreign oppressors.[9]

Juntas patrióticas, created by the jefe político, the administrative representative of the state governor, organized the fiestas. On them served all state and local officeholders and employees, including schoolteachers and members of the *fuerzas vivas* (village notables such as the town doctor and chief merchants). Like the *mayordomías* responsible for religious fiestas, the juntas funded the event and organized the preparations—cleaning the streets, beautifying the town square, and planting flowers. Personal contributions paid for music, decorations, fireworks, costumes, and uniforms. The organizing committee adopted a program approved by the town council, or ayuntamiento, and the jefe político.

The typical fiesta began at six o'clock in the morning. As the village band struck up martial music the artillery shot off salvos and fireworks burst into the half-light of dawn. Citizens raised the national flag in the town square and unfurled national banners from the windows of public buildings. At nine o'clock in the municipal palace the jefe político met the *comitiva* (consisting of school students, public employees, and elected officials) and locally quartered soldiers. Musicians from a military band or a *cuerpo filarmónico* joined them. Filing out of the building, they made up a *paseo cívico* (procession) that marched through the principal streets to the town square. There the official ceremony began with a rousing speech from a schoolteacher eulogizing the patriot heroes—Hidalgo and Morelos, fathers of Mexican independence; Ignacio Zaragoza, military commander at the Battle of Puebla; Benito Juárez, father of the liberal republic; and Porfirio Díaz, military hero in the defeat of the French and Mexico's president. Schoolchildren sang songs. One or two selected students—usually a girl and a boy—mounted to the tribune to deliver a cornucopia of flowery rhetoric in honor of the *patria* and the brave soldiers of Puebla who had died defending national soil against the foreign invaders. Orchestral music broke the monotony of speech-making, and the ceremony ended with the singing of the national anthem.

The festivities resumed at four o'clock in the town square with a concert and the launching of helium balloons. At six o'clock students, public employees, officeholders, and soldiers paid their respects to the flag as it was lowered. In the evening all public buildings and private homes on the main streets were lit up with gaslights to honor the occasion. At eight o'clock the musicians offered another serenade in the plaza, a mixture of vocal solos, waltzes, *pasos dobles*, and martial trumpeting, and the day's celebrations ended at ten with a burst of fireworks.[10]

The fiesta became a mechanism for education in a largely illiterate society.[11] The civics lessons ranged from the act of preparation (cleaning the streets, decorating the houses, polishing the buttons on the musicians' and soldiers' uniforms, planting trees and flowers in the town square) to participation and observation. It was designed to promote patriotism by teaching a political vocabulary of a few fundamental words—*patria, independencia, constitución, unión,* and *progreso*—all of them fresh and tentative in a country where the nominal independence achieved in 1821 had been followed by decades of divisive civil war. The state appropriated space to teach this vocabulary. Streets, parks, squares, and schools lost their Catholic nomenclature and assumed the names of liberal heroes and historical-political concepts (La Reforma, La Constitución, La Independencia).[12] The festival utilized this space to engage the people more deeply in learning the vocabulary.

The festival elucidated a state ideology mobilized around the future and the concepts of progress and change. The ubiquitous clock installed prominently on the town square and in all the municipal schools by Porfirian officials symbolized a new notion of time's use and mobilization, all fixed on the future. The use of schoolchildren as principal actors in the festival further appropriated the future. The equal appointment of boys and girls to oratorical performance at the festival made an ideological statement about how the future should look—an exhortative moral prescription issued to a changing but not yet compliant present. Although girls' school enrollments in Tecamachalco were growing, they still reached only two thirds of those of boys in the late Porfiriato. In 1902, 41 percent of boys and 24 percent of girls between the ages of six and fourteen were enrolled in school.[13]

Officials seized upon the theatrics of the patriotic festival to enact the historical movement of progress. In 1902, in the district seat of Tecamachalco, the Cinco de Mayo procession marched to a new hospital, named for Mucio Martínez, Puebla's governor. The build-ing of the hospital was one of several works of "improvement," along with the creation of schools, the introduction of gas lighting, and telegraph and telephone service, undertaken by the jefe político to advance "civilization" and "modernity" in Tecamachalco. To ensure that the community noted his contribution to civilization and to im-press upon everyone the meaning of progress, the jefe político led the procession to the new building, where they inaugurated it after the secretary of the ayuntamiento gave the official reading on the meaning of the Cinco de Mayo.[14]

The patriotic festival resembled the religious fiesta, with which it peacefully coexisted in late Porfirian Tecamachalco towns.[15] It imitated the religious fiesta in its use of processions, music, fire-works, and its appropriation of space for didactic purposes. The pa-triotic heroes had the aura of saints. The *patria* was most often symbolized and honored in the form of an altar, and the oratory re-lied on Catholic imagery—the "temple of the *patria*," for instance, although its direct origins were possibly Masonic. Furthermore, mechanisms of insertion associated with the festival resembled those of the sixteenth-century Christian friars. First, architects of the festi-val focused on youth, inducting schoolchildren into the patriotic cul-ture. Second, they put the organization and implementation of the fiesta into the hands of the local notables. Members of the ayunta-mientos in the outlying towns were not interlopers but hacienda administrators, merchants, shopkeepers, artisans, rancheros, and well-to-do peasants.

The mechanisms of insertion mitigated the impositional charac-ter of the festival. The patriotic fiesta, like the religious festival, served to confirm village identity, cohesion, and power structures. Such func-tions proved important in a region subject to long-standing competi-tion within and between villages and haciendas over scarce land, water, and other resources.[16] In the nineteenth century the patriotic festival became useful to legitimate alterations in local power struc-tures. Fragmentation of haciendas, privatization of communally held village lands, and commercialization resulted in the emergence of a ranchero class and social differentiation within the peasantry.[17] The railroad from Puebla city to Oaxaca cut through Tecamachalco and encouraged not only these changes but also commercialization of haciendas, whose interests were represented in the ayuntamientos of important headtowns.[18]

Because these changes were neither abrupt nor extensive they suggested the potential for widening the circles to include a new pa-triotic sociability and its liberal vocabulary. Tecamachalco did not undergo sudden and acute polarization of "haves" and "have-nots," which would have limited possibilities for cohesive ritual. Nor did the colonial Catholic order reassert its dominion. Hacienda owners were mostly absentee and only a small minority of the population lived on the large estates. Unlike much of western Mexico, the church did not recuperate organizational strength in Tecamachalco in the late nineteenth century.[19] Although popular religiosity remained strong, there were few priests, and those who ministered cooperated with officials, turning over vital statistics to build the civil registry. No evidence suggests that local elites celebrated themselves and their power by building new shrines or sponsoring religious pilgrimages. Their lack of interest in enhancing their status through such a display of faith may have contributed to the growth of the new patriotic sociability.

The environment favored cultural imitation of the notables, especially in the larger towns where distinct social groups lived side by side.[20] Here the patriotic festivals were celebrated with the greatest pomp and effect, rather than in *rancherías* or in barrios where practically all families engaged in subsistence production, sharecropping, or agricultural wage labor. People from the *rancherías* or barrios might trek to the patriotic festivals of the pueblos and headtowns of which they were dependents. If the *rancherías* were within or on the boundaries of haciendas, they likely remained under the influence of older forms of collective loyalty and ritual associated with the large estate.[21]

Wealth and "culture" counted as criteria for notable status in Tecamachalco's towns. Among the most respected, high-status groups of late Porfirian *poblano* towns were its musicians. These might be associated with strictly religious functions and instruments typical of pre-Hispanic and colonial musical culture, but many took up European brass instruments and a repertoire of martial and secular music introduced through the Reform wars and the French invasion. In the Porfiriato the brass band became intimately associated with the patriotic festival.[22] Many musicians, bearers of secular culture, acquired status in part because of their travels from town to town and their transmission of new messages and cultural forms. They served for television sets and record players in the preelectronic age and, often, for books as well in the still mostly illiterate countryside. Those who introduced European opera, dance, and martial music straddled different worlds, interpreted distinct but coexisting ideologies, and related to multiple social groups. Many were strongly identified with the value set of the patriotic fiesta, for which they provided the primary entertainment. One of two leading families in Cuaucnopalan was the García family, whose members were schoolteachers and musicians. All the male children played a musical instrument and both male and female children left the village to further their studies at the Methodist school in the city of Puebla. Solid citizens of Cuaucnopalan, this family mobilized around the *patria* and the future.[23]

On the other hand, we should not exaggerate the circles actively engaged in the Porfirian patriotic festival in Tecamachalco. *Jornaleros* (the census term applied to day wage-dependent, property-poor persons) in the larger towns and the majority in impoverished hamlets and on haciendas probably remained marginal to the celebration. The literate were more likely to participate as a result of their exposure to schooling, their association with high-status occupations, or the aspirations that motivated them to learn to read and write. But the small circle of literate men shrank in early twentieth-century Tecamachalco. Only 23 percent of the men over the age of twelve were literate in 1900, and the percentage was the same in 1910 because literate men often left.[24]

In the decade before the revolution crop-damaging weather, inflation, and lack of access to land brought hardship to many and encouraged emigration. Tecamachalco lost 3 percent of its population between 1900 and 1910. Families throughout the district were increasingly burdened by the jefe político's levies for municipal improvements. These taxes, exacted from villagers in the form of monetary and labor contributions, seemed insatiable and the villagers' capacity to respond so limited that, in 1909, the *regidor* in charge of finances in the ayuntamiento of Tecamachalco simply threw up his hands and exclaimed that the inhabitants were notoriously impoverished, with no hopes for recovery, and could pay no more. In 1909, in the midst of the controversial presidential campaign that would spark the Mexican Revolution, a large majority of the junta patriótica of Tecamachalco resigned, claiming they could not or would not meet their obligations for that year's festival.[25]

THE RECONSTRUCTION OF THE PATRIOTIC FIESTA IN REVOLUTIONARY TECAMACHALCO

The revolution in Tecamachalco began as a civic, middle-class protest in 1910. In 1913 certain rancheros took up arms, and by 1915 a full-fledged agrarian revolution was under way.[26] This disparate but forceful movement challenged rancheros as well as hacendados and expressed the grievances of *rancherías*, barrios, and smaller villages against the dominating larger towns and county seats. Urban political groups hastened the process of agrarian revolution when they periodically penetrated the countryside to recruit support for their factions. In return for support they distributed land or created links between *agraristas* and agrarian-reform officials of the state or federal government. No single urban faction gained control of Puebla's countryside until the 1930s, by which time a significant battle for the redistribution of wealth and power had been waged in Tecamachalco.[27] By 1930 fully one third of the male population of Tecamachalco had benefited from land reform. They were tough and determined; when they wanted a piece of land they invaded it. When they were awarded land they did not want, they refused to accept it and occupied instead the terrain they coveted.[28]

Challenged by the less well heeled necessarily using violent methods, the middle classes, the *fuerzas vivas* of Tecamachalco's major towns, were temporarily battered. The culture of patriotism and its overlapping culture of schooling appear to have been shaken by the arrival on the scene of the "unwashed." It was not that the *agrarista* leaders were illiterate or discredited schooling. Many knew how to read and write, several had sat on the wooden benches of Porfirian schools, and many saw promotion of schooling as an attribute of public office.[29] Rather, the struggle for redistribution engaged men's souls, both those of the old guard and those of the newcomers, in more visceral, pithier matters. Rancheros and hacienda owners confronted *agraristas* through their sharecroppers and renters. Town fought town over the same land and water. *Agraristas* fought each other over ejido parcels. Village authority flew up for grabs when the new institution of the ejido created dual governing bodies in towns. It became problematic for these ardent contenders to take time out from combat, shake hands, and meet to form the juntas patrióticas.[30]

Patriotic ritual fell victim to the violence and contention wracking the area until federal teachers entered in the early 1930s and stumbled upon the festival as a mechanism for attracting people to the school and its ideology of modernization. When the federal school inspector, Jesús H. González, arrived in Tecamachalco in 1932 to supervise the few federal schools that existed and to create new ones, he had grandiose plans. The school envisioned and programmed by the central state's Secretaría de Educación Pública (SEP) was more than a place to teach writing, reading, arithmetic, and patriotism. It was programmed to effect a thoroughgoing community transformation. The school inspector saw himself as the heir of the nineteenth-century jefe político, modernizer of infrastructure, builder of civic space and consciousness, and reformer of daily customs in the interests of efficiency and health. Like his predecessor, he would open up the backward hinterland to new worlds—build roads, introduce mail service, promote commerce, scientific agriculture, and modern medicine. His productivist discourse was typical of central-state educational bureaucrats in the early 1930s: he would sanitize a degenerate race and remake it for "progress."[31]

Much to his chagrin and disappointment, his discourse rattled in the mayhem. He lacked the authority of the jefe político: like him, he needed village labor and finances to carry out his projects, but, unlike him, the school inspector could not exact compliance from the villagers. For such tasks, he lacked the sustained support of disputing local leaders. Moreover, the Constitution of 1917 outlawed compulsory unpaid labor for community improvements. The villagers of Tecamachalco showed a discriminating response to calls to civic duty. They had to perceive the direct benefit of projects to themselves individually, factionally, or collectively in order to be persuaded to sign up.[32]

To make matters worse, the 1930s were years of economic duress. Repeated droughts and freezes rendered the harvests minuscule, sent families elsewhere in search of sustenance, and left little margin of maneuver for the teacher as agronomist.[33] González wanted to eliminate the use of alcohol, and yet the production of pulque was one of the few sources of cash for the campesinos and was commercialized by the new *agraristas*. He wanted to alter the campesino home by introducing inoculation against contagious disease, a more nutritious and diversified diet, and a more hygienic and efficient organization of the household. Yet, most campesina women would not let teachers into their homes and would not attend the school's evening adult classes. He could hardly move attendance above its 1909 levels, let alone make the school the center of village life and the new ideology of modernity.To complicate matters, the schools emptied in 1935–1936 when the antireligious aspects of the federal policy of socialist education generated strong protest in Catholic Tecamachalco.[34]

In this rather resistant environment of closed doors, federal schoolteachers encountered a channel of access in the patriotic fiesta. This ritual was an expected one in the larger towns where the SEP took over schools, and yet the political disputes accompanying local revolution inhibited its celebration. Into the vacuum of civic authority stepped the schoolteacher to assume responsibility for an event in which he or she had played a principal but not determining role during the Porfiriato. Teachers found a demand for the patriotic fiesta in the smaller villages as well. Elaborating the fiesta appealed to the ancient spirit of intervillage competition, heightened by the agrarian reform process. At the same time, subordinate villages rebelled against dominant pueblos and municipal headtowns while those once submerged within haciendas sought to establish their autonomous identities. The patriotic fiesta became a symbol of community pride and independence. The school inspector and his teachers seized upon the fiesta to channel the passions of rivalry and the longings for autonomy in a pacific and civic direction.[35]

How did teachers utilize the patriotic fiesta to promote their ideology? First, the festival provided a singular way to persuade foot-dragging, skeptical, and impoverished villagers to build schoolhouses or remodel the ones they had. The motivation to build a school suddenly increased if the goal was to inaugurate it during the *fiestas patrióticas* and show it off to the villagers down the road. After all, the school building had become a symbol of civic maturity in the nineteenth century, even if it had, in many cases, begun as the jefe político's imposition and was always a tax burden. Second, as in the Porfiriato, preparing for the patriotic fiesta became a learning-by-doing experience, a lesson in the state's model of behavior. Streets had to be cleaned, roads repaired, garbage burned, and the town square beautified with greenery and flowers. Preparing for the fiesta opened an opportunity to put into practice one of the SEP's most touted campaigns—the planting of trees for adornment, fruit cultivation, and soil preservation. Third, teachers utilized the fiesta to broaden participation in the culture of schooling. They sponsored academic contests in spelling and math for schoolchildren at the festivals. These appealed to competitive instincts within the towns and certainly between them.[36]

The use of the patriotic festival to propagate the school's ideology of modernization began in small ways. In 1933, in Ocotitlán, a schoolteacher mobilized a committee that erected a flagpole and purchased a bust of Hidalgo, which they placed on a pedestal during the Cinco de Mayo ceremonies. When a group of villagers built the new schoolhouse in Zahuatlan, the teacher invited students and teachers from schools in three other towns to celebrate its inauguration with a civic festival and sports competition.[37]

The introduction of competitive, team sports—basketball and baseball—renewed and broadened interest in the festival in town after town. Few schools in Tecamachalco had flourishing gardens, chicken coops, or beehives, but all had sports fields and a Mexican flag.[38] Urban educators in the SEP hoped sports could discipline the uncontrolled impulses and rampant passions of countrypeople. They hoped athletic contests would replace bull and cockfights associated with gambling, alcohol, and bloodthirstiness and would "invigorate a decadent race."[39] However, policymakers at the national level only dimly perceived the reception basketball and baseball would have in places like Tecamachalco.[40] The games caught on among the prominent male youth of the villages, the next best thing to the political leaders who were preoccupied with more vital matters. Sports cost little money. They consumed no vital resources on which more pressing claims were being made, and they reaffirmed old principles of male dominance, physical prowess, and their conspicuous display.[41] They offered an alternative outlet for energy at a moment when male aggressiveness, escaping traditional mechanisms of social control, vented itself in an exceptional level of political violence and criminal activity.

Moreover, sports entertained—thus widening the circles participating in the patriotic festival. They lured spectators because they showed off the strength and competence of the towns' eligible young men. Young women loved them and encouraged their families to attend.[42] Even the most recalcitrant communities, when it came to school attendance, could rally around the school-sponsored fiesta when their basketball teams went at one another. To a certain degree, athletes replaced musicians as the entertaining element in the secular fiesta. Musicians were usually too expensive for small and impoverished towns or when political disputes made it difficult to raise funds.[43] The substitution captured a process of democratizing the festival. Becoming an athlete required less esoteric and costly training than did becoming a musician.

The drawing card of sports soon caught the attention of contending factions who evinced greater interest in sponsoring the festival as a mechanism of legitimization. Competitive team sports proved useful in expressing and healing intense intercommunal and intramural rivalries. Moreover, in the 1930s politicians from Puebla city quickly perceived the role athletic events could play in incorporating local powers into the state political machine they were building. Thus, local, regional, and national aspirants to power found in sports competitions a catalyst for legitimization and a mechanism of state formation.[44]

If sports appealed because they fit within existing values and legitimized emerging political structures, they also introduced new relations and values. The school inspector saw athletes as his *falange* in the transformation of customs—the shining knights in his crusade for health and abstinence from alcohol. Because those who excelled on the fields and courts became heroes at the same time they articulated the schools' messages, they opened space for the SEP's modernizing discourse.[45] In this sense they were also like many musicians of the nineteenth century—intermediaries between old and new worlds. Through team sports, athletes articulated new values of individualism, mobility, youth, and change inimical to traditional peasant society.

Implicitly undermining the prestige of the oldest men, the arbiters of peasant culture, team sports brought greater prestige and

independent space to male youth.[46] The new athletics subtly challenged the notion that status and prowess rested on land ownership
and the cultivation of the fields. Like the schools that spawned them,
sports turned the eyes and energies of their team members outward
and upward. A typical team traveled to engage in competitions.[47] Team
sports mobilized old competitive instincts between towns but encouraged a qualitatively different mobilization of human energies in new
directions. They combined teamwork with individualism and aspirations for upward mobility in a distinctly modern approach to human
development: a motivation of the self for efficient use of mind and
body in secular and autonomous ways.[48]

The introduction of sports competitions represented a new opening for childhood, adolescence, and youth, important for both boys
and girls. The revolutionary process brought a decline in parental
control over marriage choice in some parts of rural Mexico. The school
constructed within and around itself a secular space relatively free
from family control where youth began to define itself apart from
parents and in potentially new ways.[49] If athletic competitions presented a traditional gender positioning of male as actor hero and female as supportive spectator, other portions of the festival opened
areas of activity for girls convergent with a more active notion of
women's citizenship—areas such as dancing, theater, oratory, creative composition, singing, and the exhibition of craft, agricultural,
and poultry production.

The popularity of basketball and baseball provided a pretext for
multiplying the number of patriotic fiestas and opened space for teachers to introduce new notions of patriotism, national culture, and history.[50] By the end of the 1920s the SEP began to publish literature for
and about campesinos to substitute for the Porfirian readers written
for and about the urban middle class.[51] Textbooks such as *Fermín*
remade the peasant in the image of the urban reformer. The son of a
hacienda peon who had joined the Constitutionalist armies, Fermín
received land and became a modern commercial farmer. An advocate
of schooling and the local authority on agrarian law, Fermín also read
history books and newspapers and organized the *fiestas patrióticas*
in his town.[52]

Textbooks like *Fermín* articulated an inclusionary, populist ideology absent in the Porfiriato. This ideology was further constructed
in material for the patriotic fiesta. Emiliano Zapata took his place in
the pantheon of national heroes. The image of Zapata presented on
the patriotic altar had been sanitized through *corridas* (ballads), poetry, and oratory to approximate the SEP's ideal. This Zapata did not
drink *copas* (alcohol) with his *cuates* (buddies), gamble over fighting cocks, go to battle raising the banner of the Virgin of Guadalupe,

or lead a regional movement for a return to a precapitalist order. He symbolized the struggle of all Mexican peasants for land, social justice, and modernity, and he found solutions to these goals through the state.[53]

As the notion of a peasant-made revolution made its way into the fiesta, so did a more popular reconstruction of national history and culture. In the dances and songs the children performed—the *jarabe* from Guadalajara, the Yaqui Deer Dance from Sonora, the *huapango* from the Huasteca of Hidalgo, Veracruz, and Puebla—were a rehabilitation of the indigenous past and a recognition of the heterogeneity of Mexican folk cultures as the basis for a national culture.[54] Simultaneously, theater was used to draw the public to witness lessons in national history (the conspirators of Independence, the travails of the young shepherd boy Juárez) and to mobilize them for the future through instruction in new social behavior. Children performed plays on the importance of using soap (*"La Princesa Agua y el Rey Jabón"*—"The Water Princess and the Soap King") and the evils of alcohol, such as the misery a drunken father brings to his family.[55]

With the introduction of socialist education in 1935 and the intensification of the battle between church and state for the soul of the peasant, the SEP flooded the countryside with fiesta materials designed to inject a productivist, nationalist, and secular ideology. This ideology emphasized the state's identification with the struggle of the peasants against their "class enemies"—the hacienda owners and the priests, perpetrators of backwardness and misery. The Partido Nacional Revolucionario's (PNR) Committee on Social and Cultural Action sent municipal presidents instructions for cultural campaigns to be carried out in weekend rituals in accordance with the new "nationalist calendar" replacing the *fiestas religiosas*. These festivals focused on government interpretations of Mexican socialism, defense of class interests, defanaticization, hygiene, and agricultural modernization.[56]

Gathered together in their biweekly Centros de Cooperación where they found respite from the hostile ambience, the federal teachers of Tecamachalco learned the SEP's new socialist version of history, which amplified the populist, agrarian interpretation of the early 1930s. Formerly, the historical actors had been singular heroes struggling for the formation of the state. The state in turn had become the principal actor promoting progress and modernity through its authoritarian ordering of the country. Now, in the mid-1930s, a redefined history highlighted the social struggle of classes for rights, justice, and modernity. The admission of social groups mobilized to claim their rights and improve their conditions altered the old notion of an autonomous administrative state. Social groups struggled through heroes like Zapata, distinguished by their "love for the proletarian classes." The Constitution of 1917 became a document affirming collective or class rights, supplementing the individual interpretation of rights enshrined in the Constitution of 1857.[57]

This rhetoric emanated from the central state and provided succor to teachers beleaguered by village hostility and indifference. The Tecamachalquenos received it gradually and through a negotiation that subjected the state's rhetoric to censorship, selection, and reinterpretation. In 1936 the school inspector heaved a sigh of relief when, in the midst of the religious reaction against socialist education, the *fiestas patrióticas* organized by the teachers came off remarkably well.[58] He failed to note that despite official instructions to fight priests and superstition, the festivals had remained silent on the question of religion. Villagers had successfully censored the most controversial aspect of the state's ideological aggression. When President Lázaro Cárdenas, responding to a widespread national protest against socialist education, cancelled its antireligious focus in the same year, he provided space for the Tecamachalquenos to draw out the fruits of their victory. They obtained more than the right to continue their religious fiestas. The struggle against the antireligious aspects of socialist education was a metaphor for struggle against aggressive meddling with social customs. Teachers heard this message and were forced into more sensitive negotiation. They came to respect the privacy of the campesino home, appreciate the efficacy of certain herbal remedies, court the friendship of the priest, understand parental anxieties over coeducation, and readjust their teaching programs to accommodate the short and irregular school experiences of children needed at home for work.

Nor did the school inspector note that the *fiestas patrióticas* had a social meaning quite independent of their ideological content. The festival garners powerful support from the collective life of the community and tends to free itself from dependence on ideology. Most people enjoyed taking time out from the weighty work and oppressions of daily life to enjoy a basketball tournament. Adolescent girls drew their mothers into the festivities to make costumes or prepare a collective meal, not because the girls were interested in a speech about Zapata but because they looked forward to the festival as a time when they could meet young "eligibles."[59]

As much as they liked fiestas, the townsfolk quickly whittled down the SEP's demanding calendar to a few basic events. The teachers won by putting the September Independence celebration on a par with Cinco de Mayo. Villagers also accepted Mother's Day and a celebration commemorating the revolution (November 20, the Plan de Ayala, or the Carranza agrarian-reform decree). But festivals consecrated to trees, hygiene, and abstinence enjoyed a shorter run and smaller audiences. Along with most other SEP-proposed festivals, they were eventually relegated to the school yard.[60]

Just as villagers limited festivals, so the festival itself expanded to articulate new identities and identifications sculpted through the revolutionary process. The federal school won the greatest prestige as a sponsor of festivals when it mobilized local support for the national oil expropriation in 1938. In the state of Puebla this event, publicized through the press, radio, and ample printed propaganda of the PNR and the SEP, elicited strong popular support, drawing upon deep-rooted sentiments of defensive nationalism and a sense of participation in the cataclysm of revolution and reconstruction. Teachers organized kermesses, festivals, raffles, and dances in the communities to help pay the national debt.[61] This mobilization helped to heal the wounds inflicted by the battle around socialist education. In it the Tecamachalquenos joined other Mexicans in articulating an unprecedented sentiment of membership in a national collectivity.

The construction of the fiesta based on piecemeal, informal negotiations between townsfolk and teachers would have been ephemeral were it not for the consolidation of the Mexican state in the late 1930s and early 1940s. While the patriotic festival thrives on competition between towns and factions within them, the conflict accompanying power and resource redistribution in revolutionary Tecamachalco had had a debilitating effect upon the festival when compared with its celebration in the Porfiriato. In the late 1930s the consolidation of the state more clearly delineated and stabilized local lines of authority, processes for their renewal, and property ownership. *Agraristas* were absorbed into the regional branch of the Confederación Nacional Campesina and the middle classes into the municipal committees of the regional Partido Nacional Revolucionario (later called the PRM and, still later, the PRI). Scarred victors of internecine struggles assumed the reins of local government and the responsibilities of their Porfirian predecessors. Although conflicts continued well into the 1940s, political experience and the process of party and state formation had created a common civic discourse among these men, who equated the *patria* with progress, the party, the state, and schooling.[62] The municipal presidents, the officers of the *comisariados ejidales* (public-lands commissions), and the rest of the *fuerzas vivas*—rancheros, merchants, owners of the new bus companies—formed the juntas patrióticas responsible for the festivals.

In the 1940s the Tecamachalquenos embellished their festivals. The wealthier and more unified the community, the more elaborate the fiesta: a band rather than a Victrola provided the music. By popular acclaim the festival shed the Spartan character it had in the sanitizing 1930s under the teetotaling school inspector González. Expert *charros* (cowboys) sauntered along in the parade on their horses with their silver spurs and broad-rimmed, velveteen sombreros embroidered with brocade. Village women prepared great vats of mole. Villagers danced until dawn and enjoyed elaborate displays of fireworks.[63]

THE PATRIOTIC FIESTA: STATE IMPOSITION
OR HEGEMONIC ARTICULATION?

The fiesta symbolized the new state's penetration of village life. The revolution accelerated a long-term tendency weakening the resource base of local government and increasing its dependence on outside state agencies. Often fragmented between municipal, ejido, and religious authorities, local government became vulnerable to outside mediation and support. The process of agrarian reform created strong linkages between villages and the central state. The 1902 Cinco de Mayo inauguration of the hospital paled in comparison with post-1940 fiestas celebrating the opening of canals from the federal government's irrigation works at Valsequillo, the formation of a new cooperative, and the receipt of a loan from the national Banco de Credito Ejidal.[64] Again, sports teams symbolized the linkage as they traveled along the arteries of the state playing in competitions sponsored by the local, regional, and national PRI.

State penetration is not necessarily state imposition. It would be incorrect to regard municipal officeholders and those of the *comisariados ejidales* as impostors. They had fought hard, if not fairly or peaceably, for membership. To get there they had represented groups and issues. The new concepts added to the political vocabulary of the festival—the Constitution of 1917, social justice, collective rights, agrarian reform, the progressive course of history in the direction of human liberation—had real meaning to the leaders and their clientele. The convergence between the *agraristas'* notions of history, law, and process and those articulated by the patriotic festival is illustrated in a letter sent by the *ejidatarios* and political officers of the town of Cuesta Blanca to President Manuel Avila Camacho in 1941. They wrote angrily in response to the state governor's defense of a renter's complaint against their use of water he claimed for himself:

> Please do us the favor of dictating your final decision to grant this pueblo the use of the waters as clearly explained in *Article 27 of the Republic's Constitution*, which says in its first paragraph: "The nation . . . has the right to impose limits on private property dictated by the public interest." Based on this law

and protected by the most basic *justice*, we are ready to take any risk, based on the *unequivocally revolutionary* spirit of our present Government, which we hope will know how to hear the *cry of a whole people, who without the precious liquid will perish from hunger*, and will dismiss the personal interest of a single individual, who without having the necessary facts and precedent dares to claim *rights* which are not his. . . . Citizen López y Tolsa must keep in mind that the people of Cuesta Blanca will go to the point of *sacrifice before allowing their rights to be usurped. He should know that the times when we were intimidated and subjected to brute force have long since passed.* . . . We are respectful of our Supreme Government, and we know from experience and because it is *a matter of justice* that this decision will establish a precedent which will strengthen its prestige and the firm conviction that we are entering *a new era in which we are treated as Citizens conscious of our rights.* Necessity forces us to use the waters while the Supreme Government makes its favorable decision, since the time for watering the crops is here and not to do so would mean the loss of the crop. We have faith in justice.[65]

Expressing heightened tensions between themselves and the state, the villagers nonetheless composed the letter in a language mutually constructed by themselves and representatives of the state and enunciated in the patriotic festival.

State penetration of village life converged as well with the reality lived by the townsfolk. Between 1910 and 1940 life changed in Tecamachalco.[66] The revolution had unfolded there as a violent struggle for the redistribution of wealth and power. Tearing communities apart, it cut into the social fabric. These struggles played themselves out on stark lands ravaged by drought and frost, among a hungry people threatened by deadly viruses and deserting their homes in search of employment. But disintegration resulted in reorganization. A new political order was forged with new rules for access, representation, and reward. Life became more externally linked. Nothing better captured the linkage than the negotiations between villagers and the new highway between Puebla and Tehuacán. Townspeople sought jobs on the construction crews through the Secretaría de Obras Publicas, had goats and cows run over by trucks, were ordered to fence in their livestock, disputed with rancheros over rights to build feeder roads, widened trails to accommodate the new vehicles, hauled sacks of grain to the Tepeaca market on buses, and transported sick children to the hospital in Tecamachalco in the Peregrino family's taxicab.[67]

The fiesta became a ritually performed mobilization for modernity linked to the state. Ritual, writes Inga Clendinnen, not only confirms reality but also creates it.[68] Did the patriotic festival make people think these external linkages were more promising than they actually were? Perhaps, but consideration must be given to a series of interrelated political, social, and economic processes. The Mexican state, through agrarian reform, its interaction with social and political movements, the school, and its own brutal political consolidation, composed a persuasive, hegemonic discourse mobilizing people around new options as other options were eliminated. In the 1940s and 1950s there was real convergence between fiesta discourse and local history in Tecamachalco. The state delivered neither pure democracy nor great prosperity, but it did provide political stabilization and a demonstrably better life as reflected in new irrigation canals, deep-water wells installed with gas and electricity, cheap bus transportation, the highway, mechanical corngrinders, the commercialization of fruit, and inoculations and antibiotics to combat epidemics and endemic bacterial infection.[69] These decades brought population growth and little emigration. Teachers remember them as the golden age of the festival—before television, soil erosion, and exodus.

Viewing the festival as a channel for articulating hegemony emphasizes its inclusionary aspects, in contrast to Friedlander's focus on imposition, and highlights the festival's mobilizing character, in contrast to Knight's assertion that the state had little impact as a cultural creator. Hegemony, in Gramscian terms, means rule by consensus. Coercion may precede consensus and continue to be an aspect of state power, but hegemony rests on moral and intellectual persuasion.[70] It embraces an ensemble of symbols, images, and visions of the past and the future that take hold among social subjects to shape identity, memory, loyalty, and meaning, and to energize action. These ideological elements cannot simply be disseminated from the top by elites commanding institutions such as schools, clubs, and political parties.[71] Rather, the hegemonic discourse emanating from the Mexican state through the festival resulted from interactive processes involving multiple social groups and interweaving a multiplicity of discourses. Hegemony can only be constructed from a variety of cultural traditions that make up a nation: "Nationalistic sentiments hinge . . . on fusing an extant, deeply personal sense of existence with continuation of the nation."[72]

The state-building that took place in Mexico between 1917 and 1940 allowed for nation-building on an unprecedented scale. As the peasants, rancheros, and hacienda owners of Tecamachalco struggled to redefine the parameters of power and wealth, their regional arena of state-building opened a space where identity and loyalties were also constructed. The school stepped into this space to fill it with an expanded vocabulary of identification, moral behavior, and historical time. This vocabulary was itself the product of revolutionary struggle. To be sure, the Secretaría de Educación Pública appropriated and rearranged the language, but neither this appropriation nor its dissemination constituted hegemony. Teachers as agents of the state could not impose the language or make it stick. Social subjects responded to the vocabulary selectively by adopting, reinterpreting, discarding, and internalizing parts of it. Just as the state had no autonomy in inculcating the vocabulary, the social subject's autonomy in interpreting it was mediated by his or her relationship to political power, social institutions, economic resources, and events.

The successful construction of hegemonic discourse rested upon the space it allowed for regional diversity and for multiple discourses at the local level. Expressed through the patriotic festival in Tecamachalco, this construction resounded in a state-orchestrated mobilization for modernity. Respect for custom prefaced the "mobilization." A high degree of local mediation determined meaning and behavior and the pace and nature of change, as mobilization remained contingent upon local factors related to political power, social organization, and economic growth. In Tecamachalco a mestizo agrarianism succeeded in achieving political power, refurbishing the peasant household unit of production and its patriarchal mores and accelerating commercialization. Proximity to markets and cities encouraged commercial exchange and mobility. A regional state political machine institutionalized festive celebration around a productivist paradigm (for example, sports, agricultural and livestock exhibitions, and hospitals).[73] Three aspects of the festival—political vocabulary, sports, and the Mother's Day celebration—illustrate the inclusionary and mobilizing character of hegemonic discourse in Tecamachalco.

The revolutionary process democratized the festival. Where the Constitution of 1857 focused on individual rights, the Constitution of 1917 emphasized collective rights as a basis for social justice and national development. Although deeply embedded in the political culture and practice of central highland villages, corporate rights had been deliberately excluded from the nineteenth-century liberal discourse that considered them backward and immoral. By force of the peasantry's mobilization and subsequent agrarian reform, notions and practices of collectivity penetrated the discursive space of the postrevolutionary state and, linked with the notion of individual rights, expanded the meaning of patriotism from its nineteenth-century animus against foreign oppressors to a struggle against all forms of oppression. Patriotism became bound up with an interpretation of history as the progressive struggle of "the Mexican people" for "liberation"—justice and material fulfillment.

The letter of the Cuesta Blanca villagers articulated old elements in a new, expanded logic. The organization and procedures of the town meeting and the composition of a collectively authored letter (petition) to the president (king) derive from the República de los Indios, the legal fiction that had established relations between self-governing Indian villages and the paternalistic king in the Spanish colony. The villagers justified their action—utilizing water claimed by someone else and not yet legally theirs—within a traditional peasant moral economy. They expected the president (king) to understand the taking of extralegal measures to assure survival.[74] Nevertheless, the action was not simply justified by an ancient right related to customary use and need. The authors placed their actions within the context of a popular, national struggle they had waged to achieve justice, citizenship, and liberation—in short, modernity. Ideologically, they no longer engaged in a defensive, local maneuver. Their discursive context became an open-ended arena extending beyond the boundaries of the *comisariado ejidal*, the village, or the existing state. The hegemonic discourse had grown out of and fostered the construction of counterhegemonic, oppositional articulations.

Athletic competitions also served as inclusionary and mobilizing aspects of the Tecamachalco festival. They symbolized a more active investment of self and energy than had the Porfirian *cuerpo filarmónico* or its student orators. They honored values in central Mexican peasant culture (conspicuous display of virility, male dominance and female subordination, corporate solidarity) and practices (collective competition within and between villages). Sports also encouraged change (merit-based competitiveness, individual achievement, mobility, and a relatively autonomous space for youth). In Tecamachalco their meaning and function were mediated through diverse centers of power. Excelling in sports could secure an individual important "relations" for career advancement: entry into the local patriarchal structure of power, into the state political machine, or, through education, into professional, urban employment. Just as the meaning of the festival's political vocabulary varied in different parts of Mexico, so sports assumed an importance in Puebla that they may have lacked elsewhere. The regional political machine institutionalized them as a mechanism for party-building, recruitment, and legitimization. The vitality of the marketplace and proximity of cities encouraged the horizontal and vertical mobility associated with competitive team sports.[75]

Finally, the revolutionary festival was far more inclusionary of women than it had been in the nineteenth century. It engaged schoolgirls in new activities (theater, dances, and exhibits of products) and mothers in traditional ones (cooking and sewing). One of the most important festive holidays became Mother's Day. Motherhood was differently valued and understood by peasant patriarchs and state educators.[76] The former valued women in a protected, subordinate sphere of domestic activities associated with the household unit of production. The state wanted mothers to be more active and more public. The school would reach the mothers of tomorrow with the same messages of efficiency, activity, hygiene, and productivism delivered to men. The reconstitution of the peasant subsistence household through agrarian reform exacerbated the conflict over gender constructions because the reform appeared to solidify old patriarchal behaviors. But the penetration of the market both required and made possible a greater public role for peasant women in trade, production, and migration in order to meet family subsistence requirements. The introduction of the corngrinding mill freed woman's time just as cheap bus transportation made her more mobile and encouraged her increasing participation in the economy. Thus one dilemma in gender relations was how to maintain local customs of patriarchal control while allowing for new areas of women's activity and learning.[77]

The Mother's Day festival was a moment of partial resolution when the two discourses intersected. The image of the Mexican woman honored in Mother's Day celebrations in the 1940s was bathed in the pathos of suffering reminiscent of images of the Virgin in Mexican churches. Women were honored as symbols of unbounded love and sacrifice. Dramatic skits attempted to draw tears from the audience, the theater becoming a collective commiseration over life's hard knocks embodied in the stoical figure of the mother.[78] The mother personified the integrity of the campesino family and its hierarchical structure. Mother's Day theater became a communal grieving session, legitimizing village, family, and gender subordination. At the same time, the occasion celebrated women as active producers (through exhibits of their production); as students learning new secular skills and identities in a space apart from the parental home; as performers (through dancing and acting); and as citizens honored in oratory that linked their activity to sacrifice for the *patria*.

CONCLUSION

The historian must consider the anthropologist's analysis of and sensitivity toward villagers' subordination to internal and external powerholders. The Indians of Hueyapan whom Judith Friedlander studied in the 1970s were indeed disadvantaged by Mexican power structures and yet bound to listen to a manufactured "Indian-ness" at the patriotic festival and lionization of a decontextualized local hero, Emiliano Zapata. The historian analyzes the construction of this patriotic ritual over time. As a historian Alan Knight grasps the cumulative process of ritualized ideology as an interaction between social groups and state rhetoric. Both Friedlander and Knight view the state with suspicion and mistrust. Reflecting on the Mexican state in the 1970s, Friedlander sees it as an alien and unresponsive agency of domination. Knight, assessing it in the 1930s, sees it as an ineffectual and weak agency of cultural change. His denial of the state's role in changing mentalities seems overdrawn. Between 1940 and 1968 the incidence of political repression was probably less important in maintaining stability amid rapid socioeconomic growth than was the state's construction of a persuasive hegemonic discourse that hallowed tradition and encouraged change. Teachers as agents of the state contributed to the multiple authoring of that discourse.

NOTES

1. A starting point to examine this ample bibliography is Frank Cancion, "Political and Religious Organizations," in *Handbook of Middle American Indians: Social Anthropology*, vol. 6, ed. R. Wauchope and M. Nash (Austin, TX, 1967).

2. Judith Friedlander. "The Secularization of the Cargo System: An Example of Post-Revolutionary Mexico," *LARR* 16 (1981): 132–44.

3. Among the many important works of revisionist history, see the essays in David Brading, *Caudillo and Peasant in the Mexican Revolution* (Cambridge, 1982), and Arnaldo Córdova, *La ideología de la Revolución Mexicana: La formación del nuevo régimen* (México, 1972). For interpretations of the popular movement betrayed, see, among others, Arturo Warman, *We Come to Object: The Peasants of Morelos and the National State*, trans. Stephen K. Ault (Baltimore, 1980).

4. His understanding of the revolution receives its most detailed presentation in *The Mexican Revolution*, 2 vols. (Cambridge, 1986). See also "The Mexican Revolution: Bourgeois? Nationalist? Or just a 'Great Rebellion'?" *Bulletin of Latin American Research* 4, no. 2 (1985): 1–37; and "Interpretaciones recientes de la Revolución Mexicana," *Memorias del Simposio de Historiografía Mexicanista* (México, 1990), 193–210.

5. "Intellectuals in the Mexican Revolution," in *Los intelectuales y el poder en México*, ed. Roderic A. Camp, Charles A. Hale, and Josefina Zoraida Vázquez (Los Angeles and México, 1992), 141–72; and "El liberalismo mexicano desde la Reforma hasta la Revolución. Una interpretación," *HM* 35 (1985): 59–85. His argument for popular liberalism has been strengthened by the recent work of Guy P. C. Thomson, "Popular Aspects of Liberalism in Mexico, 1848–1888," *Bulletin of Latin American Research* 10, no. 3 (1991): 265–92; "Bulwarks of Patriotic Liberalism: The National Guard, Philharmonic Corps and Patriotic Juntas in Mexico, 1847–1888," *JLAS* 22 (1989): 31–68; and Florencia Mallon, "Peasant and State Formation in Nineteenth-Century Mexico: Morelos, 1848–1858," *Political Power and Social Theory* 7 (1988): 1–54, and "The Conflictual Construction of Community: Gender, Ethnicity, and Hegemony in the Sierra Norte de Puebla" (paper presented at the University of Chicago Seminar in Latin American History, May 1990). See also Jean Pierre Bastian, "El paradigma de 1789: sociedades de ideas y Revolución mexicana," *HM* 38 (1988): 79–110.

6. "Revolutionary Project, Recalcitrant People: Mexico, 1910–40," in *The Revolutionary Process in Mexico: Essays on Political and Social Change, 1880–1940*, ed. Jaime E. Rodríguez O. (Los Angeles, 1990), 230, 247–50, 255–59.

7. For the distinction between state- and nation-building, see Thomson, "Popular Aspects of Liberalism in Mexico," 265–68; and David A. Brading, "Liberal Patriotism and the Mexican Reforma," *JLAS* 10 (1988): 27–48.

8. Ministerio de Fomento, Dirección General de Estadíustica, *Censo general de la República mexicana verificada el 18 de octubre de 1900* (México, 1900); *Tercer censo de la población, México: 1910* (México, 1918); *Boletín de estadística del estado de Puebla, 1900–1911*; Vaughan, "Economic Growth and Literacy in Late Nineteenth-Century Mexico: The Case of Puebla," in *Education and Economic Development since the Industrial Revolution*, ed. Gabriel Tortella (Valencia, 1990), 89–112, and "Rural Women's Literacy and Education in the Mexican Revolution," in *Creating Spaces: Women of the Mexican Countryside, 1850–1990*, ed. Heather Fowler Salamini and Mary Kay Vaughan (Tucson, AZ, forthcoming).

9. See Ernesto LaClau and Chantal Mouffe, *Hegemony and Socialist Strategy: Towards Radical Democratic Politics* (New York, 1985), 133, on the European concept of "people" as constructed through the popularization of war against foreign armies (Hundred Years' War).

10. Archivo Municipal de Tecamachalco (hereafter cited as AMT), Gobierno, Caja 129, Expediente 58, Relativo a la manera de solemnizar en el distrito el 40 aniversario del triunfo que tuvieron las armas nacionales el 5 de mayo de 1862, Palmar del Bravo, March 3, May 3, 1902, Caltenco, April 29, 1902, Tlanepantla, May 1902, Xochitlán, May 2, 1902; Gastos que hicieron el 9 de marzo en la funcion cívica, 1896; Caja 266, Expediente 13, Relativo a la Celebración del 5 de mayo, April 29, 1909. For analysis of this festival in northern Puebla in the 1860s and 1870s, see Thomson, "Bulwarks," 61–67.

11. The didactic aspects of the Mexican religious festival receive careful discussion in Robert Ricard, *The Spiritual Conquest of Mexico* (Berkeley, CA, 1966) and is ably synthesized by Friedlander, "Secularization of the Cargo System," 136–39. The same detailed analysis of the patriotic fiesta as pedagogy does not exist. Mona Ozouf, *Festivals and the French Revolution*, trans. Alan Sheridan (Cambridge, MA, 1988), 166–71, 198–213, offers an instructive treatment of the pedagogical techniques of the festival.

12. Examples include Plaza Juan Crisóstomo Bonilla, named in honor of one of Puebla's major liberal heroes; the many streets named La Reforma, La Constitución, and La Independencia, which are located in all substantial towns; and the schools named for patriot heroes Miguel Hidalgo, Vicente Guerrero, José María Morelos y Pavón, and Josefa de Domínguez. On the pedagogy of space, see Ozouf, *Festivals*, 126–27, 147. For some pedagogical techniques in contemporary Morelos, see Friedlander, "Secularization of the Cargo System," 139–40.

13. Vaughan, "Economic Growth and Literacy," 99–100, 104–7. On the spread of new ideology by schoolteachers through primary schools, see François Xavier Guerra, *México: del antiguo régimen a la Revolución*, vol. 1 (México, 1988), 394–443.

14. AMT, Gobierno, Caja 129, Actas de Cabildo, May 3, 1902.

15. On similarities between religious and patriotic festivals, see Friedlander, "Secularization of the Cargo System," 138–41; and Klaus Jacklein, *San Felipe*

Otlaltepec: Beitrage zue ethnoanalyse der popoloca de Puebla, Mexiko (Gottingen, 1970), 271–74. On aggressive substitution in the Sierra Norte, see the Thomson essay in this volume (Chapter 15) and "Bulwarks," 32–33.

16. Philip A. Dennis, *Intervillage Conflict in Oaxaca: San Andres Zautla and Santo Tomás Mazaltepec* (New Brunswick, NJ, 1987), 29, 151–52, 155–56; Charles Gibson, "Indians under Spanish Rule," in *Colonial Spanish America*, ed. Leslie Bethell (Cambridge, 1989), 378; and William T. Sanders and Barbara J. Price, *Mesoamerica: The Evolution of a Civilization* (New York, 1968), 183.

17. *Directorio general del estado de Puebla, 1891; Tercer censo de la población: 1910*; on privatization of communal lands, see AMT, Gobierno, Caja 129, Expediente 25, "Relativo al reparto que de terreno del fundo legal del pueblo de Cuesta Blanca hizo la respectiva Junta Auxiliar," January 22, 1902; on social differentiation manifest in disputes between farmers, see AMT, Gobierno, Caja 129, Expediente 51, "Solicitud . . . vecinos Tlacotepec pidiendo que se declare de uso publico el agua pluvial que se deposita en el jaguey conocido con el nombre de Rojas," Luciano Reyes et al. to ayuntamiento, March 15, 1902.

18. See, for example, AMT, Gobierno, Caja 129, Expediente 57, April 29, 1902, and Expediente 17, May 7, 1902, on water-use privileges accorded to the hacienda and flour mill of Palemon Coutolenc.

19. On the Catholic movement in the west, see Manuel Ceballos Ramírez, "Las lecturas católicas: cincuenta años de literatura paralela, 1867–1917," in *Historia de la lectura en México* (México, 1988), 153–204; Jean Meyer, *La cristiada*, vol. 2, *El conflicto entre la iglesia y el estado, 1926/1929* (México, 1973), 31–53; Karl Schmitt, "The Díaz Conciliation Policy on State and Local Levels, 1876–1911," *HAHR* 40 (1960): 513–32; Agustín Vaca, "La política clerical en Jalisco durante el Porfiriato," in *Jalisco en la conciencia nacional*, vol. 2, ed. José María Muria, Cándido Galván, and Angélica Peregrina (Guadalajara, 1987), 471–79.

20. Maurice Agulhon, *The Republic in the Village: The People of the Var from the French Revolution to the Second Republic*, trans. Janet Lloyd (Cambridge, 1982), 121–27.

21. *Directorio general del estado de Puebla*, 1891. It seems logical that many of these rancherías would have fallen within the economic, social, and, indeed, the spatial sphere of the hacienda. Guerra develops the notion of a traditional form of collective loyalty and ritual associated with the large estate and coexisting in a polarized fashion with the emerging liberal ethos, in *México: del antiguo régimen a la Revolución*, 1:132–38. Herbert J. Nickel mentions the nature of traditional sociability on these large estates in *Morfología social de la hacienda mexicana* (México, 1988), 269–89, 307, 389. For an example of religiosity bound up with the large estate, see AMT, Presidencia, Caja 74, Juan Amador, Esteban Morales, Paulino López, Ranchería La Portilla, Tecamachalco, June 20, 1938, on the liberation of their image of the Virgin from the chapel of the Hacienda de la Rosa.

22. Thomson in this volume (Chapter 15) and "Bulwarks," 51–61. In Tecamachalco, among the prominent bands at the end of the Porfiriato were Caltepec's Cuerpo Filarmónico, Palmar del Bravo's Banda Hidalgo, and the military band of the federal army detachment quartered in the district capital (AMT, Caja 129, Expediente 58, Relativo a la manera de solemnizar en el distrito el 40 aniversario del triunfo que tuvieron las armas nacionales el 5 de mayo de 1862, March 3, 1902). Further information on Puebla's bands and musicians comes from

my interviews with Isaura Martínez, June 19, 1989, Puebla; Marco Velázquez, July 3, 1991, Puebla; Horacio Caro, July 7, 1991, Puebla.

23. Caro interview.

24. Vaughan, "Economic Growth and Literacy," 99–100, 104–9, and "Rural Women's Literacy and Education in the Mexican Revolution," appendix tables.

25. Estado de Puebla, *Memoria instructiva e documentada que el Jefe del Departamento Executivo del Estado presenta al XX Congreso Constitucional* (Puebla, 1908), 256–57; AMT, Sección Gobierno, Caja 266, Sesión pública ordinaria, Ayuntamiento, March 3, 1909; and ibid., Noticias de ingreso y egresos, February 14, 1910; Expediente 11, Actas de Cabildo, March 3, August 4, 1909.

26. AMT, Seccion Gobierno, Caja 266, Sesión pública, Actas de cabildo, March 17, April 21, June 23, and August 4, 1909; ibid., Seguridad Pública, Caja 342, José María Trejo, Presidente Auxiliar, Tenango, May 12, June 20, 1913; No. 22, Antonio Ruiz, Quecholac, September 13, 1913; Pedro Oropez, Palmar, to Jefe Político, July 2, July 3, July 14, July 19, 1913; Heliodoro Vera, Palmar, August 19, 1913.

27. For postrevolutionary state consolidation in Puebla, see Julio Glockner Rossainz, *La presencia del estado en el medio rural: Puebla (1929–1941)* (Puebla, 1982); Jesús Márquez Carrillo, "Los origenes de Avilacamachismo: Una arqueología de fuerzas en la constitución de un poder regional: el estado de Puebla, 1929–1941" (Licenciatura thesis, Universidad Autónoma de Puebla, 1983); Mary Kay Vaughan, "Actuación politica del magisterio socialista en Puebla y Sonora (1934–1939)," *Critica* 22–23 (1987): 90–100; Wil Pansters, *Politics and Power in Puebla: The Political History of a Mexican State, 1937–1987* (Amsterdam, 1990).

28. Vaughan, "Rural Women's Literacy," appendix tables. To sample the records on this topic, see Archivo de la Reforma Agraria, Estado de Puebla (hereafter cited as ARA-P), Expediente No. 174, Tecamachalco, May 8, 1931; Acervos Presidentes, Fondo Lázaro Cárdenas Ríos, AGN (hereafter cited as LCR-AGN), Expediente 404.1/9136, Rosendo Pérez, Presidente Comité Ejecutivo Agrario, Cuaucnopalan, August 5, 1938. On invasions, for example, see ARA-P, Expediente No. 174, Tecamachalco, October 30, 1925, January 1, 1926.

29. Dissident campesinos in the town of Alseseca accused a member of the ayuntamiento of being unfit to serve because, after taxing the vecinos to remodel the school, he had pocketed the proceeds for himself. (AMT, Legajo 74, Reunión de Regidores, Junta Auxiliar, Alseseca, Tecamachalco, September 6, 1938).

30. On hacienda-*agrarista* disputes, see the huge numbers documents in the following archives: LCR-AGN; AMT, Presidencia. In the latter, see Caja 74, 1938, Cayetano Santos, Municipal President, Tecamachalco, to Municipal President, Quecholac, January 21, 1938, regarding the invasions of *ejidatarios* of San Simon on the land of *ejidatarios* of Francisco I. Madero.

31. González's ideology runs through all of his bimonthly reports in SEP/AH, Departamento de Escuelas Rurales (hereafter cited as DER), Caja 905, 1932; ibid., Caja 969, 1933; ibid., Expediente 207.1, 1935; ibid., Expediente 316.1, 1936.

32. AMT, Año de 1936, Presidencia, Legajo 68, Dolores Navarro, Poblado de San Antonio La Portilla, to Municipal President, May 2, 1936; Juan López, Juez de Presidencia Auxiliar, Alseseca, to Municipal President, October 23, 1936.

33. SEP/AH, DER, Caja 905, González, Informes, July, August, November 1932; Caja 969, González, Informes, June, August 1933; Informe anual, December

1933; Expediente 207.1, González, Informe, October-November 1935; Expediente 316.1, González, Informe, April-May 1936; Plan de Trabajo, Año de 1936, January 1936; LCR-AGN, Expediente 564.1/2091, Odilón Luna, Presidente, Comisariado Ejidal, San Mateo Tlaixpan, to Cárdenas, January 18, 1940.

34. On resistance to socialist education, see Vaughan, "Rural Women's Literacy and Education in the Mexican Revolution," 10–21; SEP/AH, DER, Caja 969, González, Informes, June, September 1933; Informe, Instituto de Mejoramiento, July 28–29, 1933; Informe Anual, December 1933; Expediente 207.1, González, Informes, February-March, August-September 1935, Informe Anual, December 1935; Expediente 316.1, González, Informes, February-March, June-July 1936; LCR-AGN, Expediente 533.3/75, Fidencio Velazquez, Comisariado Ejidal, San Mateo Tlaixpan, to Cárdenas, February 25, 1935; Expediente 541/711, Fausto Molina Betancourt, SEP-Puebla, to Cárdenas, February 17, 1936.

35. SEP/AH, DER, Caja 905, González, Informe, September 1932; Informe, Instituto de Mejoramiento Profesional, Xonaca, July 28–29, 1932; Expediente 316.1, González, Informe, October-November 1935; Archivos Particulares de las Escuelas Rurales Federales (hereafter cited as APERF), Escuela Rural Federal (hereafter ERF) Santa Rosa, Informe sintético, June 12, 1932; ERF Chipiltepec, Tochtepec, Tecamachalco, Informe sintético de visita de inspección, August 17, 1933. For developments in Tlaxcala, see Elsie Rockwell, "Schools of the Revolution: Enacting and Contesting State Forms (Tlaxcala, 1910–1930)," in *Everyday Forms of State Formation: Revolution and the Negotiation of Rule in Modern Mexico*, ed. Gilbert Joseph (Durham, NC, 1994).

36. SEP/AH, DER, Caja 905, González, Informes, July, September 1932; Informe, Instituto de Mejoramiento Profesional, Xonaca, July 28–29, 1932; Caja 969, González, Informe, June, July, March 1933; Expediente 207.1, González, Informe, October-November 1935; Expediente 316.1, González, Informe, Plan de Trabajo, January 1936, Informes, February-March, April-May, June-July, August-September 1936; SEP/AH, ERF Santa Rosa, Informe sintético, June 12, 1932; ERF Chipiltepec, Tochtepec, Informe sintético, August 17, 1933.

37. SEP/AH, DER, Caja 969, Gonzalez, Informes, May, July 1933.

38. SEP/AH, DER, Expediente 316.1, SEP Cir. Num. IV-42-132, April 25, 1936; APERF, ERF Colonia Francisco I. Madero, Quecholac, "Datos escolares," November 29, 1938; ERF, Pericotepec, Tochtepec, "Datos," November 1938; ERF Chipiltepec, "Datos," November 30, 1938.

39. On invigoration of the decadent race, see SEP/AH, DER, Expediente 207.1, González, Informe, October-November 1935; on disciplining rampant passions, see Guillermo Bonilla y Segura, *Report on the Cultural Missions* (Washington, DC, 1945), 23–25; on utilizing sports to replace blood sports, see Dennis, *Intervillage Conflict*, 31, and Robert Redfield, *Folk Culture of Yucatán* (Chicago, 1941), 274–75.

40. SEP/AH, DER, Caja 905, González, Informes, April, May, August 1932. The importance of sports in winning support for the federal school, its programs, and festivals is mentioned in most reports of the school inspector. See, for example, Expediente 207.1, González, Informe Anual, 1935; on the importance in the fiesta, see Expediente 207.1, González, Informe, October-November 1935.

41. Robert Redfield, *Chan Kom: Village that Chose Progress* (Chicago, 1950), 15, 136.

42. Ibid.; Caro interview; interview with Augustina Barrojas de Caro, Puebla, July 7, 1991.

43. SEP/AH, DER, Caja 905, González, Informes, April, May, August 1932; interview with Reyna Carmona Manzano, Puebla, July 5, 1991.

44. Dennis, *Intervillage Conflict*, 90; Redfield, *Chan Kom*, 15, 136; AMT, Ano de 1935, Presidencia Municipal, Caja 65, Actividades de Asociaciones Deportivas; Secretaría de la Económia Nacional, September 1934; Asociación Guerrero, Tecamachalco, May 12, 1935.

45. See, for example, SEP/AH, DER, Caja 905, González, Informes, April, August 1932; Caja 969, González, Informe Anual, 1933.

46. González noted that they appealed to the young, not men over fifty who continued to "obstruct" the school. González, Expediente 207.1, González, Informe Anual, December 1935.

47. Interview with Victor Alba, Puebla, July 8, 1991.

48. On modernity and the body, see Michel Foucault, *Discipline and Punish: The Birth of the Prison* (New York, 1979).

49. Redfield, *Chan Kom*, 129–37; Friedrich, *Agrarian Revolt in a Mexican Village*, 49; Oscar Lewis, *Life in a Mexican Village: Tepoztlan Restudied* (Urbana, IL, 1971), 78–79; Lewis, *Life in a Mexican Village*, 383–410; and Rockwell, "Rural Schooling and the State," 22–23.

50. SEP/AH, DER, Caja 905, González, Informes, April-May, July-August 1932; Informe, Instituto de Mejoramiento, July 27–28, 1932; Expediente 316.1, González, Informes, April-May, June-July, August-September 1936.

51. For this change in textbooks in Tecamachalco, see APERF, ERF Santa Rosa, Inventario, April 5, 1932; ERF Nazareño, Roger Sanchez Parra, Inventario y Correspondencia, June 11, 1936; Entrega en los principios de los labores escolares, February 8, 1937; ERF San Juan Ocotlán, Miguel Sánchez and Benito Mendez to SEP, August 19, 1932; ERF Caltenco, Inventario general de todo lo existente en la escuela rural federal de Caltenco, Tochtepec, March 27, 1939.

52. Vaughan, "Ideological Change in Mexican Educational Policy, Programs, and Texts, 1920–1940," in *Los intelectuales y el poder en Mexico*, 515–18; Manuel Velazquez Andrade, *Fermín*, trans. Marcel Carl (México, 1933), 1–19.

53. On Zapata, see *El maestro rural*, vol. 1, March 1, 1932, no. 1, SEP, p. 9; vol. 3, December 15, 1933, pp. 34–35; SEP/AH, DER, Expediente 316.1, González, Informe, June-July 1936; Ilene O'Malley, *The Myth of the Revolution: Hero Cults and the Institutionalization of the Mexican State, 1920–1940* (Westport, CT, 1986), 42–70.

54. SEP/AH, APERF, ERF Chipiltepec, Tochtepec, Informes sintéticos, August 31, 1932, August 17, 1933; ERF Santa Rosa, Informes sintéticos, June 12, 1931, June 26, 1933; ERF San Juan Ocotlán, September 7, 1933; SEP/AH, DER, Caja 905, González, Informe Anual, December 1932; *El Maestro rural*, vol. 1, no. 1, March 1, 1932, pp. 14–15; vol. 1, no. 3, April 1, 1932, p. 21.

55. SEP/AH, DER, Caja 905, González, Informes, July, September, October 1932, Informe Anual Escolar, December 1932; Expediente 207.1, González, Informe, October-November 1935, Informe Anual, December 1935; Expediente 316.1, González, Plan de Trabajo, January 1936; APERF, ERF Santa Rosa, Informes sintéticos, June 12, 1931, September 7, 1932, June 26, 1933; ERF San Nicolás El Viejo, Tlacotepec, "Datos," November 1938; ERF Pericotepec, "Datos,"

November 25, 1938; ERF Palmarito, Informes sintéticos, May 18, July 21, 1933; ERF Chipiltepec, Informes sintéticos, August 31, 1932, August 17, 1933; ERF San Juan Ocotlán, Informes sintéticos, July 16, September 7, 1933.

56. AMT, Año de 1935, Presidencia Municipal Caja 65, PNR Comité de Acción Social y Cultural, México, Presidente José M. Davila and Vice Presidente, Antonio Mediz Bolio, to Presidente Municipal, Tecamachalco, February 1935. The SEP had another elaborate calendar that was similar to the PNR's though more densely packed with events. See Ignacio García Tellez, *Socialización de la cultura: Seis meses de acción educativa* (México, 1935), 142–44.

57. Vaughan, "Ideological Change in Mexican Educational Policy," 518–26; see also SEP/AH, DER, Expediente 316.1, González, Indicador de Actividades, January 25, 1936; Informe, October-November 1936.

58. SEP/AH, DER, González, Informe, September-October 1936.

59. Agulhon, *Republic in the Village*, 91; APERF, ERF Pericotepec, Tochtepec, "Datos," November 25, 1938; ERF Chipiltepec, Sara Robles Jímenez, "Datos que deben rendir los Directores de las Escuelas rurales federales en la República," November 30, 1938; interview with Caro; interview with Barrojas de Caro.

60. SEP/AH, DER, Caja 905, González, Tecamachalco, Informes, September-October 1932; Expediente 207.1, González, Tecamachalco, Informe, October-November 1935; Informe Anual, December 1935; APERF, ERF Santa Rosa, Tecamachalco, Informes sintéticos, June 12, 1931, September 7, 1932; Micaela Reyes Limón, Plan de Trabajo, 1939. For further evidence on festivals devoted to trees as promoted by the PNR, see ATM, Año 1935, Presidencia, Caja 65, Juan B. Tejada, Mayor de Gobierno, February 27, 1935, to Presidente Municipal, Tecamachalco; Maldonado, Presidente Municipal to Secretario General de Gobierno, Departamento de Fomento, Puebla, March 21, 1935.

61. Vaughan, "Socialist Education in the State of Puebla in the Cárdenas Period," in *El campo, la ciudad y la frontera en la historia de México*, ed. Ricardo A. Sánchez Flores, Eric Van Young, and Gisela von Wobesar (México City, forthcoming) and "Women School Teachers in the Mexican Revolution: The Story of Reyna's Braids," *Journal of Women's History* 2, no. 1 (July 1990): 162.

62. This anecdote illustrates the nurturing of a common discourse among members of the party and state. In 1938, Sacramento Joffre, campesino leader from the district of Chalchicomula, adjacent to Tecamachalco, and *secretario general* of the Liga de Comunidades Agrarias y Sindicatos Campesinos del Estado de Puebla, wrote to the Secretaría de Educación Pública to say that delegates from the town of Alseseca, Tecamachalco, had approached him asking for a teacher "porque estan creciendo en la mas completa ignorancia, con grave prejuicio para el progreso y cultura del pueblo en general." (SEP/AH, APERF, ERF Alseseca, Sacramento Joffre, Secretario General, Comité Central Ejecutivo, Liga de Comunidades Agrarias y Sindicatos Campesinos del Estado de Puebla, to SEP, Fausto Molina Betancourt, August 19, 1938). Alseseca had been one of the most divided and recalcitrant communities in relation to the school.

63. Interviews with teachers Socorro Rivera Martínez, Puebla, July 6, 1991; Caro; Reyna Manzano Carmona, Puebla, July 5, 1991; Victor Alba Hernández, Puebla, July 8, 1991.

64. On the school's role in state penetration, see Elsie Rockwell, "Schools of the Revolution"; Gilberto Loyo, *La política demográfica de México* (México, 1935),

291, 333–34; Guillermo de la Pena, "Poder local, poder regional: perspectivas socioantropológicas," in *Poder local, poder regional*, ed. Jorge Padua N. and Alain Vanneph (México, 1988), 41–46; *Herederos de promesas: agricultura, politica y ritual en los Altos de Morelos* (México, 1980), 129–30, 138, 307–12; Lewis, *Life in a Mexican Village,* 221–52; Warman, *We Come to Object*, 288–91. On the school's conscious preparation for the entry of these institutions and celebration of their relationship to the communities, see SEP/AH, DER, Expediente 207.1, González, Informe, October-November 1935.

65. LCR-AGN, Expediente 404.2/55, Aniceto Mezo, Vicente Alducín, Domingo Trujillo et al., Cuesta Blanca, to Manuel Avila Camacho, February 20, 1941. Italics added.

66. James Scott examines the impact of processes of state and market penetration on traditional peasant communities as twentieth-century modernization picks up momentum in *The Moral Economy of the Peasantry* (New Haven, CT, 1976), 203–31.

67. See AMT, Año 1935, Presidencia, Caja 65, Contract, José Peregrino and Elipidio Navarro, January 15, 1935; Carlos Maldonado to Pascual Peregrino, March 11, 1935; Eligio Avelino, Sebastian Martínez et al., La Purísima, to Presidente Municipal, Tecamachalco, March 1935; Presidencia, Año 1936, Legajo 68, Juan Tejada to Presidente Municipal, Tecamachalco, April 24, 1936; Dolores Navarro, San Antonio La Portilla, to Presidente Municipal, Tecamachalco, May 2, 1936; Presidencia, Año 1938, Caja 74, Cayetano Santos, Presidente Municipal, to Secretario General, Gobierno, Puebla, May 12, 1938; Lic. Alfonso Meneses, Oficial Mayor del Gobierno, Puebla, April 22, 1938.

68. *Ambivalent Conquests: Mayan and Spaniard in Yucatán, 1517–1570* (Cambridge, 1987), 115.

69. Irrigation, apportioned through the works at Valsequillo or through deepwater wells, run first by petroleum and then by electricity, was one of the most important improvements of the 1940s and 1950s. Because the state normally apportioned it, ample documentation exists in national and local archives. See, for example, AMT, Legajo 74, Año 1938, Presidencia, Asamblea de la 4 Convencion pro-Irrigación del Valsequillo, Tehuacan, December 3, 1938.

70. As Wil Pansters writes (*Politics and Power in Puebla*, 8–16), the concept of hegemony is a healthy complement to studies of political power that focus heavily on corporate, bureaucratic structures and clientelism (for example, Susan Kaufman Purcell, "Mexico: Clientelism, Corporatism, and Political Stability," in *Political Clientelism, Patronage, and Development*, ed. Lemarchand Eisenstadt [Beverly Hills, CA, 1981] and de la Peña, "Poder local," in *Poder local, poder regional*, 27–56). Although Gramsci's theoretical constructs were fragmentary and interspersed throughout his writings, his essays remain useful. See "State and Civil Society" and "The Modern Prince" in *Prison Notebooks: Selections*, trans. Quintin Hoare and Geoffrey Nowell Smith (London, 1971). For explanations of this notion of hegemony, see Karl Boggs, *The Two Revolutions: Gramsci and the Dilemmas of Western Marxism* (Boston, 1984), 153–98; Chantal Mouffe, "Hegemony and Ideology in Gramsci," in Mouffe, *Gramsci and Marxist Theory* (London, 1979), 68–204; Raymond Williams, *Marxism and Literature* (London, 1977), 108–27; J.V. Femia, *Gramsci's Political Thought: Hegemony, Consciousness and the Revolutionary Process* (Oxford, 1981); Jackson Lears, "The Concept of Cultural Hegemony:

Problems and Possibilities," *American Historical Review* 90, no. 3 (1985): 576–93; and Ernesto Laclau and Chantal Mouffe, *Hegemony and Socialist Strategy: Towards a Radical Democratic Politics* (London, 1986), 65–91. Gramsci linked hegemony to a particular social class (bourgeois or working class). I have substituted the postrevolutionary state for class because, although everyone seems to agree on the bourgeois nature of the postrevolutionary Mexican state's project, it is often difficult to locate the bourgeoisie in its ideological construction. My identification of hegemony with discourse is based upon the work of Laclau and Mouffe, *Hegemony*, 93–193. My application of the concept of hegemony to ideological-cultural analysis of the Mexican Revolution has been stimulated by Florencia Mallon's work, especially "The Conflictual Construction of Community," and that of Joann Martin, "Contesting Authenticity: Battles over the Representation of History in Morelos, Mexico" forthcoming in *Ethnohistory*.

71. This Althusserian notion of ideology-creating institutions (see Luis Althusser, "Ideological State Apparatuses," in Althusser, *Lenin and Philosophy and Other Essays* [New York, 1975]) inculcating ideology from above looms large in interpretations of hegemony developed by Pansters, *Politics and Power in Puebla*, 8–16; Williams, *Marxism and Literature*, 108–14; and Boggs, *Two Revolutions*, 153–98. It appears to underscore the work of Philip Corrigan and Derek Sayer, *The Great Arch: State Formation, Cultural Revolution and the Rise of Capitalism* (London, 1985). For a critique of this perspective and an elaboration of an alternative model of analysis written by scholars of Mexican primary education, see Justa Ezpeleta and Elsie Rockwell, "Escuela y clases subalternas," *Cuadernos Políticos* 37 (1983).

72. Martin, "Contesting Authenticity," citing Bruce Kapferer, *Legends of People, Myths of State: Violence, Intolerance, and Political Culture in Sri Lanka and Australia* (Washington, DC, 1988).

73. See, for example, AMT, Año de 1935, Presidencia, Caja 65, Juan B. Tejada, Oficial Mayor de Gobierno, Puebla, to Municipal President, February 27, 1935; Municipal President to Secretario General de Gobierno, Departamento de Fomento, Puebla, March 21, 1935; Tejada, Oficial Mayor de Gobierno, Puebla, to Municipal President, May 8, 1935.

74. Scott, *Moral Economy of the Peasantry*, 32–34. A fine description of the Mexican peasant moral economy in action is William Taylor, *Drinking, Homocide, and Rebellion in Colonial Mexican Villages* (Stanford, CA, 1979), 111–51.

75. For example, in Chan Kom, studied by Redfield, competitive sports enjoyed some popularity in the 1930s but then lost their luster. Redfield says that peasant parents felt that athletics were a waste of energy and time, which might have been spent in the fields, and an unnecessary dirtying of clothing. Women and girls did not feel it appropriate to attend the games. Despite these discouragements, young men continued to play in the 1940s. (*Chan Kom*, 136–37) The variables distinguishing Tecamachalco from Chan Kom would appear to be the regional PNR's institutionalization of sports, the strong support of the teacher bureaucracy for them, and the higher levels of commercial and rural-urban exchange in Puebla.

76. Vaughan, "Rural Women's Literacy"; and idem, "Women, Class and Education in Mexico, 1880–1920," *Latin American Perspectives* 4, no. 1–2 (1977): 63–80.

77. This dilemma confronted other villages in the 1940s as well. Lewis, in *Life in a Mexican Village*, sensed the cracks in traditional patriarchal familial organizations that have occurred as a result of these factors. See especially 50–79, 317–52, 383–410. Redfield makes similar observations in *Chan Kom* (126, 137–38, 143, 160) with focus on the challenge schooling posed for traditional gender roles (freedom from parental control, greater space for adolescence, girls' abandonment of the *huipil* for the dress as well as their entry into athletics, more conspicuous public activity, and freer association with the opposite sex). Redfield may emphasize the school as a factor of change more than the marketplace or state because these were not as penetrating in Chan Kom as they were in Tezpoztlán and Tecamachalco. See also Vaughan, "Rural Women's Literacy."

78. Interview with Victor Alva and Ida Garcia Manzano, Puebla, July 7, 1991.

12

Popular Reactions to the
Educational Reforms of Cardenismo

Engracia Loyo
El Colegio de México

This essay, with those both preceding and following it, forms part of the current reevaluation of the presidency of Lázaro Cárdenas (1934– 1940) and his revolutionary programs (Cardenismo). Many recent efforts have concentrated on the Cardenista endeavors at "state-building, corporatism and capitalist development." But other studies have examined the attempts to create a revolutionary culture, paralleling much recent scholarship of the French Revolution, such as that of Lynn Hunt.[*] Cárdenas's educational campaign, especially in the countryside, and his other programs such as agrarian reform have been tested by revisionists in significant case studies. Marjorie Becker, for example, analyzes the efforts of peasants in Jarácuaro, Michoacán, to challenge the official programs of Cárdenas and, in so doing, demonstrates the flexibility and political character of these campesinos. Engracia Loyo joins Mary Kay Vaughan and Elsie Rockwell in focusing particularly on the educational missions. These studies examine the cultural negotiation that occurred in the villages and, in this way, provide a Mexican complement to the French study of François Furet.[†]
Cheryl English Martin translated this essay from the Spanish.

[*]Alan Knight, "Mexico, c. 1930–46," in *The Cambridge History of Latin America*, ed. Leslie Bethell (Cambridge, 1990), 7:3–82 (the quotation comes from p. 7); Lynn Hunt, *Politics, Culture and Class in the French Revolution* (Berkeley, CA, 1984).

[†]Becker, "Black and White and Color: *Cardenismo* and the Search for a *Campesino* Ideology," *CSSH* 29 (July 1987): 453–65, and idem, *Purity, Redemption, and Other Lessons: Constructing Hegemony in Post-Revolutionary Mexico, 1934–1940* (forthcoming); see Vaughan's essay in this volume (Chapter 11). Rockwell's views are presented in "Schools of the Revolution: Enacting and Contesting State Forms (Tlaxcala, 1910–1930)," in *Everyday Forms of State Formation: Revolution and the Negotiation of Rule in Modern Mexico,* ed. Gilbert Joseph (Durham, NC, 1994). For revolutionary programs to teach literacy, see Elaine

THE MEXICAN REVOLUTION reached its culmination with President Lázaro Cárdenas (1934–1940). He brought many popular aspirations to fulfillment and enacted sweeping reforms that altered the very appearance of the country. Backed by the Six-Year Plan—originally designed by supporters of former President Plutarco Elías Calles to limit Cárdenas's actions as president but modified by radicals in the congress at the last minute—Cárdenas was able to realize the revolutionary objectives of a broad spectrum of the population. Despite its contradictions and ambiguities the plan, whose focal point was state intervention, empowered Cárdenas to regulate several fundamental aspects of national life, among them the countryside, industry, and education.

This essay refers in general terms to the educational reforms postulated in the Six-Year Plan and to the reactions that these programs provoked among groups such as entrepreneurs, landowners, parents, organized workers, students, and teachers. In particular, it singles out "popular" reactions—those of rural teachers and those of teachers *de banquillo*, who belonged to no particular organization and who were given responsibility for imparting socialist education in the course of their daily duties. The reactions of the peasant communities who felt the impact of these reforms will be considered as well.

The Cárdenas reforms have received ample study. Abundant information exists, for example, on the president's swift and spectacular land distribution. In contrast to his predecessors he believed in destroying the latifundia and in replacing the hacienda system with that of individual and collective ejidos. The expropriation of the oil industry, a clear example of state intervention designed both to regulate relations between capitalists and workers and to fulfill the goals of the Constitution of 1917, has also been the subject of numerous works.[1] General consensus sees the oil expropriation as an unpremeditated act that took everyone, foreign proprietors especially, by surprise.

In contrast, the educational reform of 1934 was long in the making. For years various sectors of the population had struggled to impose a "revolutionary" orientation on public education. Reformers considered the Constitution of 1917 ambiguous, even meaningless, in its statement that education should be entrusted to laypersons rather than clerics. They preferred to substitute a design more explicitly consistent with their radical goals.

Cantrell Lacy, "Literacy Policies and Programs in Mexico, 1920–1958" (Ph.D. dissertation, Arizona State University, 1991), 108–47, which concentrates on the Cárdenas years; and François Furet, *Interpreting the French Revolution*, trans. Elborg Forster (Cambridge, 1981).

Alberto Bremauntz, an especially passionate supporter of social-ist education and one of the deputies who did the most to push the reform through the congress, outlined some of the circumstances that influenced the movement for educational change. These included the rationalist school founded in Barcelona by Professor Francisco Ferrer Guardia of Spain and introduced into Mexico by Spanish anarchists. From the beginning of the revolution the new school gained a large following in some workers' organizations and among revolutionary teachers and intellectuals. Supporters of rationalist education believed that instruction based on science and reason could shape a new gen-eration of Mexicans free of prejudice and religious fanaticism.[2]

The Catalan anarchist Amadeo Ferres and the Spanish educator Francisco Moncaleano were the first to spread rationalist education in Mexico. Ferres founded the newspaper *El Tipografo Mexicano*, which diffused his ideas in various states throughout the republic. For his part, Moncaleano organized Sunday meetings where workers studied anarchist ideology and the principles of the rationalist school of Barcelona. These gatherings led to the creation of the Casa del Obrero Mundial in 1912. During the course of a decade, rationalist schools spread to various states, especially Yucatán and Tabasco. Schools for workers and peasants also had begun to appear at the beginning of the twentieth century.

The educational reform program, even before its formal approval, had elicited diverse reactions among various popular groups. Accord-ing to Bremauntz himself, the Fourth Convention of the Confederación Regional Obrera Mexicana (Mexican Regional Workers' Confedera-tion) in 1924 "signalled the beginning of an era that culminated in the adoption of socialist education." At that meeting, organized labor rejected "lay education" and even rationalist education, favoring in-stead schools that were "affirmative, combative, and dedicated to the eradication of prejudice."[3]

A few years later, in 1932, participants at a gathering of federal education inspectors and directors concluded that education should be directed toward the satisfaction of the economic needs of the work-ing classes, the transformation of the systems of production, and the distribution of wealth in a "frankly collectivist" manner. Those who attended meetings of the Pedagogical Congress in Jalapa in 1932, the National Congress of Students, the National Confederation of Teach-ers in April 1933, and the national convention of pro-Cárdenas stu-dents held in Morelia, Michoacán, on July 16, 1933, all concurred that education should assume a socialist orientation. When members of the Chamber of Deputies began dealing with the need for educa-tional change, they ignited a powder keg in Mexican society. While deputies debated the reforms prior to adopting them, partisans and opponents violently confronted one another—in the streets, in the press, and in the universities.

Resolutions passed by the Primer Congreso de Universitarios Mexicanos (First Congress of Mexican University People) in September 1933 divided the university population and produced genuine turmoil in society at large. Bremauntz recalled the rancorous debate was "of utmost importance because it highlighted the ideological clash between the spiritualist, Catholic and counterrevolutionary sector, represented by Licenciado Alfonso Caso, and the ideas of university reform and an explicit orientation of university education in accord with socialist doctrine."[4] Finally, the congress concluded that universities had an obligation to shape national thinking and that holders of university chairs should contribute to the triumph of socialism over capitalism.

These resolutions produced an explosion. Many students took to the streets to express their opposition to the change, not so much for its content but because they felt that the manner of its imposition violated their rights to academic freedom. Various groups took it upon themselves to go about the country urging university graduates and backers to support freedom of instruction. Confrontations with partisans of the reform often ended in violence, and the turmoil caused some institutions of higher learning, such as the Ateneo Fuente in Saltillo, to close their doors.

Students in Guadalajara occupied the university but were immediately removed. After a second attempt they were jailed, and they responded by embarking on a hunger strike. On November 15, 1933, after the rector refused to support academic freedom, a protest rally erupted. Police attempted to halt the gathering with clubs and excessive force. In response, two hundred students took over the normal school, where they were met with gunfire that left several wounded. Finally, the university was closed. Similar incidents occurred at other universities.[5]

Once the reform project became common knowledge in December 1933, public displays of support and opposition multiplied. In April of the following year students in San Luis Potosí, gathered in the Paz Theater, the largest auditorium in the state. This convention received enthusiastic support from students at the Instituto Literario (Literary Institute) in the state of Mexico, who organized a strike and took over the building. Meanwhile, socialist students organized their first national congress, meeting on May 27 in Tabasco. There, according to one witness, "the socialist apotheosis reached the level of paroxysm. They sang the *Internationale* and other revolutionary songs, applauded Marx, and raised red and black banners." Eight hundred socialist students, workers, and peasants then met in Zacatecas and heard fourteen speakers express support for the Tabasco meeting. When the government of the state of Nuevo León announced its support for the reform, students took over the University of Monterrey, sparking violent confrontations with the police. Various university faculties and schools around the country in turn went on strike to protest the repression.[6]

The congress finally approved the reform in October 1938. The revised article 3 of the constitution stipulated that "education imparted by the state shall be socialist, and in addition to excluding all religious doctrine, it shall combat fanaticism and prejudices. To this end teaching and activities will be organized in a way that youth will come to have a rational and exact concept of the universe and of society."[7]

Reaction to the change was immediate. Detractors and supporters alike turned to the press and to the street to get their views across. Daily newspapers became a tribunal, while providing an excellent platform for dissident intellectuals' attacks on the program. Articles in *Omega* and *El hombre libre* resurrected the old struggle among liberals at the Constitutional Convention of 1917. Both papers pronounced themselves in favor of parents' unrestricted freedom to determine the education of their children. Meanwhile, those who defended the responsibility of the state to safeguard the common good provided a counterpoint.

For several years various groups denounced socialist education in the press, terming it "atheistic, alienating, and antimoral." These critics considered the term "socialist" ambiguous and imprecise and the reform unconstitutional because it violated academic freedom. They also objected to the centralizing measures of the government inherent in the reform as well as its methodological shortcomings and the misinterpretations to which it was susceptible. For example, one of these newspapers informed its readers that "young people of both sexes are told in the schools that they can surrender completely to their sexual instincts." The inevitable result, according to the author of this fanciful account, would be "immoral masses, who provoke anarchy."[8]

The less reactionary newspaper *Excelsior* predicted that "the socialist thesis will form a nursery of future rebels against the established order." Nevertheless, this paper adopted a generally conciliatory tone. It opined that both detractors and proponents of the reform had proceeded "foolishly," the former because they had attributed unfounded intentions to the program and the latter because in support of the reform they proposed to disseminate Communist propaganda. The newspaper concluded that "both groups have stirred up a tempest in a teapot."[9]

The controversy did not remain confined to newspapers. Rallies and demonstrations proliferated throughout the country. In Tampico the Unión de Padres de Familia (Parents' Union) drew more than five thousand people to the Plaza de la Libertad to repudiate the reform. Likewise, in such traditionally Catholic states as Jalisco and Durango parents publicly protested the imposition of socialist education. The Federal District witnessed numerous violent confrontations when police tried to stifle marches, whose participants included women and children. Also in Mexico City, a group of university students favoring freedom of instruction stoned the offices of the official newspaper *El Nacional.* While the first congress of Veracruz socialist students was meeting in the Llave Theater in Orizaba, groups of "Catholic" youths and women interrupted the assembly with cries of, "Long live academic freedom!" and, "Long live Christ the King!"[10]

Those who sympathized with the reform showed even greater enthusiasm, although some historians have questioned the spontaneity of their demonstrations.[11] *El Nacional* described in elaborate detail an exuberant parade of organized workers that attracted more than 150,000 participants ranging in age from fifteen to eighty and "belonging to all social classes and representing the immense majority of the Mexican people." On a day "splendid with autumn serenity," six thousand teachers joined peasants, workers, students from Tabasco, and public and private employees in a demonstration that lasted for six hours "without the occurrence of any unpleasant incidents." They marched to the sound of ninety-six bands and mariachi ensembles while a heavy shower of fliers printed with revolutionary songs dropped from balconies and from an airplane. Red banners waved from the pillars of the cathedral atrium, and thousands of voices shouted, "Down with the clergy, down with reaction!" According to the same paper, rallies in favor of educational reform had been "much greater than the demonstrations of solidarity held on May 1" supporting the petroleum expropriation.[12] States such as Sonora reported similar enthusiasm.

THE DOCTRINE

Although the Six-Year Plan of 1934 amplified the features and goals of educational reform sketched out in article 3 of the constitution, it failed to define the term "socialist." It merely stated that primary and secondary education should be based "in the orientations and postulates of the socialist doctrine that the Mexican Revolution supports." In seventeen sections the authors of the reform outlined the preferred course of popular education and called for the development of a sense of "collectivity which would stimulate cooperation and solidarity, for a better distribution of wealth." Schools should be "utilitarian and active in providing for the needs of pupils and for the education of the great masses in countryside and city alike."[13]

Once the reform was approved Cárdenas, together with his secretaries of education and principal ideologues, not only supported the reform in public statements but also broadened the objectives and sphere of socialist education, always in favor of the underprivileged classes. Gradually, they assigned additional tasks to the program, proposing the intensification of the cultural project "that the revolution has undertaken for the emancipation of the working people, in order to prepare them scientifically," and the conversion of the classroom "into a definite instrument of struggle in favor of the proletarian classes."

Ignacio García Téllez, Cárdenas's first secretary of education, addressed the cultural missions. These missions were comprised of a group of teachers from different disciplines who went from one community to another giving various forms of instruction to teachers and other adults. Their principal objective was to improve the preparation of teachers in the field, but they also did important social work in many communities. They had begun work in 1923 and spread throughout the country until 1938, when their basic function changed.[14] García Téllez said that the socialist school should extend its labors beyond the classroom, make its pupils "better factors of production," and empower workers so that "at a later time" they could participate in community government.[15] For his part, the distinguished educator Rafael Ramírez, in his *Curso de educación rural* (*Course of Rural Education*), stressed that socialist education should accompany the worker in his journey to a classless society. The recent world economic depression and the flourishing of Soviet Russia convinced many people that the socialist regimen would soon be worldwide. For Ramírez, educating the people meant "agitating them in order to awaken in them a communal conscience." He added that education should socialize people, teaching neighbors to pool their efforts and resources in order to satisfy their common needs and aspirations.[16]

The magazine *El maestro rural* served as one of the principal means to publicize the reform. Its writers suggested that the socialist school be given the task of "identifying pupils with the aspirations of the proletariat, strengthening the bonds of solidarity, and creating for Mexico the possibility of pulling itself together, culturally and economically, in revolutionary fashion." Even though publicity for the reform was broadcast through a variety of media—including the cultural missions, courses of socialist orientation, information distributed by education inspectors, and a flood of printed material—many teachers confessed that the program had "taken them by surprise." They simply received word that "now all of our schools are socialist" because the constitutional reform had taken effect on December 1. Some teachers complained that they never received a program to work with, and many others agreed that "there was a lack of precision, and many contradictions in its presentation."[17]

RESPONSE OF TEACHERS AND RURAL COMMUNITIES

Socialist education offered a full range of possibilities. For teachers entrusted with the job of carrying it out, it served as a multifaceted prism that could be viewed from different angles. For this reason the program drew diverse and often contradictory responses from educators. Some teachers totally rejected it, preferring to leave the profession rather than teach in a way that violated their principles. Those on the radical left, mostly urban teachers who belonged to a particular party or union, used the program as an excuse to spread Marxist ideology. Between these two extremes a large contingent of teachers, especially those from rural areas, supported socialist education without completely understanding it. Their view was that "as long as it came from 'Tata Lázaro,' " it must be beneficial for the people. Galán Escobedo, for example, believed that the socialist school was "the most humanistic, and the one most in tune with the misfortunes of the people." He confessed that he interpreted socialist education as "a better way of life in all respects, and progress for the peasants."[18]

Rural teachers' interpretations of the new orientation in teaching and their reasons for promoting it determined the response of their communities. Reactions of rural teachers and communities to the reform are difficult to ascertain because they did not receive detailed coverage in the press or in official documents, but individual teachers did leave personal recollections. One such account relates that teachers heard of Cárdenas's plans to impose a socialist form of education that would in turn bring the prompt liberation of the proletarian masses and support them in their struggle to attain substantial social and economic improvements. The same teacher affirms that once rural teachers became convinced that socialist schools benefited the masses, they enthusiastically endorsed the program. On December 20, more than twenty thousand teachers from throughout the country demonstrated in Mexico City to show their support.[19]

Some communities experienced virtually no change with the new program—except for the singing of the national anthem in the schools. "We paid homage to the flag every Monday, whereas formerly this was only done on civic occasions." In addition, holidays such as

May 1 were now celebrated, and the agrarian hymn or the *Internationale* was sung.[20] Many communities asked teachers to continue with the same work routines as before, and it was therefore up to the teacher whether or not the school took a new direction. One instructor observed, "We had freedom to teach," and another argued that "the logical thing within socialist education was to narrate the struggles of our people."[21]

Some teachers intensified their work within the community; as they had been doing for more than a decade, they took their tasks beyond the classroom. They believed that now more than ever educators should socialize the community and promote better conditions of life. Teachers, they argued, should arrange civic gatherings aimed at finding solutions to community problems. They should also work to improve public health and combat alcoholism in addition to organizing sporting events, open-air festivals, and cooperatives. Finally, they should teach community residents how to produce more and how to construct means of communication to lift them from their age-old isolation.

In other communities, by contrast, socialist education completely altered daily life because many teachers believed that to bring the workers a better life meant subverting the established order. One teacher, Juan Ramírez Ceballos, affirms that for many of his colleagues socialist education consisted of "observing articles 2, 3, 27, 123, and 130" [of the Constitution of 1917]. In their daily tasks, therefore, they worked to eradicate fanaticism, to teach lessons in civics, to organize peasants, and to show them how to formulate land petitions. They also fomented strikes on haciendas and ranchos whose owners refused to sign collective work contracts. In response, hacendados resorted to arms. For several years groups of self-proclaimed *cristeros* [Catholics in rebellion from 1926 to 1929] promised to fight "Communists" or "enemies of religion." They roamed about the center of the country devastating towns, cutting off the ears of teachers, and burning rural schools, all in the hope of putting off labor reforms, land distribution, and popular education. One educator referred to this period as "a very difficult time for teachers. In the 1930s it appeared that the wealthy and the religious paid bandits sufficient money to intimidate teachers and to force us to abandon the places where we worked."[22]

In many places the socialist school was misunderstood and became the subject of vicious rumors that circulated throughout the community. One teacher remembers:

Education in tiny Charco Azul was making rapid progress. But one day a poisoned mind spread the rumor that the Cárdenas government was imposing socialist education. . . . [This person] added a series of stupid exaggerations, alleging, for example, that professors were going to take the children to Mexico City and from here the government would send them to Russia, where they would be killed and made into soap and other products. . . . The community began to lose faith in the teacher. . . . The people became divided. . . . After an attempt on the teacher's life, the sub-commandant of the Rural Defense joined forces with his assailants. From then on students and teachers attended night-time classes with their textbooks and notebooks—and cartridge belts full of bullets.[23]

Almost overnight once peaceful communities and villages fell prey to the menace of the *cristeros*, who roamed about persecuting teachers or attacking them in public places. Tranquil little plazas, schools, markets, and other favorite gathering places in many quiet villages now became dangerous sites. The testimony of the teacher Guadalupe Pimental is most eloquent: "The struggle was short but cruel. Some colleagues lost their lives. . . . The price for the people was very high. . . . As residents of those places we became accustomed to living in a continual state of alarm, and any kind of noise made us jump."[24]

Some teachers saw the reform as a renewed effort to dislodge the church from the central place that it occupied in rural life and to combat the fanaticism of the people. Carrying their zeal to the utmost, they became iconoclasts, destroying images, burning statues of saints, occupying churches, organizing marches in the streets, and singing "revolutionary" hymns. Community reaction to these extreme measures was equally violent. Teacher María del Carmen Cano Sandoval remembers the bloody encounter between the members of a cultural mission and the villagers of San Felipe Torres Mochas, Guanajuato. According to Cano Sandoval, public opinion became "inflamed" because peasants "wanted to take the land and become agrarians once again" and because teachers were often required to attend socialist demonstrations. On one such occasion a large contingent gathered, headed by a band and followed by the municipal government, the teachers, and then the people. Demonstrators sang songs that insulted landowners and shouted denunciations of clergy and capitalists. As a result, the residents of the town despised the teachers and did not even wish to sell them food. On the day that the cultural mission concluded its work, as teachers and students gathered in the plaza of the pueblo, one of the teachers was attacked with a machete "because he had come to incite the people to covet that which was not theirs." Other demonstrators were stoned and fired upon immediately by people who had hidden in the church. Various teachers and peasants were killed or wounded, and finally President Cárdenas had to come to the scene of the tragedy in order to restore calm.[25] In Xalostoc, in the state of Mexico, radical teachers took over the sacristy of a church and used it for a classroom. In response the priest and the faithful proceeded to stone the school. The village had traded its tranquil existence for one of constant anxiety; many feared that the *cristeros* might attack teachers in order to intimidate them.[26]

Various factors caused the reform to have greater impact in some parts of the country than in others. Local idiosyncracies, differences in religious fervor, the attitude of local officials and their relations with federal teachers, and even the enthusiasm of inspectors and teachers determined the success of the new schools. Socialist education, therefore, can best be understood when it is studied at the local level. In Puebla, for example, the traditional religiosity of the people complemented the policies of Maximinio Avila Camacho—a conservative obsessed with the need to maintain regional control over education, he was threatened by the presence of federal teachers. As a result, socialist schools more closely resembled the schools of the 1920s than the radical blueprints issued by the central offices of the Ministry of Public Education.[27]

In Jalisco, another state with deeply rooted Catholic traditions, the implementation of socialist education reopened old conflicts. Confrontations multiplied between agrarians, landlords, and other conservative elements. In Los Altos and Colotlán, teachers faced constant assaults, and many schools were burned or otherwise destroyed. Classes came to a virtual halt. In the northern part of the state, religious groups mounted a vigorous campaign against teachers, distributing in hamlets and villages anonymous fliers that incited peasants to attack the schools and threatened them with excommunication if they failed to do so. Hacendados forbade peons and sharecroppers to send their children to school. They also harassed and threatened teachers incessantly and refused to pay their salaries.[28]

In the state of Mexico, by contrast, Governor José Luis Solórzano sponsored educational change in lieu of social reform. He also hoped to improve his popular and revolutionary image while ingratiating himself with the federal government. Outside of a vigorous critique of fanaticism he initially did little to make educational reform a reality. By 1935 change had come to the schools more as a result of initiatives from the Ministry of Public Education and the federal teachers than from any actions of the local government. In 1936 and 1937, the years when socialist education reached its peak, the realignment of political forces in the state and threats from conservatives impeded its development. Nevertheless, the reform took effect in some regions despite opposition from the church and conservatives, although apparently its reception depended heavily on the teacher or to the inspector assigned to the zone.[29]

Socialist education provoked great commotion in the state of Guerrero, in part because it was energetically promoted by the inspector of Zone 7, "a fiery and talented orator who infected everyone with his enthusiasm and zeal." The inspector took great pains to ensure that teachers in his region were indoctrinated and that they were receptive to the new ideas. He therefore tried to obtain Marxist books in order to provide each teacher with a personal library. Amadeo García Pastor recalled that *Das Capital, The Communist Manifesto,* and biographies of Lenin, Marx, and Engels were required reading, that the *Internationale* was sung, parades were organized, and revolutionary verses recited. Nevertheless, when teacher accreditation courses were organized in Guerrero, violent disagreements arose between educators and students. "There was a zone of atheist teachers, another of Marxists, another of the vanguard, another of socialists." The resulting confrontations sometimes resulted in bloodshed.[30]

In Yucatán socialist education also aroused great enthusiasm among teachers and young people. According to the educator Brito Sansores, teachers collaborated closely with the authorities: "We sang the *Internationale,* the Agrarian Hymn, and other songs that spoke of labor, equality, peace, and brotherhood." The words of the Agrarian Hymn exhorted, "Let us march, agrarians, to the fields/To plant the seed of progress/Let us all march together without stumbling/ Working for the nation's peace." Another popular "revolutionary" hymn went as follows: "Sun round and red/Like a wheel of copper/ Every day you look at me/But you always see my poverty." Teachers also organized a group of socialist youth, which in turn "infected peasants, workers, merchants, professionals, and labor leaders."[31]

The educational reform, although first formulated by radical deputies in the national congress at the end of 1934, received crucial endorsement from Cárdenas. He was credited with being the father of socialist education because he actively encouraged and ultimately enacted the program. It won the applause of those who saw in it a way of creating a more equitable society or a way of preparing people for the new social order foreshadowed by the rapid pace of change around the world in the 1930s. On the other hand, socialist education was spurned by those who felt that their own interests were threatened or who, often with justification, considered it an attack on their liberty and customs.

NOTES

1. One of the many works dealing with the reforms of Lázaro Cárdenas is Tzvi Mediz, *Ideologia y praxis politica de Lázaro Cárdenas* (México, 1985).

2. On rationalist education in Mexico, see the anthology of Carlos Martínez Assad, *Los lunes rojos* (México, 1986).

3. Gilberto Guevara Niebla, *La educación socialista en México, 1934–1945* (México, 1985), 32.

4. Ibid., 43.

5. Sebastián Mayo, in *La educación socialista en México: El asaltó a la Universidad Nacional* (Buenos Aires, 1964), describes the student demonstrations and their repression.

6. Ibid., 283–91, 308–9.

7. The text is available in various works. See, for example, Guevara Niebla, *La educación socialista*, 63.

8. *El hombre libre*, October 24, 1934, cited by Adriana Sakaar Eguiarte in *La Reacción ante la educación socialista* (Unpublished thesis, V.I.A., 1981).

9. *Excelsior*, November 3, 1934, cited by Jorge Mora Forero, *La ideología educativa del régimen cardenista* (Ph.D. dissertation, El Colegio de México, 1976).

10. Ibid., 43.

11. See Victoria Lerner, *La educación socialista*, vol. 17, *Historia de la Revolución Mexicana* (México, 1982).

12. *El Nacional*, October 29, 1934, cited in Guevara Niebla, *La educación socialista*, 65–88.

13. *La educación pública en México, 1934–1940* (México, 1941).

14. Today these missions continue to carry out extension work in rural communities.

15. "La función de las Misiones Culturales ante la Reforma Educativa," no. 8, *El Maestro Rural* (April 15, 1935).

16. "La educación socialista y la escuela rural," no. 11, *El Maestro Rural* (December 15, 1934).

17. Edgar Robledo Santiago, "El maestro rural," in *Los maestros y la cultura nacional, 1920–1952* (México, 1987), 122.

18. Efren Galán Escobedo, "El compromiso del maestro rural," ibid., 47.

19. Juan Ramírez Ceballos, "Testimonios y relatos," ibid., vol. 3, p. 23.

20. This information comes from the accounts of various teachers, among them Ismael Blanco Najera.

21. Galán Escobedo, "El compromiso del maestro rural," in *Los maestros y la cultura nacional*, vol. 3 (1989), p. 47.

22. Juan Ramírez Ceballos, "Testimonio y relatos," ibid., vol. 3, p. 27.

23. José Sánchez Jiménez, "Mí participación en la gesta educativa," ibid., vol. 2, pp. 143–44.

24. María Guadalupe Pimental, "Recuerdos del 36," ibid., vol. 2, pp. 132–33.

25. María del Carmen Cano Sandoval, "Memorias de una maestra," ibid., vol. 4, pp. 149–50.

26. Ramírez Ceballos, "Testimonio," 35. Similar events occurred in the nearby villages of Santa Clara and Tultepec.

27. Mary Kay Vaughan, "Socialist Education in Puebla in the Cárdenas Period" (paper presented at the Seventh Conference of Mexican and United States Historians, Oaxaca, Mexico, October 23–26, 1985).

28. Pablo Yankelevich, *La educación socialista en Jalisco* (Guadalajara, 1985), 94–97.

29. Alicia Civera, "Política educativa del gobierno del Estado de México, 1920–1940" (Licienciatura thesis in Pedagogy, Universidad Nacional Autónoma de México, Facultad de Filosofía y Letras, Colegio de Pedagogía, 1988).

30. Amadeo García Pastor, unpublished memoirs.

31. William Brito Sansores, "Mí labor en el sector educativo," in *Los maestros y la cultura nacional*, vol. 3, pp. 73–93.

13

Burning Saints, Molding Minds: Iconoclasm, Civic Ritual, and the Failed Cultural Revolution

Adrian A. Bantjes
University of Wyoming

In the following essay Adrian Bantjes offers a Mexican case study that can be compared to the recent historiography of the French Revolution. He analyzes the modernizing rhetoric that revolutionaries used to justify their campaign to create the "new Mexican." His examination provides a parallel to the French efforts to create a "new citizen" probed by Lynn Hunt.[*] Above all, he uses Sonora under Rodolfo Elías Calles to test Mona Ozouf's study of festivals in revolutionary France. Ozouf, who developed her thesis in part from Emile Durkheim's *The Elementary Forms of Religious Life*, examined French efforts to create a civic religion that would ensure social solidarity. Part of this effort included incinerating the symbols of the old culture so that the phoenix of revolutionary culture could rise from their ashes.[†] Bantjes's analysis of official iconoclasm in which Sonora's schoolteachers collected and burned images from the churches provides a Mexican context for David Freedberg's theoretical explorations of iconoclasm.[‡] Moreover, this essay's close examination of the Sonoran experience suggests a comparison with François Furet's exercise on the political facade that often masks real society and its interests.[§]

Bantjes received his Ph.D. from the University of Texas after completing his earlier education at the University of Leiden, the Netherlands, and at El Colegio de México, Mexico City.

This research received generous support from the Institute of Latin American Studies, University of Texas at Austin, and the Netherlands-Mexican Cultural Exchange Program. I thank Alan Knight and the editors of this volume for their comments on an earlier version of this article.

[*]*Politics, Culture, and Class in the French Revolution* (Berkeley, CA, 1984).

[†]*Festivals and the French Revolution*, trans. Alan Sheridan (Cambridge, MA, 1988).

[‡]*Iconoclasts and Their Motives* (Maarsen, The Netherlands, 1985).

[§]*Interpreting the French Revolution* (Cambridge, 1981), 58.

THE MAYO INDIANS OF SOUTHERN SONORA still speak of that fateful day in 1934 when Juan Pacheco, head of the rural police of the Mayo Valley, walked into the little church at Júpare:

> He just walked into the church. At that time the church doors were never locked as they are now. He set fire to the church. It was just a little mud and cane building with one bell. It burned and fell. And he gathered up all the Little Children [saints' images in the church] and carried them away. As they came to the river and started to cross, San Juan jumped away from [Pacheco] and hopped into the river where the little bridge is now. [Pacheco] pulled out his gun to shoot San Juan, but the little *santo* ducked under the water and [Pacheco] could not harm him. That is why the cross stands under the big oak at the place where it happened. [Pacheco] went on to the place in the bush where [the Little Crosses] now stand, and there he burned up the Little Children. That is why [the Little Crosses] are in that place now. The charred bodies of the Little Children lie there. . . . Our Father . . . will burn him down for that pain. Those little bodies suffered agony. [Pacheco] and his [cause] will be destroyed by Father Sun.[1]

This event, recorded from Mayo oral tradition, remains vividly present in Mayo collective consciousness. The destruction of the church of Júpare and the burning of the saints' images were not isolated acts of revolutionary vandalism but formed part of a wider cultural clash experienced throughout Mexico in the wake of the Revolution of 1910.

Historians of the revolution tend to view developments from 1910 to 1940 primarily from a socioeconomic and political perspective. They characterize the process as an agrarian revolution, a bourgeois revolution, or a failed socialist revolution. Cultural origins and consequences of the revolution have received relatively scant attention.[2]

Cultural transformation formed an integral part of the wider revolutionary "project." The revolutionary elite envisaged effecting not only a political and social revolution but also a cultural one. The origins of this cultural blueprint preceded the armed phase of the struggle and can be traced back to Porfirian "character education," nineteenth-century liberalism, and even the Bourbon reforms, inspired by Enlightenment thought, of the late colonial period.[3]

This cultural project assumed a distinct, more urgent, and violent character as revolutionaries dramatically transformed and radicalized it. By the 1920s and 1930s the new elite, impatient with what they regarded as the retrograde habits of traditional society, sought to destroy the old Mexico and erect upon its ruins a new utopian society by means of a veritable cultural revolution. During the 1920s revolutionary leader Plutarco Elías Calles tried to impose his cultural creed but failed miserably, plunging the nation into a bloody religious civil war known as the *Cristero* rebellion, which resulted in a stalemate between the state and the Catholic resistance.

Revolutionary leaders did not abandon the cultural project. During the 1930s they made a second, more sophisticated attempt at effecting a cultural (or, as Calles called it, a "psychological") revolution. A combination of persuasion and violence, education and persecution, supplanted mere coercion. This trend appeared most notably in the numerous "laboratories of the revolution" such as Tabasco, Michoacán, and Sonora. Here the revolutionary elite employed an array of cultural weapons (iconoclasm, civic ritual, education, theater, language, art, and poetry) in their war on what they perceived as "fanaticism" and "superstition."

National revolutionary leaders such as Plutarco Elías Calles, Francisco J. Múgica, Tomás Garrido Canabal, Salvador Alvarado, Adalberto Tejeda, Lázaro Cárdenas, and Rodolfo Elías Calles all shared what has been called a developmentalist ideology.[4] They believed that only by molding minds, by creating "new men"—modern, dynamic, secular, educated—could they found a new Mexican society. They identified the major obstacles as religion and the Roman Catholic Church, both of which they associated with backwardness, superstition, and fanaticism. This essay delineates the ideology and the means by which the revolutionaries attempted to effect their cultural revolution from above.

The first phase in this process consisted of the desacralization of the old cultural order—particularly religion—through acts of revolutionary iconoclasm, satire, and religious persecution. The next step was to produce a "transfer of sacrality" away from Catholicism to a new secular or civil religion, the revolutionary religion of a new society. This transfer would be attained through civic ritual and rationalist, "socialist" education that would replace religious rites and church-controlled education.

In the northern state of Sonora the revolutionary elite attempted to generate this imagined cultural revolution. The Callista faction that dominated the state from 1929 to 1935 exhibited a fanatically anti-clerical, jacobin approach to culture. Not satisfied with factional control, nor with the opportunity of implementing their project for economic development and modernization, they sought to create a new "mystique" without which the revolution would not be complete. Governor Rodolfo Elías Calles and his jacobin followers in Sonora failed to win the hearts and minds of the people. Instead, they were forced to resort to the same coercive methods that Rodolfo's father, Plutarco, had tried before. Burning saints' images, closing churches, persecuting the clergy and the faithful all reflected the impatience of the Sonoran Callistas with a society they were not willing to

understand or accept. This so-called defanaticization campaign became a war of symbols: red and black banners were pitted against the
images of saints. The Callistas had opened Pandora's box from which
emerged the hydra of insurrection, both Catholic and secular. This
resistance would lead not only to the demise of the Callista faction in
Sonora but also to the ultimate failure of many aspects of the cultural
revolution.[5]

REVOLUTIONARY IDEOLOGY

During the 1930s, Sonora and many other states experienced a clash
between the developmentalist ideology of a modernizing revolutionary elite and the belief systems of certain "traditional" sectors of wider
civil society. The origin of this modernizing ideology has been
attributed to the experience of life on the *frontera nómada*. The harsh
struggle of *norteño* ranchers against savage Indians and the barren
wastelands of the desert supposedly generated a northern (largely
Sonoran), petty bourgeois, secular, modern world view.[6] But this
romantic notion of northern culture is somewhat problematic. True,
northern society, more literate, secular, economically diverse, and
"Americanized" than in other parts of Mexico, may have been more
receptive to radical modernizing ideology, but developmentalism was
not an exclusively northern phenomenon. Major exponents of this
ideological current, such as Alvaro Obregón, Salvador Alvarado,
Plutarco Elías Calles, and Rodolfo Elías Calles, did come from the
north, but others, including Felipe Carrillo Puerto, Adalberto Tejeda,
Tomás Garrido Canabal, Francisco J. Múgica, Lázaro Cárdenas, and
José Guadalupe Zuno, hailed from central and southern states. For
the same reason, it may also be misleading to view these men as the
product of "fragile" zones, those peripheral regions such as Sonora,
Tabasco, Veracruz, and Yucatán with close links to international
markets.[7]

     Instead, revolutionary ideology may be the product of a shared
political culture and education derived from nineteenth-century
developmentalist liberal ideology and revolutionary praxis. Many
revolutionary leaders considered themselves liberals and shared their
nineteenth-century precursors' conviction that the "feudal" hacienda,
the Roman Catholic Church, and the retrograde habits and morals of
traditional Mexico represented obstacles in the path of progress. These
revolutionaries set as their prime goal the creation of a modern egali-
tarian society based on a vibrant capitalist economy dominated by a
strong, centralized state.[8] Creating this new, modern Mexico founded,
as Calles put it, in words quite reminiscent of the old Comtian motto

used in Porfirian rhetoric, on "order and progress" demanded the purification or complete destruction of traditional society. This implied waging war on the Roman Catholic Church, "fanaticism," "superstition," ignorance, vice, and poverty, all viewed as interrelated problems.[9]

Revolutionary language clearly delineated the modernizing project. As Lynn Hunt asserts in her study of the French Revolution, such language is more than empty rhetoric; it constitutes "an instrument of political and social change," "a way of reconstituting the social and political world."[10] Like their French predecessors, Mexican leaders sought to create a "new man." They took as their "sacred duty"—compare Mona Ozouf's "transfer of sacrality"—the need to mold "new men" educated, modern, and loyal to the new state through education, civic ritual, and, if necessary, coercion.[11] Calles stated it forcefully:

> The Revolution has not ended. We must enter a new revolutionary period, which I would call the psychological revolutionary period: we must enter and take control of the consciousness of the youth, because it does and must belong to the revolution. . . . We cannot hand over the future of the fatherland and the future of the revolution to the enemy. The reactionaries mislead us when they claim that the child belongs to the home, and the youth to the family; that is an egotistic doctrine, because the child and the youth belong to the community, and it is the revolution which has a compelling obligation toward the consciousness, to banish prejudice and to form the new national soul.[12]

Education represented the heart of the modernizing project. Radical governors, many of whom had been exposed to modern pedagogy during the Porfiriato, made education their primary concern. They adhered to so-called rationalist education with its "scientific" and materialist (that is, atheistic) emphasis.[13] In practice their rationalism often meant little more than anticlericalism and dechristianization, and it spawned a violent effort to suppress the "old Mexico" and to construct a new society on the ruins of ignorance and superstition. Revolutionary anticlericalism or jacobinism, an important component of this ideological current, was a legacy of the Enlightenment and nineteenth-century liberalism. It became the principal feature of developmentalist liberalism. Many members of the revolutionary elite viewed religion as the main obstacle to the progress they desired.[14]

Callismo in the Sonora of the early 1930s must be placed in the context of this modernizing ideology. Governor Rodolfo Elías Calles endeavored to implement this revolutionary project. He was imbued with his father's dogmatic zeal and authoritarianism and eventually antagonized broad sectors of the population. He implemented an extensive modernizing program including strong support for commercial agriculture; the creation of a solid infrastructure (irrigation systems, roads, communications); the organization of agricultural producers, workers, and campesinos along protocorporatist lines in an effort to create a "strong, organized, collectivist" state; moderate, preemptive agrarian and labor reform "from above"; the expansion of the educational system; and the unleashing of a popular and brutal xenophobic campaign that led to the expulsion of thousands of Chinese.[15]

THE SONORAN DEFANATICIZATION
CAMPAIGN, 1931–1935

> "Damned is the idol and
> the hands that made it."
> FRAY JUAN DE TORQUEMADA,
> *Monarquía indiana*

The most controversial part of the governor's modernizing project was his so-called defanaticization campaign. Calles had inherited the rabid anticlericalism of his father, the jefe máximo. Both father and son staunchly opposed the Roman Catholic Church, "that confirmed enemy of progress and the Revolution."[16] The elder Calles viewed his native Sonora as a bastion of liberalism and modernity quite distinct from the more "fanatic" central and southern states. He strongly encouraged his son to suppress what he called the *curitas* ("little priests"), *viejas beatas* (sanctimonious old women), and "bad Catholic elements."[17]

Governor Calles, possibly influenced by Tomás Garrido Canabal as well as his father, embarked on a fierce campaign of religious persecution. The crusade consisted of the expulsion of all priests and ministers; the closure of churches and chapels; the extirpation of religious symbols and images (that is, fetishes, novenas, and crucifixes); a campaign of dechristianization by means of education and mass propaganda, including speeches, songs, civic ritual, and anticlerical satire; and the repression of worship. This radical anticlericalism ultimately provoked widespread Catholic and ethnic resistance, including subterfuge, civil disobedience, riots, and, finally, armed revolt.[18]

President Cárdenas (1934–1940) initially supported the anticlerical campaign. Although hardly a *comecuras* (priestbaiter) like the two Calles, Cárdenas had implemented similar anticlerical measures during the early 1930s while governor of Michoacán. He also applauded Garrido Canabal's extremist efforts in the "laboratory of the revolution"—Tabasco—to eliminate what Cárdenas called that "idolatrous cult which had subjugated the masses."[19] Moreover, as late as 1934 memos of the official party, the Partido Nacional Revolucionario (PNR), stressed the necessity of strictly applying all anticlerical legislation.[20]

The first step toward the creation of a new society entailed the destruction of all overt symbols connected with religion in an effort to undermine the wider system of meaning they represented. Only by purging priests, churches and chapels, images of saints, crosses, religious literature, and other manifestations of "fanaticism" could the revolutionaries begin the task of reconstructing the nation and educating the new citizen through a civil religion expounded in the classroom and in civic festivals. In 1931 and 1932, Sonora's government enacted legislation limiting the number of priests and ministers to one for every twenty thousand inhabitants.[21] State authorities required clergymen to register in 1932, a demand they complied with only after temporarily suspending religious services. By the end of the year state law permitted only thirteen Catholic priests and eight Protestant ministers.[22] Governor Calles, although aware that his jacobin actions might elicit negative responses from the *viejas beatas*, deported several priests to the United States on charges of preaching against federal education.[23] The bishop of Sonora, Juan María Fortino Navarrete y Guerrero, went underground in February 1932. Finally, on May 22, 1934, the Sonoran government expelled all priests.[24]

Beginning in 1931 most Sonoran churches and chapels, from the cathedral of Hermosillo to the tiny evangelist temple in Cumpas, were closed for worship and sealed by presidential or gubernatorial decree. All these buildings were "invariably flying from the steeple the Red and Black flag, the emblem of the Bolsheviki in the mind of the Mexican people."[25] During 1934 authorities and rural teachers closed or burned most of the indigenous churches in the Mayo Valley (Tesia, Pueblo Viejo de Navojoa, San Ignacio, San Pedro, El Júpare, and Masiaca), forbade religious ceremonies, and incinerated images, much to the displeasure of the Mayo Indian villagers.[26] The iconoclasm of the chief of the rural police in the Mayo Valley, who personally closed Mayo churches, torched the chapel at Júpare, and destroyed the "Little Children," is still vividly remembered today. Local schoolteachers removed the church bells from the burned ruins. These deeply sacrilegious acts not only sparked a short-lived Mayo rebellion but also generated a millenarian movement that lasted into the 1960s.[27]

The state government often handed over church-owned real estate to unions, peasant organizations, and PNR committees or converted it into offices, meeting halls, schools, *casas del pueblo* (cultural centers), or granaries. Dances were held in churches in Magdalena, Hermosillo, and elsewhere to emphasize their desecration. Some churches, such as the Capilla del Carmen in Hermosillo and the church of Alamos, were sacked, mutilated, or destroyed.[28]

Religious persecution in Sonora, as in Tabasco, often involved the deliberate destruction of religious paraphernalia and church art. Mexican jacobins sought out especially the images of saints, which they called "fetishes" or "idols"—familiar terms in revolutionary France—and regarded as so much "abracadabra" used by cynical clergymen to stupefy and exploit an ignorant, superstitious mass of semipagan peasants.[29]

Revolutionary iconoclasm must not be considered as mere vandalism but as an attempt to strike at the heart of religion's symbolic structure. R. N. Bellah defines religion as a "set of symbolic forms and acts which relate [persons] to the ultimate condition of [their] existence." Because humanity's attempts to understand the world rely to such a degree on symbols, any struggle between weltanschauungen involves an effort to eliminate the symbols of one legitimating system and replace them with new ones.[30]

Iconoclasts destroy images, according to David Freedberg, not because they believe in their inherent magic but to break the unity between signified and signifier and to demonstrate their superiority over the power of both. Iconoclasm provokes so profound a reaction exactly because these symbols form part of a wider system of meaning by which individuals orient themselves. Iconoclasm is not an act of vandalism but constitutes "a coming to a head of the conflict in the realm of ideology." Martin Warnke comments that "aggression against religious symbols . . . is [considered] as outrageous as the slaying of the innocent."[31]

Across the state, even in the smallest villages, a slim minority of teachers, mayors, and armed police officers, popularly known as *quemasantos*, or saint-burners, supervised the public burning of fetishes, an act that soon became an iconoclastic civic ritual. Popular iconoclasm was a rare phenomenon. In the Mayo Valley the federal school inspector, several teachers from Huatabampo, the chief of rural police, the coterie of the *agrarista* mayor of Huatabampo, and other Callista teachers and union leaders represented the anticlerical modernizing element. Rural teachers played a particularly important role because of their presence in even the smallest communities as the "intellectual directors of workers and peasants." Education authorities believed that teachers in the Huatabampo school district gave greater importance to the defanaticization campaign and the formation of worker and peasant organizations than to teaching.[32]

The most celebrated case of revolutionary iconoclasm concerned the statue of San Francisco Xavier in the church of Magdalena. This saint, who was believed to work miracles, was widely venerated, especially by the Pápagos but also by the Yaqui and mestizo population. The saint's day was the most important religious feast in the region, and many residents marked the occasion with an annual pilgrimage to the shrine.[33] Teachers stormed the church and burned most of its images. Afterward, authorities removed the statue of San Francisco and temporarily stored it in the Palacio de Gobierno in Hermosillo. Finally, they had it burned in the ovens of the Sonora brewery. The faithful reacted immediately: "For many days there were pilgrimages of people from the different barrios of Hermosillo, who filled little paper bags and pouches with the ashes that were extracted every day from the oven, believing that these might contain some of the ashes of the Saint." According to one account, the unknowing perpetrator of this desecration, a pious Yaqui stoker, went mad after learning what he had done and died soon thereafter.[34]

A similar fate befell the beloved statue of Nuestro Señor de Esquípulas in the church of Aconchi. According to oral tradition dating from the colonial era and reflecting typical intervillage rivalry, muleteers transporting the statue to the neighboring town of Arizpe stopped in Aconchi for the night. When they tried to resume their journey the next morning, the statue had become so heavy that the astonished muleteers had to leave it behind with the jubilant townspeople of Aconchi. The statue signified more than an image of religious veneration; it served as a symbol of the community, of its pride and sense of history. The *quemasantos* burned it in the forge of the local smithy.[35]

Local police and teachers, strongly encouraged by the state government, publicly burned religious paraphernalia throughout Sonora. Rural teachers filled out bimonthly statistical forms that included data on the number of fetishes burned. Between September 1934 and February 1935, teachers in the Alamos school district incinerated a total of twenty-six fetishes in remote villages such as Potrero de Alcantar, Los Muertos, and Las Cabras.[36] Martín S. Mercado, inspector of the Ures school district, instructed school principals that at the 1934 Manifestación Socialista Revolucionaria, "all teachers, peasants and workers, children, women and adults, must bring to the Proletarian Bonfire all saints, images, sculptures, fetishes, banners, religious vestments, books, etc. that served the Church and the Clergy to lull the people to sleep, make a pyre of all these and set fire to them while singing the Socialist Hymn, the Labor Hymn, the Marseillaise or the Mexican National Anthem."[37]

The director of federal education in Sonora, J. Lamberto Moreno, who proudly wrote his superiors in Mexico City that teachers had incinerated thousands of religious images,[38] was profoundly touched by such rituals:

As proof of the spontaneous antireligious attitude which the children of the federal schools of the state of Sonora have assumed, I permit myself the honor of informing you of the following events: When I presented myself at the Mayo Indian village of Macoyahui to conduct my inspection, thirty-five children of both sexes came to meet me, declaring that they were waiting for me to burn the fetishes which were in the village church and in their houses, fetishes which had been valiantly extracted by the teacher, Miss Antonia Montes, with the aid of the Comisariado Ejidal and the Education Committee. Once the pyre had been lit the little Indians started dancing a pascola, and to the gay sound of their autochthonous music, they started flinging the fetishes into the fire, one by one, until the pyre was converted into an enormous bonfire, which consumed those symbols of fanaticism and exploitation. . . . In the village of Tojibampo something similar occurred. Moments after my arrival, the Union of Mothers, the Education Committee and the Infant School Community organized an antireligious social ceremony, and . . . proceeded to incinerate their fetishes of wood, cloth and chrome. As the bonfire blazed up with these icons, the children sang the Socialist Hymn and the Mexican National Anthem, solemnly protesting their adherence to the revolutionary ideology currently supported by the Government of the Republic.[39]

Despite the director's enthusiasm, what he supposed were spontaneous acts of iconoclasm may well have been orchestrated in an effort to mislead and satisfy gullible outsiders. The Mayos had a reputation for their strong religiosity and, in 1935, participated in an anti-Callista rebellion, chiefly on religious grounds.

The defanaticization campaign included an effort to eradicate even the names of saints. Events that bore religious names, such as regional markets, changed titles. The municipal authorities of Navojoa renamed the annual "San Juan" sale, the "June" sale.[40]

Sonora's defanaticization campaign included the use of coercion to discourage believers from practicing their faith. The state outlawed mass, prayer, and the celebration of religious feasts, and penalized violators with large fines and imprisonment.[41] Workers and soldiers raided a secret 1935 Easter celebration at the house of Ricardo Durazo in Magdalena, arresting forty of the two hundred people present. Authorities fined the worshippers twenty-five pesos each, except Durazo, who received a stiff two-hundred-peso penalty. When the villagers of Júpare organized a fiesta to celebrate Pentecost with "fireworks, *gigantes* [giants], firecrackers, prayers, and songs," a teacher from Huatabampo ended the celebration and arrested a number of intoxicated villagers. Governor Calles ordered the closing of a Mayo church in Navojoa during the preparations for the fiesta of San Miguel, provoking a riot.[42]

Officials confiscated, meticulously registered, and destroyed privately owned religious paraphernalia. After raiding a secret mass at a private house in Magdalena authorities confiscated twelve religious paintings, four statuettes, three small medallions, one small wooden crucifix, one small glass candelabra, three candles, five candle-stumps, five devotional books, and one book without a cover.[43]

THE TRANSFER OF SACRALITY: CIVIC RITUAL

Once the old Mexico had been destroyed, the new, revolutionary man would be created while a revolutionary civil religion would replace Roman Catholicism. As the Callista elite deemed pure repression insufficient to obtain these goals, the new Mexican citizen, whether child or adult, was to be molded through "socialist" education and civic festivals, which would fill the spiritual vacuum left by the destruction of religion. This campaign to win the hearts and minds of the Sonorans involved anticlerical satire, secular civic ritual, the formation of anticlerical organizations such as the Liga Anticlerical and the Juventudes Revolucionarias (Revolutionary Youth), a radical group comparable to Garrido's Red Shirts or Cárdenas's Bloque de Jóvenes Revolucionarios, and a concerted effort to inculcate youth with rationalist attitudes.[44]

Many revolutionaries sought ultimately to create a new civil religion—that is, a set of beliefs, rites, and symbols to legitimate and provide meaning and solidarity to the new social system. The sense among revolutionaries that Roman Catholicism had given Mexican society a degree of social cohesion and solidarity is exemplified by the pathetic and unsuccessful attempt of Luis (Napoleón!) Morones, following Robespierre, to establish a schismatic Mexican church. Revolutionaries in Cardenista Michoacán appropriated elements of the Catholic liturgy and ministered the so-called socialist sacraments.[45]

The Sonoran Callistas did not seek to harness religion as a means of maintaining social solidarity. Instead, they attempted to substitute religious rites with secular, civic ritual. Although little information exists on the origin of these festivals, French revolutionary examples, familiar to the Mexican political elite, may have provided some inspiration. Historian Mona Ozouf brilliantly demonstrated for the case of France how revolutionary festivals, by transferring sacrality, filled the vacuum left by the suppression of religious ceremonies. A similar process occurred in revolutionary Mexico. The Sunday mass, followed by the customary visit to the cantina, was replaced by the PNR-sponsored *domingo cultural* (Cultural Sunday), the Mexican equivalent of the *fête décadaire*. Similarly, secular festivals such as

Labor Day replaced religious holidays.[46] The board of the Casa del Pueblo of Huatabampo occupied the local church, removed the altar and statues of saints, and proceeded to "erect a little pavilion in which, Sunday after Sunday, they held the cultural festivals." Callista union members and teachers always participated in these celebrations, while the town's wealthy citizens generally boycotted them. Such efforts managed only to generate considerable resentment.[47] Participation in civic ceremonies does not necessarily indicate the existence of a Durkheimian moral consensus. Official and popular perceptions of civic rituals differed widely, and such gatherings often served to exacerbate conflict.[48]

A typical Cultural Sunday in Hermosillo featured the play *Death to Religion* by teacher Dolores Cortés, speeches on such topics as "Science and Religion" and "Women and the Religious Problem," and the incantation of the Socialist Hymn. PNR-organized Labor Day festivities opened with the Iconoclast Hymn followed by speeches by union leaders, sports events, dances, an anticlerical play called *The Priest of Satebo*, and ended, once again, with the singing of the Socialist Hymn.[49]

Anticlerical propaganda penetrated Sonora's most remote corners, thanks to the rural teachers who functioned as agents of cultural dissemination. Education Inspector Leonardo Ramírez G. hired a troupe of circus artists called the Compañía Fronteriza to tour the Sahuaripa area enacting comedies featuring depraved priests and their lurid activities during confession. Some comedies, such as *El Padre Francisco*, were intended for an audience of children and sought to demonstrate that the devil, *el cuco* (the bogeyman), and *hechiceros* (witches) did not exist.[50] The authorities, aware of the power of popular festivals, used the 1935 Carnival in Sahuaripa as an occasion to attack the church:

> A parade was organized (with the approval of the director of education) in which participants wore masks and costumes caricaturing and ridiculing the pope and priests. . . . The persons dressed as priests performed acrobatic stunts and made themselves ridiculous in every way possible. The performance was announced as a truly socialistic festival, demonstrating scientifically the lies taught by religion.[51]

Besides such parodies, which also had been common during the French dechristianization campaign, other forms of anticlerical satire emerged.[52] Anticlerical poetry, literature, and art generally depicted priests as lascivious, corrupt, alcoholic charlatans.[53] School drawings also reflected this campaign. Teachers and students of the rural normal school of Ures crafted wood engravings depicting not only images of sturdy peasants harvesting wheat, or a bourgeois corpse clad in evening suit dangling from a tree, but also anticlerical scenes such as a priest fleeing across the U.S.-Mexican border loaded with sacks of alms, or a peasant atop a burning cathedral, with the red and black flag flying overhead.[54]

The rhetoric of anticlericalism stressed the nefarious past of papism. Orators in remote mining camps spoke out against clerical exploitation, charging that "Catholicism means misery, hypocrisy and corruption" and reminding their audience of the heinous crimes committed by the Spanish Inquisition. Just as doctors would not exist without disease, the orators declared, "the Church needs a corrupt, hypocritical and perverted humanity, otherwise it has no meaning." One public speaker in Hermosillo referred to the infamous role played by the Catholic Church in the nation's history, in particular its treasonous collaboration with Emperor Maximilian and its accumulation of vast wealth.[55]

The defanaticizing language of the revolutionary elite bears a startling resemblance to that of the French revolutionaries. This historical parallel was not lost on the Mexican jacobins nor on their foes, who compared official anticlericalism to the scourge of 1793. Postrevolutionary civic rituals featured the incantation of the Marseillaise. Rodolfo Elías Calles expounded the ideals of "equality, fraternity, and humanitarianism," while even the relatively unsophisticated General Cárdenas invoked the oratorical skills of the Comte de Mirabeau.[56]

This essay is not an exercise in automatic discourse analysis (or *Begriffsgeschichte*). Nevertheless, one must stress the remarkable similarity between the eighteenth-century *discours déchristianisateur* studied by Michel Vovelle and the language of the Callista defanaticization campaign. Many of the principal terms identified by Vovelle as elements of this discourse surface in Mexico in the 1930s: rationalism, reason, duty, regeneration, educate, destroy, equality, fraternity, sacred, progress, missionaries, doctrine, fanatics, superstition, errors, prejudice, cults, hypocrisy, ignorance, corruption, idols, ridiculous, *beata*, and so on.[57] Whether such language was inspired by the French Revolution or formed part of a wider vocabulary of secularization can only be ascertained by detailed analysis of anticlerical discourse.

EDUCATION AND ANTICLERICALISM

The ideological conflict in Sonora centered on the issue of education. The classroom became the battleground for control of the consciousness of a new generation. Rural teachers were expected to expose the fallacy and hypocrisy of religion and stress scientific truth and rationalism. Revolutionary concern with education was hardly a novel or unique phenomenon but formed part of a wider modernizing ideology.[58] Throughout the nineteenth century, education figured prominently in the Latin American elite's debate on "barbarism versus civilization."[59] Nineteenth-century developmentalist liberals, especially the *científicos* (scientists), regarded education as the key to the destruction of superstition and prejudice and the creation of a "new man," a "new citizen." A marked continuity existed between Porfirian and revolutionary educational thought. The Constitutionalist and Sonoran administrations in particular saw education as a panacea for the nation's ills.[60]

In the revolutionary laboratories of the 1920s and 1930s regional strongmen such as the younger Calles endorsed rationalist education, which they regarded as a fundamental vehicle for modernization. The state budgets of Michoacán (1930) and Tabasco (1926) testify to the importance the revolutionaries attached to education. During the Cárdenas and Garrido administrations, educational expenditures comprised 40 percent of the state budgets. Likewise, Calles spent 35 to 37 percent of Sonora's budget on education.[61] While president, Cárdenas supported a type of "socialist" education that differed little from the old rationalist, anticlerical type. He may have been influenced by his close relationship with radical Francisco J. Múgica. As governors of Michoacán, both emphasized the importance of rationalist education, anticlericalism, and "moral education," including limits on the consumption of alcohol.[62]

The 1917 constitution, in the wording of the reformed article three, showed more affinity to developmentalist jacobinism than to socialism: "State education will be socialist, and besides excluding any religious doctrine, will combat fanaticism and prejudice, to which purpose the school will organize its teaching and activities in a form that will imbue the youth with a rational and exact conception of the universe and of social life."[63]

Thus, education became the primary means of the defanaticization campaign to counter the "nefarious" results of the church's influence. Governor Calles sought to instill in the Sonoran youth "a revolutionary conscience and mystique."[64] His administration considered rationalist, scientific education and defanaticization to be essential components of the revolution, which "will be carried out by the School." Teachers would form the revolutionary vanguard: "First, the revolution was carried through in the realm of politics; it is being carried out in the economy; and now we have to bring it about in the consciousness of the *new people*. Every teacher must be a leader, and every leader must be a soldier in the vanguard battalions of workers and peasants."[65]

Educators saw the struggle against superstition as a crucial element of class struggle. The chief of the Department of Rural Education, Celso Flores Zamora, believed that "the roots of modern religion are firmly anchored in the *social oppression* of the working masses."[66] Before rationalist education could be implemented, religious education, considered "an instrument of the bourgeoisie against the worker, like fanaticism and alcoholism," would have to be suppressed. The Sonora state government outlawed Catholic schools and, according to official sources, closed sixteen of them in at least nine towns.[67]

Federal teachers, chosen to spearhead the psychological phase of the revolution, had to be purged of any elements tainted by "fanaticism and superstition." Elsewhere, in Cárdenas's Michoacán and in Yucatán, similar purges of teachers were carried out.[68] Exact figures for Sonora do not exist, but sources indicate that the state government dismissed as many as 35 percent of all teachers, men and women who, as the government put it, "do not consider themselves sincerely and honestly capable of undertaking this task . . . due to their ideology in religious matters."[69] Many teachers faced the unpleasant choice of betraying their beliefs or losing their jobs during a period of economic crisis. In Cananea several teachers resigned in protest of government plans for sex education. Others crossed the border and started religious schools in Arizona.[70]

In every school district *comités de depuración* (purge committees) of the local chapters of the new Sonoran teachers' union monitored the revolutionary zeal of teachers. Peasant and worker organizations also kept a watchful eye on their activities. Teachers were obligated to join municipal PNR committees and participate in the party's Cultural Sundays. Like the French revolutionary festivals, these events served a repressive "sorting" purpose.[71] Teachers were compelled to sign an ideological statement in which they affirmed their disposition to comply with article three of the constitution, support socialist education, and disseminate the principles of socialist doctrine. They pledged not to profess or practice Catholicism or any other religion and to combat religion by all means possible.[72]

Evaluation of federal teachers rested on a point system rating several categories: 1) revolutionary ideology (five points—one for the "ideological declaration," and two each for participation in the antireligious campaign and in the defense of the worker against exploitation); 2) social work (five points for work on the antialcohol campaign, the Mothers' Union, the Education Committee, the Bloque de la Juventud Revolucionaria, and the community in general); and

3) skills (five points for possession of a sixth-year diploma and knowledge of cooperativism, agrarian, labor, and common law and the philosophical principles of the socialist school).[73] Of the fifteen total points, only three related to education per se; the rest pertained to the ideological and social project of the developmentalist elite.

In the task of reeducating teachers, educational officials employed so-called Antidogmatic Doctrinaire Propaganda, a secular catechism attacking the Bible on scientific grounds that claimed to prove that primitive man did not know property, family, government, or religion.[74] This "scientific" knowledge trickled down into the classroom, as is shown by this description of an official visit to a Sonoran school:

> The teacher, in order to show officials how well she has taught them, asks, "Children, who is God?" to which the children reply, "He is some old man with whiskers who, they say, lives in the sky [heaven]." The teacher then asks if that is true, and all the children reply in unison, "No!" She asks why it is not true, and the children reply that it is not true because if he did live in the sky [heaven] he would fall to earth as all bodies which are heavier than air do.[75]

Plans called for extending the ideological purge beyond teachers to other federal and state employees. Several high state officials resigned in 1935 when confronted with accusations about their religious beliefs. Organized workers and peasants in the Magdalena district planned to purge the entire public administration of "fanatics."[76]

Religion and ignorance were not the only threats to the modernization process. The revolutionary elite also battled vice by organizing youth groups and promoting sports, which would not only keep the young from the "centers of vice" but also encourage a new competitive spirit and a desire to excel—important attributes of the new citizen. Teachers, sometimes aided by local authorities, attempted to close down the numerous liquor shops that dotted the countryside. Finally, in 1935, Governor Ramón Ramos, Calles's successor, took the extremely unpopular action of decreeing complete prohibition in the state. This measure had been previously attempted in 1916 by Governor Plutarco Elías Calles.[77]

CONCLUSION

The Mexican revolutionary process included a radical cultural blueprint for society, a project that an impatient modernizing elite tried to implement during the 1920s and 1930s. In Durkheimian terms this episode forms part of the broad process of Western secularization that began with the Enlightenment. Although its roots can be traced back to the Bourbon reforms and nineteenth-century liberalism, the cultural project of the revolution was particularly radical, especially its approach to religion and the Catholic Church. While the ultimate goal, the creation of "new men," remained the same, the methods utilized became more draconian and violent. The revolutionaries, convinced that persuasion and education alone would not suffice to create new citizens, sought the destruction of the old cultural order, in particular its symbols, rituals, beliefs, and institutions. Rather than senseless vandalism or the random excesses of jacobin liberalism, saint-burning, anticlerical satire, and religious persecution formed instead an integral part of a broader cultural pattern: the attempted desacralization of the old cultural order, to be followed by a transfer of sacrality toward a new, revolutionary, civil, secular, or political religion that would supplant Roman Catholicism and provide the new postrevolutionary society with the necessary social cohesion. Much as the revolution sought to destroy the political and economic institutions of the old regime (the Porfirian military, the "feudal" hacienda), it also endeavored to purge the new Mexico of the old culture of traditional Mexico.

A relatively small revolutionary cadre, consisting of Callista *políticos*, campesino and labor leaders, and, particularly, teachers, implemented the Sonoran cultural revolution. They received limited support from segments of the urban working classes and *agraristas*, who apparently collaborated with the developmentalist political elite in the hope of receiving its patronage for labor and land reforms. But little evidence exists of general popular iconoclasm, and it seems that authentic popular anticlericalism was of minor importance.

Most sectors of the population resisted attempts by the political elite to destroy traditional religion and found a revolutionary civil religion.[78] The cultural revolution never gained the type of popular support that the political or agrarian revolutions did. During the 1930s, Mexicans resisted the cultural project through petitions, street demonstrations, school boycotts, illegal masses, the violent reopening of sealed churches, and a series of armed Catholic rebellions collectively known as the Second Cristiada. In Sonora this opposition originated not only with the church but also with many individual Catholics, especially women, indigenous groups, and *serrano* communities.

The resistance of what Alan Knight calls a "recalcitrant people" provided an incentive for the state to moderate the policy of religious intolerance bequeathed by the Maximato.[79] State and federal authorities opted for a slow, face-saving rechristianization process by the late 1930s, reopening churches, tolerating religious services, and allowing priests to return. The Education Ministry admonished rural teachers to concentrate on their tasks as educators and relinquish their role as disseminators of the revolutionary creed. Socialist education was phased out, and Catholic schools were reopened. The Sonora government even repealed prohibition soon after decreeing it.

The cultural revolution proved to be the product of what François Furet calls the "illusion of politics" and merely sparked a Thermidorean "reassertion of real society."[80] The cultural project ultimately failed due to widespread resistance from broad sectors of Mexican society. By the late 1930s the revolutionary elite demonstrated that they had learned from the myriad petitions, demonstrations, acts of violence, revolts, and millenarian movements, all of which constituted a direct and clear rejection of the cultural project. As the revolution entered Thermidor, the state began dismantling the institutions that it had used to promote the cultural revolution, a campaign that had proved to be a costly and politically dangerous fiasco.

Fray Toribio de Benavente ("Motolinía"), writing in the sixteenth century, bemoaned the cultural resistance of the indigenous population of New Spain to conversion to Christianity: "The Indians hid [their] principal idols with the symbols and ornaments or vestments of the devils, some beneath the earth and others in caves and others in the hills."[81] Whereas the "spiritual conquest" of the sixteenth century ultimately succeeded, the "cultural missionaries" of the 1920s and 1930s utterly failed in their effort to purge the country of "idolatry" and "fanaticism."

NOTES

1. N. Ross Crumrine, *The Mayo Indians of Sonora: A People Who Refuse to Die* (Tucson, AZ, 1977), 21. Crumrine changed the names, places, and dates in his study, but it is clear from other sources that he referred to acts committed by Pacheco at Júpare in 1934. See his "Mechanisms of Enclavement Maintenance and Sociocultural Blocking of Modernization among the Mayo of Southern Sonora," in *Ejidos and Regions of Refuge in Northwestern Mexico,* ed. Crumrine and Phil C. Weigand, Anthropological Papers of the University of Arizona, no. 46 (Tucson, AZ, 1987), 24; Charles J. Erasmus, *Man Takes Control: Cultural Development and American Aid* (Minneapolis, MN, 1961), 276–77; and Erasmus, Solomon Miller, and Louis C. Faron, "Cultural Change in Northwest Mexico," in *Contemporary Change in Traditional Communities of Mexico and Peru* (Urbana, IL, 1978), 97.

2. For a general overview, see Alan Knight, "Revolutionary Project, Recalcitrant People," in *The Revolutionary Process in Mexico: Essays on Political and Social Change, 1880–1940,* ed. Jaime E. Rodríguez O. (Los Angeles, CA, 1990), 227–64. The best regional study is Carlos Martínez Assad, *El laboratorio de la revolución. El Tabasco garridista* (México, 1979). Other important case studies are

Marjorie Becker, "Black and White and Color: Cardenismo and the Search for a Campesino Ideology," *CSSH* 29, no. 3 (July 1987): 453–65; Mary Kay Vaughan, "El Magisterio socialista en Puebla y Sonora: Model pedagógico y fracaso escolar. Reconversión política y modernización económica," *Crítica: Revista Trimestral de la Universidad Autónoma de Puebla* (July-December 1987): 90–100; and Adrian A. Bantjes, "Politics, Class and Culture in Post-Revolutionary Mexico: Cardenismo and Sonora, 1929–1940" (Ph.D. dissertation, University of Texas, 1991). For education, see Mary Kay Vaughan, *Estado, clases sociales y educación en México (1921–1940)* (México, 1974). On the revolutionary elite, see, for example, Enrique Krauze, *Reformar desde el origen: Plutarco Elías Calles* (México, 1987).

3. Alan Knight, *The Mexican Revolution* (Cambridge, 1986), 2:501.

4. Ibid., 1:69–70.

5. In 1935, Calles's successor Governor Ramón Ramos was toppled by the Cárdenas government in the wake of an armed uprising with significant Catholic participation.

6. Hector Aguilar Camín, *La frontera nómada: Sonora y la Revolución Mexicana* (México, 1985); Barry Carr, *The Peculiarities of the Mexican North, 1880–1928: An Essay in Interpretation*, Occasional Papers, no. 4 (Glasgow, 1971), 6–7, 9–13; Jean Meyer, "Mexico: Revolution and Reconstruction in the 1920s," in *Cambridge History of Latin America, 1870–1930*, ed. Leslie Bethell (Cambridge, 1986), 5:155; and Alan Knight, "El liberalismo mexicano desde la Reforma hasta la Revolución (una interpretación)," *Historia Mexicana* 35, no. 1 (1985): 84.

7. Francisco Naranjo, *Diccionario biográfico revolucionario*, rev. ed. (México, 1985); and Martínez Assad, *El laboratorio*, 39.

8. Knight stresses a shared educational experience—see his *Mexican Revolution*, 2:238–39; ibid., 500; Jean Meyer, Enrique Krauze, and Cayetano Reyes, *Estado y sociedad con Calles* (México, 1977), 321, 328–29; and Knight, "El liberalismo," 69.

9. Krauze, *Reformar desde el origen*, 33, 58; and Charles A. Hale, *The Transformation of Liberalism in Late Nineteenth-Century Mexico* (Princeton, NJ, 1989), 96; Knight, *Mexican Revolution*, 2:501; and Meyer, *Estado y sociedad*, 321.

10. Hunt, *Politics, Culture, and Class*, 24.

11. Meyer, *Estado y sociedad*, 320, 330; Martínez Assad, *El laboratorio*, 62; and Mona Ozouf, *La fête révolutionnaire 1789–1799* (Paris, 1976), 243–44, 268.

12. Jean Meyer, *La Cristiada*, vol. 2, *El conflicto entre la iglesia y el estado 1926–1929* (México, 1973), 208; and Martínez Assad, *El laboratorio*, 83.

13. Krauze, *Reformar desde el origen*, 11–13; Plutarco Elías Calles worked as a teacher in Sonora, while both he and Múgica were brought up by teachers. Martínez Assad, *El laboratorio*, 14, 36.

14. Meyer, "Mexico: Revolution and Reconstruction," 167; Knight, *Mexican Revolution*, 2:500–501, and "El liberalismo," 85; and Meyer, *Estado y sociedad*, 320.

15. Manuel S. Corbalá, *Rodolfo Elías Calles: Perfiles de un sonorense* (Hermosillo, 1970), 154–55, 158; on the Chinese question, see Evelyn Hu-DeHart, "Sonora: Indians and Immigrants on a Developing Frontier," in *Other Mexicos: Essays on Regional Mexican History, 1876–1911*, ed. Thomas Benjamin and William McNellie (Albuquerque, NM, 1984), 201–3; José Carlos Ramírez, "La

estrategia económica de los Callistas"; Rocío Guadarrama, "La reorganización de la sociedad," in *Historia contemporánea de Sonora, 1929–1984*, 2d ed. (Hermosillo, 1988) (hereafter abbreviated as *HCS*); and Bantjes, "Politics, Class and Culture."

16. *Memoria General: Informe rendido por el C. Rodolfo Elías Calles, Gobernador Constitucional del Estado, ante la H. XXXII Legislatura local, el 16 de septiembre de 1934* (Hermosillo, 1934), 4, 15, 35.

17. Rodolfo Elías Calles to Plutarco Elías Calles, 1931, Archivo de Plutarco Elías Calles in Archivos de Plutarco Elías Calles y Fernando Contreras Torreblanca, Mexico City (hereafter cited as APEC); Plutarco to Rodolfo Elías Calles, n.d., APEC.

18. Bantjes, "Politics, Class and Culture."

19. Martínez Assad, *El laboratorio,* 54–55.

20. Instructivo PNR, 1–11–34 (dates given as day–month–year), Archivo Administrativo del Gobierno del Estado de Sonora (hereafter AAGES) 235"35"/21.

21. Rocío Guadarrama, "Los cambios en la política," *HCS,* 179–80.

22. Voetter, Guaymas, to State Department (hereafter SD), 29–2–32, Records Relating to the Internal Affairs of Mexico, U.S. State Department, 1929–1940, 812.00, reel 18 (microfilm) (hereafter abbreviated as SD/18); and Relación de los sacerdotes autorizados para ejercer sus ministerios en el Estado de Sonora, 8–11–32, Dirección General de Gobierno, Ramo de Gobernación, 2.340 (22), AGN (hereafter AGN, DGG).

23. Rodolfo to Plutarco Elías Calles, 1931, APEC; Maney, Guaymas, to SD, 4–9–31, SD/18. On priests in Nacozari, see Boyle, Agua Prieta, to SD, 29–2–32, SD/18; on Magdalena, see Robinson, Nogales, to SD, 30–4–32, SD/18; on Cananea, see Gibbs, Cananea, to Robinson, 25–3–34, Record Group 84, Consular Post Records (hereafter RG 84), Correspondence of the American Consular Agency, Cananea, 1934–35, Vol. 27, National Archives, Washington, DC.

24. Boyle to SD, 31–5–34, SD/18.

25. Joseph B. Carbajal, S.J., to Representative John P. Higgins (Massachusetts), Affidavit Roman Catholic priest, San Antonio, 8–6–35, Religious Persecution in Mexico Papers, May-July 1935, Latin American Library, Tulane University.

26. Profesor Federal Arturo Madrid Jiménez to Gobernador de Sonora, 7–6–35, AAGES 231.5"35"/38.

27. Erasmus, *Man Takes Control,* 276–77; idem, "Cultural Change in Northwest Mexico," 97; and Crumrine, *The Mayo,* 25.

28. Guadarrama, "Los cambios," *HCS,* 181–82 (for an incomplete list, see Apéndice 1), 197–99, to be supplemented by the document "Templos retirados por decreto presidencial" in AGN, DGG 2.340(22)29. The church of Guaymas, a conservative town, was still open in 1934; Ray to SD, 1–6–34, SD/18; *El Día* (Guaymas), March 4, 1967; and Gilberto Suárez Arvizu, "Fundación de la Universidad de Sonora," *VII Simposio de historia de Sonora: Memoria* (Hermosillo, 1982), 426.

29. Meyer, *La Cristiada,* 2:200–201, 203–4, 206.

30. *Beyond Belief* (New York, 1970), 21; and Clifford Geertz, *The Interpretation of Cultures* (New York, 1973), 99, 140–41.

31. *Iconoclasts and Their Motives,* 25–37; and Martin Warnke, "Bilderstürme," in *Bildersturm. Die Zerstürung des Kunstwerks,* ed. Warnke (München, 1973), 10.

32. Director de Educación Federal Fernando Ximello to Profesor Celso Flores Zamora, Jefe del Departamento de Enseñanza Rural, Informe sintético, octubre-

noviembre 1935, SEP/AH 249; and Inspector General de Educación Federico A. Corzo to Profesor Celso Flores Zamora, Jefe del Departamento de Enseñanza Rural, Informe sintético de labores, mes de octubre, 8–11–35, SEP/AH 249.

33. Robinson, Nogales, to SD, 31–7–34, SD/18; Rosalío Moisés, Jane Holden Kelley, and William Curry Holden, *A Yaqui Life: The Personal Chronicle of a Yaqui Indian* (Lincoln, NE, 1971), 6, 14, 82, 126; Muriel Thayer Painter, *With Good Heart: Yaqui Beliefs and Ceremonies in Pascua Village* (Tucson, AZ, 1986), 83, 130–31, 154.

34. José Abraham Mendívil, *Don Juan Navarrete y Guerrero: Como pastor y como hombre* (Hermosillo, 1975); David L. Raby examines the teachers' involvement in *Educación y revolución social en México (1921–1940)* (México, 1974), 162, on the basis of an interview with a witness who stated that forty teachers of the Bloque de Maestros Socialistas stormed the church and burned the religious statues. The date given, 1939, is incorrect.

35. Hector Rubén Bartolini Verdugo, *Monografía de Aconchi (Acontzi)* (Hermosillo, 1983).

36. Gobernador Constitucional Interino Emiliano Corella M. to Comisario de Policía Yécora, 26–12–34, AAGES 235"35"/4; Ray to Yepis, 19–1–35, RG 84, Correspondence American Consulate Guaymas, 1935, vol. 5, 800; report by Inspector Ramón R. Reyes, 1935, SEP/AH 211.4. See SEP/AH for numerous examples.

37. Profesor Martín S. Mercado, Inspector of the Ures School District, to Maestros Directores, 10–11–34, SEP/AH 366.6.

38. Director de Educación Federal J. Lamberto Moreno to SEP, Informe de labores de la Dirección de Educación Federal en Sonora, relativo al tercer bimestre (enero-febrero) del año escolar en curso, 1935, SEP/AH 249.

39. Director de Educación Federal J. Lamberto Moreno to Profesor Celso Flores Zamora, Jefe del Departmento de Enseñanza Rural y Primaria Foránea, 20–4–35, SEP/AH 249.

40. Presidente municipal, Navojoa, to Manuel Soto y Olea y Hermano, 1935, AAGES 235"35"/31.

41. Gobernador Constitucional Interino Emiliano Corella M. to Comisario de Policía Yécora, 26 12 34, AAGES, 235"35"/4; Gobernador Constitucional Interino Emiliano Corella M. to Presidente municipal Divisaderos, n.d., AAGES 235"35"/ 25; for arrests, see AAGES 235"35 in general, for example, ACTA, 8–1–35, AAGES 235"35"/2.

42. Director General de Educación Federal W. Dworak to Gobernador de Sonora, 24–4–35; Tesorero General de Sonora Vicente Contreras to Presidente Municipal, Magdalena, 14–6–35, both in AAGES 235"35"/29; Profesor Federal Arturo Madrid Jiménez to Gobernador de Sonora, 7–6–35, AAGES 231.5"35"/38; and Francisco Alfredo Larrañaga Robles, *Monografía del Municipio de Navojoa: 1982* (Navojoa, 1985[?]), 92–93.

43. Acta, in Director de Educación Federal Fernando Dworak to Gobernador Interino, 24–4–35, AAGES 235"35"/29.

44. Corbalá, *Rodolfo Elías Calles,* 154–55, 158.

45. Enrique Krauze, *General misionero: Lázaro Cárdenas* (México, 1987), 59.

46. Ozouf, *La fête,* 18; and Presidente municipal, Navojoa, to Manuel Soto y Olea y Hermano, 1935, AAGES 235"35"/31. There were also Cultural Saturdays.

47. Report, anonymous teacher, Huatabampo, to Secretaría de la Defensa Nacional, 1–11–35, Archivo de la Revolución Mexicana/Patronato de Historia de Sonora, no. 75; and Bantjes, "Politics, Class and Culture."

48. Recent studies of crowd behavior at civic ceremonies reach this conclusion. See Mark Harrison, *Crowds and History: Mass Phenomena in English Towns, 1790–1835* (Cambridge, 1988).

49. PNR, Domingo Cultural en Hermosillo, 29–7–34, SEP/AH 366.6; and Programa de Festejos organizados por el Comité Ejecutivo del Estado del PNR en conmemoración del "Día del Trabajo," SEP/AH 249.

50. Inspector Leonardo Ramírez G., 5a Zona, Sahuaripa, to Director General de Educación Federal, Sonora, 3–5–35, SEP/AH 211.3; Sabino Linares of the Compañía Fronteriza to Gobierno de Sonora, 14–3–35, AAGES 235"35"/27; and Inspector Federal Daniel Domínguez Duarte to Director de Educación Federal, Informe Bimestral, enero-febero de 1936, 1–3–36, SEP/AH 319, 319.12.

51. Ray to SD, 1–4–35, SD/19.

52. Alphonse Aulard, *Christianity and the French Revolution* (New York, 1966), 109; Michel Vovelle, *Religion et Révolution: La déchristianisation de l'an II* (Paris, 1976), 192; and Jean de Viguerie, *Christianisme et Révolution: Cinq leçons de la Révolution Française* (Paris, 1986), 164.

53. The following poem about the expulsion of the Sonoran clergy appeared in a 1934 teachers' magazine:

La impresión de la hora
Corrido como un cachorro
del lobo del Vaticano
dejo el pueblo mexicano
para agenciarme un socorro.

Adios beatita Lili,
tierno ensueño de mi vida
te dejo mustia y transida;
más no me culpes a mí.

Dejo el púlpito bendito
donde el pueblo embrutecí.
Como recuerdo el besito
de mi sobrina Mimi!

Me duele dejar, caramba,
el curato de Agua Prieta
pero me llevo repleta
la bolsa de pura "chamba"

Ignoro por que "detalles"
me corren de mi Sonora.
A mí y al buen "bacanora"
nos "tira" Rodolfo Calles.

El Abate Santanon, Ures, June 1934; *Alma sonorense: Organo mensual de la Federación de Maestros del estado de Sonora*, Ures, June 1934, no. 3.

54. Examples can be found in SEP/AH 366.7.

55. Speech by Pascula E. Jiménez to the Unión de Gambusinos, La Palma, 20–10–34, AAGES 235"35"/6; and "Discurso pronunciado en el Palacio de Gobierno de la Ciudad de Hermosillo, Sonora, el 1° de Mayo de 1934, con motivo del 'Día del Trabajo,' " in Arturo García Fomenti, *Desde la tribuna revolucionaria de Sonora (Escuela socialista y otros temas)* (México, 1935), 55–58.

56. According to Krauze, Cárdenas received literature on the French Revolution from his successor, Manuel Avila Camacho. See *General misionero,* 27, 36; Meyer, *La Cristiada,* 2:210.

57. Vovelle, *Religion*, 232–35, 228, 278.

58. José Bernal Rodríguez, Inspector Federal, 5a Zona, Sahuaripa, Informe Bimestral, 19–3–36, SEP/AH 319.19; and Knight, *Mexican Revolution*, 2:501.

59. E. Bradford Burns, *The Poverty of Progress: Latin America in the Nineteenth Century* (Berkeley, CA, 1980), 23.

60. François-Xavier Guerra, *Le Mexique: De l'ancien régime à la révolution* (Paris, 1985), 2:314–15; Knight, *Mexican Revolution*, 1:23, and "El liberalismo," 68; Hale, *Transformation*, 148, 152, 155; Vaughan, *Estado*, 1:9, 28–29, 2:286–87; and Knight, *Mexican Revolution*, 2:423, 463, and "El liberalismo," 69.

61. Raby, *Educación*, 206; Martínez Assad, *El laboratorio*, 80; Eduardo Ibarra and Ernesto Camou Healy, "Las instituciones educativas," *HCS*, 579.

62. Raby, *Educación*, 199, 206; Krauze, *General misionero*, 46, 49, 54–55; Manuel Diego Hernández and Alejo Maldonado Gallardo, "En torno a la historia de la Confederación Revolucionaria Michoacana del Trabajo," *Jornadas de historia de occidente: Movimientos populares en el occidente de México, siglos XIX y XX* (Jiquilpan de Juárez, 1980), 128–29; Raby, *Educación*, 51, 199, 206; Krauze, *General misionero*, 46, 54–55; Hernández and Maldonado Gallardo, "En torno a la historia," 128–29; and Victoria Lerner, *La educación socialista* (México, 1979), 14–15, 73, 75, 82, 98–99.

63. Lerner, *La educación*, 14–15, 73, 75, 82, 98–99; Raby, *Educación*, 51; the quotation is from Martínez Assad, *El laboratorio*, 86.

64. *Memoria General: Informe rendido por el C. Rodolfo Elías Calles, Gobernador Constitucional del Estado, ante la H. XXXII Legislatura local, el 16 de septiembre de 1934* (Hermosillo, 1934), 4, 15, 35; and Corbalá, *Rodolfo Elías Calles*, 154–55, 158.

65. "Discurso pronunciado en el Palacio de Gobierno de la Ciudad de Hermosillo, Sonora, el 1º de Mayo de 1934, con motivo del 'Día del Trabajo' " in García Fomenti, *Desde la tribuna*, 55–58.

66. Flores to Director de Educación Federal, 16–4–35, SEP/AH 249.

67. García Fomenti, *Desde la tribuna*, 70–71; Corbalá, *Rodolfo Elías Calles*, 154–55, 158; *El Imparcial* (Hermosillo), August 14, 1966, mentions twenty-one schools, while Corbalá, pp. 155–56, speaks of a total of sixteen: Magdalena (two), Alamos (two), Hermosillo (three), Granados, Moctezuma, Cócorit, Ciudad Obregón, Ortiz (one each), and Cananea (four). Official sources mention sixteen schools closed between 1932 and 1934. See *HCS*, 185. Another chapter of the same work mentions eighteen private schools closed, p. 579.

68. Raby, *Educación*, 211–12; Lyle Brown, "Mexican Church-State Relations, 1933–1940," *A Journal of Church and State* 7 (1964): 211, n. 36.

69. *El Imparcial*, August 14, 1966; Fernando W. Dworak, circular no. 71–53, Hermosillo, 23–4–34, RG 84, Consular Post Records, Nogales, Confidential Correspondence 1936, vol. 2.

70. For a literary treatment of the moral dilemmas involved, see Abelardo Casanova, *Pasos perdidos* (Hermosillo, 1986); Robinson to Josephus Daniels, U.S. Ambassador, Mexico City, 1–3–35; Robinson to U.S. Secretary of State (hereafter SS), 1–6–34, SD/18; Fernando W. Dworak, circular no. 71–53, Hermosillo, 23–4–34, RG 84, Consular Post Records, Nogales, Confidential Correspondence 1936, vol. 2. Such measures were not uniformly enforced. While in Hermosillo twenty-five out of eighty state and federal teachers and six private teachers were forced to

resign, none of the Nogales teachers had retired by 1934. See Gibbs, Cananea, to Robinson, 25-5-34, RG 84, Correspondence Consular Agency Cananea, 1934–35, vol. 27, concerning those who fled to Arizona.

71. Director de Educación Federal J. Lamberto Moreno to Director y Profesores de las Escuelas Rurales Federales de Estado de Sonora, circular no. 3, 25-2-35, SEP/AH 249; Guadarrama, "Los cambios," *HCS*, 186–87; and Ozouf, *La fête*, 20.

72. For Michoacán, see "Declaración ideológica," to be signed by the teacher, the education inspector, and the director of federal education, 1935, in Archivo Francisco J. Múgica, Jiquilpan de Juárez, vol. 106, 272–1; for Yucatán, see Brown, "Mexican Church-State Relations," 211, n. 36.

73. Instituto de Orientación Socialista para los Maestros Federales del Estado de Sonora, 17-6/14-7-35, SEP/AH 249.

74. *Propaganda doctrinaria antidogmática para maestros rurales*, boletín 1, 2, and 3 (Magdalena, January 1936).

75. Yepis to SS, 7–8–35, RG 84, Correspondence American Consulate Guaymas, vol. 5, 800.

76. Ray to SD, 8–1–35, SD/18; Estatutos y reglamentos del Bloque Revolucionario de Obreros y Campesinos de Magdalena, 11–11–34, SEP/AH 249.

77. Corbalá, *Rodolfo Elías Calles*, 154–55, 158; and Inspector Leonardo Ramírez G., 5a Zona, Sahuaripa, to Director General de Educación Federal, Sonora, 3–5–35, SEP/AH 211.3.

78. Bantjes, "Politics, Class and Culture."

79. Meyer, *La Cristiada*, 1:375; and Knight, "Revolutionary Project."

80. Furet, *Interpreting the French Revolution*, 58.

81. Fray Toribio de Benavente, *Historia de los Indios de la Nueva España* (Madrid, 1985), 296.

14

Misiones Culturales, *Teatro Conasupo, and Teatro Comunidad: The Evolution of Rural Theater*

Donald H. Frischmann
La Universidad de
Las Américas-Cholula

The Maya, Mexico's best-known ethnic group of several million in Yucatán and Chiapas and in neighboring Guatemala, Belize, and Honduras, have successfully preserved much of their pre-Columbian culture, including their language and folktales. One recent technique for cultural preservation uses theater (notably the *Lo'il Maxil*, or Monkey Business, acting company in San Cristóbal de Las Casas).[*] Donald Frischmann examines the development of rural theater throughout southern Mexico. He focuses not only on its use to preserve ethnic cultures but also on its role as an educative method that empowers communities through collective creation of plays. His essay contains traces of colonial evangelical theater, revolutionary educational missions, and nonformal educational theories of Augusto Boal and Paulo Freire.[†] Frischmann, who teaches Spanish literature and drama, regularly attends Mexico's annual national theater fiesta.

W ITHIN THE CULTURAL MOSAIC known as Mexico, dramatic performances have flourished since pre-Hispanic times in a myriad of forms and languages and for a variety of purposes. Two frequently

---

This essay draws on my field experience since 1983 and archival research in 1983–84 at the Mexico City offices of the Dirección General de Culturas Populares (DGCP), Secretaría de Educación Pública (SEP). I wish to express my appreciation to the individuals and theater groups who have made this study possible. To them and their campesino audiences, I respectfully dedicate these pages.

[*]Patrick Breslin, "Coping With Change: The Maya Discover the Play's the Thing," *Smithsonian* (August 1992): 78–87.

[†]Boal, *Teatro del oprimido* (Buenos Aires, 1974); and Freire, *Pedagogy of the Oppressed* (New York, 1970).

intertwined ends have been entertainment and the inculcation of well-defined spiritual and civic beliefs. Hegemonic groups have often appropriated theater to impose or support their particular worldview.

Following the decade of revolutionary violence (1910–1920), the new regime launched a concerted educational campaign. Education Secretary José Vasconcelos, with the creation of the *misiones culturales* in the 1920s, began the implementation of a clearly defined official cultural policy. The techniques for implanting this national *política cultural* drew on the pre-Hispanic and colonial traditions.

Theatrical pageantry in pre-Hispanic times served to appease the deities in order that life continue as well as to affirm the semidivine nature of the rulers.[1] Immediately after the conquest, Franciscan Pedro de Gante and other friars capitalized on ritual performance traditions in central Mexico. Their theater of evangelization became a powerful didactic instrument aimed at cultural change and the implantation of a new worldview and political order. During the early colonial period, drama and other forms of pageantry celebrated the new religion. Indigenous peoples were encouraged (or, more often, obligated) to participate.[2]

Revolutionaries found in this tradition useful procedures that they adopted and modified for their use. Once again the live performers' extraordinary power of persuasion gained official recognition. This educational campaign devoted attention and subsidies to rural theater.[3] The Ministry of Education's cultural policy fell within Nestór García Canclini's paradigm of the Populist State. In this model the state (or ruling political parties) tries to distribute elite cultural goods while at the same time vindicating the popular culture in such a way that ensures the balanced perpetuation of the system. The frequent failure of such populist cultural programs results from the state's misinterpretation of the people's culture: it fails to differentiate between the people's interests and those that have been imposed on them through education and mass media.[4] Officials have promoted these state-sponsored theater projects as "revolutionary," "popular," and "authentically rural" despite their imposition from above on campesino communities and their strong elements of demagoguery and paternalism.

State-sponsored rural cultural projects with theater as an integral component passed through four major stages: the *misiones culturales*, 1920s–1940; the Centro Regional para la Educación Fundamental de América Latina's (CREFAL) Nuestro Teatro Campesino, 1950–1964; Teatro Conasupo de Orientación Campesina, 1972–1976; and Proyecto de Arte Escénico Popular, 1977–1982.[5] Initiated as vertically imposed, paternalistic projects in the first two programs, this theater began to undergo a transition in Teatro Conasupo, ultimately becoming an authentic, popular grass-roots movement known as the Asociación Nacional de Teatro Comunidad that began developing in 1984. The turning point came as a result of the "late populist" policies both in culture and politics of the Luis Echeverría government (1970–1976).[6]

EARLY ANTECEDENTS: RURAL THEATER AND THE *MISIONES CULTURALES*, 1920–1938

The revolutionary governments in the 1920s placed a high priority on rural education. José Vasconcelos, director (1921–1924) of the new Secretaría de Educación Pública (SEP), promoted education as an apostolic mission that swept all parts of the country; his message was that teaching someone to read and write was equivalent to giving water to the thirsty and food to the hungry. He compared building a library in an isolated village to the construction of a colonial church with its cupola covered in brilliant mosaics. He made theater and the other performing arts integral components of the *misiones culturales* with an ambitious program of outreach teams dedicated to economic rehabilitation and cultural advancement of the rural population. The program called for building schools, training new teachers (usually the mission team members themselves), organizing sports and recreation programs, and offering useful instruction in personal hygiene, scientific agricultural techniques, and trades.[7]

The *misiones*, between 1930 and 1936, mobilized community forces to build some four thousand schools with adjacent open-air theaters. The sports and recreation programs, which included theater, dance, and music, had goals of liberating the people from excessive drinking and other vices and promoting "Mexicanization," the integration of all peoples into national life and culture.[8] Rural teachers had a good number of scripts immediately available. Between 1932 and 1940 some fifty were published in the rural teachers' journal *El Maestro Rural*, others were generated through contests, and still others were written and staged by local teachers. Many of the theaters that promoted class consciousness had fallen into disuse by 1938.[9]

Why did rural theater decline? Some attributed it to the lack of appropriate children's plays, while others have suggested that insufficient government financial support caused the demise.[10] But stronger causes relate to the (at best) meager attempt to incorporate campesino creativity into original works. The plays did not reflect the campesino manner of speaking, thinking, and behaving. Instead, authors—primarily city people—focused on didactic, paternalistic, excessively rhetorical and Manichaean scripts. Rural teachers adopted the pompous and affected rhetorical style of urban playwrights and politicians for their local plays and public speaking.[11] They promoted the oversimplified worldview that elevated revolutionary governments and their programs to a sacrosanct status. These characteristics became particularly pronounced during the presidency of Lázaro Cárdenas (1934–1940), whose rural development programs revolved around socialist education and agrarian reform.

The Cárdenas government placed the "rural socialist school of the Mexican Revolution" in stark opposition to the "Porfirian school," which one writer identified as "taverns and temples; the intoxication of pulque and catechism depraving the masses." In contrast, the socialist school, said its proponents, would replace "the enervating odor of wax and incense of the dark institutions of intellectual obscurity, [with] the new cultural centers, huts or white buildings, ventilated and cheerful, . . . continuously producing class consciousness, struggle against oppression, emancipating postulates; the triumph of truth over error, progress over routine, science over ignorance, justice over crime, life over death." Furthermore, the rural teacher was proclaimed as the "Apostle of the Revolution," "the Revolution's best soldier," the "teacher-worker," and the "teacher-martyr" who faced the threat of homicide or physical mutilation at the hands of the revolution's enemies.[12]

These concepts from Mexico City appeared on rural theater stages. In the scripts written during these years the forces of good found representation as socialist education, peasant land takeovers, agrarianism, scientific agriculture, literacy, and anything else that favored the working class. Many of the positive symbols employed in these plays, such as the red flag, came from the Soviet Union. On the side of evil stood alcoholism, the Catholic church, *latifundistas* (large landowners), caciques (rural bosses) and their goons (white guards), and any other remnants of the Porfirian order.[13]

An additional limiting factor came from the absence of theater specialists among the *misiones culturales* team members. As a result, rural teachers received minimal assistance in fulfilling the prescription for revolutionary theater while at the same time maintaining the interest of actors and audiences. Moreover, the itinerant nature of the missions limited the effects of these intensive, yet brief, efforts. "Often it takes six months to a year to win the whole-hearted cooperation of a village," Lloyd Hughes concluded, "and by that time the mission is ready to move on."[14] Domingo Adame judged that

much demagoguery was present in the plays that were presented. How could this contribute to community development? There were achievements: The communities built schools; they defended teachers against goon squads sent by rural bosses who saw their interests threatened; and young Indians and campesinos left their towns and villages to pursue professional studies, although they usually never returned to their places of origin. The social education project was abandoned at the end of the Cárdenas term in office. The teachers forgot about theater and the communities continued to be excluded from "development."[15]

Despite all these weaknesses in the revolutionary program, rural theater's decline in some localities resulted from the opposition from rural priests and large landowners who forced the shutdown of the *misiones culturales* in 1938. Reorganized in 1942, once again under the supervision of the Secretariat of Public Education, the revived drama program could not generate much interest in didactic drama and puppetry. Official attention and resources then turned to the *misiones cinematográficas*, which brought feature films and cartoons by pack mule to remote Indian regions.[16]

THE INADEQUATE FORMULA AGAIN: CREFAL'S NUESTRO TEATRO CAMPESINO, 1950–1964

Rural theater once again, from 1950 to 1964, received government promotion as an educational activity and tool for community development.[17] Rural teachers could select theater studies as part of their training available through adult education at the CREFAL, supported by the United Nations Educational, Scientific, and Cultural Organization (UNESCO) and the Mexican government. In addition, scholarships attracted non-Mexican teachers from several Latin American countries to CREFAL's campus in Pátzcuaro, Michoacán. The theater program had the stated goal of creating authentic rural theater in ten neighboring communities. Nevertheless, paternalism and demagoguery once again worked directly against this objective, contributing to its ultimate failure.

Prescribed formulas effectively buried any authentic rural theater. Alfred Mendoza Gutiérrez, supervisor of the Nuestro Teatro Campesino (Our Campesino Theater) program, tried, apparently with little success, to transfer to the countryside his knowledge of theatrical precepts, especially the Stanislavsky method learned in Mexico City's Instituto Nacional de Bellas Artes. Furthermore, he thought the campesinos had been "abandoned by God" as far as their theatrical potential was concerned; he declared that they could neither talk, move, nor think appropriately and thus required massive reeducation before they could appear on stage.

Beyond the director's elitist prejudices acquired in the city, the increasingly restrained cultural policies of the governments during this period further restricted creative thinking. In short, stage productions ignored rural inequities as they defended and reinforced the status quo. For example, the effects of alcoholism were no longer viewed as an obstacle to a revolutionary program but rather in more individual and community-oriented terms. Plays ignored political and socioeconomic issues for didactic law-and-order productions, comedies of errors (penned by Mendoza Gutiérrez), and "campesino" versions of foreign works such as *Snow White*. Cosmetic changes, such as substituting Pátzcuaro's famous *Viejitos* (Little Old Men) dancers for the Seven Dwarfs, contributed little to the creation of an authentic rural theater.

Only one of the ten targeted communities produced a theater group, and it was short-lived. Excessive paternalism effectively prevented the realization of the stated goals. Instead, the theatrical activity of teachers and campesinos effectively served to contain popular movements through 1) acculturation (imposition of urban theater models); 2) folklorism (out-of-context utilization of regional cultural elements); 3) massification (rural communities remained passive receivers of a finished product); 4) emphasis on respect for existing institutions; and 5) predominance of spectacle and comedy over critical ideas.

RECENT POPULISM AND COLLECTIVE CREATION: TEATRO CONASUPO DE ORIENTACIÓN CAMPESINA, 1972–1976

The Teatro Conasupo de Orientación Campesina was created in 1971 as a communications link between the rural peasantry and Conasupo, the National Company for Popular Consumption.[18] During its first phase, extension companies made up the Teatro Conasupo, touring the countryside and performing short European plays. They attracted rural audiences to give information about Conasupo's programs. In the latter phase campesinos participated as actors. With the institution of the collective creation of plays by agency representatives and local campesinos, Conasupo laid the initial groundwork for what would eventually result in a genuine form of peoples' rural theater.

The impetus for the creation of Teatro Conasupo came from the Chiapas writer Eraclio Zepeda and a group of young collaborators who, like previous cultural missionaries, viewed their work as contributing to the full realization of the agrarian goals set forth by the leaders of the revolution.[19] Their political activism found encouragement in the populism of the Echeverría government. Economic crisis in the late 1960s had given rise to frustration and protest among the middle and lower strata of the population and had spurred budding guerrilla movements and rural land invasions in the early 1970s. Echeverría's presidential campaign castigated the excessive concentration of income and the marginalization of the masses, especially peasant and Indian groups. His reform program in the countryside included rekindling in the peasantry the hope of agrarian reform and removing local conservative obstacles (bureaucracies, *latifundistas*, and political bosses). Echeverría saw the need for a communications channel to the progressive and intellectual sectors, who had been alienated by the violent repression at Tlatelolco in 1968 by the Díaz Ordaz administration.[20] Teatro Conasupo, it seemed, could provide at least nominal attention to all of these goals.

Rodolfo Valencia, artistic supervisor for Teatro Conasupo, explained that the pact between the core of theater promoters and Echeverría clearly stipulated that they should work to support the campesinos and that they would never be asked to promote any politicians. The first itinerant brigades, as they were called, recruited actors from Mexico City's Instituto Nacional de Bellas Artes, who performed medieval farces and one-act plays by Molière and Chekhov in rural communities of less than five thousand inhabitants. These brigades took advantage of the attendance at their performances to promote elements of Conasupo's programs such as crop purchases at guaranteed prices, the building of grain silos and warehouses, the use of recommended fertilizers, and the rudiments of good nutrition. As direct field agents of Conasupo, the brigades consequently had a political mission—to break traditional local market monopolies controlled by rural bosses by linking the campesinos to the Conasupo program.[21]

So that the city players might effect a greater rapport with the rural audiences, each evening's performance included a second, improvised play. The actors attempted to synthesize the concerns of the spectators through five stock commedia dell'arte characters. Don Trinquetes and Doña Trácalas donned the guises of merchants, corrupt politicians, intermediaries, or caciques to exploit the peasantry; Juan Sin Ganas (Lazy Juan) accepted his exploitation in a docile manner; and Juan Sin Miedo (Fearless Juan), although he tried to take on his enemies, initially failed because he did not know how to proceed. Nevertheless, he ultimately succeeded thanks to the advice and example of Clarín Cantaclaro (Clear Sounding Bugle), who was wise and well informed on national and international matters, particularly the Mexican legal system.

It soon became obvious that the Mexico City troupes were neither the most qualified to address rural problems nor firmly committed to the campesino cause. Rural theater reached a new crisis that determined the next step—in fact, a leap—the creation of the first Conasupo brigades of campesino actors and the implementation of a new process of collective creation.

In San Pedro Tlalcuapan, Tlaxcala, Soledad Ruiz directed the first such group, the thirty-five-member Xicoténcatl Brigade.[22] This Náhuatl-speaking group produced a repertoire of two works. One, an improvised farce entitled *El Campesino y el Rico* (*The Peasant and the Rich Man*), portrays a peasant who sells his crop at submarket prices to a middleman; his angry wife and daughter pursue the merchant and reclaim the money after a confrontation with his thugs. The other, *Xochipitzahuac* (*Slender and Delicate Flower*), an example of sacred ritual theater, involves a traditional wedding dance and fertility ritual based on Nahua mythology, with the personification of several principal deities. In fact, the community group that had been responsible for perpetuating this ceremony became the basis for the new theater brigade.

Why frame an existing ritual practice as a play for Teatro Conasupo? For one thing, focusing attention on this ceremony demonstrated to the residents of San Pedro that their traditions were indeed worthwhile, valuable, and beautiful. This sent a particularly important message in a region surrounded by urban sprawl, threatened with induced cultural change, and marked by frequent emigration to Mexico City or Puebla for economic survival. Moreover, placing this traditional text in written form for the first time would help it survive in an age of mass media. The Xicoténcatl Brigade spurred forms of political and economic organization that put the community on a new path toward self-sufficiency. Thus, the clear vision and solid commitment of Director Ruiz carried the program far beyond the paternalism and demagoguery of official cultural policies.

Two additional pioneering campesino groups appeared shortly afterward in Oaxaca under the direction of Susana Jones Arriaga. Born in the United States and holding a degree in drama from Bennington College, she has lived in Mexico since 1948. She has directed community theater in working-class neighborhoods, especially Colonia Martín Carrera, in Mexico City. Her work in rural theater has taken her to Oaxaca, Veracruz, Aguascalientes, and other locations. Since her participation in Teatro Conasupo, she has worked incessantly as a rural theater director and consultant. In 1992 she held a position on the steering committee of the Asociación Nacional de Teatro Comunidad. Many consider her the *alma*—the heart and soul—of the rural theater movement. She had come to recognize that the acting brigades of Mexico City students would not work at about the same time and for the same reasons as did Soledad Ruiz in San Pedro Tlalcuapan. She recalled: "I was the only one besides Germán Meyer and Soledad Ruiz who actually lived out in the communities . . . and I think that the most valuable gain from that experience was learning that you have to be there. And that if you're there, you can tap people's talents much more and you can recognize them because you see how they work in their daily lives. . . . There was this enormous talent to be tapped, but you had to go out and be there, you couldn't manage it long distance."[23] This experience confirmed conclusions and suggested changes in the program. "I had become convinced," she explained, "that workers' theater could only be of importance if it were the expression of the workers themselves. Other directors in the program considered that plays written and acted by 'peasants' would be amateur—in other words, bad." But she soon had an opportunity to test her ideas:

> At the end of 1973 Julia Baker, an American doctor who had established several village clinics in the mountains of Oaxaca, asked a favor of Eraclio Zepeda. She wanted a Teatro Conasupo brigade to perform in certain villages to reinforce her work there. Eraclio asked me to accompany Julia and the brigade to a town called Tonalá and to report whether it would be possible to start a brigade there. . . . I reported that it would be possible to start not only one brigade, but two: a mestizo group in Tonalá and an Indian group with the Triquis of Copala.

Jones Arriaga added that creating brigades of campesinos rather than of Mexico City acting students was an innovation that required a good deal of persuasion before Eduardo Herrera, the program administrator, accepted the idea. A visit to Tonalá to watch a performance left him unmoved, but after joining several actors and Jones Arriaga in a private home for "tea with tequila," he became a proponent of the new program. Campesino plays such as *La Lotería de la Vida* (*The Lottery of Life*) proved the success of the transition. Jones Arriaga relates that

> the campesino audience was able to see itself reflected in the actors. Many times I heard remarks such as: "Why, that boy could be Eloy's son," or, "Look, she looks like Aunt Rodolfina." This identification with the actors produced a rapport with the audience which I have seldom seen. The play, written by the players and based on themes of regional needs, traditions and attitudes, touched chords which were common to all. After each performance the villagers would invite the group to a cup of ranch coffee and many hours of friendly talk.[24]

The two groups inspired by Jones Arriaga and another directed by Germán Meyer in the mountains of Puebla were the first to approach authentic rural theater by performing original collective creations rather than works written by an outside author or the group's director. The campesinos thus became producers, not just consumers, of the artistic product.[25] This process could be facilitated by a trained adviser, called the *promotor*, who could assist with stage direction and dramaturgy, attempting only to coordinate, not interfere, in the creative process. Jones Arriaga, for example organized brainstorming sessions, helping brigade members develop themes, usually drawn from their daily experience. Then she would assist in the structuring of scenes; finally, everyone would sit down together and put the play on paper. This significant transformation in rural theater notwithstanding, some administrators remained reluctant to place the entire project in the hands of campesinos. In 1974, out of sixteen brigades, ten comprised acting students and only six, campesinos. Of the latter, five worked in Indian languages in the states of Chiapas, Tlaxcala, and Oaxaca.[26]

Despite official reticence and the objective of promoting Conasupo programs, the more isolated groups were able to pay less attention to administrative mandates and embark on more creative ventures. The new method of collective creation became the backbone of rural theater. This new technique soon reflected the influence of Brazilian Augusto Boal and his book *Teatro del Oprimido* (*Theater of the Oppressed*).[27] Boal built upon the Latin American heritage from the 1960s, which was influenced by educators such as Paulo Freire, who wanted to raise consciousness through drama, among other methods, in such a way that it would serve as a "dynamic source of learning." Boal, a close colleague of Freire, pioneered this approach in Peru's national literacy campaign during the 1960s while in exile from the military regime in Brazil. Explaining the view held by Boal, Freire, and others of the educational aspect of drama, Ross Kidd explained:

> Theater was conceptualized as a *code*—a mirroring or representation of reality used to focus and stimulate discussion. . . . The process of improvising a drama—to reflect the world as it is, how it should be, and how people might act to bring about this change—could constitute as vital a learning experience as *decodification*—reflecting on or analyzing the drama. . . . Participants would put on an improvised drama (codification) about an issue of common concern and afterwards discuss it (decodification). The discussion would open up new insights or questions which could then be further explored through improvised drama (codification).[28]

Theater no longer was conceived of as a completed product or code. Rather, it represented an open-ended process that does more than reflect reality; it shows how the real world can be changed as participants test out their ideas for transforming it.

Teatro Conasupo achieved concrete results through the process of collective creation. Ruiz and Jones Arriaga supplied information on the achievement of agency objectives. One community, San Luis Tolocholco, Tlaxcala, achieved the first goal, "to provide agricultural, commercial, and nutritional knowledge in order to attain substantial changes in the general standard of living." There the existence of the theater brigade led to the creation of a textile cooperative. Also, the brigade inspired collectivized and somewhat modernized agricultural undertakings, motivating the purchase of a tractor to replace oxen- or mule-pulled plows.

Also in Tlaxcala, communities had some success with the second goal, "to promote popular organization as a means of putting an end to violations of the law, and to the exploitation of the campesino by middlemen and caciques." Brigade actors had worked for unrigged, democratic local elections and had succeeded through continuous struggle with local authorities. At the national level several Conasupo employees were denounced by campesinos to the brigades for having offered sublegal prices for farm products. As a result, schools were created to train campesinos to fill these same positions.

Finally, the third goal, "to rescue or strengthen local cultural values so that the campesino, particularly the Indian, might retain his original group identity," found expression in the Xicoténcatl Brigade's staging of *Xochipitzahuac*. The collective creation process itself accomplished this objective by providing the campesino with a theatrical forum in which to voice his concerns. The presence of campesino actors on stage, addressing their own immediate reality, with its problems and contradictions, strengthened the sense of pride within the participants and the audiences who saw themselves portrayed with dignity.

The Triqui group of Copala, Oaxaca, according to Jones Arriaga, recorded similar successes. She described the dynamics of change and empowerment within this highly besieged ethnic group induced through the collective theater experience:

> The Play that they created told four stories about cheating. . . . [They performed it] in almost all of the twenty-odd Triqui communities (getting to many of them required a day's trek on foot). As I watched these performances progress, I noticed a subtle change take place. The teacher-actors became orators and politicians. Slowly they abandoned all movements which were unnecessary to the text. Planted in front of their audience on a hillside, or near a one-room schoolhouse, they transformed their roles into impassioned speeches. As they spoke the spectators interrupted, correcting, refuting or applauding a concept. Each of the ten "Maestros" was eloquent and convincing but Marcos Silva Ramírez commanded special attention and respect. . . . In 1976, on January 11, representatives of eighteen communities presented themselves at the meeting [to elect a leader] and, in spite of the threats, bribes and alcohol, unanimously elected their new leader, Marcos Silva Ramírez.[29]

As the above examples reveal, the technique of collective creation inspired a dialectical relationship between stage drama and social processes. Institutional rural theater moved the community closer to popular empowerment. Despite the idealism with which it was conceived, campesino participation as actors was frequently motivated, at least initially, by some form of remuneration, such as Conasupo groceries or modest stipends.[30] Whether popular theater can be produced under such circumstances is debatable. Moreover, few if any of the campesino brigades remained active once Conasupo cut the administrative umbilical cord. It seems obvious that nonorganic institutional theater does not result in the creation and development of durable rural theater movements. The exception to this rule lies in the experience gained and lessons carried forward by the directors into subsequent rural theater experiments.

The end of the Echeverría regime marked the end of support for Teatro Conasupo, which had existed from 1972 to 1976. Germán Meyer calculated that fifty-two of its brigades had given some six thousand performances before an estimated 3.25 million spectators. This new, critical rural theater abruptly found itself in a highly vulnerable position, facing changes in official cultural policies. Nevertheless, a core of advisers had become convinced that rural theater's potential contribution to the life of rural communities was too valuable to be discarded.

PROYECTO DE ARTE ESCÉNICO POPULAR, 1977–1982

The difficult challenge of finding support for a new rural theater project fell to Jones Arriaga, Valencia, and Herrera.[31] A score of their proposals were subsequently rejected by as many government agencies, including the Secretaría de Reforma Agraria. The political risks of sponsoring a more-or-less unrestricted, large-scale project of popular theater was the greatest obstacle to obtaining institutional support. Then, in early 1977, Jones Arriaga learned from a visiting friend, R. Buckminster Fuller, that a new agency of the Ministry of Education, the Dirección General de Culturas Populares (Popular Culture Division, or DGCP), might be interested in the program. After several meetings, DGCP directors Rodolfo Stavenhagen and Leonel Durán eagerly accepted the proposal made by Jones Arriaga and Herrera. Thus was born the Proyecto de Arte Escénico Popular (Popular Theater Arts Project, or PAEP) as a rural (and urban) educational and community development support program.[32]

The SEP agreed to reassign a small nucleus of rural teachers to theatrical duties for one year, to finance a three- to four-month workshop in Mexico City, and to pay living and travel expenses for the directors and their groups. Initial plans called for performances in rural communities by two itinerant groups to create interest in theater among campesino audiences; the latter were to become producers, creators, and actors in this theater of critical thought and self-questioning as a prelude to community reflection and action. The campesino actors, similar to the previous Conasupo brigades, were neither taught nor encouraged to "pretend" or "simulate" but rather to "testify" on stage. They were envisioned not as actors but as participant-characters. On stage few assumed fictional names or dressed differently from their everyday clothes. In this way rural theater was to be "a theater of constant movement" and "of action," an instrument of communication and an agent for change and social transformation.

Theater and social change became dialectically linked. A situation (for example, the loss of traditions) would generate a play that would provoke a reaction (or fail to do so) and in turn would generate another play. The rural theater set in motion social processes, thereby acquiring more relevance than the performances themselves. Like the plays of the Conasupo-sponsored brigades, this concept of theater and its methodology were highly influenced by Brazilians Boal and Freire.

The first twenty PAEP plays, according to Meyer, contained the following themes:

1) SOCIAL PROBLEMS: alcoholism, unity-organization, repression, corruption, exploitation, marketing of products, emigration, unemployment, women's issues, reassessment of culture, means of communication, education, petroleum.
2) COMMUNITY HISTORY: narration, oral tradition, historical documents.
3) POPULAR EXPRESSION: dramatized story, traditional ceremony, Christmas play (*pastorela*), dance, fireworks.
4) COMMUNITY PROGRAMS: health, nutrition.

While attempting to avoid Manichaean dramatic structures, primary and (generally numerous) secondary themes clustered around two poles: the forces of progress and the forces of regression. The former embodied what was seen as essential for the material, moral, and ethnic advancement of the community. The latter were characterized by their opposition to any change of the political or economic status quo. This conservatism represented the interests of local bosses and the mental atavism of the community. Conditioned by poverty,

exploitation, and tradition, the campesino could not carry out beneficial, transforming actions.

In comparison with Teatro Conasupo the PAEP experienced tighter
artistic and bureaucratic supervision, Jones Arriaga remarked, which
restrained the natural creativity of the campesino participants. This
control resulted through the perhaps overly structured Mexico City
workshop and more frequent field observations. Previously, the isolation of at least some of the Teatro Conasupo brigades had allowed
for more freedom and creativity on behalf of advisers and actors.
These differences may also be attributed to the nature of the groups:
local and homegrown in the case of Teatro Conasupo's campesino
brigades, heterogeneous in the case of PAEP group members. Teachers who hailed from different communities, even different states, made
up most of the latter groups. In addition the PAEP's itinerant, one-
night-stand character limited its effectiveness in any community.[33]

Unlike Teatro Conasupo, the PAEP never sent any crooked bureaucrats, merchants, or politicians packing or inspired the creation
of agricultural cooperatives or modernization. PAEP field-workers
faced a difficult challenge indeed when sitting down to evaluate their
task. Germán Meyer reflected, "When the issue is creating consciousness, what are the parameters?" Without a systematic sociological
survey of the general population, the participants themselves become
the focal group for evaluation.

This measure identified the personal transformative power of the
PAEP collective theater experience as its greatest achievement. Many
of the actors had begun their theatrical work in various degrees of
depression and with a general lack of hope for the future. The confidence and voice gained through theater expanded their outlooks,
helped adolescents grow up and meet new challenges, and enabled
some to become successful professionals. This nonpaternalistic theater experience had great meaning for the actors. Speaking of them,
Jones Arriaga observed that "campesinos have an enormous creative
capacity, and can do wonderful things if they are allowed to."[34] The
errors and limitations that characterized institutional rural theater
during this period notwithstanding, the *teatro* experience transformed
a number of lives.

During its five-year existence, the PAEP inspired more than
twenty rural theater groups, some thirty new plays, and 2,213 performances in rural communities before more than one million spectators.[35] But this program fell victim to the six-year presidential cycle.
The high inflation rate at the end of the López Portillo government in
1982 offered justification to the next administration to terminate the
PAEP. State-sponsored rural theater, it seemed, had become a thing
of the past.[36]

Despite the temporary vitality of Teatro Conasupo and the PAEP, institutional rural theater remained in a highly vulnerable position and vanished at the stroke of the Mexico City bureaucratic pen. Despite the successful experience, there had been no overt progress toward the creation of more durable and autonomous nonprofessional theater groups. Nevertheless, the PAEP left behind people of experience dedicated to rural theater. They worked through the Secretariat of Education's Unidades Regionales de Culturas Populares (Regional Field Offices of Popular Cultures, or URCP) and the Asociación Nacional de Teatro Comunidad.

DECENTRALIZATION AND THE ASOCIACIÓN NACIONAL DE TEATRO COMUNIDAD, 1984–

Once the PAEP had been terminated, several of its more persistent field directors continued to work for the Dirección General de Culturas Populares. Some, including Francisco Acosta and Maximina Zárate, joined the newly diversified URCP. Others, notably Domingo Adame and Meyer working out of Mexico City, became national advisers to theater programs. At this time both unsuccessfully lobbied for the creation of a new, large-scale SEP-sponsored rural theater project.

During the De la Madrid administration (1982–1988) the worsening economic crisis led Martha Turok, director of the DGCP, to implement a policy of decentralization, shifting more responsibilities to the regional (URCP) offices. National support for theater programs became largely symbolic as new policies mandated a search for increased community support and paid performances. There were also moments of doubt and hesitation in Mexico City. According to Francisco Acosta, after initial success in creating interest in theater in many communities near Papantla, he and partner Maximina Zárate were suddenly reassigned to research duties. Apparently, bureaucrats in the capital had again become hesitant to allow in peasant communities a theater that promoted critical thought. Despite this, Acosta and Zárate eventually received approval to resume theatrical promotion.[37]

The new policies and severe budgetary restrictions had the salutary effect of increasing the truly popular nature of rural institutional theater. Past experiences and the failures to achieve a lasting popular appropriation of the theatrical process made it clear to practiced directors that only individuals from the rural communities were capable of establishing a permanent and autonomous local theater.

Regional agencies (URCP) recruited bilingual teachers employed in Indian communities and trained them in the rudiments of

collective creation and theatrical promotion. The initial results justified the effort as grass-roots theater groups began to spring up in
communities around Oaxaca, Oaxaca; Papantla and Acayucan,
Veracruz; and Uruapan, Michoacán. These rural theater groups soon
earned recognition as the autonomous representatives of their communities, achieving a status similar to that of village bands and traditional dance groups.[38] Finally, after sixty years of state-sponsored
rural theater, the necessary though simple solution had been reached.
Paradoxically, by not increasing available resources and official personnel but through program decentralization, budget trimming, and
the collective creation process, bilingual teachers led the development at the grass-roots level of authentic rural theater. It flourished
where national paternalism and party populism had been reduced to
a minimum.

In the Veracruz region, Zárate and Acosta cite another factor that
contributed to the success of rural theater: Papantla drew on its rich,
age-old folkloric theater of indigenous dance-dramas (at least sixteen with spoken texts and dialogues still exist). This revealed the
emergence of hybrid works based not only on Freire and Boal's methods but also on folkloric tradition, incorporating dances, themes,
masks, and other autochthonous elements.[39] In Oaxaca as well, drama
groups drew on this indigenous dance-drama tradition.

The URCP-Oaxaca, under advisers Roberto Villaseñor and Luis
Cervantes, acquired particular relevance beginning in 1984 when it
hosted the First Fiesta of Indigenous, Campesino, and Popular
Theater, celebrated in the mountain village of Santiago Laxopa. The
gathering drew seven groups from Veracruz and Oaxaca. Annual
fiestas followed in Ixtlán de Juárez (1985), Totontepec (1986), both
in Oaxaca; Coxquihui, Veracruz (1987); Zitlala, Guerrero (1988);
Caltzontzin, Michoacán (1989); Ocotlán de Morelos, Oaxaca (1990);
and Amecameca, México (1991). Each fiesta attracted more theater
groups and drew other, totally independent troupes as well. The state-
sponsored project had died, but now there existed a rural theater
movement.

The next step came in 1987 with the legal incorporation of the
Asociación Nacional de Teatro Comunidad (National Association of
Community Theater, or TECOM) as a nonprofit organization. TECOM
was then free to set its own agenda and negotiate with various agencies and state-funding sources. The basic operational unit became
fixed in the community. Theater groups existed by and for the community, and their existence no longer reflected changes in official
cultural policies. The community became responsible for much of
the organization and realization of the annual theater fiestas, appropriately renamed Fiesta Nacional de Teatro Comunidad (National

Fiesta of Community Theater) in 1987. Fiesta participants, who had swollen in number to around five hundred in 1991, are housed in individual homes and fed there or in communal kitchens. Fiesta communities become coorganizers, host, and audience to this annual event. In addition, many of their own members take the stage in front of the ever-growing popular theater community. The organization has extended into Central America, the United States, and Canada. The 1990 program included Grupo Hun-Meman-Beyilac from Guatemala; Silviana Wood's Teatro del Pueblo from Tucson, Arizona; and Ondinnok, Inc., of Wendake, Wendat Indian Nation, Canada.

Domingo Adame Hernández, Francisco Acosta Báez, and Francisco Navarro Sada have served as general coordinators of TECOM since its inception. These individuals have presided over the rapid growth of the association, which at times has stretched available resources, particularly at the annual fiesta. To alleviate the cost to the immediate community, funds and donations have been solicited from municipal and state government agencies; for example, staples to feed guests are requested from Conasupo. TECOM attempts to leave behind some reminder of its commitment to the communities that host the fiesta—one hundred fruit trees in Zitlala, for instance, and a stone fountain in Ocotlán. The fiesta brings a brief boom of prosperity to itinerant vendors and local merchants, particularly those whose *tendejones* (general stores) are located near the stages. Pesos are busily swapped for refreshments and snacks that help sustain audiences during the four or five hours of nightly, on-stage programming.

Opening and closing days include special events offered by the host community, which constitute ritual framing of the five- to seven-day fiesta. Such events underscore the indigenous traditions that TECOM officially recognizes as the principal roots of rural theater. The townspeople enact traditional forms of receiving visitors at the entrance to the town. In turn, the general coordinators of TECOM must request many times the sponsorship of the fiesta through offerings of live animals to community representatives.

The reception in 1988 provided a moving example. Once the TECOM caravan arrived and parked at the outskirts of Zitlala, "Place of the Stars," in Guerrero, the reception began. Immediately, a group of eight to ten *tlacololeros* (planter dancers) went into action, cracking their whips, letting out hoots of welcome, and flagellating each other as they skipped about. Simultaneously, a group of *tecuanes* (jaguar dancers) began to engage in ritual fistfighting. Enduring whiplashes, blows, and bruises attracted the blessings of ancestral deities for TECOM's fiesta. Other traditional *danzantes* (dancers) appeared, seemingly out of nowhere, and guests suddenly found themselves enveloped in the dynamic color, music, and magic of "living indigenous theater.''[40] The autochthonous, syncretized dance-dramas of the *chivos* (goats), *muditas* (mute women), *ocho locos* (eight maniacs), *vaqueros* (cowboys), *Apaches* (Indians or Aztecs), *zopilotes* (buzzards), *mulitas* (women muleteers), and *Xochimilcas* (women from Xochimilco), each with its own accompanying musicians, performed as a prelude to the dedication of the two-meter-high TECOM cross and the cleansing ceremony.

The town's women, hair in twin braids and dressed in white blouses and wraparound skirts, suddenly moved out of the shadows, forming two long parallel lines through which TECOM groups slowly passed in procession. The visitors were enveloped in incense from both sides, had floral wreaths placed around their necks, were swept clean from head to toe with multicolored bouquets of flowers, and were showered with thousands of flower petals. Once all visitors had passed through this magical threshold they joined the community in a joyous parade—including brass bands—that wound through the town to its center. After a series of welcoming speeches the dancing resumed until midafternoon and was repeated by different groups on a rotating basis for the rest of the fiesta.

TECOM performances typically begin around sunset under more-or-less improvised spotlights and, at times, with the aid of microphones. Nightly audiences swell to as many as one thousand men, women, and children, with curious dogs and uncontrolled youngsters occasionally crossing the stage in the midst of some performance. Works at the fiesta are presented in Spanish or in any of several Indian languages. They focus on community concerns; topics such as changing cultural values, intergenerational conflicts, youth gangs, ecological destruction, emigration to the United States, and alcoholism receive critical examination through a combination of serious dramatic and comic-farcical styles. The solutions to the conflicts usually entail renewed respect for tradition, which is not narrowly interpreted but rather broadly reinterpreted in light of the inevitable changes brought about by modernization.

What becomes evident is that rural culture is not static but dynamically evolving as it constantly seeks new solutions to problems. Legends and myths regarding origins and nature deities receive considerable attention as well, and religious ritual practices offer another focal point. Indian culture thus reaffirms itself on community stages through the richness and complexity of ancient philosophies and beliefs. Although these performances are decidedly theatrical and representational in nature, the ritual framing provided by inaugural and closing ceremonies results in the inseparable blending of art and community-life celebration. This fusion has been the fundamental characteristic of Mexican Indian cultures since pre-Hispanic times, and it remains a primary objective of TECOM fiestas.

Child, adult, and mixed-generational companies provide a freshness rarely encountered in other theatrical forums. Minimal, improvised scenery and props, everyday clothing-turned-costume, the cold night air of the Sierra Madre, the unaffected laughter and applause— all combine to create the magic that sets *teatro comunidad* apart and makes it so powerfully attractive as a form of human communication and community spirit.

CONCLUSION

The extraordinary power of live theater for transmitting ideologically charged images and messages has been of particular interest to the revolutionary Mexican state. The turning point for this art form came during the Echeverría administration through a pact with the intellectual and artistic community. Through individual commitment and hard work at the local level, this institutional rural theater began to drift away from official program mandates, and the eventual result was the creation of authentic, popular community theater groups. The Asociación Nacional de Teatro Comunidad, or TECOM, was finally created to support and coordinate this change of control over rural theater.

The present-day growth of TECOM relies on daily hard work, coordination, and planning, from the evening rehearsals on the part of campesino actors to the monthly coordinators' meetings. Only in this way will the movement realize its yearly summer workshops (in research, collective creation, and staging and acting techniques) and the growing task of coordinating the annual fiesta. It now seems certain that, like its pre-Hispanic heritage of dance-dramas, living community theater will endure and become a tradition of the people in rural Mexico.

NOTES

1. Examples of cosmic pageantry can still be witnessed. One can observe the *Okosta Pol* (Dance of the [Pig's] Head) among the Yucatec Maya, and the *Calendas* among the Zapotecs of Oaxaca. Both rituals reveal syncretized Christian elements. More autochthonous performances include the *Tecuanes* (Jaguars) of Guerrero and Oaxaca. Periodic Mayan ceremonies celebrated events such as the induction of new Jaguar priests. See Munro S. Edmonson, *Heaven Born Merida and Its Destiny: The Book of Chilam Balam of Chumayel* (Austin, TX, 1986), 20–29.

2. Othón Arróniz, *Teatro de Evangelización en Nueva España* (México, 1979). See also Marilyn Ekdahl Ravicz, *Early Colonial Religious Drama in Mexico* (Washington, DC, 1970), which includes English translations of several missionary plays originally staged in Nahuatl; and Robert Ricard, *The Spiritual Conquest of Mexico* (Berkeley, CA, 1966).

3. In the introduction to *El Teatro de la Salud* (México, 1988), Abigael Bohórquez observes that "theater is yet another audiovisual medium, always effective, and, at times, more so than other forms of dissemination of ideas. Therefore, when well employed, it is a highly valuable aid not only in health education, but also in social education and the formative process in general" (p. 10).

4. Néstor García Canclini, "Políticas culturales y crisis de desarrollo: Un balance Latinoamericano," introduction to *Políticas culturales en América Latina*, ed. García Canclini (México, 1987), 27–36.

5. The latter operated initially in Mexico City's working-class neighborhoods. For a discussion of both rural and urban state-subsidized theater in twentieth-century Mexico, see Donald H. Frischmann, *El Nuevo Teatro Popular en México* (México, 1990). Recent interviews with Teatro Conasupo and Proyecto de Arte Escénico Popular participants have led me to modify some perhaps overly optimistic conclusions. While rural theater field-workers frequently have had highly idealistic objectives of creating an authentic people's theater, the multiple restrictions imposed by government funding agencies have, until recently, made this impossible.

6. Jorge Basurto, "The Late Populism of Luis Echeverría," in *Latin American Populism in Comparative Perspective*, ed. Michael L. Conniff (Albuquerque, NM, 1982), 93–111.

7. Daniel Cosío Villegas, "La Crisis de México," *Cuadernos Americanos* 6, no. 32 (March-April 1947): 46–47; and Lloyd H. Hughes, *The Mexican Cultural Mission Programme* (Paris, 1950), 9, 12–13.

8. Katherine M. Cook, *La Casa del Pueblo* (México, 1936), 144; John B. Nomland, *Teatro Mexicano Contemporáneo (1900–1950)* (México, 1967), 75; and Hughes, *Mexican Cultural Mission Programme*, 51.

9. Domingo Adame Hernández, *Análisis crítico del movimiento de teatro rural con fines sociales en México (1932–1982) y de sus perspectivas actuales* (México, 1984), 28; Concha Becerra Celis, *Teatro y poemas infantiles* (México, 1938), 14; and Nomland, *Teatro Mexicano*, 75. Both Adame and Nomland review a number of plays from this period.

10. Ramón García Ruiz, "Prólogo," in Becerra Celis, *Teatro y poemas*, 6, and in Nomland, *Teatro Mexicano*, 76.

11. Adame, *Análisis*, 37.

12. Rafael Ramos Pedrueza, *La lucha de clases a través de la historia de México* (México, 1941), 420–22.

13. Nomland, *Teatro Mexicano*, 79–80; and Adame, *Análisis*, 28–36.

14. Hughes, *Mexican Cultural Mission Programme*, 51.

15. Domingo Adame Hernández, "De los proyectos institucionales de teatro popular en México a la Asociación Nacional de Teatro Comunidad" (paper given at the Latin American Studies Association, Washington, DC, April 1991), 4–5.

16. Nomland, *Teatro Mexicano*, 29–30, 75.

17. This discussion is based on Adame, *Análisis*, 40–69.

18. Frischmann, *Nuevo Teatro Popular*, 47–137. The Compañia Nacional de Subsistencias Populares, or Conasupo, is one of several state agencies created to direct production and marketing. Conasupo purchases farm products from campesinos at guaranteed prices and sells processed, packaged groceries at modest prices. Conasupo maintains permanent retail outlets in cities and larger towns and sends mobile grocery stores into more remote areas.

19. See his "Las Brigadas Campesinas de Teatro" (interview by Manuel Galich), *Conjunto* 32 (April-June 1977): 78–85.

20. Basurto, "Late Populism," 96–100.

21. Teatro Conasupo became an important part of the state-sponsored balancing act aimed at maintaining relative calm in the countryside during a period of economic crisis. In Stefano Varese's terminology, such measures taken on the part of the state come "very close to being an open social dialectic in which, despite an inequality of conditions, the various social forces compete, expressing their own levels of consciousness and their own abilities to organize." See "Multiethnicity and Hegemonic Construction: Indian Plans and the Future," in *Ethnicities and Nations*, ed. Remo Guidieri et al. (Houston, 1988), 57–58.

22. Named for a preconquest ruler of the Tlaxcalan people. See Soledad Ruiz, "La Brigada Xicoténcatl, Grupo Teatral Campesino," *La Cabra* 1, nos. 4–5 (September 1983): 1–5.

23. Jones Arriaga interview, June 1991, Mexico City.

24. Susana Jones Arriaga, "Some Stories for My Friends" (manuscript, 1980).

25. Augusto Boal's ideas inspired a similar process in Nigeria. See Ross Kidd, "Popular Theater and Nonformal Education in the Third World: Five Strands of Experience," *International Review of Education* 30 (1984): 265–87.

26. *Cuaderno del Brigadista* (July 1974).

27. (Buenos Aires, 1974).

28. Kidd, "Popular Theater," 273–81.

29. Jones Arriaga, "Some Stories," 29–31.

30. Germán Meyer specifically credits the inspiration of Boal and Freire; see also Jones Arriaga interview.

31. This discussion summarizes Frischmann.

32. Jones Arriaga interview.

33. Ibid.

34. Ibid.

35. Rodolfo Valencia Gálvez, "El Teatro Como Instrumento de Promoción Cultural," in *Indigenismo, Pueblo y Cultura*, ed. Jan Reuter (México, 1983), 129.

36. Domingo Adame Hernández, "El Teatro Rural Patrocinado por el Estado," *Escénica* (UNAM) 1, no. 11 (October 1985): 10.

37. Francisco Acosta and Maximina Zárate interview, October 1991, Veracruz.

38. Francisco Navarro Sada, "El Teatro Comunidad," *Repertorio* (Nueva Epoca) 9, no. 11: 133.

39. Acosta-Zárate interview.

40. Professor Cayuqui Estage Noel, founder-director of the Department of Indigenous Theater Research at the University of Oaxaca, coined the term as "a practical classification with which to expound the dramatic, choreographic, ritualistic

and socialized complex of modern indigenous communities." He accurately observes that "this complex in fact displays the characteristics essential to all dramatic genres and therefore deserves to be recognized as such." I recorded this reception on videotape and welcome inquiries about it.

15

The Ceremonial and Political
Roles of Village Bands, 1846–1974

Guy P. C. Thomson
University of Warwick

Mexico resounds with music, and musicians appear everywhere. Perhaps their ubiquity accounts for the way in which they have been taken for granted. Very few previous analyses of the significance of Mexican community bands and their tunes have been attempted; Guy Thomson has undertaken a singular investigation. He does have rich materials on which to draw, including the works of anthropologists, the observations of foreign travelers, and official records. Edward Thornton Tayloe, for example, private secretary to the first U.S. minister to Mexico, Joel Poinsett, noted in his diary that on his arrival in Jalapa, "a band of thirty musicians . . . played to a large crowd collected around them."* The role of musicians in the community is shown in a consular dispatch over a century later, which reported that Manuel Flores, a violin teacher and bandleader, had been chosen municipal president for Monterrey; he later became the governor of Nuevo León.† Developing a parallel study to investigations of brass bands in Europe, Thomson relates the purchase of instruments and training of musicians to both the patronage of Liberal community leaders and membership in militia units. Bands quickly became a matter of village pride and a factor in rivalry between communities.

Thomson has published widely on the state of Puebla‡ and presently holds the position of lecturer in Latin American Studies at the

---

*C. Harvey Gardiner, ed., *Mexico, 1825–1828: The Journal and Correspondence of Edward Thornton Tayloe* (Chapel Hill, NC, 1959), 28.

†Records of the United States Department of State relating to the Internal Affairs of Mexico, 1910–1929, 812.00 Nuevo León/200 Situation in Monterrey, January 28, 1939, Record Group 59, National Archives.

‡See, for example, *Puebla de Los Angeles: Industry and Society in a Mexican City, 1700–1850* (Boulder, CO, 1989).

University of Warwick. His current research focuses on the impact of Liberalism, including band music, on Puebla's Sierra Madre region.

> At night we heard the sound of a clarionet, and flute . . . and on enquiry, discovered that a band of musicians had been organized in the adjoining village, by the owner of the hacienda. . . . The leader was quite a respectable-looking Indian, decently dressed, who played the violin; the clarionet player was fortunate in the possession of cotton drawers and a shirt; the bassoon had a pair of trousers but no shirt; the serpent [cornet] was the wildest looking Indian I ever saw, with long dishevelled black hair, and eyes worthy of his instrument; the big drum was a huge and portly old negro, who reminded me of many of our performers . . . at home; while the octave flute was an urchin of not more than twelve, the wickedest little devil imaginable, but a fellow of infinite talent and a capital performer. . . . We were favored by the self-taught amateurs with several airs from recent operas, performed in a style that would not have injured the reputation of many a military band at home.

> BRANTZ MAYER, *Mexico as It Was and as It Is*[1]

> How many times, upon hearing a melody, we relive times gone by! The memory of the village saint's day, the religious service, the dances, rockets, in short, the village festival. In our hamlets, in the most remote of our sierras, we find a band, who with poor instrumentation and worse sound, pompously interprets something far beyond its knowledge: an overture. Who, apart from the band, is really in touch with the people? The band provides the only means for leading them along the path of artistic culture!

> NABOR VÁZQUEZ, "Breve historia de las bandas de música en México"[2]

A BRASS BAND—HOWEVER TUNELESS—produces a difficult sound to ignore. The band's sheer size, rarely containing less than twenty instruments, makes it an unavoidable public spectacle, particularly with the musicians in uniform and in military formation. Beginning in the early nineteenth century, the number of brass bands in Mexico increased from a handful in the principal state capitals to thousands throughout the cities, towns, and villages of the republic.[3] Their geographical diffusion went far beyond the principal urban boundaries of modernization. "Philharmonic bands" from the 1840s onward could be found serenading sybarites in Mexico City's Alameda, leading ecclesiastical processions in Guadalajara, awakening Fourierist Utopian fantasies in Mexico City, summoning Maya rebel warriors to hear the Speaking Cross in Chan Santa Cruz, accompanying the execution by Totonac rebels of Misantla's *gente de razón*, attending the opening of bridges, and welcoming Italian colonists in remote parts of Puebla's Sierra.[4] After 1900 virtually every Mexican village had at least one brass band as a central part of community ceremonial life.

The proliferation of the brass band in Mexico resulted from three interrelated factors: 1) The brass wind band and its musical repertory reenforced the already important place of music and musicians in village ceremonial life by overcoming many of the aesthetic and technical limitations of traditional music and musical instruments; 2) the band served to embody elements within village leadership, and band membership often reflected village factionalism; and 3) the band became an important element in the village's self-image as well as in the perception of the village among outsiders. Thereby, the band exercised an important role in a village's external relations: serenading distant powerholders, honoring visiting dignitaries, enhancing the community's prestige when playing away (if it performed well), and providing a medium—the frequent exchange of bands—for regularizing relations between neighboring villages after periods of tension and conflict. Brass bands provide a focus for exploring aspects of village life, from basic problems of subsistence and occupation, through questions of ethnic and class identity, to matters of village factionalism, village self-image, and intercommunity relations. With its development in the nineteenth century, the wind band became a central public institution.

WIND MUSIC BEFORE 1850

The brass band did not step into a musical void in the villages. Small flute and drum bands, known as *chirimías* in Oaxaca and *conjuntos aztecos* in Puebla and Tlaxcala, occupied a central place in pre-Columbian ceremonial life, and musicians enjoyed considerable status and prestige. Much larger musical ensembles accompanied warriors to battle and dignified religious ceremonies. Hernán Cortés made his first expedition to Tenochtitlan attended by a small band of "five *chirimías* (an early clarinet), sackbuts (early trombones), and *dulzianas* (a kind of flute or bassoon)."[5] After the conquest the church, particularly the religious orders, encouraged the formation of bands to accompany services, processions, and dances. Musicians received special privileges, including tribute, tax, and service exemptions. The bandmasters, *maestros cantores*, frequently substituted for the priest during his absence, thereby acquiring an unmatched authority in the direction of village ceremonial life. (During the nineteenth century, brass-band directors, often themselves *maestros cantores*, aspired to retain this authority.)[6] Besides these more ambitious bands, priests tolerated the presence in their parishes of *conjuntos aztecos* that had survived the conquest and had often been reinforced with the Spanish *chirimía*. These native musicians accompanied most processions, *mayordomías*, and dances, and the *chirimía* player often doubled as a bugler to summon people to church.[7]

Colonial band music was by no means exclusively a religious affair. Small "trumpet and cornet orchestras" performed at civic festivals, especially bullfights.[8] During the eighteenth century the provincial militia paraded on Sundays to small military bands.[9] It seems likely that the viceregal court, the colonial aristocracy, and the provincial governors and intendants would have enjoyed the pleasures of wind music, which was gradually acquiring a more important place in musical repertory throughout Europe. Nevertheless, the church sponsorship of music remained preeminent.

Between Independence and the Reform laws limiting religious processions and curtailing its wealth and association life, the church possessed a near monopoly in the timing, stage managing, and financing of external ceremonial life as well as in the provision of education (in which music had long formed an important part). A description of the processions accompanying Guadalajara's *fiesta patronal* in 1846 indicates that *músicas de viento*—probably more woodwind than brass—had acquired a central place in the city's ceremonial life two decades before the French Intervention, the event normally credited with the birth and diffusion of the Mexican wind band.[10] At the 1846 celebration, four trumpeters dressed in black led a procession formed of "many thousands of Indians"; eight girls carrying the patron saint; six files of four, candle-bearing women; "a numerous band of musicians with wind instruments"; a statue of the Virgin carried by twelve girls dressed in white; and the priests. Finally, "the rear of this cortege was brought up by more musical bands."[11]

POPULAR DIFFUSION OF THE BRASS BAND

Despite its musical tradition little evidence exists of any widespread popular diffusion of wind bands in Mexico—or in Europe—until the early nineteenth century. Widespread adoption of the wind band required two developments: the application of the valve to wind instruments, immeasurably increasing their melodic potential; and the changes in forms of popular association and warfare that accompanied the French Revolution.

Until the early nineteenth century, wind instruments possessed significantly less versatility than stringed instruments. Consequently, they were confined principally to harmony and only rarely were they used to provide melody. But all this changed: "The introduction of valves . . . removed the physical drawbacks and gave the horns and trumpets an enormously increased utility. . . . All notes were [now] . . . quickly available, and the brass instruments became capable of melody—*any* melody within their compass and suitable to their genius."[12] This technical breakthrough affected different wind instruments at different times over a period of almost fifty years, beginning with the application of slides to the trumpet by a German in 1780, a valve to the horn by Irishman Charles Clagget (1740–1795), the introduction of keys to bugles in the British Army in 1810, the truly revolutionary application of a twin valve to the trumpet by Germans Bluhmel and Stolzel in 1813, and the addition of a third valve by Muller of Mayence in 1830. These technological changes culminated in the application of valves to the full range of wind instruments by Wilhelm Wieprecht during the 1830s and the invention of new valved and keyed wind instruments by Adolphe Sax during the 1840s.[13]

By the 1840s a full range of keyed and valved instruments permitted the formation of bands composed entirely of brass. It now became possible to dispense with woodwind instruments altogether, although military and civilian bands continued to combine wood and brass throughout the rest of the century. Brass instruments, in robust combination, greatly increased versatility and loudness in open-air performances, stole a march on woodwinds, and soon predominated in most bands after the 1840s.[14] The practical impact of these technical innovations meant, first, that wind instruments became easier to play and the training of musicians greatly simplified. Second, the repertory for wind instruments could be expanded almost infinitely, since almost any tune could now be played. Third, bands and ensembles of wind instruments could form independently of the strings, escaping from the cloistered confines at the back of orchestras and the narrow disciplines and repertory of the military band. The brass band could occupy the gap in musical provision between the orchestra of the elite and the string, whistle, and drum arrangements of the people that hitherto had offered the only means of bringing music to the latter.

If the "invention of the valve in brass instruments . . . [did] more to popularize music among the masses than [any] other invention which had ever preceded it," the French Revolution provided the catalyst for the diffusion of the brass band as the popular musical form.[15] Classical authorities, however they may disagree about the relative importance of different national traditions, all concur that the French Revolution transported the wind band and wind music from the restricted confines of the court and private regiment to the wider

The Juarezcitos at a *mayordomía*

Mazatec boys' band, Huauhtla

People receiving their padre, Tilantongo

A *chirimía*

audience of the people, primarily through the National Guard units—both when mobilized for war and when returned to their villages with peace.[16]

A special relationship quickly developed between the brass wind band and the military, public spaces, and workplaces. By the end of the century, in Great Britain alone, colliery and factory bands numbered in the tens of thousands.[17] Parallel developments occurred in the world colonized by Europeans. The United States experienced a similar profusion: "Bands and band music had become deeply ingrained in American life. Virtually every city, town, and village had its own bands, with membership drawn from the community. Band music was omnipresent, heard in evening concerts, parades, political rallies, social events, picnics, civic ceremonies, educational functions."[18]

In Latin America, Bernardo O'Higgins and José de San Martín organized two military bands, one composed of slaves who were later manumitted, in preparation for the campaign to liberate Chile and Peru. Chileans continued the musical effort with the establishment in 1817 of the Academy of Military Music.[19] In Mexico, on the other hand, the revolution in wind instrumentation at first made more headway within traditional religious rituals than among the *sociabilités modernes*—the professional army, political lodges, or artisans' societies—within this country that until midcentury was only lethargically becoming secularized. The Indian wind band that Brantz Mayer described in 1841 was certainly an exception in the countryside, where the smaller *conjuntos aztecos* and *chirimías* more commonly persisted. Mayer reported the apparently successful marriage between the music of the wind band and the traditional authority of the priest (or his associates, the *mayordomos de cofradías*, *maestros cantores*, and fiscal officers) over ceremony and ritual.[20]

Indeed, the pace and apparent spontaneity in the diffusion of brass bands throughout the countryside in the second half of the nineteenth century probably have their roots in this affinity between the power of the new musical form and the patronage of the traditional hierarchy of village officeholders. Certainly, this proved the case in purely musical and ceremonial terms. The dance of the Moors and Christians still performed in the villages of central Puebla illustrates the successful fusion of songs and dance arrangements from the sixteenth century with nineteenth-century polkas, marches, waltzes, and quicksteps.[21]

In addition to these cosmopolitan elements within their repertory, brass bands played more Mexican traditional and local songs and dances that were often so well known that no musical scores were necessary. This more localized repertory—composed of *sones* and *jarabes* that accompanied carnivals, more profane parts of religious ceremonies, bullfights, and public dances—derived from rhythms of Spanish and even Moorish origin that had entered Mexico during the colonial period. They had a particularly intense diffusion during the eighteenth and early nineteenth centuries. The common denominator of all these tunes, grouped within regional families—*huapangos, jarochos, mariachis*—was the *son*, defined by Thomas Stanford as "intermediate between *ruido* and *música*," that is, halfway between noise and music.[22] To return to the critical factor here for the diffusion of brass bands, local leaders, first from the church and estate owners, and then their conservative civic associates, found benefits from the promotion of wind music.

Besides the priests and their surrogates, President Antonio López de Santa Anna and the Conservatives during the early 1850s—not the Liberals (heirs of France's democratic revolution)—put the brass wind band firmly on the national, secular political agenda. Santa Anna had first grasped the powerful symbolic power of patriotic ritual during the early 1840s with the Te Deum held in Mexico's Cathedral for his leg amputated during the Pastry War against the French. In exile in Havana before his 1852 return, Santa Anna, while attending a concert in the park, was struck by Catalan composer Jaime Nunó's virtuosity as a bandleader. After his return he instituted a program to encourage military bands and appointed Nunó director of military music. Within a year the Catalan master had composed the Mexican national anthem and taken charge of organizing a national network of military bands.

On the eve of the 1854 Revolution of Ayutla, reports claimed that there were around 230 military bands in the regular army and the *milicia activa,* although probably only a few of them were properly equipped or instructed.[23] One army band received credit for inspiring bravado among their Liberal opponents during the siege of Puebla in February 1856. A company of Alvarez's Liberal *pintos* (troops) from Guerrero, impressed with the army band and lacking one of their own, recklessly stormed a mined house on the Calle de Cholula, "removing the band, returning equipped with drums, bassoons, serpents and cornets, although their audacity cost them their captain who remained there dead."[24]

Thus, it was the Conservatives who laid the foundation for brass-band music before the 1862 French Intervention, beginnings that were then consolidated during the French occupation of the mid-1860s. The result was Mexico's standard brass band. At first called the *música de viento*, from the 1850s, this term gave way to the more pompous *cuerpo filarmónico* or *sociedad filarmónico*, indicating perhaps the prevalence of brass over wood. The standard village *filarmónico* possessed between twenty and thirty instruments.[25] These instruments, mostly of foreign manufacture, had to be imported at considerable cost.[26] This brass band had a peculiar provenance; inspired at first by churchmen and Conservatives and reaching full development during the French occupation, in the end its benefits redounded to popular Liberal military commanders such as Porfirio Díaz and Juan Nepomuceno Méndez, who quickly appreciated the military and political benefits of equipping and patronizing military and civilian musicians. Liberal leaders, by the mid-1850s, determined to appropriate the popular appeal of brass-band music, inspired and controlled by their political opponents, the clergy, and the Conservative regular army. By the end of the Three Years' War (1858–1861), Liberal military commanders such as Méndez, the caudillo of the Puebla Sierra, had learned that music sheets and instruments were as important a part of electoral or military preparations as rifles, ammunition, food rations, and ballot cards.[27]

This relationship between political power and musical organization can be traced in the memoirs of José María Maldonado, a Liberal commander in the same sierra region during the early period of the French Intervention. When he was posted to command in the region in late 1862 he found that organized band music, presumably introduced by the church, was already well established in district capitals such as Zacapoaxtla and Tlatlauqui and their surrounding Nahua barrios. He was greeted on his arrival in Tlatlauqui in November 1862, to take up the *jefetura* (leadership), much as if he were a visiting bishop. "The town was decked with arches and curtains of flowers," he recalled in his memoirs, "the wind bands alternated in their sonatas and rockets announced the arrival of the Chief." Maldonado declared that his first task as jefe político was to "regularize the musical affairs of the district, establishing weekly serenades in the public square to stimulate schoolchildren and to provide some distraction to families, lifting them from the backwardness in which they languished."[28] His purpose, of course, was to remove education, music, and ceremony from exclusive clerical control. He took seriously the organization of bands during his two years in command of the Puebla Sierra. Upon assuming the *jefatura* of the district of Zacapoaxtla in 1863, he established a "philharmonic school" under a "young and intelligent" director, whom he had contracted for ten pesos less than the previous one. Soon he could announce that the "orchestra" of Zacapoaxtla played music as well as any band in the capital of the state.[29] Although this orchestra could occasionally be cajoled to dignify military parades, more often it refused to lead troops out on active campaign, insisting upon its essentially civilian and municipal function and demanding respect for the immunity of bandsmen from other municipal offices and compulsory (including military) service.[30]

For their part, the occupation forces during the French Intervention actively promoted wind band music. Indeed, the Austrians recommenced the process of organizing military bands that had been initiated by Santa Anna. In October 1865, Emperor Maximilian's government proposed a Proyecto de un Gimnasio Imperial de Música Militar to train four hundred Mexicans, whose task on graduation would be to reform and reorganize military bands throughout the Mexican empire.[31] First, financial constraints and second, military defeat in 1867 prevented this initiative from achieving its goals. Of greater importance to the future of Mexican band music, though, was the presence of the two full European military bands that had accompanied the expeditionary force. These bands had an indelible impact on Mexican musical taste, ceremony, and recreational practice.

The French Foreign Legion Band, directed by M. Jalabert, and the Austrian Legion Band, directed by J. Saverthal, not only possessed a far wider repertory than anything before them but also introduced the practice of secular, open concerts in public places. They contributed to the renowned daily *conciertos Franco-Mexicanos*, organized by the Mexican composer José María Chávez, which sought to blend Mexican and French musical traditions.[32] The significance of these two model bands is that they pioneered a central and conspicuous public arena, the town square, for secular music. The French and Austrian bandmasters, moreover, eagerly attempted to absorb—not replace—Mexican musical traditions. The birth of the *mariachi* in Jalisco, believed to be the progeny of a French bandmaster who decided to stay after the French-Austrian withdrawal in 1867, provides a good example of this successful synthesis of brass and strings, traditional Hispanic *sones*, and modern European influences.[33] By the end of the century the brass band playing in the bandstand in the square had become a central feature of cultural life throughout the republic, indicating a community's commitment to urbanity.

Nevertheless, the widespread diffusion of wind bands throughout provincial and rural Mexico during the later nineteenth century cannot be seen as simply or even primarily a consequence of the pursuit of European tastes, musical standards, and urbanity. This might have been true for district capitals with a significant number of non-Indians. Here, the brass band, with its European repertory, could comfort the *gente decente* that Europe was being recreated in Anahuac and at the same time offer a model of taste and urbanity to the lower orders. This happened, for example, on Sunday afternoons in the main square of Altotonga, the district capital of a largely Nahua area in the Sierra Madre of Veracruz. By 1900, Altotonga had two plazas, one for the market and the other set aside for "promenade and music." The latter "was laid out with shrubs and flowerbeds. . . . Here, weather permitting, the band played for two hours on Sunday afternoons, and such of the townspeople as wished to show off themselves and their best clothes walked round, or sat down on the stone seats at the side. Most of the people that came here belonged to the better-class families, but here were also some quite poor people who wore the rebozo [shaw], which no woman of quality would wear on such an occasion."[34]

The numerous military bands in the Nahua villages of Puebla's nearby Sierra district of Tlatlauqui suggest a more complex role for the brass band than that of simply providing a cultural veneer. Here the bands that Maldonado had organized during the French Intervention had reverted by the 1870s to the control of conservative families and the clergy, who managed the district through an alliance of village National Guard commanders. These village captains exercised absolute power over their jurisdictions and posed a significant threat to the political order in the Sierra throughout the presidency of Sebastián Lerdo de Tejada (1872–1876), when this deeply religious district was in virtual rebellion against national anticlerical legislation.

These village military bands had as much to do with political power as with purveying musical urbanity. They could be relied upon, for instance, to provide a fanfare of operatic overtures to welcome the arrival of Italian colonists to the district capital in 1882. The colonists enjoyed the music and danced to those pieces that they recognized until ten o'clock at night.[35] These overtures masked a certain ambivalence, for here were village bands summoned to the district capital by the jefe político to welcome Italian colonists soon to be settled on lands over which the same villages possessed ancient claims and had occupied violently on several occasions since the early 1850s.[36] Tlatlauqui's bands thus provided a means for strengthening local *cacicazgos* (political cliques) while serving as the medium through which the jefe político could tie these villages to a wider project of district administration—namely, foreign colonization—that not everyone in the villages welcomed.

Provocative questions emerge about Mexico's military brass bands. What happened to these bands in the early years of the Porfirian regime (1876–1911) following the demobilization of many troops of the Liberal army and the return to inactive status by the National Guard? Did the bandsmen and band music realize the democratizing and liberating potential suggested by the experience of discharging bands following the French Revolution and later after the Paris Commune? Was there any Mexican equivalent to the role played by National Guard infantry bands in maintaining discipline and morale, long after the military command had beaten its retreat during the siege of Paris and the Paris Commune?[37] With peace at the start of France's Third Republic, these bands returned to barracks in their villages where they exercised their musical skills and popular repertory during local civic and patriotic ceremonies. This combination of popular village radicalism and patriotism and the political opportunism of a new generation of "conservative-liberal" statesmen helped create the greater consensus and stability that France enjoyed during the Third Republic.[38] Did anything comparable occur in Mexico between the Wars of the Reform and the peace of the Porfiriato? After the Reform Wars, the French Intervention, and the La Noria and Tuxtepec Insurrections, did the returning veterans, especially the soldier-musicians, serve to broaden the public arena in their villages and to dignify and dramatize civic and patriotic ceremonies?

Too little is known yet to be able to explore this hypothesis, but some general tendencies can be detected from the fragmentary evidence in the state of Puebla. Here, Liberal military leaders formed or reorganized a large number of village bands during the Reform Wars and the French Intervention. After the restoration of the Republic in 1867, coinciding with the disamortization of village lands, many communities decided to establish "philharmonic corps," purchasing instruments with the income generated from land sales. For example, in 1876 the military commander in the Pueblo de los Reyes, district of Tetela, purchased instruments necessary to establish a wind band with 357 pesos from land adjudications and 200 pesos more as a grant from the council.[39] The Reform thus encouraged the formation both of military and civilian village bands. Given the intensity of violent conflict during the decade of the Restored Republic and the martial character of the two "Tuxtepecano" state administrations between 1876 and 1884, many National Guard bands remained in formation until General Juan N. Méndez, proponent of the patriotic, martial, and political use of brass bands, stepped down from power in 1884. One of the first acts of Puebla's new centrally imposed administration in 1885 was to demobilize the National Guard and suppress the state's military bands.[40] Since these bands belonged to local units of the National Guard with personnel recruited from the same communities, demobilization meant that entire bands returned to civilian life in the same village. These bands soon grew to reflect the great diversity of village life.

The role of these bands in community life can be pieced together from four sources: 1) newspapers that frequently published the programs of civic and patriotic ceremonies; 2) the printed *coronas fúnebres* compiled for local dignitaries and patriotic heroes, which described funeral rituals within which bands played a prominent part;

3) the correspondence of the jefes políticos, who had to deal with the conflicts of jurisdiction arising from the presence of privileged bands of musicians in tightly governed communities; and 4) the acts of band foundation, lodged in municipal archives.[41] Certain common features of these bands emerge. For instance, band directors recruited young males from the village.[42] At least half of Huitzilan's band of twenty players were in their early teens in 1867.[43] Some bandsmen were also in their seventies, suggesting that membership was more likely before or after parenthood and peak working age, a characteristic noted for the thirty-nine-member village band of Totontepec, Oaxaca.[44] Drilling children in techniques and disciplines of band music was, of course, an integral part of the nineteenth-century movement for mass education. Several sources confirm the responsiveness of the very young to musical instruction, although the much-trumpeted health benefits are debatable.[45] Allied to these educational benefits, and just as important to Puebla's Liberal leaders, was the value of young, patriotic musicians as a political clientele.[46]

Further incentive existed in Mexico for young men to join musical groups. Band membership brought freedom from compulsory community service, demands of the cargo system, military service, and local taxation. Thus, although it involved clear and potentially arduous obligations, it effectively placed a male beyond the host of other community chores, services, and duties. Parents were therefore prepared to invest a considerable amount in their children's musical education, calculating that substantial personal benefit would accrue in the long term. The extent of this investment is illustrated by an 1876 case in which the nineteen players of the municipal band of Zoquiapa, Puebla, claimed that during six years of apprenticeship, they had each paid the band director four reales per week, giving him a substantial weekly income of over ten pesos. In return they expected exemption from taxation.[47] The opportunity to escape the extensive, recurrent, and lifelong obligations of community membership might explain why bands proved attractive to non-Indians and to members of minority factions, who sought to place distance between themselves and the potentially autocratic Indian village governments.

Yet, bands did not necessarily ensure a haven of individual autonomy from corporate pressures and communal obligations. Two cases from Puebla's Sierra during the early 1870s proved this assumption false. In both instances the autocratic way in which bandmasters, backed by village authorities, disciplined former bandsmen who sought to elude the obligations of membership eventually forced these musicians to escape persecution by leaving the community.[48] Bands from small backwoods Indian communities, even if they were municipal seats, operated quite differently from those organized in the more mestizo district capitals. Two bands established in the district capitals of Tetela de Ocampo and Zacapoaxtla during the 1860s illustrate the divergent paths of development of even these more cosmopolitan ensembles. In Tetela de Ocampo, a staunchly Liberal and patriotic municipality, home of two "Tuxtepecano" state governors (Bonilla and Méndez), the band became closely involved with the organizing and honoring of the major ceremonies of the patriotic calendar and dignifying all aspects of public life: school prize-giving, elections, the appointment of a new jefe político, and the changeover in municipal offices. At least as late as 1888 the Tetela band remained a military one. In conservative Zacapoaxtla, in contrast, the band attempted to escape its military obligations as early as 1862. By 1867 it had effectively become a municipal orchestra available to dramatize religious ceremonies within—and, frequently, beyond—the constraints of the Reform laws.

The brass band was as firmly established in Mexico by 1900 as any nineteenth-century innovation. Only a few bands, however, had achieved a high musical standard, in spite of the generally ambitious repertory of even the remotest *cuerpo filarmónico*. At the turn of the century prominent bandmasters in Mexico, as in Europe and the United States, were as concerned with improving the quality of bands as they were with elevating their musical repertory.

Mexico's equivalent of the famous American bandmaster, John Philip Sousa (1854–1932), was the clarinetist Nabor Vázquez who, in a speech to the Mexico City Conservatory in 1899, outlined a strategy for improving the *charranga*, that is, the standard untutored village band. Maestro Vázquez divided Mexico's thousands of bands into three categories, each corresponding to a distinct zone on the rural-urban continuum. First-category bands could be found in the national and provincial capitals, organized by police forces, the army, and some municipalities. During the 1870s the military band of the Corps of Sappers was considered the nation's best. By the turn of the century police bands were winning all the prizes. Ramón Hernández, director of San Luis Potosí's bands, noted that the Mexico City, Toluca, Pachuca, and Jalisco police bands regularly won competitions during the first decade of the twentieth century, while the Banda de Gendarmería de Jalisco, directed by the Italian Augusto Azalli, captured first prize in a competition in Buffalo, New York, in 1905. The state of Oaxaca was also credited with a "magnificent band" under the direction of Germán Canseco.[49]

Among Vázquez's second category were the municipal orchestras of district capitals, of the kind in the Puebla Sierra described above and the band that dignified the plaza of Lagos de Moreno during the last years of the Porfiriato.[50] Vázquez was emphatic that the ordinary, or third-category, village band held the key to the over-all cultural elevation of the nation's masses. His statement deserves repeating:

> These groups take a very active and important part in diffusing and propagat-ing, among our *pueblo bajo* [lower class], every kind of music, even when it is beyond their economic and technical capabilities. Anywhere you care to look whenever a civic, religious or profane event occurs, bands—more or less nu-merous—are always to be found, usually poorly equipped; yet in spite of ev-erything, they exhibit the greatest enthusiasm, making the very best of their natural capabilities and aptitudes, without the least concern for the criticism of their audience. For they know that they are among their "aficionados," almost always workmen, peasants or muleteers, and because their admirers care little for the social and cultural mission which the band can provide, in their igno-rance they have no other sense than the love they feel for the art. . . . To achieve a genuine diffusion of art and culture, it is time that the Conservatory in its character as a professional school should have the means to control effectively the organization of bands of any category in the technical sense . . . and be-come the arbiter, with the absolute responsibility for channeling and orientat-ing the eminently social task with which the band is charged.[51]

BANDS IN TWENTIETH-CENTURY VILLAGES

When a brass band was established in a village, it did not necessarily incorporate or displace the existing ensembles (although this may have been the effect in the long run). Often, two musical groups co-existed with a clear separation of function between the traditional village musicians formed during the early colonial period, but draw-ing upon preconquest musical and instrumental traditions of the *chirimías*, and the modern brass band introduced during the mid-nineteenth century. In Mitla, Oaxaca, for example, the *chirimía* was present at most, if not all, of the fifty or so religious festivals of the community:

> Drummer and flautist, like other musicians, are exempt from other public ser-vice. They play outside the town hall, during the intervals of the music by the town band, at the festival of San Pablo, more particularly when the bulls come out, and during the fireworks of the "dwarfs," the "giants," and the climactic "castile." During the day of candlemaking [Candlemas] at a *mayordomía*, the *chirimía* play alone, on and off, in the yard of the Mayordomo. They also play the day before, *las vísperas*, and on the feast day—three days. On *las vísperas* I have seen the drummer playing alone on the church wall; but theoretically both drum and whistle should be played three times on the roof, and this is the rule for the Fridays of Lent. On Holy Thursday, for the Last Supper, the bugle,

on this occasion called *trompeta*, is played on the roof of the church. In the procession of the Mayordomo to the church, the *chirimiteros* precede the band, walking each on the side of the road, but they do not play. They walk in the place of honor, you might think, but most listlessly, and are such shabby figures that they appear wholly detached from the trim instruments who follow. It is one of the town's many pictures of old and new in juxtaposition.

For many years the *chirimía* survived the creation of the brass band, but in the 1930s it was approaching extinction. Enrique, Mitla's last *chirimitero*, was living in great poverty; he was unmarried without heirs.[52] The only other *chirimitero* in town had already joined one of the brass bands.

In Yalalag, another Zapotec, but highland, community, the place of the *chirimía* in village ceremonies remained prominent into the 1970s. Here the drum-and-pipe ensemble possessed a near monopoly upon sacred music. The brass band played in most religious processions and festivals but often in a secondary capacity, the *chirimía* always leading.[53] The close integration of the "regular" brass band and *Teponaxtle-chirimía* ensembles is also evident in Tlaxcala.[54] Again, the difference in their deployment was that the drum-and-pipe bands took precedence within the church precinct and led religious processions, while the brass band had acquired a more important secular role. The trend throughout Central Mexico has been, nevertheless, for the drum-and-flute ensembles to diminish in importance or even disappear altogether. But the death of the *chirimía* did not necessarily spell the end of indigenous music, since the brass band often absorbed much of the traditional repertory. Such is still the case in Huejuetla (Hidalgo), where "Indian villages have brass bands that play a unique Nahua version of traditional as well as more westernized tunes."[55]

In highland Chiapas no such marginalization of the traditional ensemble occurred as the brass band remained clearly identified as a ladino institution, outside the Indian community, although welcomed to accompany religious festivals. In the Tzotzil community of Chamula during the early 1970s, "a hired ladino band," playing in the kiosk close to the church, had become a necessary accompaniment to the principal village festivals, but the Chamulans dismissed brass-band music as mere " 'musika' . . . lying in another world as far as their taxonomy is concerned. . . . Although it is proper background noise for fiestas, it does not approach the domain of 'song.' " Far more important to the Chamulas were the songs of two small ensembles: the first composed of an accordion, harp, and guitar that played during the rituals of birth, marriage, and death, and the second made up of a drum and flute, which was reserved for the cult of the saints. The musicians with the greatest prestige were those who possessed the simplest instruments. Whereas the accordion, harp, and guitar band was recruited on an ad hoc basis to assist a *cargo* (office) holder for the duration of his term, the flautist and drummer had life positions that were passed on from father to son, and they were exempted from all other community obligations.[56]

Another example of what can be labeled "ceremonial bilingualism" is found in Chamula's neighboring Tzotzil community of Zinacantan.[57] For festivals here the hired brass band came from a nearby ladino town. This band also played from a kiosk for dancing in the evening. In contrast to Chamula the band entered more fully into village ritual by accompanying groups of "volunteers" (young men who had helped with the funding and organization of the festival and who often had hired the band) marching "from their homes to the church to present special offerings of candles to the saints." Nevertheless, brass-band music was as unimportant to Zinacantecos as to Chamulans. The flute-and-drum groups and the string (violin, harp, and guitar) combinations were far more prominent in village rituals, and these musicians always led processions.[58]

In spite of differences in status between musicians belonging to these two kinds of combinations (drum-and-pipe or string), musicians in both Tzotzil communities enjoyed the exclusive privilege of exemption from any other officeholding.[59] This privilege derived only partly from the constant demand for the musicians' services. Quite as important, the music they played was both sacred and exclusive to the village, embodying a particular version of the village's beliefs and history. Most of the musicians had been taught by their fathers, whose status and art they had inherited. Many of their tunes were derived from Hispanic forms introduced by the Dominican missionaries during the sixteenth century, but the content of the songs was pre-Columbian.[60] A brass band in highland Chiapas, in contrast, was made up of ladino musicians from outside the village whose repertory was more cosmopolitan and largely, although not exclusively, secular.

Elsewhere in southern Mexico, brass bands succeeded in penetrating much more deeply into the ceremonial lives of communities than in highland Chiapas. Especially in Oaxaca, where the strength of communal traditions seems to have facilitated a particularly extensive diffusion, brass bands succeeded in appropriating most of the musical and ceremonial traditions, the special privileges and symbolic importance, hitherto the preserve of the *chirimías*. How this process of musical syncretism occurred can be analyzed through the following four aspects: 1) foundations; 2) masters, musicians,

music, and mysteries; 3) ritual and ceremonial; and 4) flattery, factionalism, and conciliation.

Foundations: Bands as a Modernizing Institution

The highland Zapotec village of Talea de Castro had only one band,
established during the nineteenth century, until 1930 when a "native
Talean priest, seeking to further 'civilize' his hometown, organized a
second group of musicians, usually referred to as 'the orchestra.' "[61]
The foundation of the second band reflected the growth of village
factionalism and social differentiation, accompanying the development of coffee production. The close association between band formation, modernity, and an emerging political leadership appeared as
well in the Yucatecan Maya village of Chan Kom, where leaders, as
part of their effort "to create a pueblo," expressed the goal of bringing music to the community. Music instruction began in the village
in 1937. Three years later a teacher moved from Mérida to Chan Kom
to instruct boys in instrumental music. Further encouragement came
from the 1944 visit of a cultural mission, which included the teaching of "musical instruments and organized and carried out a cultural
program in which the young recited verses, enacted little dramas and
represented in feather headdresses their own neglected ancestors."
Four years later the village possessed two bands of brass, clarinets,
and drums. Robert Redfield rated "at least one of these bands as truly
professional, for it was employed by neighboring villages to play at
fiestas."[62] He concluded that the bands demonstrated the village's
commitment to modernity as tangible—and more audible and conspicuous—as the road or the school.
     Whatever the initial intentions, in many villages the formation of
brass bands meant little more in terms of modernization than the
arrival of bulky, initially shiny, and technically modern instruments.
The number of bands in a community (for example, San Felipe
Otlaltepec had five) seems to have had little to do with the degree of
modernity or social differentiation along class lines. Nor in San Felipe
was the proliferation of bands related to political factionalism, beyond the drama they added to ancient interbarrio rivalries. On the
other hand, in villages such as Mitla, where two bands existed, the
older one often enjoyed closer relations with the religious authority
and cargo system, while the newer band was associated with civil
authorities and secular ceremonial duties. In these circumstances
the older band—the custodian of tradition and of local, or, in the case
of Mitla, regional identity—contrasted with the more recently
formed band, which specialized in dignifying and dramatizing more

"nation-oriented," secular, and modernizing activities, such as gubernatorial visits and competitive sporting events.

Masters, Musicians, Music, and Mysteries: A Case Study

During the period 1919–1933, Mitla had two bands: one, with only twelve musicians and founded during the nineteenth century, was called the "Juarezcitos" after its master, *maestro cantor* Manuel Juárez. The Juarezcitos were more in demand for accompanying public and private religious ceremonies. The other, founded early in this century and considerably larger, with a complement of thirty musicians, was effectively the village orchestra. Directed by another *maestro cantor*, José Amador, it figured more prominently in secular ceremonials and festivities and sporting events. In spite of these different realms the two bands experienced considerable ceremonial overlapping and rivalry as well as brinkmanship between their two bandmasters, Mitla's most prominent *maestros cantores*.[63]

Manuel Juárez unquestionably saw himself as the doyen of Mitla's musical and ceremonial life through his position as master of the Juarezcitos and principal chanter of the parish. He lived in one of the few tiled, substantial houses in the center of the village. His house, along with a neighbor's (a nephew and fellow musician), possessed just beneath its eaves a unique blue-and-white frieze comprising a series of panels depicting flowers, insects, birds, animals, plants, human faces, parts of human torsos, and the devil—the equivalent, it would seem, of the European gargoyle. Many houses in the center of town evidently had once been decorated in this way. The bandmaster lamented the decline of the custom because people no longer "have the patience," suggesting that he saw himself as the guardian of village tradition. He was the most important of the community's three *maestros cantores*.

Juárez's nephew had already achieved the status of *maestro cantor*, often substituting when his uncle was away in other Zapotec towns teaching music. Juárez was also drilling his young son Moisés to chant and direct music and had recently bought him a shiny new saxophone costing 250 pesos. In a revealing incident the father asked his son to play this new instrument at a time when he should have been in school; he insisted that the boy did not have to go school when practicing his music. The following exchange made clear the exemptions for musicians.

"He won't have to be a *topil* [village messenger and odd-job man, the basic cargo through which all males except bandsmen had to pass]

. . . but will he have to be a *topilillo de iglesia* [same position, but for the church]?" anthropologist Elsie Clews Parsons inquired. "No, nothing," replied Juárez. "He won't have any other services at all. *No te engaño, Dios 'sta mirando* [I am not deceiving thee, as God is my witness]."[64] Juárez deliberately cultivated the young musician's sense of divinely ordained exemption from any subjection to the *faenas* [tasks] of church, school, or community. Indeed, Juárez's authority as bandmaster, in contrast to that of his rival Amador, owed much to his successful maintenance of the tradition of respect for the *maestro cantor*, who, through his privileged and, in Juárez's case, secretive command over music and song, served as the exclusive medium between the divine source of music and chant and the community.

This strong sense of divine ordination helps explain other aspects of Juárez's character, particularly *envidia* (envy). Much like those of the nineteenth-century masters of British military bands, the skills and musical repertory of the *maestro cantor*, in the form of tunes and songs passed from father to son, were jealously guarded, with only a few transposed to musical sheets.[65] Despite continual requests, Juárez refused to lend Parsons his music for the Dance of the Conquest, claiming that it was needed for teaching at Yalalag and further afield. *Envidia* is further demonstrated by his petulant response to the rise of his nephew as a reputable *maestro cantor*. During one of Juárez's absences his nephew had answered the town of Abicusas's request for a music teacher. On his return the Juarezcitos divided into two factions, and soon thereafter the bandmaster was reported absent from an important festival, an event without precedent.

Evidently, directing the Mitla band while the master was away was acceptable. Extravillage teaching contracts, though, Juárez regarded as his exclusively. They were potentially quite lucrative, and accepting invitations to teach other bands extended honor to the maestro. Juárez considered his position as *maestro cantor* of the Juarezcitos to be the principal village office after the parish priest. To many Zapotec villages, Juárez, with his musical skills and collection of chants and music sheets, personified Mitla and suggested a sense of regional cultural identity.

Of course, the personal, nonprofessional motive cannot be discounted for Juárez's *envidia* in the defense of his status as *maestro cantor*. His daughter, Jovita, had just married a man in the band of Lachesila, where he had been teaching. Juárez had also recently acquired *compadres* in Huilá from the family of the bugler and *maestro cantor* (Juárez's wife, Felicitas, had just become the godmother to the bugler's daughter). The fount of his authority clearly resided in his jealous possession of the village's musical mysteries, and his wealth came as a consequence. His privileged position as senior *maestro cantor* can be more fully understood when compared with that of his rival, José Amador.

Amador, master of the considerably larger band, was also a *maestro cantor* and the son of a musician, and was training his own son to succeed him. He had studied beyond Mitla in Tlacolula and probably specialized in a more modern repertory for his band, which was formed around 1905 and aspired to the status of village orchestra. He had been a highly effective *presidente municipal* during the 1920s and still exercised considerable political influence in the village. Following orders in 1932 from the state government enforcing the anticlerical laws against religious processions, for example, he chose to disregard the ban upon musical accompaniment to the changeover in *mayordomías*, one of Mitla's principal ceremonies. He evidently was encouraged as a scofflaw by the fact that the outgoing *mayordomo* was a musician in his band as well as his cousin. In 1932 he was reported to be a constant evening visitor to La Sorpresa, Mitla's principal store, where he was teaching the owner, Don Rafael, one of the few non-Indian patricians and the senior cacique, to play the big drum for the orchestra. Don Rafael perhaps had less musical than political interest in learning the drum. Once a *músico*, Rafael would be exempt from all communal services, leaving him free to run for the municipal presidency. Amador, as master of thirty musicians, could also extend Rafael's political clientele.

Amador's influence can be further illustrated by an incident during the *fiesta patronal*. While playing at the circus, the band was insulted by a young drunk. Amador had him arrested and jailed for the night.[66] This close overlap between the bandmaster's coercive authority and the municipal-level judiciary recalls a similar incident in Zapotitlan in Puebla's Sierra during the 1870s when a man was imprisoned for refusing to contribute toward maintaining the village band. He based his refusal on his objection to the poor quality of its director. As part of his punishment he had to endure a nocturnal concert directed by the injured bandmaster.[67] While Juárez's authority was traditional—based on respect for his mastery of a private musical repertory largely within traditional Catholic ceremonies— Amador's authority owed more to his involvement with secular politics and the advantage his larger band gave him in political patronage.

The privileges of these *maestros cantores* extended to the musicians making up the two bands, who were exempt from compulsory service and taxation. In return, the bands were obliged to play at communal fiestas, "including the prolonged *mayordomías*," without payment "except in food and *tepache* [popular fruit and pulque drink] and cigarettes." At weddings, funerals, and other family occasions, musicians were, of course, paid as well as fed—often more ceremonially and sumptuously than the guests. Who were these bandsmen? They did not form, as in Naranja de Tapia, a "caste apart," an outfaction unable even to perform in their own village festivals, since both bands participated fully in Mitla's ceremonial life. Were they merely bands of youths, nurtured from infancy by the *maestros cantores*, who, once they had blown their way into adulthood, drifted into private life or other cargos? This cannot be answered. But because they trained together from the age of seven, when they cut their second, trumpet-blowing teeth, they did share an esprit de corps.[68]

The sense of a closed, quasi Masonic, masculine, tobacco-saturated world emerges in a description of band practice in the village of Santo Domingo Alvarrado:

> [The band] met to practice in the large chamber where my host kept his house altar, stored corn and entertained overnight guests. . . . The instruments, twenty or more, were kept regularly in this room, hanging on the walls. The drum was beaten thrice, at intervals of a few minutes, to summon the players. The men smoked and talked beforehand and in the intervals of practice which began about nine in the evening and lasted until two in the morning, Friday night, and until midnight Saturday night. Tired guests had to make the best of it during those excruciating hours. The first night no player paid any attention to the others; the second night there was a limited amount of concerted playing. Sunday morning, after a double summons, the band played in the church, on their knees. Two women formed the congregation. Later, the musicians chatted outside and smoked the cigarettes that they were liberally supplied.[69]

Although we know little about who became bandsmen in Mitla and to what extent they constituted a distinct group, more information exists for other villages. In the Popoloco village of San Felipe Otlaltepec, the bands perhaps offered a means of subsistence in an environment of extreme scarcity. In the late 1960s, from a total population of 1,604, some 120 musicians, grouped in five large bands, made music the most important occupation after agriculture and palm weaving. These musicians included maestros, known locally as *los señores filarmónicos* (respecting the nineteenth-century usage in the Puebla region), who did not enjoy any special privileges in the conduct of religious ceremonies. One reputable master did travel far afield training other bands. San Felipe enjoyed a reputation for producing good musicians as far distant as Tlaxcala and northern Oaxaca. As a result, all five bands had no difficulty contracting musical commitments months in advance. Musicians were paid only a little more than agricultural laborers for a *tocata*. Yet, in spite of the lengthy and time-consuming training, in comparison to other occupations music was a desirable employment among *felipeños* (people of San Felipe), in part because a musician was likely to have more experience of the world beyond the village. Moreover, whereas the *felipeño* vendor of palm mats in Puebla faced the hazards and injustices of the market-place by himself, the musician traveled in a group and was better able to manage uncertainties beyond the village.

Indeed, musicians spent much of the year traveling from one vil-lage festival to another. During the festival of the Virgin of Guadalupe in 1968, all five community bands were on the road. The band of the barrio of Ocotlán at one time played at festivals in three different villages during a tour of only four days. The poverty of San Felipe encouraged the musicians to be itinerant, particularly since playing at local festivals went unpaid, while playing at neighboring village fiestas resulted in both payment and food and lodging (if only under *portales*, or town arches). But prolonged absence of barrio bands caused resentment in the village, particularly if the bandsmen were absent from local festivals and *mayordomías*. The prestige of musi-cians within the barrio suffered from too frequent absences.[70]

Ritual and Ceremonial

From the moment that the introduction of the valve permitted a quan-tum leap in the versatility of wind instruments, the brass band be-came an attractive and easily accessible means for increasing the dramatic effect of religious processions, military parades and ma-neuvers, and secular ceremonies. In Mitla at least one band accom-panied almost every ceremony, from the modest private wedding to campaign visits of candidates for the state governorship. The village bands exerted a major role in dramatizing, dignifying, and sometimes directing ceremonial life. These ceremonies separated into three cat-egories: 1) private life-cycle ceremonies (for instance, baptisms, marriages, and deaths); 2) public religious festivals and the *mayordomías* of the saints; and 3) secular ceremonies. Of course, a considerable overlap existed between the second and third catego-ries, despite the formal separation of church and state since the pro-mulgation of the Constitution of 1857.

In Mitla, when the anticlerical laws limiting external manifesta-tions of the cult were being applied more strictly, municipal authori-ties chose to enforce them only superficially. They were obliged, nevertheless, to keep a lower profile in major ceremonies, and this required "the elimination of the band in certain affairs of the church." For example, when the ayuntamiento refused in 1932 to forego the

annual procession to the town's principal spring, ritually renewing
the water supply to a fountain facing the priest's house, this ancient
procession of pre-Columbian origin went unaccompanied by musicians for the first time in living memory.[71]

Private Life-Cycle Ceremonies

With the creation of a civil registry and the high fees for church ceremonies, bands were in less demand for the accompaniment of life-
cycle ceremonies. Nevertheless, seventy years after the establishment
of a civil registry in Mitla, most people still chose a church baptism
and, if they could afford it, preferred to be married and to bury their
dead through the church. Musical accompaniment of these ceremonies added greatly to the cost. A reforming priest during the 1930s
sought to increase congregations and the use of church sacraments in
Mitla by reducing parish fees. He lessened the cost of weddings from
twelve to four pesos, prompting a small marriage boom, much to the
glee of bandmasters Manuel Juárez and José Amador. The priest
wanted to reduce the cost of these church sacraments even further by
dispensing with the bands, but he faced a powerful musical mafia in
the personnel of the two bands, which he chose not to confront.

Church weddings and funerals were elaborate ceremonies lasting
several days and involving one or the other of the bands during the
various services, processions, and festivities. The elaborate marriage
ritual that might last six days was the particular penchant of Maestro
Manuel, who composed special chants with musical accompaniments.
Perhaps as a result, the band was fêted almost more than the bride
and groom. It "played one piece . . . when the bride . . . give[s] the
groom the first bite from her bread. . . . After this . . . the band proceeds to the house of the groom to eat. Thence the band will go to the
house of the bride to bring her family . . . to the groom's house to eat.
Again the band will eat." This continued until finally, at three in the
morning toward the end of the celebrations, "the music fails . . . for
the musicians doze."[72]

The deep somber tones of the brass band provided a particularly
appropriate accompaniment for a funeral. Manuel Juárez and the
Juarezcitos exercised a near monopoly on Mitla's church funerals,
even those of the poor who could not have met the eight-peso fee.[73]
Here, as in the wedding, Manuel assumed a director's role, composing special chants and drawing on his private fund of music. He
directed the *velada funebre* (wake) throughout the night, then blessed
and sprinkled the body with water from a green-glazed pitcher

before leading the procession, with the coffin, to the church. Although the priest was present, Manuel and his band conducted most of the service and afterward led the procession through the center of town to the cemetery.

Public Religious Festivals and the Mayordomías of the Saints

The following festivals made up Mitla's calendar. A cross indicates the involvement of a *chirimía*; an asterisk, the involvement of one band; and two asterisks, the involvement of two bands.[74]

Mitla's Calendar

Festival	Date	Celebrations	Musical Partici-pants
New Year	Jan. 1	Mass; *cambio* of municipal officials	+ *
Three Kings' Day	Jan. 6	In decline and uncelebrated	
Mayordomía of San Esquipula	Jan. 15		+ *
Fiesta of San Pablo	Jan. 25	Major festival, pilgrimage, and bullfight	+ **
Candlemas	Feb. 2	Mass	
Carnival and Ash Wednesday	not celebrated		
Mayordomía of San José	Mar. 19		+ *
Mayordomía of El Señor de las Peñas	Mar. 20		+ *
Mayordomía of El Señor de las Misericordias	3d Sunday in Lent	Pilgrimage	+ *
Mayordomía of Jesús Nazareño	5th Sunday in Lent		+ *
Mayordomía of the Virgen de Dolores	6th Friday in Lent		+ *
Palm Sunday			+ **
Holy Week			+ **
Mayordomía of the Holy Cross	May 3		+ *
Mayordomía of San Isidro	May 15		+ *
Mayordomía of the Corazón de María	May 30		+ *
Mayordomía of San Juan Bautista	June 24		+ *

Mayordomía of San Pedro	June 28	+ *
Mayordomía of San Pablo	June 29	+ *
Mayordomía of the Virgen del Carmen	July 16	+ *
Fiesta Patriótica	Sept. 15–16	+ **
Mayordomía of the Virgen del Rosario		+ *
All Saints and All Souls	Oct. 31-Nov. 2	
Mayordomía of San Francisco	Dec. 4	+ *
Mayordomía of the Virgen de Juquila	Dec. 8	+ *
Mayordomía of the Virgen de la Soledad	Dec. 18	+ *
Las Posadas		*
Mayordomía de la Navidad	Dec. 25	+ *

Purely in terms of days worked, Mitla's musicians during the early 1930s were most in demand for dignifying the festivals of the saints' *mayordomías* and the annual changeover between *mayordomos*. There were twenty-one *mayordomía* ceremonies over the year, each lasting at least three days. While the *chirimía* usually accompanied the entire three-day ceremony, the presence of the band (the Juarezcitos were preferred) coincided with the high point of the festival. The *mayordomía* of San Esquipula, which coincided with Candlemas, shows the role of the band in accompanying the feast, dramatizing the procession, bearing flowery candles, and leading the procession from the mayordomo's house to the church, where they were to be blessed.

At other major religious festivals—the fiesta de San Pablo, Palm Sunday, the latter part of Holy Week, for example—both bands and *chirimías* were kept busy. Occasionally, on Palm Sunday, for instance, the two bands even played together, Juárez's band in the gallery and Amador's in the nave of the church. The entire Palm Sunday pageant had to be executed within the atrium and the church building, respecting the Reform laws that forbade processions beyond the church confines when they involved the priest in a direct capacity. These restrictions did not apply to processions accompanying the *mayordomías* because in these the priest rarely took part directly. They applied to the Good Friday celebrations in which the Juarezcitos led the procession with the image of the Lord, to meet another one led by Amador's band, containing an image of the Virgin, followed by "fifty or more of the townswomen, . . . the processions having to dodge each other in the small churchyard."[75]

Secular Ceremonies

Bands participated prominently in secular events related to the patriotic and sporting calendar and the cycles of municipal and state politics. The people of Mitla celebrated only one *fiesta patriótica*—Independence Day—when both bands played together. The celebration went as follows: "On the first day there is *el grito*, cheering, *vivas* for all patriots, and school exercises; the bands play. The following days there are ring 'races' and the *cucaña*; and at night the cinema."[76]

Far greater political significance surrounded the annual ceremony of the *cambia de varas*, the handing over of the principal civic offices and their staffs of authority of village government. Here the outgoing president paid for a mass and a band—in Mitla, the large Amador ensemble—entertaining his colleagues and the musicians at breakfast and dinner. Several processions were involved in these proceedings, always led by the band. Other rituals involving the band included the mass for the new town government; an elaborate ceremony for the handing over of accounts; the changeover between outgoing and incoming (and newly constituted) church and school committees; and major municipal fiestas to honor political visitors, including the governor. The band also led processions to the basketball court and then played throughout the contest against a team from a neighboring town. The relationship between bands and sporting events was a new area of musical endeavor and one that promised to increase in importance.

Factionalism, Flattery, and Conciliation

The association between band formation and the growth of village factionalism has been observed in villages in eastern Spain. Joaquín Barceló Verdú found that during the nineteenth century frequently two bands, even in the smallest villages, represented competing factions.[77] Studies of Mexico have also concluded that "music plays a special role in developing alliances" within villages, comparable to family and barrio organizations, work groups, and government and church organizations.[78] This rivalry would affect, on occasions, the aesthetic impact of bands, which would attempt to outplay each other in public festivals.[79] Cacophony was often the result, such as during an Ash Wednesday fiesta in 1931 in Zachila, when two brass bands accompanied the Dance of the Christians, playing two entirely different scores.[80] Such rivalry did not necessarily indicate anything more than differences in musical specialization, taste, and patronage. In the case of the five bands of San Felipe Otlaltepec, it reflected inter-barrio brinkmanship.

Elsewhere, anthropologists have suggested that class, ethnicity, and politics were important in determining band membership. In Talea de Castro, Oaxaca, the two bands closely reflected the social differentiation resulting from the development of commercial coffee production. By the 1950s, Talea's two bands, each containing around thirty members, had come to represent distinct social and cultural constituencies. The "band" comprised conservative farmers of the town, while the "orchestra" drew its members from the progressive farmers, businessmen, and coffee merchants. Many townspeople believed two bands were a luxury the town could not afford. Indeed, in 1957, during a period of uncertainty associated with the arrival of the first road connecting with the outside world, the two bands played together at a festival, and that evening there was talk of amalgamating them into a single orchestra. In the cold light of the following day, Taleans no longer considered consolidation a possibility, above all for political reasons but also because the band and orchestra represented two types of musical expression.[81]

Whereas factionalism in Zapotec communities manifested itself in the formation of rival wind bands, in Tarascan communities in Michoacán the single brass band served to represent members of the outfaction in villages dominated by single cacique clans. This appears as an intermediate practice, between the Tzotzil habit of keeping the ladino band out of the village altogether in the interests of maintaining town consensus and the proliferation of bands in Zapotec villages, indicating their capacity to tolerate and contain intra-community factionalism. "Music correlates and clearly symbolizes the politics of Naranja de Tapia," wrote Paul Friedrich. By this he means that those who fail in cacique politics go into music. Thus, from the 1930s, membership in Naranja's band (reputedly the best in Michoacán) represented the politically neutral or those opposed to the ruling *agrarista* faction. A precedent occurred in 1886 when music and making a living intersected. The disamortization of Naranja's common lands coincided with the organization of the village band. Land sales provided money for the cost of the instruments at the same time that the deterioration of the village's subsistence base made music a necessary occupation. During the 1930s musical specialization compensated for restricted access to the means of subsistence, in this instance because the ruling factions had preferential access to ejidal lands. Political ostracism might also account for what has been observed as the general characteristic of Tarascan village bands— that they rarely, if ever, perform in community fiestas in their own *municipios*.[82]

The Tarascan peripatetic band brings together three final and related themes: the band as a means of impressing higher authorities through a political serenade; the band as a symbol of village identity; and the band as a peacemaker. Its use for impressing outsiders—in particular, higher authorities—was noted by Frederick Starr at the turn of the century. He described the Pahuatlán, Hidalgo, band that traversed the Sierra to serenade the jefe político for an entire evening. The beautiful music apparently persuaded the jefe, a powerful Hidalgo politician close to the governor, to respect Pahuatlán's customary autonomy (the village had formerly been a part of Puebla) and to oust the jefe político of Tenango de Doria (a troublesome neighboring village).[83] The band of the Totontepec Mixes in 1974 engaged in a similar serenade, successfully persuading President Luis Echeverría to contribute to the completion of a road to the village.[84]

The exchange of village bands also can serve to heal political wounds after a period of intercommunity conflict. The return of bands traveling between the Yalalag in the Sierra Zapoteca and a formerly hostile neighbor signaled that normal relations had resumed.[85] Musical groups accomplished a similar role following conflict between the Zapotec communities of Zautla and Mazaltepec, although the exchange visits may have had less to do with friendship and goodwill than the need for bands to generate income by "playing away."[86] This does not detract from the evident symbolic importance of the bands and the healing power of music.

CONCLUSION

For well over a century the brass band and the Mexican peasant community have enjoyed a close affinity. Smaller dance and jazz bands have emerged over the past few decades to enrich village music, coinciding with the decline of the traditional *chirimías* and smaller guitar and violin ensembles inherited from colonial, even precolonial days. But the brass band, as the custodian of the village's ceremonial calendar and the embodiment of its identity, still survives, particularly in Oaxaca, where brass-band competitions resemble their counterparts in Britain's colliery districts in their vitality.[87] The organization of the peasant community, with its complex system of balanced rights and obligations and command over local resources, proved particularly well-suited to the economic, educational, and recreational demands of organized band music. The brass band did not fundamentally alter the traditional importance bestowed upon musicians and music in village ceremonial and political life. Nor did the new instruments and repertory, which were initially European, necessarily represent any significant acceleration in the pace of acculturation. European "marches, overtures, polkas and fantasies" imported during the nineteenth century have comfortably shared the repertory of these bands with traditional Mexican (including indigenous) songs, dances, and rhythms for well over a century.

The achievement of the brass band was to reaffirm and technically enhance the central but long-neglected place of music and musicians in village life during a century of unprecedented village change in internal structure and relationships with the outside world. The greater size of the brass band and its increased musical versatility and volubility, compared with the traditional *chirimía*, helped in the task of reorganizing villages during the periods of disruption extending from the Reform Wars through the disamortization of village lands, the revolution, the agrarian reform, and the accelerated social differentiation that villages have undergone since the 1940s. Sketchy evidence suggests that in most cases village bands only superficially acted as "agents of modernization"—that band music was a nominal "cultural veneer" or purveyor of "urbanity" and that bands were rarely simple agencies of ruling factions. Above all, brass bands have continued to satisfy the changing needs of villagers' associational and recreational lives. They have served as a locally controlled medium for absorbing external cultural and political influences. In Oaxaca by the 1950s, even if a village were unable to achieve a reputable orchestra of its own, an aspiring village politician could still consider as the summit of his achievement as a confraternity *mayordomo* the bringing of the renowned Teotítlan band to play for the *fiesta patronal*.[88]

NOTES

1. Brantz Mayer, *Mexico as It Was and as It Is* (Philadelphia, 1847), 197, describing the Hacienda de San Nicolas, Cuautla, in 1841.

2. Nabor Vásquez, "Breve historia de las bandas de música en México," in *Orientación musical* (México, 1943), 3:14.

3. Ibid., vols. 3, 4. For full reference to this and other sparse sources on the history of Mexican band music, see Sylvana Young Osorio, *Guía Bibliográfica*, vol. 2, *La música de México*, ed. Julio Estrada (México, 1984).

4. Opening bridge: Guy P. C. Thomson, "Bulwarks of Patriotic Liberalism: The National Guard, Philharmonic Corps and Patriotic Juntas in Mexico, 1847–88," *JLAS* (1990): 51–61; welcoming Italian colonists: *PO* (Puebla) 17 (1882): 22; band of "captive musicians" of Chan Santa Cruz: Luis González y González, "El Subsuelo Indígena," in *Historia moderna de México República Restaurada: Vida social*, ed. Daniel Cosío Villegas (México, 1956), 304–5; Misantla's firing-squad serenade in 1865: "La matanza se desarrolló en medio de repiques y después de la

escena fueron tendidos los cadáveres en la calle mientras la música de viento tocaba dianas frente a los restos," in Elio Masferrer Kan, "Movimientos sociales en el Totonacapan (siglo XIX)," *America Indígena* 47 (1987): 41–44; bands in Guadalajara religious processions: Rubén Villaseñor Bordes, "Guadalajara reza y se divierte," *HM* 11 (1961): 81–103; bands prompting Fourierist projects: Nicolás Pizarro, *El Monedero* (México, 1882), 143.

5. Gerónimo Baqueiro Foster, "Embriones de la música militar en el México pre-hispánico," manuscript, Baqueiro Foster Papers, Instituto Nacional de Bellas Artes (hereafter INBA), Expediente 880, 31–37.

6. Bernardo García Martínez, *Los Pueblos de la Sierra: El poder y el espacio entre los indios del norte de Puebla hasta 1700* (México, 1987), 93–94.

7. José Arturo Chamorro, *La música popular en Tlaxcala* (Puebla, 1985), 18–25.

8. Arturo Warman notes, "The enthusiasm of the Indian population for such groups was so great that the authorities had to issue instructions limiting their number around the mid-sixteenth century," *Banda de Tlayacapan*, Instituto Nacional de Antropologia e Historia (hereafter INAH) Serie de Discos no. 8, México, 1977.

9. Thomson, *Puebla de Los Angeles*, 89.

10. Most musical histories explain the introduction of the *música de viento* in Mexico as a consequence of the French Intervention, 1862–1867, when French and Austrian bandmasters dazzled the Mexican public, who sent off immediately to Paris for modern instruments, setting in motion a musical revolution. This version obviously overlooks continuities with past musical traditions and exaggerates the suddenness of the brass band's entry into Mexico. See Guillermo Orta Velázquez, *Breve historia de la música en México* (México, 1970), 336.

11. Villaseñor Bordes, "Guadalajara reza," 83.

12. Percy Scholes, *The Oxford Companion to Music* (London, 1975), 126.

13. Harvey Grace, ed., *The New Musical Educator* (London, n.d.), 4:118–19.

14. Charles Hamm, *Music in the New World* (New York, 1983), 282–83.

15. Grace, *New Musical Educator*, 119.

16. Scholes, *Oxford Companion*, 639; Henry George Farmer, *The Rise and Development of Military Music* (London, 1912) and *Memoirs of the Royal Artillery Band* (London, 1904); J. A. Kappy, *Military Music: A History of Wind-Instrumental Bands* (London, 1894); W. J. Galloway, *Musical England* (London, 1910); Edmond Neukomm, *Histoire de la musique militaire* (Paris, 1889); and Jean Georges Kastner, *Manuel général de musique militaire* (Paris, 1848) and *Les chants de l'armeé française* (Paris, 1859).

17. By the beginning of the twentieth century, it was claimed that in Lancashire and Yorkshire alone between four thousand and five thousand bands existed, with forty thousand in the whole country. Scholes, *Oxford Companion,* 127.

18. Hamm, *Music in the New World*, 279–306.

19. Eugenio Pereira Salas, "La Academia Musico-Militar de 1817," in *Boletín de la Academia Chilena de la Historia* 18 (1951): 13–20.

20. *Mexico as It Was and as It Is*, 197.

21. Beutler, *Danzas de Moros y Cristianos* (México, 1965), 146, 162, 164–65. The continuity of this midnineteenth-century cosmopolitan repertory of marches, overtures, polkas, and *fantasías* a century after the original formation of village

bands appears in the appendix of Klaus Jäcklein, *Un Pueblo Popoloco: San Felipe Otlaltepec* (México, 1974), 301–2.

22. Warman, *Banda de Tlayacapan*; and E. Thomas Stanford, "The Mexican *Son*," in *Yearbook of the International Folk Music Council* (1972), 66–86.

23. Baqueiro Foster, "Embriones de la música militar," 104–6.

24. *Memorias del Coronel Manuel Balbontín* (México, 1958), 156–57.

25. Beutler, 145–46. A band in the Nahua community of Huitzilan (Sierra de Puebla) in 1867 contained, initially, twenty members and presumably the same number of instruments. See Archivo Municipal de Tetela de Ocampo (Puebla) (hereafter AMTdeO), Gobierno Box 10, 1867–1868, Expediente 2, April 15, 1867. A set of instruments ordered from Great Britain by Bernardo O'Higgins for Chile's Academia Musico Militar during the early 1820s numbered twenty-one (two horns, two kettledrums, one trombone, one oboe, one trumpet, one serpent, one bassoon, one chinesco, one triangle, eight clarinets, one bass drum, one drum) (Pereira Salas, "La Academia Musico-Militar," 20). The *Oxford Companion* confirms that "the normal British band is that of twenty-four players (plus percussion)"—seven cornets, three flügelhorns, five saxophones, three trombones, and six tubas, in addition to drums and cymbal—on p. 127.

26. Bronislaw Malinowski and Julio de la Fuente, *Malinowski in Mexico: The Economics of a Mexican Market System* (London, 1982), 133. The British musical instrument manufacturers, Boosey and Sons, suppliers to the Empire, may also have provided the Latin American market during the nineteenth century, although French suppliers are mentioned in some of the Mexican correspondence.

27. During the 1861 election for the Puebla state governorship, General Méndez "succeeded in leading out several hundred men, offering their leaders gifts of music for their villages and other things which those Indians like." With these men behind him, the Tetela caudillo marched to the state capital, supplying the military presence necessary for ensuring the successful candidature of Francisco Ibarra y Ramos for governor. See Ramón Sánchez Flores, *Zacapoaxtla Relación Histórica* (Puebla, 1984), 153–54.

28. Ibid.

29. Archivo Municipal del Zacapoaxtla, "Borrador de la correspondencia del jefe político, 1863."

30. AMTdeO, Box of unofficial correspondence, 1866–1867, Letter of January 12, 1867, Pascual Bonilla, Zacapoaxtla, to Juan Francisco Lucas, Tetela.

31. It is evident from the language of this project that the French and Austrian expeditionary forces had brought the classic military music manual by Kastner, *Manuel général de musique militaire*, Archivo de la Defensa Nacional, Histórico 10059 fs. 162–6.

32. Orta Velázquez, *Breve historia*, 334–37.

33. Stanford, "The Mexican *Son*," 80–81.

34. "Vaquero," *Adventures in Search of a Living in Spanish America* (London, 1911), 98.

35. *PO* (Puebla) 17 (1882): 22.

36. Moisés González Navarro, *Anatomía del Poder en México 1848–1853* (México, 1977), 67.

37. Neukomm, *Musique militaire*, 202–6.

38. Theodore Zeldin, *France 1848–1945: Politics and Anger* (Oxford, 1984); and Charles Hale, *The Transformation of Liberalism in Mexico* (Princeton, 1989), 246.

39. AMTdeO, Gobierno Box 36, 1876, "Correspondencia, Pueblos de los Reyes."

40. APD 10/171/008141, Letter of August 1885, Mucío Martínez to Porfirio Díaz.

41. *Corona fúnebre que la gratitud pública coloca sobre la tumba del general Juan Crisóstomo Bonilla* (México, 1884); and AMTdeO, Box 14, Bis, Correspondencia Xochiapulco, "Crónica de las honoras fúnebres que el Ayuntamiento de Xochiapulco hizo el día dos de mayo de 1888 al finado Diputado C. Miguel Méndez."

42. Martin Wainwright, "And the Band Begins to Play," obituary of Harry Mortimer, in *The Guardian*, February 4, 1992.

43. AMTdeO, Gobierno Box 10, 1867–1869, Expediente 2.

44. Arturo Warman, *Banda de Totontepec Mixes Oaxaca* (record sleeve), INAH, México, 1975.

45. William Galloway, a tireless campaigner for the improvement of British band music at the beginning of this century, observed that musical literacy accompanied, even preceded, verbal literacy: "Children show an extraordinary facility in sight reading," he noted, adding that the breathing exercises involved in musical training had important health benefits. See *Musical England,* 37. This latter point is belied by Frederick Starr's comments on the Huauhtla band in the Sierra Mazateca, a band "consisting entirely of boys, none of them more than twenty years of age. . . . Several boys have blown themselves, through consumption, into early graves" (*In Indian Mexico: A Narrative of Travel and Labor* [Chicago, 1908], 237).

46. In 1880, during the election of General Juan N. Méndez as governor, the wind band of Zacatlán's National Guard battalion (which was accused of intimidation on polling day) was composed of boys between the ages of ten and twelve, "to the alarm of their parents." *PO* 11, no. 51 (June 26, 1880).

47. AMTdeO, Gobierno Box 36, Correspondencia Zoquiapa, Letter of January 12, 1876, Lorenzo Rodríguez to Jefe Político.

48. Thomson, "Bulwarks," 57–61.

49. Ramón Hernández, "Relación Histórica de las Bandas de Música Militar en la República," manuscript (INBA, n.d.), 3–5. Henry Farmer identified one band of international standard: "Mexico . . . has a very fine band in that of its Artillery stationed at Mexico City. They are seventy-five strong, the instrumentation being on the French model, and embracing the entire family of saxophones. They play an up-to-date repertoire and give capital renderings of such writers as Puccini and Saint-Saens." *Military Music,* viii.

50. Anne Craig, *The First Agraristas: An Oral History of a Mexican Agrarian Reform Movement* (Berkeley, 1983), 30–31.

51. Vázquez, "Breve Historia,"14–16.

52. Parsons, *Mitla: Town of the Souls* (Chicago, 1936), 191–92, 393–94.

53. Julio de la Fuente, *Yalalag, una villa zapoteca serrana* (México, 1977), 251.

54. Hugo Nutini, *San Bernardino Contla: Marriage and Family in a Tlaxcalan Municipio* (Pittsburgh, 1968); and Nutini and Betty Bell, *Ritual Kinship: The Struc-*

ture and Historical Development of the Compadrazgo System in Rural Tlaxcala (Princeton, 1980), 83–85, 108–9, 136–38, 164–65, 184–86.

55. Frans J. Schryer, *Ethnicity and Class Conflict in Rural Mexico* (Princeton, 1990), 62.

56. Gary H. Gossen, *Chamulas in the World of the Sun: Time and Space in a Maya Oral Tradition* (Cambridge, MA, 1974), 211–17; The *Handbook of Middle American Indians* confirms that "some towns have bands, but they are chiefly ladino institutions and perform only at ladino affairs" (*Ethnology,* 1:94).

57. Robert Redfield and Alfonso Villa Rojas, *Chan Kom: A Maya Village* (Chicago, 1934), 124–25.

58. Von Z. Vogt, *Zinacantecos* (Washington, DC, 1934), 16, 78–81.

59. Frank Cancian, *Economics and Prestige in a Maya Community* (Stanford, CA, 1965), 45–47.

60. Frank and Joan Harrison, "Spanish Elements in the Music of the Maya Groups of Chiapas," *Selected Reports* 1, no. 2 (Institute of Ethnomusicology, Los Angeles, 1966/70): 1–44.

61. Laura Nader, *Harmony, Ideology, Justice, and Control in a Zapotec Mountain Village* (Stanford, CA, 1990), 47. During the nineteenth century, bands were generally referred to as *músicas de viento,* or, more pompously in the Puebla Sierra, as *cuerpos filarmónicos.* By the early twentieth century, the term "orchestra" was being used to distinguish newly formed bands from the rustic nineteenth-century *charrangas.*

62. Robert Redfield, *A Village That Chose Progress: Chan Kom Revisited* (Chicago, 1950), 48, 83.

63. The *maestro cantor,* or chanter, was an influential figure in the community. Parsons states that he could "substitute for the priest in saying responsories for the dead; at house funerals he asperses the corpse." They usually had learned their prayers and chants in childhood from their fathers. Traditionally, *maestros cantores* enjoyed certain privileges, such as freedom from paying tribute and from community service. Parsons, *Mitla,* 186–87. For *maestros cantores* in Yucatán, who formed a kind of parapriesthood, see Anne C. Collins, "The *Maestros Cantores* in Yucatán," in *Anthropology and History in Yucatán,* ed. Grant D. Jones (Austin, TX, 1977), 233–47; Redfield and Villa Rojas, *Chan Kom,* 73, 367; and Alfonso Villa Rojas, *The Maya of East Central Quintana Roo* (Washington, DC, 1945), 45.

64. Parsons, *Mitla,* 410. See also 23–24.

65. William Galloway writes that until 1845, no military music was available in printed form, and "bandmasters were driven to beg, borrow, or steal from jealous colleagues." *Musical England,* 72.

66. Parsons, *Mitla,* 398–99, 406–9.

67. Thomson, "Bulwarks," 59–60.

68. The 1992 obituary of bandmaster Harry Mortimer observes that the minimum age for recruitment into wind bands was conditioned in part by the arrival of second teeth: "Young players are usually restrained until their first set of teeth have come out, to avoid awful dental accidents under the bandstand." Wainwright, "And the Band Begins to Play."

69. Parsons, *Mitla,* 190–91.

70. Jäcklein, *Un Pueblo Popoloco,* 161–63.

71. Parsons, *Mitla*, 433–34.

72. Ibid., 103–11, 185.

73. The funeral was the one private ceremony in which Mitla's bands occasionally would offer their services free of charge. In the Mixe community of Totontepec, this was proudly the case. Warman, *Banda de Totontepec Mixes Oaxaca*.

74. The following paragraphs are based on Parsons, *Mitla*, 172, 174–80, 186–87, 197–99, 249–50, 266–67, 272–83, 280.

75. Ibid., 272–73.

76. Ibid., 280.

77. *Homenaje a la música festera* (Valencia, 1974), 25.

78. Philip A. Dennis, *Intervillage Conflict* (New Brunswick, NJ, 1987), 32. The proliferation of bands in the villages of the Sierra Mazateca was as much a consequence of the Mazateco love of music as of factionalism: "Another aspect is their love of music, and almost all towns have at least one band. In the principal fiestas bands from neighbouring towns get together to compete." The Chinantecs, in contrast, seem to have approached music more as a duty than as a pleasure: "The omnipresent village bands are rather solemn, semiofficial organisations who play dutifully on ceremonial occasions." *Handbook of Middle American Indians. Ethnology*, 1:521.

79. Jäcklein, *Un Pueblo Popoloco*, 247.

80. Parsons, *Mitla*, 261.

81. Nader, *Harmony, Ideology*, 47–48.

82. Paul Friedrich, *Agrarian Revolt in a Mexican Village* (Chicago, 1977), 40, 79; idem, *Princes of Naranja: An Essay in Anthrohistorical Method* (Austin, TX, 1986), 191; *Handbook of Middle American Indians. Ethnology*, 1:770.

83. Starr, *In Indian Mexico*, 247–48.

84. Warman, *Banda de Totontepec Mixes Oaxaca*.

85. de la Fuente, *Yalálag*, 255.

86. Dennis, *Intervillage Conflict*, 32.

87. For wind-band contests in Britain, see Scholes, *Oxford Companion*, 215–16, and in Oaxaca, *Handbook of Middle American Indians. Ethnology*, 1:521.

88. Rogelio Barriaga Rivas uses this theme in his "indigenista" novel, *La Mayordomía* (México, 1952), cited in Dennis, *Intervillage Conflict*, 35–36.

Conclusion: The State as Vampire— Hegemonic Projects, Public Ritual, and Popular Culture in Mexico, 1600–1990

Eric Van Young
University of California, San Diego

Eric Van Young presents more than a summation of this volume as he combines a judicious review of major theses, a provocative commentary on what he regards as the theoretical and methodological undertakings of cultural history, and a fine-honed discussion of understated themes—regionalism and ethnicity—with examples from his current research. Above all, he raises thoughtful questions, challenges tightly held assumptions, asserts unique (usually psychoanalytic) hypotheses, and, generally, enjoys doing history as much as revelers did Carnival.

Van Young completed his Ph.D. at the University of California, Berkeley, with the dissertation that became *Hacienda and Market in Eighteenth-Century Mexico* (1981). His engaging articles, published over the past few years (and cited in the notes), have created increasing anticipation of his "The Other Rebellion," now in progress.

T AKEN TOGETHER, the introduction and fifteen nicely realized essays in this collection arc over nearly four centuries of Mexican history. There are gaps in the coverage, to be sure, with corresponding peaks of concentration shadowing them. Although this unevenness in Mexico's historiographical landscape is already mapped out, the country's relatively neglected seventeenth century and nineteenth century between Independence and the Porfiriato still have more to recommend them than just scholarly obscurity.

Whatever the periodization or the historiographical lay of the land, the long time span and broad thematic reach represented by the

Successive draft versions of this essay benefited from sympathetic but critical readings by Michael Bernstein, Steve Lewis, and Paul Vanderwood; David Ringrose answered a reference question at a crucial point late in the writing.

essays may allow us to form an interrogatory circle embracing simultaneously the perspectives of "local knowledges" about culture,
society, and politics, and their broader applicability to a general understanding of Mexican history—to think in concomitantly extended
terms, in other words, about the sweep of Mexican history in raising
a series of questions to which these essays are only partial answers.
(By local knowledges I take to mean the contingent, historical, and
even personalized understandings that groups of people and communities bring to ideas and cultural complexes shared in a general way
with other groups.) Nor is the voice of the ethnographical interlocu-
tor absent from the volume's extended conversation about the
country's cultural history, as how could it be when so many of the
authors touch upon issues of symbolic and affective meaning whose
interpretation is shaped by the increasing (and salutary) disciplinary
convergence of history and ethnography?[1] The playful blurring of
these two genres of social inquiry promises the same sorts of risks
and contingent outcomes of most games.[2] My essay attempts to combine part friendly commentary on the other authors' fine contributions, part programmatic rumination on writing cultural history, and
part interpretive run-up on the history of public culture in Mexico. I
would like first to set something of an agenda, while at the same time
contextualizing the other essays, and then move on to a more detailed but necessarily brief discussion of some of the themes raised
by the individual authors.

Despite the manifest cogency, sophistication, and descriptive richness of these essays, and the consistency with which they all touch at
least some central themes of the volume, it is a daunting chore to
tease out in a final chapter some of the broader interpretive conclusions of the collection as a whole. This task is rather different from
the one that the editors have set themselves in the introduction, which
is to construct a conceptual framework for the volume, most especially concerning the forms and functions of public ritual, and to situ-
ate that discussion within the context of cultural studies and a set of
empirical comparisons from other areas of the world, primarily early
modern Europe and the United States. It is through the lens of public
ritual and celebration that the editors and authors broach for Mexican cultural history a number of interesting theoretical and substantive issues: among others the instability of socially constituted
meanings both diachronically (over time) and synchronically (over
space), the problematics of state- and nation-building, the resilience
of popular culture, and the recalcitrance of large segments of civil
society in the face of statist projects. Lest these concerns sound too
resolutely modernist, it should be pointed out that they resonate
strongly throughout the last two or three centuries of Mexican his-

tory. Thus, for example, reconciling elite political and more broadly public concerns about the form and appropriateness of public ritual or display and group self-representation with conflicting concerns over work discipline and *buen policía* was no less a Bourbon than a Porfirian preoccupation. These may be seen as the two sides of the Bourbon political coin, as well as those of the state-building regimes, in which the regulation of public life—ritual, expressive, affective— served in essence as the means to a state-mediated primitive accumulation of capital through increasing control of workers and their labor.

Admittedly, this is a rather functionalist interpretation of the relationship between what was perceived as the riotousness of the hoi polloi and popular contestation over public space, on the one hand, and the social control that elites always yearn for in any social order, on the other—a control they justify in terms of *raison d'état*, public order, or the imperatives of modernization. But several of the essays make clear that the calculus of social order was explicit and never far from the minds of elite powerholders. What is less clear is the ideological and moral relationship—moral in its widest sense, embracing ideas about the right, the good, the true, and the beautiful—between efforts toward economic modernization and the suppression of the more exuberant sorts of popular culture or religious celebration, or whether such "reforming" projects and cultural complexes were susceptible of wide consensual validation. Thus the essays raise another major question about how beliefs and practices come to be implanted and legitimated in any society, and in Mexico in particular: whether by imposition from above (hegemony) or by some more open-ended, chaotic process of contestation and negotiation in which groups of social actors may each have a fairly open-eyed vision of what they want their culture (or their segment of it) to be like.[3]

THEMES PRESENT

Some of the volume's themes emerge clearly, as a leitmotif will in the several movements of a large orchestral piece, while others are more muted and occasional but still strong, and yet others barely audible at all. The authors and editors agree, for example, in highlighting the importance of sacrality, forms of religious sensibility, and religious observance as central threads of Mexican cultural history. But as the editors' introduction and Adrian Bantjes's essay make clear, at least the partial transfer of sacrality from systems of religious ideas and forms of worship to the cult of the nation-state marks the passage of Mexico from colony to nation. Thus, as the essays move forward chronologically, the religious theme tends to give way to that of state-building, and discussion of religious belief and ritual to that of the forces of secularization. A related theme close to the surface of many of the essays is the relationship between the Mexican state and the nation, it being self-evident that while the former has existed since Independence as a successor to the Spanish colonial regime, the latter has been constructed cumulatively over nearly two centuries.[4]

More muted but still audible (explicitly in the essays of Tony Morgan and William Beezley) is a discussion of the increasing commodification of historical memory as the modern period advances, facilitated—in a sense, compelled—by the lengthening technological reach of the Mexican state, the spread of print and other mass media, industrialization, the progressive bourgeoisification of taste in sectors of the urban population, and the ever deeper immersion of Mexico in the swirling currents of international capitalism.[5] Commodification occurred both in the sense that signs were increasingly manufactured, consciously manipulated, and broadly diffused by powerholders to naturalize their authority, to legitimate it and provide it with a genealogy, as well as in the sense that representations of forms of community came to center on the images and ownership of things, or to be imbricated with them. A more quietly treated but still audible motif, which cuts to the heart of the formal and expressive control of civic space, surfaces in the essays of Sergio Rivera, Susan Deans-Smith, Cheryl Martin, William French, Engracia Loyo, and Bantjes: popular resistance to elite or state projects in the name of preserving local knowledges and little traditions.

Several of the essays touch on the axial organizing principle of gender (Anne Staples and Mary Kay Vaughan, for example), but none except that of Deans-Smith treats it systematically, weaving it centrally into social experience and cultural representation in the ways we are coming to see as basic.[6] Virtually none of the authors gives us a gendered reading of the rituals, celebrations, processions, acts of popular cultural resistance, or hegemonic projects they describe, most of which could be interpreted as demonstrations not only of social hierarchy or resistance to it but also of male hierarchy or resistance to it.

THEMES ABSENT

Cultural issues of historical importance for Mexico are passed over in virtual silence by authors and editors alike. Two of these issues are geography and ethnicity. We need to remember that civic spaces are physical as well as metaphorical or mental and that the friction of distance is no less important than that of class or gender in explaining much about history. Thus, in looking at public rituals or celebrations (as in the Curcio-Nagy or García Ayluardo essays), we might think not only about decoding representations of social hierarchy or religious ideas but also about the use of urban or other spaces, and according to what moral and aesthetic agendas, and with what emotional impact, mundane settings were transformed into sacral or celebratory ones.[7] On a larger scale, Mexico's difficult geography and stubborn regionality surely have had a great deal to do with the constraints on hegemonic political and cultural projects originating at the center, and with the concomitant resilience of local traditions (including ethnicity). Allowing for *chilango* disdain for the provinces, space can almost be said to function as a proxy for time in the sense that cultural practice might lag behind "modern" ideas in direct proportion to distance and isolation from the center of the country; after all, "fuera de México, todo es Cuauhtitlán."

Surely we must factor ethnicity into the complex mix of Mexican cultural history, particularly as embodied in the confrontation and accommodation between indigenous and European groups. Until well into the modern history of the country (just when would depend on where one was situated geographically) it is difficult to understand what is going on politically, economically, or culturally without reference to the survival of indigenous beliefs and forms of community within the context of colonial conquest and domination, and their prevalence in large parts of Mexico. For example, what meanings did a religious ritual convey in an ethnically stratified community, whose meanings were they, and how did they fragment along ethnic lines? And how can one speak meaningfully of nation-building when the political nation was likely to have excluded, in any serious operational sense, a large percentage of the country's population, especially in the rural sector?[8]

CULTURAL HISTORY

We shall pay some attention, however briefly, to a few issues of theory and method in cultural history, which is what all these interesting contributions are doing. Rather than dealing with these considerations apart, I want to set some of them out in a preliminary fashion here as background, then allude to them as running commentary on substantive historical questions later on.

My first observation is that historians of culture need actively to problematize their sources—that is, treat them (their "texts") as problems to be mulled over rather than pristine representations of an antecedent reality to be reconstructed.[9] This good historians have always done to some degree (along with "thick description" and some other techniques we have been enjoined to take up in recent years), but perhaps not with quite the obsessive energy that characterizes certain varieties of postmodernist thinking in the human sciences in which fact cedes ground to facticity and truth to truthoid statements. As it emerges through this operation that evidence of social and cultural processes consists of little more than textualized viewpoint, we should be prepared to admit that what historical actors do not say is often just as telling as what they do say. In conveying motives, meanings, or even the most straightforward descriptions, our texts distort (or simply follow their own internal logic) or tell only part of the story, and other important explanatory elements may lie just under the surface of those texts or beyond the barriers of consciousness, perception, or language. One of the implications following from this is the fragmentation of causal statements. So while what actors tell us about themselves, or what other actors or observers tell us about them, may very well be true, it may not only be true.

This leads to my second point: that social and cultural behaviors are likely to be overdetermined, so that there may be a variety of reasons for them or functions fulfilled by them simultaneously.[10] This has already been suggested by the editors in their discussion of theories for the function of public ritual or celebration, several of which may apply all at once rather than serially: emotional venting, entertainment value, reinforcement of social hierarchy, expression of community, expression of contention, and so forth. Nor should we be surprised to see contradictions, not only in the sense that different groups may contend over meaning and dominance in the same civic or other venue but also in the sense that within a cohesive social group, or even within an individual, apparently incompatible motives and goals, to say nothing of unarticulated or unconscious ones, may vie with one another.

A third observation follows from the multivalent, potentially self-contradictory nature of civic rituals (or of other complex cultural phenomena). Typically it is not only ritual behaviors themselves that we are interested in (though they may be inherently exotic and fascinating, and their detailed description arresting), but also a sort of extended meaning to be drawn from them about other forms of cultural expression and/or the social order that gives rise to them.[11] If in the end, within the circumscribed representation of the rituals themselves, we read such performances as texts—not fixed for all time, and subject to enormous variation in practice and circumstance, but nonetheless inscribed for a given moment—it becomes extremely difficult to tease out what is not scripted, or what is addressed to the audience or other actors sotto voce or whispered from the wings. And in terms of the larger goal of finding out something about the cultural order in which the ritual complex is embedded, then, what is the range of information their (re)construction and analysis actually convey?

The editors in their introduction and Beezley in his evocative essay suggest that the relationship between ritual event and larger society is that of "encapsulation," in which public celebrations are to be seen as a microcosm of entire cultural orders, large chunks of them, or particularly telling subsets of essential organizing principles: large worlds writ small. But while we readily may grant that they are representational—that is to say, their ontological status is as proxies, or perhaps reduced images, of larger and more elusive structures—large claims for their representativeness are often open to question. In the specific context of rituals of bereavement the anthropologist Renato Rosaldo has written:

> Similarly, *rituals do not always encapsulate deep cultural wisdom.* At times they instead contain the wisdom of Polonius. Although certain rituals both reflect and create ultimate values, others simply bring people together and deliver a set of platitudes that enable them to go on with their lives. Rituals serve as vehicles for processes that occur both before and after the period of their performance [and concurrent with them, one might add]. Funeral rituals, for example, do not "contain" all the complex processes of bereavement. *Ritual and bereavement should not be collapsed into one another because they neither fully encapsulate nor fully explain one another.* Instead, rituals are often but points along a number of longer processual trajectories; hence, my image of ritual as a crossroads where distinct life processes intersect.[12]

What I take this to mean is that ritual "events" or other public collective expressions are not so much exemplars from which a standard repertoire of elements can be culled, but rather open-ended, frayed, indeterminate (because overdetermined) "happenings" responding to the circumstances of the place and moment, though they embody important cultural understandings. They may provide insights, in other words, but never blueprints.[13] The silences of onlookers or even of participants can be telling and should not be taken for affirmation.

My cookie-cutter view of cultural history and ritual events—the insistence that what is not seen, recorded, or reconstructable is certainly there—leads me back to my observations. The fourth is that if what is absent or excluded from our texts is important in getting at culture, then culture must be in many places where we cannot see it, or where it does not occur to us to look, as well as at those social loci and in those material objects to which our conventions have directed our gaze. Given the ethnographic origins of the concept of culture, and even with the recent expansion of its dominion and the advent of cultural history, it still retains more than a hint of the exotic, the quaint, the folkloric; in a word, of being what other people do. One might think of this as the "orientalist" view of culture.[14] Relatedly, we find a widespread tendency in discussions of culture not only to exemplify it in specific events or behavioral subsets but also to reify it. I take this to be the sense in which Morgan, in his essay on workers and popular culture in Porfirian Mexico City, mentions in passing that paternalistic employers were "using culture" to court favor with the workers, as though it were a discrete object, separable and residual. Parallel to this understanding of things cultural, and at least in part the product of our compulsion to compartmentalize our inquiries into human activities along established disciplinary lines, is our tendency to use culture as a black-box explanans when recourse to our other major analytical categories—economic structure or politics, for example—fails us. But I would suggest that culture is at once more subtle and more pervasive than this, that it claims our attention even where we think there is something else going on that has little or nothing to do with it, and that we ghettoize it in this fashion only at the risk of lopping off the most important part of what we study. Is economic life really any less "cultural" than religious life? Are its forms, its affective and symbolic resonances, its shared meanings and moral dimensions any less important to our understanding of it, for example, than to our successful interpretation of behavior in civic rituals?[15] Is a parliamentary debate any less a cultural system than a ritual circumcision or a baseball game? Taking culture and cultural practice this way, as a medium that pervades social orders and part social orders rather than as exotic lumps for decoding, certainly tends to make social life analytically more fluid and chaotic, thus more closely approximating the lived reality of it.

My final point is that while culture may be viewed as pervasive and ordinary, it is also local and historical. This brings us back full circle to the idea of local knowledges and suggests another caveat about whether ritual, ceremonial, festive public events actually encapsulate cultural meanings and social processes or approximate them in some other way. Thus, whether the universalistic meanings in a Corpus Christi procession or a patriotic festival would override to some significant degree the intimate histories and daily relationships in two or more localities is open to question, even if we could hope to recover the cognitive and affective processes inside the actors' heads, which is what social and cultural history in large measure attempt. But what I have in mind here is much more mundane—that cultural history becomes localized, or molded to the contours of local history, by the myriad contingencies of everyday life, including technological change, external events, and economic cycles.[16] Let us cite an example from the essays at hand. Guy Thomson, in discussing the multiple functions of village brass bands, reminds us that their popularity and wide diffusion were significantly determined by the influence of the French Revolution on military music and the invention of valved instruments in the nineteenth century, occurrences relatively remote in time and place. Beyond this, in taking an even more detailed ethnographic approach than many of the other authors, who look at ritual or symbolic expression as communitarian or class-based in origin, Thomson suggests the existence of an infrahistory of cultural expression. Echoing the observations of Marshall Sahlins, Thomson's discussion of modern bands shows the way they affect and are affected by individuals' life-course events, village factions, and political power, thus indicating the way in which cultural or symbolic production is woven into "normal" life and gives it meaning, as opposed to being segregated into a separate or rarefied "cultural" realm.

Whatever the respective weights of continuity and contingency in our centuries-long story of Mexican culture, politics, and society, something certainly made the Mexico of 1860 or 1870 in many ways quite different from that of 1810 or 1820. One prime candidate for the cause of the changes may be the ideas of universal and modern citizenship introduced with the republican era. How these ideas were diffused during the half century between Independence and the end of the Reforma is not clear—whether through marginal increases in literacy, access to education, the proliferation of print media, physical mobility, prolonged military mobilization itself, or the thickening of social networks, or all of these together. But the tension between post Independence, and especially post Reforma, state projects and the putative claims of citizenship—the latter not only in a locality but also in a nation—surely form an important backdrop to the cultural history of the period after 1850.

CIVIC INTERLUDE

Let us glimpse that tension near its origin from two sources. First, the December 1821 description of a patriotic parade held in October in the city of Salvatierra:

> In the vanguard was a body of national militiamen, composed of the most genteel youths, very well uniformed and mounted on excellent horses, with their officers dressed very luxuriously. There followed companies of dancers from the pueblos of the district, in which were admired the expertise and harmony of the dances, and the extraordinary effort with which these poor people

overcame their poverty to dress appropriately to the occasion, and to pay for the good music they brought with them.

After them followed a float, with its orchestra, paid for by the Indians (*ciudadanos naturales*) of the barrio of San Juan Bautista, arranged and painted in good taste, on its sides various hieroglyphs and mottos alluding to the benefits to be gained from Independence, and to the gratitude owing to the Most Excellent Señor Generalísimo [Agustín de Iturbide]. And on the highest part of the float, beneath a decent canopy, was seated majestically the figure of Liberty, trampling under foot the neck of prostrated despotism. Just below her were seated Mars, Prudence, and Justice, alluding to the virtues with which our immortal Generalísimo conducted such an heroic enterprise. And at the rear, reclining on a cushion, were the sciences, an allusion to the way in which these will prosper with the political liberty of the Nation, and the tranquil repose they shall enjoy. All these were dressed and bejewelled with taste and propriety by the gentlemen to whom the float was entrusted.

Immediately after [on foot] followed Fame, and after her a numerous group of young ladies dressed in white, their dresses adorned with tricolored trimmings, representing the three guarantees, and also with tricolored ribbons and flowers in their hair, carrying olive branches in their hands, and interspersed with children dressed as angels (*genios*), the uniformity and beauty of the clothes making the most beautiful sight.

Of these ladies the last four came singing patriotic songs of excellent composition, accompanied by music, which they performed with singular perfection and grace. After them came an Indian and a Spaniard richly dressed in the old style, their arms linked. And then came the city's float, on whose sides were beautifully painted: at the foremost part the imperial eagle perched majestically on a prickly pear (*nopal*); below that an image of the Church crumbling, and the arm of the Most Excellent Señor Generalísimo holding it up; to the right side Independence, pictured as two worlds tied together with a cord being gently sundered by the same Señor Excelencísimo; to the left side Union, represented by two fists affectionately held by the hand of the Señor Generalísimo, and further along on both sides a horn of Amalthea [horn of plenty]. Each of the three guarantees was explained by an epigram; and on the front the coat of arms of the city.

On the highest part of the float rode the three guarantees, represented by three pretty little girls, each dressed in the appropriate color, and decorated with much beauty and propriety, each bearing in her hands the insignia of her attributes. Below them was America, pictured as another beautiful young woman dressed with all gentility and propriety, and decked out with a quiver on her back, a bow in one hand and an arrow in the other, and adorned with all the magnificence of jewels, pearls, and the rest, proper to signify that with which the Sovereign Author has privileged this beautiful part of the globe. At the foot of the float, standing, was the Most Excellent Señor Generalísimo, her [America's] immortal liberator, represented by a young man of handsome aspect, dressed as a general, holding in one hand broken fetters and chains in the attitude of just having smashed them, and in the other hand a crown and scepter which he was just about to don. At the front of the float rode the goddess Minerva, magnificently dressed.

The float was pulled by sixteen robust youths, dressed as noble Indians in the old style, whose variety of plumage made for the most agreeable sight. Behind this float came the Ayuntamiento, with its numerous and brilliant accompaniment, led by the Alcaldes Constitucionales; and at the rear the cavalry troop of the garrison, its commander dressed and mounted with all luxury, with the necessary dragoons from this and the national militia distributed so as to impede the innumerable spectators from interfering with the parade.

After this, everyone in the parade went to a house . . . especially disposed and decorated, where they were served a plentiful and exquisite refreshment, with one served also to the soldiers, the pullers of the floats, the dancers, and the invited guests from the pueblos. A dance followed until two in the morning, two more refreshments having been served, during which the greatest order prevailed, and the greatest pleasure in the repeated acclamations (*vivas*) directed to all the worthy objects of our rejoicings.[17]

And second, let us add to this description an extract from an edict issued by Ramón Gutiérrez del Mazo, *jefe político* of Mexico City, published in the *Gaceta imperial* in January 1822:

It being as indecent as shameful that the common people (*plebe*) of both sexes relieve themselves in the streets, squares, and public places, this scandalous excess is prohibited, and [anyone caught doing so] will be immediately arrested and condemned to an appropriate penalty by the Alcalde or Regidor of the district if they do not have sufficient means to pay the fine. . . .

Fathers and mothers of families living in quarters attached to commercial establishments (*accesorías*), and school masters and mistresses and their aides, will take special care that children not go out to relieve themselves in the street, making sure that they develop a due horror at an action so contrary to the modesty and prudence fitting to be taught them at their tender age; and the said parents and teachers will be held responsible for any violation, so that they will suffer for them the payment of appropriate fines.[18]

The pivot of modernity? perhaps not. But in these two quotations, fortuitously published within days of each other, we see the emergence of elite concerns (for surely the Salvatierra city fathers designed the floats and planned the procession) to make of public celebration a didactic and inclusionary display of civic pride and optimism; indeed, as Beezley points out in his essay, the colonial project was to dominate by exclusion, the national by inclusion or metabolization.[19] The direct object of Gutiérrez del Mazo's policy was to make of the new national capital a healthier, cleaner, more orderly, and modern place. These extracts illustrate vividly what several authors of our essays suggest implicitly, and Staples explicitly— that the notion of *policía* (state regulation of public life) went hand in hand in independent Mexico with that of public ritual and ceremonial, both converging in heightened state power legitimated by affective loyalty to a nation and by material advancement; or, at least, that was the ideal scenario.

The sense of the quotations is plain enough, so we need not engage in any extended unpacking of them here. Nor is their juxtaposition intended as an indirect, smarmy comment on the peculiarities of Mexico's march toward modernity—the lags, bottlenecks, and cultural resistances that in some sense are the subject of this volume.[20] But it may be worth making two points about these extracts. First, there is clearly a high degree of continuity between the late colonial and national periods in terms of the twin avatars of state-building, the promotion of public ritual and the regulation of public space. Second, the opposition between public ritual—in this case with its near-apotheosis of Agustín de Iturbide in tandem with the celebration of the infant Mexican nation (indeed, their virtual conflation, which would lose its ironic bite if we did not know Iturbide's eventual end)—and public squalor does not exhaust the layered meanings stretched between them.[21] Another counterpoint is found deeper within each extract, that between state and civil society—between losers and winners, sacral and secular, stubborn local and popular practice dug in behind the breastworks of community versus reductionistic projects launched from the high ground of the state. We now turn to a consideration of that long history, with the important caveat that state action is only a part of the process of social and cultural change. Nonetheless, since nearly all these essays focus on the implications of the growth of state power in Mexican history in its ritual context, the emphasis is amply justified.

THE STATE AS VAMPIRE

Let us return briefly to the central streets and town plaza of Salvatierra in October 1821. Public rituals—and all rituals are in a sense public (that is, they seem to have an audience)—occasionally come with glossaries and operating instructions; more often they do not. A certain amount of decoding is therefore necessary if we are to grasp what their representations are representing and what layered meanings they convey, especially as seen through the veils of distant time. Though we are forever barred entry into the thoughts of the Indian and the Spaniard "richly dressed in the old style, their arms linked," who paraded between the tricolor-festooned, singing young ladies and the city's float celebrating Iturbide, we can puzzle over their public personae. At a guess, their old-style garb harked back to the era of the conquest: the Spaniard in doublet, hose, cape, with Renaissance-era hat; and the Indian decked out in cotton mantle, the feathered headdress of a Mexica warrior or *tlatoani*, with open sandals, though he might have affected the neoclassical Greco-Roman costume prevalent in idealized nineteenth-century iconographic representations of Aztec rulers. We are on fairly safe ground in supposing that this pair, whatever their raiment, was meant to symbolize the healing of the wound inflicted by the Spanish conquest of Mexico: their arms fraternally linked, forward they marched toward the new nation's providential destiny, connecting past and future. This would have been a particularly piquant but sanguine evocation in view of the implicit acknowledgment by Mexico's new ruling creole elite that the struggle for independence from Spain had been marked strongly by elements of race war and a well-developed, popular vindicationist ideology of Aztec *revanchisme*.[22]

Nearly a century later, as Barbara Tenenbaum vividly shows in her essay, the Mexican state was still celebrating itself with proto-*indigenista* "murals in stone" (dressed in the old style), ostentatiously punctuating the central artery of the capital, reasserting anew the public, ceremonial, and iconographic dominance of Cuauhtémoc and the Mexica over other indigenous groups.[23] The neoclassical representations of Aztec heroes on the Paseo de la Reforma in Mexico City are of generalized as opposed to specific Indians, and their dedication was accompanied by a veritable orgasm of nationalist rhetoric. This flattening, or idealization, is one aspect of what I am calling the commodification of historical memory.

In the same decades when the Porfirian regime was hyping this proto-*indigenismo* in the public sphere, it was wheeling around a hoary racist machine on real (or putative) indigenous groups that found (or put) themselves in the path of progress and hegemonic state projects. Recent work of Paul Vanderwood on the millenarian episode at Tomóchic in the early 1890s, for example, reveals the negative Indian stereotypes widely current in the late nineteenth century (applied to the Tomochitecos, though most of the "rebels" were in fact mestizos), and suffusing the work of such Liberal paladins as José María Luis Mora and Justo Sierra. The popular press of the time (especially the *capitalino* press) was replete with journalistic evocations of Indian barbarism and the omnipresent specter of caste war. In 1890 the Mexico City daily *El Universal* invoked a comparison with savage frontier Indians in reproving small children for prankish behavior, and speakers at the dedication of the Cuauhtémoc monument on the Paseo de la Reforma conjured up the horrors of Indian caste war against the background of a real caste war in Yucatán. A few years earlier, in 1886, *El Monitor Republicano*, another *capitalino* newspaper, resurrected the colonial doctrine of a "just" war to legitimate the regime's warfare against the Sonoran Yaquis.[24]

None of this was new, of course, but stretched far back into colonial times, offering yet another in a series of continuities in Mexican cultural history. In the colonial period, Indians for the most part were viewed by those in authority not only as children of diminished intellectual capacity but also as ignorant, lazy, drunken, vicious sodomites naturally prone to suggestion, extreme violence, and religious backsliding.[25] Nor did this complex of attitudes toward indigenous people have much to do with Enlightenment thought, with its mania for classification, though the Enlightenment may have laid an ideological patina over the basic conceptual arsenal.[26] It goes back much further in the history of European-native encounter, finding its roots not only in the radical otherness of American native cultures in the eyes of the Europeans but also in the daily praxis of exploitation and asymmetrical power relations. Indeed, I am tempted to remark that the exploitation seems ontologically prior to the ethnic elements. Whatever the case, in Mexico the apparent contradiction is composed of two sides of the same coin. The multivocality of the concept "Indian" is turned at one and the same time to nation- or state-building, to the invention of tradition, and to the construction of an imagined community, while it is also employed to squash resistance to the state's project and destroy a real community. Through this appropriation of Indianness the Porfirian state may be seen as a kind of ideological vampire, sucking the life from real people to ensure its own immortality and mummifying the past to control the present and guarantee the future.

The mention of the Salvatierra float and the Paseo de la Reforma monuments raises both the issues of ethnicity and geography mentioned above and substantially passed over in most of the essays in this volume. Certainly this discussion hardly scratches the surface of the ethnic dimension in Mexican cultural history—one of the major features distinguishing it from, say, European cultural history but uniting it to the study of other colonial societies dominated by Europeans. This set of distinctions has retained a remarkable salience throughout most of Mexican history, and actually until the present (witness the events of 1994 in Chiapas), when demographic submersion has done more to resolve the "Indian problem" than anything else, and when in fact the post-Revolutionary cult of official *indigenismo*, foreshadowed by the Porfirian regime, has long since stood the whole issue on its head. Nonetheless, until well into this century indigenous people formed an important cultural and political grouping. A generation after the two Spanish and Indian gentlemen walked together arm in arm through the streets of Salvatierra, Staples relates, the municipal fathers of Tlacotalpan, Veracruz, passed an ordinance (1855) clearly aimed at keeping Indians off the sidewalks in favor of the *gente decente*, even if the enactment was ostensibly race blind. We may be permitted some doubts, then, at Beezley's suggestion that sometime in the middle to late nineteenth century the "Indian problem" was transmuted into the "campesino problem."[27]

It is possible to introduce more concretely the largely missing ethnic dimension into these provocative treatments of Mexican public ritual, civil society, and state development (always excepting Tenenbaum's essay, which is less about ethnicity than about national mythologizing). Let me cite one example among many. Beezley's essay on Porfirian Guadalajara mentions early on that during the middle decades of the nineteenth century (at about the time when the Tlacotalpan city fathers were trying to keep Indians off their sidewalks) the Mexico City municipal authorities looked with a jaundiced eye upon popular festivities associated with the liturgical calendar. One of the popular customs they most disapproved was the wearing of masks by revelers, presumably because the anonymity and impunity thus afforded might encourage crime. From the authorities' perspective we might readily concede the point, but there may have been another motive behind their concerns. What could a mask hide most effectively? Gender?—unlikely. Individual identity?—possibly, but still problematic where people had any personal familiarity with one another, as between urban barrio authorities and neighborhood residents. One answer is that masks hid phenotype and ethnicity, as pressing a concern to those trying to "whiten" and modernize the nation and its civic spaces as criminality on the local or national level, especially where elite fears of caste war and projections of dark-skinned hostility were fed by the actuality of regional brigandage or insurgencies (that of Manuel Lozada, for example, in the Nayarit area during the 1850s and 1860s) that incorporated elements of ethnic resistance.[28] To hide phenotype or ethnicity would be to blur the sense of who was celebrating as well as erode the boundaries of the civic or political nation—less a matter of social control, perhaps, than moral discourse.

A second facet of the celebration of Cuauhtémoc and the other Mexica monarchs on the Paseo de la Reforma, more muted but less ironic than the ethnic one, is the dominance of Tenochtitlán over other indigenous city-states, and more generally by the Valley of Mexico over local and provincial realities and histories. As we pass from the ethnic to the spatial dimension of Mexican cultural history, we see the same vampirism manifesting itself as the antientropic impulse of the state toward centralization in nearly all aspects of life. The discursive tradition paralleling this centripetal drive recently has been analyzed by Carlos Monsiváis; in considering the fate of Mexican regions he leans simultaneously to the playful and the melancholy, reminding us of Hamlet's contemplation of Yorick's skull.[29] He points to the strong association of regions with "provinces," and of both with "backwardness." Indeed, the dyad of urban civilization and provincial barbarism echoes in spatial terms what we have just discussed in ethnic terms, and for much the same reason—that cities were viewed, during the colonial period and even beyond it, as islands or bridgeheads in a vast sea of people of color, embodying not only some modicum of physical security but also the centers of political and economic power and the traditions of Mediterranean sociability. Monsiváis adds that, at least from the center of the country, Mexican regions and their localities have been viewed as perpetually underage in both the sense that they have been seen as minors (errant children disputing the patriarchal or imperial power of the center) and from an evolutionary perspective (as flies in amber, museums of archaism, the repositories of traditional cultural values "glorifying failure"). Some states—or some historical incarnations of the Mexican state—have been stronger than others, to be sure, but where increased centralization has failed it generally has not been for want of trying or for lack of an ideological umbrella to cover its grosser realities.

My formulation of the problem, taking off from an analysis of the history of Mexican regionality and regionalism over the long haul, has taken the tack that most state projects, at least since the late Bourbon regime, have tried in the name of modernization to replace strong regional and weak class structures with weak regional and strong class structures.[30] For a number of reasons, the colonial period and the nineteenth century left Mexico with a weak regional integration and limited opportunities for market development, economies of scale, or real economic growth, which allowed only a low degree of social division of labor and therefore a weak class structure and vertical, or sociopolitical, articulation. One way of conceptualizing this spatial problematic is through recourse to the idea of energy exchanges between man and his environment;[31] through thinking about the efficiency of energy transmission, whether in the form of goods and services, taxes, information, or political decisions; and about what geographers call the friction of distance. The frameworks of these exchanges, whether institutionalized or ad hoc, are at the center of many of the questions that concern historians and others: not only market relationships and production arrangements but also the structures of the state, the burgeoning of nationalism, and the homogenization of culture.

Taking seriously the energy-exchange model and its spatial dimension opens up interesting questions for large-scale thinking about the history of Mexico, many of which are reflected in the essays in this volume. For example, one of the constant preoccupations of students of Mexican history and of national political and cultural discourse within the country itself is the growth of the Mexican state, particularly since the Revolution of 1910. Indeed, in the triumphalist interpretation the entire economic and political development of the nineteenth century, or Mexican history even further back, may be seen as a long and chaotic prolegomenon to the emergence of the modern post-Revolutionary state.[32] While we might characterize this narrative as simplistic or even teleological, there is something to be said for it. Political and military struggles over the control and constitution of the Mexican state may be viewed as attempts to construct or capture an instrumentality to reduce the friction of distance and therefore increase the efficiency of energy extraction by the center. Whether members of the active political public in the nineteenth century considered themselves liberals or conservatives had a good deal to do with whether they thought that the growth of markets should be antecedent to the growth of the state, or whether affairs should be the other way around. Similarly, the growth of modern Mexican nationalism has had much to do with the breaking down of the many regional pointillisms through more efficient systems of transport, market mechanisms, military logistics, and media of information exchange.

Seen from this vantage point, the growth of state power since the early nineteenth century, and the impetus toward economic development that went along with it as both effect and legitimizing ideology, may be seen as a process whereby Mexico's strong regional structure was weakened and its weak class structure strengthened. The class structure of a developed capitalist system is arguably a more efficient mechanism for extracting energy from the environment than a highly regionalized economy, with the outcome that the social groups controlling the high ground of the state, and their pet projects, are the beneficiaries of the net energy gain. The process of state-building has not been without its costs or setbacks. Assuming for the moment a degree of congruity between colonial regions and Mexican federal states, these latter entities have tried at various times to block the emergent hegemony of the central state.[33] In the post-Revolutionary period the forward progress of the central state against the forces of regional control of resources is especially well illustrated by the development of irrigation and power projects centering on great river basins.[34] On the ideological front, myth-building and state-building were essential concomitants for the rooting of nationalism and national identity beginning in the nineteenth century, while a Mexican national historiography was tentatively constructed out of the building blocks of regional history.[35]

These issues of the relationship of peripheries to center comprise at least part of the historical subtext of many of the essays in this volume. At times centralizing projects have been advanced with the complicity of provincial elites, popular groups, and working people, at other times in the face of their resistance; in some fundamental sense complicity and resistance can even coexist in the same social group, community, or individual at the same time. Nor is this tension limited exclusively to central state or regional relations, but it should be conceived of as more broadly spatial, operating in smaller socio-cultural theaters, no matter what the scale or institutional entities involved. Indeed, Mexico has seen a long history of centrifugal struggles even at the local level (of peripheries at the periphery), as for example the tendency during the colonial period and even in the nineteenth century for outlying districts at the *municipio* level to assert their independence against their *cabeceras* (district head-towns), and for these latter to exert their dominance over smaller settlements.[36]

These spatial or political tensions might well intersect the trajectory of more obviously symbolic or affective life in the arena of religious and patriotic festivals. Vaughan shows that the Tecamachalco area's subordinate settlements used patriotic fiestas as channels for the expression of civic pride and independence. This prompts the observation that public ritual may not be exclusively a form of social (that is, vertical) domination but also of spatial (that is, horizontal) domination. Furthermore, as forms of sociability change over generations, the function of public ritual may also change, and with it the spatial dimension in the relationship between ritual and subordination. For example, Morgan points out that religious celebrations played a relatively minor role in binding together workers and capital in Porfirian Mexico City but a much larger role in the provinces in the same era. In this instance, space might be seen to function as a proxy for time.

The relationship between temporal and spatial dimensions of the festive or ritual world comes through even more clearly in French's essay, when he makes the point that the labor mobilizations associated with capital intensification, specifically in late nineteenth-century mining development in northern Mexico, brought customs from rural areas to centers of urban and industrial concentration. From this perspective the microhistory of popular culture and resistance would present a sort of archaeology of celebratory custom—a temporally layered repertoire of "archaic" practice introduced into modern venues and confronted with elite and state attempts to impose invented hegemonic usages. We tend to think of this dissonance predominantly in the Thompsonian vein of time and work-discipline,[37] but there may be other interesting ways to think about these issues, as for example in terms of rates of cultural sedimentation and/or co-optation. In any case, this is one reason why breaking down the regions in Mexico vis-à-vis the center is such an important state project: it presumably yields ever increasing control over both capital and labor, resulting in the same sort of vampirism as the appropriation of history and ritual.

THE ENCHANTMENTS OF RITUAL

When we asked above whether or not public ritual celebration can be said to encapsulate a society's cultural practices and beliefs, we raised the issue of how such observances achieve representation—how their codes are constructed. The question of what these public ritual representations do is a different matter. Though some common interpretive threads may be teased out, there is no completely consistent formulation among the essays in this volume as to the social or cultural functions of public ritual in Mexican history. That this is hardly surprising in view of the richly overdetermined nature of ritual life the essays amply attest.

Linda Curcio-Nagy, for example, stresses the integrationist aspects of the baroque Corpus Christi procession, which may be construed as expressions of overarching and unifying community sentiment embracing social groups that under normal circumstances might be at odds with each other because of political, ethnic, economic, or other differing interests and identifications. She also notes that the colonial elite actively promoted the "acculturative" function of festivals in the face of their own fears of popular resistance and disorder, as a way of turning the recently colonized into good colonial subjects. For a much later period, noting that the disencryption required of audiences viewing twentieth-century improvised campesino theater often tended to open a space for political discussion and conscientization among country people, Donald Frischmann asks whether secular (civic) ritual did not have the same impact. Clara García Ayluardo stresses with Curcio-Nagy the cross-class, unifying nature of public ceremonial within a framework of religious transcendence (the capacity of such rituals, in other words, to activate *communitas* in Victor Turner's sense), yet she seems also to suggest that *cofradía* activities reinforced rather than muted principles of social hierarchy and differentiation.[38]

Martin, as well as Curcio-Nagy and García Ayluardo, finds colonial religious processions to have been occasions for elite ostentation and the reinforcement of elite authority, embodying prevailing ideas of precedence and privilege.[39] Martin also interprets late colonial civic rituals as "lessons of subordination" originating in a failure by dominant local groups to exert effective control over the turbulent lower orders by other means. Vaughan sees rural festivals principally as elements in a hegemonic discourse rather than a subversive one (that is, of broad social consensus rather than contention), a view of Mexican village fiestas as instruments of self-domination, but adding the important qualification that the domination thus achieved by local and national powerholders over subaltern groups is volatile and negotiated. Nonetheless, she explains how festivals in the post-Revolutionary period were turned to good use by local schoolteachers to inculcate their ideology, producing intracommunity solidarity and intercommunity competition and differentiation as important secondary effects. Finally, all the authors, even those dealing principally with the more open-ended forms of display or celebration and their interplay with the hegemonic projects of the Mexican elite (Rivera, Staples, Tenenbaum, Beezley, French, and Thomson) rather than with sacred or secular ritual events strictly speaking, would doubtless acknowledge the affective (that is, escape-valve) and entertainment aspects of such performative time-outs in everyday life.[40]

In our preoccupation with decoding the latent functions of ritual, it is easy to downplay or ignore the centrality of its manifest expressive content—an actual belief in the efficacy of divine or saintly intervention in human affairs, the propitiatory or re-equilibrating power of human ritual expression itself to put the world aright, or the devotion to community, monarch, or state. Indeed, the theology (that is, the explicit ideological content and rationality) of ritual and celebration is somewhat stinted by most of the authors of these essays (Bantjes and Vaughan being exceptions) in favor of a more distanced, analytical, or interpretive view of the social and cultural function of such public performative acts. But while we disaggregate types or levels of meaning in these processes for analytical clarity, we do so at the risk of emptying out the experience of the historical actors to the point that we begin to wonder why people engaged in these silly behaviors in the first place.[41] In the affective or expressive realm, apart from the variety of their functional effects, rituals provide collective, public venues for magical thinking and also connect us with the past. Vaughan astutely notes the high degree of similarity in Mexican cultural history between religious and patriotic festivals and their ritual elements. We must wonder whether rituals ever can be truly secularized, since they are meant to invoke as much as to represent; that is to say, there is as much about them of collective wishes as of collective statements: of who we want to be or how the world should be, as opposed to who we are or how the world exists at any given moment. Furthermore, as the editors point out in the introduction, if rituals and public celebration fuse the individual to the collective and represent the past to the present (witness the Indian and the Spaniard of the Salvatierra float), they also portray and speak for the present to the past. In this sense, pasts are not only molted and molded but also spoken to. The practice of representing present to past is prominent in Mexican culture, as the traditional celebration of the Day of the Dead and the vivid, day-to-day presence of Mexico's history in song, in monument, and in ideology make clear.[42]

The powerful social and cultural valences of ritual and public celebration have made of them a contentious terrain—of state action, of co-optation, of the stubborn back-pressures of civil society—through much of Mexican history. Predictably, the volume's authors differ in their overall evaluation of these historical processes. Some paint a decidedly more positive or optimistic picture in which, if the triumphalism of the "official" version of the history of the Mexican state is somewhat muted, at least that history is portrayed as far from an unmitigated disaster for popular culture, local traditions, and civil society. Others take a decidedly darker view, with the Mexican state, whether autonomous or substantially the creature of conscious elite policy, as juggernaut. The positive view would appear to be the position of Vaughan, who writes of "multiple discourses" at the local level and of the advent of state-sponsored patriotic and other festivals in the post-Revolutionary period as a negotiated penetration willed at both national and local levels. Bantjes, on the other hand, espouses the darker vision of the defanaticization campaign in Sonora and the popular reaction to it, stressing that in this instance jacobin modernizers ran ahead of the majority of local populations. Rivera offers yet a third interpretation of the stress between popular cultural expression and state policy in the later colonial period, emphasizing the Bakhtinian aspects of popular practice, though we wonder if the tone then was not in fact a good deal edgier, more conflictual, and even more depressive than ludic.

In any case, the state drive to convert, co-opt, control, or suppress elements of religious ritual and other forms of popular cultural expression goes back to well before the nineteenth-century era of liberalism and industrialization, or of the politically voracious Porfirian and Revolutionary regimes. In the essay by Curcio-Nagy, for example, we note the difference in attitude toward public ritual display by the Habsburg and Bourbon states, the former leaning to corporatism and inclusion, the latter to bureaucratic regulation and social surveillance.[43] García Ayluardo sees overt signs of Bourbon regalism in the regulation of religious ceremonial and the activities of corporations (including confraternities). Martin's discussion of the urban culture of colonial Chihuahua stresses the co-optation or replacement of popular public observances with those celebrating the monarchical regime.

In the post-Independence period, as several authors observe, the drive to secularize public celebration and ritual continued. The nineteenth century, as we have said above, saw an increasingly sharp disagreement between church and state as to the public exercise of religious ritual. In general terms, the contraction of the public religious matrix during the century meant that individuals had to go to religion rather than religion coming to them. Parallel to this trend and impinging upon it was the effort of the authorities to sanitize popular cultural expression and take back the very streets in which it found its performance venue.[44] Staples notes the popular tendency to see the street as an extension of living and working spaces, as against the efforts of the state to police life and enforce order there. In the colonial period, as Rivera points out, the street as a sort of public tabula rasa—for promiscuous class contact and the expression of popular culture—was transformed by ritual practice (decoration, procession) into a different sort of space, one whose affective and semiotic potentials depended upon the tensions or contradictions between the everyday and the privileged claims of ritual itself. This "fun as risk" is anathema to modernizing states, whether in the sacred or secular realms, so that the state's efforts to flatten out ambiguities in the use of public spaces and to make itself the sole arbiter of the meanings of those uses must be seen as at the heart of most state projects.

These modalities of state self-invention continued their advance from the Porfirian period into the Revolutionary era. Beezley tells us that in the mid-1890s patriotic celebrations tended to be changed from evening torchlight affairs to daytime ones because of the association of torchlight processions with earlier protestations in favor of political liberty, and the resulting desire of the Porfirian "smart set" to tame these possibly riotous occasions or forestall them altogether. He reminds us that parallel to this the Porfirian regime "tamed" the church, struck a political *concordat* with it, countenanced the return of the Jesuit Order, and finally oversaw the official dedication of the nation to the Virgin of Guadalupe in 1895. Also during the Mexican *fin de siècle*, as Morgan tells us in his description of workers and employers in Mexico City, forms of popular culture were captured and domesticated by paternalistic bosses, thus replicating on a smaller scale the way the state co-opted and controlled ritual and celebration. Frischmann carries the story forward to the creation by José Vasconcelos (as secretary of education in the early 1920s) of secular *misiones culturales* in the countryside, which resonated strongly with the practices of colonial evangelization. In the period after 1910, as Bantjes, Loyo, Vaughan, and Frischmann all point out, schoolteachers were often the central agents of these projects at the local level, especially in the countryside, whether as iconoclasts, bearers of rationalist educational philosophies, socialist pedagogues, or heroes of rural dramatic spectacles, respectively.

RESISTANCE AND POPULAR CULTURE

These co-optations and other state actions may be seen as the ritual and celebratory analog of a long-term political process—its flesh made word, so to speak—in which state-making and nation-building reinforced each other in complex ways. Yet most of the authors here also point to stubborn back-pressures against this *étatisme*, or what we generally refer to as popular cultural and political resistance. The basic question at issue here for several centuries has been: Whose culture is it, anyway—the people's, the elite's, or the state's? Moreover, the question of what constitutes resistance has become a thorny one in the human sciences of late, particularly with the advent of subaltern studies and, before that, with the turn of social and cultural historians to looking at the history of popular groups and their ways of thinking (*mentalités*).[45] For example, does a subversive reading by popular groups of ritual elements within an established framework whose boundaries the protesters do not violate constitute resistance or the acceptance of an effective hegemony dominated by elites or the state?

Whatever view we take of this matter on a theoretical level, it is certainly the case that the people often appear recalcitrant and the elite and/or the state by turn (or simultaneously) seem arrogant, paranoid, fearful, or beleaguered. Even though the packed Catholic liturgical calendar ostensibly originated with the church and its "great tradition" theology, it has been adopted enthusiastically by the popular classes in Mexico, with the addition of the famous *San Lunes* (Saint Monday), a day devoted to sleeping off the hangovers from the weekend and about which employers have complained for generations that little or no work gets done. Was the popular attachment to such celebrations a reaction to the imposition of work discipline in a society still functioning on assumptions about looser peasant work rhythms? Along parallel lines French points to the publicly indecorous behavior of working-class people in Porfirian Parral as a form of symbolic contestation of middle-class morality and the structures of authority supporting it, at the same time that it asserted the claims of popular culture.[46] Jumping ahead a bit in time, Loyo takes as her theme the popular response to the Cardenista educational reforms of the 1930s, tracing the resistance to those reforms by more conservative social sectors—precisely the sort of popular back-pressure I have been suggesting.[47]

We may cite a final example from Frischmann's essay on twentieth-century rural theater, in which he notes beginning in the early 1930s the progressive appropriation of state-subsidized dramatic groups to the purpose of a genuinely popular cultural and political expression. By the time we arrive at the more recent Teatro Conasupo, Frischmann tells us, one of the stock commedia dell'arte characters is Juan Sin Miedo, a campesino willing to take on his class enemies but not possessing a knowledge of the politico-legal system sufficient to the task. Juan's reliance on the expertise of his ally Clarín Cantaclaro in the ways of the Mexican legal system, however, eventually leads to his triumph. The strong resonances here with Indian mastery of the colonial courts and other legal institutions are almost too obvious to bear mention. As I suggested above, we need to keep in mind that resistance within an institutional or well-established cultural framework may be construed as a form of co-opted resistance, or it may not, depending upon the respective viewpoints of historical subject and observer.[48]

One of the most important loci of contestation over cultural forms and meanings remains the workplace, especially as Mexico has become ever more urbanized and industrialized. Viewed from a certain vantage point, even where it is not explicit, the subtext of most of these essays is the history of labor. If poverty has always been seen as the rookery of crime, then the workplace may be seen as the rookery of cultural attitudes. This points up the continuing importance of writing for Mexico a "new" cultural history of labor, the sort of historiographical enterprise already well advanced (perhaps even now passing out of fashion) for Europe and the United States. The essays by Deans-Smith, Morgan, and French certainly move in this direction. Aside from volition—that is, the will of popular groups to hang onto their own culture and identity and reproduce them—there were in the early modern period certain "objective" forces ranged against the sort of social homogenization and cultural bowdlerization embodied in the colonial state's efforts to regulate the moral lives of workers and censor popular religious expression. In the capital's Real Fábrica de Tabacos, as Deans-Smith points out, these factors included ethnic division and cultural plurality within the work force itself, spatial dispersion, and labor organization. French, on the other hand, points to the common social and cultural attitudes arising from the work experience. We wonder whether the forge of the workplace did not do more in disciplining and homogenizing workers than overt state efforts to regulate the use of public spaces.[49] Morgan's view is altogether darker. In exploring the transformative power of capital in the workplace with the advent of larger industrial forms of organization, he points to new stresses on the paternalist system, new expectations from all groups, new demands on workers, new uses of time and place, and new forms of sociability. He describes a sort of trade-off between the Díaz regime and urban industrial workers, in which the latter lost access to the political system but gained "bread and circuses." However, with the advent of Francisco Madero and the Revolution, this produced a lack of worker support for the regime.

THE POWER OF REMEMBERING

This volume finally deals as much with forms of collective memory and their progressive commodification as it does with the advance of state power, the contestation over the scope, style, and meanings of public ritual observance, or the erosion of local knowledges in Mexican history. The agents of this mnemonic imperialism—the state, the church, the capitalist world order, and local elites as cultural *compradors*—flit through most of the essays. I have already raised the point, along with Beezley, about the tendency for "invented traditions" to be commodified (that is, adapted to wants, made serviceable), particularly with the advent of literacy and mass media, and of transportation systems and communication; and most of the other essays deal with this phenomenon at some length. Indeed, commodification is in large measure a necessary condition of such invention.

When we think of commodities, we are likely to summon up images of "things"—mountains of soybeans, or oceans of canola oil. What commodities have in common are homogeneity, portability, blandness, divisibility, and a certain alienated quality. Hegemonic projects embody a drive to introject these characteristics into public discourses and private understandings—to monopolize sign production, to lobotomize local understandings or co-opt them into quaintness in order to fill museums or make them into tourist attractions, to flatten and homogenize ideological content, and to fabricate genealogies to naturalize the commodified memory. Myths, national holidays, textbooks, public monuments, compulsory military service, street signs, advertising: these are the instrumentalities or weapons of commodification. But this is of necessity a hard-fought campaign, popular back-pressures and pockets of stubborn cultural guerrilla resistance tending to make final pacification an unrealizable goal.

From this perspective all modern states are Asiatic, their public architecture and monuments a form of frozen energy, built because they can be built and because the building itself reifies and reinforces state power. The "nationalist mythologizers" who in Tenenbaum's account succeeded the "francophile progressives" knew this very well, as demonstrated by Vicente Riva Palacio, who praised public art as an instrument of social and political control. Thus, while Mexico City's Passion of Cuauhtémoc and Vindication of Hidalgo are monumental evocations of high symbolism and ecstatic nationalism, they are also in some sense commodities—infinitely divisible, portable, and readily and universally comprehensible.

The essays of Morgan and Beezley have some interesting things to say about the commodification of memory that picked up momentum with the relatively late advent of large-scale industrial capitalism in Mexico. New, secular celebrations and representations now increasingly elbowed aside traditional religious ones, thus comprising the discursive analog of the aggressive, even violent defanaticization campaign that Bantjes describes for the post-Revolutionary period in Sonora. Morgan discusses the advent of advertising in tandem with the growing consumer culture in the industrializing national capital, though he does not make clear how this functioned in relation to public ritual and spectacle, whether as counterrepresentation or surrogate representation. Much of his account centers on the entrepreneurial showmanship of Ernesto Pugibet and his Buen Tono cigarette enterprise. The competitive gimmickry and advertising of the tobacco companies strikes us as similar to corporate self-representations in traditional public ritual, as seen in the Curcio-Nagy and García Ayluardo essays, but with a difference: the essential passivity of the intended audience and its ingestive consumer tumescence (a pining for "la rubia que todos quieren" [Cerveza Superior]).[50] Beezley notes in his essay that the floats so much a part of public celebration after 1895 often centered on the display of "things," this more material sort of commodification resonating with the conversion of participants to observers and consumers. At the same time, he remarks, the embourgeoisement of sectors of the Mexican urban population in the late Victorian period distanced them from rituals of all sorts, even those marking events in the family life cycle, while the two-dimensional photograph boomed in popularity as a mnemonic artifact. In a speculative mode, Beezley goes a step further, positing that as former celebrants were being converted into spectators, they themselves were being commodified, in a sense—a process we might now call "massification." His point, as I take it, is that the conversion was not only a function of changes in the physical environment of the city—the advent of electric light, and population growth, though these factors were important—but also principally a project of state ideological control.

CONCLUSION

These essays have surveyed and mapped a broad territory: geographically from the vast Mexican north to the near south of the country, with the capital perhaps overrepresented; temporally from the sixteenth century to the 1990s. Though forms of ritual expression have ostensibly been our principal concern, the essayists have ranged over or touched upon a much wider variety of very concrete human activities: labor, public art, education, iconoclasm, musical and theatrical expression, popular protest, law and public policy, consumer culture, and laughter, not to mention several perennials of the structurally minded, including the development of capitalism, the growth of the Mexican state, and the transition to modernity.

Perhaps the most consistent theme to emerge from the essays as a whole, aside from the expressive and political power of ritual celebration and other forms of public performance, is the dialogue between the Mexican state and the Mexican people over who shall control those forms of expression. When this dyad—state versus people—is committed to paper it seems overly Manichean. One of the most important tasks of social and cultural historians is to deconstruct these terms, so that "the state" is disaggregated into the many groups that really contend at any given historical moment for access to the levers of power, and "the people" can be seen whole in their multiplicity, not as a homologous magnitude. Nonetheless, there is a good deal of analytic power in this formulation, schematic though it may be. The Mexican state certainly has not had everything its own way over the last couple of centuries; if it had, Mexico today might look more like Switzerland or one of the Scandinavian countries. The control it has tried to exert over exuberant little traditions has in part, and at times, left a remarkably deep imprint on Mexican culture and will become even more profound in the future, whether or not the neoliberal project of the 1990s succeeds or not. But just as suburban housing developments start out internally standardized and then differentiate over the course of decades—people remodel, relandscape, take better or worse care of their homes—so the initially homogeneous understandings of appropriated or invented traditions and representations will tend to redifferentiate over time, generating new and stubborn local knowledges whose voices clamor to be heard in the dialogue of cultural history.

NOTES

1. For stimulating essays addressing the issues currently under debate in ethnography and social or cultural history see John and Jean Comaroff, *Ethnography and the Historical Imagination* (Boulder, CO, 1992); Emiko Ohnuki-Tierney, ed., *Culture through Time: Anthropological Approaches* (Stanford, CA, 1990); and James Clifford and George E. Marcus, eds., *Writing Culture: The Poetics and Politics of Ethnography* (Berkeley, CA, 1986). Bryan D. Palmer challenges this approach in *Descent into Discourse: The Reification of Language and the Writing of Social History* (Philadelphia, 1990).

2. The term "blurred genres" comes from Clifford Geertz's essay with the same title in *Local Knowledge: Further Essays in Interpretive Anthropology* (New York, 1983), 21ff.

3. For an introduction see Walter L. Adamson, *Hegemony and Revolution: A Study of Antonio Gramsci's Political and Cultural Theory* (Berkeley, CA, 1980). James C. Scott marshals a trenchant critique of Gramscian and post-Gramscian concepts of hegemony in *Domination and the Arts of Resistance: Hidden Transcripts* (New Haven, CT, 1990); and for an evaluation of Scott's work see Eric Van Young, "The Cuautla Lazarus: Double Subjectives in Reading Texts on Popular Collective Action," *Colonial Latin American Review* 2 (1993): 3–26.

4. David A. Brading, *The First America: The Spanish Monarchy, Creole Patriots, and the Liberal State, 1492–1866* (New York, 1991).

5. For the Porfirian era see William Beezley, *Judas at the Jockey Club and Other Episodes of Porfirian Mexico* (Lincoln, NE, 1987); and Stephen Haber, *Industry and Underdevelopment: The Industrialization of Mexico, 1890–1940* (Stanford, CA, 1989). For a discussion of material culture and the social meanings in the colonies see my essay, "Material Life in the Colonial Latin American Countryside," in Louisa S. Hoberman and Susan M. Socolow, eds., *Rural Society in Colonial Latin America* (Durham, NC, forthcoming).

6. See Marjorie R. Becker, *Setting the Virgin on Fire: Lázaro Cárdenas, Michoacán Peasants, and the Redemption of the Mexican Revolution* (Berkeley, CA, forthcoming).

7. For a deconstruction of local settings and social action see Clothilde Puertolas, "The Festival of San Fermines" (Ph.D. diss., University of California, San Diego, 1989); and Rhys Isaac, *The Transformation of Virginia, 1740–1790* (Chapel Hill, NC, 1982).

8. See Alan Knight, "Racism, Revolution, and *Indigenismo*: Mexico, 1910–1940," in Richard Graham, ed., *The Idea of Race in Latin America, 1870–1940* (Austin, TX, 1990), 71–113.

9. For further discussion see Van Young, "The Cuautla Lazarus."

10. The term "overdetermination" was originally drawn from psychology early in the present century; see Burness E. Moore and Bernard D. Fine, eds., *A Glossary of Psychoanalytic Terms and Concepts*, 2d ed. (New York, 1968), 69.

11. Victor Turner, *The Ritual Process* (Chicago, 1969).

12. Renato Rosaldo, *Culture and Truth: The Remaking of Social Analysis* (Boston, 1989), 20 (emphasis added).

13. Inga Clendinnen's philosophically brilliant reading of Mexica culture in *Aztecs: An Interpretation* (New York, 1991) adopts the culture-as-encapsulation stance (pp. 4–5).

14. With apologies to Edward Said, *Orientalism* (New York, 1979). James Clifford has developed this point in *The Predicament of Culture: Twentieth-Century Ethnography, Literature, and Art* (Cambridge, MA, 1988). See also George Marcus and Michael Fischer, *Anthropology as Cultural Critique: An Experimental Moment in the Human Sciences* (Chicago, 1986).

15. See my "Dreamscape with Figures and Fences: Cultural Contention and Discourse in the Late Colonial Mexican Countryside," in Serge Gruzinsky and Nathan Wachtel, eds., *Le Nouveau Monde—Mondes Nouveaux* (Paris, forthcoming).

16. Marshall Sahlins, *Islands of History* (Chicago, 1987), 1.

17. *Gaceta imperial de México*, December 27, 1821, describing a parade that took place in October in Salvatierra.

18. Continuation of a decree published earlier, now in ibid., January 7, 1822.

19. For a comparative discussion of the "problem of the Indian" see Thomas M. Davies, Jr., *Indian Integration in Peru: A Half Century of Experience, 1900–1948* (Lincoln, NE, 1974).

20. Parisian streets also flowed with mud and refuse, and the hygienic habits of many of the French capital's residents closely approximated those of the Mexicans; see *Journal des débats,* November 1, 1826. Sewer workers and other Parisians were regularly carried off by asphyxiation from the deadly miasmas of the sewers; see Louis Chevalier, *Laboring Classes and Dangerous Classes in Paris during the First Half of the Nineteenth Century*, trans. Frank Jellinek (Princeton, NJ, 1981).

21. Timothy E. Anna, *The Mexican Empire of Iturbide* (Lincoln, NE, 1990); Javier Ocampo, *Las ideas de un día: El pueblo mexicano ante la consumación de su Independencia* (Mexico City, 1969).

22. See my book in progress, "The Other Rebellion"; and for the 1810 sedition case against José María González del Pliego, the Indian notary of the village of Ocoyoacac, near Tenango del Valle, see AGN, ramo Criminal, vol. 207, exp. 22, fols. 306r–327v, 1810.

23. See Tenenbaum's "Murals in Stone: The Paseo de la Reforma and Porfirian Mexico, 1873–1910," in Ricardo Sánchez, Eric Van Young, and Gisela von Wobeser, eds., *La ciudad y el campo en la historia de México: Memoria de la VII Reunión de Historiadores Mexicanos y Norteamericanos* (Mexico City, 1992), 1:369–79.

24. Paul Vanderwood, "Indios, Fanáticos, Bandidos: Labelling the Millenarian Movement at Tomóchic, Mexico," in Lewis Knafla, ed., *Criminal Justice History: An International Annual, 1992* (Westport, CT, 1993), 161–89; idem, "Region and Rebellion: The Case of the Papigochic," in Van Young, ed., *Mexico's Regions: Comparative History and Development* (San Diego, 1992), 167–90. The journalistic references come from Vanderwood, "Indios, Fanáticos, Bandidos."

25. Eric Van Young, "In the Gloomy Caverns of Paganism: Popular Culture, the Bourbon State, and Rebellion in Mexico, 1800–1821," in Christon I. Archer,

ed., *The Mexican Wars of Independence, Empire, and Early Republic* (Lincoln, NE, forthcoming); idem, "Religion and Popular Ideology in Mexico, 1810–1821," in Steve Kaplan, ed., *Indigenous and Popular Responses to Western Christianity* (New York, forthcoming).

26. For Enlightenment "typophilia" (my coinage) of European intellectual traditions toward non-European cultures see Mary Louise Pratt, *Imperial Eyes: Travel Writing and Transculturation* (London, 1992). See also Anthony Pagden, *The Fall of Natural Man: The American Indian and the Origins of Comparative Ethnology* (New York, 1982); and Juan A. Ortega y Medina, *Imagología del bueno y del mal salvaje* (Mexico City, 1987).

27. Knight, "Racism, Revolution, and *Indigenismo*."

28. Paul Vanderwood, *Disorder and Progress: Bandits, Police, and Mexican Development*, ed. rev. and enl. (Wilmington, DE, 1992), 64–65; Jean Meyer, *Esperando a Lozada* (Guadalajara, 1984); and on these issues generally, Gilbert M. Joseph, "On the Trail of Latin American Bandits: A Re-examination of Peasant Resistance," *LARR* 25 (1990): 7–53.

29. Carlos Monsiváis, " 'Just Over That Hill': Notes on Centralism and Regional Cultures," in Van Young, ed., *Mexico's Regions*, 247–54.

30. This discussion draws on my "Introduction: Are Regions Good to Think?," in *Mexico's Regions*, 1–36; and my "Haciendo historia regional: Consideraciones metodológicas y teóricas," in Pérez Herrero, comp., *Región e historia en México* (Mexico City, 1991). An English version of this essay will be published as "Doing Regional History: A Theoretical Discussion and Some Mexican Cases," in *Conference of Latin Americanist Geographers Yearbook, 1994*, David J. Robinson, ed., forthcoming.

31. Richard N. Adams, *Energy and Structure: A Theory of Social Power* (Austin, TX, 1975).

32. See John Friedmann, Nathan Gardels, and Adrian Pennink, "The Politics of Space: Five Centuries of Regional Development in Mexico," *International Journal of Urban and Regional Research* 4 (1980): 319–49.

33. Marcello Carmagnani, "Finanzas y estado en México, 1820–1880," *Ibero-Americanisches Archiv* 9 (1983): 277–317; Mario Cerutti, "Monterrey and its *Ambito Regional*, 1850–1910: Historical Context and Methodological Recommendations," in Van Young, *Mexico's Regions*, 145–66.

34. David Barkin and Timothy King, *Regional Economic Development: The River Basin Approach in Mexico* (New York, 1979); Clifton L. Kroeber, *Man, Land, and Water: Mexico's Farmlands Irrigation Policies, 1885–1911* (Berkeley, CA, 1985).

35. David J. Robinson, "The Language and Significance of Place in Latin America," in John A. Agnew and James S. Duncan, eds., *The Power of Place: Bringing Together Geographical and Sociological Imaginations* (Boston, 1989); David A. Brading, *The Origins of Mexican Nationalism* (Cambridge, 1985); Ignacio del Río, "De la pertinencia del enfoque regional en la investigación histórica sobre México," *Históricas* 27 (1989): 21–32. Compare Paul Vanderwood, "Building Blocks but Yet No Building: Regional History and the Mexican Revolution," *Mexican Studies/Estudios Mexicanos* 3 (1987): 421–32.

36. Compare Charles Gibson, *The Aztecs under Spanish Rule: A History of the Indians of the Valley of Mexico, 1519–1810* (Stanford, CA, 1964), and James

Lockhart, *The Nahuas after the Conquest: A Social and Cultural History of the Indians of Central Mexico, Sixteenth through Eighteenth Centuries* (Stanford, CA, 1992). See also "Charles Gibson and the Ethnohistory of Postconquest Central Mexico," in James Lockhart, *Nahuas and Spaniards: Postconquest Central Mexican History and Philology* (Stanford, CA, 1991), 159–82.

37. E. P. Thompson, "Time, Work-Discipline, and Industrial Capitalism," *PP* 38 (1967): 56–97.

38. On the notion of *communitas* see Turner, *Dramas, Fields, and Metaphors: Symbolic Action in Human Society* (Ithaca, NY, 1975), esp. 231–71. For a general treatment see Pilar Gonzalbo Aispurú, "Las fiestas novohispanas: Espectáculo y ejemplo," *Mexican Studies/Estudios Mexicanos* 9 (1993): 19–45.

39. See James Scott, *Domination and the Arts of Resistance*, esp. 45–69; and Robert Darnton, *The Great Cat Massacre and Other Episodes in French Cultural History* (New York, 1984).

40. On religious ritual as venting see Emmanuel Le Roy Ladurie, *Carnival in Romans*, trans. Mary Feeney (New York, 1979); and for ritual as expressive of social conflict or inversion see Barbara A. Babcock, ed., *The Reversible World: Symbolic Inversion in Art and Society* (Ithaca, NY, 1978), and Natalie Z. Davis, *Society and Culture in Early Modern France* (Stanford, CA, 1975).

41. For a treatment of public religious ritual that attempts to integrate social and cultural meanings see Robert Anthony Orsi, *The Madonna of 115th Street: Faith and Community in Italian Harlem, 1880–1950* (New Haven, CT, 1985). Paul Vanderwood brought this study to my attention.

42. See Hugo Nutini, *Todos Santos in Rural Tlaxcala: A Syncretic, Expressive, and Symbolic Analysis of the Cult of the Dead* (Princeton, NJ, 1988).

43. Venturing to characterize state structures in terms of neurotic stances, we might speak of Habsburg hysteria and Bourbon obsessiveness or anality.

44. See David A. Brading, "Tridentine Catholicism and Enlightened Despotism in Bourbon Mexico," *JLAS* 15 (1983): 1–22; and my "Religion and Popular Ideology in Mexico, 1810–1821," in Kaplan, ed., *Indigenous and Popular Responses to Western Christianity*.

45. See Howard Kaminsky, "From *Mentalité* to Mentality: The Implications of a Novelty," in Mark D. Szuchman, ed., *The Middle Period in Latin America: Values and Attitudes in the 17th–19th Centuries* (Boulder, CO, 1989), 19–32.

46. The editors in their introduction to this volume point to the moral dimension of state formation and the exercise of power, concluding in their gloss on the work of Philip Corrigan and Derek Sayer (*The Great Arch*) that "state power works within us." Even if only understood as metaphorical, this association between the "moralization" of popular culture and the exercise of state power—the hegemonizing of bourgeois morality, as it were, and its introjection into the cultural understandings of popular groups—raises intriguing parallels with the tenets of classical psychoanalytic theory, according to which we might understand the state as a sort of institutionalized (bourgeois) superego. Freud had some interesting observations about the evolution of "civilization" and its relationship to the moral sense (embodied by the superego), essentially concluding that the costs of civilization in terms of instinctual repressions might be higher than the benefits; see Sigmund Freud, *Civilization and Its Discontents*, trans. and ed. James Strachey (New York, 1962); and on the state, especially, see 42ff.

47. For a discussion cast in terms of Philip Corrigan and Derek Sayer's *The Great Arch: English State Formation as Cultural Revolution* (New York, 1985), and James C. Scott's *Weapons of the Weak: Everyday Forms of Peasant Resistance* (New Haven, CT, 1985) and *Domination and the Arts of Resistance*, see Alan Knight, "Hegemony, Resistance, and Popular Culture in Revolutionary Mexico," in Gilbert M. Joseph, ed., *Everyday Forms of State Formation: Revolution and the Negotiation of Rule in Modern Mexico* (Durham, NC, forthcoming).

48. This issue can be framed within Steve Stern's concept of "resistant adaptation" developed in "New Approaches to the Study of Peasant Rebellion and Consciousness: Implications of the Andean Experience," in Steve J. Stern, ed., *Resistance, Rebellion, and Consciousness in the Andean Peasant World, 18th to 20th Centuries* (Madison, WI, 1987), 3–25; see also Eric Van Young, *Hacienda and Market in Eighteenth-Century Mexico: The Rural Economy of the Guadalajara Region, 1675–1820* (Berkeley, CA, 1981), 294–342. On Indian use of New Spain's court system to defend individual and collective interests see Woodrow W. Borah, *Justice by Insurance: The General Indian Court of Colonial Mexico and the Legal Aides of the Half-Real* (Berkeley, CA, 1983).

49. See Doris Ladd, *The Making of a Strike: Mexican Silver Workers' Struggles in Real Del Monte, 1766–1775* (Lincoln, NE, 1988).

50. The term "consumer tumescence" comes from Jean-Christophe Agnew, "Coming Up for Air: Consumer Culture in Historical Perspective," paper presented at the 82d Annual Meeting of the Organization of American Historians, St. Louis, 1989.

Latin American Silhouettes
Studies in History and Culture

William H. Beezley and
Judith Ewell
Editors

Volumes Published

William H. Beezley and Judith Ewell, eds., *The Human Tradition in Latin America: The Twentieth Century* (1987). Cloth ISBN 0-8420-2283-X Paper ISBN 0-8420-2284-8

Judith Ewell and William H. Beezley, eds., *The Human Tradition in Latin America: The Nineteenth Century* (1989). Cloth ISBN 0-8420-2331-3 Paper ISBN 0-8420-2332-1

David G. LaFrance, *The Mexican Revolution in Puebla, 1908–1913: The Maderista Movement and the Failure of Liberal Reform* (1989). ISBN 0-8420-2293-7

Mark A. Burkholder, *Politics of a Colonial Career: José Baquíjano and the Audiencia of Lima*, 2d ed. (1990). Cloth ISBN 0-8420-2353-4 Paper ISBN 0-8420-2352-6

Kenneth M. Coleman and George C. Herring, eds. (with Foreword by Daniel Oduber), *Understanding the Central American Crisis: Sources of Conflict, U.S. Policy, and Options for Peace* (1991). Cloth ISBN 0-8420-2382-8 Paper ISBN 0-8420-2383-6

Carlos B. Gil, ed., *Hope and Frustration: Interviews with Leaders of Mexico's Political Opposition* (1992). Cloth ISBN 0-8420-2395-X Paper ISBN 0-8420-2396-8

Charles Bergquist, Ricardo Peñaranda, and Gonzalo Sánchez, eds., *Violence in Colombia: The Contemporary Crisis in Historical Perspective* (1992). Cloth ISBN 0-8420-2369-0 Paper ISBN 0-8420-2376-3

Heidi Zogbaum, *B. Traven: A Vision of Mexico* (1992). ISBN 0-8420-2392-5

Jaime E. Rodríguez O., ed., *Patterns of Contention in Mexican History* (1992). ISBN 0-8420-2399-2

Louis A. Pérez, Jr., ed., *Slaves, Sugar, and Colonial Society: Travel Accounts of Cuba, 1801–1899* (1992). Cloth ISBN 0-8420-2354-2 Paper ISBN 0-8420-2415-8

Peter Blanchard, *Slavery and Abolition in Early Republican Peru* (1992). Cloth ISBN 0-8420-2400-X   Paper ISBN 0-8420-2429-8

Paul J. Vanderwood, *Disorder and Progress: Bandits, Police, and Mexican Development*. Revised and Enlarged Edition (1992). Cloth ISBN 0-8420-2438-7   Paper ISBN 0-8420-2439-5

Sandra McGee Deutsch and Ronald H. Dolkart, eds., *The Argentine Right: Its History and Intellectual Origins, 1910 to the Present* (1993). Cloth ISBN 0-8420-2418-2   Paper ISBN 0-8420-2419-0

Jaime E. Rodríguez O., ed., *The Evolution of the Mexican Political System* (1993). ISBN 0-8420-2448-4

Steve Ellner, *Organized Labor in Venezuela, 1958–1991: Behavior and Concerns in a Democratic Setting* (1993). ISBN 0-8420-2443-3

Paul J. Dosal, *Doing Business with the Dictators: A Political History of United Fruit in Guatemala, 1899–1944* (1993). ISBN 0-8420-2475-1

Marquis James, *Merchant Adventurer: The Story of W. R. Grace* (1993). ISBN 0-8420-2444-1

John Charles Chasteen and Joseph S. Tulchin, eds., *Problems in Modern Latin American History: A Reader* (1994). Cloth ISBN 0-8420-2327-5 Paper ISBN 0-8420-2328-3

Marguerite Guzmán Bouvard, *Revolutionizing Motherhood: The Mothers of the Plaza de Mayo* (1994). Cloth ISBN 0-8420-2486-7 Paper ISBN 0-8420-2487-5

William H. Beezley, Cheryl English Martin, and William E. French, eds., *Rituals of Rule, Rituals of Resistance: Public Celebrations and Popular Culture in Mexico* (1994). Cloth ISBN 0-8420-2416-6 Paper ISBN 0-8420-2417-4